THE

# HISTORY OF NORTH AMERICA

GUY CARLETON LEE, Ph. D.

OF

JOHNS HOPKINS AND COLUMBIAN UNIVERSITIES, EDITOR

WILLIAM PENN

HANNAH PENN

Water-color facsimiles after the original paintings by Joseph Wright in Independence Hall, Philadelphia.

# The Colonization of the Middle States and Maryland

*Frederick Robertson Jones, Ph.D.*

HERITAGE BOOKS
2011

# HERITAGE BOOKS
*AN IMPRINT OF HERITAGE BOOKS, INC.*

Books, CDs, and more—Worldwide

For our listing of thousands of titles see our website
at
www.HeritageBooks.com

A Facsimile Reprint
Published 2011 by
HERITAGE BOOKS, INC.
Publishing Division
100 Railroad Ave. #104
Westminster, Maryland 21157

Copyright © 1904 George Barrie & Sons
*Entered at Stationer's Hall, London.*

Index Copyright © 2000 Heritage Books, Inc.

Previously published as:
*The History of North America
Volume IV*

— Publisher's Notice —
In reprints such as this, it is often not possible to remove blemishes from the original. We feel the contents of this book warrant its reissue despite these blemishes and hope you will agree and read it with pleasure.

International Standard Book Numbers
Paperbound: 978-0-7884-1588-3
Clothbound: 978-0-7884-8648-7

# EDITOR'S INTRODUCTION

THE history of American colonization is to most persons the record of the activities of the Cavalier and the Puritan. Little thought is given to the story of the Dutchmen who strove to create a New Netherland, or to that of the Swedes who warred with the Dutch and the English in the Delaware country, nor, indeed, is much general interest shown in the accounts of the foundation of New Jersey, Delaware, or Maryland.

True, there is existent more or less local interest in sectional history, and certain of the sons and daughters of the Middle States, alive to the importance of their section during the period of colonization, have striven to perfect the historical records of their several States and to place a knowledge of them in the hands of the public. But when we sum up this local interest and its effect we find that even in New York, New Jersey, Pennsylvania, Delaware, and Maryland public regard for the history of the Middle colonies does not bulk so large as the general, and we may say popular, interest in the history of the colonies of the East and of the South during the early period of their existence. When, therefore, the general reader considers this period, embracing as it does the initial years of American colonization, his mind fastens more often upon Plymouth Rock and Jamestown than upon Manhattan and St. Mary's; and when he studies the advanced or later stage of the period of colonization, it is not to New Haven, New York, Philadelphia, and Baltimore that he turns, but to Boston and Charleston.

The general indifference to matters of sectional history is, it is happily true, giving way before the efforts of such learned and progressive bodies as the historical societies of New York, Pennsylvania, and Maryland; but, nevertheless, the bulk of the people of the Middle States remain as uninterested as were the bulk of the people of the Middle colonies in the stirring events of their history, in the unsurpassed record of those who laid surely and strongly the foundations of such great States as New York and Pennsylvania. It is difficult to assign adequate reason for such attitude on the part of those who may well be ranked among the most progressive and intelligent people of the United States. We may well be puzzled as to a solution of our perplexity when we ask ourselves to-day: Can any section of the United States boast of a city that surpasses New York in importance? or of four cities that together can outrank New York, Philadelphia, Pittsburg, and Baltimore? And we might have asked ourselves in the period of State building: Does any section possess greater and wealthier towns than that of the Middle colonies? But we need not confine our questions to those concerning material prosperity. Were not the men of the Middle colonies the peers of those of any section of the British possessions? If the South had Washington, the Middle colonies had Franklin; if the South spoke of Jefferson, the Middle colonies might well boast of Hamilton; and if the New England colonies declared the fame of Adams and Hancock, had not the Middle colonies Jay and Morris; and Maryland was not behind its sister colonies in the possession of great men.

Did New England or the South possess a more worthy colonizer than William Penn? a more interest-compelling figure than Peter Stuyvesant? or a more far-sighted proprietor than Cecil Calvert? Then, too, was the history of New York, the Jerseys, and Pennsylvania less worthy of record than that of the colonies of the South and of New England? If we turn to Massachusetts because of Lexington

and Concord, and to the South because of Yorktown and
Cowpens, why not to the Middle colonies for the record
of Ticonderoga, Saratoga, and Valley Forge? In fact, in
nothing were the Middle colonies surpassed by those of the
Northeast and the South.

What, then, is the reason for the lack of interest in the
history of the Middle States, which stand to-day as did their
forerunners—the Middle colonies—unsurpassed in men
and resources, and a glorious past? The reply seems to us
to be unmistakable, though complex: The Middle colonies
and States, though always earnest and resultful in action,
have been slow to advertise their deeds. Then, too, interest has centred in the South and in New England. The
South, separated from New England in thought and action,
was the land of Romance; this attribution coupled with
the notoriety given to the section by the agitation concerning its peculiar institution, the character of Southern leaders
and the strength and success with which they maintained
any position assumed by them, combined to centre attention
upon the South and to bring the section into disproportionate
prominence.

The South, however, differed widely from New England
in that its praise as well as its dispraise came from those
not of its soil and in almost every instance not resident
within its borders. Because of this lack of local panegyrists it is second to New England in the attention that has
been paid to its history in special and general works upon
American colonization.

New England possessed the radicalism of the South without her picturesqueness. Though not so rich in natural
resources, she was filled with the spirit of endeavor; but
radicalism, resources, and progressiveness would not have
given New England her historical prominence had it not
been that she has possessed scores of authors and speakers
who have, in season and out of season, sounded the praises
of their section and its leaders. Traditions of the period
of New England colonization have been made the basis

of numberless publications. Literary industry and ability have magnified the importance of New England in the creation and progress of the United States, and have made the history of New England a household word not only in the section discussed and in the South, but in the Middle States, where local history has until recent years been but slightly studied and not generally known. The result is that all the country is familiar with the history of the Puritan, but few are they who know the history of the Quaker or that of those sturdy colonists who followed the Dutch on the Hudson or brought to naught the plans of Calvert.

This particularization of section is unfortunate, for if the foundation of Boston is important, so is that of New York; and if New Haven is the basis of history, so, too, is Baltimore. If Massachusetts has claim upon the attention of the Pennsylvanian, how much more so has Pennsylvania itself or Delaware or New Jersey? And what more profitable historical study to a native of New York than the record of the growth of his own State? In fact, the Middle colonies have as much claim to general study as any of those communities which before 1776 fringed the Atlantic seaboard. But the men of the Middle colonies have left their deeds to be related by others, and these have not given their heart to the task. Those men who laid the foundations of New York, Pennsylvania, Maryland, New Jersey, and Delaware were too busy with their personal work, too busy with their labor in advancing colonial, and, later, national, interests to spread abroad praise of themselves or to contest with their neighbors to the south or east for control or place. The descendants of the colonists have in great measure followed the example of their ancestors.

This must not be understood as disparaging the work of the historical students of the Middle States, which has claims to serious attention and high praise. But, though scholarly, this work has not aroused that popular interest which has been created by the work of the men of New England, neither has it spread abroad the fame of the Middle colonies as the fame of New England and the South has been disseminated through the nation and the world.

To-day there are signs of a revival of interest in the history of the colonization of the Middle States. Readers are turning to its record, but they search and find not, for the literature of the colonization period is all too scanty. There seems to be lacking a work that gives a detailed, comprehensive, and readable description of the colonization period in the territory from which has been created the States of New York, New Jersey, Delaware, Pennsylvania, and Maryland. In view of this fact, the plan of THE HISTORY OF NORTH AMERICA allowed generous space to this period, and *The Colonization of the Middle States and Maryland*, the present volume, is the result. Professor Frederick Robertson Jones, its author, has from the mass of available source material succeeded in preparing a sympathetic and comprehensive study of his subject. His volume approaches the ideal of a scholarly and readable history, presenting in succinct form a wealth of detail.

GUY CARLETON LEE.

*Johns Hopkins University.*

# AUTHOR'S PREFACE

According to the charter of the great joint-stock company granted by James I. in 1606, the jurisdiction of the London branch, or Virginia Company, was to extend from thirty-four to forty-one degrees of north latitude, while that of the Plymouth branch, or North Virginia Company, was to stretch from forty-five down to thirty-eight degrees. The region between the thirty-eighth and the forty-first parallels was thus open to colonization by both companies, with the stipulation that neither company should establish a settlement within one hundred English miles of a previous settlement made by the other. Roughly speaking, this domain included all that part of the Atlantic seaboard extending from the latitude of the extreme southern boundary of Maryland (thirty-seven degrees fifty-three minutes) to that of the southernmost boundary of Connecticut (forty-one degrees). The only colonial settlements of importance within the present jurisdiction of the Middle States and Maryland that were not approximately within these limits were the towns and villages situated in the Hudson and Mohawk valleys, and at the extreme eastern end of Long Island. Of these, Albany, Schenectady, Esopus, and Southold were of the most consequence during the colonial period. The history of the Middle States and Maryland is thus identical, for the most part, with an account of the development of this belt of debatable land.

The colonies within this zone, since they lay between New England on the north and east and Virginia on the south, were greatly influenced by the religious, political, social, and economic institutions of both these sections. Territorial proximity to one or the other of them resulted in the dominance of its characteristic institutions, as against those of other neighboring colonies. Maryland responded more readily to the influence of Virginia, for example, while New York and New Jersey borrowed more largely from New England. From one to the other of the two extremes, there was a gradual and almost imperceptible transition. Undoubtedly, the main factors in establishing these differences were economic and physical. Reference is made here, however, only to the influences exerted by the colonists of Virginia and New England upon the settlers of the territory in question.

This does not mean that the Middle colonies as a group had no life, no institutions, no development peculiarly their own, that they were merely the resultant of the two forces exerted upon either side of them. On the contrary, this group of colonies had a history of its own essentially unique and unquestionably distinct from that of the Southern colonies and that of New England.

The fact is not so obvious, however, that it appeals at once to the casual observer or even, possibly, to the historian; and this may be the reason why the Middle colonies have never received historical treatment as a territorial unit. Each of them has had its representative historians, at whom no one can level the criticism of inertia. Some of their histories are admirably done and stand as monuments of scholarly attainment. The scope of these, however, is no broader, for the most part, than a single State, and in some instances it is limited to the confines of a county or a town. As a result, the local history of each colony has been adequately and even generously treated, while the intercolonial history has been neglected entirely.

The object of the present narrative is to show, first, that the Middle colonies possessed important characteristics and interests in common. For they afforded, to a greater extent than any other part of the English colonial possessions in North America, a place of refuge for the oppressed of all lands and creeds; and nothing is more characteristic of them, during the period under consideration, than the general toleration of the religious beliefs of all classes. This policy entailed, furthermore, the serious problem of assimilating a population of many nationalities. To work this conglomerate mass into a form fit for incorporation into the prospective Nation was a task different from that of any other section. Secondly, on account of these common characteristics and interests, and on account of the fact that the colonies were constantly brought into contact with one another through their many boundary disputes, they present a territorial and political unity that admits of a special and independent study.

Particular emphasis has likewise been laid upon certain other matters of intercolonial importance: namely, the growing ascendency of England over France until the successful issue of the French and Indian War; the importance of contemporary European politics whenever it throws light upon colonial events; and the causes of the American Revolution in so far as they had their roots in the early colonial period.

The narrative ends with the repeal of the Stamp Act and the passage of the Declaratory Act, when the first phase of the Revolutionary period may very well be said to have closed. The plan of the work has not admitted of footnotes. Consequently, bibliographical citations have been limited to those authorities from which important material has been quoted. Rather than make the few references to sources that insertion in the body of the text would permit, it has been considered preferable to omit them entirely.

Grateful acknowledgment is due to a friend and associate, Mr. Gordon Hall Gerould, of the Department of English, Bryn Mawr College, for reading the proofs of this book; likewise, to Miss Ala Bibb Jones, of Philadelphia, for valuable assistance in collecting materials.

FREDERICK ROBERTSON JONES.

*Bryn Mawr College, Pennsylvania.*

# CONTENTS

| CHAPTER | PAGES |
|---|---|
| EDITOR'S INTRODUCTION . . . . . . . . . | v–ix |
| AUTHOR'S PREFACE . . . . . . . . . . . | xi–xiii |

I  EARLY DUTCH SETTLEMENTS ON THE HUDSON, 1613–1647 . . . . . . . . . . 3–37

Holland falls heir to Spain's commercial supremacy. Early Dutch trading posts. Dutch East India Company. Explorations of Henry Hudson. Fort Nassau. Manhattan and Fort Amsterdam. Adrian Block. Treaty of Tawasentha. Dutch West India Company. First English protest against Dutch colonization in America. Fort Orange. First colonists. Walloons settle on Staten Island. Peter Minuit, director. Manhattan purchased. Indian troubles. Ominous difficulties with the English of New England. French schemes against New Netherland. The charter of "privileges and exemptions." The patroonship. Wouter van Twiller, director. William Kieft, director. New Netherland prospers. Aggressive policy toward the Indians. Struggle at New Amsterdam for popular government. Popular Assembly. Massacre of Indians at Pavonia. Kieft *versus* Dominie Bogardus. Kieft removed. Peter Stuyvesant, director. His contest with Kuyter and Melyn. Kieft sails for Holland. Drowned in Bristol Channel.

II  DUTCH AND SWEDISH SETTLEMENTS ON THE DELAWARE, 1623–1647 . . . . . . 39–55

Topography and colonization. Dutch and English claims to the Delaware. Expedition of Walloons sails for South River. Charter granted to Godyn and Blommaert. Colonists sail from Holland under De Vries. Zwaanendal the Unfortunate. De Vries's account of the massacre of the colonists. Patroons sell out to Dutch West India Company. Gustavus Adolphus

MIDDLE STATES AND MARYLAND

CHAPTER  PAGES

charters Swedish West India Company. Chancellor Oxenstiern draws up a plan for a company to settle and trade with America. William Usselincx appointed first director. Oxenstiern forms the Swedish South Company. Peter Minuit commissioned governor of the Swedish colony on the Delaware. Fort Christina. Swedes discouraged. Timely arrival of a relief expedition. Dutch colonists under Swedish flag. English attempts at settlement on the Delaware. Failure of the New Haven attempt. John Printz, Governor of New Sweden. Lutheran, the established church of New Sweden. John Campanius. Dutch and Swedes clash on the Delaware. Peter Stuyvesant assumes control of Dutch affairs.

III CLASH OF NATIONALITIES ON THE DELAWARE, 1621–1647 . . . . . . . . 57–73
Three-cornered struggle for the possession of the Delaware. Respective claims of the Dutch, Swedes, and English. Superiority of Dutch claim. Indefiniteness of early charters and land grants. Lord Baltimore's patent. Invalidity of Swedish claim. Renewed English attempts at settlement on the Delaware. English remonstrances to Dutch for trading on the Delaware. Serious clash between the Swedes and the English of New Haven. The quarrel reaches a climax. Stuyvesant meets at Hartford the Commissioners of the United Colonies of New England. An arbitration commission appointed. Commission makes a colorless award. Renewal of quarrel between Dutch and English with regard to Delaware territory. An expedition against New Netherland planned. An English arbitration commission visits Manhattan and confers with Stuyvesant. Complete failure of the mission.

IV MAINTENANCE OF THE STATUS QUO . . . 75–89
Reasons why open hostilities did not break out at once between the Dutch, Swedes, and English for the possession of the Delaware. Overwhelming power of English in comparison with that of the Dutch. Superiority of Dutch resources to those of the Swedes. Correspondence between Governor Winthrop and Peter Stuyvesant. International relations of the English, Dutch, and Swedes. "Unity of faith" of the three nationalities. The "ancient and loving union" between the three nations. "Their common dangers from their common enemies." The "known malice of the barbarians" to the three nationalities. Charges and counter charges of undue influence with Indians. Doubt on part

CHAPTER   PAGES

of Dutch, Swedes, and English as to the validity of their territorial claims in America. Want of unity on the part of the English colonies. Dissensions between the colonies comprising the United Colonies of New England. Summary of reasons for the delay in the outbreak of hostilities between the Dutch, Swedes, and English in America.

V   DUTCH CONQUEST OF NEW SWEDEN, 1647–1655 . . . . . . . . . . . . . 91–115

Peter Stuyvesant, Director-general of New Netherland. Deplorable condition of the colony upon his assumption of power. He asserts the power of the West India Company. Finances. Demand for a measure of popular government. "The Nine." Stuyvesant quarrels with the patroons. Brant van Slechtenhorst. Swedes on the Delaware pick quarrel with the Dutch. Printz *versus* Hudde. Swedes maltreat Dutch. Outrages reported to Stuyvesant. He adopts a conciliatory policy. Stuyvesant sends a commission to New Sweden. Stuyvesant visits Fort Nassau on South River. Attempts to settle boundary dispute by compromise. Unsuccessful. Erects Fort Casimir. Swedes protest. John Rysingh becomes Deputy Governor of New Sweden. Fort Casimir treacherously captured by the Swedes. Dutch swear allegiance to Sweden. Dutch retaliation. Stuyvesant ordered to "revenge the injury" and to "drive the Swedes from every side of the river." Stuyvesant prepares fleet and armament. The fleet sails up the Delaware. Fort Trinity captured. The surrender of Fort Christina. The Dutch pillage the Swedes. Fall of New Sweden. Swedes protest against Dutch aggression. Captain Derck Smidt. Jacquet in charge of the conquered colony. New Amstel.

VI  ENGLISH CONQUEST OF NEW NETHERLAND, 1655–1664 . . . . . . . . . . . 117–146

Passage of the first English Navigation Act. War between England and Holland. Stuyvesant prepares to defend New Netherland from a possible attack by New England. Stuyvesant's troubles. A burgher government conceded to New Amsterdam. Stuyvesant's relations with the English residents of Long Island. A *landdag* held at New Amsterdam. The director-general approved by the Dutch West India Company. Gravesend notoriously disaffected. Stuyvesant's triumph complete. The territorial claims of the Earl of Stirling and Sir Edmund Plowden. Stuyvesant practically

CHAPTER  PAGES

abandons all claim to New England territory. The capture of the *San Beninio*. Quarrel with New England. Overthrow of New Netherland imminent. Averted for a decade by end of war between Holland and England. Boundary dispute between New Netherland and Connecticut. Stuyvesant visits Boston and appears before the Commissioners of the United Colonies. The Duke of York organizes secret expedition against New Netherland. Hostile fleet appears before New Amsterdam. Stuyvesant commanded to surrender. Fall of New Netherland.

VII THE DUTCH UNDER ENGLISH RULE, 1664–
1685 . . . . . . . . . . . . 147–178

Capture of New Netherland an act of English spoliation. New Amsterdam occupied by English. "The Duke's Laws." Hostilities again precipitated between Holland and England. Peace of Breda formally cedes New Netherland to English. Witchcraft delusions. Determination of boundaries. Abolition of "burgher" distinctions. Troubles with the English towns on Long Island. War between Holland and England. Dutch fleet appears before New York. Colony recaptured by the Dutch. New Netherland prepares for an attack by New England. New Netherland restored to the English. New patent issued to the Duke of York. Mail route established. Andros lays claim to part of Connecticut. End of King Philip's war. Disaffection of the Iroquois. Andros clashes with Philip Carteret as to sovereignty over East Jersey. A legislative assembly summoned. "The Charter of Liberties and Privileges." New York divided into twelve counties. Establishment of courts.

VIII MIGRATION OF THE OPPRESSED . . . 179–209

*Walloons*—Settle on North, South, and Fresh Rivers. Beginning of Albany. Settle in Esopus. Kingston and New Paltz founded. *Puritans*—Religious controversies in New England bring many Puritans to New Netherland. Puritans in Maryland. Their intolerance. *Huguenots*—Welcomed in all parts of Dutch and English America. Many settle in New York. New Rochelle. Importance of the Huguenot advent. *Quakers*—Persecuted by Stuyvesant. Trouble in Maryland. Settlements in New Jersey. Penn's "Holy Experiment." *Mennonites*—Similar in belief to Quakers. Company formed to settle on South River. Numerous settlements in Pennsylvania. Pastorius. *Lutherans*—Oppressed by Stuyvesant.

CHAPTER  PAGES

Freedom of worship. Pennsylvania, the stronghold of Lutheranism. Torkillus. Campanius. Mühlenberg purifies and reorganizes the sect. *Jews*—Settle principally in New York and Philadelphia and seaport towns. Haym Salomon. Immigration of Portuguese Jews from Brazil; from Dutch Curaçoa. Finally permitted to settle in New Netherland. Granted civil rights. *Waldenses*—Settle on Staten Island. Settlements in Pennsylvania. *Labadists*—Their doctrines. Colony settles in Maryland. *Roman Catholics*—Settle at St. Mary's, Maryland. Adverse legislation against the Roman Catholics. Jesuits in Maryland. Roman Catholics disfranchised in Maryland. *Palatines*—Located on the Hudson. Removal to Schoharie and Mohawk valleys. Palatine Bridge. German Flats. Settlements in Maryland. The "Pennsylvania Dutch." *Acadians*—Exiled and distributed among colonies. The exiles in Maryland. *Moravians*—Settle first in Georgia. Found Bethlehem and Nazareth, Pennsylvania. *Tunkers*—Settle at Germantown, Pennsylvania. The "Harmless People."

IX  LORD BALTIMORE'S EXPERIMENT, 1632–1685 . . . . . . . . . . . 211–239

George Calvert plans an "asylum for conscience." The charter of Avalon. Beginnings of Maryland. Cecilius Calvert's charter. Virginia opposes the charter. Leonard Calvert leads an expedition to St. Mary's. Quarrel between Lord Baltimore and Claiborne. A naval battle. Claiborne and Ingle rebellion. Baltimore's government overthrown. The first Assembly. The government remodelled. Seat of government changed to Annapolis. The colony restored to its allegiance to the proprietary. Passage of the Act of Toleration. Puritan commissioners seize the government. Proprietary rights practically abolished. Act of Toleration repealed. Régime of religious intolerance. Proprietary reinstated in government. Act of Toleration made perpetual. Fendall's rebellion. Boundary disputes. Herman's map of Maryland. Governor Calvert and William Penn confer with regard to boundary disputes. A partial settlement.

X  EVOLUTION OF NEW JERSEY, 1614–1685 . 241–262

Early grants. Dutch settle Jersey City and Bergen. Colonists from New Haven settle parts of West Jersey. The Delaware Company's settlement. Bergen a municipality. The "Elizabeth Town Patent." Albania. New Jersey part

MIDDLE STATES AND MARYLAND

CHAPTER                                                              PAGES

of grant to the Duke of York. Territory between North and
South Rivers granted to Lord John Berkeley and Sir George
Carteret. Philip Carteret leads an expedition to New Jersey.
The "Concessions and Agreements." A New England
exodus. Newark founded. The "Fundamental Agree-
ment." Trouble with the Indians. First Assembly meets
at Elizabethtown. Land titles in dispute. The Monmouth
Patent. East and West Jersey definitely separated. The
Jerseys again under the Dutch. Restored to the English by
the Treaty of Westminster. Quarrel between Andros and
Governor Carteret as to territorial jurisdiction. William
Penn interests himself in West Jersey. Liberty of person
and freedom of conscience declared. Land purchased from
Indians. Fenwick leads an expedition of colonists to the Delaware. Founds Salem. The "Quintipartite Deed." Boun-
daries determined between East and West Jersey. The
"First" or "Yorkshire Tenth." The "Second" or
"London Tenth." Burlington settled. The Byllinge-
Jennings dispute. "Certain Fundamental Principles" of gov-
ernment. Dispute about excise with New York. Settled in
favor of West Jersey. The Duke of York relinquishes claim
to West Jersey. East Jersey likewise made independent of
New York. The Council of Proprietors. East Jersey at
odds with its governor. James II. attacks charters of East and
West Jersey. Placed under jurisdiction of New York.

XI  PENN'S "HOLY EXPERIMENT," 1681–1685 . 263–281
Cromwell and religious toleration. William Penn becomes
a Quaker. Decides to alleviate condition of Friends by establishing a colony in America. Penn's charter. Boundaries
of the grant. "Lower Counties" secured. Colony named
"Pennsylvania." First colonists arrive. Penn's "Frame of
Government." Penn visits province. The "Holy Experiment" fairly launched. Chester founded. An Assembly
held. The Great Law of Pennsylvania. Penn selects site
of Philadelphia. Draws plans for city. The Shackamaxon
Treaty. The first General Assembly. The Lower Counties annexed to the province. The Great Law. Penn
visits Lord Baltimore in Maryland. Second Assembly.
Acts of the Assembly. The Bill of Settlement. Beginning of struggle for power by Assembly. First meeting
under new Frame of Government. Immigration to Pennsylvania. State of province. First school. Penn returns
to England. Executive power intrusted to the Provincial

Council. Dissensions in the province. Thomas Lloyd impeached; elected president of the Council. Dissatisfaction in Lower Counties; they are separated from the province.

XII  THE REVOLUTION OF 1688 . . . . . 283–308

Louis XIV. plots the overthrow of New York. Plan of James II. for union of the northern colonies. Repudiation of Charter of Liberties. Andros becomes governor of all New England. Government of New York and the Jerseys merged into that of New England. Boston the capital. Liberty of conscience accorded. Freedom of press curtailed. Conference with the Iroquois at Albany. The rule of Andros in New England insufferable. Revolution of 1688. Immediate effect of accession of William and Mary upon the American colonies. Andros arrested in Boston. Penn accused of sympathy with the Jacobite plots. Severance of political union between the Jerseys and New York. Rebellion in New York. The anti-Catholic movement. An insurrection. Jacob Leisler, dictator of New York; he addresses William and Mary; summons a committee of safety. A popular convention. Disturbances at Albany. Leisler's power absolute. The French send raiding parties into English colonies. Schenectady massacre. The first American Congress. Abortive expedition to Canada against the French and Indians. People rebel against Leisler. A representative Assembly called. Leisler compelled to surrender; charged with treason and murder, he is executed, with Milborne. Revolution in Maryland. The "Papist Plot." John Coode's revolt. The capture of St. Mary's. The Protestant "Associators." Maryland becomes a royal province. Church of England established.

XIII  THE MIDDLE COLONIES AFTER THE FLIGHT
OF JAMES II., 1692–1714 . . . . . . 309–334

New York's puppet governors. Negotiations with the Mohawks at Albany. Military expedition into Canada. The Leislerians and the anti-Leislerians. Pennsylvania and Delaware added to New York government. Penn reinstated in his proprietary. New charter granted. Proprietary, Churchman, and Lloyd parties. The Lower Counties definitively separated from Pennsylvania. Foundation of Trinity Church, New York. Prevalence of piracy. Captain Kidd. Affairs in the Jerseys. School Act. Internal troubles. Patents of East and West Jersey surrendered to Queen Anne. Distinction

| CHAPTER | PAGES |

between East and West Jersey ceases. Consolidation with New York. Assemblies distinct. Quarrels between the governor and the Assembly. Bills of credit. Anne's law regulating the currency. Maryland as a royal province. New York negro plot of 1712.

XIV GROWTH OF AN ARISTOCRATIC COLONY,
1714–1754 . . . . . . . . . . 335–367
Solid growth of New York. Slavery. Trade and Commerce. Disagreements between the governor and the Assembly. Conference with Indian sachems at Albany. Congress of governors at Albany. Chief Justice Morris removed from office. Struggle for popular rights. Bradford's *Gazette* *versus* Zenger's *Weekly Journal*. Libels. Trial and acquittal of Zenger. Triumph of freedom of the press. Negro plot of 1741. King George's War. The capture of Louisburg. Saratoga destroyed. Peace of Aix-la-Chapelle. Quarrels between the governor and the Assembly. Parliament plans to assume supreme control of the colonies. King's College chartered. College of New Jersey founded. Queen's College established.

XV GROWTH OF A DEMOCRATIC PROVINCE,
1714–1754 . . . . . . . . . . 369–381
An era of good feeling. Bills of credit issued. Governor Cosby clashes with the Assembly. A rapid succession of executives. New Jersey separated from New York. Treaty with Indians at Easton, Pennsylvania. Kaleidoscopic change of administrations. William Franklin the last of the royal governors of New Jersey. Progress of the colony. Schools and churches erected. Dutch manners and habits prevail in parts of New Jersey. English and French tastes predominate. The professions. New Jersey agricultural. Social pleasures.

XVI GROWTH OF A QUAKER COMMONWEALTH,
1714–1754 . . . . . . . . . . 383–420
Disgraceful conduct of Governor Evans. The Assembly refuses to pass a militia law. Governor Evans attempts to prevent the free navigation of the Delaware. Death of William Penn. State of Pennsylvania at Penn's death. Governor Keith meets the Assemblies of Lower Counties and province. Relations with the Indians. A militia law passed. Paper currency issued. Governor Keith defies the proprietary.

Good will between the governor and the Assembly. New issues of paper money. John Penn visits the colony. Boundary dispute with Maryland becomes critical. The Scotch-Irish. Quakers oppose war measures. Benjamin Franklin. Favors paper money. *Pennsylvania Gazette* and *Poor Richard's Almanac*. University of Pennsylvania founded. The Bradfords and printing. More bills of credit issued. Scruples of the Quakers against war. French invade Pennsylvania.

XVII DEVELOPMENT OF MARYLAND, 1714–
1754 . . . . . . . . . . . . 421–444

Sir Lionel Copley, first royal governor. Severe measures against the Roman Catholics. Capital changed from St. Mary's to Annapolis. John Coode. Maryland little affected by Queen Anne's War. Benedict Leonard Calvert abjures the Roman Catholic faith. Province restored to the proprietary. Progress of the province. Towns "staked out." Baltimore founded. Urgency of the Maryland-Pennsylvania boundary difficulties. Baltimore Hundred in dispute. Petty boundary warfare carried on. Boundary commissioners appointed by Maryland and Pennsylvania. Border warfare. Provisional boundary line agreed upon. Commissioners again appointed to settle the dispute. The survey on Fenwick's Island. Difficulties encountered. Thomas Fenwick. Condition of the province at outbreak of French and Indian War. Marked industrial improvement. Social conditions.

XVIII THE FRENCH AND INDIAN WAR, 1754–
1763 . . . . . . . . . . . 445–473

Peace of Aix-la-Chapelle of the nature of a truce. The final struggle. The Albany Convention. Plans for a federal union proposed. Analysis of the plan adopted. Rejected by the Board of Trade and by the colonies. Reasons for failure. War between France and Great Britain. Three expeditions planned against France in America. Congress of colonial governors at Alexandria. Braddock's expedition. French plan of defence. Capture of Fort Du Quesne. The war in the north. Plan of Louis XIV. to conquer New York. Johnson's successes. Forts William Henry and Edward. Massacre of garrison of Fort William Henry. Louisburg captured. British defeated in advance upon Ticonderoga. Fort Frontenac captured. Pitt at the helm. French give way upon all sides. Surrender of Quebec. End of French power in America. Interest of colonies in the war.

| CHAPTER | PAGES |
|---|---|

Financing the war. The Quakers and non-resistance. Maryland's slight interest in the war. Establishment of northern boundary between Maryland and Pennsylvania. Importance of Mason and Dixon's boundary line. New York's part in the war. Bills of credit issued. New Jersey's participation in the war. Terms of the Treaty of Paris. Significance of the accession of George III.

XIX ASSUMPTION OF PARLIAMENTARY CONTROL, 1763–1765 . . . . . . . 475–507

Prophecies of Vergennes and Choiseul. The spirit of unity among the colonies. Colonies financially embarrassed. Reimbursement in specie. Conflicting theories of sovereignty. British government decides the colonies must bear part of financial burden caused by war. Revenues of the colonies. Grenville decides upon Parliamentary taxation of colonies for revenue. The Stamp Act passed. Native Americans appointed stamp collectors. Opposition to Stamp Act in colonies. The "Sons of Liberty." Attitude of New York. A crisis in New England. Attacks upon the stamp collectors. The Stamp Act Congress. A declaration of rights and grievances. Arrival of stamps in New York. Non-importation agreements. The Stamp Act riot. Maryland's stamp collector driven from the province. Arrival of stamped paper for Maryland. Maryland Assembly passes resolutions declaratory of "the constitutional rights and privileges of the freemen" of the province. Benjamin Franklin examined by a Parliamentary committee. The *Royal Charlotte*, bringing stamps for New Jersey, Maryland, and Pennsylvania, meets with unexpected opposition. Lawyers' opposition in New Jersey. The Sons of Liberty active in the colony. Changes in British ministry. The Stamp Act repealed. Principle of taxation maintained by British ministry. The Declaratory Act. Statues in honor of George III. and Pitt voted in New York. Rejoicings throughout the colonies. Significance of the repeal of the Stamp Act. Importance of the Middle colonies in the coming struggle for independence. Summary.

CHRONOLOGICAL TABLE . . . . . . . . . 509–518

LIST OF ILLUSTRATIONS . . . . . . . . . 519–523

# THE COLONIZATION
## OF THE
## MIDDLE STATES AND MARYLAND

JONES

# CHAPTER I

## EARLY DUTCH SETTLEMENTS ON THE HUDSON, 1613–1647

"THOSE Dutch are strong people. They raised their land out of a marsh, and went on for a long period of time breeding cows and making cheese, and might have gone on with their cows and cheese till doomsday. But Spain comes over and says: 'We want you to believe in St. Ignatius.' 'Very sorry,' replied the Dutch, 'but we can't.' 'God! but you *must*,' says Spain; and they went about with guns and swords to make the Dutch believe in St. Ignatius. Never made them believe in him, but did succeed in breaking their own vertebral column forever, and raising the Dutch into a great nation."

Thus does Carlyle devote a number of teeth of his Teutonic saw to the Spanish, whose persecution of the Dutch made possible the extension of the latter's commercial power to America. Emerging strong from the fight for religious liberty; compelled by the physical condition of their soil to become a maritime nation—the Dutch studied the weak and strong points of Spain, and studying, saw, and seeing, soon overcame her.

"Brave Little Holland" fell heir to Spain's commercial supremacy and turned it to a far better account than that decaying nation had done. Not until the passage of Oliver Cromwell's Acts of Trade in the middle of the seventeenth century was Holland's commercial supremacy threatened.

She was the carrier of the larger part of the world's commerce; consequently she was the first to see the anomalies of the commercial principles of mercantilism. While England and other countries were making ineffectual laws prohibitory of the exportation of the precious metals, Holland was removing all restrictions to their natural flow. It was perfectly evident to her that commerce was not a gambling scheme by which one country lost and the other gained; or that the gain or loss depended upon the astuteness or the reverse of the gambling nations. It soon became evident to a commercial nation like Holland that commerce was an advantage to both trading nations; that one received fair value for its superfluity of commodities while, at the same time, it received those commodities from abroad which were in great demand.

It was perfectly reasonable then that Holland, the destined carrier of the world's commerce, should take early advantage of the discoveries of the Spanish, Portuguese, English, and French explorers of the century succeeding the landfall of Columbus. During the years 1497 and 1498, John and Sebastian Cabot, having discovered Newfoundland, sailed along the coast of North America from Labrador past what was to become the port of New York, and may have proceeded as far south as the coast of what is now Florida. They claimed for their sovereign, Henry VII. of England, under whose commission they sailed, the "entire territory which they occasionally saw at a distance." This discovery became the sole historical basis for the English claim to the Hudson River valley in the struggle of the nations that took place during the third quarter of the seventeenth century.

In the spring of 1524, the Florentine, Giovanni da Verrazano, coasting north from the Carolinas under the French flag of Francis I., probably entered the harbor of what is now New York. He gives a very interesting description of that bay, but made no landing. The first Dutch ships to venture upon American seas were sent out in 1510. In that year, Charles V. had granted an island in America to the Sieur Beveren, who "dispatched two armed vessels in search of his new estate." Furthermore, in 1512, Anthony Molock ventured to the Cape Verd Islands in a Dutch vessel. We may say, in fact, that by the time Charles V. came into possession of the Low Countries, Dutch vessels were no uncommon sight on the waters of the New World.

The year 1566 was a very important one for Holland, commercially as well as politically. That year, Philip II. of Spain determined to root out the Reformation from the Low Countries. As a result, in 1567 seven of the eleven provinces of the Spanish Netherlands revolted. This lost to Holland the advantages she had enjoyed as a part of a great and powerful commercial nation. For, by an edict, the subjects of Spain and Portugal were prohibited from trading with the rebellious provinces.

The loss to the Low Countries was only temporary, however, for in the end it led to the development of the Dutch East India trade. This, in turn, was largely instrumental in causing ventures to be made in the western seas. In fact, two citizens of Amsterdam sent several vessels to the West Indies in the latter part of 1597. The next year the city of Amsterdam despatched more ships to the same waters. Furthermore, it is held that in the same year several Dutchmen in the employ of the Greenland Company actually built two small forts for protection against the Indians during the winter months on territory destined to become New Netherland. One of these forts is said to have been built on North River and the other on South River—that is, on what are now Hudson and Delaware Rivers.

In 1602, the States General obliged the various trading companies to incorporate under the title of the East India Company. This was done for political as well as commercial reasons. And what is more to the purpose, its incorporation was one of the most important reasons for the formation of that later trading association, the Dutch West India Company. It was not until the early fall of 1609, however, that the Dutch made a serious attempt to extend their influence to American waters, and then it was under the leadership of an Englishman. It was Henry Hudson's third unsuccessful attempt to find a northwest passage to China. The first and second attempts had been made under the English flag, and the third was under that of Holland. After trying ineffectually to discover a route to China in the latitudes of Newfoundland, Penobscot Bay, Cape Cod, and Chesapeake and Delaware Bays, he anchored in the waters of "The Great North River of New Netherland." This was on the morning of September 4th. After sailing up the river almost as far as the site of Albany in his endeavor to discover a route to China, Hudson returned to England, and shortly after his arrival there he severed his connection with the Dutch East India Company.

The conditions in Holland were ripe for taking advantage of the explorations of Henry Hudson. The Dutch had harried the Spaniards, their tyrants, even in "the remotest recesses of their extensive possessions." Jacob Heemskerk dealt a crushing blow to their maritime supremacy in 1607. As a result of this victory, Spain was more than ready to conclude a truce in the following year. In fact, the independence of the Dutch was practically if not technically recognized and the nation was free to push forward its commerce.

It did not take the practical Dutchman long to realize the great prospect opened up to him in America. For twoscore years and more he had not had the opportunity of directing his trading energies into the proper channels. The Spanish duel had entirely occupied his time. Now, however, the opportunity was offered and the place and the materials. Europe needed furs and needed them badly. The supply had been drawn from Russia at considerable cost and in limited quantities. Now they could be had in America in abundance and in exchange for the merest baubles.

Because of this, an expedition was sent out by some Amsterdam merchants in 1610. The ships were loaded with a varied cargo of goods that would most likely attract the eye of the savage or appeal to his practical sense. So successful was the expedition that others were sent out at frequent intervals during the next five years. They also proved very remunerative.

The Dutch showed their practical sense in the selection made for the first sites of their trading posts. The magnificent harbor approaches to New York City would have impressed the explorer of any nation as admirably suited to a commercial station. But the early Dutch settlers were commercial only to the extent of buying furs from the Indians at small cost and shipping them to Holland for manufacture. In consequence, the magnificence of the harbor did not impress the early Dutch settlers as much as did the possibilities for traffic afforded by Hudson River. Here was a great river piercing the very territorial centre of the fur-trading Indians and navigable for Dutch ships at least one hundred and sixty-six miles. Not far from the mouth of the river was an island about thirteen and one-half miles long and varying in width from a few hundred yards at each end to two and one-quarter miles, the whole comprising about twenty-two square miles or fourteen thousand and eighty acres. The shores of this island were swept by the great river and its tributary and a continuation of the great sound. The water upon three sides was naturally adapted to harbor purposes. The island was admirably situated for commanding the traffic of North River and its tributaries. In fact, it is probable that Adrian Block, another Dutch explorer, visited Manhattan, made a landing, and established a trading station as early as 1611. This was protected by two small forts.

By reason of its favorable position, Manhattan soon became the headquarters of the traders under the superintendence of Hendrick Christiansen. Under his guidance, the whole country was scoured, even to the exploring of the smallest creeks and rivulets, in the hope of promoting the fur trade. Christiansen was interrupted in his efforts by a most portentous event. In 1613, Captain Samuel Argall, of Virginia, returning from an attack upon Port Royal in Acadia, decided to stop over at Manhattan. By way of asserting the priority of his own claim to Manhattan, he compelled the Dutch trader "to submit himself and his plantation to the king of England and to agree to pay tribute in token of his dependence on the English crown."

No doubt this interruption to the Dutch fur traffic led to a movement to secure the exclusive right to the trade of the new country. In answer to a formal petition, the States General passed an ordinance, March 27, 1614, having that end in view. This gave a practical monopoly of the fur traffic to any persons making new discoveries. The monopoly was to last four voyages. The ordinance caused considerable activity among Dutch merchants, particularly those of Amsterdam and Hoorn. Five ships were sent out almost immediately under Adrian Block, Hendrick Christiansen, and Captain Cornelius Jacobsen May.

Block's vessel was burned shortly after reaching Manhattan. He constructed a yacht and continued his explorations along East River, and up Connecticut River as far as latitude forty-one degrees forty-eight minutes—calling it Fresh River. May explored southward as far as the Delaware capes. On their return, these three explorers made a report to the States General and submitted a map in which the new country is called "New Netherland" for the first time (October 11, 1614). A special grant was made in favor of the interested parties, and the trading association was named the United Netherlands Company.

Active preparations were now made to promote the enterprise to its fullest capacity. A trading house thirty-six by twenty-six feet was erected on an island at the head of navigation on the west shore of the great river, just below the present city of Albany. A strong stockade fifty feet square was built around the house, and the whole was encircled by a moat eighteen feet wide. A primitive battery of two pieces of cannon and eleven stone guns mounted on swivels was manned by a garrison of ten or twelve men.

Almost at the same time, Christiansen erected another fort on an elevated spot on the southern extremity of the island of Manhattan, nearly on the site of an insignificant establishment erected in 1613. Thus were established in 1614 Fort Nassau, at the head of navigation, and Fort Amsterdam at the mouth of the Hudson. The post at the mouth of the river was the centre of the activities of the Dutch. Here the ships of the new company came every year to bring supplies and trading goods. Here the traders at the advance post up the river brought peltries and carried back the trinkets and cloths for the Indians. The ships returned to Holland heavily freighted with valuable furs. Fort Amsterdam became the factor between Holland and the fierce Indian tribes like the Mohawks. Fort Nassau was the advance post, finely situated for tapping the fur resources of the upper Hudson, Mohawk, and Champlain valleys— even from "the distant castles of the Five Nations to the hunting grounds of the Minquas."

The mission of the Dutch in America was trade. Successful trade necessitates peaceful relations between the parties engaged in trafficking. This was the constant object of the first Dutch settlers. It is evidenced in the very earliest relations between the Dutch and the Indians. One particular event proved of continental and international importance. This was the treaty of Tawasentha, between the Dutch on the one hand and the powerful Iroquois and their allies on the other hand. This treaty with the Five Nations was momentous in its consequences, not only to the Dutch colony, but to the whole country. On a hill called Tawassgunshu by the Indians, on the banks of the Tawasentha, or Norman's Kill, this treaty of alliance and peace was consummated. The belt of peace was held as a sign of union; the calumet was smoked, and the tomahawk was buried; and the Dutch promised to build a church over the buried tomahawk to prevent its being dug up.

Here, two miles below the present site of Albany, after the abandonment of Fort Nassau, the Dutch under Jacob Eelkens had already built a fortified trading house. The treaty was agreed to the same year, 1617, and remained unchanged for twenty-eight years. It was renewed in 1645, and was continued without any breach on either side till the English gained the country.

This was the auspicious beginning of those friendly relations between the Dutch and the Iroquois confederation. England, on the conquest of New Netherland, received it as an important legacy. During the entire continuance of that mighty duel between England and France in two continents, the advantages of that primitive treaty were manifest. The French, under Champlain, had aroused the animosity of these Indians. The Iroquois stood as a barrier between the two combating forces. When the Iroquois were not definitely leagued with the English they were, for the most part, neutral. Where the two great contestants were so evenly matched in many respects as were the English and French in America, this powerful neutral confederation held the balance of power. Speculation is dangerous, but it is safe to assume that had the Iroquois been enemies of the English rather than friends or neutrals, the final expulsion of the French from North America would have been indefinitely delayed; and, as a consequence, the independence of the thirteen English colonies. It is impossible to exaggerate the importance of the neutrality of the Iroquois in this great struggle. It is well not to underrate the importance of this treaty of Tawasentha, which led gradually to that friendly neutrality.

The exclusive grant to the New Netherland Company expired by its own limitations on January 1, 1618, and the States General refused to grant a renewal. The success of the East India Company led to a movement for the establishment of a West India Company. As early as 1602 the suggestion had been made that such a company would prove a success. William Usselincx, a man well versed in Spanish-American trade, was the principal projector.

It is very interesting to note what were some of the reasons urged for the formation of such a company. Stress was laid upon the Dutch grievances against the Spaniards; the fertility of the soil and the friendliness of the people of the newly discovered land; the desire of the Indians to be allied with the Dutch against the Spaniards; that these Indians were not the savages most Europeans thought them; the abundance of the salt to be had for the taking; and last, the urgent calls to Christianize these same savages. All were invited to subscribe to the stocks of the venture. In fact, the project met with general approval. A charter was drawn up, and was being duly considered by their high mightinesses, when peace or truce proposals were received from the archduke which temporarily interrupted the progress of the scheme.

The return of the expedition of Henry Hudson in 1609 revived the agitation for the incorporation of the new Company. But conflicting interests of those engaged in the monopolistic trade of New Netherland resulted in neutralizing the efforts of all contestants. Further agitation for the old monopolistic privileges would have proved fruitless, however, for in 1621 was chartered that "great armed commercial association," the Dutch West India Company. It was modelled after its predecessor, the Dutch East India Company. In fact, the former was designed to coöperate with the latter in the charter-avowed objects of extending national commerce, of promoting colonization, of crushing piracy, but, above all, of humbling the pride and might of Spain. For executive efficiency, the Company was divided into five branches, or chambers. These were established in the different cities of the Netherlands, and their managers were styled Lords Directors. The Amsterdam branch was the most important, and to it were assigned all affairs relating to New Netherland. The general supervision of the Company was in the hands of a board of Nineteen

Delegates. After 1629, nine of these were from the branch at Amsterdam; four from Zealand; two from Meuse; and one each from Friesland, the North Department, and Groningen. The nineteenth was appointed by the States General.

Even a most cursory review of the privileges of this corporation would indicate its enormous latent power. It had exclusive control of the trade of Africa from the Tropic of Cancer to the Cape of Good Hope and the coast of America from the Straits of Magellan to the extreme north. It was authorized to form alliances offensive and defensive with Indian tribes, and was obligated to advance in every way possible the material welfare of the lands taken up for commercial and colonization purposes. The Company was given power to make laws and to administer them; to build forts; to declare war and to make peace with the consent of the States General. With the approval of the States General, the Company could appoint a director-general and all other necessary officers, whether civil, military, or judicial; the only qualification being that they should swear allegiance to the States General as well as to the Company. This director-general and his council had judicial, legislative, and executive power. Some supposed an appeal to Holland was permitted, but that privilege was never recognized in practice. The will of the Company was to be law, as expressed in its instructions and ordinances, marine or military. In cases not provided for, the Roman Law, the imperial statutes of Charles V., the "edicts, resolutions, and customs of the Fatherland were to be received as the paramount rule of action."

The States General guaranteed freedom of navigation and traffic within the territorial limits prescribed in the charter. Also, the same power agreed to furnish a million of guilders and, in case of necessity, a certain minutely defined naval armament. The naval armament was to be furnished only on condition that the Company should maintain a much larger naval establishment and support the whole. The combined forces were to be under an admiral appointed and instructed by the States General.

The charter was purely that of a commercial company with the belligerent end in view of taking every opportunity of dealing Spain a severe blow; and it contained no provisions favorable to individual freedom; nor did it provide for the welfare of prospective colonists in America. It must be said, however, that in this respect it did not differ from the patents establishing the only existing colonies in America at that time, namely, Florida, Canada, and Virginia.

These, then, were the powers of the governing corporation that controlled the affairs and guided the destinies of New Netherland until the passing of the Dutch sovereignty. Not until two years after its incorporation—that is, in 1623—did the Company begin operations. Serious obstacles had arisen and it was found desirable to amplify the charter. Also, various explanations were added. The approval of the States General was finally secured on June 21, 1623.

Amidst all these preparations a most ominous note of warning was sounded. During the two years in which the West India Company's charter was in an embryonic state, Dutch private merchants continued to make remunerative trips to Manhattan and other North American points. The authority to make these ventures was had under a provision continuing the old license under which traders had previously engaged in trafficking with the New World.

The remunerative quality of this trade did not fail to excite jealousy on the part of Englishmen who were interested in Virginia and New England. From the time of the voyage of the Cabots, England had asserted an unostentatious claim to the whole North American coast, from the Spanish possessions in the south to those of the French in the north. At this time, 1621, this claim was being asserted with considerable vigor by those interested in the English colonies on the triple grounds of "first discovery, occupation, and possession." In support of this contention, these individuals exhibited their charters and letters patent.

The knowledge that a great and powerful Dutch commercial company had been chartered led those especially interested in English claims in America to bestir themselves in taking definite action. They presented a remonstrance to James I., who, through the Privy Council, instructed the British ambassador at The Hague to make representations with reference to these proposed invasions of English rights. There is little doubt but that this protest was the first "official assertion by the British government of the illegality of the Dutch settlement on the continent."

The British ambassador made the protest in a perfunctory manner, and the States General received it in an equally perfunctory manner. In fact, it could not be shown that the Dutch had actually made any settlements within the bounds of the territory under dispute, although it was found that they had made discoveries. The wrangle—if, indeed, this mere formal protest could be properly so called—was terminated for the time being by the death of James I. The incident is important not so much by reason of any immediate danger of the English taking material steps to assume possible possession of New Netherland as for its bearing upon subsequent Dutch-English relations. When taken in the light of the Argall incident of 1613,—to which reference has been made,—together with subsequent incidents of like character, the protest assumes an importance out of all due proportion to its bearing upon the period under discussion. It is but one of the links in the chain of evidence adduced to support a continuous English claim to the territory settled by the Dutch under the name New Netherland. The validity of this claim and the relative merits of that of the Dutch are subjects that will be treated at length in another chapter.

By 1623, the West India Company had finished its preparations and had drawn up the articles of agreement between the managers and other adventurers. The territory was made into a province and "invested with the armorial bearings of an earl." The first colony to New

Netherland sent out by the Dutch West India Company was under the auspices of the chamber of Amsterdam, under whose superintendence the province was placed. In March, 1623, the two-hundred-and-sixty-ton ship *New Netherland* sailed from Holland, and after a voyage of two months arrived off Manhattan. The colonists were, for the most part, Walloons. They were of French extraction, dwelling in the southern provinces of Holland, and had originally intended to immigrate to Virginia, but had been refused advantageous terms. The expedition was under the superintendence of Cornelius Jacobsen May.

At the mouth of the Hudson were found two vessels—a Frenchman and the Dutch yacht *Mackerel*. The latter had been despatched the preceding year for purposes of reconnaissance. It had traded with the Indians up the Hudson and had returned in time to meet the first colonists. The captain of the French vessel insisted on taking possession of the territory in the name of the French king, but he was persuaded from doing so by a timely display of cannon by the *Mackerel*.

The passengers of the *New Netherland* were distributed at strategic points in the three great river valleys. Eight men were left at Manhattan; two families and six men were sent to Fresh River (now the Connecticut); a party was settled on the west shore of Long Island; and several families were settled at a spot in the vicinity of the present town of Gloucester, New Jersey, where they erected Fort Nassau. The last-mentioned was the first settlement of Europeans on the Delaware, or South River, as it was then called. A majority of the colonists, however, or about eighteen families, under the leadership of Adrian Joris, a director under May, continued up Hudson River. They erected Fort Orange upon the site laid out the preceding year. This site was on the west bank of the river, a few miles north of the redoubt which had been erected in 1618 on Tawasentha Creek—about thirty-six Dutch miles from the island of Manhattan.

These families were not colonists in the strict sense of the word. They had no well-defined intention of settling down and cultivating the soil. They were rather Company servants engaged in the purchase and preparation of furs for shipment. Some of them returned home after the expiration of their term of service. It was not until several years later that colonists began to come in earnest. By the end of the first year, Joris returned with a cargo of valuable furs. In 1625, Peter Eversen Hulft, of Amsterdam, sent out three vessels at his own risk, laden with seeds, stock, and farming implements. When William Verhulst assumed direction of the colony in the same year, the population had grown approximately to two hundred persons.

The colony was now beginning to assume a more permanent aspect. This was particularly true in the following year, 1626, when Peter Minuit, of Wesel in Westphalia, came out as Director-general of New Netherland. A colony of Walloons, in the meantime, had settled at first on Staten Island. Later on, they removed to the northwest extremity of Long Island at a point called Wahlebocht, or the "bay of the foreigners"—now corrupted into Wallabout. Subsequently, these settlers spread westward to the extremity of the island which was called "Breukelen"—now Brooklyn—after a Dutch village of that name on the river Veght in the province of Utrecht.

The government of the colony was now placed in the hands of Minuit and his council of five. This council, with the director-general, had manifold powers. It exercised supreme executive, legislative, and judicial authority, both civil and criminal—subject, of course, to the Company in Holland. The prosecuting officer was the *schout fiscal*, who played the triple rôle of sheriff, attorney-general, and supervisor of customs.

Minuit signalized the beginning of his administration by purchasing Manhattan from the Indians (1626). There were about twenty-two thousand acres, for which the thrifty Dutchmen paid in truck the sum of sixty guilders, or, in the

Hooghe Mogende Heeren

Hier is gisteren t'Schip t'wapen van Amsterdam aengekomen is den 23 September uyt Nieu Nederlant geseylt uyt de Reviere Mauritius: rapporteert dat ons volck daer kloeck is, in vrede leven. Sijne Vrouwen hebben oock kinderen aldaer gebaert, hebben t'eylant Manhattes van de wilden gekocht, voor de waerde van 60. guld: is groot 11000 morgen. Hebben alle koren gesaeyt met gesaeyt, ende half Augusto gemayt. Daer van sijnde de monsterkens van zomerkoren, als taruwe, Rogge, Haver, Gerst, Boeckweyt, Knarisaet, Boontjens en Vlas.

Het Cargasoen van't sz schip is.

7246 Bever vellen
178½ Otter vellen
675. Otter vellen
48. Mincke vellen
36 Catlosse vellen
33 Mincken
34 Ratte vellekens:

Veele Eycken balcken, en Noten gout

Hier mede

Hooge Mogende Heeren, sijt de Almogende in Ghnade bevolen

In Amsterdam den 5en novem a° 1626.

Uwe Hoo: Mo: Dienstwillighe

P. Schaghen

Letter stating that Manhattan Island had been purchased from the "wild men" for the value of sixty guilders. *From the original in the Royal Archives at The Hague, Holland.*

money of to-day, about $120. The Indians did not understand the European principle of alienation of land. Therefore, many transactions similar to this transference of Manhattan smacked somewhat of the shrewd bargain.

About the same time, Eghquaons, or Staten Island, and Governor's Island were secured in very much the same way. On the south point of the newly acquired Manhattan a block house was erected. Red cedar palisades surrounded it, and it appeared formidable enough to the Dutch to be called Fort Amsterdam. It served likewise as the executive building, and may be called the first capital of New Netherland. The island was then a "mass of tangled, frowning forest, fringed with melancholy marshes." Near the site of Canal Street "the primeval forest resounded nightly with the growl of bears, the wailing of panthers, and the yelp of wolves, while serpents lurked in the dense underbrush."

No sooner had the little colony been fairly launched than it began to have a foretaste of the difficulties that were in store for it in the future. Troubles with the Indians were fortunately few, and those that were encountered were due to the indiscretions of the Dutch themselves. On the other hand, the little colony was in no manner responsible for the jealousy of the English and the silent schemings of the French. A word concerning each of these difficulties:

Between the Mohawks and the Mohegans there was deadly enmity. The Mohawks were Iroquois, and the Mohegans were Algonquins. The former dwelt on the west side and the latter on the east side of the great river. In 1626 a war party of Mohegans crossed to Fort Orange and induced the commander, Krieckebeeck, to lead six men of the garrison in an attack upon the Mohawks. The Mohawks did not wait to be attacked, but did the attacking. Krieckebeeck was slain with an arrow; three of his men were tomahawked, and the Mohegans were put to flight with great slaughter. The Dutch say Tymen Bonwensen "was eaten by the savages after he had been well roasted." The Mohawks justified their actions on the ground that they had been wantonly attacked and had merely defended themselves. The new commander saw the strength of the defence, renewed the old treaty of alliance, and the incident was closed. It was thought advisable, however, to remove the families from Fort Orange to Manhattan, and to replace them with a garrison of sixteen men under Krol, one of the recently arrived "consolers of the sick." This Indian trouble had both a good and a bad result. It taught the Dutch not to meddle in intertribal quarrels; but it no doubt kept settlers away for about two years. And because of it the little colony on the Delaware was deserted and operations were suspended on the Connecticut.

The trouble with the English was at the time of a very mild character, but in the light of subsequent events it was one of those ominous clouds that forebode a storm. We must not lose sight of the fact that during this time protests from the colonists in New England continued to pour in at the English court. The English had been settled at New Plymouth for six or seven years. It was not long before the thrifty Yankee and the commercial Dutchman heard of each other through the Indians. Director Minuit transmitted a very courteous letter to Governor Bradford, of New Plymouth, offering to engage in a mutually remunerative commerce. Governor Bradford replied just as courteously but naively asserted the English claims to New Netherland by warning the Dutch against vessels belonging to the other English plantations which were commissioned to capture and expel all strangers trading within the limits of forty degrees. To this communication the authorities at Fort Amsterdam replied courteously, though firmly maintaining their right to the territory in question. They cited the fact that for twenty-six years they had authority to trade in that territory direct from the States General and the Prince of Orange. This claim of legality to their title was accompanied by a runlet of sugar and two Holland cheeses. The latter were thankfully though cautiously received. Bradford suggested an arbitration commission to consider the mutual advantages of trade agreement. The Dutch eagerly accepted this invitation, and Isaac de Razier was sent as ambassador and arrived "honorably attended with a noise of trumpets." This was "the first meeting in the solitude of the New World between friendly colonists of two allied European nations." As a result, a brisk trade sprang up between the English and the Dutch colonists.

The question of jurisdiction, however, was only settled temporarily. The Company obtained from Charles I. in 1627 an order in council declaring that by the treaty of Southampton all English ports were open to the Dutch. This protected Dutch vessels trading in New Netherland from seizure by English cruisers.

In the meantime, the French were planning the extension of their power in America. In 1624, Richelieu, with consummate genius having overcome all obstacles, had taken upon himself the sole direction of the policy of the government of Louis XIII. That policy now began to assume a certain degree of consistency. For the most part, it was necessarily concerned with domestic and European affairs. But Richelieu was not unmindful of the future importance of America, and outlined a policy of large extensions of power in that direction. Little or no headway was made toward the carrying out of this policy until the reign of Louis XIV. By reason of alleged priority of discovery, the French laid claim to the territories settled by the English and Dutch and protests were made against the possession of such territories by these two nations. The little colony was thus threatened not only by the indiscretions of its own citizens, but particularly by France and England, which were unanimous in their assertion that the territory did not belong to the Dutch. This French claim was but another warning added to that already sounded by the English.

In 1627 the Dutch won a series of brilliant victories over the navy of Spain. The prosperity of New Netherland was profoundly affected by these victories. Especially by that one in which a Spanish silver fleet of nineteen vessels was captured, with booty equal to about $30,000,000, by Admiral Peter Petersen Heym in command of the ships of the Dutch West India Company. Great wealth was thus thrown into its coffers. It declared dividends equal to fifty per cent of its capital, and its prosperity gave a woefully needed impulse to the permanent colonization of New Netherland. Nearly seven years had elapsed since the incorporation of the Company, and nearly five years since it began active operations. Nevertheless, that part of the charter which bound the corporation to "advance settlement and encourage population" had been ignored. Practically the only inhabitants of New Netherland were the servants of the Company who were engaged in the fur trade. Scarcely any soil had been reclaimed, and the only exports were furs. The Company saw that its sole source of income was from the fur trade. That state of affairs was unsatisfactory when it was realized what an extremely fertile and well-favored country New Netherland was. The cost of the establishment was out of proportion to the returns, and the internal affairs of the colony were exceedingly irregular.

These facts had been before the Assembly of the Nineteen, the governing body of the Company, for some time, and colonial, seignioral, and manorial schemes for developing the colony and making it a more prosperous investment were discussed at some length and with much heat. At one of the meetings, when the commissioners for the States General and other notables were in attendance, a draft of a "charter of privileges and exemptions" was drawn up which was considered advantageous to all parties interested or who might become interested as colonizers. The report was referred to a committee for examination and for later reference to the Nineteen. Heym's victory occurred just at the right time. By it the committee was greatly influenced in its consideration of the draft. Finally, after numerous amendments and frequent references to the committee, the Nineteen agreed to the draft, June 7, 1629. Shortly afterward it was ratified by the States General.

This was the famous charter of "privileges and exemptions." It consisted of thirty-one headings and is the charter that founded the patroonship of New Netherland. "This charter, which transplanted to the free soil of America the feudal tenure and feudal burdens of continental Europe, is remarkable principally as a characteristic of the era in which it was produced. It bears all the marks of the social system which prevailed at the time, not only among the Dutch, but among the other nations which had adopted the civil law. The colonies were but 'transcripts' of the 'lordships' and 'seigneuries' so common at this period and which the French were establishing contemporaneously in their possessions north of New Netherland, where most of the feudal appendages of high and low jurisdiction, mutation fines, preëmption rights, exclusive monopolies of mines, minerals, watercourses, hunting, fishing, fowling, and grinding, which we find enumerated in the charter to patroons, form part of the civil law of the country to-day." There is no doubt, however, that the charter was extremely faulty. It was too thoroughly aristocratic and placed a premium upon slavery and servitude. Agriculture was fettered and manufactures were prohibited. On the other hand, the rights of the Indian to the soil were respected, the building of churches and schools was enjoined, landholding by freemen was encouraged, and the colonists were exempted from taxation for ten years.

The charter provided that any member of the Company who, within the next four years, should settle in New Netherland along the Hudson or any adjacent river fifty grown-up persons, should be given a grant of land. This estate he was to hold as "patroon," or lord of the manor. The grant might have a frontage of either sixteen miles or eight miles, depending upon whether it extended along one side of the river or both sides. No definite limits were fixed as to the distance the estate should extend back from the river.

The patroon held his estate in fee, and could devise it at death. He was chief magistrate and had supreme authority in cases involving fifty guilders or less. In other cases, appeal could be made to the director and council at New Amsterdam. This provision was easily evaded by requiring a promise from the colonists to forego this right. During the period of exemption from taxation the colonists could not move from one estate to another. Land was to be cleared, houses and barns were to be built, and cattle and tools were to be furnished—all by the patroon. For this advance of capital, the patroon received a fixed rent, payable usually in kind, and also a percentage of the increase of stock and a part of the crop. In addition, the patroon had a first option upon the sale of the farmer's produce. The latter must grind his grain at the patroon's mills and must get a license to hunt and fish. Should he die intestate, the patroon became his legal heir.

There were numerous aggravating trade restrictions. The Company reserved to itself a monopoly of the fur trade. The patroons could trade with whomsoever they wished, but were compelled to do so through the port of New Amsterdam as a factor, where an export duty of five per cent was collected by the Company. The manufacture of cotton or woollen cloths was prohibited. This was done as a concession to the Dutch manufacturers. Slavery was permitted and even encouraged. The Indians were to be paid for their land. Certain Dutch writers have made much of this fact, but it is not entitled to stress. The English of the Atlantic Colonies, with the exception of the acquisition of the territory of the Pequods by conquest, invariably gave an equivalent acceptable to the Indians for land acquired from them. The Dutch, it may be added, did the same and may therefore receive the same credit, but no more.

The charter was in substance thoroughly undemocratic. It attempted to introduce a feudal system where such a system was totally out of keeping with the natural conditions. It could not prove attractive to men who had enjoyed the privileges of freedom, whatever attraction it might have to Dutch merchants who expected thereby to raise their social standing by means of landed possessions and territorial rights, which mere trading in cotton and gin could not accomplish for them.

Samuel Godyn and Samuel Blommaert, two of the Company's board of directors, secured the first manor under the new charter. This grant and the one in the following year, 1630, lay upon both sides of Delaware Bay in what is now Delaware and New Jersey.

Kilian van Rensselaer, a lapidary of Amsterdam and a director of the West India Company, was led by the flattering reports of Krol to invest in lands in the vicinity of Fort Orange under the terms of the new charter. Purchase was made in 1630 of a tract of land on the west side of North River. It extended northward from Barren Island to Smack's Island and "two days journey into the interior." This together with subsequent purchases included the greater portion of the land now contained in Albany, Rensselaer, and Columbia Counties, except Fort Orange itself, which remained in the possession of the Company. The colony was called Rensselaerwyck, and the first colonists consisted mostly of farmers who were well provided with cattle and agricultural implements. Wolfert Gerritsen was overseer of farms, and Gillis Hosset was special agent for Rensselaer. It was at the suggestion of Hosset that much more land, north and south of Fort Orange, was subsequently purchased.

Michael Pauw, another director, took advantage of the new charter. In the summer of 1630 he bought from the natives the whole of Staten Island and the territory including the Hoboken and the Jersey City of to-day. The purchase of Staten Island was approved by Director-general Minuit, July 15, 1631. The name Pavonia was given to the manor, and the colony maintained itself on the New Jersey side of the river for about seven years. In the end, however, it did not prove profitable and Pauw sold out to the Company.

The patroon system soon brought on a conflict with the Company. Van Rensselaer formed a stock company to develop his holdings. By agreement he was to have no rank or authority superior to his associates except such as went with the title "patroon." His partners were bound to do "fealty and homage for the fief on his demise in the name and on behalf of his son and heirs." The object of the patroons seems to have been, at this time, the development of the Indian trade rather than the development of the country. By the fifteenth article of their charter they claimed the right to trade with the Indians, not only along the coast, but in the interior—in fact, at any point where the Company did not have representatives at the time the charter was granted in 1629. The fur trade was simply irresistible to the patroons. They were shortly accused of trading in fur on their own private account and thus interfering with what the other directors claimed to be their "vested rights." Mutual recriminations followed, until the competition forced a revision of the Articles of Freedom. As a result the privileges of the patroons were somewhat curtailed. This did not settle the difficulties. The patroons continued to encroach upon the rights of the Company, and, in the end, blocked the attainment of the very object for which the patroon system had been created—that is, the growth of an agricultural colony.

The quarrel was referred to the States General, and incidentally Director-general Peter Minuit was recalled in 1631. This was due, no doubt, in part to the fact that the vast alienations of the public domain had taken place during his administration. He was thought to be too favorably disposed toward the patroons. Minuit looked upon his recall as unfair and unwarranted treatment. The struggle over the appointment of a successor lasted two years, and colonization and settlement were retarded in consequence.

In 1633 Wouter van Twiller, or "Walter the Doubter," as Irving calls him, came over as director-general. The appointment was a great surprise, for Van Twiller's sole distinction, apart from being a clerk in the employ of the Company at Amsterdam, was the fact of his having married the niece of Kilian van Rensselaer and that one of the Rensselaers had married his sister. Van Twiller was a man of no wide reach of intelligence. He had been given up to the routine of the office, and his appointment seems to have been a clear case of nepotism. He arrived at Manhattan in April, 1633, in the warship *Southberg*, of twenty guns, accompanied by one hundred and four soldiers. With him came Dominie Everardus Bogardus, the first clergyman, and Adam Roelandson, the first schoolmaster, of the province. No sooner was Van Twiller installed in his new government, and had assumed its responsibilities, than he began to experience its difficulties. Troubles with the ubiquitous Yankees, with the treacherous Indians, and with his own recalcitrant Dutch, began to surround him. His conduct amidst those difficulties brings down upon him the ridiculous description of Irving: "With all his reflective habits, he never made up his mind on a subject. . . . His habits were regular. He daily took his four stated meals appropriating exactly an hour to each; he smoked and doubted eight hours, and he slept the remaining twelve of the four and twenty. Such was the renowned Wouter van Twiller,—a true philosopher, for his mind was either elevated above, or tranquilly settled below, the cares and perplexities of this world."

In spite of what Irving has to say about the "doubting" propensities of Van Twiller, the colony presented at least the appearance of prosperity under his administration. At New Amsterdam, the fort was reconstructed and a guard-house and barracks were built. At the same time that a plain wooden church was constructed to take the place of the "loft used for religious purposes," a house was erected for the "midwife." Also a dwelling and a stable were built for the use of Dominie Bogardus, and "mansions" were constructed for the Honorable Mr. Gerritsen and the director-general. There were also erected a bakehouse, a boathouse, a goat's stable, houses for the smith, cooper, and corporal, a corn grist mill, and the inseparable brewery. Improvements were made, likewise on South River and at Pavonia, while at Fort Orange the inhabitants rejoiced in the possession of an "elegant large house, with balustrades and eight small dwellings for the people." In truth, Van Twiller had large ideas of the resources of the Dutch West India Company. Those resources were largely apparent, however, and Van Twiller lost sight of the fact that the chief essential to the prosperity of the colony was agricultural settlers. Hardly one had as yet been sent over to reclaim the wilderness.

Van Twiller had difficulties at home and abroad. The trouble was principally with the Raritan Indians, although open hostilities broke out between the Dutch at Fort Good Hope on Fresh River and the Pequods. The origin of the trouble with the Raritans is in doubt. In 1634, Van Twiller succeeded in concluding an advantageous peace with them. However, this misunderstanding led to more serious Indian troubles in the next administration.

The trouble at home was the old question as to the respective rights of the patroons and the Company under the charter of 1629. Each interpreted the charter differently. The Company would confine the patroons exclusively to agriculture. The patroons claimed that they had already expended a "ton of gold" on their three colonies and that their charter gave them the right to unrestricted trade along the coast and in the rivers, and, as successors to the "Lords Sachems from whom they purchased," also the right to exclusive commerce and jurisdiction within their patroonships. The matter was brought before the Company, the Nineteen, and finally before the States General, and was not settled until several years later.

The administration of Van Twiller closed with two additional quarrels—one with the minister and the other with the schout fiscal [sheriff]. The cause of the trouble between Van Twiller and Bogardus is not known. Can it be traced to the bibulous habits of both? The clergyman is represented as calling the director "a child of the Devil, a consummate villain . . . and to whom he should give such a shake on the following sabbath, from the pulpit, as would make him shudder." On the other hand, the minister is represented as "having demeaned himself towards the director in a manner unbecoming a heathen much less a christian, letting alone a preacher of the gospel."

The schout fiscal, Lubbertus van Dincklagen, criticised the director-general for what he called his irregular conduct. He no doubt referred to both his official and personal conduct. Similar criticism was levelled by the schout fiscal at Bogardus. In fact, drunkenness seems to have been not at all uncommon. The explorer De Vries wrote that "he was astonished that the West India Company should send such fools to the colony, who knew nothing but how to drink themselves drunk . . . that the company would soon go to destruction." In fact, Van Dincklagen's predecessor in office, Notelman, was "somewhat of a bowser and when dry would not keep from his wine." It was for that reason that he was recalled and Van Dincklagen, "an honorable man and a doctor of laws," was appointed in his stead.

Van Twiller arraigned the schout fiscal, condemned him to lose his wages,—which were three years in arrears,—and shipped him off to Holland. This was virtually depriving him of his office, which he held direct from the chamber of Amsterdam. Van Dincklagen returned in the summer of 1636, and memorialized the States General. He demanded a redress of his grievances and called attention to the maladministration in New Netherland. Bogardus was included in his accusations. The States General continued to urge matters so strongly that the Assembly of the Nineteen removed Van Twiller in 1637 under charges. Nevertheless, he feathered his nest before leaving office by securing many acres of desirable land from the Indians.

William Kieft was commissioned director-general, September 2, 1637. He arrived at Manhattan on the 28th of March in the year following. One of his first steps was the organization of a council. His method of retaining entire control was as simple as it was unique. There were exactly two in the council, Kieft and the Huguenot physician Jean de la Montagne. Kieft gave the Huguenot one vote and kept two for himself. This council managed the general affairs of the government. And badly, indeed, did they need managing. The fort was tumbling down and could keep nothing in or out. The guns were off their carriages, and were serving the very prosaic purpose of furnishing rustic benches for the town loafers. All the vessels except two were falling in pieces, and these two were as yet not completed. The property of the company was decaying, its fields lay untilled, while those of the late director blossomed as a rose. In the fur trade, the Company got the worthless hides, while its servants and the patroons and the Yankees got the best.

Kieft tried to rectify these conditions. All persons were admonished to abstain from "fighting, swearing, and other immoralities." "The tapping of beer during divine service or after ten o'clock at night was strictly forbidden." Kieft was an adept at fighting with edicts and proclamations. Such long-range methods suited his style of belligerency. His proclamations, moreover, resounded with a detonation thunderous in direct proportion to the distance of the objects against whom they were directed. If, perchance, it was the Swedes on the Delaware under Minuit, or the Yankees on the Connecticut, both those valleys resounded with the reverberatory sounds of Kieft's proclamations—growing in intensity as they lengthened the distance from Manhattan. People with less temerity would have succumbed forthwith. But he always ended up by graciously permitting the objects of his verbal fusillades to continue to exist where they had settled.

A new era began in 1638. In September of that year the monopoly of the New Netherland trade, which the West India Company had enjoyed for sixteen years, was abolished. This was done on the initiative of the Company, after consultation with the States General. The fur trade and the right to lands in fee were thrown open to every person—citizen or alien. The Company retained the sole monopoly of carrying settlers and their commodities. The prohibition on manufactures was also renewed. Immigration was encouraged in many ways—free transportation was provided, and also the use of well-stocked farms for six years on the payment of a very moderate yearly rental. The stock was to be returned at the end of that period, but all increase was to be retained. Money and commodities were lent when necessary.

The beneficial results were almost instantaneous. Not only did the poor come over, but also the wealthy with great numbers of stock and dependent settlers. The population was also recruited from New England and Virginia. The first of the well-to-do Hollanders came with De Vries, Christmas, 1638, and built homes on Staten Island. The next year Thomas Belcher settled on the present site of Brooklyn borough on Long Island, and Antoine Jansen, a Huguenot, settled at Gravesend. The authorities in Holland began to take a new interest in the colony. On July 17, 1640, a new charter was agreed upon, entitled "Freedoms and Exemptions for all Patroons, Masters and private persons who should plant colonies in, or convey cattle to New Netherland." The charter essentially modified the one already granted. It did not affect the reform legislation of 1638, but further enlarged the liberties of the ordinary citizens by cutting down the privileges of the patroons.

Kieft's administration was characterized by his aggressive policy toward the Indians, which led indirectly to a demand on the part of the settlers for a share in the government of the province. His first blunder was in 1639. A demand for tribute was made upon the Indians in return for imaginary protection. At the same time, an effort was used to prevent the sale of firearms to them. The Raritans were the first victims. They refused point-blank to render tribute to any man. As a result, several Indians were killed and their crops destroyed. The Raritans took speedy revenge by totally destroying De Vries's colony on Staten Island. Bounties were placed on the heads of the Raritans, and the services of some red men were enlisted on the side of the Dutch. Matters went from bad to worse. Kieft was compelled to summon the leading men to an assembly at Fort Amsterdam, August 28, 1641. Twelve men were selected to consider the question of Indian relations. They were all Dutchmen, and De Vries was president. In speaking of Kieft's summoning of the leading men of the colony to an assembly, O'Callaghan says: "It was the first time that their existence as a component part of the body politic had been recognized or their influence acknowledged." The advice of the Twelve was practically for war, but with the qualification that the hunting season should mark the opening of hostilities, and that prior to their beginning certain concessions should be made by Kieft. In January, 1642, after months of wrangling, the Twelve finally consented to an expedition. But not until after they had obtained the promise of the concessions from the director. He promised a reconstruction of the council and that at least four of its members should be chosen by a popular vote; a removal of restrictions on trade; the exclusion of New England cows and sheep; and the increase of the currency. The director never carried out his promises. He dismissed the Twelve and forbade, on pain of corporal punishment, public meetings of the people without his order, as tending to dangerous consequences. Van der Donck states very plainly that Kieft allowed the twelve representatives to be chosen merely to serve him as a cat's-paw; that they had neither vote nor voice in the council and were of no moment when their opinions differed from that of the director-general, who looked upon himself as a sovereign in the country.

Kieft had been put in personal command of the expedition, which was to be furnished with munitions of war from the Company's stores. It set out for Westchester County, but its march ended in a ridiculous failure. The Indians, however, were scared into signing a treaty which stipulated the delivery of the murderer of Claes Smit, who had been the victim of the Raritan raid upon De Vries's colony. This provision of the treaty was never carried out.

Coincident with these political events in New Netherland, religious controversies stirred New England. These sent a wave of migration to Kieft's dominions. Francis Doughty came for "freedom of conscience," which he missed in New England. While preaching at Cohasset, he had been dragged from his pulpit and ejected for holding that "Abraham's children ought to have been baptized." He and a large party of followers settled on Long Island. John Throgmorton, with thirty-five English families, settled on East River. He and Hugh Peters could not agree, and the former was driven out "for the free exercise" of his religion. Anne Hutchinson came also and settled not far from Throgmorton's party. This influx of immigrants was recognized by the appointment of an English secretary as an important officer. De Vries said the next thing should be a respectable church, and as an evidence of good faith he immediately subscribed one hundred guilders toward one. Subscriptions were completed a few days later at the wedding feast of Dominie Bogardus's daughter—"after the fourth or fifth round of drinking." The religious element of the colony was recruited at the same time by the coming of Dominie Johannes Megapolensis. He settled at Rensselaerwyck, and was the first clergyman for that patroonship.

The remainder of the unfortunate rule of Kieft centres around three important events—two of them very disastrous to New Netherland, and all three closely connected and having as their result the recall of that unpopular and inefficient director-general. These three important events are: continued war with the neighboring Indians; the incessant struggle on the part of the people of New Amsterdam for a voice in the government; and the ousting of the Dutch by the English from the Connecticut valley and adjacent parts. The last will be considered in its proper place in a subsequent chapter.

The war with the Algonquins was due to Kieft's rashness, stupidity, and inefficiency. His bad treatment of these friendly tribes led to a horrible massacre of Indians and their subsequent retaliation, until many of the Dutch were compelled to flee to Holland or take refuge in the towns. The trouble originated in January, 1643. A beaver-skin coat was stolen from a drunken Indian at Hackensack. In retaliation, the Indian and his friends slew an unoffending colonist, Van Voorst. The tribe of the murderer offered two hundred fathoms of wampum in compensation. De Vries tried to persuade Kieft to accept the atonement; he refused, demanding the surrender of the murderer. The chiefs claimed that they were unable to deliver him, he having fled up the river. Kieft ordered Pacham, chief of the Haverstraws, to deliver up the fugitive.

This had not been done in February when a band of ninety Mohawks swooped down upon the river tribes, demanding tribute. As such a demand was usually accompanied with slaughter, the terrified Algonquins fled toward the Dutch settlement asking protection. De Vries saw it was a fine opportunity for diplomacy. But Kieft saw in it only an opportunity for wreaking vengeance for the murder of Smit and Van Voorst. Secretary Van Tienhoven and Corporal Hans Stein were sent over to Pavonia to spy out the position of the Indians. On the night of February 25th and 26th, two parties left Fort Amsterdam "after having the blessing of heaven invoked on the expedition," and fell upon the sleeping, unsuspecting, friendly Indians to whom a few days before they had sworn friendship. The following is a graphic account of the affair by De Vries, an eyewitness:

"I remained that night at the Director's and took a seat in the kitchen near the fire. At midnight, I heard loud shrieks and went out to the parapet of the fort, and looked toward Pavonia. I saw nothing but the flashing of the

Document signed by Peter Stuyvesant. *From the original in the Myers Collection, Lenox Branch of the New York Public Library.*

guns. I heard no more the cries of the Indians. They were butchered in their sleep!"

Eighty Indians were slaughtered at Pavonia and forty at Corlear's Hook by the second party. "Sucklings were torn from their mothers' breasts, butchered before their parents' eyes, and their mangled limbs thrown quivering into the river or the flames. Babes were hacked to pieces while fastened to little boards,—their primitive cradles,—others were thrown alive into the river, and when their parents, impelled by nature, rushed in to save them, the soldiers prevented them landing and thus both parents and offspring sank into one watery grave. Children of half a dozen years; decrepit men of threescore and ten, shared the same fate. Those who escaped and begged for shelter next morning, were killed in cold blood, or thrown into the river."—"Some came running to us," says De Vries, "from the country, having their hands cut off; some lost both arms and legs; some were supporting their entrails with their hands, while others were mangled in other horrid ways, too horrible to be conceived. And these miserable wretches as well as many of the Dutch were all the time under the impression that the attack had proceeded from the terrible Mohawks."

This crime has hardly a parallel in the annals of savage atrocities—directed, as it was, upon friendly villages of harmless, unsuspecting Indians. The massacre of the sleeping Dutch of Schenectady forty-seven years later by French and Indians was not its equal. There, sixty persons were killed. Peter Schuyler, Mayor of Albany at the time (1690), made a mistake when, writing to Massachusetts for aid, he said: "it was a dreadful massacre and murder, the like of which has never been committed in these parts of America." He had either forgotten or refused to recall the massacre of the Indians at Pavonia and Corlear's Hook by men of his own race just forty-seven years before.

The eleven river tribes immediately combined and retaliated upon the Dutch. Property was destroyed, colonists were put to death, and the actual destruction of the province was imminent. At the same time a state bordering upon anarchy existed in New Amsterdam. A truce was patched up between the factions, but it was not long maintained. The situation became even more serious. The colonists threatened to send Kieft to Holland for trial. At this point the director thought it well to appeal once more to the people. He asked that five or six persons be elected from among themselves to consider such propositions as he should submit for the general good. A board of Eight men was chosen, and it met two days afterward, September 15, 1643. The board decided to make war upon the river tribes, but to keep peace with the Long Island Indians.

The Indians, as usual, did not wait to be attacked. They "swept with fire and slaughter in every direction." Kieft asked for help from Connecticut, but it was not given. The colony was practically rescued by the opportune arrival of one hundred and thirty Dutch soldiers, who had been sent from Curaçoa, in the West Indies, by Peter Stuyvesant [Stuijvesant]. The tide was turned. This, added to Captain John Underhill's destruction of the Algonquin stronghold in March, 1644, broke up the formidable league of Indians. Before the end of April, the Long Island and Westchester Indians had sued for peace. The war terminated before the close of the summer.

On October 28th of the same year, the Eight sent home a complaint to the directors of the Company. The address was couched in the most condemnatory terms. Famine threatened. They laid before the States General a statement of their weakness and of the strength of the Indians. Likewise, the fact that before Kieft began his persecutions of the Indians they had "lived as lambs among us." The States General was warned against Kieft and the report he had prepared, concerning which it was said: "If we are correctly informed by those who have seen it, it contains as many lies as lines."—"It is impossible ever to settle the country until a different system be introduced here, and a new Governor be sent out with more people, who shall settle themselves in suitable places, one near the other, in form of villages and hamlets, and elect from among themselves a bailiff, a schout, and a *schepen*, who shall be empowered to send deputies to vote on public affairs with the Director and Council; so that hereafter the country may not be again brought into similar danger."

Both these demands were granted in some degree by a measure of local government and the recall of Kieft. It was decided to vest the government in three persons, to be called the Supreme Council. These three were to be the director-general, a vice-director, and a fiscal, or treasurer. Delegates from the commonalty were to meet every six months at Manhattan "for the common advancement of the welfare of the inhabitants." For the social well-being of the colony there were instituted other measures, namely: the introduction of negroes from Brazil; allowance of general trade with that country; prohibition of the sale of firearms to the Indians; and the appropriation for local uses of the revenue drawn from tariffs on exports and imports.

By 1645, Kieft had signed treaties with the minor tribes of Indians and with the Mohawks at Fort Orange. The latter treaty was confirmed at Fort Amsterdam on the 30th of August—the Mohawks appearing as arbitrators for the Five Nations. September 6th was appointed as a day of thanksgiving "to proclaim the good tidings."

Before Kieft's withdrawal, he came into conflict with Dominie Bogardus. "What," asked Bogardus, in one of his sermons, "are the great men of this country but vessels of wrath and fountains of woe and trouble? They think of nothing but to plunder the property of others, to dismiss, to banish, to transport to Holland." Kieft accused the dominie of drunkenness and sedition, and attempted to drown his voice by the rattle of drum and the firing of cannon.

Upon the arrival of his successor, Kieft handed over the administration of the colony amid universal rejoicings. His administration had ended practically in 1646, although it was 1647 before he was superseded. Serious complaints, charging him with nothing less than tyranny, extortion, murder, theft, and other "heinous crimes," had been transmitted to the directors of the West India Company. A vote of thanks was refused him, and two of the Eight, Joachim Kuyter and Cornelius Melyn, petitioned for a judicial inquiry beginning with 1639. This was refused by Peter Stuyvesant, the new director-general, who looked upon it as of the nature of an attack upon the sacredness of the directorship. Their complaints were dismissed, consequently, and counter charges were preferred against them. Melyn was indicted for rebellion, sentenced to seven years' banishment, to pay a fine of thirty guilders, and to forfeit all benefits derived from the Company. Kuyter was indicted for counselling treachery against the Indians, and was sentenced to banishment for three years, and to pay a fine of one hundred and fifty guilders. Kieft, Melyn, Kuyter, and Bogardus all sailed on the ship *Princess* for Holland. Kieft carried with him a fortune of four hundred thousand guilders, and also Kuyter and Melyn as prisoners. The vessel was wrecked in Bristol Channel, and Kieft and Bogardus, together with seventy-nine other persons, were drowned. Kieft is said to have remarked, in the midst of the danger: "Friends, I have been unjust toward you; can you forgive me?" Thus ended most tragically the careers of the two most turbulent spirits in New Netherland. Kuyter and Melyn were rescued and reached Holland in safety. There they presented their case before the States General.

The States General suspended Stuyvesant's sentence, cited him to appear at The Hague to defend it, and granted the appellants enjoyment of the full rights of colonists in New Netherland. In the spring of 1649 Melyn returned to Manhattan in triumph with these documents. He demanded that his triumph should be made as public as his disgrace had been. His demand was yielded to, and the decision was read and explained by the authorities before the people assembled in the church within Fort Amsterdam. Stuyvesant yielded. "I honor the States, and shall obey their

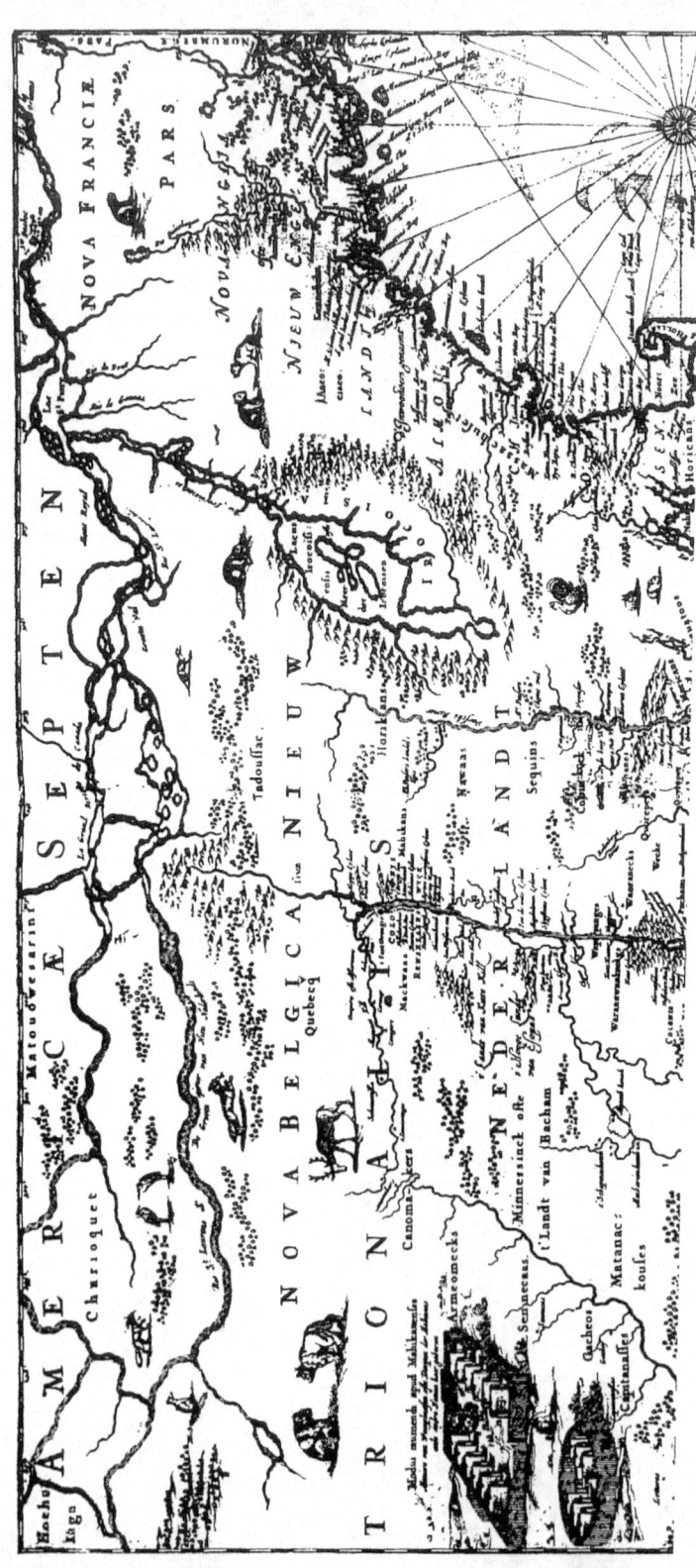

Nicolas J. Visscher's map, issued about 1655, showing the second published view of Manhattan Island as it appeared in 1640. *From the original in the New York Public Library, Lenox Branch.*

commands," said he; "I shall send an attorney to sustain the sentence." Stuyvesant's enmity did not stop with Melyn himself. The latter's son-in-law, Jacob Loper, was refused permission to trade in South River. Melyn failed, however, to secure a reversal or a mitigation of his sentence, and returned to Holland to seek "tardy justice in the Fatherland." He returned again in midwinter of 1650 with a new letter of safe conduct from the States General. Again he became the object of persecution by Stuyvesant, who had the ship in which he sailed together with its cargo confiscated, although neither belonged to him. Summoned to Manhattan on new charges, he refused to appear, and a house and lot of his in New Amsterdam were confiscated. The persecutions continued until 1655, when he removed to New Haven and took the oath of fidelity to its government. In 1661, he sold out his patroonship in Long Island to the Company, received indemnity for his losses, and was given "full amnesty with regard to all disputes." With this settlement he returned to New Amsterdam.

These unfortunate internal strifes did not absolutely prevent the colony's expanding when once peace with the Indians was restored. Brooklyn set up a municipal government in 1646 and Long Island was prosperous.

## CHAPTER II

### DUTCH AND SWEDISH SETTLEMENTS ON THE DELAWARE, 1623-1647

COINCIDENT with the settlement of the Hudson River valley, the Dutch attempted to plant colonies along Connecticut River and more especially along the shores of Delaware River and Delaware Bay. To these early settlers, Hudson River was North River, the Connecticut was Fresh River, and the Delaware was South River. The topographical conditions that attracted Dutch traders to North River also attracted them to Fresh River and to South River. In each one of the three cases there was a long navigable river affording easy communication with the interior and consequently with the fur-trading Indians. All three river valleys were densely wooded, and peopled with Indians who were very friendly disposed toward the whites, who brought them trinkets, domestic utensils, ammunition, firearms, and, more especially, fire-water. The importance of the fur trade in its bearing upon Dutch settlement must never be underestimated. The Dutch did not come to America primarily to settle down and conquer the wilderness. None of the early settlements were of a permanent character. Those who came were mostly men and servants of the great Dutch trading company. The habitations erected were of the most temporary character, and were deserted for others just as soon as new places promised greater advantages incident to a traffic in furs. In fact, the Dutch were at first exploiters, not of the soil, but of the Indians and their furs. The topography of these three river valleys was preëminently adapted to an industry of this character.

The first attempts at settlement on the Delaware were made by the Dutch. Their claim to the territory was based upon the discoveries of Henry Hudson in 1609 (August 28th), and the explorations of Cornelius May. There was opposed, however, the indefinite English claim to the territory as a part of Virginia, based upon the fifteenth century discoveries of the Cabots. Delaware Bay had been visited likewise in 1610 by Sir Samuel Argall, afterward Deputy Governor of Virginia, who named the bay after Lord De La Warr. In 1611, the latter visited the bay himself on his voyage homeward. It was not, however, until 1614 that May sailed for Manhattan, encouraged by the Ordinance of that year. Five ships had been fitted out by merchants of Amsterdam—the *Fortune*, belonging to Hoorn and commanded by Cornelius May; the *Tiger*, commanded by Hendrick Christiansen; the *Fox*, commanded by Captain de With; the *Nightingale*, commanded by Captain Volkersten; and another vessel named the *Fortune*, commanded by Adrian Block. While Block was exploring Long Island Sound, May was cruising southward and finally arrived at Delaware Bay. The east cape May named after himself, and to the west cape he at first gave the name Cornelius, also after himself. This, however, upon second thought he changed to Henlopen, the name of a town in Friesland. Shortly after May's voyage, Captain Hendricksen, in the yacht *Restless* (built at Manhattan), explored Delaware Bay and River as far north as the Schuylkill. Based upon the explorations of these men, the merchants of Amsterdam obtained from the States General a monopoly of the trade along the coasts and rivers thus explored. The grant was entitled the United New Netherland Company, and was inclusive of South or Delaware River. The monopoly was to last for five voyages within the period of three years commencing the first day of January, 1615. The decree was dated at The Hague, October 11, 1614. James I. of England had granted most of the territory eight years before to the North Virginia Company. The monopoly ceased by limitation in 1618, and an application for renewal was only partially granted. No advantage was taken of the monopoly on the Delaware or its branches.

It was not until 1623 that an attempt was made to establish a colony on the Delaware. It was under the auspices of the Dutch West India Company. It was organized in 1621 and consisted chiefly of Walloons. A vessel was fitted out called the *New Netherland* (a ship of two hundred and sixty tons), and sailed March, 1623, under the superintendence of Captain May. After a voyage of two months, the expedition arrived at Manhattan. Several families of the expedition were sent to the Delaware, and erected a second Fort Nassau at a place near Gloucester Point—on the east bank of the river opposite the land now covered by Philadelphia. Captain May accompanied the settlers, but it is not known how long he remained. The fort was very soon abandoned, and the Indians took possession of it. This was the case when De Vries visited the site in 1633. No further attempt was made by the Dutch to occupy the Delaware until 1631. In that year a colony was established.

This unfortunate colony was the offspring of the famous feudal charter of "Privileges and Exemptions" granted by the Dutch West India Company, June 7, 1629, and establishing the system of patroonship so characteristic of Dutch colonization in America. The first patroonship granted under this charter was dated June 19, 1629, and was to Samuel Godyn, a merchant of Amsterdam, and Samuel Blommaert, both members of the Company's board of directors. The grant lay on the west shore of Delaware Bay, extending from Cape Henlopen inland thirty-two miles, and was two miles in breadth. In July, 1630, the purchase was ratified at Fort Amsterdam by Minuit, then Governor of New Netherland, and his council. It is the oldest deed for land in Delaware, and comprised the water line of Sussex and Kent Counties. The year following, May 5th, Peter Heyn and Gillis Hossett purchased a district sixteen miles square on what is now the New Jersey shore—including Cape May. This purchase was attested at Manhattan in the following June. Representatives had been sent out prior to this to examine the country and purchase lands from the Indians. An Indian village at that time stood on the site of what is now Lewes, and this site was no doubt included in the grant. Godyn and Blommaert formed a partnership with five other directors, including Van Rensselaer and the historian De Laet, to increase their capital. Captain David Pieters de Vries, of Hoorn, "a bold and skilfull seaman, and master of artillery in the service of the United Provinces," was offered a "commandership" and employment as "second patroon." He declined this offer and was made a full patroon (October 16th). His services were considered necessary by reason of his experience and business ability. A ship of eighteen guns, commanded by Pieter Heyes, and a yacht, the *Walrus*, were sent out on December 12, 1630, under command of De Vries, with thirty colonists. They carried material for whaling and for tobacco and grain planting, also tools and cattle. One vessel was captured by pirates and the other arrived in Delaware Bay some time probably in April, 1631. A landing was made in what is now Lewes Creek, Sussex County—then called Hoornkill. A house was erected and encircled with palisades. It was called Fort Oplandt. It is said that from the number of swans which De Vries had seen he called the place Zwaanendal, or "Valley of Swans." The arms of Holland were affixed to a pillar, and the water in the neighborhood was called Godyn's Bay. Says Bancroft: "The voyage of Heyes was the cradling of a State. That Delaware exists as a separate commonwealth is due to this colony." In the course of the year, De Vries returned to Holland, leaving Gillis Hossett, the commissary of the expedition, in command. Through the representations of De Vries, in whom the patroons had great confidence, a second expedition was fitted out. But before it sailed news was received of an appalling calamity that had befallen the unfortunate colony of Zwaanendal: the fort had been destroyed and the colonists slain.

This was the account that De Vries learned on his arrival from one of the Indians whose confidence he gained:

The Dutch arms that had been erected upon the taking possession of the country in the name of Holland consisted of a piece of tin on which the coat of arms of the United Provinces had been traced. One of the Indian chiefs, attracted by the glittering tin and not knowing its significance, tore it down and made it into a tobacco pipe. The Dutch foolishly looked upon this as a national insult, and set up such a clamor that the Indians put the chief to death for the sake of making amends. The family and friends of the murdered chief wreaked a fearful revenge upon the little colony. They slew all the colonists—including a large bulldog, the guardian of the peace. They had more trouble in putting the bulldog to death than they had in the case of the colonists, for it took twenty-five arrows skilfully shot before he rendered up the ghost.

When De Vries arrived on his second trip, therefore, he found nothing but charred timbers and bleaching skeletons. He regained the confidence of the Indians, though with difficulty, and tried to retrieve the fortunes of the colony, but without success. Whales were scarce, and he had no disposition to plant corn. Food was necessary, and the expedition returned to Holland. The patroons had been quarrelling and the partnership was soon dissolved, so the land titles on both sides of the bay were sold back to the Company for fifteen thousand six hundred guilders. "Thus," says De Vries, "terminated our first colony, to our great loss."

But the Dutch were not destined to be the first colonizers of what is now the State of Delaware. That honor belongs to the Swedes. In fact, as early as 1624, William Usselincx, a merchant of Antwerp and the original projector of the Dutch West India Company, had drawn up a plan for the promotion of a similar company in Sweden. The scheme, from which originated the settlement of Delaware, was approved by Gustavus Adolphus, then King of Sweden, perhaps because it promised to be the means of planting Christianity among the heathen; perhaps because by it there was a possibility of extending the dominions of Sweden, of enriching its treasury, and of establishing a lucrative foreign trade. A company called the Swedish West India Company was formed and a charter was granted to it on July 2, 1626. Usselincx's description created a perfect furor among all ranks in Sweden. Subscription books were opened and there was great rivalry in securing stock, Gustavus Adolphus himself pledging the royal treasury to the extent of four hundred thousand Swedish dollars. The project was in a fair way to be executed when the Thirty Years' War and afterward the death of the king at Lützen, November 16, 1632, caused a complete collapse of the undertaking. No attempt was made at that time by the Swedes to settle America—notwithstanding Campanius to the contrary. The project is important, however, in that it was afterward carried into effect in 1638.

A short time before his death, Gustavus Adolphus, while at Nuremberg, had drawn up a plan for a company to settle and trade with America. On the 10th of April, 1633, Chancellor Oxenstiern signed and published this plan. He appointed as first director of the company William Usselincx. But it was Peter Minuit, former Director-general of New Netherland, who was to lead the first Swedish colony to America. He had quarrelled with the Dutch West India Company, and offered his services to the crown of Sweden. He laid before Oxenstiern a plan for the settlement on the Delaware and offered to conduct the expedition. The patent which had been granted in 1626, during the reign of Gustavus Adolphus, was renewed, and its privileges extended to the citizens of Germany. Oxenstiern presented the case to Queen Christina, and Minuit was commissioned governor of the expedition.

The exact time of the sailing of the expedition is not known, but it was probably in the fall of the year 1637, for in the spring of 1638 we find that Kieft, the Dutch director-general at New Amsterdam, officially protested against the Swedish settlement. The expedition consisted of an armed ship, the *Key of Kalmar*, and a transport ship, the *Griffin*. There were about fifty persons, many of whom were criminals sent out as indented servants. They were well stocked with food, munitions of war, merchandise for trading purposes, and presents for the Indians. A clergyman, Reorus Torkillus, accompanied the expedition. The vessels, sailing by way of the West Indies, stopped at Jamestown, Virginia, for ten days. After renewing the supply of water and wood, they proceeded to the Delaware, where they arrived in March, 1638. Shortly after entering the bay, the adventurers landed at a point of land in what is now Kent County, Delaware, and called it Paradise Point. From here they proceeded up the Delaware, and finally, on March 29, 1638, made a landing on Minqua Kill, the Christina, at a point now within the city of Wilmington. Minuit bought several acres of land from the Indians for a copper kettle and some trifles, erected a fort and trading house, and garrisoned it with twenty-four soldiers and began a small plantation. The fort was named Fort Christina, the creek Christina Creek, and the settlement was called Christinaham.

To avoid possible collision with the Dutch at New Amsterdam, Minuit proceeded with as much secrecy as possible. But, despite this, his arrival was soon known by the Dutch at Fort Nassau, and on April 28th the assistant commissary at that fort notified Kieft of the presence of the Swedes. At the same time, the commissary sent Peter May to demand of Minuit his license and commission. The demand was refused. Jan Jansen, the clerk at Fort Nassau, was then ordered to make a formal protest should Minuit commit any acts disadvantageous to the Dutch. Kieft's declaration against Minuit is a marvel of bombast in view of the fact that the latter knew that the former was powerless to enforce it, being without money or troops. "If," ran the protest, "you proceed with building of forts, and cultivating the lands, and trading in furs, or engage further in anything to our prejudice, we protest against all expenses, damages, and losses, and will not be answerable for any mishaps, effusion of blood, troubles, and disasters which your company might suffer in future, while we are resolved to defend our rights in all such manner as we shall deem proper."

Minuit paid no attention to Kieft's protest, but kept quietly at work and finished Fort Christina. Furthermore, shortly afterward the land from Cape Henlopen to the Falls of Trenton was purchased by the Swedes from the Indians. Part of this land had already been sold eight years before by the Indians to Godyn. In fact, De Vries's unfortunate colony of Zwaanendal was within the boundaries of the grant.

The Swedish colony prospered during the first year, in spite of the Dutch opposition. Thirty thousand skins were exported, and the Dutch were constantly undersold. Within two years came a change, and the little colony became discouraged. The Swedish Company had failed to send additional supplies for the Indian trade, provisions were exhausted, trade declined, and sickness prevailed. In the spring of 1640 the colonists resolved to remove to New Amsterdam. The day before their contemplated departure, however, the Dutch ship *Fredenburg* arrived from Sweden with supplies. The ship sailed under the Swedish flag, although her passengers and crew were Hollanders—Jacob Powelson being the captain. The succor was most unexpected. The prosperity of the Swedish colony had attracted notice in other parts of Europe, and a company had been formed in Holland to make settlements under the patronage of the Swedish Company The *Fredenburg* had been sent out by this Dutch company. She sailed from Holland in January and arrived in South River some time during the latter part of April or the first of May. She was freighted with colonists, stock, and all supplies necessary for a colonial establishment. A despatch was produced from Chancellor Oxenstiern and his brother, requesting the colonists to receive the emigrants in a friendly manner. Information was given at the same time that two other vessels would be sent out in the spring.

These Dutch colonists were settled a few miles from Fort Christina. The terms of their charter gave them permission "to form a settlement, at least five German miles below Fort Christina, on both sides of South River, and take up as much land as they could place in actual cultivation in ten years." The charter was a very liberal one and had been given at first to Gothardt de Redden, William de Horst, and others; but later to Henry Hockhammer and others. They were given full power over the land, and with the consent of the governor of the colony could remove to other land if dissatisfied with what they had taken up originally. Three florins for each family were to be paid to the Swedish crown in recognition of its sovereignty. They were given the right to conduct their own judicial affairs and to elect their own officers. They were to submit their statutes and ordinances to the governor for confirmation. A large amount of religious toleration was granted, but all were required to "live in peace, abstaining from every useless dispute, from all scandal and all abuse." Ministers and schoolmasters who were interested in the conversion of the pagan inhabitants must be employed in numbers demanded by the population. Freedom in commerce and manufacturing was granted them, but the commerce must be carried on in Swedish bottoms. Gothenburg was to be the factor between New Sweden and Europe. For ten years they were to be exempted from import duties. After that time they were to pay five per cent on all exports and imports and were also to contribute toward the expenses of keeping up the new colony. The relationship between master and servant was set forth very clearly. Whoever discovered mines of minerals could, with the consent of the governor, retain a monopoly of them for ten years. After that time preference was still allowed the discoverer on payment of an annual quitrent. Property was to be exempt from taxation, and fines were not to exceed forty rix-dollars [one hundred florins of the empire].

This was, in effect, a Dutch colony within a Swedish colony. It is supposed to have been located in the neighborhood of St. George's and Appoquinimink Hundreds in New Castle County—probably not over three miles from the Swedish settlement. This would seem to be so from the instructions of Governor John Printz, who protested that the new settlement was considerably within the five-mile limit specified in the charter of his colony. Jost de Bogardt was probably the first governor of the Dutch settlement. He was to receive two hundred rix-dollars per annum as salary, which was to be increased by one hundred florins if, in the future, he showed new proofs of his attachment and of his zeal to promote the welfare of the colony and of the crown. We have no information as to whether his salary was increased or remained the same.

These emigrants were received joyfully. There was no evidence of jealousy, and the spirits of the Swedes were revived. They postponed indefinitely their departure for Manhattan and went to work with a renewed vigor. In the autumn of the same year, 1640, Peter Hollender and Moens Kling arrived from Sweden with three ships loaded with supplies for the colonists. Hollender, who had been an officer in the Swedish army, had been appointed deputy governor of the colony. New Sweden was now given a new lease of life and prospered well. New lands were taken up and new settlements were made. The next year, 1641, Peter Minuit, the first Governor of New Sweden, died, and in 1642 was succeeded by Hollender. Little is known of Hollender's character. He made very little impress upon the struggling little Swedish colony, returning to Sweden within a year and a half.

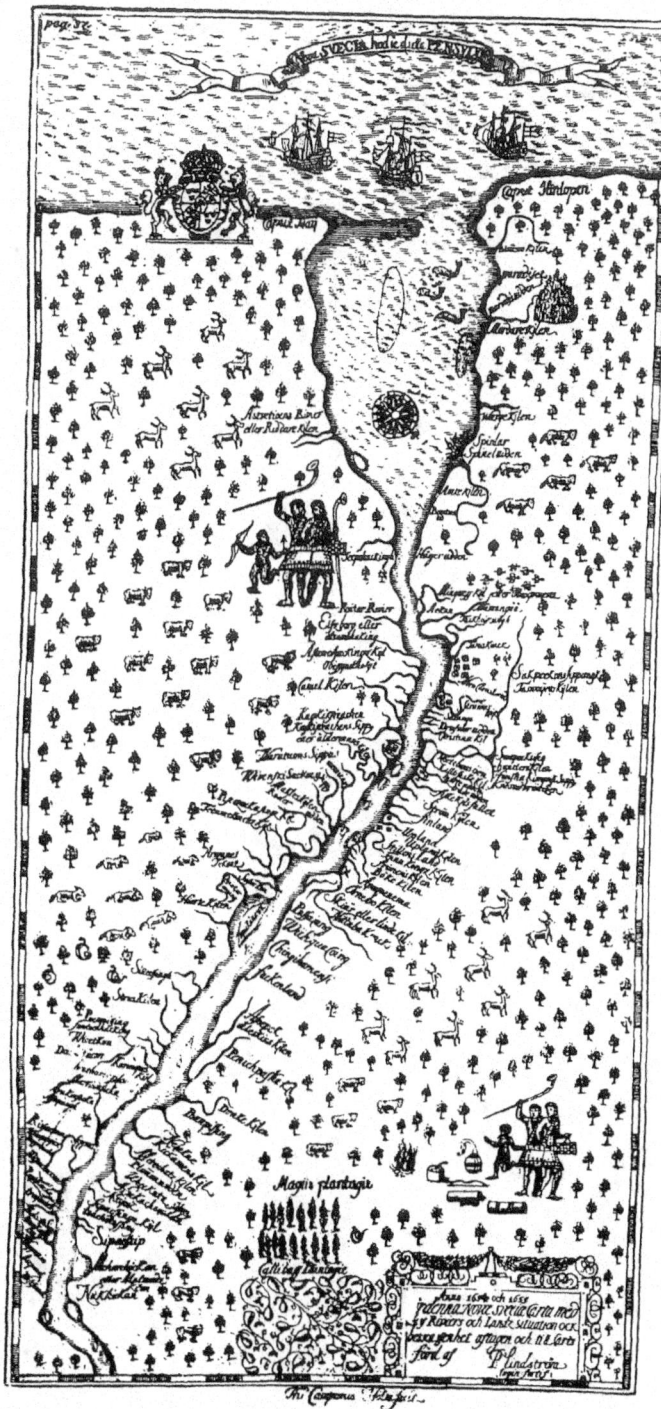

Engraved copy of Lindström's map of New Sweden. *The original of which is in the Royal Library, Stockholm.*

It was during this period that a company of English colonists of the New Haven colony attempted the settlement of the Delaware and the Schuylkill. Some of the leading colonists of New Haven were London merchants, and were among the wealthiest of the early settlers of New England. Following out their original commercial schemes, they began to establish coastwise trade with Barbadoes, Virginia, and nearer points. As early as the winter of 1638–1639, the colonists of New Haven learned from George Lamberton, one of their citizens, of the valuable fur trade in which the Dutch and Swedes on the Delaware were engaged. Seizing at once the opportunity of gain, the leading colonists, the governor, and the minister of New Haven formed the Delaware Company. Toward the end of 1640 the company sent out a vessel to the Delaware under Captain Turner. Under his supervision, most of the southwestern coast of what is now called New Jersey was purchased from the Indians, as well as a piece of land on the present site of Philadelphia, just opposite Fort Nassau and belonging to the Dutch.

On August 30, 1641, the New Haven town meeting assumed control of these purchases. When the fifty families, the first settlers, passed New Amsterdam, Governor Kieft made a formal though unavailing protest. Most of the settlers took up a position on Varkin's Kill, near the Salem, New Jersey, of to-day. A fortified trading house was occupied on the Philadelphia site [Passayunk]. The Dutch and the Swedes took measures to oust the "interlopers," and as a result of this opposition the settlement proved a failure. Most of the settlers returned to New Haven during 1643, and the failure of the venture came near proving the financial wreck of its New Haven promoters. The attempts, however, were not discontinued, for we shall find that coincident with efforts to collect damages from the Dutch for the destruction of the first venture preparations were made and carried out for other enterprises in the same territory.

So important had New Sweden become in the estimation of the home authorities, that on August 16, 1642, John Printz, a lieutenant-colonel of cavalry, was appointed governor. His instructions were dated at Stockholm a day earlier, and in them the boundaries of New Sweden were stated to extend "from the borders of the sea to Cape Henlopen, in returning southwest toward Godyn's Bay, and thence toward the Great River, as far as Minqua's Kill, where is constructed Fort Christina, and from thence, again toward South River, and the whole to a place which the savages called Santickon . . . the whole may be in length about thirty German miles," etc. From this it would seem that the boundaries claimed by the Swedes extended from Cape Henlopen to Trenton, New Jersey, comprising not only the whole of Delaware, but a part of Pennsylvania. Printz was to develop industry and trade, and live in amity as far as possible with his Dutch and English neighbors. The friendship of the latter in Virginia was to be particularly cultivated, inasmuch as the Swedes must depend for supplies to a large extent upon that colony. The Dutch colony under Swedish sovereignty was to be carefully fostered; but if they had settled nearer Fort Christina than their charter allowed, they were to be required to remove the full distance. The Indians were to be treated "with humanity and mildness," and "neither violence nor injustice" was to be done them. They were to be instructed in the Christian religion, and goods were to be sold to them cheaper than to the Dutch at Fort Nassau or to the English near by. The latter was advised for the purpose of winning the Indians over to the Swedish alliance. Printz was to build himself a residence, and erect fortifications at Cape Henlopen, James's Island [part of Camden, New Jersey], and other favorable places were to be fortified in such a way as to "shut up" South River.

However, agriculture with particular attention to grain and tobacco, sheep and cattle breeding, and salt manufacture, were not to be neglected in any respect whatever. At the same time, "metals or minerals" were to be sought, and investigations were to be made as to the possible use of the great quantities of timber in the colony. Also, as to whether oil could be pressed from the nut trees and whether whale fisheries and silkworm culture might not be developed to advantage. The "laws and customs of Sweden" were to apply to all judicial cases, while the governor was given power to imprison for major offences or even to exact the death penalty; but, in every case, only after a fair trial before the leading persons of the colony best versed in judicial procedure. The Lutheran Church was to be established—and divine services were to be performed "according to the true Confession of Augsburg, the Council of Upsala, and the ceremonies of the Swedish Church." Nevertheless, the Dutch in New Sweden were not to be interfered with in the use of their own Reformed faith.

Printz's commission was for three years, and his salary was to be one thousand two hundred silver dollars [eight hundred rix-dollars] beginning January 1, 1643. After the expiration of the three years, he was to be permitted to return after having appointed a temporary successor. A tax of two thousand six hundred and nineteen rix-dollars was allowed from the excises on tobacco for the expenses of the colony. The total budget was to be in the aggregate three thousand and twenty rix-dollars per annum. Half of the governor's salary was to be in excise; the lieutenant was to receive sixteen rix-dollars per month; the sergeant-major, ten; the corporal, six; the gunner, eight; the trumpeter, six; the drummer, five. In addition, the twenty-four soldiers were to receive four rix-dollars each; the paymaster, ten; the secretary, eight; the barber [surgeon], ten; the provost, six, etc.

Printz and his party arrived at Fort Christina, February 15, 1643, in two vessels—the *Renown* and the *Stork*. In the expedition was John Campanius—celebrated in the history of New Sweden as Campanius, the first to translate the catechism of Luther into an Indian dialect. He also kept a journal of the time he spent in New Sweden. This formed the basis of Thomas Campanius's—his grandson—*Description of the Province of New Sweden*. The elder Campanius was born at Stockholm on August 15, 1601, and on February 3, 1642, was appointed by the government pastor of the congregation in New Sweden. He held this position for six years, after which he returned to Sweden, where he died on September 17, 1683. Shortly after landing, Printz began to plan the erection of his residence and the fortifications. On Tinicum Island, not far above Chester, Pennsylvania, he erected Fort Gothenburg and his residence. The fort is spoken of as being "pretty strong," and the residence, Printz Hall, as being "very handsome." On the same island a church was likewise erected and consecrated by Campanius, September 4, 1646.

Another fort, Elfsberg or Elsinburg, was built on the east shore of the Delaware south of the present town of Salem, New Jersey. Hudde says: "It was usually garrisoned by twelve men and commanded by a lieutenant. It had eight iron and brass guns, and one potshoof." Fort Gothenburg commanded the Dutch Fort Nassau, and Fort Elsinburg is said to have been erected for the purpose of obliging the Dutch vessels to lower their colors on sailing up the Delaware. Certain it is that De Vries, of "Zwaanendal the Unfortunate," was fired upon (October, 1643) as he sailed up the river, and ordered to strike his colors. De Vries describes Printz, the captain of the fort, as one "who weighed upwards of four hundred pounds, and drank three drinks at every meal." Hazard, however, in his *Annals* claims that this man was not the governor but his relative. The Dutch must have been negligent in their protection of their rights, for they did not attempt to prevent Printz's erecting a fort (Fort Manayunk or Schuylkill) on an island near the mouth of the Schuylkill, thus shutting up that river. Nor did they prevent his building a "strong house" or "New Fort" at Kingsessing, and a somewhat more substantial affair named "Korsholm" at Passayunk, in somewhat the same neighborhood. By the erection of these forts, the Swedes were enabled to control the fur trade of the Schuylkill—without which, as Hudde, commissioner in command of Fort Nassau, claimed, the possession of Delaware River at that point was valueless. The evidence of inefficiency in the Dutch cause and even of traitorous conduct against Jan Jansen, who was in charge of the Dutch interests on the Delaware, October 12, 1645, accumulated to such an extent that he was removed from his position. Andreas Hudde was appointed in his place. Jan Jansen had permitted the erection of these Swedish forts and "strong houses," although they were clearly opposed to the Dutch interests on the Delaware. In fact, he had even lent the Swedes one of the Dutch Company's carpenters for the erection of one of the forts.—(*Albany Records*, Acrelius.)

The real beginning of serious dispute between the Dutch and the Swedes about the possession of the Delaware was in the early part of 1646. In December, 1645, by the carelessness of a servant, Fort Gothenburg was burned, the goods contained therein were lost, and its magazine was blown up—thus weakening the Swedes. Hudde was an entirely different man from his predecessor. He was thoroughly faithful to his employers. He was active and pertinacious, whereas Jan Jansen was lazy and wavering. He determined to extend the Dutch influence even in the face of Swedish forts and protests. A Captain Blancke, newly arrived in a sloop from Manhattan, was ordered to ascend the Schuylkill and trade with the Indians as he had intended doing. Printz made a formal protest and threatened to seize the vessel and cargo. Blancke—none too brave—thereupon retired, fearing loss of his property. His vessel and cargo were his own private property, and had they been forfeited he would have found it difficult to recover them. Hudde himself made an attempt to trade with the Indians of the Schuylkill, but was no more successful than was Blancke.

Hudde's next move was to follow out instructions from Manhattan and ascend the Delaware above the falls in quest of minerals. In this too, however, he was forestalled by the Indians, who claimed that the Swedes had told them that the Dutch from Manhattan were plotting their destruction; that two hundred and fifty men would be sent to kill all the savages below the falls and erect a fort to prevent their being assisted by their friends from the upper river. Then again, on the 25th of September (1646), Hudde purchased land from an Indian proprietor in pursuance of instructions from Manhattan "to purchase some land from the savages situated on the west shore, about a mile distant from Fort Nassau to the north." Vincent (*History of Delaware*) holds that as a Dutch mile was equivalent to four English miles, the land taken up must have been a part of that upon which the city of Philadelphia now stands. No sooner had the arms of the Dutch West India Company been erected upon a pole than Hendrick Huyghens, the Swedish commissioner, pulled them down. This, of course, brought vigorous protests from Hudde, with counter ones from Printz. Hudde's last protest was sent by a sergeant on October 22d, but Printz is said to have received the protest most contemptuously and had the sergeant thrown out of doors with still less ceremony.

The quarrel between the two little colonies grew warmer and warmer. An abortive attack of the Indians upon the Dutch was credited by Hudde to the diabolical machinations of the Swedes. "Printz," said he, "leaves nothing untried to render the Dutch suspected by both savages and Christians." Likewise, when Hudde asserted the priority of the Dutch claim to the Delaware, Printz replied "that the devil was the oldest possessor of hell, but that he sometimes admitted a younger one." In addition, Printz was accused of further tampering with the Minqua Indians—furnishing them with guns and powder. He stopped the Dutch vessel *Siren*, confiscated a quantity of powder and shot, and committed other less belligerent acts.

Right in the thick of the quarrel, however, a man became Director-general of New Netherland, in place of Kieft, who could out-bluster Printz and whose bluster was accompanied by deeds to the extent made possible by his very limited possession of the sinews of war. Peter Stuyvesant arrived at New Amsterdam on the 11th of May, 1647, and began his administration six days later. He it was who was to change the balance of power on the Delaware as between the Dutch and the Swedes by throwing his personality into the scale. Stuyvesant moved cautiously at first and almost diplomatically, which is saying a great deal in his case. But move he did, and the manner of that movement and the causes leading up to it will be the subjects under consideration in a subsequent chapter.

## CHAPTER III

*CLASH OF NATIONALITIES ON THE DELAWARE, 1621-1647*

THE early struggle for the possession of the Delaware was a three-cornered one. The Dutch, the Swedes, and the English were the contestants, and the claims of each may be defended with a certain show of historical justice. There is no doubt as to the mere historical facts. But when it comes to an estimate of the evidence, difficulty is experienced at once. It is easy enough to say that discoveries were made by John and Sebastian Cabot (1498), by Verrazano (1524), by Sir Humphrey Gilbert (1583), by Henry Hudson (1609), and that they included the territories under consideration. It is just as easy to assert that the same territories were a part of the London and Plymouth grants (1606), the patent of the Council for New England (1620), the Maryland grant to Lord Baltimore (1632), the Palatine grant of New Albion (1634), the old Dutch monopoly of 1614, the grant to the Dutch West India Company (1621), the grant to Lord Lennox and Lord Mulgrave on the dissolution of the Council for New England (1635), or the grant to the Swedish West India Company. But it is quite a different matter to decide as to the merits of each case from the point of view of actual historical right to sovereignty. The relative merits of "first discovery," "earliest settlement," "bona fide purchase," "actual development," must be determined in the conflicting claims before a useful expression of opinion can be given. Even further difficulty will be experienced on account of the absolute want of definiteness of boundaries in the old charters, patents, grants, and deeds. European geography was sadly enough neglected, but in the case of the New World there was an almost total absence of anything approaching geographical accuracy in the different charters and patents even in those parts where discovery and exploration would seem to have furnished the necessary materials. Monarchs gave charters right and left, not only without a due regard for the claims of other nations, but seemingly even without a due regard for the territorial boundaries of grants already given by themselves. Consequently, we have not only the conflicting territorial claims of friendly or hostile monarchs, but even the spectacle of threatened hostilities between the representatives of the same monarch by reason of their claiming the same territory and having their claims backed up by formal patents. For example, not only did the Swedes and the Dutch come to blows over their respective claims to the Delaware, but William Penn and Lord Baltimore, some years later, almost came to blows over parts of the same territory. Even at the time when the Swedes and the Dutch fought over the possession of the Delaware, they both combined to drive the English out of the same territory; while the English, on their part, quarrelled among themselves as to which of their own patents properly covered the disputed territory. The Virginians claimed it to be a part of their grant; Lord Baltimore asserted his proprietorship over it; the English of New Haven and Boston actually tried to colonize it; while Sir Edmund Plowden, calling himself Earl Palatine of New Albion, tried to drive the Dutch and Swedes from the same territory, for he considered it a part of his dominions granted by Charles I.

The truth of the matter is that something more than right of first discovery, priority of grant, charter, or patent, and even than right of first occupancy, should constitute the most substantial claim to ownership and sovereignty. To be sure, these claims to ownership should have their due weight, but in themselves merely they are not sufficient. The real test is actual occupation of the territory with the intention permanently to develop the territory as occupied and some degree of evidence that that intention is being fulfilled. Sebastian Cabot may have sailed along the coast of America as far south as Cape Hatteras in 1498, and may even have sailed into New York Bay, but that fact did not give England a just claim to the Hudson and the Delaware as against the claim of the Dutch. Verrazano no doubt sailed into New York Bay in 1524, and coasted along the continent to the south, but that fact did not give his master Francis I. a just claim to the Delaware and the Hudson for France as against either the Dutch or English claim. And what is more to the point, although there is no doubting the importance of Henry Hudson's sailing up North River in 1609 as far as the Albany of to-day, yet that discovery, reinforced as it was by the later explorations of Block and May, did not give the Dutch an undisputed title to the lands explored. If the Dutch claim to the possession of New Netherland had been based upon nothing more substantial than that discovery, then it could not be supported as against the English claim.

The Delaware of the Swedes and the Dutch occupied that neutral belt of territory between the two branches of the great joint stock company chartered by James I. in 1606, and known as the London and Plymouth Companies from the city headquarters of their management. The London Company had jurisdiction from thirty-four to thirty-eight degrees north latitude; the Plymouth Company, from forty-five down to forty-one degrees. The provision was made that the intervening territory between thirty-eight and forty-one degrees was to go to whichever company should first plant a self-supporting colony. Now, the Swedish and Dutch settlements upon the Delaware were made entirely within this neutral belt. Consequently, when from twenty-three to thirty-two years after this grant was made the Dutch and Swedes permanently located themselves on the Delaware, they did so within territory already claimed and allotted by the English. The English, however, made no attempts at settlement on the river during this period.

A part of this territory was likewise included in the new charter granted to the London or Virginia Company in 1609, when the old charter's bounds were made to comprise the coast line two hundred miles north and two hundred miles south of Point Comfort. Furthermore, reference has been made to the fact that in 1613 when Captain Argall, of Virginia, was returning from a predatory visit to the French settlement at Port Royal in Acadia, he stopped at Manhattan. He claimed that a grant of land there had been made him by the Virginia Company. He forced Christiansen, representing the Dutch power, to recognize the sovereignty of the King of England and the authority of the Governor of Virginia, and to agree to the payment of tribute in recognition of his dependence on the English crown.

In 1621, as we have seen, through representations of the Virginia Company, the English Privy Council instructed its ambassador at The Hague, Sir Dudley Carleton, to protest against the Dutch occupancy of the Hudson and Delaware valleys. In these instructions, dated December 15, 1621, the English claimed the territory in question *jure primæ occupationis*. The remonstrance was delivered to the States General the following year, but nothing came of it.

On June 20, 1632, Charles I. granted a charter to Cecilius Calvert, Lord Baltimore, in recognition of George Calvert's services to James I.; but more particularly, probably, through the intercession of his Catholic queen, Henrietta Maria, who was interested in securing a home for the persecuted followers of her faith. The boundaries of this grant were well defined. Its limits were to the fortieth parallel of north latitude and on the south to the southern border of what is now Delaware. The eastern boundary was the ocean and Delaware Bay and River. This, of course, embraced all the present State of Delaware and a part of Pennsylvania.

The English claim to the Delaware was asserted anew in 1633, when De Vries visited Virginia to obtain corn. He was given a cordial welcome, but was told at the same time that South River belonged to the English, and it was added, though erroneously, that Lord Delaware had taken possession of it some years ago.

On June 21, 1634, Charles I. granted to Sir Edmund Plowden and eight other petitioners all Long Island and forty leagues square of the adjoining continent. This was the County Palatine of New Albion. The charter was so defined as to include not only New Jersey, but also Maryland, Delaware, and Pennsylvania. The eastern side of the "forty leagues square" extended along the coast from Sandy Hook to Cape May. Sir Edmund, the earl of this county palatine, made futile attempts until the day of his death, in 1659, to wrest his earldom from the unsympathetic Swedes and Dutch then firmly settled on the Delaware. It should be mentioned that Vincent (*History of Delaware*, 142) holds that this grant did not include Delaware, but appertained exclusively to New Jersey.

In 1638, the first Swedish colonizing enterprise in the ships *Key of Kalmar* and *Griffin*, under the command of Peter Minuit, called at Jamestown, Virginia. This afforded the English another opportunity to assert their claim to the Delaware. In a letter to Secretary Windebanke, dated May 8, 1638, Jerome Hawley, the secretary of Virginia, described in some detail the visit of the Swedes. He mentioned their determination to make a settlement on the Delaware under a commission from the young Queen of Sweden. At the close of the letter, he reasserted the English claim to the Delaware. He likewise suggested that the Swedes and others might be prevented from settling on the Delaware by the English colonists in Virginia and by the use of visiting English ships—certainly without any "charges upon his majesty." During this whole period there is only one instance recorded when the English are said to have relinquished their claim to the Delaware.

About 1632, Charles I., upon application of the Swedish ambassador, John Oxenstiern, is said to have relinquished to the Swedes all claims to the Delaware. This recognition of the Swedish claim was said to have been by reason of the right of first discovery. There is no evidence of a documentary character to support this agreement. It is little or nothing more than tradition. Acrelius mentions the circumstance, but assigns a later date to it. Therefore, it may be said with approximate historical exactness that from the beginning of exploration in the Hudson and Delaware valleys to the overthrow of New Netherland there was not a time when the English did not assert their claim to the territory in question. As to the justice of their claim, that is another matter: it was based upon right of first discovery; and whatever may be said as to its merits, there can be no difference of opinion as to the continuous assertion of it in the most positive terms. Attempts of other nations to establish colonies in the two valleys were invariably subjects of protest by the English.

We have already seen that the boundaries of New Netherland were defined by the Dutch in 1614. That the southern limit was South River, or the Delaware, and the northern limit the forty-fifth parallel. We have likewise noted the failure of the first two Dutch attempts at colonization upon the Delaware—Fort Nassau in 1623, and Zwaanendal in 1631. And we have seen, furthermore, that it was not until 1638 that the first Swedish settlement was made at Fort Christina.

From this survey it is perfectly clear that from the point of view of "right of discovery" and "priority of claim" the English had a decided advantage over the Dutch. And, moreover, that from both those points of view and, in addition, "priority of occupancy," the Dutch had an indisputably clearer title to the territory than had the Swedes. The latter were clearly interlopers, although at first possibly innocent ones. As between the English and Dutch claims, the advantage is undoubtedly with the latter. Although the

English claim to first discovery and priority of claim is without question, yet it was the Dutch who first took actual possession of the territory in dispute. The English made no serious attempts to colonize the Delaware until the unfortunate intrusion of the New Haven company at Varkin's Kill and Passayunk in 1641. It was not until the Dutch had shown the value of the territory from the point of view of the fur trade that the Swedes came and the English of Virginia and New England began to turn a covetous eye toward those parts. It was the coming of the English that practically precipitated the triangular clash on the Delaware.

The New England claim included all the territory between forty and forty-eight degrees of north latitude. Roughly speaking, this extended from about the latitude of Philadelphia to near the mouth of the St. Lawrence. Lord Baltimore's claim extended from the thirty-eighth to the fortieth degree of north latitude. This shut out the Dutch and Swedes completely.

As early as 1642 the Director-general and Council of New Netherland, learning of the English settlements on the Delaware opposite Fort Nassau and on the Schuylkill, took definite action having in view their expulsion. The settlements were considered of "ominous consequence, disrespectful to their High Mightinesses, and injurious to the interests of the West India Company, as by it their commerce on the South River might be eventually ruined." In view of these facts, it was resolved "that it is our duty to drive these English from thence, in the best manner possible." Accordingly, April 22d, instructions were issued to Jan Jansen, commissary or governor on the Delaware. Upon the arrival of the yachts *Real* and *St. Martin* he was to proceed to the Schuylkill with a body of men and require the English to show their authority for daring to encroach upon "the Dutch rights and privileges, territory, and commerce." On failure to show the proper authority, the English were to be driven away as peaceably as possible. Should they make a show of resistance, they were to be secured and brought to New Amsterdam. The English improvements were to be levelled "on the spot," but care was to be had that no personal property was injured. An accurate inventory of the personal property was to be taken in the presence of the English.

Jan Jansen undoubtedly carried out his instructions and expelled the English from the Schuylkill. The New Haven records declare that in spite of the English purchases on both sides of the river, Governor Kieft sent armed men without warning or protest and forcibly burned the trading house. Furthermore, that their goods were seized and held for a while and that they themselves were kept prisoners. The damage done was estimated at £100, for which no satisfaction could be secured as late as 1650.

As we have seen, no sooner had Printz become settled as governor of the Swedish colony than he proceeded to expel the colonists of New Haven under Lamberton from their remaining settlements upon the Delaware. Testimony to this effect was given before the court of New Haven (August 2, 1643) by John Thickpenny, one of the colonists who had been arrested with Lamberton. According to Thickpenny's deposition, this expulsion of the English from Varkin's Kill was not unaccompanied with treachery. While Lamberton's pinnace, the *Cock*, was anchored about three miles above Fort Elsinburg, a letter arrived from Printz. The letter was brought by two Swedes, Tim the barber [surgeon] and Godfrey the merchant's man. Printz stated that the Indians had stolen a gold chain from his wife. That, as those Indians were about to trade with Lamberton, he desired his good offices in getting the chain back. Lamberton was requested to stay on board until the next morning, when he would recognize the thief by a certain mark on his face. No Indians came aboard. But when Lamberton called upon Printz at the latter's request, in company with John Woollen, the Indian interpreter, and John Thickpenny, all three were arrested. Woollen was placed in irons. Printz's wife and Tim the barber tried

# FRIENDS,

HESE are to Satisfie you, or any other who are Sober, and are any wise minded to go along with me, and Plant within my COLONY, That we shall no doubt find, but that New CESAREA or New JERSEY, which is the Place which I did Purchase: Together with the Government thereof, is a Healthy Pleasant, and Plentiful Country: According to the Report of many Honest Men, Friends, and others who has been there, and the Character given thereof, by John Ogilby in his AMERICA, which I herewith send. The Method I intend for the Planting of all, or so much thereof, as I shall reserve to my self, my Heirs and Assigns for ever. Is thus:

1. WHoever is minded to Purchase to them and their Heirs for ever, may for Five Pound have a Thousand Acres, and so Ten Thousand Acres; and thereby be made Propriators or Free-Holders.

2. Who is minded to Carry themselves, (and not Purchase) with their Families at their own Charges, are to have the Freedom of the Country when they Arrive, and one hundred Acres for every Head they carry above the Age of Fourteen, to them and their Heirs for ever. At the yearly Rent of a Peny for every Acre, to Me, my Heirs and Assigns for ever.

3. Who are minded to go as Servants, who must be Carried at my Charges, or any other Propriator, or Purchasors, or Carries themselves with Servants at their own Charges as aforesaid; they are to Serve 4 years, and then to be made Free of the Country: Their Masters are to give them a Suit of Cloaths, and other things sutable; a Cow, a Hog, and so much Wheat as the Law there in that Case allows; with Working Tools to begin with: And then he is to have of me, or his Master out of his Propriety, a hundred Acres, Paying the yearly Rent of a Peny for every Acre: To me and my Heirs for ever, or to his Master and his Heirs.

And as for the Planting of the Whole, with Ease, Satisfaction and Profit, as well to the Poor as the Rich: this Method is intended, and approved of by many that are preparing to go with me, which I intend will be about the middle of the next Month call'd April, or the end thereof without fail, if the Lord please.

First, 10000. Acres being pitch'd Upon, and divided according to every mans Propriety; then Lots shall be cast, and when every one knows where his Lot lies, there being also a place Chosen and set out for a Town or City to be Built, in which every Purchaser must have a Part, by reason of Delaware River for Trade. Then every one must joyn their Hands, first in Building the Houses, and next in Improving the Land, casting Lots whose Houses shall be first built, and whose Land first Improved: And as the Land is Improved so it shall be for the Use of all the Hands and their Families which are joyned in this Community, until the whole 10000. Acres be Improved; Then every one to have his own Lot to his own Use: And so this Method to be used till the Country be Planted.

If any like not this Method, they may be left to Improve their Propriety alone. If any happen to go who is not Able to get a Livehood here, nor to Pay their Debts out of their Stocks, the Governor and his Council shall take care, upon notice given thereof by the Creditors, that such shall make Satisfaction out of their Estates, as the Lord shall give a Blessing to their Labours, and an Increase of their Substance. Provided the Creditors hinder not their Passage, but give the Governor and his Council a Particular of their Debts.

The Government is to be, by a Governor and 12 Council to be Chosen every year, 6 of the Council to go out, and 6 to come in; whereby every Proprietor may be made capable of Government, and know the Affairs of the Country, and Priviledges of the People.

The Government to stand upon these two Basis, or Leges, viz. 1. The Defence of the Royal Law of God, his Name and true Worship, which is in Spirit and in Truth. 2. The Good, Peace and Welfare, of every Individual Person.

This 8th. of the 1st. Month.
1675

I am a Real Friend and Well-wisher to all Men
J. Fenwick

Fenwick's address to those minded to plant within his Colony of New Cesarea, or New Jersey. *From the original in possession of the Historical Society of Pennsylvania.*

to get Woollen intoxicated. He was given all the wine and beer he could drink—no mean quantity—and immediately taken before Printz. That worthy made great professions of love for Woollen and "made large promises to do him good." This was done with the object in view of persuading Woollen to say "that George Lamberton had hired the Indians to cut off the Swedes." Woollen refused to make the statement. Printz then "drank to him again," and said "he would make him a man, give him a plantation, and build him a house, and that he would not want for gold and silver." Woollen again refused. The governor became much enraged, swore vigorously, and, clapping the irons upon Woollen, threw him into prison.

Lamberton finally regained his liberty by paying Printz a "weight of beaver." All the English who refused to take the oath of allegiance to the crown of Sweden were expelled. Lamberton reported these outrages to the court of New Haven. The court requested Governor Winthrop to demand satisfaction of both the Dutch and Swedish governments. Lamberton was commissioned to treat with the Swedish government about reparation for the losses sustained. This he did not succeed in doing, however, for in 1647, while on a voyage to England, he was lost at sea.

Governor Winthrop carried out the instructions of the New Haven court. He wrote Printz with reference to his treatment of Lamberton. Printz denied the whole matter, "using at the same time large expressions" of his respect for the English and particularly for the New Haven colony. He took occasion at the same time to forward copies, on oath, of the examinations taken in the case and also a copy of all the proceedings between the Swedes and the New Haven colonists settled on the Delaware. Winthrop laid these documents before the General Court of the United Colonies of New England. The court met at Boston on the 7th of March and had cognizance of just such disputes. Printz requested to be shown a copy of the New England patent. It was reported that he said he would allow the

English to proceed with their settlement on the Delaware should a new commission be given them by the commissioners of the United Colonies. The commission was issued.

The next incident in these petty international disputes was more vexatious than serious. An expedition had been sent from Boston in 1644 to discover the great Lake Lyconnia. It was supposed to lie in the northwest of the land included in the New England patent, and might be reached by sailing up the Delaware. The ultimate object was the development of a new trade in beavers. The expedition was well provisioned and well fitted for exploration purposes. Letters were carried to Printz, the Swedish governor, and Jan Jansen, the Dutch governor, on the Delaware. The Dutch allowed the expedition to proceed, but at the same time made a protest as a matter of record. On the other hand, the Swedish fort brought them to by a shot from a cannon. William Aspinwall, the leader of the expedition, landed and remonstrated with the Swedish governor for having treated him so badly. The latter acknowledged his fault and promised amends. The amends turned out to be of the nature of a bill for forty shillings—the price of the shot fired at them. The bill was paid. Both the Dutch and Swedish governors now allowed the expedition to proceed. Neither, however, permitted the English to engage in trade, even going so far as to appoint a pinnace each to attend them. The master of the English vessel proved "such a drunken sot, and so complied with the Dutch and Swedes, that they feared that when they had left the vessel to have gone up the lake in a small boat, he in his drunkenness would have betrayed their goods to the Dutch." Fearing such treachery, the adventurers gave up the expedition and returned home. A second similar expedition from Boston fared more disastrously. After having secured a supply of beaver, they were suddenly attacked by the Indians. The master and three others were killed. A man and a boy were captured. The former, Redman by name, knew the Indian language and lived among the Indians for over a month. He received a part of the stolen goods. Printz persuaded certain Indians to capture him, and when he was taken they sent him on to Boston. He was tried for betraying his companions, but was acquitted.

Governor Eaton, of New Haven, complained loudly of the outrages suffered by the English on the Delaware at the hands of the Dutch and Swedes. He addressed a letter to Governor Kieft at Manhattan, dated August 12, 1646, embodying these complaints. The distance from New Haven to Manhattan seems to have deadened the sound of his "yammering"; at least, in so far as the Dutch attention to them is a true test of their audibility. The protests were made, but the Dutch gave no proofs by their acts of having heard them.

In 1649 and 1650, during the administration of Peter Stuyvesant, this quarrel between the Dutch and the English of New Haven reached a climax. Governor Eaton, of New Haven, complained to the Commissioners of the United Colonies of New England at their meeting in Boston in 1649. The commissioners, however, were not very favorably disposed toward the New Haven attempt to colonize the Delaware. They held that the plantations in New England were already very much undermanned, and that consequently the men for colonization purposes could not be spared. Nevertheless, they addressed a letter to Stuyvesant, stating that previous replies of the Dutch authorities at Manhattan to the commissioners' complaints relative to the outrages upon the Delaware had not been at all satisfactory. Furthermore, "they asserted the right of the English to the tracts on the Delaware, and that whilst the people of New Haven would neither encroach nor in any way disturb the peace of the Dutch, they must not fail in maintaining the rights and interests of the English."

At this point, Stuyvesant proved himself to be a diplomat such as hardly anyone gives him the credit of being. He agreed to meet the Commissioners of the United Colonies at Hartford for the purpose of arranging amicably the difficulties about the settlement of the Delaware. The meeting was held at the request of the commissioners. A short account of this very interesting event will not be out of place.

Stuyvesant reached Hartford on the 23d of September, 1650, after a four days' journey. He travelled in great state and was courteously received along the entire route. The negotiations were carried on in writing, in order "that all inconvenience by verbal speaking either through hastiness or otherwise" might be prevented. A number of important questions in dispute were settled at once. Other questions were left for arbitration. Two arbitration commissioners were appointed by each party. The United Colonies appointed Simon Bradstreet, of Massachusetts Bay Colony, and Thomas Prince, of Plymouth Colony. Stuyvesant selected Captain Thomas Willett, a merchant of Plymouth, and Ensign George Baxter, his English secretary. Stuyvesant's instructions to his representatives were exceedingly liberal. The four points submitted to the consideration of the arbitrators were: "first, the settlement of differences; secondly, a provisional boundary between the English and the Dutch; thirdly, a course to be pursued concerning fugitives; fourthly, a neighborly union between New England and New Netherland, as near as may be agreed upon." In substance, they had full power to settle "any differences between the two nations," to end and determine them as they "might deem just and right." Likewise, they were clothed " with power to enter into such terms of accord for provisional limits and leagues of love and union betwixt the two nations in those parts as to them should seem just and right." Similar instructions were given to the arbitrators of the United Colonies.

When the arbitrators met, the New Haven grievances were presented to them. Stuyvesant was not prepared to reply to the charges made, by reason of the fact that the alleged outrages had been committed during the incumbency of his predecessor, Kieft. Consequently, the arbitrators suspended judgment on those grievances in order to afford Stuyvesant time to lay the matter before the West India Company so that due reparation might be made. Nevertheless, Stuyvesant did not weaken in the slightest degree the claim of the Dutch to the Delaware. On the contrary, he continued to protest most vigorously against any other claim. Neither of the claimants would abate one jot from its original claims. The arbitrators, therefore, finding no basis for a just settlement or for even a satisfactory compromise of the dispute, decided to make a thoroughly colorless award. Both parties were to remain in *statu quo prius*. They were to "plead and improve their just interests on the Delaware for planting and trading as they shall see cause;" but that "all proceedings there, as in other places, were to be carried on in love and peace," till the right might be "further considered and greatly issued either in Europe or here by the two states of England and Holland." The award, of course, settled nothing as to the possession of the Delaware. Nevertheless, it was duly signed on September 19, 1650, by the arbitrators in the presence of all of the commissioners. Stuyvesant agreed to abide by the decision.

The absence of clashes between the Dutch and the English upon the Delaware for several months led Stuyvesant into the belief that his Hartford treaty had proved a success. If he ever indulged such a thought, he was rather rudely shaken in the possession of it, for the appetite of the New Haven people for the rich and fertile banks of the Delaware had merely been whetted by their brief occupation of them. Fifty citizens of that colony embarked in a chartered vessel under a commission from Governor Eaton and sailed for the Delaware. They touched at New Amsterdam and presented letters to Stuyvesant. The director-general was taken completely by surprise upon learning their destination. He asked to see their commission, and upon receiving it declined to return it. The master of the vessel and four others were arrested, thrown into prison, and kept there until they pledged themselves to abandon their expedition and return home. Stuyvesant took occasion at the same time to warn them that if he should find them trading on the Delaware, their goods would be seized and themselves sent prisoners to Holland. He also wrote to Governor Eaton, April 11, 1651, protesting in very strong language against the infraction of the provisional agreement. To emphasize his determination to preserve the Dutch rights on the Delaware intact, he declared that he would oppose all intruders " with force of arms and martial opposition, even unto bloodshed."

The prospective colonists considered themselves badly used by Stuyvesant. They promptly complained to the Commissioners of the United Colonies at their next meeting, stating their pecuniary loss to have been £300. In addition, they demanded satisfaction for their imprisonment as well as protection in the settlement of the lands they claimed as justly theirs.

The commissioners were very cautious. They did not think it advisable to precipitate hostilities, at least for the time being. To mollify the injured New Haven colonists, however, the commissioners decided that if they should fit out an expedition of from one hundred to one hundred and fifty men at their own expense, the United Colonies would protect them from the Dutch. The conditions imposed, however, were so very onerous that one gets the impression that the commissioners did not expect the New Haven people to comply with them. The expedition must be undertaken within twelve months; it was to be made up of able-bodied men, fully equipped with arms and ammunition and transported in vessels "fit for such an enterprise;" finally, the whole expedition must be approved in all its details by the magistrates of New Haven. Then, after all the requirements had been fulfilled to the satisfaction of the commissioners, if they "carried themselves peaceably," the United Colonies would furnish them with a sufficient number of soldiers for their defence. They were to bear the whole expense, however, of such protection, and their lands and other property were to be held as surety for the payment of the debt.

The representations made to Stuyvesant were of far greater importance. He was informed that he had broken the Hartford treaty, which permitted the English colonists to settle on their Delaware lands. Furthermore, that he had shown "no just title to the Delaware," and was in no position, consequently, to dictate who should settle there. At the same time, they wrote to their London agent, Mr. Edward Winslow, complaining of the conduct of the Dutch and of the dishonor placed upon the English nation by submitting to such outrages. They pointed out also the duty of preserving the English title to so considerable a place as Delaware. They claimed that the Dutch should be compelled to pay damages to those who had suffered injuries in person and estate. The commissioners disclosed a certain degree of uncertainty in their own minds as to the validity of their title to the Delaware. They were not quite sure that their neglect to improve the Delaware lands had not invalidated their title to those lands. To satisfy themselves on this point, the commissioners directed their agent to learn how Parliament or the Council of State regarded their claim to the lands under old patents when those lands had not been improved. They were desirous of knowing, likewise, if Parliament had made any later grants of those lands, and, if so, whether the rights of *bona fide* purchasers under the old patents had been regarded.

The people of New Haven were persistent in their determination to maintain their rights on the Delaware. They went so far as to ask Captain Mason, a man of " known courage and military skill," to remove with them to the Delaware and take the management of the Company. He was upon the point of accepting when the General Court of Connecticut unanimously requested him to remain at home, inasmuch as his services were deemed indispensable. He yielded to the wishes of the General Court, and the project was abandoned.

It was two years before the English of New Haven or the United Colonies again made a serious move in the direction of the Delaware. In April, 1653, at the request of Stuyvesant, the English appointed three commissioners to repair to Manhattan. They were to discuss more particularly immediate New England and New Netherland difficulties; yet matters concerning Delaware River were not to be overlooked entirely. Inasmuch as this conference concerns the wider interests of New Netherland, a fuller account of it will be given in a subsequent chapter. It is of interest to us at this point as being an important incident in the course of events leading up to the final contest between the Dutch and the English for the possession of the Hudson and Delaware River valleys. This conference was not attended with much success. For some cause, the commissioners left Manhattan in haste, greatly to the surprise of Stuyvesant. In their letter to Governor Stuyvesant, May 2, 1653, the commissioners reiterated all their previous complaints. They said "that to this day they have received nothing but dilatory exceptions, offensive affronts, and unpleasant answers, as well in the South River Bay, called Delaware, as upon the Fresh River, called Connecticut." In answer to this arraignment, Stuyvesant addressed a long letter to the court at Boston, in which he completely unmasked. He said, "the question is under whose jurisdiction were these lands on South River before they were bought, built, and inhabitated" by the New Haven colonists? Furthermore, that his refusal to permit the English to settle on the Delaware was in strict accordance with his express orders. Thus his whole treatment of the last New Haven expedition was proper in every respect and, in truth, even courteous. That, far from throwing the messengers of the expedition into prison, he had had them entertained most civilly indeed at the house of Martin Crygar, the captain-lieutenant of the town.

We have followed this trouble between the English and the Dutch for the possession of the Delaware from its very inception to 1653, when it becomes merged into the greater fight for the possession of the whole of New Netherland. A thorough knowledge of the facts is indispensable in getting a correct idea of the case made out by both the English and the Dutch in support of their titles to the territory included within the bounds of New Netherland. The subject will be taken up again for consideration when we come to treat of the English conquest of New Netherland.

## CHAPTER IV

### *MAINTENANCE OF THE STATUS QUO*

THE reader will no doubt wonder why at some time prior to 1655 during the continuance of this triangular clash between the Dutch, the Swedes, and the English for the possession of the Delaware, open and actual hostilities did not break out? Why the Dutch of New Netherland, who were much stronger than the Swedes of New Sweden, did not declare war upon the latter and exterminate them? This they could have done with the greatest ease at any time prior to the actual overthrow of New Sweden by Stuyvesant in 1655. Or, it may be asked, why did not the English declare war against New Netherland? The English on the North American continent far outclassed the Dutch in population, wealth, and in the stability of their settlements. New Netherland was completely hedged in by the English of New England, of Virginia, and of Maryland. Not only was this true, but many English colonists had settled in the territory immediately bordering upon the Dutch settlements. This territory was in most instances acknowledged to be Dutch territory. For instance, we find the English settled all along the northern shore of Long Island and along the southwestern coast of what is now Connecticut, but what was then regarded as Dutch territory. Not only was this so, but we find the population of New Netherland itself containing such a large percentage of English settlers, that from very early times Kieft, then Director-general of New Netherland, found it absolutely necessary to create an English secretaryship as one of the colonial offices. In brief, we may say that New Netherland was not only hedged about by the ubiquitous English but was thoroughly honeycombed by them.

There was no time from the beginning of the trouble between the Dutch and the English in America when the English of the United Colonies alone could not have annihilated the little Dutch colony. Then why, we may ask again, did not England conquer the Dutch and the Swedish colonies when so many excellent causes of hostilities presented themselves continuously—the Lamberton affair and the arrest of the messengers of the New Haven expedition at New Amsterdam, for instance? Or, at least, why did not the Dutch take advantage of their numerous opportunities to open hostilities with the Swedes—the insult to the Dutch arms and Printz's treatment of the Dutch upon the Delaware being cases in point? But neither the English nor the Dutch took advantage of their superior physical powers to crush wantonly a weaker colony. We must look for the explanation in the politics of both Europe and America. Stuyvesant sums up very aptly some of the most important reasons in his correspondence with Governor Winthrop.

When the quarrel between the Dutch and the New Haven people concerning the occupation of the Delaware by the latter was rapidly reaching a critical point, Governor Winthrop took occasion to address a letter to Peter Stuyvesant. He expressed his regret at the misunderstanding which existed between the latter and Governor Eaton. He also expressed his desire that all further provocation on either side be avoided. Stuyvesant gave immediate attention to this communication from a gentleman "whose personal worth and integrity secured him universal respect." In his reply under date of April 3, 1648, he took occasion to defend his reputation from the scandalous attacks of the New Haven people. He said he had been greatly wounded in reputation by those reports which taxed him with attempting to raise the Mohawks against the English.

It was contrary to the rules and principles of Christianity even to entertain so "devilish and wicked a device," much less to put it in practice. While at Fort Orange, he had endeavored to establish, according to his bounden duty to God and his neighbor, a firm peace not only between the Mohawks and all the other Indian tribes and the Dutch, but also between those and " his brethren the English and French." This, he held, proved the sincerity of his professions as against the slanders of Mr. Winthrop's countrymen. Furthermore, "for Christianity's sake, for love and union," he was willing to overlook these wrongs and was ready to support Governor Winthrop in anything he might consider expedient " for a union in the bonds of Christian love and friendly neighborhood."

In a second communication, dated May 24th, he renewed his offer to meet in Connecticut, at an early day, the governors of Massachusetts Bay and New Plymouth colonies and the Commissioners of the United Colonies. The purpose of the meeting, he stated, to be "to reconcile the past, to prevent future differences; and to establish a joint league, offensive and defensive." The necessity of the "joint league" he urged on the grounds of: "first, their unity of faith; secondly, the ancient and loving union between both nations in Europe; thirdly, their common dangers from their common enemies; fourthly, the known malice of the barbarians to both the Dutch and English."

In this correspondence Stuyvesant gives us what might be called a summary of the reasons why open hostilities had not broken out between the English and the Dutch and, we might add, the Swedes in America. A brief review of the international relations of these three nations during the century intervening between the accession of Philip II. to the throne of Spain (1556) and the passage of the English Navigation Acts in 1651 will show the significance of Stuyvesant's statements.

First, as to their "unity of faith." By the end of the first quarter of the sixteenth century, Protestantism had been introduced into all three nations. In England, the Reformation may be said to have commenced with the divorce of Henry VIII. from Catharine of Aragon, his marriage to Anne Boleyn (1533), and the consequent rupture with Rome. The Reformation was checked temporarily by the passage of the bill of the Six Articles in 1539, but was practically completed during the reign of Edward VI. (1547–1553). Then came the restoration of Romanism in the reign of Mary Tudor (1553–1558) and the subsequent recovery of Protestantism in the reign of Elizabeth (1558–1603). The Act of Supremacy (1559), the growth of Puritanism, and the Spanish Armada (1588), definitely fixed England in her Protestantism before the end of Elizabeth's reign. Certainly from the beginning of the English successful colonization of America (1607), and throughout the colonial period, Protestantism may be said to have been the paramount faith in England. Particularly is this true of the period immediately under discussion (1623–1655), which includes the greater part of the period of Puritan supremacy. There was, of course, the reactionary tendency toward Roman Catholicism in the reign of Charles II., and more particularly in that of James II. The second revolution, the placing of William and Mary on the throne, and the Act of Settlement (1701), gave to Protestantism its certain status. The accession of the Protestant Hanoverians (1714) completed the movement.

The doctrines of Luther found an easy entrance into the Provinces. From 1521 to 1555, they were brought in by foreign merchants, "together with whose commodities," writes the old Jesuit historian Strada, "this plague often sails." The German and Swiss soldiers whom Charles V. brought to the country; the English exiles, driven away by the persecutions of Mary Tudor; the proximity of the Provinces to Germany and France; the spirit and occupation of the people; and, in fact, the whole atmosphere of the country—all combined to make easy the introduction of Protestantism into the Provinces. The Inquisition, Alva's atrocities, and the schemings of Philip II., not only failed to extirpate Protestantism from the Netherlands but caused it to take still deeper root. The declaration of Dutch Independence was formally issued at The Hague on the 26th of July, 1581, and was followed by the great prosperity of the United Provinces. At length, April 9, 1609, a truce for twelve years was agreed to between the Dutch Republic and Spain. The former's freedom and independence were unconditionally recognized. There were no conditions concerning religion. . Thus, at the beginning of Dutch colonization in America, Protestantism was firmly established in Holland. The end of the twelve years' truce brought on war, but the supremacy of the Protestant faith was never threatened for a moment in the Netherlands. The final negotiations of peace between Spain and the United Provinces took place in 1648 and were followed shortly by the prosperity and preëminence of the Dutch Republic.

Luther's doctrines were first introduced into Sweden in 1519, by two brothers, Olaus and Laurentius Petri, who had studied under the "great apostle of reform" at Wittenberg. Through the Petris, Gustavus Vasa entered into a correspondence with Luther, and at the great Diet at Westerås in 1527 the Reformation was formally introduced. There were several reactions in Sweden toward Roman Catholicism,—especially during the reign of John III. (1568-1592), —but in every instance the reaction was in connection with the prospective union with Poland. The accession of Gustavus Adolphus, in 1611, assured the firm establishment of Protestantism in Sweden.

This review of ecclesiastical conditions in England, Holland, and Sweden during the period of the rivalry of the three nations for the possession of the Delaware and Hudson valleys emphasizes the importance of Stuyvesant's first reason for the necessity of peace and union. It may be held very justly, however, that it was not so much "unity of faith" that made these nations tolerant of each other as it was unity in their opposition to Rome. England was first Episcopalian, then Presbyterian or Calvinistic, and again Episcopalian; while Holland was Calvinistic and Arminian, and Sweden was largely Lutheran. At times there was almost as much hostility between the different Protestant sects as between those same sects and Roman Catholicism. It was their mutual dislike of Rome that united them.

This "unity of faith" or unity of opposition to Roman Catholicism brought forward the second argument of Stuyvesant for peace and union, namely, "the ancient and loving union" between these nations in Europe. During the period of which we are treating, England, Holland, and Sweden had been for the most part either in open military alliance against Spain and the Empire or had secretly rendered each other assistance. From 1623 to 1651, at least the people of the several countries sympathized at all times with the struggles of the others for religious freedom and ecclesiastical independence.

The policies of the Dutch and Swedish colonial governors were outlined and dictated from Europe. These policies were governed almost entirely by the political and economic conditions existing in Europe. The same cannot be said so truly of the English colonial governments. New England always acted more or less independently of the home government. This at first was attributable to a want of interest on the part of the latter. Later, however, it was due to the great English revolution and the unsettled condition of English politics. The English colonies were left largely to shift for themselves. Nevertheless, in international affairs —in matters of importance between them and their neighbors of foreign nationality—the colonial governments did not move upon their own initiative. For this reason, whatever attitude the English, Dutch, and Swedish colonial governments assumed toward each other, it was the result of the policy determined by their respective home governments. It was the political, religious, and economic conditions of affairs in Europe that determined their policies. The wars

Map of the town of Mannados, or Manhattan, as it was in Septem as "The Duke's Plan." *From the MS. in the Geograp*

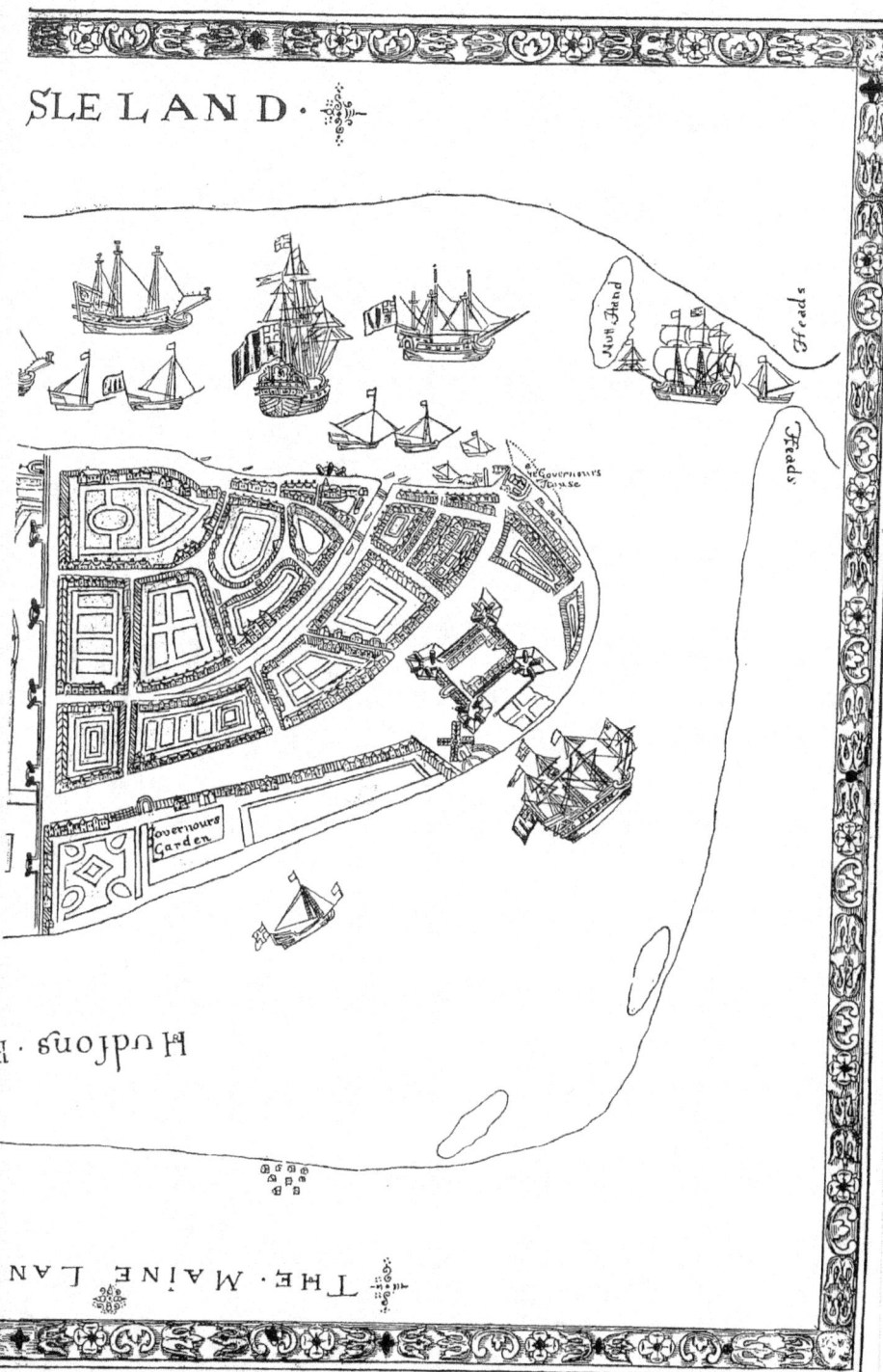

ber, 1661. The earliest extant English map of New York, known
hical and Topographical Collection in the British Museum.

of the Reformation being the all-absorbing international events of the period, the paramount issue then was, of course, Roman Catholic or Protestant supremacy.

The close association of England and the Netherlands began in Elizabeth's reign. The Emperor Charles V. had abdicated and Philip II. had succeeded him as King of Spain in 1556. Philip began his persecution of the Netherlands almost immediately, and later was morally supported in his policy by his wife, Mary Tudor of England. In 1569, during the reign of Elizabeth, England was engaged in a quarrel with Alva as head of the Spanish government in the Netherlands. It resulted in almost the destruction of the Flemish trade. From 1572 to 1580, Elizabeth carried on against Spain a piratical war under the leadership of Drake. This was largely in consequence of the ruthless war waged against Protestantism in the Netherlands by Philip II. Toward the close of the year 1575, envoys were sent to Elizabeth to solicit her aid, and, under certain conditions, to offer her the sovereignty of Holland and Zealand. She was not ready to fight Spain openly, and could not be induced to grant the Hollanders a loan. Ten years later the same offer was made and again declined. This time, however, Elizabeth despatched troops to the Netherlands and sent her favorite, the Earl of Leicester, to command. At the same time, she played the Netherlands false by intriguing with the Spaniards.

In 1596, the English and Dutch, under the command of Lord Admiral Howard and the Earl of Essex, captured and plundered Cadiz. The Spanish navy was crippled, the city was destroyed, and millions in plunder were taken. The most important alliance, however, occurred in 1625, during the Thirty Years' War. The representatives of the princes of the Empire induced three nations of the Reformed faith—England, Holland, and Denmark—to ally themselves for the purpose of assisting their oppressed brethren. England sent subsidies, Holland supplied troops, and the command of the delivering army was confided to Christian IV., King of Denmark. Three years later (1628), Gustavus Adolphus first made his sensational entrance into the war in Germany; and in 1631 he was assisted by England with money and with about six thousand English and Scotch volunteers. We may say, then, that almost from the accession of Elizabeth, in 1558, down to the passage of the Navigation Acts, in 1651, under Cromwell, England and the Netherlands had a friendly understanding. Seldom during that period were the two nations at odds, and frequently were they openly allied in defence of Protestantism. Sweden fought in defence of the same principles that had actuated England and Holland. The community of religious and political interests among England, Holland, and Sweden—but particularly between England and Holland—was the main reason for the tolerant spirit of the colonial governments of the three nations. At home, they were friends and even allies. They were fighting a great war for religious and political liberty, and they did not want to take steps with reference to each other that might be considered unfriendly, let alone hostile. A false move in North America on the part of any one of the colonial governments might have caused disastrous results in Europe. Politics were so nearly balanced there that a hasty move on the part of any one of the Protestant allies might have destroyed the equilibrium.

Stuyvesant's third plea for peace and unity between the Dutch and English in America was "their common dangers from their common enemies." At the time Stuyvesant wrote there is no questioning the importance of the European danger. During this period and for more than half a century prior to it, the common enemies of England and the Netherlands were Spain and Austria. From 1560 to about 1660, there is scarcely a decade when England was not hostile to Spain, either openly or covertly. During the greater part of that century the same may be said of the Netherlands and Spain. The common enemy of England and Holland at the time Stuyvesant wrote was Spain. Stuyvesant wrote this letter to Governor Winthrop, it will be recalled, on May 24, 1648. The Peace of Westphalia was not signed until the 24th of October, 1648. From 1618, when Ferdinand precipitated hostilities in Bohemia, until the signature of the Peace in 1648, the Protestant and Roman Catholic nations were engaged in a great struggle for supremacy and, in some cases, even for existence. This period of the Thirty Years' War includes the first part of the period of the struggle for the possession of the Hudson and the Delaware valleys by the English, the Dutch, and the Swedes settled in America. These three nations were, at the same time, fighting in Europe in defence of religious and political liberty. Their common danger was imperial tyranny and their common enemy was Spain.

Stuyvesant's fourth reason for urging peace and union as between the Dutch and English colonies in America was the "known malice of the barbarians" to both of those nations. The danger from the Indians was particularly great at that time. They continuously threatened the very existence of the white settlements until the overthrow of King Philip in 1676. The danger was indeed great, and the white settlers could ill afford to waste their strength in an intercolonial war. The Iroquois confederation was always a source of great danger. Although they were at that time on friendly terms with both the Dutch and the English, yet no one could tell when their friendship might turn into enmity. Stuyvesant himself had been accused by the English of New Haven of attempting to raise the Mohawks against the English. His indignant denial of the accusation shows how seriously he regarded the danger of an Indian uprising against the domination of the whites. There is no doubt whatever of his entire innocence. He was righteously indignant at the accusation and considered it a vicious slander.

The Dutch on the Delaware, in turn, made a like accusation against the Swedes. Reference has already been made to the quarrel between Hudde and Printz—Hudde claimed that an abortive attack of the Indians upon the

Dutch was due to Printz's unchristian schemings. The accusations and counter accusations were only the beginning of many similar disputes among the English, the French, and the Dutch colonial governments. Such accusations characterized all intercolonial disputes down to the end of the American Revolution. Each nation accused every other nation of stirring up or attempting to stir up the Indians against the other colonies. The indictment was frequently not without foundation in fact. This was particularly true in the great French-English duel for supremacy in America that began with King William's War in 1690 and ended with the close of the French and Indian War in 1763. We shall find that one of the main causes of the hostilities between the Dutch of New Amsterdam and the English of New England was the mutual recrimination with respect to tampering with the Indians. Both claimed that the other had secretly induced the Indians to go upon the warpath and had sold them guns and ammunition for that purpose.

Viewing the question in the light of subsequent developments, we are able to add to these four pleas made by Stuyvesant for peace and unity certain other important reasons why "peace and unity" were sustained. At least, why they were sustained as between the Dutch and the Swedes until 1655, and as between the Dutch and the English until 1664. The four pleas urged by Stuyvesant explain satisfactorily why hostilities between the three rivals did not originate with the home governments. As long as the latter were at peace with one another, and particularly as long as they were open allies in a common cause, their colonial policies would be friendly; at least, not overtly hostile. But the policy of the home country could not always control the acts of the colony. There were very good reasons for this, and among them might be mentioned: the great distance of the colony from the home government; the great struggle of the Thirty Years' War that covered the first half of the period under discussion and demanded the whole attention of the nations engaged in it; and lastly, the necessity of giving the colonial government a considerable degree of latitude in the management of its own affairs. There were times when the colonists of all three nations had to act and act promptly without instructions from their home governments. There were times when the very existence of the colony demanded such action, even when the action threatened to lead to international complications.

From this it would seem that the colonial governments of the three colonies might have been led very easily into a war with one another, despite the peace policy of the home governments. The very reasonable defence could have been made that the exigencies of the situation demanded prompt action and that a delay for instructions from the home government might have proved disastrous. Several times the colonial governments were upon the eve of taking just such action, but were prevented from doing so by the satisfactory solution of the problem at hand.

In addition, then, to Stuyvesant's fourth plea for peace there were three important reasons why it was sustained. These three reasons, like his fourth plea, were local in character. While the first three pleas of Stuyvesant will explain the policy of peace on the part of the home governments, it will take his fourth plea in conjunction with these others to explain the policy of peace sustained by the colonial governments.

In the first place, the English, Dutch, and Swedish colonists had some doubt themselves as to the validity of their individual claims to definite tracts of land in the disputed territory. This was particularly true in the case of the English colonists of New Haven and their claims to certain lands in the Delaware valley. Their doubt as to the validity of their own claims was not, of course, admitted to the rival nationalities. But we find several communications with the home government in which the request is made that an opinion be given upon the validity of their claims. A typical illustration to which reference has already been made will be sufficient for our purpose. We will recall that Stuyvesant imprisoned the messengers of the New Haven expedition that stopped at New Amsterdam to pay him their respects in 1651. The United Colonies of New England mollified the people of New Haven by empty promises and wrote Stuyvesant a rather bombastic letter. In addition, a letter was written to the agent of the United Colonies at London, Mr. Edward Winslow, complaining of the conduct of the Dutch. After pointing out the desirability of defending the English title to the Delaware valley, the commissioners naïvely call attention to the very grave weakness of that same title. They were not quite sure that their neglect to improve the lands in dispute had not invalidated their title to them. To make this point very clear, the agent was requested to feel the pulse of Parliament or of the Council of State to discover how their claims were regarded; whether or not their failure to improve the lands in dispute had invalidated their title to them under the old patents. They wanted to know, likewise, whether any later grants of the lands in question had been made by Parliament; and if so, whether the rights of *bona fide* purchasers under the old patents had been regarded.

When the contesting colonists were not by any means sure of the validity of their titles to the lands in dispute, they would have committed a gross error had they recklessly begun hostilities. They could not have depended upon the support of the home government in the event that their titles to the land in dispute proved invalid. Not one of the colonial governments had the courage born of a conviction that its title to the land in dispute was indisputable. This was particularly true in the case of the English and the Swedes. We have already remarked that the title of Holland in the Delaware valley was much clearer than those of her two rivals.

In the second place, had the English title to the settlements on the Delaware been entirely valid, the chances are that the English colonies could not have united upon a common plan of action. There was a most decided want of community of interest between the New England colonies and the Southern colonies. New England differed from Virginia and Maryland so essentially,—religiously, politically, and socially,—that there was not the proper foundation at that time for unity of action even against colonists of another nation. Puritan New England had little in common with Cavalier Virginia. It must be borne in mind that this clash between the three nationalities in the three river valleys approximately coincided with the great struggle in England between Charles I. and Parliament, and later, after the execution of the king, between the Cavalier and the Puritan interests. Charles I. became king in 1625 and was beheaded in 1649. The Commonwealth lasted from 1649 to 1653, and the Protectorate from 1653 to the Restoration in 1660. The clash between the English and the Dutch on the Connecticut began in 1635; between the Dutch and the Swedes on the Delaware, in 1638; and between the Dutch, the Swedes, and the English on the Delaware, in 1641. New Sweden was conquered by the Dutch in 1655, and New Netherland was conquered by the English in 1664. From 1635 to 1664, then, we may say that the rival nations contested for the possession of the three river valleys. Thus we see that with the exception of the last four or five years of this period the issue between the Puritans and the Cavaliers was very tightly drawn. Virginia was Cavalier, New England was Puritan. Their sympathies in the great English revolution were respectively Cavalier and Puritan. They probably could not have united in a movement to oust the Dutch and the Swedes from the three river valleys had they been left by the home government to follow their own inclinations in the matter. As evidence of this fact we have but to point to the failure of the various schemes for a consolidation of the English colonies in America before the great issue of the American Revolution afforded the necessary foundation for united action. Andros's scheme of unification in 1688; the New York

Colonial Congress fiasco of 1690; Benjamin Franklin's Plan of Union at the Albany Convention in 1754; Braddock's brow-beating Congress at Alexandria in 1755—all failed to accomplish the end sought. Unification of the English colonies in America was the object in view, but the mutual jealousies between colony and colony and the mutual distrust of the colonies and of the mother country prevented the successful culmination of these various plans for unification.

In the third place, there were dissensions between the four colonies comprising the United Colonies of New England. These colonies united were strong enough without the help of the other colonies to wage a successful war of conquest against the Dutch and the Swedes. The New England Confederation was formed at Boston in May, 1643, by delegates from Plymouth, Massachusetts Bay, Connecticut, and New Haven Colonies. From that time until its practical dissolution in 1684, the records of the United Colonies are full of evidences of the disagreements, jealousies, and mutual recriminations of these four Puritan colonies.

The facts that have been thus brought forward in the course of this discussion should go a long way toward answering satisfactorily the questions asked at the beginning of the chapter. Namely, why, prior to 1655, did not the Dutch, the English, and the Swedes resort to open and declared warfare in their triangular contest for the possession of the Delaware valley? Why did not the Dutch of New Netherland declare war upon the Swedes of New Sweden and exterminate them? Why did not the English wage war against the Dutch? Why was each of the three colonial governments so tolerant of the other two? Answers to these questions have been found in the seven reasons just adduced, namely: first, their unity of faith; secondly, the traditional political union of their respective home countries—especially as between the English and the Dutch; thirdly, their common danger from their common enemies;

fourthly, the known hostility of the Indians toward them; fifthly, their doubts as to the validity of their individual titles to the disputed territory; sixthly, the want of a community of interest among the different English colonies; seventhly, the jealousies existing among the colonies composing the New England Confederation.

## CHAPTER V

### DUTCH CONQUEST OF NEW SWEDEN, 1647–1655

WHEN Peter Stuyvesant assumed control of the government of New Netherland on the 11th of May, 1647, everyone felt instinctively that a man of character had succeeded the worthless Kieft, by whom New Netherland had been brought to the verge of ruin. A fourth part of the city of New Amsterdam, it is said, consisted of grog shops and houses where nothing could be got but tobacco and beer. Needless to say, drunkenness and broils were of common occurrence. Religion and education were neglected. A church begun in 1642 was unfinished—the director-general appropriating to his own use the fines and forfeitures set aside for its completion. No attempt was made to Christianize the savage. Harvard College was founded in 1636, but by 1646 not even a common primary school had been established in New Netherland. The funds that had been collected for a schoolhouse in New Amsterdam had been misappropriated. Agriculture was neglected. Scarcely fifty "bouweries" existed outside of Long Island. In 1643, the population of New Netherland numbered three thousand, while in 1646 it had dwindled to about one thousand. The whole province could not furnish more than three hundred men capable of bearing arms. The Indians had lost one thousand six hundred of their people in the war of 1641 and were in a dangerous mood. The government was disorganized and the people were discontented. Smuggling had almost ruined legitimate trade and had cut off the usual source of government revenue. The patroons and the Company were at odds over conflicting claims of jurisdiction. The very existence of New Netherland was threatened by the rival English colonies.

It must be admitted, however, in extenuation of Kieft's policy, that he had a most difficult task in the administration of the government of his province. He was far distant from the source of his military supplies, and had but a handful of soldiers crowded in a dilapidated fort with which to sustain his power and to repel attacks. The population was small, "turbulent and unreliable." The province was surrounded by savages ever on the alert for "rapine and murder," and was threatened by the English in New England and by the Swedes on the Delaware. The States General had all it could do to maintain its independence, while the Company regarded the province merely as a source of commercial gain. The former could not spare the time to supervise the affairs of the colony and the latter merely exploited it, giving in return very little support. With dissensions within, with attacks from without, and with an absence of hearty support from the governing powers, Kieft's task was indeed not an easy one. Yet, there is little doubt but that not a few of his difficulties were caused by his want of tact, by his imprudence, by his rashness, and by his arbitrary actions. It may be said truthfully that many of his embarrassments here cited were largely of his own creation: it was more the man than his environment. He brought the colony to its lowest ebb. We shall see what changes were brought about under his successor.

Such was the condition of affairs when Peter Stuyvesant, the last Director-general of New Netherland, assumed control of the government. For several years prior to his coming he had been in the Company's service as director of its colony at Curaçoa. There he had distinguished himself by his energy and bravery. He had lost a leg in an attack on the Portuguese settlement at St. Martin's, and it was on his return to Europe for surgical aid that he was placed in charge of New Netherland while still retaining his former commission. His very first speech, as well as his whole personal bearing, was indicative of what manner of man he was. "I shall govern you as a father his children, for the advantage of the chartered West India Company, and these burghers, and this land," said he, in summing up his view of the situation and his relation to it. It is said that he put on airs and strutted about, like a peacock, with great state and pomp. Some of the representative citizens on going to welcome him were left to wait for several hours bareheaded, while he "as if he were the Czar of Muscovy remained covered." The transmission of the government from Kieft to himself was made as spectacular as possible. The whole community was called to witness the ceremony.

Stuyvesant was born about 1602, and was the son of a clergyman, the Rev. Balthazar Stuyvesant. He had a college education and considered himself well versed in Latin. Upon leaving college, he entered the army. He married Judith Bayard, the granddaughter of a French Protestant clergyman. This clergyman was Nicholas Bayard, who, after the Massacre of St. Bartholomew's, in 1572, escaped to the Netherlands. As to Peter Stuyvesant's personality, we have an admirable description by the veracious Diedrich Knickerbocker: "A valiant, weather-beaten, mettlesome, obstinate, leathern-sided, lion-hearted, generous-spirited old governor." His manner was most autocratic and his speech was very abrupt—often offensively so. He was diligent in furthering the interests of his superiors; and when he had decided as to what those interests were, he was very prompt in action. He was not the one to brook opposition, and his arbitrary conduct again precipitated the old struggle between the settlers and the director-general.

His first act was to organize his council, and almost his second act was to begin issuing proclamations. This he did with quite as much zeal as Kieft had shown. Sabbath breaking, brawling, and drunkenness were forbidden. Liquors could not be sold, except to travellers, before two o'clock on Sundays, when there was no preaching, otherwise not before four o'clock, and after nine o'clock in the evening. The selling of liquor to savages was forbidden at all times. The most stringent regulations against smuggling were proclaimed, and a new excise duty on wines and liquors was levied. The people protested without avail against these exactions. It was "like the crowning of Rehoboam," they said; "if their yoke was heavy under Kieft, it was still heavier under Stuyvesant." These regulations and many others of a petty character gave rise subsequently to a powerful opposition to his administration. The excuse for such exactions might have been the emptiness of the provincial treasury; but no excuse was offered. The finances of the colony were in a very disorganized condition. The war had ruined the farmers and they were consequently unable to stand taxation. To supplement the resources of the treasury, the Company's yachts *Cat* and *Love* were despatched on a cruise. As Holland was at war with Spain, it was hoped some of the enemy's richly laden galleons might be captured.

There seemed to be a most manifest unwillingness on the part of the people to furnish the funds necessary for the carrying out of some of the most pressing of Stuyvesant's instructions. The fort needed repairs, and the Indians had not been given the presents promised them at the close of the war. The director-general was helpless, being without money or goods. In the midst of his difficulties, he called his Council together and told it the exact condition of affairs. He was advised very tactfully that the only way to get the funds needed was to yield to the popular demand for representation. The people could then express their wishes and make known their wants; otherwise, they were not willing to be taxed without their consent. In accordance with the advice of the Council, an election was held in September, 1647, at which the people of Manhattan, Breukelen, Amersfoort, and Pavonia chose eighteen of their "most notable, reasonable, honest, and respectable" citizens. Of these, according to the custom of Holland, the director and his Council were to select nine men "as good and faithful interlocutors and trustees of the commonalty." When invited to do so, they were permitted to "advise and assist" in promoting the general welfare of the province.

The charter of concessions was dated September 25, 1647. O'Callaghan says of it, "meagre though it was in privileges and concessions, it deserves notice as marking the glimmering of popular freedom at this remote day." Of the Nine Men, three were selected from among the merchants, three from the citizens, and three from the farmers. Prior to the Indian war, the privilege had been granted the citizens of electing a Board, first of twelve and later of eight men. We will recall the fact that under Kieft the former was extinguished as soon as it demanded an extension of political power; whilst the latter was completely ignored by the director-general in all important matters of State. The Nine Men, however, were given a little more authority. They were to be consulted on all matters of importance. They were given limited judiciary powers—sitting in council in rotation to judge civil cases. Those who contemned their decision or appealed from it were fined.

Stuyvesant carefully hedged these meagre privileges. The director-general could attend the meetings in person and act as president or could appoint one of his Council to act in his stead. Only in the first election was the selection to be made by the voters. Later, the Nine Men were to nominate their successors. In each year, six of the nine were to retire, but were eligible for reëlection. This provision is found in Section IV of the charter. Annually, in December, six were to leave their seats, and from the most notable citizens twelve were to be nominated, who, "with the Nine assembled, shall be communicated to Us, without Our being *required to call in future the whole commonalty together.*" Out of the twelve the director and Council were to select six. The Nine Men thus formed a self-perpetuating body.

Stuyvesant so constructed the charter that they might fall more and more under his influence. In this, however, he was not altogether successful. The Nine contrived to act more or less independently, and represented as best they could the interests of the people. These were but the beginnings of constitutional government, yet the advance over the administration of Kieft was very marked. It is significant that this representation was a clear concession in return for taxation.

This popular body being organized, Stuyvesant lost no time in calling their special attention to the sad condition of the fort, to the want of a suitable church edifice, to the disgraceful state of public education in New Amsterdam, and to the mean appearance of the city itself. Most of the houses in New Amsterdam were built of wood and thatched with straw. Many of the chimneys were of wood. This statement was communicated to the Nine Men in writing, Stuyvesant being confined to his room by an attack of influenza, which was epidemic in New Netherland at that time. Most of the propositions made by the director-general were approved and a tax was voted. The Nine refused, however, to provide means for repairing the fort, holding very justly that the Company had agreed by the charter of 1629 to maintain the defences. This, they held, was no more than right, inasmuch as the people were required to pay customs, duties, excises, and tolls at the Company's mill.

Stuyvesant's relations with the Nine Men were very soon complicated by the larger issues that characterized his administration. He was shrewd, intelligent, sound in mind and judgment, but his abrupt, autocratic, imperious manner led him into many difficulties. This manner was due to some extent to his military training, but for the most part it was born in him. He could no more rid himself of it than he could replace his wooden leg with a sound one of flesh, blood, and bone. From the beginning of his administration—or *reign*, for that word more nearly characterizes his attitude toward the people—in 1647 to its overthrow

First engraved view of New Amsterdam, showing Manhattan Island as it was in 1630. From a copperplate published at Amsterdam in 1651, now in the New York Public Library, Lenox Branch.

by the English in 1664 he was in the midst of a continuous round of disputes. This period of New Netherland history might be treated very aptly under the headings of his different quarrels. First, he quarrelled with the colonial patroons; then, with the English in New England; then, with the Swedes on South River; and finally, with his own people of New Netherland. However, he was not able to isolate these disputes in such a manner that he might have but one on his hands at a time. He was either not adroit enough to do this, or uncontrollable circumstances made it impossible. Probably it was due to both these circumstances that he frequently had two or three quarrels on his hands at one time. With his people he quarrelled almost incessantly. The insatiably land-hungry Yankees continuously pressed over the territorial boundaries of New Netherland. The Swedes loudly proclaimed their rights to lands on South River in exact proportion to the lack of validity of their titles. The colonial patroons continued as of yore to infringe upon the privileges of the Company in every way that Dutch ingenuity assisted by distance from the governmental centre could suggest. Frequently, then, at the same time Stuyvesant would be engaged in disputes with the English and the Swedes about territorial claims; with the colonial patroons in regard to the respective merits of Company and patroonship privilege; and with his own people as to what were the prerogatives of the director and the privileges of the people. When it was not all these disputes together, it was a combination of some two or three of them. Attacked on South River by the Swedes; the object of anathemas hurled at him from New England; hectored by the silent schemings for aggrandizement on the part of the Colonial patroons; and execrated by a large part of the commonalty—it is no wonder that the governor frequently lost his temper, which was none too amiable at the best. The wonder is that he succeeded in keeping his head above the waters of the deluge that continually threatened to engulf him. A less valorous man would have succumbed long before the English tidal wave finally swamped him in 1664.

An account of Stuyvesant's quarrels, then, is a history of his administration. His dispute with New England and his more important troubles with his own people we shall consider in the next chapter. After a brief statement of his attempts at preserving the privileges of the Company against the unwarranted encroachment of the colonial patroons, we shall consider at some length the immediate difficulties that led to the final overthrow of the Swedish power on South River. The quarrel between the Dutch and the Swedes on South River has been brought up to the year 1647, when the assumption of power by Stuyvesant introduced a most vigorous policy in the maintenance of Dutch rights to the territory on that river. Before continuing this subject, however, let us turn for a moment's notice to the dispute between Stuyvesant and the colonial patroons. The scene of the narrative lies for the most part in the north of New Netherland.

By the terms of Stuyvesant's commission, which the States General issued to him on July 28, 1646, he was required to promote the affairs of and to maintain in good order "everything for the service of the United Netherland and the General West India Company." Most of Stuyvesant's troubles with the patroons and with the commonalty may be traced to his honest determination to carry out these instructions of his commission. He was determined to maintain the prerogative of the West India Company at all hazards, whether against the people of the province, the lordly patroons, the Swedes, or the English. For the most part, he was impersonal in his enforcement of these prerogatives. Even his imperious bearing and his lordly self-esteem might be credited in part to his realization of the fact that he represented the privileges of the West India Company on the one hand and the sovereignty of the States General on the other. Occupying somewhat the position of a feudal lord, he had to pay some heed to the rather shadowy power of the States General and much more heed to the very material power of the West India Company. The patroons were of the character of feudal chiefs, over whom the director-general was required to assert "an authority which they refused to acknowledge." The interests of the Company were Stuyvesant's first concern, and whoever or whatever opposed these interests he attacked most uncompromisingly. In this he was no respecter of persons, as is evidenced by his frequent clashes with those high in official power. This is very aptly illustrated in an incident that occurred on his voyage to New Netherland to assume the directorship. His little fleet had captured a Spanish ship and he invited Van Dincklagen, his vice-director, to consult with him as to the best disposal of the prize. Van Dyck, the treasurer, very naturally supposing his attendance was expected, entered the cabin. But no sooner had he put his foot inside than Stuyvesant gave him a push none too gentle, at the same time exclaiming: "Get out of here! when I want you I'll call for you!"

From the moment when the patroons first planted colonies in New Netherland, jealousies arose between them and the directors of the West India Company. The continuance of the patroon colonies was opposed. They were considered injurious to the country. For this reason, Pavonia and Zwaanendal were repurchased in 1634 and the patroon of Rensselaerwyck was requested to cede to the Company his privileges and possessions. Failing to secure Rensselaerwyck, the directors next attempted to circumscribe the jurisdictions and to weaken the power of the patroons. The two representatives of these conflicting interests of the Company and the patroon were respectively Stuyvesant and Brant van Slechtenhorst. To the latter was intrusted the immediate management of Rensselaerwyck, with the official titles of Director of the Colony, President of the Court of Justice, and "Superintendent of all the bouweries, farms, mills and other property belonging to the patroon." He knew full well the chartered prerogatives of his patroon, and was determined to brook no interference with them from any outside authority. The director-general might issue as many proclamations as he saw fit, but he would not recognize them unless they were endorsed by his own superior, the patroon.

It was perfectly evident that where two such men as Van Slechtenhorst and Stuyvesant came together with two such conflicting claims to authority there was bound to be an explosion. It came almost within a month of the former's assumption of the superintendency of Rensselaerwyck. Stuyvesant proclaimed the first Wednesday in May, 1648, as a day for fasting and for public worship in the churches of New Netherland. A copy of the proclamation was forwarded to Rensselaerwyck and arrived April 26th. It was not received in "that spirit of submissive obedience which the Director General demanded for all of his orders." It was considered an invasion of the prerogative of the patroon, and Van Slechtenhorst protested against it. Stuyvesant considered this act as dangerously approaching treason, and the thought with him was coincident with action. He gathered up a military escort and proceeded to Fort Orange. Upon his arrival and departure he was honored by several salutes from the patroon's three pieces of cannon. So say the records, at least, and in addition we are informed that Van Slechtenhorst purchased twenty pounds of powder, spent twenty guilders for beer and victuals, and provided the "Heer General" upon his departure with "divers young fowls and pork."

Van Slechtenhorst was summoned before the director-general and charged with infringing the Company's sovereignty. The former was a foeman worthy of the old general's steel. He replied: "Your complaints are unjust; I have more reason to complain, on behalf of my patroons, against you." In answer to this, Stuyvesant drew up a long list of protests and ordered Van Slechtenhorst to correct all the abuses mentioned. The latter denied *in toto* the director-general's right to interfere in the affairs of the patroonship and refused point-blank to be governed by his proclamations. Retort followed retort until the departure of Stuyvesant. No sooner had that departure been made than Van Slechtenhorst continued to conduct affairs in direct opposition to the commands of Stuyvesant. This exasperated the director-general beyond measure. A squad of soldiers was sent to Fort Orange with orders to arrest Van Slechtenhorst if necessary, in the most civil manner possible, and serve upon him a summons to appear at Fort Amsterdam to answer for his conduct. These soldiers were not very well qualified to carry out instructions demanding such tact. They destroyed the patroon's timber and killed his deer, and they were insolent to the commander. This rude conduct, together with their instructions to pull down houses within close proximity to the fort, aroused the ire of even the Indians. They demanded if "Wooden Leg, in whom they had confided as their protector, intended to tear down the houses which were to shelter them in stormy and wintry weather?" If land were all he wanted, his soldiers could accompany them home, and they would be given plenty of land in the Minqua country.

Van Slechtenhorst was ordered peremptorily to appear at a court to be held in April at New Amsterdam. He refused to obey the commands of the director-general and made a long and angry protest. The dispute continued with varying degrees of intensity until 1651, when it again reached a climax. A call for a subsidy brought a protest from Rensselaerwyck, and Van Slechtenhorst was sent to New Amsterdam to remonstrate with the director and Council against it. Shortly after his arrival he was arrested and detained four months before he made his escape. The trouble grew more serious, until the following year, 1652, witnessed the close of what O'Callaghan calls "Van Slechtenhorst's reign." On April 18th, nine armed soldiers burst into his house and, without any preliminaries, dragged him to Fort Orange a prisoner, "against all his protests, where neither his children, his master, nor his friends, were allowed to speak to him," whilst "his furs, his clothes, and his meat were left hanging on the door-posts, and his house and papers were abandoned to the mercy of his enemies." He was then carried to New Amsterdam, "to be tormented, in his sickness and old age, with unheard-of and insufferable persecutions, by those serving a Christian government, professing the same religion, and living under the same authority." The patroon and co-directors of Rensselaerwyck sent on December 16, 1652, a vigorous protest to the Amsterdam Chamber, complaining of what they termed Stuyvesant's high-handed measures. The directors replied in vague terms, and the patroon immediately addressed a memorial to the States General, demanding justice and redress. The Amsterdam Chamber, after considerable delay, replied to some of the charges brought against Stuyvesant, their agent in New Netherland. The directors then taking the offensive made counter charges against the agents of the patroon. In the end, the dispute was settled entirely to the satisfaction of the director-general. He was sustained at every point.

While these events were occurring on North River, Dutch interests on South River were not altogether neglected by the authorities at New Amsterdam. The Dutch settlements on South River, however, might have fallen into a state of utter decay had it not been for the loyal efforts of one man, Commissary Hudde. He, as we have seen, infused great activity into affairs in that quarter and appears to have made every endeavor to extend Dutch influence and dominion. He found it by no means an easy task, however, for in that vicinity the Swedish Company was more powerful than the Dutch Company. The Swedes were extremely arrogant and evidently desired to pick a quarrel, with the end in view of driving the Dutch from the river. Printz, the Governor of New Sweden, was as zealous in the interests of the Swedes as was Hudde in the interests of the Dutch. He had been tampering with the Minquas and had endeavored to obtain their consent to the erection of a fort in their country, by means of which he expected to secure from thirty to forty thousand beavers annually.

With this end in view he had fortified the mouth of the Schuylkill—the highway to the Minquas' territory. On hearing this, the Indians of Passayunk invited the Dutch to build a trading post at that point. Furthermore, to show their sincerity, they had warned the Swedes away and had planted on the ground, with their own hands, the standard of the Prince of Orange. Hudde proceeded without delay to put the project into execution. No sooner had Fort Beversreede been completed, April 27, 1648, than Hendrick Huyghens, the Swedish commissary, arrived with seven or eight men, and demanded by what authority Hudde had erected that building? "By order of my masters and the previous consent of the savages," was the reply. Moens Kling, the commander of the Swedish fort in the vicinity, arrived later with twenty-four armed men. They were ordered to lay down their muskets and take up their axes, whereupon they cut down every tree near the place—even the fruit trees which Hudde had lately planted.

Intelligence of this violence soon reached New Amsterdam, and Vice-director Van Dincklagen and Jean de la Montagne were commissioned by the Council to investigate the affair. They arrived on the 7th of June, 1648, and several days later, in the presence of Printz, made a protest against his illegal occupation of the Schuylkill. The commissioners did little else than meet the Indians and have them confirm past and present purchases of land. Far from exerting a restraining influence upon Printz, the visit seemed to exasperate him to further deeds of violence. It is not necessary to mention in detail the numerous disputes that took place between the Dutch and the Swedes in the neighborhood of the Schuylkill. They were nearly all of minor importance, but at the same time they were exceedingly irritating to Dutch pride.

Many of these petty incidents were recited to Stuyvesant by Hudde when the latter, in response to a summons, visited Manhattan in September of 1648. He returned in October and continued to issue protests against the encroachments of the Swedes; for the desire for peace on the part of his superiors seems to have limited him to paper warfare. The manner of addressing Printz in these protests not inaccurately gives us an idea of the tone of their contents. Now the protest would begin: "To the noble governor, De Heer John Printz—Sir Governor;" then it would read: "Noble and valiant John Printz;" while later it would run: "Honorable and obliging good friend—accept my cordial salutation;" or: "Noble honorable lord, John Printz." Hudde could do little else than to hurl protests at Printz. To vindicate Dutch honor and to maintain Dutch rights, to defend Forts Nassau and Beversreede, such weapons of warfare were rather ineffectual. Hudde had but six able-bodied men at this time on the river. The Swedes had it all much their own way.

On November 9, 1648, Secretary Van Tienhoven addressed a letter to Stuyvesant from Fort Beversreede suggesting that it would be advisable for the latter to make a trip to South River and look into the situation for himself. Stuyvesant did not find the opportunity to make the trip until July, 1651. The Dutch West India Company had finally come to a realization of the necessity of settling the differences respecting the jurisdiction on South River with Christina, Queen of Sweden. In a letter of instructions to Stuyvesant, dated March 21, 1651, the directors of the Company had already informed him of their intention to arrange matters with the Swedes. "In the mean time," the instructions read, "your honor will endeavor to maintain the rights of the company, in all justice and equity, while we again recommend that your honor will conduct himself with that discretion and circumspection by which all complaints, disputes, and coolness between friends and allies may be avoided." This letter explains satisfactorily the spirit of compromise with which Stuyvesant began and carried out his visit to South River. It is also another incident in addition to those already cited in a preceding chapter explanatory of the maintenance of the status quo.

Stuyvesant arrived at Fort Nassau on South River, accompanied by Dominie Grasmeer and a large suite of officers. He grasped fully the wisdom of terminating the feuds between the Dutch and Swedes and arriving at an understanding with Printz. In this way their mutual enemy, the English, might be kept out of that territory. With this object in view, he communicated with Printz immediately upon his arrival. He explained the Dutch title to the lands in dispute, and demanded an exhibition of the Swedish title. The Dutch title was stated to rest on right of first European discovery and occupation and upon actual purchase from the Indians many years before the arrival of the Swedes. Printz merely replied that the Swedish limits were "wide and broad enough." He was not able to show his titles. He claimed that they were at Stockholm. One of the chief sachems, Wappan-zewan, afterward informed Stuyvesant, however, that Printz was endeavoring at that very time to purchase from him the lands upon which the Swedes were settled. Printz had maintained that he had already purchased these lands. The Indians thereupon conveyed to Stuyvesant, whom they called "the Grand Sachem of the Manhattans," the title to the lands in dispute.

Stuyvesant succeeded in doing little toward carrying out his mission except calling a council of Indian chiefs to meet at Fort Nassau. After a solemn conference, the chiefs presented to the Dutch "as a free gift" large tracts of land. The only conditions made were by Chief Pemenatta, who insisted that the Dutch should repair his gun when out of order and give the Indians a little maize when they required it. Fort Nassau, situated on the Jersey shore, being inconveniently far up the river, was demolished and a new fort called Casimir was erected on the opposite bank of the river, about four miles from Fort Christina. Printz protested most vigorously against the erection of the new fort, but was nevertheless willing to arrive at some friendly understanding with Stuyvesant before the latter's departure. Both men " mutually promised to cause no difficulties or hostilities to each other, but to keep neighborly friendship and correspondence together and act as friends and allies." Having accomplished very little toward the amicable settlement of affairs on South River, Stuyvesant and his suite returned to New Amsterdam.

The finances of the Company at New Amsterdam were very much disorganized by reason of this expedition. The absolute necessities of the government could not be met for the winter and this new debt paid at the same time. The ancient expedient of paying off debts at fifty per cent was resorted to. A certificate was given for the other half, to be paid in goods the following year. The expedition did not meet with the unqualified approval of the directors of the West India Company. In a letter addressed to Stuyvesant and dated April 4, 1652, they expressed their surprise at the trip being made at all. They were not quite sure that the demolition of Fort Nassau was an act of prudence. They were at a loss to know for what reason the new fort had been named Casimir—it being more nearly a Swedish name than a Dutch name. The project of building another fort on the east bank of South River was left to his discretion. He was warned to be on his guard lest the new fort be surprised and captured by the Swedes.

Temporarily, at least, a better state of feeling seemed to exist between the Dutch and the Swedes on South River. For some time prior to the building of Fort Casimir, the Swedes had received no help from the mother country. Printz, apprehensive of danger from the near vicinity of the Dutch, or having become discouraged by the neglect of the home authorities, or by reason of his unpopularity, petitioned his government for permission to return home. Without waiting for this permission, which arrived December 12, 1653, he returned to Sweden, having left his son-in-law, John Pappegoya, in temporary charge of affairs. The people of New Sweden then petitioned Stuyvesant to take them under his protection.  Stuyvesant declined, however, to accede to their request until he could learn the views of the Amsterdam Chamber.  His superiors addressed a communication to him on November 4, 1653, urging him to conduct himself "with all possible prudence toward the Swedes . . . carefully avoiding everything which might give them offence, as it would be highly improper to increase, at this critical period, the number of our enemies."  With regard to the petition of the Swedes to be taken under the Dutch sovereignty, they rather encouraged the project, at the same time stating their willingness to protect all who would be obedient to the Dutch laws.  Nevertheless, they left further action in the matter to the director-general's discretion.  Stuyvesant, however, did not encourage the colonists to change their allegiance.  This was the last opportunity of peaceably acquiring New Sweden, for in the fall of 1654 the Swedish Company made a new effort to improve the condition of its colony.  It was time something was done, for the colony had dwindled to sixteen persons.

Affairs on South River, however, reached a crisis when John Rysingh, formerly secretary of the College of Commerce in Sweden, arrived, May 31, 1654, as a deputy governor.  He was accompanied by about three hundred persons and was to succeed Printz as governor upon the latter's departure from New Sweden.  He received his appointment from the General College of Commerce, to which the government of Sweden had given the management of its affairs on South River.  He was instructed to avoid a conflict with Stuyvesant and was particularly warned against making any hostile demonstration against Fort Casimir.  But no sooner had he appeared before the fort than, in violation of his instructions, he demanded its surrender and, in fact, the surrender of the whole river.  Van Tienhoven called upon the commander, Gerrit Bikker, to defend the fort.  "What can I do?" the latter replied, in despair; "there is no powder."  Shortly after, two guns loaded with

shot were fired over the fort as a signal, and almost at the
same time Swen Schute rushed into the fort at the head of
twenty or thirty men and took possession of it. Bikker
offered no resistance whatever, but instead welcomed them
as friends and struck his flag. The Dutch soldiers were
then driven from the fort, and their goods, together with
those of Bikker, were confiscated. Practically everything in
the fort was taken. Bikker, in a letter to Stuyvesant, said:
"I could hardly, by entreaties, bring it so far as to bear
that I with my wife and children were not likewise shut
out almost naked." Van Tienhoven and another commissioner were permitted to go to Rysingh to demand an
explanation of his conduct. Rysingh replied most curtly
that he had acted in pursuance of orders from the crown
of Sweden; that the Swedish ambassadors at The Hague
had been assured by the States General and the West India
Company that the erection of the Dutch fort on Swedish
soil had not been authorized; and that if the Dutch were in
the way of the Swedes, then he was to "drive them off."
After vouchsafing this explanation, Rysingh gave Van Tienhoven a resounding slap on the breast, saying at the same
time: "Go! tell your Governor that!"

Of the ten or twelve Dutch soldiers in the fort, seven or
eight, with Van Tienhoven, were sent to Manhattan. The
others, with Bikker and most of the colonists, after taking
an oath of allegiance to Sweden, were permitted to remain.
The name of the fort was changed to Fort Trinity, because, according to Swedish accounts, it was captured on
Trinity Sunday. Bikker sent Stuyvesant an account of
the capture of the fort, as did also Rysingh in a letter dated
May 27, 1654. It was soon rebuilt under the superintendence of Peter Lindstrom, the Swedish engineer. Lindstrom
also prepared a large map for the Swedish government,
embracing both sides of Delaware River as far as Trenton.

The news of this piece of treachery, committed as it
was in time of peace and in direct opposition to special instructions, aroused the indignation of the Dutch at New

Amsterdam. Stuyvesant was in the midst of his preparations for the defence of New Netherland against an expected attack by the English. Consequently, he was not able to retaliate immediately. This bit of Swedish folly had, however, as a sequel the overthrow of New Sweden and the appropriation of the territory by the Dutch. Stuyvesant did retaliate shortly by capturing a Swedish ship, the *Golden Shark*, in charge of Hendrick van Elswyck, and bound for South River. The ship had entered the harbor of Manhattan by mistake, and the captain had sent a boat to Manhattan to secure a pilot to take him to South River. Van Elswyck was sent to South River to invite Rysingh to visit New Amsterdam to confer with Stuyvesant for the settlement of "unexpected differences." He was promised a cordial reception, comfortable lodging, and courteous treatment. He declined the invitation and failed to send a representative, although especially requested to do so. Stuyvesant then confiscated the vessel and cargo, notwithstanding a formal protest from Van Elswyck.

The news of the treacherous capture of Fort Casimir soon reached Holland. On November 16, 1654, the Amsterdam directors ordered Stuyvesant to "exert every nerve to revenge that injury, not only by restoring affairs to their former situation, but by driving the Swedes from every side of the river, *as they did with us*." Two armed ships, the *King Solomon* and the *Great Christopher*, were fitted out, and the drum was beaten daily in the streets of Amsterdam to invite volunteers to embark in them on the proposed expedition for the conquest of New Sweden. Stuyvesant was likewise given permission to press into service a sufficient number of ships to complete the expedition. He was instructed to leave nothing untried to apprehend Bikker, for it was difficult to say which was the more contemptible—the capture of the fort by the Swedes, or its cowardly surrender by the Dutch commander.

Stuyvesant now had a free hand to act, and it was necessary to do so at once before reinforcements could reach the

Swedes. The unfortunate war between the Dutch Republic and the English Commonwealth, which began July 8, 1652, ended in 1654. The day the news of peace reached Manhattan (July 16th), was set apart as a day of general thanksgiving. Little danger was now apprehended in the direction of New England. Furthermore, affairs were in a rather unsettled condition in Sweden. Axel Oxenstiern, the faithful chancellor of Gustavus Adolphus and his daughter, Queen Christina, who had done so much for the settlement of South River, died in August, 1654. In the same year Christina abdicated the throne of Sweden in favor of her cousin, Karl X. Gustaf—better known as Charles X. After the Peace of Münster, Holland had no longer any particular reason for avoiding interference with Sweden.

The winter of 1654 passed, however, without anything overt being done. Protests and counter protests passed between the Swedes and the Dutch relative to the capture and confiscation of the ship *Golden Shark* and its cargo. In the spring of 1655, the directors engaged from the Burgomasters of Amsterdam one of their "largest and best vessels," the *Vigilance*, of thirty-six guns. In this they sent out an additional force of two hundred men. Upon the arrival of the *Vigilance* at New Amsterdam, the expedition was commanded to start with all "possible despatch and prudence," even though Stuyvesant had not yet returned from a voyage he had undertaken to the West Indies. Secrecy was enjoined, inasmuch as the directors had learned that immense preparations were being made in Sweden to reinforce the colony on South River. Upon the river itself, however, the Swedes were under slight apprehension as to their security and did not learn of the military preparations of their enemy until the punitive expedition was about to start.

Stuyvesant, having returned from Barbadoes on August 16th, proclaimed the 25th of the same month as a "general fast, thanks, and prayer day" for the success of the expedition. A call for volunteers was made and a pension promised everyone who should be wounded in the service. Pilots were engaged and all longshoremen were impressed into the service. Each merchantman was ordered to furnish two of its crew and a proportionate share of provisions and ammunition. Three river yachts were chartered, and a French privateer, *L'Espérance,* just arrived at New Amsterdam, was likewise engaged. In the midst of the preparations, a question of some importance arose: "Should the Jews be enlisted?" Stuyvesant was not long in settling the question. "In the celebrated emporium of New Amsterdam," he decided, "Jews are not called to take part in such duties." They were declared exempt, though they were perfectly willing to serve. In lieu of service, a tax of sixty-five stuivers a month was levied upon every Jew between the ages of sixteen and sixty.

On the 5th of September, Sunday, after the usual morning service, every possible preparation having been made, the little fleet set sail. It consisted of seven vessels, with a force on board of from six to seven hundred men. Stuyvesant himself was in command and was accompanied by Vice-director De Sille and Dominie Megapolensis as chaplain. The next afternoon, the fleet anchored safely before Fort Elsinburg, which was found in ruins and deserted. Here Stuyvesant consumed several days in reviewing his fleet and in dividing it into five sections, each under its own colors. By Friday morning, between eight and nine o'clock, the expedition was landed above Fort Trinity, within gunshot. Stuyvesant immediately despatched Captain-lieutenant Derck Smidt with a drummer to demand the surrender of the fort. Swen Schute, the commander, requested time to communicate with Rysingh, but was not accorded the privilege. Meanwhile, the Dutch cut off communication between Fort Trinity and Fort Christina, and the Swedes were again summoned to surrender. At Schute's request a parley was granted, and the representatives of the two forces met "in the valley midway between the fort and the Dutch battery." Nothing came of the interview, and the third and last order

to surrender was given.  Another delay was requested and
granted, the Dutch battery construction not being sufficiently
far advanced to proceed with the attack.

The next morning, September 11th, the Swedish commander, seeing the folly of further resistance, went on board
the *Balance*, upon which was Stuyvesant, and capitulated.
The terms of the capitulation were liberal.  The commander was permitted to remove all the artillery of the
crown at his pleasure; twelve men, with colors flying and
with their full arms and accoutrements, were permitted to
march out with the commander as his life guard, but the
rest only with their side arms; and the commander and
his officers were to retain their personal property.  About
noon the Dutch troops marched into the fort.  About thirty
Swedes took the oath of allegiance to New Netherland
prescribed by Stuyvesant and asked leave to move to New
Amsterdam.  The next day being Sunday, Dominie Megapolensis preached a sermon of thanksgiving to the "army
of occupation."

The capture of Fort Trinity was accomplished with so
little noise that the event was not known to Rysingh at
Fort Christina until the day after the event occurred.  In
fact, out of nine or ten of his best men who had been sent
to reinforce Schute all except two were captured by the
Dutch advance guard.  Van Elswyck was now sent to persuade Stuyvesant not to move on Fort Christina, but without
success.  Rysingh, now realizing that Fort Christina was
to be attacked, employed all his forces during the night to
strengthen his position.  On the following morning, the
Dutch threw up a battery and intrenched themselves on
the opposite bank of Christina Creek.  By the 15th they had
invested the fort on all sides.  The fleet was then brought
into the mouth of the creek and cannon was mounted
in strategic places.  Stuyvesant then commanded Rysingh
"either to evacuate the country, or to remain there under
Dutch protection."  The Swedish commander stoutly refused to do either.  But he could not hold out long against

# VRYHEDEN

### By de Vergaderinghe van de Negenthiene vande Geoctroyeerde West-Indische Compagnie vergunt aen allen den ghenen / die eenighe Colonien in Nieu-Nederlandt sullen planten.

*In het licht ghegheven*

Om bekent te maken wat Profijten ende Voordeelen aldaer in Nieu-Nederlandt, voor de Coloniers ende der selver Patroonen ende Meesters, midtsgaders de Participanten, die de Colonien aldaer planten, zijn becomen.

*Westindjen Kan syn Nederlands groot gewin*
*Verkleynt s'vijands Macht brengt silver platen in.*

### T'AMSTELREDAM,

By Marten Iansz Brandt Boeckvercooper / woonende by de nieuwe Kerck / in de Gereformeerde Catechismus. Anno 1630.

Title-page of the *Charter of Liberties and Exemptions*, dated 1629, which attempted to transplant to America the feudal tenure and burdens of Continental Europe. *From the original in the New York Public Library, Lenox Branch.*

so superior a force. His powder was practically exhausted and he had but thirty men for the defence. In the meantime, the Dutch troops were pillaging the Swedes who lived outside the fort, and, to add to his trouble, Rysingh's own garrison began to show signs of mutiny. Most of them were worn out by constant watching, some were sick; there had been some desertions, and Stuyvesant threatened to give them no quarter if they stubbornly held out much longer. Twenty-four hours were allowed in which to capitulate. This occurred on the 25th of September, after a siege of fourteen days. The Swedes marched out "with their arms, colors flying, matches lighted, drums beating, and fifes playing." The Dutch then took possession of the fort, hauled down the Swedish flag, and hoisted their own.

The terms of the capitulation permitted all Swedes who desired to leave the country to do so, and the Dutch were to furnish the means of transportation. Those who desired to remain would be protected in their "persons, property, or conscience." Permission was given to Rysingh and Van Elswyck to land either in France or England. Stuyvesant lent the former three hundred pounds, Flemish, to be repaid within six months at Amsterdam—the property of the crown and Company being held as security.

Immediately after the surrender, Stuyvesant, following out his instructions, offered to return the fort to Rysingh on certain "honorable and fair conditions." Rysingh, however, declined the offer. The Dutch were accused of committing many outrages on the inhabitants after the fall of the fort. There is considerable evidence to support this contention. In one of Rysingh's remonstrances to Stuyvesant, he says "women were violently torn from their houses, whole buildings were destroyed; that oxen, cows and swine, and other creatures were butchered, the horses wantonly shot, the plantations destroyed, and the whole country was left so desolate that scarce any means remained for the subsistence of the inhabitants." He is supported in this statement by Acrelius. A Dutch mob attacked Rysingh himself and stole most of his private property. There is no evidence to show that these atrocities were committed with the connivance or even the knowledge of Stuyvesant.

Rysingh and Van Elswyck were conveyed to Manhattan in the *Balance*. Later, they were sent to Europe and landed in England, where they gave the Swedish minister the first information of the overthrow of the Swedish power on the Delaware. In New Amsterdam a long and heated correspondence was carried on between Rysingh and Stuyvesant. The former claimed that Stuyvesant broke the terms of capitulation in several important particulars. On Stuyvesant's departure for Manhattan, Captain Derck Smidt was temporarily placed in command of the Dutch interests on South River. Later, November 29th, John Paul Jacquet was given a commission as permanent vice-director.

Thus fell New Sweden, the immediate result of a rash act of an injudicious governor. Had Rysingh not attacked Fort Casimir in disobedience to the express instructions of his government, the Swedish power might have been prolonged for a time longer. In the end, however, it was doomed to give way to the far superior forces of the Dutch or the English. In 1656, the States General and Sweden made the conquest a matter of international negotiations. The Swedes protested against the Dutch aggression, but in the end the matter was dropped. In the same year the interests of the West India Company on South River were sold to the city of Amsterdam. The colony of New Amstel was erected and control passed from New Netherland. For seventeen years the Dutch and the Swedes had occupied the river jointly. Such, however, had been their jealousies arising from a mutual "thirst for power" that the country had made little or no advance. The Swedes had made more progress than the Dutch, notwithstanding the neglect of the mother country, but it was not what it should have been even under the circumstances. The clash between the three nationalities, Dutch, Swedes, and English, in one of the three great river valleys of the East, resulted in the complete victory of the Dutch over the Swedes. The scene of the next conflict will be North River, and in place of the Swedes the Dutch will have as opponents the far more powerful English.

A

# Brief Description

OF

## NEW-YORK:

Formerly Called

### New-Netherlands.

With the Places thereunto Adjoyning.

Together with the

Manner of its Scituation, Fertility of the Soyle, Healthfulness of the Climate, and the Commodities thence produced.

ALSO

Some Directions and Advice to such as shall go thither: An Account of what Commodities they shall take with them; The Profit and Pleasure that may accrew to them thereby.

LIKEWISE

A Brief RELATION of the Customs of the Indians there.

By *DANIEL DENTON.*

*LONDON,*

Printed for *John Hancock* at the first Shop in *Popes-Head-Alley* in *Cornhil* at the three Bibles, and *William Bradley* at the three Bibles

---

THE

# HISTORY

Of the PROVINCE of

## NEW-YORK,

FROM THE

First Discovery to the Year M.DCC.XXXII.

To which is annexed,

A Description of the Country, with a short Account of the Inhabitants, their Trade, Religious and Political State, and the Constitution of the Courts of Justice in that Colony.

> Lo! swarming o'er the new discover'd World,
> Gay Colonies extend; the calm Retreat
> Of undeserv'd Distress.
> ———— Bound by social Freedom, firm they rise;
> Of Britain's Empire the Support and Strength.   TROMSON.
>
> Nec minor est Virtus, quam quærere, parta tueri.

By WILLIAM SMITH, A.M.

LONDON:

Printed for THOMAS WILCOX, Bookseller at *Virgil's Head*, opposite the New Church in the Strand.
M.DCC.LVII.

---

Title-pages of the earliest separate printed account in English of New York, and of the first comprehensive account of the colony. From the originals in the Columbia University Library.

## CHAPTER VI

### ENGLISH CONQUEST OF NEW NETHERLAND, 1655–1664

THE passage of the first Navigation Act, in October, 1651, by the English Parliament marked a change in the English commercial policy that was productive of momentous results. It brought about an estrangement between England and her North American colonies that led eventually to the independence of thirteen of the latter. It brought about also an estrangement between England and her ancient friend and ally, Holland, that resulted in the ruin of the Dutch naval and commercial power and the establishment of the supremacy of that of England.

By the middle of the seventeenth century the Dutch enjoyed the greater part of the carrying trade between Europe and the West Indies, and Holland had become the commercial centre of Europe. Three-fourths of the carrying trade of England was done in Dutch bottoms and by Dutch sailors. The commerce of Holland followed the tricolored flag of the United Provinces over every sea. Her colonial outposts were scattered throughout Asia, Africa, and America. England witnessed this marvellous growth of Dutch trade, and was filled with jealousy and alarm upon comparing it with the rapid decay of her own. "Already her ships began to lie idle at her quays, and her mariners to seek employment in the vessels of the Dutch." Even while the negotiations with St. John were being carried on, the States General concluded a commercial treaty with Denmark which was very much opposed to the best commercial interests of England. Then, again, after the triumph of the Parliamentary cause over the personal rule of the Stuarts, many royalists had found refuge in Virginia, Barbadoes, and other West Indian settlements. Thus it happened that after the rest of the dependencies of England had been brought to a recognition of the new government, the white population of these other colonies might be said to have been in a state of open rebellion. Barbadoes had, for example, actually received Lord Willoughby as governor under a commission from Charles II., who was at that time a fugitive in Holland. It went so far as to proclaim Charles king.

It was thus largely by reason of these circumstances, taken advantage of by persons wishing to injure Cromwell through the expense of a foreign war or to revenge themselves for slights and injuries received at the hands of the Dutch, that Parliament passed the Trade and Navigation Act. The act decreed that no merchandise of Asia, Africa, or America should be imported into England or any of her dependencies except in English-built ships, belonging either to English or English-colonial subjects. Furthermore, that the ships must have English commanders and be manned by crews three-fourths of whom, at least, were English. It was further decreed that no products of Europe should be brought to England, unless in English vessels or in those of the country in which the imported cargoes were produced. This act was also accompanied by the issuance of letters of reprisal to some English merchants who considered themselves aggrieved by the Dutch.

These measures affected the Dutch with particular severity, and one of the consequences was undoubtedly the war with Holland that broke out the year following. Their immediate effect was the lopping off of one of the principal sources of Dutch commercial supremacy and the capture of eighty Dutch ships as prizes. The Dutch were now as eager to court English friendship as a few months before they had been disinclined to accept it. In the following

December they sent ambassadors to the English Commonwealth to protest against these hostile measures. They were instructed, likewise, to propose a treaty providing for a free trade to the West Indies and Virginia and for a settlement of the boundaries between the English and Dutch colonies in America. Neither of these propositions was acceptable to England. The Dutch had forbidden the English to trade with the Dutch colonies, and now the Dutch were prohibited from engaging in trade with the English colonies. With regard to the colonial boundary proposition, the very ominous reply was made that the English had been the "first planters of the northern continent of America," and now had settlements from the "southernmost part of Virginia, in 37° N. Lat., to New Foundland in 52°." The English maintained very naïvely, furthermore, that they knew of no plantations of the Dutch within those bounds except a small number on Hudson River. Consequently, they were convinced that it was not necessary at the present time to settle the boundaries, but that it might be done at a more convenient time in the future. The English did, however, offer to reopen the negotiations on a basis of free trade on both sides. But the Dutch ambassadors were not instructed to offer reciprocal trade. Holland was hampered by two enormous commercial monopolies, and to these was intrusted the government of her colonies. The West India Company controlled New Netherland and, of course, was not inclined to support a proposition that would dispossess her of valuable privileges. The negotiations consequently proved fruitless, and the ambassadors were recalled.

The two nations soon came to blows. Even while the negotiations were still pending, Van Tromp encountered the British fleet under Blake in the Downs, and a bloody but indecisive battle followed. This led to a declaration of war on July 8, 1652. A series of brilliant naval engagements followed. For some time neither nation seemed to have the advantage. Van Tromp, defeated by Blake, gave way to De Ruyter, but was later reinstated in command. Van Tromp then defeated Blake off the Naze, November 28th, and cruised the Channel with a broom at his mast head implying that he had swept the English from the seas. But his exultation was premature. The next year (1653) saw Blake able to fight a drawn battle of two days' duration, and June 3d of that year saw the complete defeat of the Dutch admiral. The next year witnessed the death of Van Tromp and the complete ruin of the naval power of Holland. The Dutch merchant shipping likewise had suffered so severely that the States were driven to treat for peace. Cromwell, who had recently turned out the Long Parliament, was very glad to close a war between two Protestant powers that had so many things in common. The treaty was signed in 1654, and Denmark, the Hanseatic towns, and the Swiss provinces were parties to it. The supremacy of the English flag in the British seas was recognized; the Navigation Act was accepted; and the infant Prince of Orange was excluded from the stadholdership.

While all the United Provinces were in a state of turmoil as a result of the war with the English Commonwealth, the States General did not neglect to take precautions for the protection of New Netherland. Stuyvesant was instructed to keep a careful watch over the English colonies. By reason of the superior power of the English in America it was deemed impolitic to precipitate actual hostilities. Broils with the people of New England were to be studiously avoided, and their friendship, particularly that of the English of Virginia, was to be carefully cultivated. If, however, New England was determined to fight and should precipitate hostilities, then the aid of the Indians was to be solicited and any other means of defence was to be employed. Nevertheless, as a measure of precaution, Stuyvesant was instructed to arm and drill all freemen, soldiers, and sailors; to appoint officers and places of rendezvous; to get together a supply of munitions of war; and to inspect the fortifications at New Amsterdam, Fort Orange, and Fort Casimir. Proper military precautions were not neglected on Manhattan. A wall was built across the island at the northern limit of the city to keep out hostile forces landing at the north. This was the beginning of the Wall Street of to-day. A line of round palisades, six inches in diameter and twelve feet in height, was also constructed. It was backed by a sloping earthwork four feet in height.

The news of the war created but little less excitement in New England than it had created in New Netherland. All wondered what policy the Dutch would pursue in America. The Puritan colonies sympathized with Parliament and had very vaguely defined ideas of an annexation of New Netherland. Stuyvesant saw the danger, and to counteract their schemes put himself in communication with the governments of New England and Virginia. He expressed the friendly feelings of the West India Company and of the authorities of New Netherland, and proposed that peace should be maintained in spite of the war between their mother countries. The governors of Connecticut and New Haven were never very friendly to Stuyvesant. This very poorly concealed hostility on the part of the two New England colonies, aggravated by the European war and the domestic troubles at New Amsterdam, made Stuyvesant's position at this crisis a most precarious one indeed. To appreciate fully his troubles with New Netherland, it will be advisable to take up the thread of the narrative of his domestic troubles at the point we left off in the preceding chapter. After that has been done, the account of the difficulties with New England may be continued until their climax in the English conquest of New Netherland in 1664.

Stuyvesant found his troubles at New Amsterdam as vexatious as those upon South River. His choleric temperament and exaggerated view of the importance of his official position led him into constant quarrels. No sooner was he free from one than another claimed his energies. The Kuyter-Melyn affair was hardly disposed of when he found himself involved in a quarrel with the Nine Men. Troubles had been accumulating some time before they reached a climax. Kieft had failed to collect debts due to the Company to the extent of thirty thousand guilders. Stuyvesant caused distress by suddenly demanding payment. On the other hand, the people complained that their own claims for wages and grain against the Company had not been paid. Stuyvesant's commercial policy was unwise, and his usual method of punishment when attempts were made to evade the high customs duties was confiscation of goods. This resulted in popular discontent in Holland and an avoidance of Manhattan as a port of entry by ships engaged in the West India trade. There was so much complaint, that the Nine Men were obliged to interfere. They determined to send a delegation to Holland, who should represent truthfully the condition of the colony and ask for certain very much needed reforms. They were encouraged in this determination by Melyn's success, which showed conclusively that the States General was willing to listen to the colonists and was desirous of affording them encouragement.

Stuyvesant at first commended the project strongly, but it soon appeared that his commendation was based on the understanding that the whole proceedings should be in his name. To this the Nine Men would not assent. They then requested the privilege of presenting the matter to the people. When this privilege in turn was denied, several leaders of the popular party took the liberty of going from house to house to get an expression of opinion. "From this time," wrote a contemporary, "the breast of the Director General became inflamed with rage" against all who were concerned in the affair, although they were esteemed as "honestest, fittest, most experienced, and most godly in the community." Intrigues were set on foot to divide the popular party, and prosecutions were begun against some of the more prominent of the leaders.

The Nine Men were not to be bullied in this manner. They were led in their determination to take a bold stand in defence of the rights of the people by Adrian van der

Donck, a member of the Council and formerly Sheriff of Rensselaerwyck. To Van der Donck was assigned the task of keeping a journal of events preparatory to drawing up a remonstrance. Stuyvesant, learning of this, seized Van der Donck's papers and had him thrown into prison. He was accused of conduct tending to bring the sovereign authority into contempt. After a stormy session of a council of Stuyvesant's own choosing, Van der Donck was expelled from the Council. The vice-director, Van Dincklagen, alone opposed this action.

Van der Donck now became a political martyr, and Stuyvesant's persecution of him only confirmed the Nine Men in their determination to obtain a redress of their grievances from the States General. They prepared a memorial asking for three things: first, that the States General should assume the direct government of New Netherland; secondly, that it should give New Amsterdam a suitable municipal government; thirdly, that it should determine the boundaries of New Netherland so that the people might "dwell in peace and quietness, and enjoy their liberty, as well in the trade and commerce as in intercourse and settled limits." They pointed to the government of New England as a good example to be followed, and asked that the franchise enjoyed in Holland should be enjoyed in New Netherland and that the government of the provinces should resemble the "laudable government" of their fatherland.

This memorial and an accompanying remonstrance appear to have been drawn up by Van der Donck, and were signed by the Nine Men on July 26, 1649. Van der Donck and two others were chosen to go to The Hague to present the popular cause. A fortnight before their departure, Cornelius van Tienhoven, the secretary of the province, set sail for the same destination as the personal representative of the director. Wishing to avoid the scene of Kieft's shipwreck, his vessel sailed by the way of the north of Ireland. The ship containing the popular delegates, on the contrary, took a direct course and reached Holland first, much to the chagrin of Van Tienhoven. Once there, their efforts were seconded by Cornelius Melyn, Wouter van Twiller, and Dominie Backarus, the lately resigned successor of Dominie Bogardus. Sixty-eight specifications were submitted to the States General of "excessive and most prejudicial neglect" on the part of the Company. On April 11, 1650, a committee of the States General reported a provisional order for the settlement of the whole controversy. Stuyvesant was condemned for bringing on the disastrous Indian war, and was forbidden to begin hostilities with the Indians or with the English without the authority of the States General. No arms or ammunition were to be sold to the Indians, and the inhabitants were to be enrolled as a militia. Three clergymen and several good schoolmasters were to be provided for the province. The commonalty was to be convoked for the purpose of selecting two members of the Council. The machinery of taxation was to be determined by the commonalty.

The States General was not inclined to oppose the West India Company to the extent of assuming the government of New Netherland. Consequently the first article of the Nine Men's petition was not granted. As to the second article, there was no objection to New Amsterdam's setting up a municipal government, with a schout, two burgomasters, and five schepens. Stuyvesant was to be called to Holland to give an account of his conduct. As to the third article, there was no objection to a commission for settling boundaries.

The Amsterdam Chamber opposed this provisional order in every particular, and it was referred back to the committee. Stuyvesant was thus encouraged by the Company to continue his arbitrary acts. Vice-director Van Dincklagen, for opposition to the policy of Stuyvesant, was expelled from the Council, arrested, and imprisoned for several days. The Nine Men were forbidden the use of the pew assigned to them by the consistory of the church. When any vacancy occurred in their body, Stuyvesant refused to allow it to be

De Staten Generael der
Vereenighde Nederlanden,

Edele, Eerentfeste, Hooggeleerde, Wijse,
Voorsichtige Heeren; Den Heer Taerdt
Pensionaris vande Provintie van Hollandt ende
Westvrieslandt heeft in onse Vergaderinge
gecommuniceert sekere Missive vande
Secretaris de Wilde, geschreven tot Amsford,
dan den 24ᵉ deses, Waerbij den selven Heer Taerdt
Pensionaris geadviseert, wesende de confir-
matie vande Recuperatie van Nieuw Nederlandt;
Waerop bij ons gedelibereert sijnde, Hebben wij
goetgevonden de Resolutien, die wij in de modus
deses toesenden, met versoeck dat deselve de
saecke soodanigh wille beleijden, dat t'gene
inde voors: onse Resolutie is vervat, door
sijne directie aldaer moge werden uijtgewerckt;
Waertoe ons verlatende, Bevelen wij in de
in Godes Heijlige protectie; Inden Haege den
25ᵉ October 1673.

Ter ordonnantie vande hooghgem.ᵉ
Heeren Staten Generael,

H. Fagel.

Document, dated 1673, relative to the surrender of New York to the
Dutch. *From the original in the New York Public Library.*

filled. Several times the Nine petitioned the States General anew—once September 13, 1650, and again December 22d of the same year. Finally, in 1652, largely as a result of the opposition of the other Dutch Chambers to Amsterdam's greed, the export duty on tobacco was removed, the importation of slaves from Africa was permitted, the charges for emigrant passages reduced, and a burgher government was conceded to New Amsterdam. This municipal government was to be as nearly like that of the city of Amsterdam as possible. As a matter of fact, however, Stuyvesant retained in his own hands the appointment of the schout, burgomaster, and schepens, and continued to claim the right to make binding ordinances and interdicts issued on his own personal responsibility. It was not until February 2, 1653, that Stuyvesant issued a proclamation making effective the instructions of the Amsterdam Chamber to set up a municipal government. The same year, the States General recalled Stuyvesant, ordering him to proceed to Holland to render an account of his administration. The Amsterdam Chamber was amazed at this recall and succeeded in having it revoked. Hostilities with England were fast approaching and an experienced soldier was needed at New Amsterdam.

In these bitter disputes with his own countrymen, Stuyvesant was strenuously supported by the English residents. As early as 1649 they had been employed in the interests of the director and his Council to counteract the demands of the people for a more liberal government. The English residents of Long Island were among those most active in the support of the administration. They were to a large extent under the political domination of George Baxter, of Gravesend, who was Stuyvesant's English secretary of state. When Secretary Van Tienhoven, as Stuyvesant's personal representative, was sent to Holland, in 1649, to oppose the popular delegates in their appeal to the States General, he carried with him a mass of exculpatory documents. Among these was a letter to the Amsterdam Chamber from the magistrates of the English settlement at Gravesend. In it they declared their confidence in Stuyvesant's "wisdom and justice in the administration of the commonweal." The very next year, another letter signed by Baxter and the magistrates at Gravesend was addressed to the Amsterdam Chamber. It was even more submissive than the other. They "thankfully" acknowledged the benefits which they had enjoyed under the rule of the Company, who, they asserted, was the "rightful owner of this place." Furthermore, that the delegates who had returned from Holland were given up to "schisms, factions, and intestine commotions." That this could best be prevented "by supporting and maintaining our present governor against these malignants, and by our superiors in Holland discrediting the false reports of discontented persons." A third letter, dated September 14, 1651, from the magistrates at Gravesend and Hempstead, and signed by the ever faithful Baxter, breathed the same sycophantic spirit as the other two. They opposed any change whatever being made in the government of the province; they believed in the desirableness of a strongly centralized government; and they opposed a popular election of the governor, which they conceived would bring anarchy and ruin down upon all. Stuyvesant thus found himself in the most extraordinary position of depending upon his alien subjects for support while nine-tenths of his own countrymen were bitterly opposed to him. This extraordinary condition of affairs tended only to aggravate matters, for it gave moral support to the Company in its continued opposition to the spirit of popular freedom among the Dutch colonists. Van der Donck expressed very aptly the consensus of opinion with respect to Stuyvesant when he wrote: "Our great Muscovy duke keeps on as of old—something like the wolf, the longer he lives, the worse he bites."

Stuyvesant was to reap retributive justice, however, at the hands of these very English subjects of Long Island within less than two years. Toward the latter part of November, 1653, when provincial affairs were in a most critical situation, the English of Long Island showed strong symptoms of disaffection. Holland was engaged in a war with England, and Cromwell was threatening an attack upon New Netherland in conjunction with the New England Confederation. Stuyvesant's treasury was bankrupt, the fort was in a dilapidated condition, and his Dutch subjects were disaffected. The burghers of New Amsterdam would not agree to pass the ordinances necessary for the defence of the city until Stuyvesant should agree to their demands for certain municipal reforms. He succeeded in setting matters right by surrendering to the city the excises upon liquors consumed within New Amsterdam. This was done on condition that the burghers and schepens should furnish subsidies for the maintenance of the city works, and for the support of the civil and ecclesiastical officers.

These concessions were not granted, however, before the disaffection had spread to Long Island. The West India Company, fearing treachery among the English alien residents during the war with England, instructed Stuyvesant to appoint none but Dutchmen to the public offices. Notwithstanding the sycophantic letters to the Amsterdam Chamber, Gravesend was now foremost in opposing the provincial government. As before, Gravesend was under the influence of George Baxter, the former confidential agent of Stuyvesant and one of the Dutch arbiters in the treaty of Hartford. He and the Gravesend men were now just as much opposed to a "strongly centralized government" as formerly they had supported it. They now stood in dread of "tyranny more and feared anarchy less." For the expression of such treasonable thoughts, they had on the former occasion called the Dutch "malignants."

The Long Island colonists had suffered numerous losses from the Indians and from pirates. This moved them in the summer of 1653 to take some measures for their security. Several minor meetings led finally to a popular convention, or *landdag*, at New Amsterdam, December 10, 1653, for the discussion of public affairs. It was the most important popular convention that had ever assembled at New

Amsterdam. Stuyvesant at first opposed the meeting, but was informed that it would take place, and "he might do as he pleased and prevent it if he could." He consequently made the best of it and gave a reluctant sanction to what he could not prevent. The conduct of the English delegates in a former meeting, he said, "smelt of rebellion, of contempt of his high authority and commission." Of the towns participating in this convention, four were Dutch and four English, the former being represented by ten Dutch and the latter by nine English delegates. To Baxter, who had had experience in preparing State papers, was given the duty of drawing up the remonstrance. After a loyal preface in which the authority of the States General and the West India Company was distinctly recognized, the remonstrance grouped the grievances of the people under six heads: first, the fear of the establishment of an arbitrary government; secondly, the belief that the people must look after their own defence against the Indians, the protection afforded by the provincial government being grossly inadequate; thirdly, the appointment of officers and magistrates without the consent or nomination of the people, quite contrary to the laws of the Netherlands; fourthly, the unreasonable enforcement of long forgotten orders and proclamations of the director and Council, made originally without the knowledge or consent of the people, and now raked up for the "confusion and punishment" of those who could not be supposed to know them; fifthly, the neglect to make promised grants on the faith of which large improvements had been made, thus creating the suspicion that innovations were in contemplation different from former stipulations; sixthly, the granting of large tracts of land to favored individuals, to the great injury of the province.

The nineteen delegates signed this remonstrance. It was then sent to Stuyvesant with the request that he "answer on each point or article, in such wise" as to afford satisfaction, or to make it possible to proceed further as "God shall direct our steps." This remonstrance was a blow at

Stuyvesant. A categorical answer he did not return, but did vouchsafe a long reply bristling with sarcastic remarks and weighed down by evasions, subterfuges, and insidious attempts to create national prejudices. He held that Breukelen, Midwout, and Amersfoort were without jurisdiction and had no right to send delegates to a popular convention. That the other members were a few unqualified delegates who had no right to address the director or anybody else. That the colonies of Manhattan, Rensselaerwyck, Staten Island, and the settlements of Beverwyck and South River had been too sensible and prudent to "subscribe to all that had been projected by an Englishman." In fact, he did not believe George Baxter himself understood what he meant. What did they know about arbitrary government? "If their rule were to become a cynosure—if the nomination and election of magistrates were to be left to the populace, who were the most interested, then each would vote for one of his own stamp—the thief for a thief; the rogue, the tippler, the smuggler, for a brother in iniquity, that he might enjoy greater latitude in his vices and frauds."

The delegates were not to be silenced by this tirade. In a rejoinder, they appealed to the "Law of Nature" which permits all men to assemble for the protection of their liberties and their property. They asserted, furthermore, that unless the director answered categorically the six points of their remonstrance, they would appeal to the States General and the West India Company.

The old general's wrath now waxed hot. He held the act of the convention "smelt of rebellion," and ordered the delegates to disperse on pain of his highest displeasure. What had the "Law of Nature" to do with public meetings for the protection of public liberty! only magistrates, not common people, had a right thus to assemble. "We derive our authority from God and the Company, not from a few ignorant subjects, and we alone can call the inhabitants together." This was Stuyvesant's farewell slap.

The popular voice, however, was not to be stifled without a protest. Letters were addressed to the West India Company by the burgomasters and schepens of New Amsterdam, by the magistrates of Gravesend, and by Baxter and others, explaining the unhappy state of affairs. They were intrusted to François le Bleeuw, an advocate, who proceeded to Holland with instructions to "use every legitimate means to procure the reforms" demanded by the people. The mission was a total failure, and Le Bleeuw was forbidden to return to New Netherland. In a letter dated May 18, 1654, the West India Company emphatically approved Stuyvesant's conduct. "We are unable to discover in the whole remonstrance," they wrote, "one single point to justify complaint. You ought to have acted with more vigor against the ringleaders of the gang, and not have condescended to answer protest with protests, and then to have passed all by without further notice." Stuyvesant was ordered to punish the ringleaders for the purpose of deterring others from following their example. He was to punish the Gravesend rabble summarily and in a most exemplary manner. The burgomasters and schepens of New Amsterdam were charged to conduct themselves "quietly and peaceably" and to submit themselves to the government placed over them; to hold no "particular convention" with the English on matters of State which did not concern them; or worse, to attempt an "alteration in the state and its government."

Following out these instructions, Stuyvesant removed from the magistracy George Baxter and James Hubbard, who had sat in the convention as delegates from Gravesend. This town had now become notoriously disaffected. Many English residents of Long Island, in fact, began to mutter threats of mutiny. The report was spread early in 1655 by Baxter, who had just returned from New England, that the Protector had ordered the taking of the island from the Dutch by force if necessary. This gave Baxter and Hubbard the opportunity for which they had been looking. They hoisted the English flag at Gravesend, and read a seditious paper in which they declared that "we, as freeborn British subjects, claim and assume to ourselves the laws of our nation and Republic of England over the place, as to our persons and property, in love and harmony, according to the general peace between the two States in Europe and this country." While they were engaged in reading this bit of interesting literature, a party of Stuyvesant's soldiers appeared on the spot and arrested both Baxter and Hubbard. They were taken to New Amsterdam and kept in prison for nearly a year. Gravesend now became tranquil, and Stuyvesant's triumph was complete. Thus failed for the time being one of the earliest and most notable attempts on the part of the people to gain a certain measure of popular control in the affairs of the province. Nevertheless, the people continued to look forward to the time when government by the people would cease to be a dream and would become a reality. In the meantime, they had to content themselves with placing every obstacle in the way of a tyrannical administration and with indulging the "hope of obtaining English liberties by submitting to English jurisdiction."

The dispute between the Dutch and the English of New England in its relation to the possession of the Delaware, which we have detailed from its inception down to the precipitate withdrawal from New Amsterdam of the delegates of the latter in May of 1653, was aggravated by contemporary wrangles between the Dutch and the English of Long Island and the Southern colonies. On the dissolution of the Council for New England in 1635, Charles I. had granted Long Island to William Alexander, Earl of Stirling, then Secretary of State for Scotland. Two attempts were made by his agents to take possession of the island,—one in 1637, and one in 1640,—but both proved unsuccessful. At the beginning of Stuyvesant's administration in 1647, Lord Stirling's widow made another attempt. She sent Andrew Forrester, a Scotchman, with power of attorney to take possession of the island. Announcing himself as Governor of Long Island, he appeared at Manhattan and demanded to see Stuyvesant's commission. The latter was completely taken aback by Forrester's assurance. He soon recovered his composure, however, and packed his opponent off to Holland a prisoner, where he might defend himself if he could. But the ship put into an English port and Forrester escaped. He did not return to America.

The next year, 1648, Sir Edmund Plowden, the titular Earl Palatine of New Albion, paid a second visit to Manhattan. His first visit had been made in 1643, during the administration of Kieft. He claimed most of the territory between Cape May, Sandy Hook, and Delaware River, under an absurd patent issued at Dublin by the Viceroy of Ireland. Kieft had disregarded entirely Plowden's claims, and they were treated in no wise less contemptuously by Stuyvesant. The Viceroy of Ireland had no authority whatever to grant territorial rights in America. Plowden had been living in Virginia for seven years and had lost all his property. He went to Boston from Manhattan and thence to London. He did not return to worry Stuyvesant again, but seems to have been content with publishing a pamphlet, *Description of the Province of New Albion*, in lieu of actual possession of the same. Fendall's Maryland claim was based upon more solid grounds than those of Stirling and Plowden, and in another chapter will be given the consideration due it.

Stuyvesant realized the very great importance of a peaceful settlement of the boundary disputes with New England. The Hartford Convention of 1650 had been planned to that end. Of this treaty, with especial reference to South River, we have spoken in a preceding chapter. It only remains to speak of the treaty in its particular bearing upon the territorial disputes between New Netherland and New England. The board of arbitration speedily decided that the Long Island boundary between the Dutch and English jurisdictions should be a line drawn from the extreme western part of Oyster Bay to the Atlantic Ocean. On the mainland it was to extend from the west shore of Greenwich Bay, about four miles from Stamford, north twenty miles—provided it did not run within ten miles of "Hudson's River." The Dutch were not to settle within six miles of the line, and Greenwich was to be under Dutch jurisdiction. Both sides of the Connecticut were decided to belong to the English, but the Dutch were to keep possession of the lands near Hartford actually in their possession or actually determined by metes and bounds.

By this treaty, Stuyvesant practically abandoned all claim to New England territory. Open opposition to the treaty developed in New Netherland. The fact that both of the Dutch referees were Englishmen was considered an insult or at least a slight. Complaints were sent to Holland that more territory had been surrendered than might have formed fifty colonies. Van der Donck wrote: "All the arbitrators were English and they pulled the wool over the director's eyes." "He never imagined that such hard pills would be given him to digest," wrote another. "New England speaks of him in terms of great praise, . . . because he hath allowed himself to be entrapped by her courtesy." Stuyvesant himself, when he heard of the award, is said to have exclaimed: "I've been betrayed! I've been betrayed!" It is a fact that, when he reported the negotiations to the Amsterdam Chamber, he did not send a copy of the Hartford treaty. A certified copy did not reach the Chamber until 1656, when it was sent to the States General and ratified on February 22d. The West India Company was instructed to see to it that the treaty was ratified by England. This was not done, and the matter remained in suspense until the restoration of Charles II. Although the treaty was decidedly in the interests of New England as against those of New Netherland, yet there is no doubt but that Stuyvesant did the best he could under the circumstances. Had the treaty not been negotiated, it is altogether probable that New Amsterdam would have fallen before the advance of the English some time before 1664. The ratification of the treaty is very good evidence that this view of the situation was taken by both the States General and the West India Company.

The treaty did not, however, prevent continued encroachments upon Dutch territory by the English of Massachusetts and Connecticut. In 1653, the English seized Fort Good Hope on the Connecticut, and six years later, 1659, Massachusetts attempted to make several settlements on the banks of the Hudson. Both these acts were plainly direct breaches of the Hartford Convention. The former event is worthy of more than passing comment, inasmuch as it marked practically the end of Dutch pretensions upon the Connecticut.

The Dutch claim to Connecticut River was based upon the navigation of that river as far as Hartford by Adrian Block in 1614. Dutch traders made their appearance there in 1622, and in 1623 a small fort or trading post is said to have been projected. No Dutch settlements were made, however, and Fort Good Hope was not finished by Jacob van Curler until June, 1633. Prior to this, however, in 1630, the territory is alleged to have been conveyed to Lord Warwick by the Council for New England. He, in turn, two years later, made grants to Lord Saye and Sele, Lord Brooke, Saltonstall, and Winthrop. In 1635, English colonists settled Hartford, Windsor, and Wethersfield. From this date, the association of the English and the Dutch on the Connecticut became close, and disputes inevitably arose.

The climax was reached in 1654, when the cupidity of Connecticut was finally gratified by the formal capture of Fort Good Hope. It had already been seized, July 7th, the year before, by the eccentric John Underhill, who posted a notice on the unoccupied fort declaring that he did so "with the permission of the General Court of Hartford." Underhill's activity in collecting testimony in support of charges against Stuyvesant had led to his arrest and brief imprisonment at New Amsterdam. On his release he had raised the Parliamentary flag at Hempstead and Flushing and was compelled to escape to New England. He secured the equivalent of letters of marque from Providence Plantations, giving him authority to capture Dutch vessels. Construing his commission liberally, his first exploit was the seizure of the fort. "Thus was the last vestige of Dutch dominion in New England wiped out."

Two other causes of irritation between the Dutch and English colonists were the onerous customs regulations of New Netherland and the attitude of both toward the Indians. At the beginning of Stuyvesant's administration, the commissioners of the United Colonies had protested against the Dutch traders selling guns and ammunition to the Indians. Also, a complaint was made of the high duties imposed upon imports and exports. The colonial duties were indeed injuriously high, and Stuyvesant enforced them to the letter. This led to an incident that was the cause of considerable friction. Secretary Van Tienhoven happened to visit New Haven in 1647 and found there an Amsterdam ship, the *San Beninio*. It had been trading for about a month without a license from the West India Company as required. Two of the owners of the cargo applied for permission to trade at Manhattan, and later the permission was sent to New Haven. Stuyvesant learned in a most accidental manner that the ship was to sail for Virginia. No offer having been made to pay the proper duties, such action constituted an open violation of the colonial revenue laws. Stuyvesant determined to seize the vessel. He despatched a company of soldiers on board the *Zwoll*, a vessel recently sold to some merchants of New Haven, under the pretext of conveying it to the new owner. Instructions were given to capture the *San Beninio*. The strategy was an entire success. The vessel was seized in New Haven harbor "on the Lord's day" and brought direct to Manhattan and confiscated.

This bold act naturally caused great excitement in New Haven. The people of that place had tried to stop the ship, but having been taken by surprise they made the attempt too late. Eaton protested most vigorously against this outrage and retaliated by taking into his service three of the West India Company's delinquent servants who had fled from Manhattan. At the same time he addressed a very sharp letter to the director, lecturing him for his shortcomings. Stuyvesant resented what he termed Eaton's "ripping up all my faults as if I were a schoolboy, and not one of like degree with himself." This he followed up by issuing in turn a retaliatory proclamation promising a safe domicile to slaves, debtors, and prisoners. "If any person," ran the proclamation, "noble or ignoble, freeman or slave, debtor or creditor, yea, to the lowest prisoner included, run away from the colony of New Haven, or seek refuge in our limits, he shall remain free, under our protection, on taking the oath of allegiance." This impolitic act placed the director in a false position both at home and abroad. His own countrymen condemned it as tending to make New Netherland a refuge for criminals and vagabonds. The Company deemed it unwise to give England needless offence. The proclamation was annulled the next year, 1648, after the fugitives had returned to New Amsterdam on Stuyvesant's personal promise to pardon them.

Stuyvesant and the commissioners of the United Colonies were almost constantly in correspondence about some fancied or real grievance. In 1653, during the war between England and Holland, Stuyvesant was accused of inciting the Indians to make a concerted attack upon the English. He did not wait for the commissioners to act, but met the accusations with a prompt and vigorous denial. Furthermore, he offered to defend himself at Boston or at New Amsterdam. The commissioners accordingly sent agents to Manhattan. These agents behaved in a most undiplomatic manner—acting as inquisitors and seeking to collect only evidence incriminating the Dutch. Stuyvesant kept himself under wonderful control. He made five propositions that gave evidence of his desire to live in amity with the New England colonists: first, neighborly friendship, without regard to the hostilities in Europe; secondly, continuance of trade and commerce as before; thirdly, mutual justice against fraudulent debtors; fourthly, a defensive and offensive alliance against the enemies of both the Dutch and English provinces; fifthly, the negotiation of these points by Dutch plenipotentiaries with the commissioners in case the agents lacked full and final powers to act.

The New England agents, however, repelled Stuyvesant's friendly overtures, and, after issuing a defiant manifesto, left New Amsterdam abruptly without assigning any reason other than a desire to reach Boston in time for an election. They had ample time, nevertheless, on their way home to stop at Flushing, Stamford, and New Haven to collect hearsay evidence to sustain their charges against the New Netherland authorities. On reaching Boston, they submitted their testimony and at the same time made certain belligerent recommendations. Six out of eight of the commissioners were for instant war. Immediate hostilities, however, were averted by the refusal of Massachusetts to engage in war. For this attitude, Massachusetts was blamed roundly by Connecticut and New Haven. Both these colonies were bent on war and considered themselves strong enough to subdue New Netherland without the aid of Massachusetts. Excited meetings were held at Stamford and Fairfield, volunteers were raised, and an appeal was made to Oliver Cromwell.

Animosity was excited also in London by the publication of an infamous pamphlet entitled *The Second Part of the Amboyna Tragedy*. It purported to be a "Faithful account of a bloody, treacherous, and cruel plot of the Dutch in America, purporting the total ruin and murder of all the English colonists in New England; and extracted from the various letters lately written from New England to different merchants in London." The Amsterdam Chamber immediately issued a Dutch translation of this pamphlet, characterizing it as "an infamous, lying libel, at which the Devil in Hell would have been startled."

Cromwell, now Protector, seized upon this condition of affairs as a good opportunity to make the move that he had been contemplating for some time. Though negotiations for peace with the United Provinces were in progress, he permitted himself to be persuaded by the agents of New Haven and Connecticut to send four ships of war to America. This little fleet, upon which two hundred soldiers were embarked, was under the command of Major Robert Sedgwick and Captain John Leverett. They carried instructions authorizing them to call upon the governors of the New England colonies to join in "vindicating the English right and extirpating the Dutch."

Cromwell's letters roused New England to action. Connecticut promised two hundred men, and even five hundred, "rather than the design should fail." Plymouth promised to furnish fifty men, stating at the same time, however, that it concurred in hostile measures against the Dutch only in behalf of the "national quarrel." In command of their forces, Plymouth placed Captain Miles Standish and Captain Thomas Willett. The latter was one of Stuyvesant's two negotiators of the Hartford treaty. New Haven raised one hundred and thirty-three men. Massachusetts, however, was less zealous, but did allow three hundred volunteers to enlist. This would have made a total force of eight hundred and eighty-three men, but Plymouth failed to furnish its quota in time, thus reducing the number to eight hundred and thirty-three. Stuyvesant could not cope with this force, and the overthrow of New Netherland seemed to be at hand. The director was full of apprehension. He did not believe even the Dutch in the country districts would support him in case of a sudden attack. His English subjects he knew would take up arms against him and join the enemy, in spite of the fact that they had sworn allegiance. "To invite them to aid us," he said, "would be bringing the Trojan horse within our walls. What can we do?" he asked, "we have no gunners, no musketeers, no sailors, and scarcely one thousand six hundred pounds of powder."

In the meantime, however, the peace negotiations between Holland and England had been brought to a successful issue. Just as Sedgwick's fleet was on the point of sailing from Boston, news reached Boston and New Amsterdam that a peace had been agreed upon. There was joy at New Amsterdam. The hostile forces intended to conquer New Netherland were diverted for the purpose of dislodging the French from the coast of Maine. The 12th of August was appointed by Stuyvesant as a day of general thanksgiving. He called upon the people to praise the Lord, who had secured their gates and blessed their possessions with peace, "even here, where the threatened torch of war was lighted, where the waves reached our lips, and subsided only through the power of the Almighty." For ten years longer, New Netherland was to remain under the sovereignty of the Dutch.

The events were already occurring that were to lead ultimately to the overthrow of Dutch power in America. On the 3d of September, 1658, Oliver Cromwell died and the reins of government fell quietly into the weak hands of his eldest son, Richard. It was very evident to all that the restoration of the Stuarts was near at hand. But the restoration of Charles II. did not produce in England more friendly feeling toward the Dutch. Although Charles was entertained magnificently at The Hague on his way from Breda to London, and although he swore lasting friendship for Holland, yet the English Parliament took the first opportunity to make still more obnoxious the Navigation Act of 1651. The two nations had become commercial rivals, and it soon became evident to the Dutch that another crisis was near at hand and that little more could be expected from Charles than from the Protector.

One of Charles's first acts affecting colonial affairs was the granting of a most liberal charter to Connecticut. This charter annexed New Haven to Connecticut and simply ignored the existence of New Netherland. At the time of the Restoration it was clear to some of the shrewdest of the

English statesmen that the moment for the employment of a stronger colonial policy had arrived. The colonies were ordered to "carefully and faithfully execute" the Navigation Act. The colonies answered that this could not be done so long as the Dutch were in control of New Netherland. The Dutch possessions were central and separated the English possessions like a wedge. The New England colonists coveted the lucrative fur trade of the Hudson. Furthermore, control of the region was necessary for the military command of the eastern part of the continent. All these arguments were presented to Charles by busy intriguers with the ardor born of individual interest.

Connecticut now began to plan for the acquirement of all of the rights and privileges granted by its new charter. The West India Company saw clearly the trend of affairs, and instructed Stuyvesant to effect, if possible, a definite settlement with Connecticut. The director accordingly visited Boston and appeared before the commissioners of the United Colonies. Stuyvesant was completely baffled in his attempt, and the conference ended without the accomplishment of the object desired. Stuyvesant next sent envoys to Hartford who inquired: "If Connecticut extends to the Pacific Ocean, where lies New Netherland?" The Hartford men replied most nonchalantly: "We know not, unless you can show us your charter." The conference thus ended as unsatisfactorily as had the one in Boston. It was perfectly plain to Stuyvesant that this attitude on the part of Connecticut boded ill for New Netherland. He wrote to the Company, asking that soldiers and supplies be sent, otherwise, he said, "we declare that it is wholly out of our power to keep the sinking ship afloat any longer."

Matters went from bad to worse. In 1663, John Scott, a bold adventurer, arrived in America and assumed the presidency of a rebellious league of Long Island towns including Hempstead, Gravesend, Flushing, Oyster Bay, Middelburg, and Jamaica. He had come over with letters of recommendation from Charles to the New England governors.

Connecticut immediately took up his cause and supported his seizure of parts of Long Island. Affairs had now reached such a critical state that Stuyvesant called a landdag to meet April 10, 1664, to consider what should be done. All realized that little could be done, and this gloomy view of the state of affairs was very shortly to be drastically verified.

Charles II. now made up his mind to seize New Netherland. Lord Stirling's old patent to Long Island was purchased for £3,500 and the rights under it granted to the king's brother, James, Duke of York. The patent covered the whole of New Netherland and a part of Connecticut. The duke lost no time in making good his pretensions. As Lord High Admiral, he despatched a fleet of four ships with about four hundred and fifty regular troops with their officers to take possession of New Netherland. The expedition was intrusted to Colonel Richard Nicolls, who was to be the duke's deputy governor after the Dutch possessions were secured. The expedition had been organized in deepest secrecy, lest Holland should be afforded the opportunity of sending a fleet to the defence of the province. In spite of these precautions, however, Stuyvesant received intelligence of the expedition early in July. The governor prepared as best he could. He was making satisfactory headway with his defences, when news came from the West India directors that there was no cause for apprehension, that the fleet had been sent out for an entirely different purpose. Efforts were now relaxed, some warships about to sail for Curaçoa were permitted to go, and Stuyvesant left for Fort Orange.

There was sufficient truth in the report to help to lull suspicions at New Amsterdam. The fleet reached New England in July, and the commissioners on board at once demanded the assistance of Massachusetts in the project. But the people of Massachusetts were "full of excuses," fearing that the overthrow of New Netherland would give Charles a freer hand in putting down his enemies in New

England. Connecticut, on the other hand, was alacrity itself and offered, without delay, her military forces.

News of the final destination of the fleet was brought to Stuyvesant while he was absent in the northern part of the Dutch territory. He hurriedly returned and made every effort to redeem the precious time lost. But it was too late. Within a few days after his arrival, the English squadron sailed up the Lower Bay and anchored just below the Narrows. A company of soldiers was sent ashore, and seized the block house on Staten Island. The next morning, Saturday, August 30, 1664, Stuyvesant was ordered to surrender. His cause was a hopeless one. He had only about one hundred and fifty regular soldiers, and but two hundred and fifty citizens capable of bearing arms, and many of these were disaffected. There were but twenty guns mounted at Fort Amsterdam and the supply of powder was inadequate. Both river banks were defenceless. The ships of the enemy carried at least one hundred and twenty guns and there was a total of nearly one thousand men on board, but Stuyvesant determined to make a stout resistance. He consulted with his burgomasters and schepens, but found them strongly inclined to offer no resistance. Non-resistance was, in fact, openly advocated. The demand on Rensselaerwyck for aid was answered by the statement that they had all they could do to protect themselves against immediate attack by the Indians. The Dutch on Long Island refused aid, saying they had their own families and property to protect.

Nicolls now addressed a letter to Winthrop, authorizing him to offer Stuyvesant in the king's name most favorable conditions to all the inhabitants. Winthrop, who, with other commissioners from New England, had joined the English squadron, delivered this letter to Stuyvesant under a flag of truce and urged him to surrender. This he refused to do, saying, "such a course would be disapproved in the Fatherland—it would discourage the people." Nevertheless, Nicolls's letter, when read to the Council and the burgomasters, produced a most favorable impression. The latter requested that it be read to the citizens who were collected in crowds outside the place of meeting, as "all which regarded the public welfare ought to be made public." Stuyvesant refused to accede to this request, and on its being doggedly insisted upon he angrily tore the letter in pieces. The citizens then left their work on the fortifications and through three of their representatives demanded the reading of the letter. Complaints were now uttered against the Company's misgovernment, and resistance was declared to be idle. "The letter! the letter!" was the general cry. Stuyvesant now saw that "to offer resistance against so many would be as idle as to gape before an oven." He feared a mutiny and yielded. The fragments of the letter were collected and a copy read to the people. It read as follows:

"Mr. Winthrop:
"As to those particulars you spoke to me, I do assure you that if the Manhadoes be delivered up to his Majesty, I shall not hinder, but any people from the Netherlands may freely come and plant there or thereabouts; and such vessels of their own country may freely come thither, and any of them may as freely return home, in vessels of their own country; and this and much more is contained in the privilege of his Majesty's English subjects; and thus much you may, by what means you please, assure the Governor from, Sir, your very affectionate servant,
"Richard Nicolls."

Stuyvesant's sceptre had now evidently departed from him. There was nothing for him to do but to reply to Nicolls's demand to surrender by a justification of the Dutch title to New Netherland. But Nicolls was there not to discuss titles, but to carry out instructions. "On Thursday," he said, "I shall speak with you at the Manhattans." In answer to a statement that he would be welcome if he came as a friend, he replied: "I shall come with ships and soldiers. Hoist a white flag at the fort, and I may consider your proposition."

It was now perfectly evident to Nicolls that Stuyvesant was averse to surrender. As two of the English ships passed in front of Fort Amsterdam, the old director stood on one of the angles of the fort with an artilleryman at his side who was prepared to fire at the foe at the word of command. The director seemed eager to give the order to fire. It is a heroic picture, that does not fade from the mind easily. On the request of Dominie Megapolensis, he did not give the command. The people of the town were thrown into a panic at the approach of the enemy. Stuyvesant was implored to submit. "He would rather be carried a corpse to his grave," was his reply. He was now presented with a remonstrance suggested by Dominie Megapolensis and signed by ninety-three of the leading citizens, among whom was Balthazar Stuyvesant, the director's own son.

Stuyvesant's position was altogether hopeless. The enemy, constantly reinforced by people from New England, pressed upon him in front. At his rear were his own thoroughly disaffected burghers. The fort could not withstand the enemy three days at the longest. The city itself was practically defenceless. The supply of powder would not last a day, and the stock of provisions was equally low. The soldiers were inclined to be mutinous, and were heard to say: "Now we hope to pepper those devilish traders who have so long salted us; we know where booty is to be found, and where the young women live who wear gold chains." Surrender was the only course to adopt. Six representatives each were appointed by Stuyvesant, and Nicolls and articles of capitulation were drawn up and agreed upon, September 6, 1664. They were signed by Nicolls immediately, but Stuyvesant and his Council did not sign them until the following Monday—two days after. There were twenty-three articles in the capitulation. The only difference of opinion was respecting the Dutch soldiers, whom the English refused to transport to Holland. The Dutch

PETER STUYVESANT

*From the painting in possession of Peter Stuyvesant, Esq.*

were to enjoy security in their property, inheritance customs, liberty of conscience, and church discipline. For the time being, the municipal officers of Manhattan were not to be changed. The town was to continue to choose deputies, who were to have a free voice in all public affairs. The enforcement of the Navigation Act was to be delayed six months, during which time there was to be free intercourse with Holland. Public records were to be respected.

Monday morning, September 8th, at eight o'clock, the Dutch forces, led by Stuyvesant, marched out of Fort Amsterdam with all the honors of war and proceeded down Beaver Lane to the landing, with drums beating, colors flying, and matches lighted. At the same time, an English corporal's guard occupied the vacated fort. Colonel Nicolls and Sir Robert Carr, at the head of two companies of soldiers, entered the city, and Sir George Cartwright took possession of the gates and occupied the town hall. The English flag was raised above Fort Amsterdam, and Nicolls was proclaimed deputy governor for the Duke of York by the burgomasters. The fort's name was changed to Fort James, and the names of the city and province were changed to New York—in compliment to the duke.

Fort Orange on North River and New Amstel on South River surrendered next, after all the privileges of the Articles of Capitulation had been promised their defenders. The name of the former was changed to Fort Albany, after the Scottish title of the Duke of York. New Amstel offered resistance to Sir Robert Carr, who was sent to accept its capitulation. The fort was then stormed and plundered, and three of the Dutch were killed and ten wounded. Carr then broke every promise he had made. The inhabitants were plundered and the Dutch soldiers were sent "to be sold as slaves in Virginia." The treaty with the Iroquois was renewed and they were promised the same advantages as they had been given by the Dutch. This alliance continued practically unbroken until the beginning of the American Revolution.

Thus came to an end the Dutch power in America. The act of spoliation by which it was accomplished is without palliation. In time of profound peace and scarcely without warning the possessions of a friendly power were violently seized. It was done at the direct instigation of a king who, when a fugitive without a home and without a country, was entertained most hospitably by the very nation whose sovereignty he thus violated. However fortunate this act of Charles II. may be considered from the point of view of subsequent developments, it cannot be defended by any rule of international ethics—whether of the seventeenth century or of the twentieth. O'Callaghan, quoting from Butler, says: "In the history of the royal ingrate by whom it was planned, and for whose benefit it was perpetrated, there are few acts more base, none more characteristic."

## CHAPTER VII

*THE DUTCH UNDER ENGLISH RULE, 1664–1685*

REGARDED from the point of view of political morality, history has but one voice—that of the severest condemnation—in characterizing those unscrupulous schemers who were directly instrumental in despoiling Holland of her possessions in North America. There were undoubtedly great underlying causes, such as commercial jealousy and a desire for territorial unification, that would have brought about this same result in course of time. Nevertheless, the commission of this act of spoliation would have been indefinitely postponed had it not been for the malign influence of two powerful individuals. To Sir George Downing and the Duke of York belongs the discredit of having planned and consummated this outrage. They planned it in secret and accomplished it with a studied deceit toward a friendly power. Through the prudence of Clarendon, England and Holland had agreed upon a treaty of peace and alliance, September 4, 1662. These friendly relations might possibly have continued had it not been for the "private interest and private pique" of the duke and Downing. The latter was envoy at The Hague. O'Callaghan well describes him as "keen, bold, subtle, active, and observant, but imperious and unscrupulous, naturally preferring menace to persuasion, reckless of the means employed or the risk incurred in the pursuit of a proposed object, disliking and distrusting the Dutch, and forearmed with a fierce determination not to be foiled or overreached." The Duke of York had private interests to subserve and a personal pique to avenge. As Governor of the Royal African Company he was brought into direct rivalry with the Dutch. Furthermore, by reason of libellous remarks made about him in Holland, he disliked the Dutch as much as did Downing.

Whatever may be said as to the political equities of the conquest of New Netherland, there can be but unanimity of opinion as to its importance to England. By this conquest England became the mistress of all the Atlantic coast between Acadia and Florida. Furthermore, the navigation laws of England, which could not be made effective in America so long as Holland controlled so important a colony, could now be enforced without hindrance.

The change of sovereignty did not retard the material development of the province. Nor did it curtail the popular privileges that had been wrested from the unwilling hands of Peter Stuyvesant. The terms of capitulation had been extremely liberal, when we recall the fact that they had been granted by a conqueror. The King of England had merely resumed possession of a province occupied and improved by a foreign people. The duke's policy was to make the territory a paying investment. To accomplish this it was necessary for him to prevail upon the inhabitants to remain by offering them liberal inducements to do so. These terms they accepted in good faith and quietly submitted to the change of rulers.

At the time of the conquest, according to Chevalier Lambrechtsen, New Netherland consisted of three cities and thirty villages. Exclusive of Indians its population was about ten thousand souls, while that of New Amsterdam was one thousand six hundred. The people of the province enjoyed a fair measure of freedom and protection. There were numerous flourishing farms, or bouweries. The Dutch and their alien neighbors, on the whole, lived in harmony; and, theoretically at least, a comparatively high standard of justice was administered to all impartially. All were fairly adequately protected by constitutional guaranties. New Netherland had welcomed from the earliest times the oppressed of all nations. The knowledge of the traditional Dutch policy of religious toleration drew many men of many creeds and tongues to New Amsterdam. This policy, despite the rule of the Company forbidding the setting up of any church except the Dutch Reformed, had been carried out consistently by Director Kieft and had not been set aside entirely by Stuyvesant. Thus Walloons, Waldenses, Huguenots, Swedes, Roman Catholics, German Lutherans, Anabaptists, and English Quakers settled alongside the supporters of the Reformed Faith. An asylum had been furnished the exiled Puritans of New England, and during Stuyvesant's rule there had been a great influx of sects from many parts of Europe. This was not due primarily to a liberal policy on the part of the Company, as we have seen. An exception to this uniformly tolerant policy toward the sects must be made in the case of Stuyvesant. Whether from a zealousness to carry out to the letter the instructions of the Company or from a lack of appreciation of the equities of the situation, Stuyvesant attempted to inaugurate a different policy from that of Kieft in his attitude toward the sects. Several Lutherans were imprisoned for attending private meetings. A few humble Baptists at Flushing, on Long Island, were fined and expelled. A number of Long Island Quakers who had been expelled from Boston were treated in a most barbarous manner by Stuyvesant; and the town officers of Flushing, who protested against such savage cruelty, were drastically punished. But these acts of persecution were certainly isolated cases and were condemned by public opinion; moreover, they were unanimously condemned by the Amsterdam Chamber, and Stuyvesant received a rebuke. "The consciences of men ought to be free and unshackled, so long as they continue moderate, peaceable, inoffensive, and not hostile to government. Such have been the maxims of prudence and toleration by which the magistrates of this city have been governed; and the consequences have been that the oppressed and persecuted from every country have found among us an asylum from distress. Follow in the same steps and you will be blest." Stuyvesant did not interfere again with liberty of conscience.

The last nine years of Dutch sovereignty in New Netherland were, in fact, a period of growth and prosperity. Yet, in comparison with the advance made by the English colonies, this growth was not notable. At the Restoration of Charles II., the population of New England could not have been less than fifty thousand, while that of Virginia and Maryland was about thirty-five thousand and fifteen thousand respectively. A number of reasons have been assigned in preceding pages for this disparity in population between the colonies of these nationalities. One important obstacle to the rapid growth of New Netherland during this period has not, however, been considered. Beginning with 1655, New Netherland experienced all the horrors of Indian uprisings. Terror seized the land and most of the farmers fled to Manhattan. These Indian troubles interfered with the peaceful prosecution of the vocations of the inhabitants of the parts visited by the scourge of war. Furthermore, inasmuch as they rendered a large immigration to the colony smaller than it might have been under entirely favorable circumstances, it will not be out of place at this point to give a brief account of the most important of these outbreaks.

The relations between the Dutch and the savages had continued generally friendly for ten years after Kieft's treaty with the latter at Fort Amsterdam in 1645. The blame of the Indian massacre of 1655 seems to rest entirely on one Dutchman, Hendrick van Dyck, who had been schout fiscal of the province. Van Dyck detected an Indian squaw stealing peaches from his orchard, and shot and killed her. Her tribe's people burned to avenge her death, and in this they were supported by the neighboring savages. On September 15th, before the break of day, about one thousand nine hundred Algonquins landed from sixty-four canoes and thronged the streets of New Amsterdam. They came from Esopus and Hackensack, Tappan and Stamford, on the pretence of looking for Mohawks. They at first offered no violence to anyone and satisfied themselves with breaking into several houses. The council, the city magistrates, and some of the principal inhabitants held a parley with the chief sachems in Fort Amsterdam. As a result of this meeting the savages promised to leave Manhattan at sundown, but broke their word. Van Dyck was shot through the heart, and a neighbor who came to his rescue was tomahawked. Matters were in a critical condition, indeed, until the soldiers and militia, sallying from Fort Amsterdam, drove the savages from Manhattan. They passed over to the Jersey shore, laid Hoboken and Pavonia in ashes, and killed or captured most of the inhabitants. Staten Island was next devastated. In three days one hundred of the inhabitants had been killed, one hundred and fifty had been taken prisoners, and three hundred had lost their homes. Twenty-eight bouweries and several plantations had been destroyed, and the damages were computed at two hundred thousand guilders.

These Indian troubles continued intermittently. Stuyvesant held a conference with the Indians at Esopus, May, 1658, and a peace was agreed upon. The troubles were renewed, however, in the fall. Again the white men were to blame. Some tipsy Indians who were making night hideous at Esopus were fired upon by some frightened settlers, and two or three of the Indians were wounded. This foolish act led to a war in which several Dutch settlers were burned at the stake. It became necessary to call in the assistance of the Mohawks, and it was not until July, 1660, that peace was made. But hostilities soon broke out afresh. Stuyvesant shipped some of the Indian prisoners to Curaçoa. This gave a new cause for war. It was not long in coming. In June, 1663, two villages near Esopus were burned, and the inhabitants—men, women, and children—massacred. The war that followed lasted nearly a year, and in the end the Indians were thoroughly defeated. In May, 1664, the last treaty of peace was entered into between the Dutch and the Algonquins.

These Indian wars, covering as they did nearly ten years of Stuyvesant's administration, somewhat retarded the rapid growth of the province. Nevertheless, New Netherland experienced unexampled prosperity, and the bad effect of the wars was negative rather than positive. The war that Kieft provoked in 1643 had imperilled the existence of the province, but these later wars had merely slackened its growth. Settlers were planting homes north and west of Fort Orange. In 1661, Arendt van Corlear was authorized to buy the "Great Flats," where later Schenectady was laid out.

Such was the condition of New Netherland when it fell into the hands of the English. About a year after the surrender, Stuyvesant was summoned to Holland to render an account of his conduct to the States General. He met with a rather cold reception, and was blamed by the West India Company for consequences for which it was primarily responsible. A request on Stuyvesant's part for justification of his conduct met with a prompt and hearty response. Testimony in his behalf came in such abundance from the leading men of New York that the ex-director was in the end triumphantly sustained by the government. After the Treaty of Breda, in 1667, finally conceded New York to the English, Stuyvesant set about obtaining a relaxation of the English navigation laws in favor of the colony by allowing it a direct commerce with Holland. After having secured certain very valuable trade concessions from the King of England, Stuyvesant returned to New York and spent the remainder of his days in peaceful retirement on his farm, the Great Bouwerie. Here, in 1682, at the ripe age of eighty, he died.

The Duke of York hoped to realize £30,000 a year from the conquered province. To bring about a materialization of this hope it was necessary to secure a person of undoubted ability as governor. The duke found in Colonel Richard Nicolls the qualities necessary to fill the requirements. He was sincere, courageous, sensible, prudent, and liberal-minded; moreover, he possessed great ability and was somewhat of a scholar, being fond of the classics and speaking Dutch and French with fluency. Wherever he went, his popularity was instantaneous, and New York was not an exception. He disturbed no one in property or person. After a year had passed, the local government of burgomasters, schepens, and schout was replaced by a mayor, aldermen, and sheriff.

Nicolls was the personal representative of the Duke of York and had authority to make all laws and to carry on the government. He immediately appointed English councillors and an English secretary. Once in a while, one or two of the former Dutch councillors were summoned for advice. An English garrison was stationed at Albany. The religious situation was changed but little. Services after the order of the Church of England were now established in addition to those previously held.

In March of 1665 the governor promulgated on his own and the duke's authority a code of laws known as "The Duke's Laws." It was a body of laws for the government of the new province, and none could complain of it as wanting in liberality. It was alphabetically arranged, collated, and digested out of the several laws then in force in the English colonies. It exhibited many traces of Connecticut and Massachusetts legislation. Governor Nicolls imagined it "could not but be satisfactory even to the most factious republicans." Immigrants came into New York from the neighboring colonies of New England, on the strength of the promulgation of these laws. All civil and criminal cases were to be tried where the cause of action arose. Cases involving less than £5 were to be arbitrated, voluntarily if possible, but forcibly if necessary. When the amount involved was between £5 and £20, the case was to be tried before the "Sessions," from which there was no appeal. At the death of anyone, the constable and two overseers personally investigated the manner of death and inquired as to whether a will had been left. No letters of administration were to be granted until the third session after the death of the person, except to his widow or child. Of the surplus of the personal estate, one-third was to go to the widow and the other two-thirds to the children—the eldest son retaining a double portion. "No Christian" was to keep a slave, "except persons adjudged thereto by authority, or such as have willingly" sold themselves. No person was to brew beer except those who were skilled in the art. The death penalty was to be exacted in the cases of those who denied the "true God or His attributes;" and of those who committed any wilful or premeditated murder. Other capital offences were highway robbery, poisoning, bestiality, kidnapping, false testimony resulting in death, treason, and conspiracy against the public peace. Children above the age of sixteen who should strike their parents were to be executed unless they had done so in self-defence.

A church was to be built in every parish. There was to be no travelling on Sunday, and misdemeanors such as "swearing, profaneness, Sabbath breaking, drunkenness," etc., were to be reported by the churchwardens twice a year. None but skilled persons were to be permitted to practise medicine. Perjury was to be punished by standing in the pillory and by the offender's rendering double damage to the injured person. Apprentices and servants who ran away from their masters were to serve double the time of their absence. Innkeepers were compelled to secure certificates of good character from the constable and two overseers of the parish, and they were not to "suffer any one to drink excessively in their houses after nine o'clock at night, under a penalty of 2s. 6d." In general, the Code confirmed the patroons in their estates, which were now called "manors." Trial by jury was introduced and the criminal code was amended. Religious liberty was guaranteed to all Christians.

To give the appearance of popular sanction to this Code, Governor Nicolls observed the formality of summoning a meeting of two delegates from each town, to be chosen by a majority of the taxpayers. The convention met at Hempstead on the 28th of February, 1665. It consisted of thirty-four delegates—two from each of the English and Dutch towns on Long Island and two from Westchester. No deputies were summoned from New York, Esopus, Bergen, or any other town in the province, for reasons that later will be made clear. The following places sent two delegates each: New Utrecht, Gravesend, Flatlands, Flatbush, Bushwick, Brooklyn, Newtown, Flushing, Jamaica, Hempstead, Oyster Bay, Huntingdon, Brookhaven, Southold, Southampton, Easthampton, and Westchester.

The governor opened the meeting by reading the duke's patent and his own commission. The delegates objected to some of the clauses of the Code, and Nicolls accepted several amendments. But when they asked for the privilege of choosing their own magistrates, the governor exhibited his instructions "wherein the choice of all the officers of justice was solely to be made by the governor." He then informed the delegates that if they desired a larger share in the government than he could allow, they "must go to the king for it." The delegates thus found that they were not a popular representative body having the power to make laws, but were only agents to accept those already prepared for them. The Code was "promulgated" the next day, March 1, 1665.

This Code, with the alterations and additions made to it from time to time by the governor and council, continued to be the law of the colony until 1683. In that year the first colonial legislature met, and for a short time the people were given a share in the legislative powers. The Code did not by any means provide a constitutional government for the people of New York. The will of the duke's governor was almost supreme in the colony. Fortunately, Nicolls was liberal and well endowed with admirable characteristics. The Code was intended ultimately to apply to the whole province and, in fact, several of its provisions went into general operation at once. Long Island, however, seems to have been the main object of its application. The majority of the inhabitants of the Hudson valley were Dutch and hardly understood the English language. Consequently, only by degrees could their institutions be altered with justice. Nicolls thought it prudent not to enforce the Code in New York, Esopus, Albany, and Schenectady.

In the meantime, hostilities were precipitated between England and Holland. In November, 1664, the Dutch government had denounced the conquest of New Netherland as "an erroneous proceeding, opposed to all right and reason, contrary to mutual correspondence and good neighborhood, and a notorious infraction of the treaty lately concluded." It furthermore demanded "prompt restitution and reparation." This Charles refused to make. He claimed that New Netherland had been settled and occupied by the English prior to the Dutch. Furthermore, that the former had merely permitted the Dutch nation at the outset to settle there and that such permission had not conferred upon the Dutch a just title to the lands thus appropriated. Without stopping to argue the question or to demonstrate the absurdity of this claim, the Dutch reply was that New Netherland "must be restored." Secret orders were sent to De Ruyter, who was in command of the Dutch squadron on the coast of Africa, to capture the English possessions there. Likewise, to make reprisals upon the English at Barbadoes, New Netherland, Newfoundland, and, in fact, wherever found. The king and the Duke of York were evidently both disposed to hostilities. Letters of reprisal were issued against the United Provinces, and, without any declaration of war, one hundred and thirty Dutch merchant vessels were seized in the English ports.

Intelligence of this condition of affairs reached Nicolls by way of Boston. He began to make preparations for defence. All the estates of the West India Company were sequestered and, after the declaration of war, were confiscated together with the property of the Dutch who had not taken the oath of allegiance. War was formally declared between Holland and England in March, 1665, and the aid of France was asked in conformity with the treaty of 1662. The citizens of New York were now called together to devise plans for defence. The governor offered to contribute palisades and weapons and, moreover, promised not to compel any inhabitant to fight against his own nation. No enthusiasm was elicited. The Dutch seemed not unwilling that the colony should again pass into the hands of their countrymen. They did not, however, oppose Nicolls openly or express their wish for Dutch success. No categorical answer was given. Some of the people said the defences of the town were sufficient; others, that they could not work before they had their arms restored to them. The town was indeed in no condition to resist De Ruyter's squadron, should it appear before New York. Nicolls himself frankly acknowledged this in a letter to Lord Arlington, dated July 31, 1665.

Early in 1666, the condition of affairs became much more complicated. Louis XIV. of France, who had declared the Dutch claim to New Netherland to be valid, now reluctantly declared war against England. The part that France took in the war was, however, rather insignificant. The Dutch were compelled to rely mostly upon their navy. During the war, the naval honors were fairly evenly divided. In one naval engagement the Dutch suffered a complete defeat; twenty of their first-rate men-of-war were captured or sunk, and three of their admirals and four thousand men were killed. On the other hand, De Ruyter and Cornelius de Witt appeared upon the English coast, sailed up the Thames, captured Sheerness, and destroyed a great number of ships of the line. De Ruyter also ravaged the whole seacoast from the mouth of the Thames to Land's End. The inhabitants on the coast were terrified, and all England felt a bitter sense of her degradation.

Negotiations for peace between the hostile nations had already been begun at Breda. As a result of this last victory, these negotiations were now carried on upon terms much more advantageous to Holland. They were speedily concluded and the Peace of Breda was signed on St. Bartholomew's Day, 1667. By this peace, New Netherland was formally ceded to the English in exchange for Surinam [Dutch Guiana] in South America and the island of Poleron, one of the Banda group, near the Moluccas. The Dutch, on the whole, were well pleased with the terms of the peace and there was considerable rejoicing at The Hague. The West India Company's shareholders and the regents of the city of Amsterdam were, of course, somewhat dissatisfied. The feeling in England was not unanimous. Although the church bells rang in London, yet there were no bonfires—"partly," says Pepys, "from the dearness of firing, but principally from the little content most people have in the peace." Official intelligence of the Peace of Breda reached New York on New Year's, 1668. Nicolls announced the good news by warrants, addressed to each justice, requiring a general proclamation of the event. For the next seven years at least, New York was to enjoy free trade with the Netherlands. A new order of things opened with the proclamation of peace. Stuyvesant's success at London in gaining a certain measure of commercial freedom encouraged the merchants to engage in new enterprises.

Two important events should be chronicled before bringing the administration of Nicolls to a close. One was the trial and acquittal of two persons accused of witchcraft, and the other was the determination of the boundaries of the colony. Both redound to the credit of the administration of Governor Nicolls.

All the New England penalties against witchcraft had been omitted from the "Duke's Laws." Consequently, when Ralph Hall and his wife Mary were presented by the authorities of Brookhaven, October 2, 1665, for practising "some detestable and wicked arts, commonly called witchcraft and sorcery," the court was at first at a loss to know how to proceed against them. Finally, it was decided that they should be indicted for murder by means of witchcraft.

The case was tried before Nicolls's first Court of Assizes. Twelve jurymen sat on the case. One of these was Jacob Leisler, afterward so prominent in the affairs of the colony. The jury found that there were "some suspicions by the evidence" of what the woman was charged with, but that there was nothing "considerable of value to take away her life." As for the man, there was "nothing considerable to charge him with." Hall was put under bonds for his wife's good behavior while she remained in the colony and for her periodical appearance at court. After three years, however, Governor Nicolls finally dismissed the case. How notable a contrast between the liberality and common sense that characterized the treatment of this case and the bigotry, superstition, and cruelties that characterized the Salem trials! No one was hanged in New York in 1665, and the accused received an impartial trial. At Salem in Massachusetts, in 1692, nineteen were hanged, one was pressed to death by weight of stones, eight were condemned, one hundred and fifty were in prison, and two hundred more were accused by the "afflicted." All were prejudged by a packed jury presided over by hysterical judges and encouraged by bigoted and fanatical clergymen.

One of the most important events of Nicolls's administration was the determination of the boundaries of the province. We have seen that Rensslaerwyck, Fort Orange, and Esopus submitted to Colonel Cartwright with hardly a show of resistance; but that New Amstel on the Delaware under its commandant, Alexander Hinnoyossa, offered a determined but ineffectual resistance to Sir Robert Carr. The Duke of York's patent extended only to the east bank of the Delaware, and, according to the charter Charles I. gave Lord Baltimore, the whole western shore was part of Maryland. The duke, however, paid no attention to this prior right and practically annexed the whole western shore of Delaware Bay. In fact, the royal commissioners had been instructed by the king to reduce to his obedience the Dutch wherever seated within his claimed dominions in

North America. It was claimed that the Maryland people were in some way overawed by the city of Amsterdam, which owned the Delaware settlements, and that unless they were secured the acquisition of New York would be of small advantage to the king. The "Territories" on the Delaware consequently remained a part of New York until 1682, when they were given to William Penn.

The royal commissioners next turned their attention to a still more delicate task. The Connecticut charter of 1662 included not only New Haven in its jurisdiction but also a large part of New Netherland. By the Duke of York's charter of 1664, New York began at Connecticut River, and included not only Long Island and the New Haven colony but even Hartford itself. New Haven at first stoutly refused to be swallowed up by Connecticut, because the latter's charter had been surreptitiously obtained "contrary to righteousness, amity, and peace." As soon, however, as it saw that it must submit to New York if it did not to Connecticut, it readily decided upon the latter alternative.

The Connecticut authorities now saw they were dependent upon the recommendations that Nicolls might make to the Duke of York and to the king. Should he insist upon Connecticut River as the western boundary line of New York, he would probably be supported in his contentions. It was clearly good policy for Connecticut to conciliate the royal commissioners; so five hundred bushels of corn and some horses were presented to them, and agents were appointed to go with Governor Winthrop to New York to discuss the question of boundaries with the commissioners, Nicolls, Cartwright, and Samuel Maverick. Nicolls was not inclined to press his claims beyond what was reasonable. An agreement satisfactory to all interested parties was finally reached. The southern boundary of Connecticut was to be the Sound, and Long Island was to be a part of New York. Nicolls himself pleaded the cause of Connecticut with respect to her western boundary. He held that to insist upon

# By His Excellency

Coll. *Benjamin Fletcher* Captain General and Governour in Chief of His Majesties Province of *New-York*, &c.

# A PROCLAMATION

WHEREAS The *French* and *Indians* of *Canada* have lately Invaded the Country of the Indians of the Five Nations in Amity with the Subjects of the Crown of *England*, and have destroyed their Indian Corn. To the end that the said *Indians* that have so suffered the loss of their Corn, may be supplyed with what is necessary for their Maintenance for the Year ensuing, I have therefore, by and with the Advice and Consent of His Majestics Council for this Province, Prohibited the Transportation of Indian Corn and Peas from the County of *Albany*, *Ulster* and *Dutches County*, to any other County or Place down the River, until the first day of *April* now next ensuing. And all Masters of Sloops, and other Vessels are hereby prohibited accordingly, as they will answer the contrary at their peril.

Given at Fort William Henry the Twelfth Day of September, in the Eighth Year of the Reign of our Soveraign Lord WILLIAM the Third, by the Grace of God, King of England, Scotland, France and Ireland, Defender of the Faith, &c. Annoq; Domini 1696.

Ben. Fletcher.

## God Save the KING

---

*Printed by* William Bradford, *Printer to the Kings most Excellent Majesty*, at the Bible in the City of New-York, 1696.

Early broadside relating to King William's War, issued September 12, 1696. From the original in the New York Public Library.

Connecticut River as the eastern boundary of New York would "cast dishonor upon his majesty" and would result in the "utter ruin of that colony and a manifest breach of their late patent." Furthermore, that in the delicate relations which the commissioners sustained to New England, it would be good public policy to make the settlement of this boundary dispute a "leading case of equal justice." Consequently, it was agreed that the boundary line should run from the head of Mamaroneck Creek to the north-northwest until it reached the Massachusetts line, keeping always "about twenty miles from any part of Hudson's River." The first day of December, 1664, the agreement was ratified by the royal commissioners and signed by Winthrop and his colleagues.

There is little doubt but that Connecticut secured a distinct advantage in this boundary agreement. Its commissioners may not have been guilty of the trickery claimed by Broadhead (*History of the State of New York*, ii, 56), nor may they have been so guileless as suggested by Fiske (*Dutch and Quaker Colonies in America*, ii, 6); but certain it is that the final agreement was less advantageous to New York than had been the boundary settlement of 1650 between the Dutch and the English colonies. The line should have started near Stamford and should have run due north. The line established started about ten miles from the Hudson, crossed the Hudson near Peekskill, and ended thirty-five miles west of that river. The error was soon detected, and the boundary was changed to nearly its present position in 1683. The boundary decision was not ratified by the Duke of York or by the king. Considerable time elapsed before the affair was finally closed.

To Long Island, Nicolls gave the name Yorkshire, and divided it into three ridings. Nantucket and Martha's Vineyard remained a part of New York until 1692, when they were ceded to Massachusetts. The island of Pemaquid and a part of the mainland between Kennebec and St. Croix Rivers were also a part of the duke's grant.

They also were turned over to Massachusetts, together with all the rest of Maine, after the accession of William and Mary.

After the Peace of Breda, the duke yielded to Nicolls's many requests to be relieved of the governorship of the province. On the 28th of August, 1668, he embarked for England "with every demonstration of respect and regret from those who, receiving him as a conqueror, bade him farewell as a friend." He had used his extraordinary powers prudently and had always acted with the "integrity of a true gentleman." Maverick, in writing to Lord Arlington, said of him, "by his prudent management of affairs he had kept persons of different judgments and of diverse natures in peace and quietness, during a time when a great part of the world was at war; and furthermore, that no one had ever arrived at a better understanding with the Indians than had he." Nicolls took part in the third naval war between the English and the Dutch and was killed at the battle of Solebay, May 28, 1672, having reached the forty-seventh year of his age.

His successor in the government of New York was Colonel Francis Lovelace. He was a man of respectable abilities and of worthy character, but much inferior to his predecessor in both respects. He was by no means enterprising, and was content to continue the policy of Nicolls. This was fortunate. He lacked energy and decision, but was upright and good-natured and of "generous mind, and noble." Lovelace was a court favorite. His zeal in the interests of Charles II. had resulted in his imprisonment in the Tower by Richard Cromwell on the charge of high treason. He had been enrolled as a knight of the "Royal Oak" at the Restoration and later had been made a gentleman of the king's Privy Chamber. His task as Governor of New York was to finish as quietly as possible the work of bringing the Dutch under English authority. To accomplish this, he fostered social relations between the settlers of the two nationalities. He protected the Reformed Church in all its privileges and granted the Lutherans and Presbyterians religious freedom. In his encouragement of religious toleration he was supported by the Duke of York, who, by conviction a Roman Catholic, sympathized with all who dissented from the Church of England.

One of Lovelace's first popular acts was the abolition in 1668 of the classes of "great burghers" and "small burghers" instituted by Stuyvesant in 1657. This division into classes was an imitation of a Dutch custom, but had proved very unpopular. Members of the council, burgomasters, schepens, officers of the militia, ministers of the Gospel and their descendants, and the descendants of militia officers, in a male line, were great burghers. Others could be enrolled in this class upon the payment of fifty guilders. All other persons born in the city were small burghers. Likewise, all who had been resident there a year and six weeks; or who had married daughters of burghers; or who were salaried servants of the West India Company; or who kept a shop or were engaged in a permanent business in the city. Transient residents of the city could be enrolled in this class on the payment of twenty-five guilders. The great burghers were eligible to public offices. In cases of conviction for a capital offence, they were exempt from confiscation or attainder. The privileges granted to small burghers were mostly of a commercial character, tending to add to the facilities for trading.—(O'Callaghan, *History of New Netherland*, ii, 341.)

The new governor, like Stuyvesant and Nicolls, was soon to experience the restive character of the English towns on Long Island. The government of New Netherland, unlike those of New England, was an autocracy, and had been continued as such after the English conquest. The continuance of this form of government had been very distasteful to the English towns on Long Island, and they fretted under it. This was especially true of those towns that had been in alliance with Connecticut. These towns had reluctantly submitted to the dominance of New York, preferring to retain their former political connections. At the conquest, they had been led to expect from the proclamation of the royal commissioners that they would be admitted to the ordinary privileges and immunities of British subjects. They expected to be given the power of participating in the government—of choosing their own representatives to a general assembly with the power of making laws. Witness their chagrin and disappointment, however, when they discovered that the "Duke's Laws" granted them none of those anticipated privileges. They expressed their indignation at what they termed the "servile submission" of their delegates at the Hempstead convention. They considered some of the laws established by the Code as arbitrary and oppressive, and some of those made by Lovelace as still more onerous. In November, 1669, petitions from three towns were presented to Governor Lovelace, asking for a legislature chosen by the freeholders. Nicolls had refused a similar request at the Hempstead convention in the spring of 1665, and Lovelace, likewise, had no authority to grant it. He merely replied that "nothing was required of them but obedience and submission to the law of the Government, as appeared by His Royal Highness's Commission which had often been read to them."

The trouble reached a climax in 1670. In October of that year the Court of Assizes ordered a tax levied on the Long Island towns for the repair of Fort James. Those towns, however, having had their petition for a representative assembly rejected the year before, were in no mood to submit to this tax. They claimed it was contrary to the principle of "taxation by consent," which had been maintained in Holland since 1477 and asserted in England since 1265. They had paid a direct tax of a penny a pound to defray the expenses of their own town governments and had, in addition, paid the duke's customs duties. Submission to this last tax, however, would form a bad precedent. They were not represented in the Court of Assizes; and if that body could levy a tax to rebuild a palisade, it could likewise levy one to support the garrison and they knew not what else. Southold, Southampton, and Easthampton agreed to contribute provided they might have the privileges enjoyed by the king's subjects in New England. Huntingdon refused because it was deprived of the liberties of Englishmen. Jamaica held the tax inconsistent with the British Constitution, but declared its willingness to bear the tax in patience if it was the king's express purpose to "disprivilege" it. Flushing and Hempstead concurred with Jamaica. These remonstrances were adjudged "false, scandalous, illegal, and seditious, tending only to disaffect all the peaceable and well-meaning subjects" of the king in the province. Lovelace ordered the remonstrances burned publicly before the town hall in the city of New York, and at the same time ordered criminal proceedings to be begun against the principal seditionaries. It was easier to burn "seditious" remonstrances than to remove the cause of their being made. Long Island continued for some time disaffected and was more or less a thorn in the side of the duke's administration. An appeal to the king was made by several of the towns, and it is worthy of note that when the war between Holland and England reached its height "benevolences" were asked instead of taxes.

In the meantime political conditions in Europe were so readjusting themselves as to portend important changes in New York. The remarkable success of the armies of Louis XIV. in Flanders led to the formation of the Triple Alliance between England, Holland, and Sweden against France. As a result, Louis was compelled to suspend his conquests and make peace with Spain. The Triple Alliance was very popular in England. Bishop Burnet said it was certainly "the masterpiece of King Charles's life; and if he had stuck to it, it would have been both the strength and the glory of his reign. It disposed his people to forgive all that was past and to renew their confidence in him, which was much shaken by the whole conduct of the Dutch war." The movements of the French as a result of the war caused much excitement in New York. In the summer of June, 1671, the move made by Courcelles toward New York caused a panic in the province. Some of the people made preparations to move away before the French could reach them. But the cause of the excitement soon changed from the French to the Dutch. French gold and a French woman, combined with a hatred for the Dutch and a probable desire to establish the Roman Catholic faith in England, led Charles II. to break away from the Triple Alliance. A secret treaty was concluded at Dover in May, 1670, between Charles and Louis. A second but open treaty was likewise negotiated in January, 1671. By the terms of the latter treaty, the United Provinces were to be dismembered and all except Holland were to be annexed to England and France.

War broke out in 1672. The war was to be fought by England on the sea and by France on land. Accordingly, the navy of the former captured the Dutch Smyrna fleet even before war was declared, and an immense army of the latter very shortly invaded Holland. "No clap of thunder," wrote Temple, "could more astonish the world" than the capture of the Smyrna fleet.

News of the war led Lovelace to make prompt preparations for the defence of New York. He was directed by the king to put the whole province in a condition of defence and be warned against private men-of-war. The warning was timely. While De Ruyter and Cornelius van Tromp were defending Holland against the attacks of the English and French squadrons, a Dutch fleet of fifteen ships under Cornelius Evertsen was cruising in the West Indies for the purpose of harassing the English. Joined by a fleet under Jacob Binckes and enlarged by prizes, the combined forces resolved to sail for New York. The fleet, consisting of twenty-three vessels, carrying one thousand six hundred men in addition to their crews, anchored under Staten Island, August 7, 1673. Governor Lovelace was absent in New England, but his presence would not have changed the result. On the 9th of August, after shots had been exchanged between the fleet and Fort James, New York was formally surrendered to the Dutch.

There was once more a general change of names and a reëstablishment of old boundary lines. "New Netherland" was restored; Fort James was changed to "Willem Hendrick," in honor of the Prince of Orange; and New York City was changed to "New Orange"; Kingston [Esopus] became "Zwaanenburg"; Albany became "Willemstadt," and its block house, "Fort Nassau"; New Jersey became "Achter Koll," or "Back Bay." A council of war appointed Anthony Colve, a captain of infantry, Governor of New Netherland. His commission described his government as extending from fifteen miles south of Cape Henlopen to the east end of Long Island and Shelter Island; thence through the middle of the Sound to Greenwich and northerly according to the boundary line established by the treaty of Hartford in 1650. The western boundary was Delaware Bay and River. Pemaquid, Martha's Vineyard, and Nantucket were not included. A large part of the territory submitted to the change peacefully and some towns even gladly. The eastern Long Island towns, Southampton, Easthampton, Brookhaven, Southold, and Huntingdon, yielded unwillingly. Lovelace learned of the surrender while in New England, and, hastening over to Long Island, tried to raise its militia for the purpose of retrieving the calamity. Later, he was enticed over to New York, arrested for debt, stripped of his property, and then given permission to leave the province six weeks after he had paid his debts. However, as there seemed to be no present or remote prospect of his paying his debts and there seemed to be no other reason for keeping him, he was allowed to embark in the fleet for Holland.

Colve displayed remarkable energy in putting the defences in shape to resist a possible attack from England or New England. There seemed to be no immediate danger from the former source. In New England, on the contrary, there was every indication of an approaching conflict. A protest by Southampton against the Dutch conquest met with a ready sympathy from the New England Confederation. First, Connecticut sent troops over to Long Island; then Massachusetts decided to take action after meeting with losses on the high seas at the hands of the Dutch; Plymouth declared there was "just ground for a war," and Rhode Island put her harbors in a state of defence against attacks by the Dutch. Had all the New England colonies united in an attack upon Manhattan, Colve's situation would have been precarious in the extreme. By the spring of 1674, however, the fort was nearly completed, and mounted one hundred and ninety guns. To make the fort effective, Colve found it necessary to pull down a large number of buildings that had been built too close to its walls. Those who suffered by this wholesale destruction and removal were assigned new lots and recompensed out of a tax levied for the purpose. To pay the expenses of these repairs extraordinary duties were levied and a large amount of English and French property found in the city was confiscated.

Colve then turned his attention to the eastern end of Long Island. An expedition was sent to Shelter Island with the intention of reducing to subjection the towns that were proving refractory. Fitz John Winthrop with the Connecticut forces had reached Southold. Forces were likewise hurried from Southampton and Easthampton, and it was decided to make a stand against Colve's men at Southold. The Dutch forces appeared before the town and demanded its surrender. In case of refusal, the town was threatened "with fire and sword." The answer was returned that the Dutch commander would be received "as a person that disturbs his majesty's subjects." Thereupon shots were exchanged without any damage being done. The Dutch, finding the English too strong for them, returned to Manhattan.

While these events were occurring in New Netherland, the war between Holland and England was rapidly drawing to a close. The attack upon Southold had occurred on March 6, 1674. The Treaty of Westminster, by which the war was brought to a close, had been signed on February 19, 1674. In Holland, just prior to the treaty, the States General had decided to grant the request of the burgomasters and schepens of New Orange to assume the government of the province of New Netherland. Joris Andringa, secretary to the provincial fleet, was appointed governor to succeed Colve. The Treaty of Westminster, however, changed all these plans. Four days after the appointment of Andringa as Governor of New Netherland, the States General had offered to restore the province to England. This offer was not a voluntary one, but was dictated by necessity. The success of France in the war threatened the interests of the House of Hapsburg in Spain and Austria. Holland, consequently, found herself in the odd position of being opposed by her former friends and supported by her former enemies. Spain succeeded in persuading Holland to make peace with England. Charles was willing to come to terms on condition that conquests should be mutually restored as they were prior to the war. Furthermore, that Holland should pay England a liberal war indemnity. The treaty was signed on February 19, 1674, and proclaimed at the City Hall of New Orange on the 11th of July following.

The Duke of York's proprietorship over New York was decided by the crown lawyers to have been extinguished by the Dutch conquest. The sovereign Dutch States General had treated directly with Charles II. as sovereign, and as such the latter was sole proprietor of the ceded province. Consequently, a new patent was issued to the Duke of York. New Jersey, all territory west of Connecticut River, Long Island and adjacent islands, and Pemaquid were included in this entirely new grant. Nicolls's arrangements with Winthrop and the rights of Berkeley and Carteret were completely ignored.

At the time of the transference of New York to the English, the province contained scarcely twelve thousand white persons. Schenectady was the remotest settlement on the Mohawk. The population was quite cosmopolitan —the names indicating immigrants from Prussia, Germany, Switzerland, Bohemia, Norway, and Denmark. In an engraving in the *Description of New Netherland*, by Arnoldus Montanus, 1671, we have what purports to be a picture of New York as it was at that time. Inness calls it a "nondescript sketch of little worth." There is an account of the city, likewise, in Daniel Denton's *Brief Description of New York*, London, 1670. The houses were sharp-gabled structures of one and two stories. The fort and the church were not far from the bay. Denton describes the city as "built most of brick and stone and covered with red and black tile; and the land being high, it gives at a distance a pleasing aspect to the spectator." The king's cosmographer, John Ogilby, gives a more elaborate picture of the city, but he seems to have compiled it chiefly from Denton and Montanus rather than from observation. The climate necessitated thick clothing in winter, and the account by Knickerbocker of the manifold petticoats and trousers is not far from correct. The tavern was a prominent feature of the town life. A fair called the Kirmess brought the population together for a succession of holidays. The most important act of Lovelace's administration was the establishment of a regular monthly post service between New York and Boston. The order was issued on December 10, 1672, and was the first regular mail service in America. In a letter to Winthrop, dated December 27th, Lovelace wrote that the first change of horses would be at Hartford. All letters outward were to be "postpaid," and those coming to New York were to be post prepaid likewise. The mail was to start on the first Monday of each month and return the same month. The regulations established by Lovelace were quite simple and interesting. The first post was to have started on New Year's Day, 1673, but was kept back until the Albany news reached New York. It was not until January 22d that the start was finally made. The route led through Harlem, Pelham Manor, Greenwich, Stamford, New Haven, Hartford, and Springfield. The postman crossed bodies of water in boats, followed Indian trails, bridle paths, and watercourses. Wagon roads were the exception. Letters were placed in sealed bags, according to their destination. Only "by-letters" were placed in an open bag. The interests of this postal service had called Lovelace to New England when New York was recaptured by the Dutch. The first Merchants' Exchange was also established during Lovelace's administration. It met Friday mornings, near the site where now Broad Street is crossed by Exchange Place. Lovelace encouraged shipbuilding, and in partnership with some others he built two ships—one being "a very stronge and handsome vessel but costly" named the *Good Fame*.

Lovelace having fallen out of favor, it was necessary for the duke to appoint a new governor of New York. His choice fell upon Major Edmund Andros, an officer in Prince Rupert's regiment of dragoons, a member of the royal household, and commander of the king's forces in Barbadoes. He had fought with distinction in the wars in Holland. The Duke of York accordingly commissioned him "Lieutenant and Governor," July 1, 1674. His commission was similar to those of Nicolls and Lovelace. Andros was born in London in 1637, and was of an excellent family. He was a moderate Episcopalian, unblemished in his private character and fairly well educated. He spoke Dutch and French fluently and had undoubted administrative ability. He lacked tact and sympathy, and in enforcing the unjust mandates of his unscrupulous superiors he earned the reputation of being a conscienceless tyrant.

Andros arrived in New York on the 22d of October, and on the 10th of November he assumed the government and appointed officers. The transfer caused less friction than might have been expected. By his instructions, Andros was required to administer justice to the Dutch and English with all "possible equality"; to observe the laws of Nicolls and Lovelace; and to permit all persons to worship as they saw fit. In some matters, however, Andros showed that crude want of tact that characterized him throughout his official career. Manning, who surrendered the province to the Dutch fleet, was degraded and declared incapable of filling any office of trust. John Burroughs, town clerk of Newtown, was publicly disgraced for representing the grievances under which his fellow townsmen suffered. When Cornelius Steenwyck, Johannes van Brugh, Johannes de Peyster, Nicholas Bayard, Aegidius Luyck, William Beekman, Jacob Kip, and Anthony de Milt, representing many prominent burghers of New York, objected to taking the oath of allegiance without the modification permitted by Nicolls, Andros clapped them all into prison. They were charged with mutinous and inflammatory behavior, but were released on bonds. Later, they were tried on the less serious charge of having engaged in trade without having taken the oath of allegiance. Seven were convicted, but on their yielding all penalties were remitted. Then again, in 1678, Jacob Milborne was arrested as "a mutinous person" and fined £45.

On the other hand, there is no doubting Andros's indomitable courage and loyalty to the interests of his superiors. When the Long Island towns, Southold, Easthampton, and Southampton, claimed to be under the jurisdiction of Connecticut, Andros compelled them to submit to his administration without further ado by threatening to deal with them as if in rebellion. He laid claim to all of Connecticut west of Connecticut River, and requested the General Court of that colony to turn the territory over to him. On the 8th of July, 1675, he reënforced his claim upon the territory in question by appearing before Saybrook with three sloops-of-war. The Connecticut authorities, however, were prepared for his arrival. Captain Bull was in charge of the fort. All the major could do was to have read aloud the duke's patent, to which was read in reply the Connecticut General Court's manifesto in which Andros was referred to as a disturber of the peace. Andros was thus

compelled to withdraw most ignominiously, although the
garrison respected his feelings sufficiently to salute him
upon his departure. On his return, he landed at Southold
and from there despatched soldiers to look after his interests
in the islands of Nantucket and Martha's Vineyard.

The Indians, in the meantime, were beginning to give
trouble. King Philip's war broke out in the summer of
1675. Andros's visit to Saybrook was in part the result
of this Indian outbreak. His attention was, however, soon
turned to an Indian question of far greater moment than
King Philip's war. The Iroquois had never forgotten the
attack made upon them at Ticonderoga by the French under
Champlain. They took every opportunity of striking a blow
at the French in Canada. We have already seen how the
latter, in 1666, under Courcelles, then governor, attempted
to chastise the Iroquois league. Courcelles penetrated the
Mohawk country as far as Schenectady, and at another time
destroyed the rather extensive fortifications of the Iroquois.
All these aggressive attempts of the French to rid themselves
of the fury of the league failed. The French authorities
then turned their efforts toward gaining the friendship of
the Indians. Through the Jesuit missionaries, they made
some headway in winning over the Oneidas, Onondagas,
Cayugas, and Senecas. The Mohawks were beyond redemption.

Andros soon saw the seriousness of the situation. The
Duke of York seems to have favored the efforts of the
Jesuits; but Andros saw that an alliance between the French
and the Long House would mean the paramount supremacy
of France in American affairs. He decided to visit the
Indian country. After making brief stops at Esopus and
Albany, the governor penetrated the wilderness sixteen
miles to Schenectady—then a little Dutch village marking
the "remotest western outpost of civilization." From here
he journeyed to the three principal "castles" of the Mohawks. The first was situated on the west bank of Schoharie Creek at its junction with the Mohawk; the second,

at Canajoharie; and the third, on the site occupied by the town of Danube in Herkimer County. Leaving the Mohawk country, the party penetrated the Oneida country as far as a stronghold known as Nundadasis, contiguous to the site of the city of Utica. Here was held a congress of the principal chiefs of the Iroquois league. Presents were exchanged, the pipe of peace was smoked, and the Long House swore eternal friendship for the English and enmity for the French. The ancient Dutch treaties were renewed and Andros was formally given the title "Corlear," which he had first received at the third Mohawk castle. Arendt van Corlear, the founder of Schenectady, had signified to the Indians Dutch power and Dutch friendship. The most important result of this conference was the organization, in August, 1675, of a local board of Commissioners for Indian Affairs. This had its headquarters at Albany. Robert Livingston, the town clerk of Albany, was made secretary of this board.

Sir George Carteret had claimed that when the king regranted him East Jersey after the Treaty of Westminster, he was continued as lord proprietor. The Duke of York, on the other hand, claimed that Carteret was but a lord of the manor, and as such under the sovereignty of New York. Philip Carteret, representing the widow of Sir George Carteret, acted upon the former assumption, called an assembly, and declared Elizabethtown a free port. Andros was instructed by the duke to seize vessels clearing from any other port than New York. Philip Carteret denied Andros's right to assert, in any respect whatever, sovereignty over Jersey soil and in this he was supported by his assembly. This resulted in Andros's first deposing Carteret, and then in causing his arrest, which was accomplished in a most brutal manner. After a four weeks' imprisonment he was brought to trial before a jury and acquitted, much to the chagrin and open anger of his persecutor. At first Carteret was not permitted to assume any authority in East Jersey, either civil or military. Later, however, he was escorted back by Andros himself and partly reëstablished in his rights. Lady Carteret, upon hearing of these violent proceedings against her representative and against her rights, had the matter brought to the attention of the Duke of York. The duke, fearing the Carteret power at court, mendaciously denied responsibility for the action taken by Andros. Following up this statement, he furthermore formally relinquished his claim upon East Jersey and confirmed it in the proprietorship of Sir George Carteret's heir.

Many other complaints of Andros's conduct likewise reached England in 1680. In addition to his tactless management of the East Jersey affair, it was urged that he unduly favored Dutch shipping, and permitted the people of Boston to traffic in furs with the Mohawks. In consequence, he was summoned by the duke to justify his conduct. He sailed in January, 1681, leaving Lieutenant-governor Anthony Brockholls in charge of affairs. The duke sent over John Lewin to investigate the conduct of Andros in his administration of the affairs of the province. His report was entirely favorable. Andros was vindicated and received a substantial token of his vindication in being made a gentleman of the king's privy chamber. He did not return until he was sent out as governor-general of all the northern colonies.

Brockholls at once experienced trouble. For some unaccountable reason, Andros had neglected to renew by a special ordinance the customs duties imposed in 1677 and expiring in November, 1680. After the governor's departure, the merchants refused to pay any duties on imports. The lieutenant-governor was not sure he had authority to renew the duties, and the council advised him that he could not collect them without specific orders from the Duke of York. The whole dispute was precipitated when William Dyer, collector of the port, was arrested for traitorously exercising "regal power and authority" by demanding the payment of taxes not legally due. He was brought to trial, but appealed to the courts in England. There, he was examined by the king's legal advisers and received a material vindication of his conduct in being made surveyor-general of customs in America.

Brockholls was now persuaded to present to the duke a petition for a legislative assembly. The demand was urgent, it was held, because the people "were groaning under inexpressible burdens of an arbitrary and absolute power" by which "revenue had been exacted, their trade crippled, and their liberties enthralled." Pressure for money led the duke to grant the petition. The condition he made was that the colony should raise sufficient funds to pay the public debts and maintain the government suitably.

The calling of the first assembly was left to the successor of Andros. On September 30, 1682, the duke commissioned Colonel Thomas Dongan Governor of New York. He was born in 1634, and was a younger son of an Irish baronet. He was a Roman Catholic and held a colonelcy in the royal army. He had fought in France, had been lieutenant-governor in Tangier; was energetic and covetous, yet "a man of integrity, moderation and genteel manners." He arrived in New York on August 28, 1683, amid universal rejoicing. He was instructed to summon a General Assembly, to consist of not more than eighteen persons, who were to be chosen by all the freeholders. The Assembly was to "have free liberty to consult and debate for all laws." The duke alone could exercise the right of veto over its acts.

After a hurried visit to Albany, the governor issued a formal summons for the Assembly, bearing the date September 13, 1683. The Assembly met in Fort James, October 17th. There were eighteen delegates in all: Schenectady sending one; Albany and Rensselaerwyck, two; Esopus, two; New York and Harlem, four; Staten Island, one; each of the three ridings [districts] of Yorkshire [Long Island], two; Martha's Vineyard and Nantucket, one; Pemaquid, one. The session lasted three weeks, and fourteen acts were passed. The first and by far the most important of these acts was "The Charter of Liberties and

Privileges." It declared that under the king and lord proprietor the supreme legislative authority was to reside in the governor, Council, and the people represented in a General Assembly. The Assembly was to meet at least once in three years, and every freeholder was to have the privilege of electing the representative without any "manner of constraint or imposition." A majority of votes was to determine the election. The usual Parliamentary privileges were conferred upon the members of the assembly, and the most liberal provisions of English law were declared to extend to the inhabitants of New York. Freedom of conscience and religion was guaranteed to all peaceable persons who professed "faith in God by Jesus Christ." No manner of taxes were to be laid upon any excuse whatever except by the act of the governor, Council, and Assembly. An accompanying act was passed granting the duke and his heirs certain duties on imports. This charter was proclaimed on October 31, 1683. "In no other colony in America had the principle of representation of the people as a condition of taxation been so clearly asserted by statute at that day." In fact, March 3, 1685, when the duke had become king, he objected to the words "the people" as being "not used in any other constitution in America."

A second act, passed on the 1st of November, divided New York into twelve counties—New York, Westchester, Ulster, Dutchess, Orange, Albany, Richmond, Kings, Queens, Suffolk—within the present limits of the State. In addition there were Dukes, including Nantucket, Martha's Vineyard and dependencies, and Cornwall, including Pemaquid and adjacent territory.

A third act established four distinct tribunals in New York: town courts, to be held monthly for the trial of small offences; county courts (Courts of Sessions), to be held quarterly or half-yearly; a general Court of Oyer and Terminer, to sit twice a year in each county and having original and appellate jurisdiction; and a Court of Chancery, to be the supreme court and composed of the Council and the governor or a chancellor to represent him. Any person could appeal from the judgment of this court to the king. A naturalization law was passed at the same time.

In December, these acts of the Assembly were sent to England for the duke's approval, but before he had affixed his signature to them an important event occurred which brought with it many momentous changes. Early in February, Charles II. was stricken with apoplexy and died on the 6th of that month. He was succeeded by his brother the Duke of York, as James II. This accession boded ill for popular rights in the colonies. New York became a royal province, and the attitude of its former proprietor toward it was changed. James the king was a different man from James the duke. He held that the "Charter of Privileges" tended too much to restrain the governor and to abridge the king's power. Consequently, he did not sign the charter nor did he repeal it, but held it in abeyance until he should devise another plan of colonial government. The results of his attempts to materialize this plan we shall have occasion to consider in a subsequent chapter.

## CHAPTER VIII

### MIGRATION OF THE OPPRESSED

WE have thus far spoken of the English, Dutch, and Swedes because to them belongs the major credit of colonizing the territory now known as the Middle States. We must not, however, lose sight of the lesser divisions of emigration that became fused into the conglomerate population of the Middle States. In the present chapter we propose to treat in detail those groups that for one reason or another cannot properly be classified under the general headings of English, Dutch, or Swedish. We may begin with the Walloons. These people had passed through the fire of persecution. They inhabited originally the southern Belgic provinces of Hainault, Namur, Luxemburg, Limburg, and part of the ancient bishopric of Liège, and spoke the old French language. At the union of the northern provinces of the Netherlands in 1579, the Roman Catholic southern provinces declined to be parties to it. Many of their inhabitants, nevertheless, had accepted the principles of the Reformation. Against these Protestant Walloons, the Spanish government directed with unrelenting fury all the engines of the Inquisition. In consequence, they emigrated by thousands to Holland, where they knew that the persecuted of every race and creed could find safe asylum. They carried with them a knowledge of those arts in which they were highly proficient and thus added greatly to Holland's reputation as a manufacturing nation.

Hearing of the New World and the wide range given to ambitious and industrious people, these refugees determined to try their fortunes in America. Accordingly they petitioned for the privilege of migrating to Virginia. But satisfactory arrangements could not be made with the Virginia Company, and thus their first attempt failed. Shortly after, the Dutch government learned of their desire to migrate and, knowing from experience what desirable citizens they made, determined to send them out under the auspices of the Dutch West India Company. Accordingly, when in March, 1623, the *New Netherland* sailed for the New World, she conveyed a company of thirty families, most of whom were Walloons. The superintendence of the expedition was intrusted to the experienced Cornelius Jacobsen May, of Hoorn. He was to remain in New Netherland as the first director of the colony. The second in command was Adrian Joris, of Thienpont.

After a voyage of two months, they arrived safely at Manhattan. Here May left a party of eight men, while other parties were sent to establish colonies on South and Fresh Rivers. Most of the immigrants, however, settled on the west bank of Hudson River, at a point where, the year before, Fort Orange had been begun. Here eighteen families, under the leadership of Adrian Joris, took up their homes. They finished the fort and set to work immediately tilling the soil and constructing themselves "some huts of bark." Shortly after, some of the neighboring Indians, the Mohicans and some of the Iroquois, visited the settlement, bringing Joris valuable presents. A covenant of friendship was entered into between them, which was sacredly kept for several years. This was the beginning of Albany, now the capital of New York. Yet another party settled on the shore of Long Island at a deep bay near the present site of the Brooklyn Navy Yard. The name "Wallabout," or Walloon Bay, is commemorative of the nationality of some of these early settlers.

In 1660 still another expedition of the oppressed Walloons, who had temporarily sought refuge along the banks

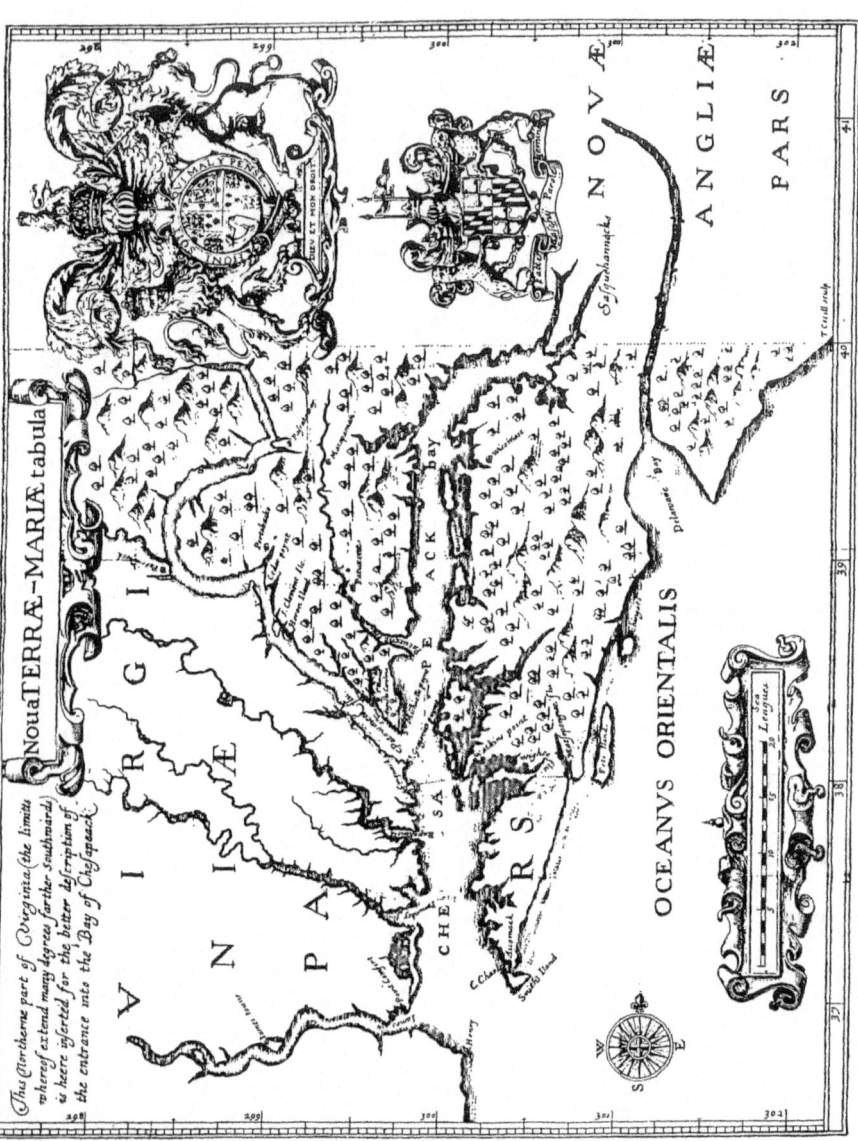

Map of Maryland in 1635. From the original in the New York Public Library, Lenox Branch

of the Rhine, came to America. Under the leadership of
Louis du Bois, they settled in Esopus and began the towns
of Kingston and New Paltz.

The persecution of the Puritans by the king and the
Established Church of England, instead of extirpating this
sect, had the contrary effect of strengthening their faith and
adding to their numbers. So severely were they persecuted
in the time of James I., that rather than give up their principles they decided to exile themselves from their native
country. They had often heard extolled the liberality of
Holland, where, it was said, there was religious toleration
for all. So, early in 1608, a party of about one hundred in
all set out for that country to dwell among strange people.
Their leaders were John Robinson, their minister, and William Brewster, their ruling elder. First they settled at
Amsterdam, where they remained for a few months. The
following year, however, they went to Leyden and were
joined there by other refugees. By hard work and indomitable pluck they at length won a competent and comfortable
living. They remained in Leyden twelve years, having been
treated all the while by the Dutch with marked kindness and
generous consideration.

Nevertheless, they continued to feel that they were aliens
and longed for a spot where they could establish their own
schools and churches. Their treatment by the Hollanders
had been so uniformly kind, it is not strange that when once
they decided to emigrate to the New World, they sought to
do so under the auspices of their benefactors. Accordingly
in 1620, their leader, the Rev. John Robinson, addressed himself to the Amsterdam merchants, promising four hundred
families from Leyden and England to colonize New Netherland. They wished, said Robinson, "to plant there the
true and pure Christian religion, to convert the savages of
those countries to the true knowledge and understanding
of the Christian faith, and, through the grace of the Lord,
and to the glory of the Netherlands government, to colonize and establish a new empire." The only stipulation

they made was that in case of attack by another power the United Provinces should protect them.

These overtures were gladly listened to by the Amsterdam company, for they desired to establish a substantial colony in New Netherland. They foresaw that the large number of settlers the Puritans promised, judging from the good record they had made in the Fatherland, could hardly prove other than successful. They offered the Puritans attractive inducements to emigrate, promising, in fact, to transport them free of cost to North River and to furnish every family with cattle. As to assuring them protection against a foreign foe, that, they decided, was beyond their jurisdiction. They referred the whole matter to Prince Maurice, who in turn referred it to the States General. But the statesmen of the Netherlands were too deeply involved in large and ambitious designs to pass favorably upon the petition of the Amsterdam company. They were shaping the constitution of the West India Company, whose powers and capital were to be so great that the States General fondly hoped it might be instrumental in dealing its ancient enemy Spain a death blow. Inasmuch as all matters relating to colonization would come under the jurisdiction of this Company, it was decided that this petition should be deferred.

Aside from this, a more powerful consideration swayed the States General. A war with Spain was expected, and it was desired to keep on friendly terms with England. It knew that the English denied the Dutch title to North River and Manhattan. It was clear, therefore, that to plant an English colony on disputed territory and guarantee it protection could only end in a quarrel. England might not object to Holland's extending a helping hand to English refugees in Holland; when, however, that hand reached across the ocean and assumed to protect them in what King James considered English territory, that might prove another question. Therefore, the petition of the Puritans was finally rejected and, instead of their migrating to America under the protection of the Dutch, they went under the auspices of the London Company.

The Puritan movement was, however, to be felt in the Dutch province, for dissensions in New England drove not a few of the English colonists to New Netherland, where they found the freedom which in vain they had sought in the colonies on Massachusetts Bay. Early in 1642 came the Rev. Francis Doughty and Richard Smith with a party of other seekers after freedom of worship. They were followed shortly by John Throgmorton and thirty-five English families, who settled on East River and built homes for themselves. In 1642 Anne Hutchinson, not feeling secure from the Massachusetts authorities, even in Rhode Island, emigrated to New Netherland with all her family. All these Puritan emigrants to New Netherland were received kindly by Kieft, the director-general. He granted them lands on which to settle and establish for themselves homes, and he accorded them all the privileges which the Dutch inhabitants enjoyed.

Other refugee Puritans settled in Virginia, where they lived in peace until 1643, when the Assembly passed an act expelling all Nonconformists from that colony. Many of these sought and found refuge in Maryland, where freedom of conscience was granted them. There nothing was demanded of them but obedience to the laws, fidelity to the proprietary, and the usual quitrents. These conditions they gladly accepted. Their largest settlement they called Providence. For a time they were content in their new home and dwelt peaceably with their Roman Catholic fellow colonists. Eventually, however, they made sorry returns for the hospitality which Lord Baltimore had accorded them. In conjunction with other malcontents they complained to the English Parliament "that Maryland was but a nursery of Jesuits and that the poor Protestants were everywhere suppressed." This charge was easily proved utterly baseless.

When Oliver Cromwell declared himself Protector, the confusion which followed in the colonies gave Baltimore's enemies the opportunity for which they had been long looking. Bennett and Claiborne placed themselves at the head of a party of men from Virginia and Maryland. They forced the governor, Stone, to resign, and put in his place a Captain William Fuller, who, with a Puritan Council, was to administer affairs. Then followed a régime of intolerance. An Assembly was called, but no Roman Catholic was eligible to office or could cast a vote. The Toleration Act of 1649 was repealed, and another, called "An Act Concerning Religion," was proclaimed. This act denied protection to all Roman Catholics in the exercise of their religion. Later, Brownists, Quakers, Anabaptists, " and other miscellaneous Protestant sects" were included within the operation of the act. In fact, none but the Puritans could look for protection from the newly established government.

The Reformation in France from the very beginning had gained steadily, until not only many of the middle classes but many of the aristocracy and even some of the clergy supported it. They built schools and churches of their own, and increased numerically in spite of persecution. The Huguenots, whose greatest strength lay in the class composed of skilled artisans, scholars, and merchants, were the most moral, industrious, and intelligent of the French population. They had found a friend in Henry IV., who in 1598 proclaimed the Edict of Nantes, which granted them many privileges and more especially freedom of conscience. This edict remained in force until its revocation in 1685, during the reign of Louis XIV.

The migration of French Protestants had been going on for several years; it now became so vast that the industrial welfare of the nation was threatened. Louis forbade all Protestants to leave the country. In spite of this decree, however, the exodus was very little diminished. Protestants fled in disguise; and many Catholics, pitying them, helped them on their way. The neighboring Protestant nations eagerly opened their arms to their oppressed brethren. Money was raised to assist them to reach an asylum. Holland exempted them from taxation for twelve years, and all Protestant countries offered them immediate naturalization.

Many of these Huguenots went first to Holland and England, but finally found their way across the ocean to the American colonies of their benefactors. There they were received with great kindness and consideration, and eventually did much to enrich their adopted homes. Many of them found their way to New York, where they joined the ranks of the army of the oppressed from many countries. Settling here upon the land sold them by Jacob Leisler, they began New Rochelle, so named in honor of the French town from which so many of them had come.

Two hundred thousand Huguenots, driven from their homes by Louis XIV., could not help impressing their character to a very marked extent upon the people among whom they settled. Particularly was this true in America, where, the habits and institutions being new and plastic, every nationality represented had more or less to do with moulding American life and thought. The Huguenots brought to the New World their French arts, which were then unknown in America. They brought, likewise, their talents and their knowledge of mercantile affairs. The advent of such a people could not fail to be beneficial to the colonies.

George Fox, the founder of the Society of Friends, was born at what is now called Fenny Drayton, Leicestershire, England, July, 1624. Without doubt the character of his parents had much influence upon his development. His father, Christopher Fox, a weaver, was so renowned among his neighbors for his uprightness that he was called by them "righteous Christer." His mother, also, was a woman of great piety and sweetness of character. In his boyhood he was employed by a shoemaker, who also dealt in wool, and for a time George tended the sheep,—"a fit emblem of his future service in the Church of Christ," says William Penn. Although a member of the Church of England, the worldliness of the ministers and members of that church was early realized by him. He felt that the life had completely

departed from the Church service, and that at that time it was
nothing more than a shell. These things greatly distressed
him. He felt something must be done, but knew not what.
The friends to whom he applied for advice and enlightenment gave him no aid. One advised him to get married,
in order to soothe his mind; another—a priest—told him to
use tobacco and take to the singing of psalms. His friends
giving him no comfort, his trouble increased, but in the
midst of all the darkness he says he heard a voice which
said: "There is one, even Christ Jesus, that can speak to
thy conditions." From that time on, he felt that he was the
man called of God "to awaken men from their lifeless forms
and dogmas to a sense of the vital importance of an inward,
living, spiritual, religion."

He did not intend to found a new sect, but only wanted
to purge the Church of England of its falsities. He refused to take oaths, quoting the Bible injunction "swear
not at all"; neither would he raise his hat as was the custom,
contending that at the name of God alone should that be
done. Also, he refused to address any man with the plural
pronoun, believing it incompatible with the Biblical idea of
simplicity and truth. Because of these things he gave great
offence to his fellow men, and for preaching them he frequently found himself imprisoned. Upon one occasion,
when arrested, having admonished Justice Bennett, before
whom he was brought, "to tremble at the word of the
Lord," the justice, tradition avers, dubbed Fox and his followers "Quakers." Although persecuted for their own
peculiarities, the Quakers frequently had to answer for the
absurdities of other newly risen sects. But persecution did
not disturb them; in fact, "they courted it."

The news of the new sect reached America, where the
movement was watched with alarm. In Massachusetts, it
is said, a day of fast and prayer was held "on account of
the news of the doings in England of a strange people called
Quakers." Shortly after this, however, in spite of prayer
and fasting, to Boston's horror, two Quaker women came

to town. They were immediately imprisoned, their books were burned, and as soon as possible they were shipped back to England. But others came, notwithstanding, and all Massachusetts was soon in a fever of excitement. The Quakers were absolutely antagonistic to the settlers of Massachusetts, and trouble naturally followed their advent in that colony. They were imprisoned and whipped, and finally four of them, one a woman, were hanged on Boston Common.

A party of Quakers, expelled from Boston by the authorities, came to New Amsterdam in August, 1657. Here, contrary to precedents, they were treated very little better than in Boston. Stuyvesant was then in power. He was somewhat narrow and bigoted and had given, as we have had occasion to mention, the West India Company serious trouble by his intolerance and persecution of all creeds save his own. He made no exception to the Quakers and, in fact, his treatment of them was even more severe than usual. Some were imprisoned, while Robert Hodgson was both imprisoned and fined. Having no money, he was sentenced to two years' hard labor at a wheelbarrow. He refused to carry out his sentence, declaring himself innocent of any crime. He was repeatedly whipped with a piece of tarred rope in the hands of a negro. To this outrage was added two days and nights on bread and water and still another whipping. By this time the people were aroused, and offered to pay his fine if he were released. Hodgson refused this offer, believing "a principle was at stake and he would rather die." Finally, however, public sentiment became too strong even for Stuyvesant, and the Quaker was released.

Some of the Quakers who had sought refuge in Maryland from the persecutions received in New England and Virginia gave the authorities of the former colony considerable trouble. They refused to bear arms or take oaths and, not content with confining these views to themselves, they tried hard to proselyte others. In 1658, two of their number, Josiah Cole and Thomas Thruston, were arrested for refusing to take the oath of fidelity. Later, on "account of their insolent behavior, in standing presumptuously covered," they were forever banished. Also, an order was passed that all Quaker "vagabonds and idlers" should leave Maryland, and if they ventured to return should be whipped from constable to constable out of the province. Those who had entertained Cole and Thruston, together with a man who had refused to assist in the arrest of the latter, were whipped. This order, however, was in force only during Fendall's rule. There is no record of Quakers having been whipped later. Although they were fined for refusing to bear arms or to contribute funds toward the militia, they were treated for the most part leniently and found comparative comfort in the Maryland colony. They increased so rapidly that in 1661 they had stated times for meetings, and in 1672 were visited by their founder, George Fox, who attended several of their meetings.

It is probable that the first settlement of Friends in New Jersey was made along the banks of Raritan River in 1663. In 1670, a meeting house was built at Shrewsbury. The proprietorship of New Jersey had been held jointly by Lord John Berkeley of Stratton and Sir George Carteret, but in 1673 the latter sold out his interest in the colony to a Quaker, John Fenwick, in trust for another Quaker, Edward Byllinge. Trouble arose between the two Friends on account of the transaction, which was finally referred to William Penn for settlement. To Fenwick, Penn granted one-tenth of the land and a sum of money, and he was to hand over to Byllinge the remaining nine-tenths of the purchase. After considerable hesitancy, Fenwick finally yielded to Penn's decision and surrendered to Byllinge his nine-tenths. He himself, in company with some other emigrants, sailed to Delaware River, and on its eastern shore founded the town of Salem, June, 1675. For this he was subsequently put in Fort James, by Andros, for poaching on the Duke of York's territory. Edward Byllinge had now become financially embarrassed, and surrendered his share in

# A CHARACTER Of the PROVINCE of MARY-LAND,

Wherein is Described in four distinct Parts, (Viz.)

I. The Scituation, and plenty of the Province.
II. The Laws, Customs, and natural Demeanor of the Inhabitant.
III. The worst and best Usage of a Mary-Land Servant, opened in view.
IV. The Traffique, and vendable Commodities of the Countrey.

ALSO

A small *Treatise* on the wilde and naked I N D I A N S (or *Susquehanokes*) of *Mary-Land*, their Customs, Manners, Absurdities, & Religion.

Together with a Collection of Historical LETTERS.

By GEORGE ALSOP.

London, Printed by T. J. for Peter Dring, at the sign of the Sun in the Poultrey: 1666.

Title-page of Alsop's *Character of the Province of Maryland.* From the original in the New York Public Library, Lenox Branch.

the land to William Penn and two other Quakers, Gawaine Laurie and Nicholas Lucas. These trustees determined to establish a refuge in their part of New Jersey for all religious sects, particularly Quakers. In their statement it is set forth that no person should " be called in question or molested for his conscience or for worshipping according to his conscience."

To this asylum in 1677 sailed a ship from England laden with two hundred and thirty Friends. Sailing up Delaware River, they landed and founded a village which they called Burlington, after the town in Yorkshire whence a large number of them came. They made a treaty with the Indians, and won, by their kindness, the friendship of the red men. The colony grew in numbers and prospered. The progress of the Quaker colony in West Jersey was watched with interest by one of the founders—William Penn. It had long been his dream to found an asylum in the New World where both religious and civil liberty could be enjoyed by the people. It was to be a place where Quakers and the persecuted of all sects could find peace and the liberty of worshipping God according to their own consciences. The evident prosperity of the colony in West Jersey encouraged him to believe that the same experiment could be made successful if carried out on a larger scale. The financial condition of England at this time gave him the opportunity he craved. The government owed the estate of his father a large sum of money, £16,000, but owing to the poverty of the nation there was nothing with which to pay the debt. Penn, therefore, requested the king, in lieu of the money, to grant him a tract of land in America. There were some who objected to this plan. They prophesied trouble to the crown should it be carried out. Nevertheless, in spite of objections, on March 4, 1681, a charter was granted Penn recognizing him as the sole proprietor of the territory called Pennsylvania. He wrote his frame of government and formed his code of laws. In one of these, his determination to make Pennsylvania a haven for the oppressed found expression. It stated "that all persons living in this province, who confess and acknowledge the one Almighty and Eternal God to be the Creator, Upholder and Ruler of the world, and that hold themselves obliged in conscience to live peaceably and justly in civil society, shall in no wise be molested or prejudiced for their religious persuasion or practice in matters of faith and worship; nor shall they be compelled at any time to frequent or maintain any religious worship, place, or ministry whatever." In addition to the territory granted him, Penn purchased of the Duke of York that country later known as the "Lower Counties." Penn now saw the realization of his dream, his "Holy Experiment" had begun.

The fame of this land along the Delaware, where all religions could live peaceably, spread among the countries of Europe, and many persons prepared to go to Pennsylvania. In the course of the first year more than twenty ships sailed for Delaware River, carrying perhaps three thousand passengers. In 1682, Penn also sailed for his new colony and reached Pennsylvania in October, landing at New Castle. The freedom of conscience which the laws of Pennsylvania offered to all sects alike not only brought a great number of Quakers to its shores, but likewise the oppressed of many other sects.

Among them were the Mennonites, or Anabaptists, who in their belief were very similar to the Quakers. Like them, they refused to bear arms or take oaths. In 1662, peculiar articles of agreement had been signed between the burgomasters of Amsterdam and a society of Mennonites. A grant of land at Hornkill on South River was made to this sect. A company was formed, and one hundred and seventeen articles of association were agreed upon for the settlement. During the first five years after their arrival, they were to live in common. At the end of that time, the property was to be divided and each head of a family was to receive his proportional share. Worthless persons were to be expelled by a vote of two-thirds of the members. The colonists were plundered of all their effects by the English in 1664, after the conquest. The marauding party took "what belonged to the Quaking Society of Plockhoy, to a very naile." After William Penn's "Holy Experiment" was fairly under way, other Mennonites, persecuted alike by Protestants and Catholics, left their homes in Germany and Switzerland and settled in Pennsylvania alongside of the Quakers, to whom they were so near akin in religious belief. The first permanent society in North America was organized at Germantown, Pennsylvania, in 1683, and these were followed by many others from various portions of Germany. Their leader was Francis Daniel Pastorius. He was an enthusiastic scholar, "studying science, philosophy, jurisprudence, or whatever came to hand, and reading eight or ten languages." In 1712, they purchased some land in Lancaster County.

At the beginning of the history of New Amsterdam, we find that oppressed and persecuted sects of every kind found there an asylum where they worshipped God according to their own consciences. After a time, however, the influx gradually became so great that Stuyvesant, a rabid Calvinist, began to fear for the supremacy of the established Dutch Reformed Church. Among the sects which had found a refuge in New Amsterdam was the Lutheran. By 1656 it had increased to such numbers that, instead of being content with continuing the former custom of worshipping in private homes, its members desired a church of their own. They accordingly petitioned Stuyvesant to permit them to build a church and to send for a pastor of their denomination. This request the director refused. They then addressed themselves to the West India Company, where again they met with a refusal.

Later, Megapolensis and Drisius, the Dutch ministers, made complaint that instead of coming to hear them preach the Lutherans preferred to hold conventicles in their own homes. Stuyvesant, thereupon, issued a proclamation prohibiting all unlicensed persons from preaching or "holding conventicles not in harmony with the established religion as set forth by the Synod of Dort." Anyone violating this ordinance was to be fined one hundred pounds, Flemish, and all who attended such meetings would be fined twenty-five pounds. Immediately, there followed fines and imprisonment for the Lutherans. They thereupon complained to the authorities in Holland, and the zealous Stuyvesant received a prompt rebuke from the West India Company. In spite of this, when Ernestus Goetwater came to New Amsterdam in 1657 with a commission from the Lutheran Consistory at Amsterdam to preach and organize a church for the Lutherans, he was arrested and ordered back to Holland. In 1659, the West India Company, again hearing complaints about the harshness of Dutch clergymen in their treatment of Lutheran pastors, wrote to Megapolensis and Drisius that, unless they ceased a "too overbearing preciseness," the directors would permit the Lutherans to build a church of their own. When the Dutch came under the mastery of the English, during Francis Lovelace's administration, the Lutherans were encouraged to bring over their own minister from Holland and were permitted to worship after their own fashion without being persecuted.

Many of the Lutherans came to Pennsylvania and settled. Swedish Lutherans came in 1636 and 1637 and joined the Swedish settlement on the Delaware. Reorus Torkillus was their first pastor. He was succeeded by Campanius, who did missionary work among the Indians and translated Luther's Catechism into the Delaware dialect. The first Lutheran church in Pennsylvania was built in 1646. In 1733, three of the Pennsylvania congregations sent to Germany for pastors. In 1742, Henry Melchior Mühlenberg was sent to them. Mühlenberg was born in 1711, in Hanover, Germany. He has been called "the patriarch of the Lutheran Church in America." Before Mühlenberg came to Pennsylvania, the German Lutherans, now numerous in the province, had gradually become very indifferent to religious affairs. Many were so utterly indifferent, in fact, that

## SIR GEORGE CALVERT

First Baron Baltimore.

*From a copy in the State House at Annapolis after the original by Daniel Mytens the Elder, now in possession of the Earl of Verulam at Gorhambury, England.*

it became proverbial to speak of their belonging to the "Pennsylvania Church."

Many emigrants came to the province without their own ministers, and having no one to teach them they grew decidedly lax in their religious observances. Many false teachers arose among them in the years immediately preceding Mühlenberg's arrival. He found the Church needed a thorough reorganization. Drunkenness was very common. He writes of Pennsylvania in 1754: "It teems with a wicked, frivolous rabble and vagabonds of preachers and students, and the Devil is raging and carrying on his slanders and calamities against the poor Hallenses." Mühlenberg set to work, and during his long ministry did much by his faithfulness and kindness to bring about a better organization and a better religious feeling among the Lutherans.

As early as 1603 the Jews were permitted to settle in Holland, where they prospered and made money, adding much to the wealth of their adopted country. When the Dutch West India Company was formed, we find that many of the Jewish citizens subscribed to the Company's stock and several of them were made directors. A large number of them went first to Brazil, when the Dutch took possession of that country. Later, however, when the Dutch were driven out by an uprising of the people, the Jews, confident no longer of safety, again sought refuge under the Dutch. This time they found their way to America. These were joined by Jews from the Dutch island of Curaçoa.

The Jews for the most part settled in New Amsterdam and other places along the seaboard. Many of them found their way to Philadelphia, where some of them became estimable citizens. Among them was Haym Salomon, who did much toward financing the American Revolution. He negotiated the war subsidies secured from France and Holland, and served as paymaster-general for the forces of the latter country in the United States. Furthermore, he advanced money to the agents and ministers of the United States in foreign countries, as well as to statesmen and others at home. The United States borrowed $600,000 of him in specie, of which $400,000 had not been paid at the time of his death. His descendants have attempted repeatedly to induce Congress to repay the loan, but without success.

Stuyvesant looked with anxiety upon the arrival of so many Jews into his dominion. He succeeded in making it so uncomfortable for them that many left and sought refuge in Rhode Island. He had written a remonstrance to the Dutch West India Company and had pleaded "that none of the Jewish nation be permitted to infest New Netherland." Instead of complying with his request, the Company rebuked the director for his unfairness. Furthermore, the States General, by an act of July 15, 1655, expressly gave the Jews permission to trade to New Netherland, and to reside there on the simple condition that they should support their own poor.

When the Dutch were conquered by the English, and the Duke of York came into possession of New Netherland, this policy of toleration was continued. As a result of this, the Jewish population rapidly increased and many of them became rich. In 1748, they enjoyed all rights that other citizens possessed, save that of voting for the members of the legislature. The Assembly of 1737 put itself on record in regard to this privilege. A contested election case came up before the Assembly, and one of the parties protested that the Jews had been allowed to vote. The question was settled by the Assembly deciding that Jews had no right to vote in New York, since the same privilege was not granted them in England.

The Waldensian Church is probably the oldest Protestant church in the world. The Waldensian valleys are in the north of Italy in the midst of the Cottian Alps, about thirty miles southwest of the city of Turin, the capital of Piedmont. The history of the Waldenses is that of repeated persecutions by the Roman Catholics. In 1655 occurred their most severe persecution. An army, composed partly of French troops of Louis XIV. and partly of Irish soldiers, entered the valleys and treated the people with frightful barbarity. Destruction was spread on every side. Invited by the Elector Palatine, some of the persecuted Waldenses made their way to the Palatinate, while others went on to Holland. Still others wishing to go to the Delaware, Jacob Alricks was directed to purchase all the land between South River and the corner of North River. During the administration of Stuyvesant, in 1662, many Waldenses settled on Staten Island. Later, a number settled in what is now Pennsylvania.

Jean de Labadie, a Frenchman, was the founder of the sect to which has been given his name. He was born in 1610, and was educated by the Jesuits at Bordéaux. He left the Jesuits in 1639. Later, he became a Calvinist, but in the end, finding no sect quite to his mind, he founded one. Labadie's doctrines were a combination of mysticism and Calvinism. He held that illumination by the Holy Ghost was the means of salvation, even superseding the Bible. He rejected infant baptism and the observance of the Sabbath, and taught communism in property. On account of their peculiar doctrines, the Labadists were expelled from Holland and ultimately settled at Wiewerd in Friesland.

In 1679 they sent two of their members, Peter Sluyter and Jasper Dankers, to America "to look for a suitable spot to plant a colony." They landed in New York and there made a disciple of Ephraim Herman, eldest son of Augustine Herman, who owned a vast tract of land in what is now Cecil County, Maryland. In company with Ephraim Herman, they visited the elder Herman at his large estate at the head of Chesapeake Bay, which he called, in honor of his fatherland, Bohemia Manor. There they were kindly received, and, though for a time they continued their journey down the peninsula, they soon returned to the manor and purchased of Augustine Herman three or four thousand acres of land. They then journeyed back to Wiewerd, but in

1683 returned again to the land they had purchased. They brought with them a colony of fellow believers and settled upon this land. Peter Sluyter set himself at the head of affairs and ruled in a rather arbitrary manner. In 1698 the colony was divided, and in 1722 Sluyter died.

George Calvert, the first Lord Baltimore, having embraced the Roman Catholic religion, determined to found a colony in America where all the persecuted of his faith in England could find a refuge and could enjoy the privilege of worshipping as they pleased. At that time the Catholics in England were fined £20 a month for not attending the services of the Established Church. This law was not always strictly enforced, but large sums were frequently extorted by the government from the Catholics by way of compromise.

George Calvert died before receiving the charter of the grant of land which he had received from the king. It was left to his son, Cecilius Calvert, to carry out the plan which his father had conceived. Again receiving a grant to the territory north of the Potomac, he called it Maryland in honor of Queen Henrietta Maria. In 1633, he sent his brother Leonard with a party of three hundred persons to colonize his new possessions. They landed at the mouth of the Potomac and founded the town of St. Mary's. Lord Baltimore wished to make Maryland an asylum for the oppressed not only of his own sect but of other sects besides. Consequently his charter granted religious freedom to all, and permitted the people from the first to take part in making their own laws.

In the other English colonies, the Catholics were usually deprived of many of the privileges granted to their fellow citizens. Even in Pennsylvania, where one would look for religious toleration, they were legislated against after Penn regained his province. In the third charter, issued in 1696, there appeared an oath of allegiance required of all persons about to become public officers. This oath imposed a rejection of the doctrines taught by the Roman Catholic Church.

# A LAW
## OF
# MARYLAND
### Concerning
# RELIGION.

Oraſmuch as in a well-governed and Chriſtian Commonwealth, Matters concerning Religion and the Honour of God ought to be in the firſt place to be taken into ſerious conſideration, and endeavoured to be ſettled. Be it therefore Ordained and Enacted by the Right Honourable *CÆCILIUS* Lord Baron of *Baltimore*, abſolute Lord and Proprietary of this Province, with the Advice and Conſent of the Upper and Lower Houſe of this General Aſſembly, That whatſoever perſon or perſons within this Province and the Iſlands thereunto belonging, ſhall from henceforth blaſpheme GOD, that is curſe him; or ſhall deny our Saviour JESUS CHRIST to be the Son of God; or ſhall deny the Holy Trinity, the Father, Son, & Holy Ghoſts; or the Godhead of any of the ſaid Three Perſons of the Trinity, or the Unity of the Godhead, or ſhall uſe or utter any reproachful ſpeeches, words, or language, concerning the Holy Trinity, or any of the ſaid three Perſons thereof, ſhall be puniſhed with death, and confiſcation or forfeiture of all his or her Lands and Goods to the Lord Proprietary and his Heirs.

And be it alſo enacted by the Authority, and with the advice and aſſent aforeſaid, That whatſoever perſon or perſons ſhall from henceforth uſe or utter any reproachful words or ſpeeches concerning the bleſſed Virgin *MARY*, the Mother of our Saviour, or the holy Apoſtles or Evangeliſts, or any of them, ſhall in ſuch caſe for the firſt Offence forfeit to the ſaid Lord Proprietary and his Heirs, Lords and Proprietaries of this Province, the ſum of Five pounds Sterling, or the value thereof to be levied on the goods and chattels of every ſuch perſon ſo offending; but in caſe ſuch offender or offenders ſhall not then have goods and chattels ſufficient for the ſatisfying of ſuch forfeiture, or that the ſame be not otherwiſe ſpeedily ſatisfied, that then ſuch offender or offenders ſhall be publickly whipt, and be impriſoned during the pleaſure of the Lord Proprietary, or the Lieutenant or Chief Governor of this Province for the time being: And that every ſuch offender and offenders for every ſecond offence ſhall forfeit Ten Pounds Sterling, or the value thereof to be levied as aforeſaid; or in caſe ſuch offender or offenders ſhall not then have goods and chattels within this Province ſufficient for that purpoſe, then to be publickly and ſeverely whipt and impriſoned as before is expreſſed: and that every perſon or perſons before mentioned, offending herein the third time, ſhall for ſuch third offence, forfeit all his or her lands and goods, and be for ever baniſht and expelled out of this Province.

And be it alſo further Enacted by the ſame Authority, advice, and aſſent, That whatſoever perſon or perſons ſhall from henceforth upon any occaſion of offence, or otherwiſe in a reproachful manner or way, declare, call, or denominate, any perſon or perſons whatſoever, inhabiting, reſiding, trafficking, trading, or commercing within this Province, or within any the Ports, Harbours, Creeks or Havens to the ſame belonging, an Hereticke, Schiſmatick, Idolater, Puritan, Presbyterian, Independant, Popiſh Prieſt, Jeſuit, Jeſuited Papiſt, Lutheran, Calviniſt, Anabaptiſt, Browniſt, Antinomian, Roundhead, Separatiſt, or other name or term in a reproachfull manner relating to matter of Religion, ſhall for every ſuch offence forfeit and loſe the ſum of Ten ſhillings Sterling, or the value thereof, to be levied of the goods and chattels of every ſuch offender and offenders, the one half thereof to be forfeited and paid unto the perſon & perſons of whom ſuch reproachful words are, or ſhall be ſpoken or uttered, and the other half thereof to the Lord Proprietary and his Heirs, Lords and Proprietaries of this Province: But if ſuch perſon or perſons who ſhall at any time utter or ſpeak any ſuch reproachful words or language, ſhall not have goods or chattels ſufficient and overt within this Province to be taken to ſatisfy the penalty aforeſaid, or that the ſame be not otherwiſe ſpeedily ſatisfied, that then the perſon and perſons ſo offending ſhall be publickly whipt, and ſhall ſuffer impriſonment without Bail or Mainpriſe untill he, ſhe, or they, reſpectively, ſhall ſatisfie the party offended or grieved by ſuch reproachful Language, by asking him or her reſpectively forgiveneſs publickly, for ſuch his offence, before the Magiſtrate or chief Officer or Officers of the Town or place where ſuch offence ſhall be given.

And be it further likewiſe enacted by the authority and conſent aforeſaid, that every perſon and perſons within this Province, that ſhall at any time hereafter prophane the Sabbath, or Lords day, called Sunday, by frequent ſwearing, drunkenneſs, or by any uncivil or diſorderly Recreation, or by working on that day when abſolute neceſſity doth not require, ſhall for every ſuch firſt offence forfeit two ſhillings ſix pence Sterling, or the value thereof; and for the ſecond offence five ſhillings Sterling, or the value thereof; and for the third offence, and for every time he ſhall offend in like manner afterwards, Ten ſhillings Sterling, or the value thereof; and in caſe ſuch offender or offenders ſhall not have ſufficient goods or chattels within this Province to ſatisfy any of the aforeſaid penalties reſpectively hereby impoſed for prophaning the Sabbath or Lords day called Sunday as aforeſaid, then in every ſuch caſe the party ſo offending ſhall for the firſt and ſecond offence in that kind be impriſoned till he or ſhe ſhall publickly in open Court before the chief Commander, Judge or Magiſtrate of that County, Town, or Precinct wherein ſuch offence ſhall be committed, acknowledge the ſcandal and offence he hath in that reſpect given, againſt God, and the good and civil Government of this Province : and for the third offence and for every time after ſhall alſo be publickly whipt.

And whereas the inforcing of the Conſcience in matter of Religion hath frequently fallen out to be of dangerous conſequence in thoſe Commonwealths where it hath been practiſed, and for the more quiet and peaceable Government of this Province, and the better to preſerve mutual love & unity amongſt the Inhabitants here, Be it therefore alſo by the Lord Proprietary with the advice and aſſent of this Aſſembly, ordained and enacted, except as in this preſent Act is before declared and ſet forth, that no perſon or perſons whatſoever within this Province, or the Iſlands, Ports, Harbors, Creeks, or Havens thereunto belonging, profeſſing to believe in Jeſus Chriſt, ſhall from henceforth be any ways troubled, moleſted, or diſcountenanced, for, or in reſpect of his or her Religion nor in the free exerciſe thereof within this Province or the Iſlands thereunto belonging, nor any way compell'd to the belief or exerciſe of any other Religion, againſt his or her conſent, ſo as they be not unfaithfull to the Lord Propretary, or moleſt or conſpire againſt the civil Government, eſtabliſhed or to be eſtabliſhed in this Province under him and his Heirs. And that all and every perſon and perſons that ſhall preſume contrary to this Act and the true intent & meaning thereof, directly or indirectly, either in perſon or eſtate, willfully to wrong, diſturb, or trouble, or moleſt any perſon or perſons whatſoever within this Province, profeſſing to believe in Jeſus Chriſt, for or in reſpect of his or her Religion, or the free exerciſe thereof within this Province, otherwiſe then is provided for in this Act, that ſuch perſon or perſons ſo offending ſhall be compell'd to pay treble damages to the party ſo wronged or moleſted, and for every ſuch offence ſhall alſo forfeit Twenty ſhillings Sterling in Money, or the value thereof, half thereof for the uſe of the Lord Proprietary and his Heirs, Lords and Proprietaries of this Province, and the other half thereof for the uſe of the Party ſo wronged or moleſted as aforeſaid; or if the party ſo offending as aforeſaid, ſhall refuſe or be unable to recompence the party ſo wronged, or to ſatisfy ſuch fine or forfeiture, then ſuch offender ſhall be ſeverely puniſhed by publick whipping and impriſonment during the pleaſure of the Lord Proprietary or his Lieutenant or chief Governor of this Province for the time being, without Bail or Mainpriſe.

And be it further alſo enacted by the authority and conſent aforeſaid, that the Sheriff or other Officer or Officers from time to time to be appointed and authorized for that purpoſe of the County, Town, or Precinct where every particular offence in this preſent Act contained, ſhall happen at any time to be committed, and whereupon there is hereby a forfeiture, fine, or penalty impoſed, ſha l from time to time diſtrain, and ſeize the goods and eſtate of every ſuch perſon ſo offending as aforeſaid againſt this preſent Act or any part thereof, and ſell the ſame or any part thereof for the full ſatisfaction of ſuch forfeiture, fine, or penalty as aforeſaid, reſtoring to the party ſo offending, the remainder or over plus of the ſaid goods or eſtate, after ſuch ſatisfaction ſo made as aforeſaid.

Broadside : a law of Maryland concerning religion (the Maryland Toleration Act). *From the original in the New York Public Library, Lenox Branch.*

This, of course, was equivalent to exclusion from office of all Catholics. However, there were but few of that faith in Pennsylvania at that time.

Leisler, who had usurped power in New York after the overthrow of Andros, made the anti-Catholic feeling in the colony an excuse for many of his high-handed acts. The reign of James II. had filled the hearts of the colonists with a dread of Roman Catholic supremacy. Dongan had been a Catholic and had placed men of that faith in office. Nevertheless, he was a broad-minded man, and it is probable the Catholics had no more than their share of preferment. At any rate, there were not enough Catholics in New York to warrant a charge of conspiracy being brought against them, nor the annoyances to which they were subjected during Leisler's usurpation. When Sloughter became Governor of New York, the charter, annulled during the reign of James II., was reënacted with the exception "of the right to worship according to the Romish Religion."

In Maryland, Jesuit priests, who had gone out to work among the Indians, received as gifts from them large tracts of land which, of course, became the property of the Jesuit order. The priests, moreover, dwelling in the wilderness, were freed from the statute law. They even claimed not to be amenable to the common law and held themselves answerable only to the canon law and to ecclesiastical tribunals. This view did not fit in with Lord Baltimore's idea that all colonists were subject to the same laws. He foresaw that the enforcement of this principle was likely to bring him into conflict with the Jesuit order. Nevertheless, he took a prompt and a decisive step. He petitioned Rome to remove the Jesuits from the missions and put in their places prefect and secular priests. This request was granted, and an order removing the Jesuit priests was issued by the Propaganda. Then again, in the new "Conditions of Plantation," which he issued in 1641, two of the sections provided that "no lands should be granted to, or held by, any corporation or society, ecclesiastical or temporal, without special license from the Proprietary."

To bring about a final settlement of the affair, the Jesuits, the governor, and Secretary Lewger met in conference. As a result, the whole question of the attitude of the Roman Catholic Church in Maryland toward the proprietary government was submitted to the Provincial of England. A memorial was sent at the same time to the Propaganda, protesting against the hardship of removing those who had " borne all the burden and heat of the day, just as they were beginning to reap some fruit of their labors." Shortly after, Father Moore, the Provincial, decided the dispute in favor of Lord Baltimore and executed a release of all the lands acquired by the society from the Indians. Lord Baltimore, having carried his point, the order for the removal of the Jesuit priests was thereupon rescinded (Browne).

Many of the Puritans, driven from other colonies, found a refuge in Maryland, where they repaid the proprietary's kindness by hatching numerous plots against his authority. After Cromwell dissolved Parliament and proclaimed himself Protector, although the oath of allegiance to the proprietary remained the same, the Puritans refused to take it by reason of Baltimore's being a Catholic. We have already referred to the fact that Bennett and Claiborne, glad of an excuse to injure the proprietor, gathered a force from Virginia and Maryland and took possession of the government at St. Mary's. A General Assembly was called, but no Catholic was allowed to cast a vote, or be elected a member. The statute of 1649 was repealed, which granted religious freedom to all Christians, and instead a law was passed which denied permission to Catholics to worship in Maryland. The Assembly went even further and declared that Lord Baltimore no longer had any rights whatever in the colony he himself had founded. The rank injustice of this act can be realized when we recall the fact that the proprietor had invited to his province many of the people who now turned against him. Protestant Dissenters and

Quakers were exempted from all penalties and disabilities, and were given the privilege of having separate meeting houses, provided they paid a poll tax of £40 to support the Establishment,—the Protestant Episcopal Church. As for the Catholics, it is perhaps needless to add that they were not included in this amnesty.

Let us now turn our attention to the persecuted of another European nationality, who, as a result of the devastation of their country by Louis XIV., poured into America in a steady stream, beginning with the year 1708. They were the Palatines of the Rhenish Palatinate.

There were two Palatinates, the Upper, or Bavarian, and the Lower, or Palatinate of the Rhine. Only the latter need concern us. This Palatinate became Protestant in the year 1559, when Frederick III. marked his accession to the electoral dignity by definitely associating himself and his house with the Reformed or Calvinistic Church. By reason of its location it was early brought in contact with the Lutheran and Calvinistic doctrines.

The personal religion of the Elector of the Palatinate was indeed a matter of importance, for the attempt was sometimes made by the ruler to force his religion upon the country. Consequently, when John William, of the House of Neuburg, became Elector in 1690, he tried to bring the Palatinate and its people under allegiance to the Roman See. The bigotry of John William and his persecutions were among the causes of the exodus of the Palatines from their homes. Of greater importance, however, than this were the devastations of the Palatinate in 1674 and 1688 and the War of the Grand Alliance and the War of the Spanish Succession that swept over that unhappy country from 1689 to 1713.

The Revocation of the Edict of Nantes by Louis XIV., October 22, 1685, drove many Huguenots to the Palatinate. This brought the wrath of that king down upon the little electorate. He ordered his generals to make the Palatinate a desert. Three days were given for the inhabitants to leave

the country. Thousands fled to other parts of Europe. The
Palatinate was laid waste. During the War of the Spanish
Succession the Palatinate again suffered desolation. In fact,
the depredations of Marshal Villars, in 1707, were so widespread that the inhabitants could no longer exist upon the
land. It was then that the great exodus began that brought
so many Palatines to America.

The exodus was conducted as secretly as possible, for the
elector opposed the movement. As a result, we have no
trustworthy account of the first emigrations, but it is quite
probable the fugitives went to New Jersey. Among the
first pioneers, however, was a noteworthy company of forty-
one members. They went first to England, in 1708, and
thence to America. They were under the leadership of the
clergyman Kockerthal, and came over to New York with
Lord Lovelace. The greater part of this company were
farmers. All were Lutherans. At a later date, Kockerthal made a trip to the Palatinate and brought back others
of his countrymen. The severe winter of 1708–1709 in
the Palatinate drove others from their homes, and of these
some came to America.

When the Palatinate exodus really began in earnest, thousands suddenly swept down upon England and Holland.
One of the emigrants says of it: "A migrating epidemic
seized on the stricken people and, as a wave, thirty thousand
Germans washed along the shores of England. Israel was
not more astounded at the armored carcasses of the Egyptians lying on the banks of the Red Sea, than were the people
of England at this immense slide of humanity." The government of England was forced to care for this impoverished
army of refugees. They began to arrive in London in May,
1709, and before the end of October thirteen thousand had
arrived. London was unable to provide for their wants.
The question then arose of what should be done with
them. The Parish Laws of England would not permit their
being absorbed in the counties of England. Finally, the
question was settled by sending them to America, provision

being made by the English government for their transportation and for subsistence upon their arrival.

At this time there was a vacancy in the governorship of New York. Robert Hunter was appointed to fill it. He proposed to the Lords of Trade in November, 1709, to take over with him to New York three thousand of the Palatines, to be employed in the production of naval stores. It was thought, furthermore, that the pines in the Hudson and Mohawk valleys could furnish England forever with tar and turpentine. Hunter thought the Palatines would add greatly to the defence of New York against the French and Indians. The government granted Hunter £10,000 for the project.

In January, 1710, Hunter set out for New York with these Palatines in ten ships. It is estimated that there were at least three thousand of them. So crowded were the ships that at least five hundred died on the way. Delayed by storms and contrary winds, they did not arrive at New York until June. One of the ships, the *Herbert*, was cast away on the east end of Long Island, but only a loss of goods was suffered. The wreck of this ship gave rise to the well-known legend of the " Palatine Ship and Light." Tradition avers that the vessel was decoyed ashore with false beacons by the islanders, who rifled and burned it. As this legend runs, "a light is at times seen from the Island upon the surface of the ocean, which in its form has suggested to the imagination a resemblance to a burning ship under full sail; and it is called the Palatine Light and Palatine Ship." —(Cobb, *Story of the Palatines.*)

When Hunter arrived off New York, the authorities, thinking there might be contagious diseases aboard, decided to build huts for them on Nutten Island, now Governor's Island. They remained here for five months. The authorities put the Palatine boys out as apprentices. Many of them were orphans, and among them was John Peter Zenger, of whom we shall later hear much. The children were scattered over New York, Robert Livingston taking seven for himself. This action on the part of the authorities caused considerable discontent among the Palatines. Hunter sent surveyors along Mohawk and Schoharie Rivers to lay out settlements. They soon reported that the lands along the Schoharie were good, but that there were no pines.

Consequently, in October, 1710, Hunter, for £266, purchased six thousand acres of land along Hudson River from Robert Livingston. This area not being sufficient, an additional tract of land, belonging to the crown, of eight hundred acres on the west side of the river was purchased. Most of the Palatines were settled in five villages on these tracts of land. Later, this number was increased to seven. About four hundred of the emigrants, mostly widows, single women, and children, remained in New York. These villages were familiarly known to the Palatines as East Camp and West Camp, names which still exist. The east side tract stretched sixteen miles along the Hudson and twenty-four miles to the eastward to the Massachusetts line. Its population was one thousand two hundred, but the number of the able-bodied men capable of working was not large. Winter came on without their being prepared, and there was much suffering from want of proper and sufficient food.

The Palatines soon looked upon their lot as but very little short of slavery. They were ill treated by the agents of the governor. They became disgusted with the manufacture of tar. They complained that the land allotted to them was insufficient to permit provision for their children who might survive them. The people in the immediate neighborhood aroused their discontent by glowing descriptions of the fine lands along the Schoharie. Very soon the Palatines became mutinous, and Governor Hunter was called upon the scene. The malcontents plainly told him the land was unfit for them and that they wished to remove to the Schoharie. They claimed that they had been cheated by the agents; that many of England's promises to them had not been kept; that they were willing to fulfil their contract, but positively refused to remain where they were any longer. The governor set forth the difficulty of settling on the Schoharie by reason of the danger from the Indians.

Seemingly, peace was established, but as soon as the governor departed conditions grew worse than they had been before. Hunter's patience being quite exhausted, he sent some soldiers under Colonel Nicholson to coerce them into submission. Some of the settlers having armed themselves, they were forthwith arrested and disarmed by the soldiers. The mutinous Palatines then betook themselves quietly to the villages. For the time being the insurrection was at an end. They worked all through the following summer, and only occasional murmurs arose.

In the fall, Hunter established a court over them and stationed troops in the immediate vicinity. But in 1712 his funds ran out and he was compelled to suspend all work. The Palatines were given permission to scatter wherever they wished, on condition that they did not go outside of New York and New Jersey. They immediately took advantage of this concession. There was no general plan of action. Perhaps a third remained where they were, but the majority of them betook themselves toward "the promised land of Schoharie." They had already sent out a party of seven men under Weisler to the Schoharie, to spy out the land and to deal with the Indians. They reported on the condition of the country, and within two weeks preparations were made for a general exodus.

In due time, they arrived on the Schoharie and settled in seven villages named in honor of their seven leaders. They soon experienced troubles with Colonel Nicholas Bayard and other claimants with respect to their titles to the land. It was not, in fact, until 1725, five years after Hunter's departure for England, that their titles to the land were confirmed. Prior to this settlement, however, there were numberless disputes between the Palatines and other claimants to the soil. When Sheriff Adams attempted to make arrests he found himself confronted with a mob of women, led by Magdalena Zeh. The sheriff was knocked down, beaten, and dragged through the vilest puddles of their barnyards. He was then put on a rail and ridden "Skimmington" through the settlements, a distance of seven miles or more. Finally, he was left on a bridge, well out on the road to Albany.

When Burnet became governor, he was directed to look after the Palatines and to settle them upon lands of which a disposition had not as yet been made. The governor considered the advisability of settling them in the Mohawk valley, where they would prove a barrier against the French. This plan was not at all displeasing to at least some of the Palatines. There were three divisions among them: one division wished to stay where they were; another wished to emigrate to Pennsylvania; and a third wished to go to the Mohawk. The Palatines along the banks of the Mohawk were joined in 1722 by the major part of a shipload of their fellow countrymen newly arrived in New York. This increased the number in the Mohawk valley to over three hundred persons. A patent of one hundred acres was granted to these Palatines in 1725. It was a free grant, subject only to the usual quitrents. For thirty years, under this patent, they lived unmolested and prospered greatly in this fertile valley of the Mohawk. Settlements grew up and forts and trading posts were established. Among these settlements were the two towns of Palatine and Palatine Bridge. Many of those who came over in 1722 settled in the neighborhood of the latter town. The level meadows along the south side of Mohawk River came to be called the "German Flats." They were unsurpassed in fertility. Just opposite, on the north side of the river, was the settlement of Herkimer, named after the most celebrated general of the Palatines. On all sides of the German Flats, Palatine settlements sprang up.

The signal failure of Hunter's philanthropic scheme cannot be blamed upon the Palatines. Hunter miscalculated the tar and turpentine producing capacity of the pines along the Hudson. Even if the English treasury had continued

Annapolis. January 13. 1755

Sir

I could not help embracing the Opportunity by Captain Rutherford of acknowledging the Receipt of Your favour of the 7th Inst. I need not express to You how much I am concerned at the Account You sent me of Your Assembly's Obstinacy; I cannot but approve of Your sending a Belt to the Six Nations in behalf of this Province tho' for want of being before acquainted therewith I have writ with Governor Dinwiddie to Mr Delancey desiring him to have a Belt delivered as from us in case He should think proper to send any Message to the Six Nations; You will be kind enough to acquaint me at Scarroyady's Return with the Event of his Journey, & You will I hope excuse the Brevity of this & attribute it to my being just about to depart for the Camp where I propose to tarry about a Month if nothing extraordinary & unexpected requires my Return to Annapolis.

I am with the greatest Regard
Sir Your most humb. obedt Servt
Horo Sharpe

P.S. I should be glad to learn how Matters are at Venango.

Autograph letter, dated January 13, 1755, from Horatio Sharpe, Governor of Maryland, to Robert Hunter Morris, Governor of Pennsylvania. From the original in the Emmet Collection.

to support Hunter and if the settlers had remained docile, the scheme could not have succeeded. The pines along the Hudson were not tar-bearing trees. Then, again, the English government shamefully abandoned the governor and his wards. The £10,000 granted him was exhausted even before the Palatines reached the Hudson. After that, he had to support the colonists out of his own pocket. He paid Livingston for the land with his own money. In all, he lost £20,000 in the scheme. Later, he went to England to make a personal appeal to the government for reimbursement, but we have no record that justice was ever done him.

Palatines settled in Maryland, in what is now Frederick County, as early as 1710. To encourage their immigration the Assembly exempted them from paying public levies. They did not come in large numbers, however, until 1729 or 1730. Charles Calvert offered many advantages to persuade them to settle in Maryland. In 1735, Daniel Dulaney offered inducements to them if a hundred families would settle on some of his land. In 1749, provision was made for a much larger number of them. The immigration increased so rapidly that in 1774 Frederick County had a population of nearly fifty thousand. This was about one-seventh of the population of the whole province.

The Palatines on the Schoharie having heard flattering reports of the fertile lands on the Tulpehocken and the Swatara, about one-third of them emigrated to Pennsylvania. Governor Keith did what he could to encourage them to take up lands in those parts. At least sixty families emigrated in the spring of 1723, and still other families left in 1728. To the first settlement they gave the name Heidelberg. All were treated with the kindest consideration by the Pennsylvania authorities. This treatment led many others to settle along the Susquehanna and its tributaries. For twenty years beginning with 1717 there was a steady stream of Palatines coming into Pennsylvania. Many of them came directly from the Palatinate. By 1740, their number must have been at least fifty thousand. Coming over without any means whatever, they were often sold in Philadelphia at auction to serve for a term of years. They thus received the name "Redemptioners." They usually gave three or five years of service, which brought about £10 at auction. Many afterward became wealthy. In 1755, the Pennsylvania Assembly passed a bill limiting the emigration of Palatines, but it was vetoed by the governor on the ground of its being inhuman.

This mass of German settlers in Pennsylvania, being thrown so close together, naturally retained their customs. Being so far from the place of their birth, their language soon degenerated into a patois—a mixture of South German with English. This dialect or patois is commonly called "Pennsylvania Dutch." It is still spoken by some of the inhabitants of central Pennsylvania. It flourishes around the cities of Lancaster, York, Reading, Allentown, Easton, Lebanon, and Harrisburg.

Jonathan Dickson, in writing about the Palatines, says: "We had a parcel,"—meaning the Palatines,—"who came out about five years ago and proved quiet and industrious." The Palatines, and likewise the other German settlers, were industrious, economical, patriotic, and religious. Their eagerness to work overcame all opposition to their migration into a country. They possessed moral earnestness, soberness of mind, persistency, and staying qualities. They were determined to improve themselves and their fortune, and to enjoy freedom of worship. Benjamin Franklin, in 1766, said the Germans made up one-third of the one hundred and sixty thousand whites in Pennsylvania. Furthermore, that they were "a people who brought with them the greatest of all wealth—industry and integrity and characters that had been supervised and developed by years of suffering and persecution."

Governor Thomas, in his address to the Council, said: "This province has been for some years the asylum of the distressed Protestants of the Palatinate and other parts of Germany, and I believe it may with truth be said that the present flourishing condition of it is in a great measure owing to the industry of those people; and should any discouragement divert them from coming hither, it may well be apprehended that the value of your lands will fall and your advance to wealth be much slower." Among these German settlers and their descendants were men prominent in the French and Indian War, and in the Revolutionary War. They sent whole companies to the front. Their frontier settlements were bravely defended against the enemy. They saved many an interior town from the ravagings and burnings of the enemy. They delved into the soil and opened up iron mines, and established forges and furnaces. Forests were cut down, and in their places settlements and farm lands sprang up. They supplied the needs of the ever increasing new arrivals and paved the way for other settlements to the west of them.

The Treaty of Utrecht, 1713, gave the province of Acadia to England. But the people were mostly French, and the English government was really only a military occupation of the peninsula. At the time of the French and Indian War there were more than sixteen thousand inhabitants in the province. The governor, Lawrence, pretending to fear an insurrection, urged Braddock and the colonial governors to strengthen the English rule over the French inhabitants. Accordingly, an expedition was fitted out with Lawrence at the head. In less than a month the English were complete masters of the province.

The French inhabitants, however, outnumbered the English, and, in order to balance the unequal population, Lawrence and some others in authority concocted the scheme of driving the French from their homes. Their estates were confiscated, their towns were burned, and they themselves were driven into exile and scattered throughout the English colonies. The history of civilized nations hardly furnishes a parallel to this wanton and wicked destruction of an inoffensive colony. In 1755, many of them were sent to Annapolis, Maryland, and from there to the different counties of the province. Their lot was a hard one. They were treated as prisoners of war, and yet were deprived of the hope of exchange or release. People could not be induced to employ them, and yet were "irritated at their wretchedness and destitution." Their only friend in the province seems to have been a merchant of Oxford, Talbot County, Maryland, Henry Callister, who assisted them in many ways.

In 1734, on account of the persecutions to which they were subjected at home, some Moravians came to America, and settled in Georgia. There they remained until 1740, when the Spanish war broke out; and as their religion would not permit them to bear arms, they went to Pennsylvania, where they founded Bethlehem and, later on, Nazareth.

The Tunkers are a sect of German-American Baptists—called by themselves "Brethren." Their name is sometimes erroneously spelled "Dunkers" and "Dunkards," but it comes from the German *tunken*, "to dip." The sect is said to have been founded by Alexander Mack, at Schwarzenau in Westphalia, in 1708. They came to America because of persecutions in Germany and settled in Germantown, and chose Joseph Becker, a weaver, to be their minister. The "Sieben Taeger," or German Seventh Day Baptists, are an offshoot of the Tunkers. They settled in 1732 at Ephrata, Lancaster County, Pennsylvania, under Conrad Beissel. They dressed like monks and nuns, and used a vegetable diet. They might marry, but if they did so they were obliged to leave the settlement at Ephrata. Some of them afterward moved to Ohio, Indiana, Maryland, Virginia, and several other States. The denomination is now well-nigh extinct. The Tunkers have increased in numbers. This denomination should not be confused with the Mennonite, the Amish, the Schwenkfelder, and other peace sects, though these sects have one common quality: the quiet and peaceable lives led by their members. Because of this they have sometimes been called "the Harmless People."

We have thus shown to what a great extent the Middle colonies furnished the oppressed of many lands and many creeds a safe retreat from the persecutions to which they had been subjected in their native countries. In no other part of North America was liberty of conscience granted to the same degree during the colonial period. The victims of a relentless persecution for the sake of their religious beliefs, the Dutch had adopted a policy of broad toleration for all sects. They made it the policy of the government of New Netherland, and the English followed their good example after the conquest of that province. In consequence, New York harbored a mixed population of many creeds,—Walloons, Puritans, Huguenots, Quakers, Lutherans, Jews, Waldenses, Roman Catholics, and Palatines. Lord Baltimore's experiment was in behalf of the persecuted Roman Catholics; but other colonists were welcomed, and we find settled within the borders of Maryland, Labadists, Puritans, and Palatines. William Penn's "Holy Experiment" was primarily in behalf of the oppressed Friends; but the persecuted of all creeds were invited to Pennsylvania upon an equality with the followers of George Fox. Accordingly, Mennonites, Lutherans, Waldenses, Palatines, Moravians, and Tunkers came in great numbers. Likewise, New Jersey was settled largely by the Friends, but the oppressed of other colonies were welcomed within its borders. Undoubtedly there were some persecutions, as we have shown in the case of Stuyvesant against the Quakers, the Lutherans, and the Jews, and the Puritans against the Roman Catholics in Maryland. For the most part, however, such oppression was decidedly the exception to the rule and attracts our attention because of that fact. Nothing, therefore, we may say, is more characteristic of the Middle colonies during the period under consideration than the uniform toleration of the religious beliefs of all classes of the population. The Middle colonies in this respect present a pleasing contrast to the other sections of the country during this period.

## CHAPTER IX

### LORD BALTIMORE'S EXPERIMENT, 1632-1685

CHESAPEAKE BAY, which divides Maryland into the Eastern and Western Shore, is the largest bay or inlet in the territory of the United States. It extends two hundred miles north and south and varies in width from ten to twenty miles. The land gradually rises toward the west. The central portions of the State and the mountainous valleys beyond are very fertile. The greatest elevation is in the mountains of the Blue and Alleghany Ridges, which traverse the extreme western portions of the State from northeast to southwest.

It is a peculiarity of the present State of Maryland that, though small and narrow, it unites a great variety of soil, climate, geological structure, flora, and fauna. Chesapeake Bay itself "draws tribute from an extraordinary range of country and climate. While one of its arms touches the foot of the Catskill, and almost reaches to the Adirondacks, another pierces to the heart of the Alleghanies due westward, and a third flows with a turbulent stream through the Blue Ridge hard by the Peak of Otter." It is difficult to overestimate the importance of Chesapeake Bay in the development of Maryland. It was the greatest source of wealth to the colonists. One could travel by means of it from place to place with ease. This was a most important condition when we come to consider the fact that the roads of the country were undeveloped and, in most cases, even unbuilt. Out of the waters of the bay they brought fish, oysters, and crabs; on its banks they found all kinds of fowl. It was, indeed, the first settlers' most valuable possession. No one took up lands that did not border on its waters. In a word, we may say that the numerous tributaries of the Chesapeake, navigable in many instances to their very sources; the unsurpassed fertility of the soil drained by its waters; the unexcelled means of sustaining life offered by the bay itself—all combined to make this part of the eastern seaboard no less well adapted for colonization purposes than the valleys of the Hudson and the Delaware.

Roman Catholics, persecuted in England, looked for a home in a remote possession of Great Britain where they might worship free from persecution. George Calvert, the first Baron of Baltimore, projected the plan of opening an "asylum for conscience." He was prevented by death from the execution of his plan, but his son, Cecilius Calvert, carried it on. The elder Calvert seems to have taken a profound interest in the plans for American colonization at quite an early date. He was one of the councillors of the New England Company and, in 1609, was a member of the Virginia Company. Afterward, at the revocation of the charter of the latter, he was appointed one of the Provisional Council for the government of the province. In 1620 he purchased from Sir William Vaughan a patent covering the southeastern peninsula of Newfoundland. This was the charter of Avalon, and, differing but slightly from that of Maryland, evidently served as a model for it. In 1627, Baltimore visited his colony, and the following year brought over a part of his family and some colonists, making in all about a hundred souls. The hostility of the French from without and the Puritans from within to no little extent caused the failure of this colonizing attempt. Calvert's fortune was seriously impaired and his health fatally undermined as a result of the experiment.

In the meantime, however, Calvert, now Lord Baltimore, had received information of the flourishing condition of the

Charles Calvert, third Lord Baltimore. *From the painting by Thomas Sully after an original attributed to Van Dyke but probably by Kneller, now in the Philadelphia Academy of the Fine Arts. The Sully is now in possession of the Maryland Historical Society.*

Virginia colony. On October 1, 1629, he arrived at Jamestown with his wife and several children and some forty colonists, in search of a desirable situation to make a settlement. The colonists there gave him by no means a cordial reception, having, no doubt, received some intimation of his colonial designs. He was tendered the oaths of supremacy and allegiance, but being a Catholic he refused to take them. He recognized only the Pope as spiritual head. Nevertheless, to avoid provoking bad feeling, he offered to take a modified form of the oath. They were unwilling to accept this offer. The Virginia Council could not admit one to their settlement who would not acknowledge all the prerogatives of his majesty, and so requested him to depart in the next ship. He was offered insults and some of the rabble even attempted to do him personal violence.

Disappointed in finding a residence in Virginia, Lord Baltimore now turned his attention to the neighboring territory. His eyes fell upon the region along Chesapeake Bay, as yet unsettled. Its situation and fertility led him to a closer inspection. Here he decided to try to obtain a home for religious freedom. He left for England, leaving his wife and children behind. Upon his arrival, he found a letter from the king advising him to "desist from further prosecuting his designs and to return to his native country." The king would not permit him to return to America, but granted him permission to send for his wife and children. The vessel on which they sailed was cast away and they were lost.

On his return to England, Lord Baltimore had made an application for a grant of territory lying to the southward of James River, in Virginia, between that river and the bounds of Carolina. Charles granted his request, on account of his past services, his unimpeachable reputation, and the favor with which he was held by himself and his father, James I., before him.

The charter was prepared and signed in February, 1631. The territory comprised the northern part of North Carolina

and the southern part of Virginia as far north as James
River. Francis West, once governor, William Claiborne,
secretary, and William Tucker, one of the Council of
Virginia, objected to the planting of the colony within the
limits of Virginia. To avoid any difficulty, Lord Baltimore requested his majesty to grant him in lieu thereof
some part of the continent to the northward. The request
was granted. Lord Baltimore drew up a charter, modelled
on that of Avalon, with his own hand, leaving a blank for
the name. It is said he intended the name should be
"Crescentia," or the land of Crescence, most probably as a
name of "good omen for its growth and prosperity." Again,
others hold that it may have been in honor of Crescentius, a
consul, who in the tenth century attempted to throw off the
German yoke and to restore the ancient republic. Charles
asked his lordship what he should call the colony. Lord
Baltimore replied that he should like to name it in honor
of the king, but was deprived of that privilege inasmuch as
his name had already been given to Carolina. Charles suggested "Mariana," but Lord Baltimore objected, saying it
was the name of a Jesuit priest who had written condemning
monarchy. Charles then proposed " Terra Mariæ," in honor
of Queen Henrietta Maria. This name was consequently
inserted in the charter. Before the patent had received the
impression of the Great Seal, Lord Baltimore died, April
15, 1632. His health seems to have been broken by the
rigors of the inhospitable climate of Newfoundland. His
eldest son, Cecilius Calvert, succeeded him. To him
the Maryland charter was issued, and it bears the date
of June 20, 1632.

This charter was of the most liberal character. By its
provisions, Baltimore and his heirs were made the proprietaries of the territory, which, like the See of Durham in
England, was to be a palatinate. This made it equivalent
to a principality, and the prerogatives of its proprietor were
well-nigh regal, the crown reserving to itself merely a
feudal supremacy. The proprietor was only required to

pay to the king a yearly rent of two Indian arrows, in acknowledgment of his feudal subordination. In addition to this, he bound himself to pay a fifth portion of whatever gold or silver might be discovered in the province. He owned the soil and was, in fact, absolute lord of the land and water within the boundaries of his province. He could erect towns, cities, and ports, and could levy taxes and collect tolls and duties. He could exercise both the civil and military powers of a sovereign. For example, he could confer titles and dignities under a system of subinfeudation; he could make war or peace; call out the whole fighting population and declare martial law. He could constitute courts, from which there was to be no appeal, and could appoint judges, magistrates, and other civil officers. He could even make the laws with the assent of the majority of the freemen, or of their representatives. In cases of emergency, he could enact laws himself, provided they did not impair life, limb, or property. Furthermore, he could execute the laws and pardon offenders. His subjects were exempted from regal taxation. When doubtful points were at issue, it was provided that in their interpretation they should be construed in the sense most favorable to the proprietary.

Certain rights were guaranteed to the colonists. They and their descendants were to remain English subjects, and their right to go and come from England was not to be abridged in any way. They could acquire, hold, and alienate all kinds of property in England, and they were given the privilege of trading freely with English or foreign ports. They were given the privilege of accepting or rejecting laws proposed by the proprietary.

The boundaries of the province were, in turn, precisely defined. Its northern limit was the fortieth parallel; its western and southwestern limit was a line running south from this parallel to the furthest source of the Potomac and thence by the western bank of that river to Chesapeake Bay; its southern boundary was a line crossing the bay and peninsula to the ocean; its eastern boundary was the ocean, and

Delaware Bay and River. This included, of course, the present State of Delaware, a part of Pennsylvania, and probably a part of West Virginia.

The Virginia colonists opposed the Maryland charter most bitterly. Some of the members of the old Virginia Company protested against it as an invasion of their own charter rights; others were not at all pleased at having Maryland as a neighbor. The protests, nevertheless, were unavailing. The Privy Council, after a formal hearing, decided in favor of Baltimore. Those who continued to think they had grievances could have them righted by the ordinary processes of the law.

Cecilius Calvert now fitted out two vessels, the *Ark* and the *Dove*, to transport the colonists to their new home. The *Ark* was of three hundred and fifty tons burden and had been used to carry the first Lord Baltimore, his family, and his colonists to Avalon. The *Dove* was a small vessel of but fifty tons burden. Upon these two vessels were loaded the supplies and implements for the new colony. There were about twenty gentlemen and over two hundred laboring men and handicraftsmen in the expedition. Probably most of the "gentlemen" were Roman Catholics and most of the laborers and servants were Protestants. Baltimore remained behind, to defend his charter against open and covert attacks. He placed the expedition under the command of his brother, Leonard Calvert. His younger brother, George, was likewise one of the company. The *Ark* left Gravesend on the 18th of October, 1633, stopped at the Isle of Wight to take on board two Jesuit fathers, Andrew White and John Althain, and other colonists, and finally sailed for America on the 22d of November. They touched at Barbadoes, and on the 24th of February arrived at Point Comfort, Virginia. Stopping here for over a week, they sailed northwest and shortly reached the Potomac. Near the mouth of this river, on an island to which they gave the name St. Clement's, the colonists planted a cross and celebrated their first Mass. It was on the day of the

Feast of the Annunciation, March 25, 1634, but New Year's Day according to the calendar of that day.

From here the colonists sailed up the Potomac until they reached a small tributary having a good harbor. This they fixed upon as the site of their settlement. Henry Fleete, a Virginian, who was familiar with the country, acted as guide to the expedition. From Father White's letter to Mutius Vetellesetis, dated April, 1634, we have a most interesting account of the determination of the site of St. Mary's by a member of the expedition. "The first island we came to we called St. Clement's Island. . . . Going about nine leagues (that is, about twenty-seven miles) from St. Clement's, we sailed into the mouth of a river on the north side of the Potomac, which we named St. George's. This river (or rather, arm of the sea), like the Thames, runs from south to north about twenty miles before you come to fresh water. At its mouth are two harbors capable of containing three hundred ships of the largest size. We consecrated one of these to St. George; the other, which is more inland, to the blessed Virgin Mary." At the latter point they landed and found an Indian town called Yoacomaco. They made a peaceful arrangement with the Indians to live in one part of the town and the Indians in the other, and that at the end of the harvest time they—the Indians—should leave, which they did. This the Indians very readily agreed to, inasmuch as they had already determined to abandon their lands and seek safer homes elsewhere, having been harried to desperation by the hostile Susquehannas to the north of them. Thus upon the 27th of March, 1634, they took possession and called the town "Saint Maries."

The little colony was soon to experience trouble from a quarter where it should have least expected it. Virginia thought its rights had been invaded by the charter which the king had granted Lord Baltimore. In consequence, as St. Mary's grew and gave promise of prosperity, the enmity of some Virginians increased almost in direct proportion.

Then, again, they objected to the proximity of what they termed "Popish" settlements, and were likewise jealous of the privileges of the free trade with foreign ports which had been granted to the new colony but had been denied them.

Virginia's jealousy and animosity for twenty years centred around the claim of one man—William Claiborne's claim to Kent Island. It has been said by many historians that Virginia had established settlements under the authority of Claiborne before the charter was granted to Baltimore. That consequently, as the country granted to Baltimore was previously settled by Claiborne, the former's grant was void. "But it seems," says Bozman (*History of Maryland*, i, 263), "to be extraordinary, that although history recognizes this objection as being frequently made, yet it furnishes no authentic proof of the fact on which it is founded."

Claiborne had first gone out to Virginia as a surveyor to the Virginia colony in 1621, "to survey the planters' land and make a map of the country." He acquired much real property, and after the revocation of the Virginia charter became a member of the Council. He was likewise appointed secretary of state for Virginia by the commission which appointed Sir John Harvey governor whenever the place should be made vacant. While secretary, Claiborne had a fine opportunity for accomplishing his designs. He had, in the meantime, embarked on several commercial enterprises. He had been in the habit of carrying on a trade with the Indians along the shores of the Chesapeake, and Virginia gave him authority later to explore and make discoveries along that bay. It was in connection with this traffic that he acted as agent for a firm of London merchants, Cloberry and Company. This authority thus conferred upon him by Virginia gave him even better opportunities for enriching himself. It appears that he established trading posts along the northern part of the bay. The first was probably on the Isle of Kent.

When, in 1629, Lord Baltimore visited Virginia, he, it may be presumed, mentioned his intention of obtaining a grant along the Chesapeake. Claiborne was probably alarmed at this project, for his trading posts were in this territory and any settlements he had made he considered to be under Virginia authority. Claiborne, therefore, obtained from King Charles, May 16, 1631, a license "to trade in all seas, etc., in or near about those parts of America." For the more effectual execution of this license, command was also given to the governor to permit Claiborne and his company "freely to repair and trade to and trade in all the aforesaid parts, as they should think fit and their occasion should require." Claiborne secured this license by representing to Sir William Alexander, the king's secretary of state for Scotland, that he wished to promote a trade between New England, Nova Scotia, and Virginia. About ten months afterward, Claiborne applied for a commission from Harvey, Governor of Virginia, "to sail and traffic unto the adjoining plantations of the Dutch seated upon this territory of America." A commission was granted him on March 8, 1632. By it he was authorized to trade with the Dutch and English plantations, and, in fact, wheresover he desired. By the same commission, all representatives of the English government were ordered to render him any assistance within their power.

It is quite obvious, from these two commissions, that neither mentions specifically or even refers in definite terms to any plantations or settlements, or to any traffic in the Chesapeake. It would seem, then, that if Claiborne had formed any settlements on the Isle of Kent or at the mouth of the Susquehanna, they were unauthorized settlements made under his license to trade and make discoveries in the Chesapeake. When Lord Baltimore visited Virginia, it did not occur to him that these were really authorized settlements. Nor did it occur to him that they would be brought forward as objections when he should apply for a charter. Consequently, when he applied for this charter after returning to England, he was probably honest when he represented the territory as hitherto unsettled.

We have already referred to the fact that shortly after Baltimore's grant the planters of Virginia sent a petition to the king, which was acted upon in the Star Chamber, July 3, 1633. It was decided that Lord Baltimore should remain in possession of this grant and that the planters "be left to their remedies at law, if they had such." No doubt Claiborne took an active part in having this petition presented to the king. Although he had received a license to trade, this gave him no "right to the soil or to any jurisdiction over it." Nor could he support his title on the ground of prior occupancy. His license from the king went no further than a permission to trade, which might have been granted to a citizen of a foreign State. Claiborne had, it is true, established a trading post on an island to which he gave the name Kent Island instead of Winston's Island as Captain John Smith had named it. Here he erected some buildings—the capital being furnished by the London merchants. For lack of support by these merchants and by reason of fear of the Indians, the post was almost upon the point of extinction when the Maryland colonists established themselves at St. Mary's.

Claiborne was soon notified that Kent Island was within the limits of the Maryland patent. Nevertheless, he refused to recognize the authority of Lord Baltimore. Furthermore, for the purpose of annoying and hurting the latter's colony, he incited the Indians against it by telling them the colonists were Spaniards and had come to destroy them. The matter was, of course, reported to Lord Baltimore at once by one of his vessels returning to England. On the 4th of September he instructed Leonard Calvert that if Claiborne would not recognize his authority, he was to seize and hold him prisoner at St. Mary's and, if possible, take possession of the Isle of Kent. The king at the same time ordered Governor Harvey to afford the Marylanders protection against the Indians, to allow them free trade with Virginia, and to assist them in all ways possible. He likewise commanded Baltimore not to interfere with Claiborne in the

Sir

London Feb'y the 9th 1765 —

On consideration of your and Col: Richard Tilghman's request, and of the Petition of Solomon Holton, & that you and the Col: recommend him as a proper Object for My Clemency, I do accept him as such, and you have My Consent to remit to Solomon Holton two Thirds of the Fine amerced upon him of one hundred Pounds by the County Court.

Touching the Petition of Mrs Hamson Widow and on behalf of her son and by you recommended, in Consideration of her Merit and Young Family in Distress, — — — I yield favour on her Behalf and you have hereby My direction and Consent, and which you are to Edward Lloyd Esqr My Receiver General to make known, as My Orders and Consent to him on My Behalf, to Issue and to Grant a Lease on the Behalf of her son an Orphan for the Term of twenty six years on the old Conditions, with exemption for three Lives, only for the aforesaid number of years, and this, My Direction is his Sufft Warrant to me for his so doing.

Yours truly
F C Baltimore

To Horatio Sharpe Esqr My Lieutt Govr
at Annapolis Maryland —

Letter of Frederick Calvert, sixth, and last, Lord Baltimore. *From the original in possession of the Historical Society of Pennsylvania.*

exercise of his privileges on Kent Island, thinking, no doubt, that the island was not within the boundary of the Maryland patent.

Friendly letters passed between Lord Baltimore and Governor Harvey of Virginia with regard to the affair, but Claiborne, in spite of this, did all he could to discourage the new colony. He thought by doing this at the very beginning he could exasperate the newcomers to such an extent that they would abandon the enterprise. Affairs shortly came to a crisis. In 1635, the *Long Tail*, a pinnace belonging to Claiborne, was captured by Captain Thomas Cornwaleys for being a Virginia boat trading in the Chesapeake waters without a Maryland license. Claiborne retaliated by fitting out a boat, the *Cockatrice*, with thirty men from Kent Island, which he placed under the command of Lieutenant Ratcliffe Warren. Two pinnaces, the *St. Margaret* and the *St. Helen*, were thereupon fitted out by Governor Leonard Calvert and placed under the command of Captain Thomas Cornwaleys, with orders to proceed to Kent Island and subdue the rebellion. The hostile vessels met, it seems, on the 23d of April, 1635, in Pocomoke River, on the eastern shore of the bay, and fought the first naval battle upon the inland waters of America. Claiborne's men fired the first shot, killing William Ashmore of the Maryland force and wounding several others. Cornwaleys's men returned the fire, killing Lieutenant Warren, John Bellson, and William Dawson. The *Cockatrice* then surrendered, and the men were taken prisoners. Among those captured was a certain Thomas Smith, "gentleman," who was probably second in command. We shall have occasion to recur to him in another connection. On the 10th of May another conflict took place in the harbor of the Pocomoke, and there was, probably, further bloodshed.

The Virginians were very indignant at this treatment of Claiborne's men, and believing Governor Harvey to be in sympathy with Governor Calvert's course they rebelled and refused to recognize his authority. Harvey was compelled to sail for England. After his defeat on the Pocomoke, Claiborne gave up for a time at least his resistance to Calvert and soon after took refuge in Virginia. Governor Calvert made a requisition on the Virginia authorities for the surrender of Claiborne, claiming he was a fugitive from justice. The Virginia authorities refused to comply with this request. Claiborne soon after left for England for the purpose of having his affairs adjusted there. George Evelyn, who took his place, assumed charge of Kent and Palmer Islands and recognized the authority of Calvert. After repeated petitions to the king, but finding no redress for his supposed wrongs, Claiborne returned to Virginia, where he found his property had been forfeited to the government. He petitioned the Assembly to restore his estate, but his request was refused. By the latter part of the year 1637, Kent Island had been reduced to obedience. Measures were then taken to extend the civil authority over that part of the province. On December 30, 1637, Governor Calvert issued a commission to Captain George Evelyn, appointing him commander of the island. In spite of this pacific move, however, in February, 1638, the islanders became so unruly that the governor and Council were compelled to send out an armed force to subdue its inhabitants. As no reference is made to the hostilities that followed, it is inferred that a satisfactory adjustment of the trouble was effected. In 1640, Claiborne petitioned anew to have his confiscated property restored to him, but this was again refused.

While the colonists were experiencing considerable trouble with the Indians and were arming themselves to protect their interests and their lives, an additional burden was laid upon their shoulders. Captain Richard Ingle, an associate of Claiborne, and, as some termed him, "a pirate and a rebel," was discovered hovering about the settlement with an armed ship. It was perfectly plain from his movements that he was endeavoring to strengthen the hands of the disaffected. Just prior to this, in April, 1643, Governor Calvert had sailed for England to confer with Lord Baltimore with regard to the state of affairs in Maryland. He appointed Giles Brent to act as governor in his stead during his absence. Brent ordered Ingle's arrest. He was captured, but soon escaped and joined Claiborne in his designs against the peace of the province. Governor Calvert returned in September, 1644, and found the province considerably stirred up; in fact, Claiborne was actively engaged in hostilities. Consequently, on January 1, 1645, a proclamation was issued declaring Claiborne and Richard Thompson, a planter, enemies of the province, and prohibiting them from trading with Kent Island.

About 1642, Claiborne had been appointed treasurer for life of the province of Virginia. The trouble at home between Parliament and the king was reflected in the provinces. Claiborne, seeing the king's power waning, was not slow to go over to the winning side. Lord Baltimore, on the contrary, who had always been a friend of the king and had received many favors at his hand, was faithful to him. This fidelity to his king made Lord Baltimore's possessions in the New World insecure, and Claiborne immediately took advantage of it. He seized Kent Island in 1645 without trouble. With Ingle he invaded the Western Shore. St. Mary's was seized shortly afterward, and Governor Calvert fled to Virginia for help. But it availed little, for the insurgents overthrew the proprietary government, and for nearly two years Claiborne and his faction held complete sway.

During Claiborne's supremacy those who were faithful to the governor suffered in many ways. Many were driven into exile, and those who remained were placed under heavy fines and their property taken from them. Even the missionaries to the Indians did not escape. They were sent to England in chains, where they were imprisoned a long time. Their missionary stations were broken up. Among those captured was the venerable Father White, one of the pioneer colonists. He was sent to England a prisoner and was tried on a charge of treason, but secured his acquittal. On account of his age and infirmity he was not permitted by his ecclesiastical superiors to return to the province. He died in England in 1656. Ingle returned to England after this rebellion in Maryland, and was there prosecuted by Captain Cornwaleys for his robberies.

While Maryland was experiencing these troubles from without, it was not by any means neglectful of its internal economy. Its first Assembly met at St. Mary's, February 26, 1635. Leonard Calvert was president of the Assembly, and it was apparently composed of all the freemen in the colony. It was evidently intended to be purely democratic—an assembly of the whole people. Some suppose the word "freemen" mentioned in the writ of summons meant only those who held property. But a vote of the Assembly of 1642 seems to prove that the term "freemen," in the first years of the colony at least, designated a "citizen above the age of majority, and not held to personal service." An instance is given of a Thomas Weston, who, being called, stated that he was no freeman, as he had no possessions and no certain dwelling place. By a vote, however, it was decided that he was a freeman, and as such was entitled to a vote. Men were allowed to vote either in person or by proxy.

This first Assembly drew up a body of laws and forwarded it to the proprietary for his approval. It was rejected, probably on the ground that under the charter the proprietary had the authority to make laws with the assent of the freemen, not *vice versa*. This threw the province back upon the common law of England during the two years following. This body of laws, together with the record of the proceedings of the Assembly, has not survived the ravages of time. On the other hand, we have the record of the second Assembly, which met on January 25, 1638. It was made up, likewise, of all the freemen of the colony. If not present in person, they were represented by proxies. The governor presided and was joined by councillors appointed by the proprietary. The freemen were summoned in the usual way by writ, and those omitted could present themselves at the meeting of the Assembly and claim their seats. The usual Parliamentary privilege of freedom from arrest for minor crimes during the sessions of the Assembly was accorded the members.

The Assembly was now, in turn, given the opportunity of returning in kind the proprietary's veto of their body of laws of the first Assembly. A draft of laws he had sent over was read, and rejected by a large majority. A serious deadlock was threatened. The governor's commission did not give him the power of punishing capital offences except under the laws of the province. Some held that the laws of England would become operative, while others held "that such enormous offences could hardly be committed without mutiny, and then they might be punished by martial law." A case in point was awaiting decision. Thomas Smith, to whom we have referred as second in command of Claiborne's forces at the naval engagement on Pocomoke River, had, in the meantime, been arrested for piracy and murder. "There was no grand jury to indict him, no court to try him, and no law to try him under." The case was, nevertheless, proceeded with in this manner: in the afternoon of the 14th of March, 1638, the whole Assembly, being impanelled as a grand jury, brought in the indictment. Thereupon it resolved itself into a high court of justice, and appointed Secretary Lewger as attorney-general. The prisoner, upon being arraigned, pleaded not guilty; he was, nevertheless, impartially tried and found guilty. The governor pronounced the death sentence. This sentence is interesting in that it shows the persistency of the old legal forms. It is as follows:

"Thomas Smith, you have been indicted for felony and piracy; to your indictment you have pleaded not guilty; and you have been tried by the freemen in this General Assembly, who have found you guilty, and pronounce this sentence upon you: that you shall be carried from hence to the place from whence you came, and thence to the place of execution, and shall be there hanged by the neck until you be dead, and that all your lands, goods and chattels, shall be forfeited to the lord proprietor, saving that your wife shall have her dower, and God have mercy upon your soul."

It is recorded that the prisoner then demanded his clergy, but the privilege was denied him, the governor holding that it could not be allowed in his crime. Furthermore, that even if it could be allowed it was then too late after judgment.

At the next session of the Assembly, the government was remodelled. Writs of summons were displaced by writs of election. Burgesses selected from every hundred took the place of the popular assembly. The House of Assembly was to meet triennially, and was made up of the burgesses together with the governor and Council. More frequent sessions could be held if specially summoned by the governor. The proprietary retained, however, the very dangerous privilege of summoning members by special writ. Such members had equal privilege of voting with the regularly elected burgesses. If summoned in sufficient numbers they could, of course, annul the popular will. However, unfair advantage does not seem to have been taken of this provision. Another peculiar provision was retained: that those freemen who had failed to vote for the burgesses elected might appear in person and claim their seats. Some of them availed themselves of the privilege. During this session, four acts were passed of the character of a Bill of Rights. Freedom of worship was secured, allegiance to the king was affirmed, the liberties of Englishmen were assured to the freemen, and the territorial rights of the proprietary were confirmed. Next, civil and criminal courts were established, provision was made for justices of the peace and other officers, a code of laws was enacted, commerce and agriculture were regulated, and arrangements were made for the meeting and inspection of the militia. For some reason or other, these acts failed of passing to a third reading, and it was not until the next session that the "colony was equipped with all the machinery of a representative popular government" (Browne).

In the meantime, the colony increased rapidly in population. New colonists came in a steady stream and took up new manors, plantations, and homesteads. As soon as the population of a district had increased sufficiently, it was erected into a hundred. Such, for instance, was St. George's Hundred, established in January, 1638, and placed under the command of a high constable. Many of the settlers came as "servants" and paid for their passage by terms of service of from three to five years. Most of them were farmers and artisans, but not a few of them were men of good families. At the expiration of their terms of service, "servants" acquired all the rights and privileges of freemen. In addition, many craftsmen came out at their own expense and received land allotments larger than those received by the others. It may be said, in general, that the character of the majority of these early settlers in Maryland was much above the level of the average colonists in America at this time. They were for the most part of the kind most beneficial to a young and struggling colony. Some came with their entire families, intending to settle upon the land permanently. The younger men came with the determination of making a place of responsibility for themselves in the colony. The terms of colonization were exceedingly liberal. No extraordinary religious or political tests were required of anyone.

In 1649, a rival settlement to St. Mary's was established within the bounds of Baltimore's grant. The Congregational or Independent Church had been established in Virginia in 1642. Notwithstanding the laws made against the members of this denomination, they increased in numbers until they had about one hundred and eighteen members. Thinking they were increasing too rapidly, the Virginia authorities broke up their conventicle and scattered their membership. Their pastor, Mr. Harrison, went to Boston, and their elder, Mr. Durand, went to Maryland. Soon after the latter had settled in Maryland, some of the members of the church followed him (1649). They established themselves at a place they called Providence, but afterward changed to Anne Arundel. This was most probably on or near the spot on which the city of Annapolis now stands.

St. Mary's, the first settlement in Maryland, had always been the seat of government, but when Francis Nicholson became governor (July, 1694), he ordered the Assembly to meet at Anne Arundel town instead of St. Mary's (September 21, 1694). In a subsequent chapter we shall show how the inhabitants were greatly excited over this change, knowing as they did that it meant the ruin of their town. We shall find that they appealed to the Assembly in vain to reconsider its action. The seat of government was changed to "Anne Arundel town," and the Assembly held its first session in the house of Major Dorsey, February 28, 1694. In the next session they gave the town the name of Annapolis and made provision for the erection of public buildings and a parish church.

The news of Governor Calvert's having fled to Virginia after the invasion of Claiborne and Ingle had proved successful soon reached England. The proprietary, Lord Baltimore, on learning the news, was in despair and seems to have considered his province as lost to him. He sent instructions to his brother to realize whatever he could from the general wreck and ruin. But the governor, being on the spot, did not consider all lost. Claiborne and Ingle were already proving themselves obnoxious to the colonists, and then, again, the proprietary had a staunch supporter in Sir William Berkeley, the royal Governor of Virginia. Governor Calvert merely bided his time. The auspicious moment arrived toward the latter part of the year 1646. He raised a small force composed of Virginians and fugitives from Maryland, pledging the proprietary's and his own estates to pay them. With this ridiculously small force he

Letter of Cecil Calvert, second Lord Baltimore. *From the original in possession of the Historical Society of Pennsylvania.*

retook St. Mary's without any resistance, and soon brought back the whole Western Shore to its allegiance to the proprietary. Kent Island offered some resistance, but it likewise submitted after a while. A general amnesty was proclaimed to all who had taken part in the insurrection, on the sole condition that they take the oath of fidelity. Ingle and an associate, Durford, only were excepted.

Governor Leonard Calvert died in Maryland, June 9, 1647, and Thomas Greene succeeded him. Greene did not prove a success, and in 1648 Baltimore removed him and appointed William Stone governor. Stone was a Protestant, and it was probable that his appointment was dictated by a desire on the part of the proprietary to remove a source of discontent. Maryland was represented as being a stronghold of Popery in which Protestants were persecuted and oppressed. The new governor was bound by his oath of office to protect every person of every faith in the free exercise of his religious views. Finally, the very next year, 1649, the famous Act of Toleration was passed. It was entitled "An Act Concerning Religion." It laid fines upon those who spoke lightly of the Virgin Mary, Apostles, and Evangelists, while the penalty of death was to be exacted of those who blasphemed any Person of the Holy Trinity. Those who reviled another on account of his religious persuasion by calling him Puritan, Jesuit, Papist, and the like, were to be punished. Swearing, drunkenness, disorderly recreation, unnecessary work on the Sabbath, were forbidden. The clauses of the act guaranteeing liberty of conscience are well worth quoting: "whereas the enforcing of the conscience in matters of religion hath frequently fallen out to be of dangerous consequences;"—"and the better to preserve mutual love and amity among the inhabitants of the Province;" it was provided that no person believing in Jesus Christ should be in any ways "troubled, molested, or discountenanced for or in respect of his or her religion, nor in the free exercise thereof." Heavy penalties were provided for infractions of this last provision of the act.

The execution of Charles I. in 1649 placed the future of the province very much in doubt. Baltimore did not oppose the new order of things, and seemed to be on good terms with Parliament and the English leaders. This is evidenced by the fact that Charles II. in 1650, while a fugitive in the island of Jersey, declared Baltimore a rebel and gave the government of Maryland to Sir William Davenant, the English poet and dramatist. It is said that he actually set sail for America, but was captured in the English Channel and sent back by a Parliamentary cruiser. Virginia had proclaimed Charles II. king, and had enacted the death penalty for anyone who should dispute his title. This act brought a fleet from Parliament to reduce the colony to subjection. Ingle, who was then in England, tried to involve Maryland in the hostilities at the same time, but Baltimore proved to the satisfaction of the Parliamentary government that there was no revolt in that colony against the new order of things. His representations were successful, and Maryland was stricken out of the instructions issued to the Parliamentary Commissioners, to whom was intrusted the duty of reducing to subjection the recalcitrant colonies. Nevertheless, probably through the machinations of William Claiborne and Richard Bennett, the expression "the plantations within the Chesapeake Bay" was finally inserted in the commission dated September 26, 1651. After the subjection of Virginia, the Parliamentary Commissioners turned their attention to Maryland. At first they deposed Stone, but afterward reinstated him. Then they took action that practically abolished the rights of the proprietary. Baltimore sought redress, but was unsuccessful for the time being.

Cromwell having expelled the Rump Parliament, April 20, 1653, and having declared himself Protector, Stone proclaimed him such in Maryland. That province was, however, a proprietary government by virtue of its charter, but was now held under the Protectorate. Cromwell did not object to this, but Claiborne and Bennett, for reasons of their own, gathered together a force composed partly of Marylanders and partly of Virginians, and compelling Stone to resign appointed a Providence Puritan, Captain William Fuller, in his place. Writs were now issued by the Commissioners, of whom Claiborne and Bennett were two, which were religiously intolerant. No Roman Catholic was allowed to vote or to be elected as a burgess. They repealed the Toleration Act of 1649, and enacted in its stead one of their own making, which they called "An Act Concerning Religion." By its provisions, none who professed Roman Catholicism might receive protection. Moreover, those who professed a belief in that religion were not to be permitted to worship according to its forms. No Protestants professing faith in Christ were to be interfered with, "provided that this liberty was not extended to popery or prelacy, or to such as under the profession of Christ hold forth and practise licentiousness." Roman Catholics and the Churchmen, together with the Brownists, Quakers, Anabaptists, and some other Protestant sects, were deprived of the freedom of worship which they had previously enjoyed to a greater or lesser degree. "Surely," says Browne, "this toleration might have been expressed in briefer phrase."

Lord Baltimore's territorial rights were next attacked. The whole province was thrown open to all who desired to take up land, without any reference to the proprietary or his representatives. Baltimore complained to Cromwell, who directed Bennett to desist from interfering with the Marylanders. But, prior to this, Baltimore had rebuked Stone for so promptly complying with the request to resign. Stone, smarting under this rebuke, collected a force and advanced upon Providence. Fuller, in command of the Puritans, met him with a force of one hundred and seventy-five men, supported by two ships in the river. The captains, being Puritans, naturally consented to help Fuller. A battle was fought on a narrow neck of land in the harbor of the Severn, March 25, 1655. Stone's one hundred and thirty-five men were defeated. In spite of his promise of quarter, Fuller executed four of the captives in cold blood. Stone and five others were condemned to death, but through the intercessions of the soldiers and some of the women their lives were spared. Stone, though severely wounded, was kept in confinement for some time. The Puritans seized the great seal and the records and confiscated the property of the conquered force.

The whole question of the rights of Baltimore was again referred to the Protector and the Commissioners for Plantations, and a decision was once more rendered in the proprietary's favor. He now, in turn, lodged a complaint against Bennett and Claiborne for the massacre at Providence. Baltimore was fully sustained in all his rights, sovereign and territorial, and his authority throughout the province was reëstablished. The Toleration Act of 1649 was reënacted and this time was made perpetual. The agreement was signed and sealed on March 24, 1658. A general pardon was granted to all those who had supported the insurrection, and for the oath of fidelity was substituted merely an obligation to be loyal to the government of the proprietary. This obligation read as follows: "I, A. B., do promise and engage to submit to the authority of the right honourable Cecilius Lord Baltimore and his heirs, within this province of Maryland, according to his patent of the said province, and to his present lieutenant and other officers here by his lordship appointed, to whom I will be aiding and assisting, and will not obey or assist any here in opposition to them." Those who did not care to take the obligation upon themselves were accorded the privilege of leaving the province within a year. All cases in dispute were referred to the Lord Protector and the Council. No one was to rest under a disability of any kind for taking part in the recent troubles. The turbulent Claiborne, from this time, drops out of the history of Maryland.

Prior to this final happy adjustment of the dispute, Captain Josiah Fendall had been appointed Governor of Maryland by Lord Baltimore. Philip Calvert, Lord Baltimore's brother, was appointed secretary of the province, and instructions were issued to the new governor. Fendall had not been long in office before he began scheming to enlarge his authority at the expense of that of the proprietary. He early set forth the claim that he held his authority solely from the Assembly itself. Through his influence the Assembly was reorganized, all former acts were repealed, and it was made a felony to change the government thus created. Fendall practically renounced his allegiance to the proprietary and surrendered his commission. A new one was issued him by the Assembly. Thus, by a few arbitrary acts, the whole constitution of the province was changed and the proprietary's entire authority taken from him.

As soon as Baltimore learned of Fendall's treachery, he appointed (1659) his brother, Philip Calvert, illegitimate son of Sir George Calvert, the first Lord Baltimore, governor in Fendall's stead. An order from the king was secured, directing Sir William Berkeley, the royal Governor of Virginia, to assist in reëstablishing the proprietary government. Those who had been unwittingly drawn into the plot were to be pardoned. Fendall and Fuller, however, were on no account to be spared. As soon as Philip Calvert's commission was shown, the rebellion collapsed completely. Fendall tried to make trouble for Baltimore by stirring up a rebellion in Charles County, but failed miserably. Afterward he and other leaders in the plot surrendered themselves. They were found guilty of treason and sentenced to banishment and forfeiture of their estates. Later, upon Fendall's pleading abjectly for pardon his sentence was considerably mitigated.

The legislative machinery as now constituted consisted of the governor and Council sitting as an Upper House and the delegates sitting as a Lower House. This bicameral form of government had been introduced in 1650 at a session of the Assembly, which enacted "that the present Assembly, during the continuance thereof, be held by way of upper and lower house, to sit in two distinct houses, apart, for the more convenient dispatch of business therein to be consulted of." The assent of both Houses was necessary to the passage of a bill. The Upper House, being appointed by the proprietary, represented his interests. The Lower House, elected by the people, in turn represented their interests. Although the establishment of this bicameral form of government granted the people a great increase of popular privileges, yet the proprietary not only confirmed it but forbade its change. Later, he gave the freemen the additional privilege of initiating laws subject to his veto, whereas his charter conferred upon him the privilege of initiating laws subject to their adoption by the Assembly. However, the governor and Council continued to exercise the charter privilege, under certain restrictions, of enacting ordinances having the force of law. The Council, likewise, transacted executive business. The government as thus established continued without material change until the Revolution.

Besides that with Virginia, two other boundary disputes engaged the proprietary's attention prior to the deposition of James II. The first was with the Dutch and the Swedes on Delaware River and Bay, and came very early in the history of the province. The second was with William Penn, and came upon the eve of the second English Revolution. Both these disputes are of considerable importance, inasmuch as they were carried on with considerable acerbity by all the parties interested. These disputes, likewise, fill many pages of the history of the colonies engaged in them. After the English conquest of New Netherland and after the territories on the Delaware had become a part of Pennsylvania, both disputes were merged into the one with William Penn. A brief survey of these disputes will not, consequently, be out of place at this point.

In 1638, as we have seen, the Swedes made their first permanent settlement within what was then claimed to be the limits of Maryland. From that time, however, they continued to make settlements on the west bank of Delaware River without hindrance from the Maryland authorities.

Nor were they in any manner seriously disturbed until 1655, when they were subdued by the Dutch. The Dutch, likewise, had made settlements along the Delaware, but they had died out one by one until the tragic massacre of the inhabitants of Zwaanendal by the Indians in 1631. Nevertheless, other Dutch attempts at colonization followed.

While the Dutch and the Swedes were squabbling over this section, the Maryland authorities warned both that they were trespassing on Baltimore's territory. The further demand was made that they should acknowledge his authority, quit the province, or take the consequences, which, it was intimated, would be serious. Stuyvesant thereupon sent Augustine Herman and Resolved Waldron to discuss the affair with the Maryland authorities. Nothing, however, came of the conference, for neither party was willing to concede anything. Manifestoes were exchanged, after which the envoys departed, Waldron to report to Stuyvesant, and Herman to take up a permanent residence in Maryland under a manorial grant from Lord Baltimore.

So important a personage was Augustine Herman in the affairs of New Netherland and Maryland, and so important a service did he render the latter province in particular, that it will not be out of place to pause in our narrative long enough to record the principal events in his interesting career. Born in the city of Prague, Bohemia, about 1608, he had played the rôles of "soldier, scholar, artist, merchant, land-surveyor, speculator, and manorial proprietor" before his death in 1686. Having served through several campaigns in the army of Count Albert von Wallenstein, he was present, in all probability, at the battle of Lützen, when that general was defeated by the Swedes and Gustavus Adolphus was killed.

Probably as early as 1633, Herman emigrated to New Amsterdam, where for several years he represented the firm of Gabry and Sons, merchants of Amsterdam. He soon became prominent in the affairs of New Netherland, for, shortly after his arrival, we find him despatched to the

Dutch settlements on South River in the interests of some land purchase venture. As a result of an unfortunate investment in a small privateer called *La Garce*, he experienced financial reverses in 1651. Two years later, however, he made a satisfactory settlement with his creditors. He opposed the policy of the Dutch West India Company, and, as one of the Nine Men, supported Adrian van der Donck's "Remonstrance" to the States General. Later, he was arrested by Stuyvesant on a trivial charge, but was soon discharged from custody. As a result of a trick played by George Baxter, he and a companion were arrested in 1652 for conspiring against the Rhode Island government. They had considerable difficulty in establishing their innocence.

By 1659, Herman seems to have made his peace with Stuyvesant, for it was then that he and Resolved Waldron were sent as a commission to Maryland. They were to reach some agreement with Governor Fendall by which the boundaries between the Maryland and the New Netherland possessions on South River might be permanently established. No doubt Herman owed his appointment to his knowledge of surveying, his linguistic attainments, and his business ability.

Fortunately, Herman kept a journal of this expedition to Maryland (*New York Colonial Documents*, ii). Accompanied by soldiers and guides, the two commissioners made their way on foot and by canoe to Patuxent, where they spent several days in conference with Governor Fendall and Philip Calvert. From Patuxent they sailed down Chesapeake Bay and secured an interview with the Governor of Virginia. Later, they returned to Maryland, and it was then that Herman offered to make a survey and draw a map of the whole province in consideration of a manorial grant. Lord Baltimore accepted the terms of the offer. Herman spent about ten years on this survey, and received a grant of about five thousand acres of land in recognition of his valuable services. It was situated on Elk River, and for the most part was in the present Cecil County. From

Augustine Hermann. *From the original painting in possession of Mrs. Hermann Massey.*

time to time, he increased his holdings to between twenty and thirty thousand acres. The original grant he named "Manor of Nova Bohemia." About 1662 he removed his household from New Amsterdam, and on the 19th of June of the same year he received his first patent from the proprietary.

Herman's large map of Maryland, with a medallion portrait of himself, was published by Faithorne in London about 1670. A copy of it is preserved in the British Museum, and it is highly commended by contemporaries. A representation of the Alleghany Mountains, near the present city of Cumberland, Maryland, appears in one corner of the map. A note in explanation of the illustration gives us a very good idea of the crude conception of the geographical extent of the North American continent prevailing at that time. "These mighty high and great Mountaines trending N. E. and S. W., and W. S. W., is supposed to be the very middle Ridg of Northern America and the only Naturall Cause of the fierceness and Extreame Stormy Cold Winds that comes N. W. from thence all over this Continent and makes Frost."

Herman erected his manor house on a stream which he called Bohemia River, near the head of Chesapeake Bay. Here he lived in great style and was the most important personage in that part of the colony for nearly a quarter of a century. The following inscription appears on a stone on his manor:

> "Augustine Herman, Bohemian,
> The First Founder &
> Seater of Bohemian Manor
> Anno 1661."

The old Bohemia Manor House was burned in 1815. Many valuable historical documents and mementos were destroyed.

In the meantime, the relations between Maryland and the Dutch on the Delaware became so strained that, in 1659,

Lord Baltimore contemplated resorting to force. He soon found, however, that he could expect no aid from Virginia or New England. Nor had it, in fact, been definitely decided whether or not New Amstel was within the fortieth parallel. Until that question should be definitely determined, Baltimore decided it would not be well to be too hasty. Hostilities were consequently very wisely deferred.

In 1663, Governor Charles Calvert, eldest son of the second Lord Baltimore, Cecilius Calvert, who had in 1661 succeeded Philip Calvert, visited the Dutch authorities at New Amsterdam and tried to arrange a settlement of the boundary question, but was not successful. In 1664, King Charles settled the matter—or rather unsettled it—by granting his brother James, the Duke of York, all the territory extending from the west bank of the Connecticut to the eastern shore of the Delaware. As we have seen, James sent a military force to take possession of his grant, but it was some time before the whole Dutch power was finally overthrown and himself firmly established in its possession.

In 1682 William Penn and Charles Calvert, now the third Lord Baltimore, had a conference to discuss the dispute which had arisen concerning the boundary between their respective grants. Penn exhibited his patent dated 1681, and Baltimore produced his charter antedating Penn's grant by half a century. Baltimore claimed as his northern boundary the fortieth parallel, "which," said he to Penn, "by your patent, is your southern bounds, as Watkin's Point is mine." Penn, while acknowledging this, tried to persuade Baltimore to agree upon thirty-nine degrees five minutes as his northern boundary. Baltimore, of course, refused to agree to this. Another meeting was held at New Castle, May, 1683, but with no better results. Fearing the consequences of Penn's representations to the king, Baltimore left for England to present his case in person. He had little reason to believe that he would receive consideration, for James II., who had succeeded his brother as king in 1685, was endeavoring by every means possible to concentrate in himself not only all the power in England but likewise in the colonies.

After repeated requests on the part of Penn, the English Privy Council, November 7, 1685, decided a part of the boundary disputes. The peninsula was to be divided between Baltimore and Penn by a meridian line running north from the latitude of Cape Henlopen. With this decision, Charles Calvert, who had succeeded Cecilius to the title and possessions in 1675, was very much disappointed. Inasmuch as James II. was a Roman Catholic, Baltimore thought his proprietary interests would not suffer. Such was not the case, for James regarded his colonial possessions merely as fruitful objects of exploitation. Consequently, he promoted the interests of Lord Baltimore only to the extent that they were not antagonistic to his own. In 1691 William III. assumed the government of the province, but the proprietary was, however, allowed to retain the income from his provincial possessions. In 1741 his heirs were restored "to all their rights as fully as the legislature thought fit that any proprietor should enjoy them."

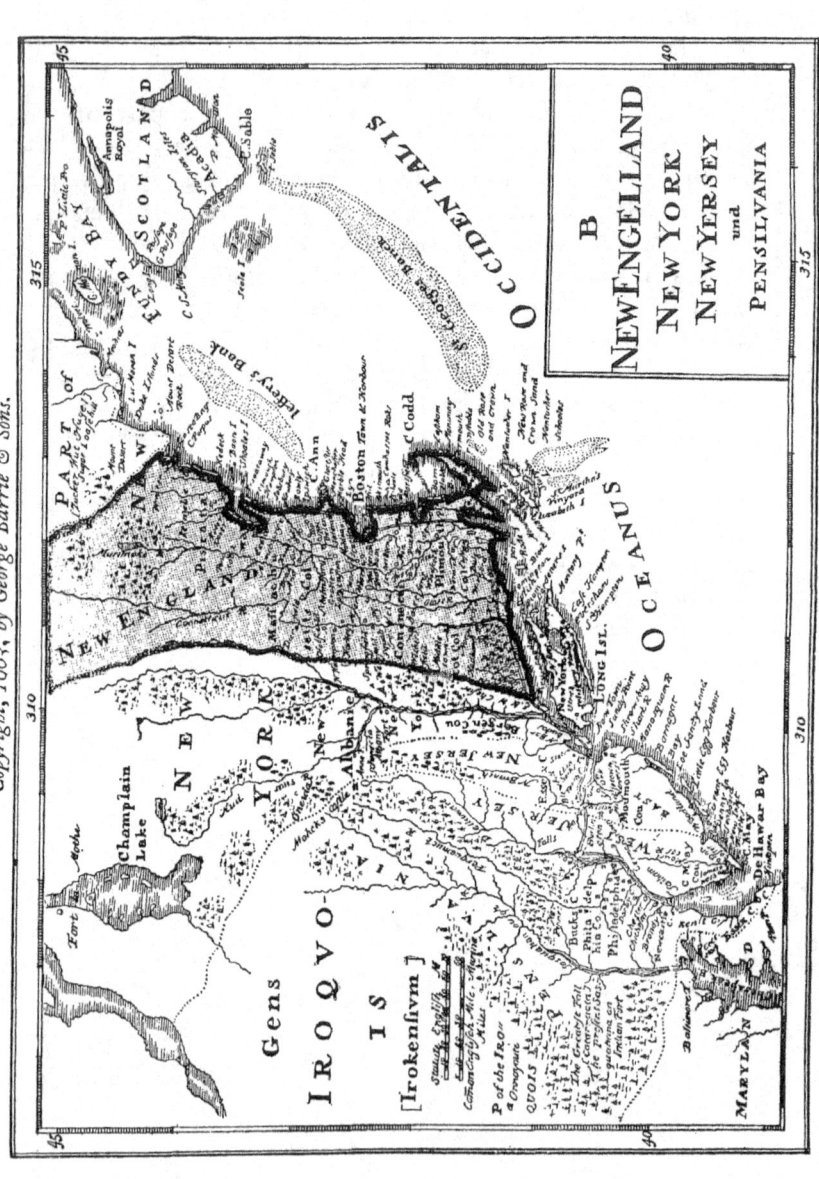

Early German map, dating probably from the latter part of the seventeenth century, showing the dividing line between East and West Jersey. From the original in the private collection of Julius F. Sachse, Esq.

# CHAPTER X

## *EVOLUTION OF NEW JERSEY, 1614-1685*

THE early history of the territory now comprised within the bounds of the present State of New Jersey is inextricably bound up with that of New Netherland and, after the English conquest, with that of New York. First settled by the Dutch both on North River and on South River, this territory was nevertheless embraced within the patent of the Council for New England (1620)—the successor to the Plymouth Company. Though settled and still claimed by the Dutch, and though a part of the patent of the Council for New England, the territory was nevertheless included within the very indefinite Palatine grant of New Albion (1634). The very next year (1635) it was again assigned to Lord Mulgrave on the dissolution of the Council for New England. Not until June, 1664, in fact, was even the semblance of an independent existence conferred upon it. On June 23d and 24th of that year, even before the actual conquest of New Netherland, the Duke of York executed deeds of lease and release to Lord John Berkeley of Stratton and Sir George Carteret, granting them the territory now comprised practically within the limits of New Jersey. Even then, from time to time, it was claimed by the governors of New York either to be subsidiary to the latter province or actually a part of it. The attitude assumed by Governor Sir Edmund Andros, of New York, in 1680 toward Captain Philip Carteret, Governor of New Jersey, and the practical annexation of New Jersey to New York in 1702, during the reign of Queen Anne and the governorship of Viscount Cornbury, are cases in point.

An attempt had been made by the Dutch in 1614 to form a settlement on the present site of Jersey City, and some fortifications against the Indians had been constructed. But it was not until after the establishment of a settlement by the Dutch at New Amsterdam that plantations were started in earnest on the western side of the bay. Bergen was begun about 1617, but it was a mere trading place for the Indians during its first years. For mutual protection against the Indians the farmhouses were built in close proximity, while the farm lands lay in the surrounding districts. This group of farmhouses formed the village of Bergen. Smith (*History of New Jersey*, 61), thinks a few Norwegians and Danes may have been concerned with the Dutch in the original settlement, the name " Bergen " being derived from a city in Norway. It is probable, however, that the name was not applied before 1660, and then it may have referred to the high ground upon which the village was located. Or, what is more probable, it may have been named for Bergen in the north of Holland, because of the same affection for home that led to the adoption of the names of other Holland towns for the new settlements.

Settlements sprang up later in West Jersey than in East Jersey. Colonists from New Haven were among the pioneer settlers of the former. Their object in this instance was solely commercial. In fact, it might be said that the inhabitants of this colony were always on the lookout for new trading posts for the purpose of developing their trade with the Indians. During the winter of 1638–1639, George Lamberton, of New Haven, having carried on a lucrative fur trade with the Indians on Delaware River, reported that fact to his fellow citizens of New Haven. They, likewise, determined to secure a share of this trade now exclusively enjoyed by the Dutch and the Swedes. A " Delaware Company " was formed, consisting of the governor, the minister, and all the principal inhabitants of the colony. In 1640, Captain Turner was sent to the Delaware in charge of a vessel to spy out the land and to purchase lands along the banks of Delaware Bay from the Indians. He was specifically warned against interfering with the Dutch and the Swedes. The spirit of these injunctions Turner disobeyed. He purchased from the Indians nearly all the southwestern part of Jersey and also a strip of land on the present site of Philadelphia. Nevertheless, the officials of New Haven, at a town meeting, August 30, 1641, approved the action of the "Delaware Company."

The first instalment of settlers sent to this territory consisted of fifty families. Most of these families settled on Varkin's Kill, near the present site of Salem, New Jersey. The Swedes and the Dutch protested most vehemently against these so-called "squatters." We have already recorded in a preceding chapter in considerable detail how the settlements were broken up by the open hostility of the Dutch and the Swedes on the Delaware. Many of the colonists returned to their New England homes during the winter of 1643 and the spring succeeding. This failure crippled New Haven financially, but its inhabitants for a long time continued to claim the lands they had purchased on the Delaware. Another attempt to settle these lands was made in 1651, but Peter Stuyvesant, then Director-general of New Netherland, blocked it. The Dutch conquest of New Sweden practically put an end to the immediate attempts of New Haven to colonize the Delaware.

In the meantime, Bergen, having grown to considerable proportions, was incorporated in 1661. Tielman van Vleeck was appointed sheriff, and a subaltern bench of justice was then established. The latter was composed of the sheriff and two schepens, and was probably the first legal tribunal established in New Jersey. Steps were taken that year also for the erection of a sawmill. In 1662, a well was dug, four hundred and seventeen guilders were subscribed toward the erection of a church, and in 1664 a block house was ordered to be built. Soon after the incorporation of the town, palisaded forts were erected for the protection of its inhabitants. Likewise, at this time, a Reformed Dutch church was organized. This congregation worshipped for twenty years in a log schoolhouse, but in 1682 a more substantial edifice was erected. This church is the oldest in New Jersey.

In 1664, John Bailey, Daniel Denton, and Luke Watson, of Jamaica, Long Island, purchased of certain Staten Island Indian chiefs a tract of land, on a part of which Elizabeth now stands. Having petitioned Governor Richard Nicolls, of New York, a deed to these lands was granted to John Baker of New York, John Ogden of Northampton, John Bailey and Luke Watson and their associates. The deed was dated at Fort James, New York, the 2d of December, and is commonly called the "Elizabeth Town Patent." This grant was made before the title of Lord John Berkeley and Sir George Carteret was known. The Indians received for this Elizabethtown tract: "Twenty fathom of trayden Cloth, two made Cotes, two gunnes, two kettles, ten barres of Lead, twenty handfulls of Powder, foure hundred fathom of white wampom, or two hundred fathom of black wampom." The whole was valued at £36 14s. The grantors were Mattano, Manamowaone, and Cowescomen, the deed being signed only by Mattano.

When the Duke of York took possession of New Netherland and the surrounding territory, he specified it by three names, to comprehend all his titles. The province itself was called "New York." Long Island was called "Yorkshire." The region between the Hudson and the Delaware was called "Albania." Little is known of this last territorial division except of that portion of it that was contiguous to Manhattan. Albania offered the greatest attraction to settlers, for it could be improved more readily than the other colonies. There was plenty of fertile land; the rivers were long and wide, and the seacoast was extensive; and hopes of rich mines were held.

While Governor Nicolls was engaged in settling the boundary dispute with Connecticut, the Duke of York was taking steps to dismember the province of New York. To Lord John Berkeley and to Sir George Carteret, even before the conquest of New Netherland, the duke had given the whole territory between North and South Rivers. Berkeley, who was a brother of Sir William Berkeley, Governor of Virginia, had been the duke's own governor and was afterward made treasurer of his household. He is described as a "bold and insolent man, popishly inclined, not incorrupt, and very arbitrary." Carteret, who was treasurer of the Admiralty Board, had been governor of the island of Jersey at the Restoration, and was made chamberlain of the king's household. As Governor of Jersey he had received Charles while Prince of Wales, and had defended the island against Cromwell's forces, and had been the last commander on British soil to honor the king's flag. He is described as the "most passionate man in the world."

To these favorites, then, the Duke of York, on the 23d and 24th of June, 1664, had granted all that valuable territory now practically coincident with New Jersey. The territory was called "Nova Cæsarea," or New Jersey, in commemoration of Carteret's defence of the island of Jersey in 1649. Toward the end of July, 1665, Captain Philip Carteret arrived at New York with about thirty emigrants in the ship *Philip*. He was the cousin of Sir George, and had been commissioned as governor of the new province. Early in August he landed in New Jersey at the head of his followers, carrying a hoe on his shoulder and thereby intimating his "intentions of becoming a planter with them." He established himself on the north bank of "the Kills," and named the settlement Elizabethtown, after Elizabeth, the wife of Sir George Carteret.

The grant of Nova Cæsarea to Berkeley and Carteret is said to have been given in consideration of a "competent sum of money." By its terms, the grant included all that "tract of land adjacent to New England and lying and being to the westward of Long Island and Manhattan Island; and bounded on the east part by the main sea, and part by Hudson's river; and hath upon the west, Delaware bay or river; and extendeth southward to the main ocean as far as Cape May, at the mouth of Delaware bay; and to the northward as far as the northernmost branch of the said bay or river of Delaware; which is in forty-one degrees and forty minutes of latitude, and crosseth over thence in a straight line to Hudson's river, in forty-one degrees of latitude; which said tract of land is hereafter to be called Nova Cæsarea or New Jersey, and also all rivers, mines, minerals, woods, fishings, hawkings, huntings, and fowlings, and all other royalties, profits, commodities, and hereditaments whatsoever to the said land and premises, belonging or in any wise appertaining, with their and every of their appurtenances in as full and ample manner as the same is granted unto the said Duke of York by the before recited letters patent." These letters patent, in addition to other rights, had conferred on the Duke of York that most important one of government. The power of hearing and determining appeals was reserved to the king. Chalmers says: "relying on the greatness of his connection, the duke seems to have been little solicitous to procure the royal privileges conferred on the proprietors of Maryland and Carolina, whose charters conferred almost unlimited authority. And while as counts-palatine they exercised every act of government in their own names, because they were invested with the ample powers possessed by the prætors of the Roman provinces, he ruled his territory in the name of the king."

On February 10, 1665, Berkeley and Carteret published *The Concessions and Agreements of the Lords Proprietors of the Province of Nova Cæsarea, or New Jersey.* The "Concessions and Agreements" were of the nature of a constitution and were very liberal in their terms. Under them the government of the province was placed in the hands of a governor, a Council, and an Assembly. The Council was to be chosen by the chief executive and was to be composed of not less than six and of not more than twelve persons, while the Assembly was to consist of twelve persons who were to be chosen annually by the freemen. The governor and Council were given the power of appointing all officers. They were to execute the laws and were to exercise a supervision over the courts appointed by the Assembly. All laws not against the English statutes or against the proprietors were to be passed by the Assembly. Such laws were to be published by the governor and his Council. They were to remain in force one year, during which time the Lords Proprietors could take them up for consideration.

One hundred and fifty acres of land were given to every freeman coming over with the first governor, provided he owned "a good musket, bore twelve bullets to the pound, bandeliers and match convenient, and six months' provisions for himself." Likewise, for every manservant or slave brought over and similarly provided for, the freeman was to receive an additional one hundred and fifty acres of land. Slaves and Christian servants were to receive seventy-five acres at the expiration of their terms of service. Liberty of conscience was guaranteed. In each parish, two hundred acres were to be put aside for the ministers, who were to be supported by the Assembly. These "Concessions," as they were called, were looked upon by the citizens of New Jersey as a charter of their liberties and as of much higher authority than the Acts of the Assembly.

When Governor Philip Carteret arrived in New Jersey, he found four families who had settled round Elizabethtown under the Long Island patent. Their claim to the soil hindered, at first, all harmonious coöperation with the governor in his efforts for the progress of the new settlement. Subsequently, however, the governor and Council, compromising, came to an understanding with these claimants, by which the local privileges granted them by Governor Nicolls were confirmed. Carteret's treatment of the claims of these settlers is but one of many evidences of his desire to induce settlers to remain in the province and to persuade others to immigrate there. Very shortly after his arrival, he sent men to New England to induce settlers to come to New Jersey. In this he was quite successful, for the invitation resulted in bringing to Elizabethtown and the surrounding neighborhood many new settlers. The ship that brought Carteret to New Jersey returned to England to bring back more people and goods. Several other vessels during the ensuing years made trips for similar purposes. Within two years, thirty-three inhabitants of Bergen, sixty-five of Elizabethtown, thirteen from Woodbridge, twenty-four from Navesink, two from Middletown, and two from along the Delaware, subscribed to the oath of allegiance.

Governor Carteret's offer of full civil and religious liberty to all prospective colonists attracted the attention of members of Congregational Churches in Milford, Guilford, Branford, and New Haven. A committee, with Robert Treat at its head, was sent to Governor Carteret to confer with him concerning the matter. Furthermore, they were instructed to examine carefully the lands offered them and to decide for themselves from actual personal observation whether or not it would be advisable to accept the offer. They first examined the New Haven property on the Delaware and decided upon the site of Burlington. Afterward, however, from suggestions on the part of Governor Carteret, they were induced to settle on Passaic River.

In May of 1666, the remnant of the old New Haven colony of 1638, under the leadership of Robert Treat and Matthew Gilbert, sailed up Passaic River. They came with "their families, their beloved pastor, their church records and communion service, their deacons and their household goods." They settled at a place they at first called Milford, from the home of Robert Treat. The name was soon changed, however, to Newark, after the English home of the Rev. Abraham Pierson, a minister at Branford in the New Haven colony, whose flock migrated almost bodily with him to New Jersey.

Before leaving Branford for their new home on the Passaic, the emigrants adopted the "Fundamental Agreement": "1st. That none shall be admitted freemen or free Burgesses within our Town, upon Passaick River, in the province of New Jersey, but such planters as are members of some or other of the Congregational Churches; nor shall any but such be chosen to Magistracy or to carry on any part of Civil Judicature, or as deputies or assistants to have power to Vote in establishing Laws and making or Repealing them, or to any Chief Military Trust or office. Nor shall any But such church members have any Vote in any such elections; Tho' all others admitted to Be planters have Right to their proper Inheritances, and do and shall enjoy all other Civil Liberties and Privileges, according to Laws, Orders, Grants, which are or hereafter shall Be Made for this Town. 2d. We shall with Care and Diligence provide for the maintenance of the purity of Religion in the Congregational Churches." These articles were subscribed by twenty-three heads of families. Some time after the colonists had been settled in Newark, the Fundamental Agreement was slightly revised. The most important change in the phraseology was that "the planters agree to submit to such magistrates as shall be annually chosen by the Friends from among themselves and to such Laws as we had in the place whence we came." To this revision, sixty-four men put their names—twenty-three were from Branford, and the remainder from New Haven, Milford, and Guilford. That illiteracy was not at all prevalent among these settlers is very evident from the fact that out of the sixty-four signers of the document only six were obliged to make their marks.

The New England settlers experienced some little trouble with the Indians before they succeeded in settling peaceably upon the lands granted them by Governor Carteret. They hoped that Carteret would clear the lands of all claims by the Indians; but this Carteret was not authorized to do. The Indians objected to the first settlers taking up the lands, and detained them on their vessels until a satisfactory understanding was reached. This objection arose mainly from Robert Treat's failure to deliver a letter which Carteret had written to the Indians. Finally, a satisfactory agreement was made on board the vessel. The new settlers promised to give the Indians "fifty double hands of powder, one hundred bars of lead, twenty axes, twenty coats, ten guns, twenty pistols, ten kettles, ten swords, four blankets, four barrels of beer, ten pairs of breeches, fifty knives, twenty hoes, eight hundred and fifty fathoms of wampum, twenty ankers of liquors or something equivalent, and three troopers' coats."

In summing up the importance of this transplantation of a New England colony to New Jersey soil, Levermore (*The Republic of New Haven*, 120) says most aptly: "It seems to me that, after 1666, the New Haven of Davenport and Eaton must be looked for upon the banks, not of the Quinnipiac, but of the Passaic. The men, the methods, the laws, the officers, that made New Haven Town what it was in 1640, disappeared from the Connecticut Colony, but came to full life again immediately in New Jersey. . . . Newark was not so much the product as the continuation of New Haven."

The first Assembly of New Jersey met at Elizabethtown on May 26, 1668, and remained in session five days. There were burgesses from Elizabethtown, Bergen, Woodbridge, Newark, Shrewsbury, and Middletown. A bill of "pains and penalties" was passed, resembling in many respects the Levitical laws. A second meeting of the Assembly in the following November considered the very vexed question of the validity of land titles granted by Governor Nicolls. As to his own grants, Carteret was always very careful to see to it that the titles of lands were purchased from the Indians. Although the number of Indians in the neighborhood was not large, yet they were sufficiently numerous to cause considerable annoyance to the whites if they were so inclined. The governor consequently ordered all newcomers to purchase of the Indians, but if they had previously purchased they were merely to pay their proper proportions.

This policy was undoubtedly a good one, for there was very little trouble between the Indians and the whites in New Jersey.

On the other hand, much trouble arose about the Monmouth Patent, which included Middletown, Shrewsbury, and other settlements. By Nicolls's grant, these settlements had power to pass such laws as they thought wise. In pursuance of this privilege, they held a local Assembly, June, 1667. They refused to recognize laws passed at the first session of the General Assembly. Furthermore, the deputies refused to swear fidelity and allegiance to the New Jersey proprietors, and when commissioners tried to collect assessments they met with a prompt refusal. The settlements demanded exemption from any such claims, citing their grants from Nicolls in support of this contention. At a meeting of the General Assembly, November, 1671, Middletown and Shrewsbury were declared guilty of contempt.

The trouble, unfortunately, did not stop here. On May 14, 1672, the representatives of Bergen, Newark, Woodbridge, Elizabethtown, and Piscataway met to elect a president. This meeting was not in accord with Philip Carteret's wishes. The choice of president of this Assembly fell on James Carteret, said to be an illegitimate son of Sir George Carteret. He claimed to have a warrant from his father. This meeting declared him not only president of the Assembly but of the whole province. This was open and declared rebellion. Governor Carteret then accepted his Council's advice to depart for England, leaving John Berry in charge. When the governor arrived in England, he stated the condition of affairs to the Lords Proprietors. As a result, James Carteret was ordered immediately to Carolina; and the New Jersey authorities were required to recognize Nicolls's grants to the insurgent settlements. As a result of the publishing of these orders, after Carteret's return in 1674 peace was soon established throughout the province. In July, 1674, Lord Berkeley was induced to give up his grant in order that a more definite boundary settlement might be established between his own territory and that of Sir George Carteret. The deed of division was executed on July 1, 1676. From this time till 1702, the two provinces of East and West Jersey were separate and independent.

After the reconquest of New Netherland by the Dutch in 1673, Elizabethtown, Woodbridge, Newark, and Piscataway surrendered to the New Amsterdam military tribunal. This consisted of the commanders Cornelius Evertsen and Jacob Binckes and Captains Anthony Colve, Boes, and Van Zyle. The ownership of all lands by the English was legalized and confirmed and placed on an equality with the right of ownership enjoyed by the Dutch. Citizens conducting themselves rightly were to be exempt from bearing arms against England. The laws of the Netherlands determining the descent of property were to be enforced, yet the citizens might freely dispose of their possessions. Liberty of conscience was not to be interfered with. These terms were entirely satisfactory to the people. Each town was directed to nominate, by a plurality of votes, six persons for schepens, or magistrates. Likewise, two deputies for the purpose of nominating three persons for schouts and three for secretaries. From the nominations thus made the Council selected three magistrates for each town, and a schout and a secretary for the six towns collectively.

The Dutch authorities somewhat doubted the loyalty of the English, so they sent commissioners to visit the villages of New Jersey and take the oath of each inhabitant. A report was made to the authorities of all those who had taken the oath and of those who had not. A code of laws was promulgated on November 18th, considerably milder than the drastic Levitical code of 1668. It remained in force only until the Treaty of Westminster, February 19, 1674, when New Netherland was finally ceded to England. After that treaty New Jersey once more passed into the hands of the English.

Reference has been made to the decision of the crown lawyers that the provinces belonging to the Duke of York before the Dutch Conquest reverted to the king after the Treaty of Westminster. Charles II., however, June 29, 1674, issued a new patent to his brother. Chalmers claims that the Duke of York was really pleased with this decision, because he got back New Jersey, the loss of which was deeply deplored by Governor Nicolls. The new patent ignored the claims of Berkeley and Carteret. The latter protested vigorously and sought the aid of Charles II., with whom he was a favorite. Sir George Carteret was completely successful, and in July, 1674, he received not only his own former grant but the eastern part of New Jersey as well. No notice was taken of the western part of the territory, which Berkeley had sold to some Quakers for £1,000. This caused some territorial entanglements which were not unravelled until two years later by the " Quintipartite Deed."

When in October, 1674, Sir Edmund Andros assumed the governorship of New York, he did not assert his full authority over New Jersey. Nevertheless, he assumed an overlordship over the province and gave William Dyer power to collect the customs the duke had established throughout his territory. We have seen that this led to a serious clash between Andros and Carteret in 1676, which was not settled until the New Jersey proprietor was finally sustained in his independence by the king. The relations between the two governors became more and more strained until 1680, when Carteret was arrested, imprisoned, tried, and acquitted, and then deposed from the governorship of his province at the command of Andros. The Duke of York repudiated Andros's brutal activity, and in 1680 relinquished all claims to New Jersey. Andros's action in this matter is generally accredited with being the major cause of his recall.

Let us now turn our attention for a moment to West Jersey. Berkeley had sold his half-interest to John Fenwick on the 18th of March, 1673. The latter had been a member of the Parliamentary army and had afterward turned Quaker. In this purchase Fenwick was associated with Edward Byllinge, likewise a Quaker. These men wished to establish an asylum in America where they could worship with freedom from persecution. In the deed of purchase, Fenwick was named trustee for Byllinge. Shortly after, a land dispute arose between these two men, and William Penn was called in as arbitrator. He awarded nine-tenths of the purchase to Byllinge and one-tenth to Fenwick, together with a sum of money. Fenwick at first refused to accept this settlement. Later, however, when Byllinge became financially involved, Fenwick, as his trustee, handed over the nine-tenths to William Penn, Gawaine Laurie, and Nicholas Lucas. The transference of title was signed February 10, 1674. Soon after, Fenwick's one-tenth likewise passed under the control of these men. The most prominent of these purchasers was William Penn. Through his influence two land purchasing and colonizing associations were formed. One of these consisted of Yorkshire Friends and the other of London Friends. In 1677 commissioners were sent out to govern the province.

In June, 1675, Fenwick sailed up the Delaware with his children, relatives, settlers, and servants, and landed at the mouth of a creek called by the Dutch Varkin's Kill, or "Hog's Creek," near the Swedish settlement of Elsinburg. Fenwick named the place Salem, "peace." These high-handed proceedings aroused the ire of Governor Andros, who demanded by what authority Fenwick settled there. Following this up, the former had an order passed by the Council, December 5, 1675, that Fenwick be not received as owner of lands on the Delaware. Furthermore, Fenwick was charged with granting land, and dispossessing owners of their lands. Having refused to obey a peremptory order to submit himself to the jurisdiction of New York, orders were next issued for his arrest. Being brought a prisoner to New York in December, 1676, a special court was summoned the following month to try his case. He was compelled to give a bond for £500 not to act in a public capacity and a similar bond to prosecute his case before the king. Thereupon he was released and permitted to return to Salem. Immediately upon his arrival he assumed all the privileges of proprietorship, appointed officials, and made preparations for defence. Affairs were conducted in this manner until 1678, when Andros made some minor provisions for a local government.

We have referred to the first boundary settlement between East and West Jersey. The second was called the "Quintipartite" from the number of persons concerned in it. They were Sir George Carteret, William Penn, Gawaine Laurie, Nicholas Lucas, and Edward Byllinge. The purpose of the conference was to readjust the boundary between East and West Jersey. It was felt that the previous boundary between the two provinces, a line running from Barnegat to "a certain creek on Delaware River next adjoining to and below" Rancocas Creek, south of Burlington, was too indefinite and very unfair. The new boundary was to run from Little Egg Harbor to the forty-first degree of latitude on Hudson River. Thence it was to extend in a straight line to the northernmost branch of Delaware River. From that point it was to extend southward to the most southerly line of Little Egg Harbor. The "Deed" was executed on July 1, 1676, and was an attempt to divide East and West Jersey into two equal parts. Later, in 1687, we find Keith trying to carry out this intention of an equal division. He ran the line from Egg Harbor northwardly to the south branch of Raritan River. Had he extended the line to Delaware River as the "Deed" called for, West Jersey would have contained about fifty-four thousand acres less than East Jersey.

When Sir George Carteret died, in 1680, he left his property in East Jersey to the Earl of Sandwich and others in trust for the benefit of his creditors. The property was sold in 1680, but for some reason or other a transfer was never made; so in 1681 the property was finally sold to the highest bidder. William Penn, with eleven associates, most of whom had already been interested in West Jersey, were the purchasers, paying £3,400. Afterward, each of these twelve men sold half of his interest to twelve others, making twenty-four proprietors of the province.

The crowning glory of the Quaker movement in Jersey was that document of liberty known as *The Concessions and Agreements of the Proprietors, Freeholders, and Inhabitants of the Province of West Jersey in America.* This was first published on March 3, 1677. Penn is held to be the author of this very democratic document. The people had complete control of all local affairs, while the proprietors had but little power in the government. At first the people and proprietors elected ten men as commissioners. Later, each ten of the hundred electors selected a commissioner. The Assembly was chosen very much in the same manner as the commissioners. The people selected their own justices and constables. Equal taxation and religious toleration were among the rights guaranteed to the people. It was declared that "No Men or number of Men upon Earth hath power or Authority to rule over Men's consciences in religious Matters." Before anyone could be deprived of "Life, Limb, Liberty, Estate, Property, or any way hurt in his Privileges, Freedom, or Franchises," he was tried by a jury consisting of "Twelve good and lawful Men of his Neighborhood." Perjury was punished severely, while in cases of murder and treason the sentence was left to the General Assembly "to determine as they in the Wisdom of the Lord shall judge meet and expedient." One found guilty of bribing the Assembly was ever afterward ineligible as a member of the General Assembly. These "Concessions" were read before and after every session of the General Assembly and to the people four times a year in every court in the province. The document is probably the "first example of Quaker legislation." The settlers on Fenwick's "tenth" were not to enjoy the privileges of the code.

Mention has been made of the fact that the Quakers organized two companies, one in Yorkshire and one in

A
Brief Account of the
# PROVINCE
OF
## EAST NEW JARSEY
IN
## AMERICA
Published by the
### SCOTS PROPRIETORS
Having INTEREST there.

For the Information of such, as may have a Desire to Transport themselves, or their Families thither.

WHEREIN

The Nature and Advantage of, and Interest in a Foreign Plantation to this Country is Demonstrated.

EDINBURGH,
Printed by JOHN REID. Anno DOM. 1683.

---

# THE
# HISTORY
OF
## THE COLONY
OF
NOVA-CÆSARIA, OR NEW-JERSEY;

CONTAINING,

AN ACCOUNT OF ITS FIRST SETTLEMENT, PROGRESSIVE IMPROVEMENTS,

THE ORIGINAL AND PRESENT CONSTITUTION, AND OTHER EVENTS,

TO THE YEAR 1721.

WITH

SOME PARTICULARS SINCE;

AND

A SHORT VIEW OF ITS PRESENT STATE.

By SAMUEL SMITH.

BURLINGTON, IN NEW-JERSEY:
Printed and Sold by JAMES PARKER: Sold also by DAVID HALL, in PHILADELPHIA. MDCCLXV.

Title-pages of one of the earliest tracts, and of the first comprehensive account of New Jersey.
*From the originals in the New York Public Library, Lenox Branch.*

London, having as their object the purchase of land in the New World for settlement purposes. In 1677 the proprietors sent commissioners to buy land from the natives, and in the same year members of both companies, together with others, sailed on the ship *Kent* from London. It is said that Charles II., while cruising for pleasure on the Thames, came across them while they were on the point of embarkation to America. On learning who they were and what was their purpose, he gave them his blessing. The expedition reached New Castle, August 16, 1677, and proceeded thence to Raccoon Creek, where a landing was made. There were in all two hundred and thirty persons. After an exploration of the territory, the Yorkshire commissioners chose the territory from the falls of the Delaware southward as the scene of their future activities. The London commissioners selected what is now the site of Gloucester. The former is known as the first or Yorkshire "tenth," and the latter as the second or London "tenth."

When the Yorkshire commissioners found that the London commissioners were going to settle so near them, they proposed that the two combine and lay out a town for mutual protection against the Indians. The Yorkshire Company claimed the larger share, as their land was the best in the woods. The London Company, being few and realizing they would be at the mercy of the Indians, reluctantly agreed. A surveyor was employed to divide the site on which they had determined to locate the town. A main street was surveyed, on each side of which lots were laid out. The Yorkshire Company took the easternmost lots, while the other lots fell to the share of the London Company. At first the new town received the name of New Beverly, but afterward it was called Bridlington, and still later the name was changed to Burlington.

The proprietors of West Jersey appointed Edward Byllinge governor, who in turn appointed Samuel Jennings as his deputy. Jennings arrived in September, 1681. He was an approved minister of the Quakers, and his experience, candor, probity, and ability rendered him useful to the whole society of that people in the province. Although his temper was hasty, he was always obliging and even affectionate. In spite of this, he was not always treated kindly and fairly.

The Assembly of May, 1683, decided that both the title and government were purchased by William Penn and his associates. Fearing that Byllinge might release Jennings from his office as deputy governor, the Assembly appointed him governor. Jennings was sent to England for the confirmation of his election and to consult with Byllinge. Thomas Olive, speaker of the General Assembly, was appointed deputy governor *pro tem*. This action of the Assembly precipitated the Byllinge-Jennings dispute, which was finally put in the hands of George Fox, George Whitehead, and twelve other prominent Quakers to decide. A decision was rendered in October, 1684. Byllinge was declared to be the lawful governor and the power of the General Assembly to choose a chief executive was denied.

Deputy Governor Jennings and the Assembly shortly afterward agreed upon "Certain Fundamental Principles" of government. There were ten articles in all and they breathed the spirit of democracy. They provided for annual elections of the Assembly by the free people of the province. The governor was given the privilege of calling the Assembly in extraordinary session if he deemed it necessary. The governor was denied the power of raising military forces or of making war unless ordered to do so by the Assembly. He was likewise denied the power of making or enacting any laws whatsoever. Should he attempt to do so, he was to be declared an enemy of the people. The Assembly should not be prorogued without its own consent before the expiration of a whole year from the day of election. The consent of the Assembly was necessary before the governor and council could levy a tax or raise any sum of money whatever. All officers of State were to be nominated by the Assembly and were to be solely responsible to that body. The governor could not make treaties, send ambassadors, or enter into alliances without the Assembly's consent. No tax or custom could be voted for a longer time than for one whole year. There was to be freedom of conscience and worship, and no one was to be debarred from office by his religious belief.

A dispute that had arisen between the settlers of New Jersey and the Governor of New York now reached a critical stage. Very early in the history of the settlement, the governor had levied a tax of ten per cent on imported goods brought to Hoorn Kill. There was, in addition, a tax on exports. When settlers began to arrive on the Delaware they were charged five per cent on the invoice value of their goods and not on their net cost. The right of the agents of the Duke of York to collect these duties was questioned, and through their friends in England the colonists made a most vigorous protest. Chiefly through the instrumentality of William Penn, the Duke of York finally consented to put the question in the hands of a commission for decision. The commission, after considerable time had elapsed, in turn referred it to Sir William Jones, whose opinion was to be final. The verdict was against the duke, and in August, 1680, he declared West Jersey free from the obnoxious duties. On the 6th of that month, the duke furthermore granted to William Penn and others a complete release of West Jersey.

Furthermore, two months later, East Jersey was released and thus both the Jerseys became independent of New York. Later, as we have seen, Penn and eleven associates purchased the Carteret interests in East Jersey, and on the 14th of March, 1682, a new grant was made them, which was fuller and more explicit than its predecessors. Finally, on November 23, 1683, King Charles II. formally recognized the proprietors' right of soil and government. The twenty-four proprietors formed a "Council of Proprietors." They were given power to appoint, oversee, and displace all officers necessary for the management of their property. Robert Barclay, a Scotch Quaker, was appointed governor.

He was of unblemished character and had considerable influence with the king. Grahame says of him: "He was admired by scholars and philosophers for the stretch of his learning and the strength and subtility of his understanding, and endeared to the members of his religious fraternity by the liveliness of his zeal, the excellence of his character, and the services which his pen had rendered to their cause." He was allowed to exercise his authority through a deputy. He chose Thomas Rudyard, a prominent lawyer of London.

Before the two Jerseys succeeded in shaking off their dependence upon New York, and while West Jersey was engaged in its disputes with the Duke of York, East Jersey was at odds with its governor. Philip Carteret convened the Assembly at Elizabeth in October, 1681. The governor claimed the proprietor had the authority to alter the concessions of 1665. The Assembly just as emphatically denied the proprietor this authority and sent the governor and Council the following communication: "It is the opinion of this House that we are now about ours and the Country's businesse. Everything is beautifull in season. This House expects those Acts already before you should be passed and returned back to this House." To this the governor and Council made reply: "True wisdome would teach you better manners than to Stile Yorselves the Generall Assembly. Doubtless there was no want of Ignorance and Disloyalty where this Bratt had its educac'on insomuch as that the generall assembly consists of the Governor Councell and Deputies, ergo, the Deputies no generall assembly. It was Lucifer's Pride that putt him upon settling himselfe where God never intended to sett him and his Presumption produced or was forerunner of his fall. . . . Everything being beautiful in its season and so we bid you farewell." Thus was dissolved the last Assembly under the administration of Governor Carteret.

The death of Charles II. brought about very important changes in both East and West Jersey. James II., upon his accession, aimed at three things: first, the concentration of his power in the American colonies; secondly, the abolition of popular government; thirdly, the reduction of the colonies to absolute dependency. He issued *quo warranto* proceedings in the courts to cancel the charters of East and West Jersey, as well as those of other colonies. To Sir Edmund Andros was assigned the task of establishing a centralized government. James was told his revenues might be increased by strengthening his power over East and West Jersey and other provinces. He set about doing this, regardless of the three charters he had granted while Duke of York. The proprietors remonstrated. They petitioned against the action of the Governor of New York in seizing vessels trading to New Jersey. They told the king that he had not granted them New Jersey out of benevolence, but that £12,000 had been expended for it. As to not paying so much custom as New York, they replied that New Jersey was a separate government—that New York laws were not binding in New Jersey. But if the king desired, they would put the duty as high as it was in New York. And finally, if the king wanted a change in government, they would let him appoint one of their number as governor of both East and West Jersey.

The only request the king granted them was the appointment of an officer at Perth Amboy to collect the customs. This was, however, strictly in the line of his own interests. Nothing could keep James from involving New Jersey with the other colonies, whose charters and constitutions he had resolved to annul. This persistency led the proprietors of East and West Jersey to offer to surrender their rights, thinking that by so doing they might obtain from the king a reconfirmation of this grant. Gawaine Laurie had been appointed Deputy Governor of East Jersey in 1686, but he was shortly succeeded by Lord Neil Campbell. The latter did not remain long in the province, but appointed Andrew Hamilton as his substitute.

In April, 1688, during Hamilton's administration, the proprietors surrendered their rights to James II. East and

West Jersey were annexed to Governor Andros's dominion and Francis Nicholson was appointed lieutenant-governor. Andros created considerable surprise by retaining all the officials in office. The change in government was thus only nominal, the actual administration of affairs being confided to the governor's lieutenant. Andros's control over the Jerseys, however, was not long, for James II. was compelled to flee from England and William of Orange succeeded him, as William III.

# CHAPTER XI

### PENN'S "HOLY EXPERIMENT," 1681–1685

IT may be significant that at the height of Cromwell's power Quakerism first made its appearance. It was the most extreme form of Protestantism of the day, and Cromwell was a most liberal-minded statesman in his treatment of religious sects. It was he, for example, who first encouraged the Jews to return to England after a practical banishment of three hundred and fifty years; and it was he who encouraged an enlargement of their political privileges in at least one of the colonies. This large-minded tolerance can be best appreciated when we understand to what extent the attitude of the Quakers in social and political matters frequently subjected them to punishment. There were many who refused to pay tithes, or to testify under oath, or to lift their hats in the presence of a magistrate. Their lack of ecclesiastical organization frequently led to their being confounded with fanatical enthusiasts. Many of them courted persecution by reason of their missionary zeal, and their unfortunate confusion with the fanatics instilled in the minds of the people a feeling of horror at the spread of their doctrines. Nevertheless, Cromwell was not disposed to annoy them, and, as a matter of fact, he counted a number of prominent Quakers among his friends.

One of the most notable conversions to Quakerism after the Restoration was that of William Penn. He was born in London, October 14, 1644. His father, Sir William Penn, had been a vice-admiral of Cromwell's fleet, but, having made his peace with Charles II., he was knighted and continued in the enjoyment of his former honors. Sir William had lent the king a considerable sum of money, which by 1681, with accumulated interest, amounted to about £16,000, and as the exchequer was always low this obligation was not cancelled until long after. Even then it was not settled in money, but by the transfer of a large tract of land in America to his son. Young William received his early education at Chigwell and under a private tutor on Tower Hill. At sixteen he was sent to Christ Church, Oxford, and while an undergraduate there showed a decided leaning toward the Puritans. After hearing Thomas Loe preach, he was greatly influenced by the teachings of the Quakers, and it was at Oxford that he and other students became converted to the doctrines of that sect. His father had high ambitions for his son and was exceedingly alarmed at his religious tendencies, consequently in 1661 he was taken away from Oxford—or, as some claim, "sent down"—and placed with some fashionable friends at Paris in the hope of diverting his mind. This plan seemed for a while to prove successful; for after studying hard at a Huguenot college in Saumur for a year or more, and after travelling a year in Italy, Penn returned to England, a man of the world. Again, however, he heard Loe preach, and this time he made a final decision to throw aside his worldly prospects, disappoint his father, and cast his lot with the Quakers.

After studying law at Lincoln's Inn, he happened to visit Ireland, and at Cork was imprisoned for attending a Quaker meeting. This was by no means the first time he underwent imprisonment for his religious views, but the influence of his father usually secured his release. Sir William would have forgiven his son almost anything, even his objectionable manner of speech, but he could not brook young Penn's refusal to lift his hat not only to himself but to the Duke of York or even to the king. This was quite too much for the old gentleman's endurance, and he turned his son out of doors. Afterward father and son became reconciled through the entreaties of Lady Penn and the representations of influential friends who admired in the young man his lofty character and his dauntless courage. Sir William died in 1670.

Penn's accession to the Quakers was a great help to that sect. He was well born, well educated, eloquent, and possessed of a considerable fortune. He did much to differentiate the sect from the fanatical rabble with which it had been unjustly confused, and in other ways he used all his influence to better the condition of the Friends. He often pleaded with the king and judges to release them from prison, and at times was successful, but, as a rule, the persecution was as vigorous as ever.

Penn had often thought of establishing a colony for the Quakers in America, and it was with this end in view that he had obtained a part of the New Jersey grant. Friends flocked to this colony in large numbers, and so successful did the venture prove that Penn thought even more seriously than ever of establishing an asylum of his own in the New World. The government, which owed his father £16,000, failing to satisfy the debt, Penn proposed that he be granted a province in America by way of settlement. This proposition was accepted and the terms of the charter were drawn up and signed by the king on March 4, 1681.

Penn thus became proprietor of a large domain. He drew up the charter himself in imitation of that of Maryland, although in at least two very important respects it differed from it. Unlike the Maryland charter, this did not grant exemption from crown or Parliamentary taxation. Also, laws enacted by the Pennsylvania legislative body were required to be sent to England for the royal approval, while those of Maryland when confirmed by the proprietor were not subject to this revision. The eastern boundary of Penn's province was the Delaware. The line began twelve miles north of New Castle and, extending northward to the forty-third degree of latitude, ran westward five degrees.

The southern boundary was partly an arc of a circle having a radius of twelve miles north of New Castle and with that town as its centre. At the supposed intersection of this arc and the fortieth degree of north latitude, the line was to run thence by a straight line westward to the limits of the longitude mentioned as the western end of the northern boundary. By a provision of the charter, Penn was to pay to the king two beaver skins, which were to be delivered at Windsor Castle on the first day of January in every year. This tribute was paid by the Penns until 1780. In order to have an entrance to the Delaware, Penn bought of the Duke of York that strip of territory afterward known as the "Lower Counties," comprising New Castle, Kent, and Sussex of what is now the State of Delaware. In all, the duke made three conveyances in August, 1682. He released all his rights to the province by the first; the town of New Castle and the land lying within a twelve-mile circuit of the courthouse were granted by the second; and the land beginning twelve miles south of New Castle and extending southward to Cape Henlopen was granted by the third conveyance. Profiting by the trouble experienced with the New England colonies, especial care was taken with Penn's charter to define the proprietor's powers and to preserve the supremacy of the crown. Though drawn up by Penn, it was revised by Lord Chief Justice North and the attorney-general, Sir William Jones. The revisers added the important clauses to which reference has been made.

Penn proposed at first to call his province New Wales, for, as he wrote in a private letter, it was a pretty hilly country. But, it is said, the secretary, who was a Welshman, objected to this name. Penn then suggested Sylvania, and to this the king added "Penn," out of honor for William's father, the admiral. Penn modestly objected to this, fearing it would be considered a piece of vanity on his part. He even offered the under-secretaries twenty guineas to change the name, but the offer was refused and the province was called Pennsylvania.

Penn himself gives us a most interesting account of the naming of his province. It appears in a letter to his friend Robert Turner, and bears the date March 5, 1681—the day after he came into possession of the charter. After formally greeting his friend, Penn adds that "after many waitings, watchings, solicitings, and disputes in council, this day my country was confirmed to me under the great seal of England, with large powers and privileges, by the name of Pennsylvania, a name the king would give it, in honour of my father. I chose New Wales, being, as this, a pretty hilly country, but Penn being Welsh for *a head*, as Penmanmoire, in Wales, and Penrith in Cumberland, and Penn in Buckinghamshire, the highest land in England, called this Pennsylvania, which is, *the high* or *head woodlands;* for I proposed, when the secretary, a Welshman, refused to have it called New Wales, *Sylvania*, and they added *Penn* to it, and though I much opposed it, and went to the king to have it struck out and altered, he said it was past, and would take it upon him; nor could twenty guineas move the undersecretaries to vary the name, for I feared lest it should be looked on as a vanity in me, and not as a respect in the king, as it truly was, to my father, whom he often mentions with praise."

In the autumn of 1681, a vessel from London and one from Bristol started out for Penn's province, with colonists and three commissioners aboard. A third vessel—the *Amity*, from London—did not leave England until April of the next year. The *John and Sarah*, from London, was the first vessel to arrive, and the *Bristol Factor* soon followed on December 11th. The latter vessel anchored at what is Chester now, but then called Upland. That night the vessel was caught in the ice, and the emigrants were compelled to land and spend the winter at that place. The inhabitants offered them the best hospitality they could. There was not, however, sufficient room for all, and some were compelled to find shelter by digging caves in the ground or by making earthen huts. Some of the colonists were still living in this manner when Penn arrived the next year. There were, perhaps, at this time two thousand persons in the province.

Less than a month after the king had signed the patent, Penn sent his cousin, Colonel William Markham, as deputy governor, to take possession of the country. He was instructed to call a council of nine to assist him in the administration of the government and to determine the boundary lines with Maryland. Courts were to be established and the peace was to be maintained. In addition to the king's declaration announcing the grant of the patent and a command to render obedience, Markham carried a most interesting letter addressed to the colonists already settled in the province. It shows better than anything else Penn's liberal intentions on assuming the proprietorship of the colony.

"My friends," wrote he, "I wish you all happiness, here and hereafter. These are to let you know that it hath pleased God, in his providence, to cast you within my lot and care. It is a business that, though I never undertook before, yet God has given me an understanding of my duty, and an honest mind to do it uprightly. I hope you will not be troubled at your change and the king's choice, for you are now fixed at the mercy of no governor that comes to make his fortune great; you shall be governed by laws of your own making, and live a free, and, if you will, a sober and industrious people. I shall not usurp the right of any, or oppress his person. God has furnished me with a better resolution, and has given me his grace to keep it. In short, whatever sober and free men can reasonably desire for the security and improvement of their own happiness, I shall heartily comply with, and in five months I resolve, if it please God, to see you. In the mean time pray submit to the commands of my deputy, so far as they are consistent with the law, and pay him those dues (that formerly you paid to the order of the governor of New York) for my use and benefit, and so I beseech God to direct you in the way of righteousness, and therein prosper you and your children after you. I am your true friend,—William Penn."

Penn's frame of government was completed and published in the spring of 1682. In the preamble he sets forth his ideas about the origin, nature, and object of government. It is of divine origin, he claimed. "Its object is to encourage the well disposed, to shield virtue and reward merit, to foster art and promote learning." The sovereign power was to reside in the governor and the freemen of the province. The people were to elect two bodies to legislate, the Council and the Assembly. The proprietor reserved only for himself the right to preside at the Council and to have three votes. His deputy or agent was to have the same prerogative. Seventy-two persons were to be chosen by universal suffrage for three years to form a Council. One-third of these were to retire every year, and their places were to be filled by others newly elected. This popular body was to prepare and propose bills, and to it likewise were intrusted the execution of the laws and the preservation of peace. It could likewise " decide upon the sites of new towns and cities, build forts, harbors, and markets, make and repair roads, inspect the public treasury, erect courts of Justice, establish primary schools, and reward the fruits of useful inventions and discoveries."

For the more efficient transaction of business, the members of this body were to be divided into four grand committees: one on plantations; one on justice and safety; one on trade and treasury; and another on manners, education, and arts. Authority to convene and prorogue the Assembly was granted the governor and Council. During the first year every freeman was to have a seat in the Assembly. After that time, however, its membership was to be limited to a representative body of two hundred until the population justified an increase, but the number was not to exceed five hundred. Annual elections were to be held and voting was to be by ballot. The Assembly had the power to confirm but not to initiate legislation. It could not appoint the justices and sheriffs, but could draw up a list of nominees from which the governor was to choose one-half. The first draft which Penn made of his charter was somewhat different from the one he finally gave out and of which we have just given a synopsis. The first draft made the Assembly similar to the English House of Commons. It was to have the same privileges, and, in fact, Magna Charta and all confirmatory laws were to form a part of the fundamental law. Penn signed the second draft of the Frame of Government on the 25th of April, 1682.

In August, 1682, Penn fitted out the vessel *Welcome*, of three hundred tons, to convey him to his province, but it was the 1st of September before he and his hundred fellow passengers finally set sail. During the voyage smallpox broke out among the passengers. The attack was mild at first, but later proved to be of such a virulent type that more than thirty died on the voyage. Penn devoted himself constantly to the alleviation of the sufferings of his fellow voyagers.

Nine weeks after sailing, toward the end of October, they anchored in the harbor of New Castle. Here they were welcomed by the Swedes, English, and Dutch who had preceded them to the new country. The day after he arrived, Penn assembled the people in the courthouse and formally took possession of the province. He made a speech, asserting as the reason of his coming "a desire to found a free and virtuous State in which the people should rule themselves." He spoke to them of the constitution which he had made for Pennsylvania and likewise promised the inhabitants of the territory which he had purchased from the Duke of York the same privileges. The representatives of the Duke of York gave Penn the key of the fort and presented him with "turf and twig, and water and soil of the River Delaware."

Penn then journeyed on to Upland, a Swedish settlement founded probably about forty years before. Landing at the village on Sunday, October 29, 1682, Penn turned to his friend Thomas Pearson, and said: "Providence has brought us here safe. Thou hast been the companion of my perils. What wilt thou that I call this place?" Pearson, coming from the city of Chester, England, replied: "Call it Chester." Here an assembly was held, which passed the sixty-one statutes known as the Great Law of Pennsylvania. Penn now felt that his "Holy Experiment" was fairly well launched.

Penn had instructed his commissioners, who had preceded him the year before, to select a site for the capital of the province. After a careful investigation, his surveyor reported that the best place for the city was "the land lying at the junction of Delaware and Schuylkill Rivers, both of which were navigable." Here there was clay for brick and near by there were stone and marble quarries. Besides, the neighboring lands were not swampy. This land was owned by three Swedish brothers, Svenson by name, and was covered with a dense forest. The land for the new city, consisting of three hundred and sixty acres, was given by the three brothers upon condition that two hundred acres should be given to each of them in another part of the city together with a yearly rent of one half-bushel of wheat for each one hundred acres.

According to Penn's design, Philadelphia was to cover twelve square miles. He drew the plan of the city on paper, with the streets, docks, and open spaces. Two streets were to front the two rivers and were to be connected by an avenue one hundred feet in width. Streets and gardens were to adorn this avenue. Running at a right angle with this there was to be a broad street of equal width to be called High Street. This plan divided the city into four sections. In the centre there was to be reserved a public square of ten acres, and in the middle of each of the four sections there was to be a similar square of eight acres. Parallel with High Street there were to be eight streets fifty feet in width. Penn's desire was to have a "green country town," and to make this possible he encouraged the building of houses surrounded with gardens.

Penn was charmed with the country, and so expressed himself in a letter. "O how sweet," wrote he, "is the quiet of these parts, freed from the anxious and troublesome solicitations, hurries, and perplexities of woeful Europe!" Continuing, he says the land is like "the best vales of England watered by brooks; the air, sweet; the heavens, serene like the south of France; the seasons, mild and temperate; vegetable productions abundant, chestnut, walnut, plums, muscatel grapes, wheat and other grain; a variety of animals, elk, deer, squirrel, and turkeys weighing forty or fifty pounds, water-birds and fish of divers kinds, no want of horses; and flowers lovely for colour, greatness, figure, and variety. . . . The stories of our necessity [have been] either the fear of our friends or the scarecrows of our enemies; for the greatest hardship we have suffered hath been salt meat, which by fowl in winter and fish in summer, together with some poultry, lamb, mutton, veal, and plenty of venison, the best part of the year has been made very passable." As regards the climate, however, Penn has another story to tell. He writes "the weather often changeth without notice, and is constant almost in its inconstancy."— (Clarkson's *Life of Penn*, i, 350, 402.)

Penn now turned his attention to the Indians. He had the year before addressed them a most friendly letter at the same time he had addressed the people through his deputy governor, Colonel Markham. Upon Penn's arrival in his province, he soon won the love and the admiration of the Indians by going among them freely. He was present at their feasts, and watched the young men in their dances. They gave him the name of the great Onas. His treaty with a tribe of the Delaware or Lenape Indians was one of the most famous events of his first visit to the New World. Shackamaxon, meaning "the place of the eels," was the site of this most famous meeting. This spot had been used as a meeting place by the Indians even before

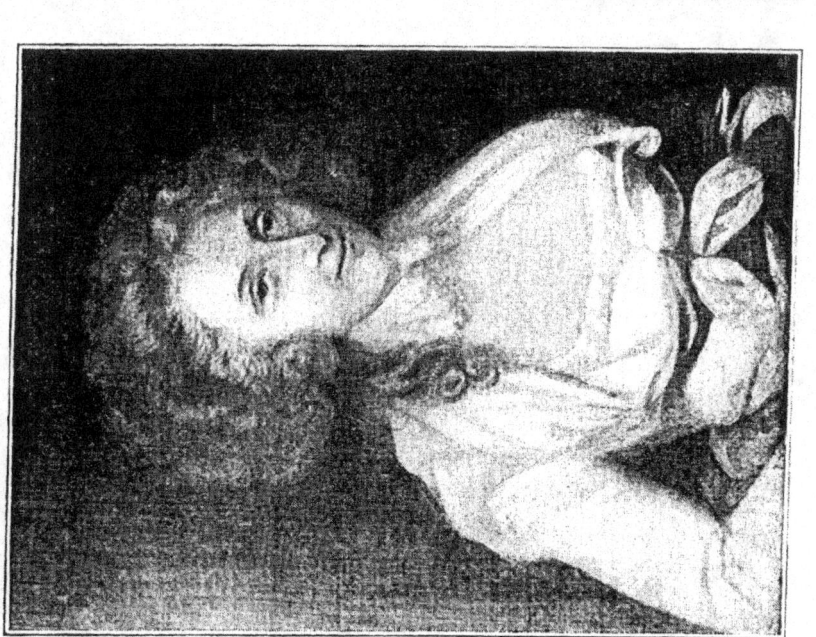

Mrs. Franklin, his second wife.     William Franklin, Governor of New Jersey.

From the original paintings in possession of *Dr. Thomas Hewson Bache, of Philadelphia.*

the arrival of the white men. A large elm tree grew in this space, and under this Penn stood and received the Indians. Colonel Markham was at his right. After the reception, the chief sachem Taiminent advanced a few steps, put on his head a chaplet into which was twisted a small horn, his symbol of authority, and sat down. On his right were the older sachems, while the middle-aged warriors arranged themselves around them in the form of a crescent. The younger men formed the outer circle. When all were seated, Taiminent announced their readiness to listen to the governor.

Penn thereupon arose and said: "The Great Spirit who ruled the heavens and the earth, the father of all men, bore witness to the sincerity of his wishes to dwell with them in peace and friendship, and to serve them with all his power. Himself and followers had met them unarmed, because their religion forbade the use of hostile weapons against their fellow creatures; they came not to injure others, that was offensive to the Great Spirit, but to do good, in which he delighted; having met in the broad pathway of truth and benevolence, they ought to disdain deception and to regulate their conduct by candor, fraternity, and love."

He then explained his treaty to them, and requested the sachems to sign it for themselves and their children. They used no oaths or seals, but the treaty was ratified both by the Quakers and the Indians with "yea."

Before leaving Chester, Penn's most important act had been the issuance of writs to the sheriffs of New Castle, Kent, Sussex, Chester, Philadelphia, and Bucks Counties, requiring them to summon all freeholders to assemble to elect representatives in the General Assembly that was to meet within a month. Before the fall of New Netherland, Sussex County was called "Hoornkill." Later, it received the name "Whorekill," and then "Deal." On December 25, 1682, Penn changed it to "Sussex." At the same time, "Jones" County was changed to "Kent." The Provincial Council was not organized until March of the following year. The Assembly met at Chester on the 14th of December, 1682. Only sixteen of the forty-two members were present. Nicholas Moore was elected speaker, and three committees were appointed. One of the committees was on elections and privileges, another for the preparation of bills, and a third on justice and grievances. A number of rules were adopted for the government of the Assembly. Any member could have access to all committees except those of secrecy. No member could leave on a journey during the session, except by express permission from the speaker. Any member who should strive to pervert the meaning of a question was to be expelled. No member might speak more than twice on a question, once before and once after it was put, and all long speeches without special point were to be stopped by the speaker. Any member could offer a bill, public or private, except a tax bill. The use of the names of the members and the use of all personalities were to be debarred from debate.

It is significant that at this first election of Assemblymen undue influences were used to elect a member from New Castle. The sheriff of that county employed unlawful means to procure the election of Abraham Mann. It is even more significant, perhaps, that after testimony was taken Mann was expelled and his opponent, John Moll, put in his place by a unanimous vote. Although the session lasted but three days, yet laws of importance were passed. The first annexed the Lower Counties to the province, and the second provided a naturalization law. Penn presented to the Assembly copies of the laws which had been prepared and published in England. These were adopted by the Assembly.

The most important action of this Assembly was, however, the enactment of " The Great Law." It contained sixty-nine sections and was presented by Penn. The code was entitled: " THE GREAT LAW, *or, the body of Laws of the province of Pennsylvania and territories thereunto belonging, passed at an assembly at Chester, alias Upland, the 7th day of the 10th month, December, 1682.*" March, of course, at that date was the first month. The first section contained the celebrated provision for "liberty of conscience." It read, in part, as follows:

"It is enacted by the authority aforesaid, that no person now or at any time hereafter living in this province, who shall confess and acknowledge one Almighty God to be the creator, upholder, and ruler of the world, and that professeth him or herself obliged in conscience to live peaceably and justly under the civil government, shall in anywise be molested or prejudiced for his or her conscientious persuasion or practice, nor shall he or she at any time be compelled to frequent or maintain any religious worship, place, or ministry whatever, contrary to his or her mind, but shall freely and fully enjoy his or her Christian liberty in that respect, without any interruption or reflection; and if any person shall abuse or deride any other for his or her different persuasion and practice in matter of religion, such shall be looked upon as a disturber of the peace, and be punished accordingly."

Every Christian twenty-one years old and "unstained by crime" was an elector, and was eligible for election to the Assembly. Every child twelve years old was to be taught some useful trade. Legal fees were to be low and published in every court of justice. Persons wrongfully imprisoned were to have double damages from the prosecutor.

After a visit to Lord Baltimore, when an ineffectual attempt was made to negotiate a settlement of the boundaries between the provinces of Pennsylvania and Maryland, Penn made preparations for the second Assembly. In addition to convoking the Assembly, he ordered the election of twelve men from each county to serve as delegates in the Provincial Council to be held at Philadelphia. The people departed from a literal observance of the writ by electing twelve men in all from each county. They petitioned at the same time that three of these might represent them in the Council and nine in the Assembly. Although Penn granted the petition, yet the change was not agreeable to at least one member. Nicholas Moore maintained that the change was grossly unconstitutional and that the action of the Council was treasonable. For this "unreasonable and impudent" conduct he was called before the governor and Council and severely reprimanded.

Exclusive of the Bill of Settlement, which was the result of Penn's submission of a new frame of government, the most important action taken by this Assembly [1683] was that relating to the excise. An excise tax and another on exports and imports were passed. In addition, Penn was asked to accept the revenues coming from a tax of twopence a gallon on all imported liquors, a penny on cider, and twenty shillings on every hundred pounds' worth of goods imported in merchandise, with the exception of molasses. Penn explained, however, that the collection of this duty would be difficult and costly, and proposed instead that at least £500 should be raised by voluntary subscriptions for the support of the government. "But some of the collectors were strangers, and had little influence; others were a little too great to be much imposed upon, many more were rich, and still others preferred their own ease to the people's good."

This Assembly likewise put itself on record as opposing a life tenure of offices by appointees of the governor, but as favoring Penn's power of appointment during his lifetime. Furthermore, the basis of representation was increased, the four grand committees of the Council and the governor's treble vote were abolished, and the time for holding the annual elections for members of the Council and Assembly was changed to the 10th of March. Two peculiar bills were introduced, but failed to become laws. One compelled young men to marry, and the other specified that only two kinds of clothes should be worn,—one suit for summer and one for winter.

This Assembly is chiefly notable, however, for the action taken leading to a decided enlargement of the scope of its authority. It was suggested that the House be allowed the privilege of proposing to the governor and the Provincial Council "such things as might tend to the benefit of the

# The FRAME of the GOVERNMENT
## OF THE
## Province of Pennsilvania
## IN
## AMERICA:

Together with certain

# LAWS

Agreed upon in England
## BY THE
# GOVERNOUR
## AND
Divers FREE-MEN of the aforesaid
## PROVINCE.

To be further Explained and Confirmed there by the first *Provincial Council* and *General Assembly* that shall be held, if they see meet.

Printed in the Year MDCLXXXII.

# THE
# FRAME
OF THE
## Government of Pennsilvania
IN
## AMERICA, &c.

**To all People,** *to whom these Presents shall come:*

**W**HEREAS **King Charles** the Second, by his Letters Patents, under the **Great Seal** of *England*, for the Considerations therein mentioned, hath been graciously pleased to Give and Grant unto Me **William Penn** *(by the Name of* **William Penn Esquire,** Son and Heir of **Sir William Penn** deceased*)* and to My **Heirs** and **Assigns** forever, *All that Tract of Land or Province, called* **Pennsilvania,** *in* America, *with divers great Powers, Preheminencies, Royalties, Jurisdictions and Authorities necessary for the Well-being and Government thereof.*

**Now know Ye,** That for the *Well-being* and *Government* of the said *Province,* and for the *Encouragement* of all the **Free-men** and **Planters** that may be therein concerned, in pursuance of the Powers aforementioned, I the said **William Penn** have *Declared,* *Granted* and *Confirmed,* and by these Presents for **Me**, my **Heirs** and **Assigns** do *Declare, Grant* and *Confirm* unto all the **Free-men, Planters** and **Adventurers** of, in and to the said Province These **Liberties, Franchises** and **Properties** to be held, enjoyed and kept by the **Free-men, Planters** and **Inhabitants** of and in the said *Province* of **Pennsilvania** forever.

*Imprimis,* That the *Government* of this *Province* shall, according to the *Powers* of the *Patent,* consist of the **Governour** and **Free-men** of the said *Province,* in the Form of a **Provincial Council** and **General Assembly,** by whom all *Laws* shall be made, Officers chosen and publick Affairs Transacted, as is hereafter respectively declared; That is to say,

II. That the **Free-men** of the said *Province* shall on the *Twentieth* day of the *Twelfth* Moneth, which shall be in this present Year *One Thousand Six Hundred Eighty and Two,* Meet and Assembly in some fit place, of which timely Notice shall be beforehand given by the **Governour** or his *Deputy,* and then and there shall chuse out of themselves **Seventy Two** Persons of most Note for their *Wisdom, Virtue* and *Ability,* who shall meet on the Tenth day of the First Moneth next ensuing, and alwayes be called and act as the **Provincial Council** of the said *Province.*

B                                                                III,

Title and first page of Penn's *Frame of Government.* From the original
in possession of the Historical Society of Pennsylvania.

Province." Penn conferred with his Council about the matter and decided to submit a new frame of government. After a lengthy debate, and with several important revisions, the Assembly adopted the Bill of Settlement, April 2, 1683. There were present when the bill was adopted fourteen members of the Council,—not counting Penn,—forty-three members of the Assembly, and four inhabitants of Philadelphia. The House was given greater legislative power, and it was provided that all bills should be published twenty days before the meeting of the Assembly, thus diminishing the danger of hasty legislation.

The new frame of government was shortly to be tested. The first meeting of the Assembly under its provisions was held in May, 1684. Two Philadelphians contested sharply for the honors of the speakership. Nicholas Moore, who afterward became chief justice, succeeded in winning the honor. It was he who had been reprimanded by the governor and Council during the second session of the Assembly. Twenty bills that had been previously passed by the council were enacted. One of these bills had as its object the protection of the proprietor and of his rights. A heavy penalty was to be inflicted upon anyone who should attempt to incite the people to hatred of him, or to dispossess him of his rights.

The first three years after Penn's arrival witnessed a great flow of immigrants into Pennsylvania. They came from various places in England, Wales, Holland, and Germany. Most of them, though not all, were Quakers. They were mostly husbandmen, tradesmen, and mechanics. Some had money when they came, but most had it to make in the New World. Some even brought the frames of their dwellings with them. They came so fast and in such large numbers that Penn deemed it wise to buy more land of the Indians. The records show that one purchase included land "as far back as a man could walk in three days." Penn, indeed, had good reason to feel contented with the success of his "Holy Experiment." Within three years from the time Philadelphia was founded, its population had reached two thousand five hundred, while there were more than eight thousand people in the whole province. New Netherland had not exceeded this growth during the whole first half-century of its existence. Penn had planned a school almost as soon as the colony was founded. In December, 1683, Enoch Flower began to teach in a hut divided into two apartments. "To learn to read," it cost "four shillings a quarter; to write, six shillings; boarding a scholar, to wit, diet, lodging, washing, and schooling, £10 a whole year." It was six years afterward when the public school was opened. George Keith was master, and his stipend was £50 per year, "besides a house for his family and school rooms."

Receiving news of the severe illness of his wife, and other matters requiring his presence in England, Penn decided to return. Before leaving, he called the Indians together at Pennsbury Manor, his country seat on the Delaware, and told them of his contemplated voyage. He asked them to live in peace with themselves and with the whites during his absence. He requested them not to drink too much fire-water, and at the same time forbade his own people to sell them brandy and firearms. He likewise sent a circular letter to the Quakers of the province, " urging them to be watchful over themselves, helpful to one another, circumspect and zealous." After concluding a treaty of peace with the Indians, Penn sailed in August, 1684, on the brig *Endeavor*, and arrived at his home in Sussex early in October. He found that the persecution of the Nonconformists had increased during the time of his absence, and he immediately set himself at work to try to obtain pardons for his friends and the adoption of Acts of Toleration. While in England, his wife died, and in 1696 he married Hannah Callowhill, of Bristol.

In Penn's absence, the executive power was intrusted to the Provincial Council. To Thomas Lloyd, a Welsh Friend, was given the great seal, in his capacity of president of the

Council. Lloyd first assumed that official dignity at a meeting of the Council at New Castle, August 18, 1684. At the preceding meeting, held in Sussex County on the 14th, Penn himself presided. William Markham was made secretary, and a surveyor-general, commissioners of the land office, and provincial judges were selected. Penn had not been absent long before troubles and quarrels arose in the province. Chief Justice Moore had been impeached by the Assembly for violence, partiality, and negligence, but had been acquitted on a technical error in the form of procedure. Nevertheless, the Assembly succeeded for the time being in having all places of trust closed to him. Patrick Robinson, clerk of the Provincial Court, was declared a public enemy for having refused to produce the minutes of the Assembly. An ineffectual attempt was made to disqualify him for office. A justice of the peace was dismissed from office, charged with uttering treasonable words against the king, and other officials were accused of extortion. It was furthermore charged that "gross immoralities were practised among the lower class of people inhabiting the caves on the bank of the Delaware." On the other hand, peace with the Indians had been kept, land improved and sold, laws enforced, courts established, and elections "regularly held and quietly conducted."

No doubt, one of the chief causes of trouble was that Penn's relation to the colony was of a twofold character. He was both governor and land owner. Those who were pressed, however mildly, for payment of their long overdue quitrents became angered, and expressed their resentment by electing representatives who opposed the government and made every effort to reduce its power. The Provincial Council, not proving effective, had transferred its executive power to five commissioners. Because two of these would not act, the Council resumed its executive powers and discharged its duties until new commissioners were appointed in February, 1688. At the meeting of the Assembly in 1688 ill feeling arose because, contrary to custom, the speaker was not presented to the commissioners and Council for confirmation. The Assembly then transacted its business behind closed doors.

Finding that government by commissions was a failure, Penn in 1688 appointed a single deputy, Captain John Blackwell, at one time an officer under Cromwell. This experiment also was far from a success. Blackwell was in the province only thirteen months, but during that time the colony was in one continuous political uproar. The deputy governor arrested the speaker of the former Assembly for trying to impeach Chief Justice Moore. He imprisoned and suspended David Lloyd, clerk of the Supreme Court, for refusing to hand over to him the records of that court. Doubting the constitutionality of all laws enacted during Penn's absence, he suspended them. In attempting to establish a militia, he was opposed by the Quakers. Thomas Lloyd was impeached for stirring up discontent and for refusing to sign the acts of the government. One member of the Council was debarred therefrom for not properly addressing the governor, and another was arraigned for publishing a copy of the constitution. Blackwell, in short, stirred up such an opposition to himself that he realized that his usefulness was at an end and requested his recall.

To provide for the vacant deputy governorship, Penn sent two commissions, which were to be presented to the Council for alternative choice. By one commission, the Council was empowered to select three persons, of whom the one receiving the largest number of votes was to act in place of a deputy governor until Penn should appoint one to act permanently in that capacity. By the other commission, the Council itself was to act in the place of the deputy and was given the privilege of electing its own president. Both these commissions were dated September 25, 1689. The Council decided upon the second plan, and Thomas Lloyd was elected president at a session of the Council held January 2, 1690. The Lower Counties were dissatisfied, fearing they would be neglected in the distribution of offices. They claimed that Philadelphia had robbed them of much of their business and that they had borne more than their share of taxation. As they could arrive at no satisfactory understanding, these three counties were cut off from the province, and Markham was made their lieutenant-governor. To this separation Penn assented reluctantly, foreseeing that it would cause future trouble.

A new danger arose. Penn feared that the dissensions in the province might be made a pretext in England for depriving him of his patent. His known friendship for James II. caused him considerable annoyance, and his enemies used it to stir up additional trouble in the province.

## CHAPTER XII

### *THE REVOLUTION OF 1688*

Louis XIV., with the "wily and indomitable" Frontenac, was plotting the overthrow of New York. Frontenac was to return to America with one thousand regulars, fall upon Albany, sail down the Hudson, and unite at New York with a French fleet. This would cut the Iroquois off from their supply of firearms and would make them an easy conquest. After that, New England would also be an easy capture. But when Frontenac landed in Canada, he found he had been anticipated by the Iroquois, who had laid waste all southern Canada, with Montreal as a centre, and had captured a magazine of rifles and ammunition. Consequently, Frontenac had to give up the conquest of New York and New England and turn his whole attention to the Iroquois. This put off the war temporarily. But James II. saw that it had to come, and set on foot a momentous scheme that had great results, among which may be mentioned the ultimate welfare of America, and the overthrow of Andros, if not, in truth, the overthrow of James himself.

When James II. became king, he brought to the throne a greater knowledge of England's American colonies than any other English king. This was owing to his long and varied experience, while Duke of York, as a colonial proprietor. As a Catholic, he determined to do all in his power to establish the Roman Catholic religion in England and in the colonies. Furthermore, immediately upon his accession to the throne, he determined to concentrate in himself all power, both in England and America. We have seen that, with this object in view, he had revoked the charter of New York which as Duke of York he had granted freely. The people of New York had rejoiced greatly when James was proclaimed king. They hoped that since he had interested himself so much in that colony while duke, this interest would be continued when he became king. Nor did his interest in the colony wane in the slightest, but it manifested itself in quite a different way from what the colonists expected.

In 1686, James's plan for the unification of all the English northern colonies took form at Whitehall. It was determined that in order to render them more capable of defending their borders against the French in Canada, these colonies should be united under one head. Then, again, two other reasons for unification should be urged in addition to the pressing necessity for defence against the French: first, the advisability of cementing a strong alliance with the Iroquois League; and secondly, the determination of James to strengthen his arbitrary power. It must be kept in mind always that the last mentioned was the all-controlling reason with the king. Everything else was subsidiary. To make his own power at home and in the colonies absolute, it was necessary to checkmate the French in their aggression upon the American borders. To accomplish this, it was indispensable that the northern colonies should present a united front to the French, and that the Iroquois League should be propitiated. The one controlling thought with James, we may repeat, was his extreme selfishness and his conscienceless determination to make his power absolute whatever might be the results.

Circumstances seemed to favor his plans. Massachusetts had been worsted in its quarrel with Charles II. and its charter had been annulled on a writ of *quo warranto* in

SIR WILLIAM KEITH
Governor of Pennsylvania.

LADY KEITH

1685. Plymouth had never secured a charter. Writs of *quo warranto* had been issued against the charter of Connecticut in 1685. The charter of Rhode Island had been proceeded against in the same way in 1686, though Andros did not get possession of the document any more than he did of the charter of Connecticut.

When James finally decided upon this consolidation of New England, he looked about him for a man to put at the head of affairs to carry out his arbitrary rule. His choice lay between Colonel Thomas Dongan, Governor of New York, and Sir Edmund Andros. He finally decided upon the latter, whom he had previously sent out as Governor of New York. Dongan, although a Catholic, was displaced. From his long American experience, "his administrative ability, his irreproachable private character, and, above all, his soldierly notions of prompt obedience to orders," Andros was just the agent to execute the king's arbitrary designs. Although fond of prelacy, he was not a Roman Catholic. He reached Boston on the 20th of December, 1686, as captain-general and governor of all New England, which included Massachusetts Bay, New Plymouth, New Hampshire, Maine, and the Narragansett country, or the King's Province. He was given the authority to make laws and levy taxes, with the consent of a council appointed by the crown. He was to allow no printing presses, except by special license. He was to encourage episcopacy, and to sustain authority by force. Personal liberty and the customs of the country were to be disregarded. None might leave the colony without a special permit. Probate fees were to be increased almost twenty-fold. Two companies of soldiers, mostly Irish Romanists, were raised in London and placed at Andros's disposal, in order that he might be able more effectively to execute the king's orders. The governor was to receive £1,200 as his salary.

New York, because of its peculiar relations to the Iroquois and to Canada, its great extent of territory, and its wealth, had demonstrated that a separate government was for it a necessity. But James II., pleased with the result of the consolidation of the New England colonies, determined, in spite of New York's claim to a separate government, to take a further step. New York and the Jerseys were to be included in the unification scheme. In this way, all the territory which the patent of James I., of 1620, had named "New England in America" would be brought, for the first time, under one royal English governor. Pennsylvania, possibly because the king stood in need of Penn's good will, was not to be included in the union. But all the rest of British North America, between Delaware Bay and Passamaquoddy Bay, and stretching across the continent from the Atlantic to the Pacific, was to be made a political whole under the governorship of one man, to be chosen by the king. Later, action was taken likewise against the charters of Maryland and Carolina, but the proceedings in these cases were not carried to an issue.

With this end in view, James revoked New York's half-granted charter and annexed that colony to New England. Dongan was notified of the change, and instructed to deliver to Andros the seal and records of the province. The former was assured that James was entirely satisfied with his services in the "most important British possession in America," and that he would be rewarded upon his return to England. On Saturday, the 11th of August, 1688, the new governor-general reached New York in state. He was received by Colonel Bayard's regiment of foot and a troop of horse. The king's new commission was read in Fort James, and then published at the City Hall. Immediately afterward, Andros sent for and received from Dongan the seal of the late government of New York. This he broke in the presence of the members of the Council, according to the king's instructions. In its stead, the great seal of United New England was thenceforth to be used. A proclamation was at once issued retaining in office all persons not removed by order of the king, and directing that the taxes be continued.

It was planned that Andros should have a Council composed of forty-two of the principal men from the colonies included in his "Dominion of New England in America." No place was fixed upon by the king as the capital of this dominion, but Andros quietly assumed that Boston would serve his purpose best. The governor was to communicate to his Council such of the royal instructions as he should find convenient. These councillors were to enjoy freedom of debate, and seven of them were necessary to constitute a quorum. In extraordinary emergencies, however, a smaller number was given permission to transact business. By the advice and consent of a majority of the Council, laws could be made and taxes imposed. The governor was authorized to suspend any councillor for good and sufficient cause; and he was required to nominate to the Plantation Committee persons fit to supply vacancies. In all appointments, whether councillors, judges, sheriffs, or any legal officers whatsoever, the governor-general was always to observe the greatest precautions. Especial care was to be taken that men of estate and ability thoroughly in harmony with the government should be selected. "Necessitous people" or people heavily in debt were to be ignored. All laws within the colonies at the time of unification were to remain in force until the governor and his Council should make others. Liberty of conscience in all religious matters was to be guaranteed to all law-abiding persons, in accordance with the king's declaration of April 4, 1687. Nothing was said about the Church of England in the instructions sent to Andros. Captain Francis Nicholson, commander of a company of the king's regulars stationed at Boston, was commissioned lieutenant-governor.

Almost immediately upon Andros's landing at Boston, Indian affairs claimed his attention. The day he reached New York he announced his arrival to the Marquis de Denonville, who represented French interests in Canada. He maintained that the Indians of the Five Nations were British subjects, and requested that the French should do them no injury. As Indian affairs were not running smoothly enough to suit Andros, he determined to go to Albany. He was accompanied by several of his councillors and fifty soldiers, and after reaching Albany he was joined by Nicholson, the lieutenant-governor, who came from Boston *via* Springfield. The Five Nations sent delegates to Albany to meet Andros and his councillors, and an interview was held in the town house. Here Andros was welcomed by the orator of the Mohawks, Sindacksegie. The next day, the meeting being continued, Andros addressed the Indians as " Children " and assured them they need now have no fears, inasmuch as the French and the English were friends. The Iroquois promised to have nothing to do with the French, but to treat them as friends, as Andros requested. The Mohawks expressed the desire that the old covenant that had been made with their ancestors be kept firm. " Then we were called Brethren, and that was also well kept; therefore, let the name Brethren continue, without any alteration." They requested Andros to endeavor to secure the release of the Indians who had been carried off as prisoners to France. " The Governor of Canada," said the Indian, " is pleasant with his eye, and speaks fair with his lips; but his heart is corrupt, and we find that the old covenant made with this government has been kept inviolate." Andros promised to do what he could to secure the return of the prisoners from France, and the following day—the 21st of September, 1688—the conference ended.

After a stay of two months in New York and Albany, Andros returned to Boston in October, 1688, to prevent if possible a second Indian war. The Indians of Maine had given considerable trouble near Casco Bay, and volunteer troops had been sent thither from Boston without orders from the governor-general. Andros took with him such of the New York records as he deemed necessary to have at hand during his absence. Nicholson was left in charge of affairs in New York, with the local councillors as advisers. The

A list of Debtors to the Estate of Coll. Francis Lovelace In the books of Isar: Bedlow deced: Inhabiting in Gravesend upon Long Island

| | |
|---|---|
| Catalina Barents | 77 : — |
| Micha Spicer | 208 : 8 |
| George Cumens | 127 : — |
| Richard Harbel | 113 : 4 |
| Charles Morgan | 80 : 12 |
| Capt Wilkins | 141 : 10 |
| Samuell Spicer | 320 : — |

**By the Governour**

You are hereby desired and required to give notice to ye above persons of yo Towne, That they appeare and pay to Mr Philipp Wells in ye sort ye summes herein mencioned being ye ballance of their Accts in Mr Isaak Bedloo's books, Or to summon them in his Maties Name to answer their neglect at ye Next Genall Court of Assizes to be held in this City, beginning ye 4th day of ye next month in default att their Perill. when also you are to make a returne of this Warrt. Given under my hand in New Yorke this 25th of Sept. 1676.

To ye Constable and Overss of Gravesend

ANDROSS

Manuscript list of debtors to the estate of Colonel Francis Lovelace, signed by Sir Edmund Andros. *From the original in the Emmet Collection.*

people of New York did not relish this tyrannical treatment. In the first place, they were most vehemently opposed to the annexation of New York to New England. Geographically, politically, and socially, New York was unlike the New England colonies. Annexation ignored their "natural and proper sentiments of local patriotism." However, they were not to be deprived of their identity much longer. Outside forces were working in their favor. England was on the verge of a political upheaval.

The rule of Andros in New England was insufferable. Here he carried things with a high hand. Unusual taxes were imposed without authority, little regard was had for the English common law, the press was closely muzzled, the writ of *habeas corpus* was suspended, and land titles were questioned that the officials might exact fees for new patents. The public records of all the defunct New England colonies were lodged in Boston, and those who desired to consult them were compelled to make a tedious and costly journey to that city. All deeds and wills, likewise, were registered there, and excessive fees were charged for their registry. The colonial representative assemblies were abolished, and the power of taxation was taken from the town meetings and given to the governor-general. When the Rev. John Wise protested in behalf of his town of Ipswich against this last act, he was thrown into prison and fined a sum equal to $1,000 in money of to-day, and then deprived of his ministerial orders.

The New England people could endure Andros no longer. Increase Mather, president of Harvard College, headed a commission that was sent over to England to protest against Andros's tyrannical acts. Mather presented addresses of thanks which he had brought from New England, and afterward submitted complaints of the "enslaved and perishing estate" of the inhabitants, by reason of the misgovernment of Andros. He was kindly received by James. But all final action was prevented by the Revolution of 1688.

James II.'s arbitrary rule and predilection for the Roman Catholic religion caused first dissatisfaction among his subjects and finally rebellion. The opinion that the King of England should be a Protestant was held alike by Episcopalians and Dissenters. Religious sects and political parties combined against the Catholic king. With one accord they turned to the Calvinist husband of Princess Mary as their "Deliverer." An invitation was accordingly sent to William of Orange, the Stadholder of the Dutch Republic, imploring him to come to their rescue. The long pent-up rebellion burst forth when on the 5th of November, 1688, William's expedition landed at Brixham, in Devonshire. Before the end of November, Englishmen of every rank and influence gathered round the standard of the Prince of Orange. James, at last realizing his danger, disbanded the royal army, threw the great seal into the Thames, and finally, with William's connivance, embarked for France on December 23d. Before Christmas, the last Stuart king had become a royal guest of Louis XIV. of France, and in England there was a vacant throne. William and Mary accepted the proffered crown on February 13, 1689, and were proclaimed King and Queen of England. Their first act was the confirmation of all Protestants in the offices they held on the preceding 1st of December. This proclamation did not, however, affect the English colonies.

When the news reached America late in March, 1689, that William and Mary had accepted the throne, it was hailed with uncontrolled joy. On April 18th, armed yeomanry began to pour into Boston. Andros now realized that the end of his rule had come. He tried to get aboard a frigate in the harbor, thinking thereby to escape to New York, where he might find refuge. But the Yankees were too quick for him. He was caught and thrown into jail, together with Chief Justice Joseph Dudley, who had insulted the people of New England by telling them that the only liberty left them was that of not being sold for slaves. Massachusetts restored its old government. Plymouth,

Rhode Island, and Connecticut quietly did the same. Andros was sent to England for trial the next year, but the colonists' complaints were dismissed. He governed Virginia from 1692 to 1698. From 1704 to 1706, he was governor of the island of Jersey. He afterward removed to London, where he died on February 24, 1714.

Thus came to an inglorious end the tyrannical rule of Sir Edmund Andros as governor-general of United New England. It is difficult to form a correct estimate of his character, though there cannot be two opinions as to his ability. He was probably better fitted for the post to which James appointed him than any other man of the time. The estimate put upon his character by early New England writers cannot be accepted without considerable qualification. They almost to a man denounced Andros as a "mere bigot, and minion, and tyrant, with hardly a redeeming trait." But he simply carried out to the letter the instructions of a bigoted and tyrannical king. Broadhead's estimate of him, though far from correct, is certainly more liberal: "He was not to blame because James had directed New England to be governed without an Assembly, by himself and his councillors. Andros's duty was to execute his sovereign's commands; and this he did with characteristic energy—faithfully, fearlessly, and sometimes harshly." Neither was he to blame for the fact that New York, which had always been peculiarly free in her government, had lost that freedom and had been annexed to James's New England colony. This was the result of the king's plan, and Andros, unfortunately for himself, was the man chosen to govern the new dominion and carry out that plan. "For everything done by each of his subordinates, the governor was held responsible. Most of his own acts were able and statesmanlike, though some of them were arbitrary and provoking. The real fault of Andros was that he administered his government too loyally to his sovereign, and too much like a brave soldier. What is called loyalty often depends on fashion or accident. Instead of conciliating, Andros wounded;

and James, seeing the injury his viceroy was doing him in
New England, was obliged to rebuke his excessive zeal."—
(Broadhead, *History of New York*, ii, 526–527.)

Shortly after William's accession to the throne, he prepared a short letter addressed to the American colonies, enjoining them to retain all James's arrangements undisturbed until he should have the opportunity of putting into operation his own plans. This did not please Increase Mather, who saw that if the letter was delivered promptly it might result in sustaining Andros in power for a longer time. Aided by Sir William Phipps, Mather succeeded in having delayed the transmission of this letter of the 12th of January. It did not reach Boston until May 29th, by which time Massachusetts was in rebellion and Andros was in prison. On learning of this state of affairs, Phipps, who had brought other official letters in addition to the one mentioned above, opened them. The same afternoon, William and Mary were proclaimed king and queen at Boston, "with greater ceremony than had been known." The Massachusetts authorities thereupon decided to continue Andros and his colleagues close prisoners without bail.

This New England revolution, starting at Boston, extended rapidly to the Chesapeake. Its object was Protestant liberty. Massachusetts at once restored its old government, just as if its charter had not been annulled. The other New England colonies followed suit—Plymouth, Rhode Island, and Connecticut resumed their old governments as if nothing had happened. The revolution restored to England her legislative privileges, "vindicated her chartered rights," and guaranteed to her legislative body the sole privilege of taxation. Like results were either secured to the colonial governments or doggedly claimed by them.

Penn, who was in England at the time of William and Mary's accession to the throne, received orders to have the new sovereigns proclaimed in Pennsylvania. However, the proclamation was not forwarded immediately, and the delay gave the enemies of Penn an opportunity to prefer charges against him. He was accused of sympathy with the Jacobite plots, because of his friendship for James II. On account of these accusations he was forced to live for some time almost like a prisoner.

The announcement of the overthrow of the government of Andros, and the success of the English Revolution, resulted in a severance of the political union between the Jerseys and New York. Thereafter, for twelve years, the political condition of the former bordered on anarchy. Nevertheless, during the entire period the Puritans in East Jersey and the Quakers in West Jersey appear to have managed their local affairs, through their town organizations, safely and orderly.

The first news of William's invasion of England had been brought to New York on a coasting vessel from Virginia in February, 1689. Nicholson could hardly believe the report, but shortly afterward Leisler received confirmation of it from Maryland. Nicholson suppressed the news for a time, as he feared trouble, but it was despatched to Andros in Maine by both land and water. New York, for a time after the news of the accession of William and Mary had been reported, refused to take action until orders had been received from the king. Finally, however, in June, the accession of both monarchs was proclaimed. If in Massachusetts the announcement had led to immediate revolt, in New York it led to open, armed, and, for a while, completely successful rebellion.

In this critical state of affairs, had Nicholson been equal to his position he might have saved New York from the unfortunate incidents that now pressed upon it in rapid succession. "But the lieutenant-governor," says Broadhead, "was a regular parade soldier. Without the directing mind of Andros, he shrank into insignificance." Had Andros been at Fort James instead of being locked up in a Boston jail, or had he been killed in the Massachusetts insurrection —everything might have gone well, for a time at least. But Andros being neither dead nor alive in so far as a practical connection with New York affairs was concerned, Nicholson did not know what to do. He was afraid either to assume responsibility or not to assume it; and thus caught fast midway between prompt action and criminal inactivity, he hesitated, and, hesitating, lost everything. Of course, technically, Nicholson was in a peculiar position. He had received no official notification and directions from William, and could not recognize an English sovereign of whose accession he had not been officially notified—at least, so he thought. Yet Nicholson knew William and Mary had been proclaimed in Boston on the arrival of Phipps with the Privy Council's despatches for Andros. He had likewise received the London *Gazette* announcing their accession, and might have been justified in violating official forms in view of the critical condition of affairs in New York. But Nicholson took no such responsibility upon himself. He was a fair example of a "straightforward English official bound by red tape." Not having instructions from his immediate chief, he refused to act without them.

This critical state of affairs in the province was very much complicated when, on the 27th of April, news was received of the declaration of war made upon Great Britain and Holland by Louis XIV. Although the announcement was premature,—war not being declared until May 7th,—yet it had all the force of a certainty. War had been anticipated for several years, and there seemed to have been premonition of the bloody struggle that lasted eight years and is known in America as King William's War and in Europe as the War of the League of Augsburg. William, as Stadholder of the United Provinces, on May 12, 1689, entered into an offensive and defensive alliance with the Emperor of Germany against Louis. As King of England, on May 17th, he declared war against France, and on December 30th England joined the Grand Alliance. Spain followed on June 6, 1690, and Victor Amadeus, Duke of Savoy, on October 20th. War continued until 1697, when it was brought to a close by the Peace of Ryswick.

## THE REVOLUTION OF 1688 295

Conditions never seemed more ripe for a French invasion of New York than now. Louis was still the most powerful factor in European politics, and his spirit of Catholic propagandism was an important element with which to reckon. There were the elements for an anti-Catholic panic in New York. James had planned the establishment of the Roman Catholic Church in the American colonies. The two regiments of regular troops were composed of Romanists, and one of these had been commanded by Nicholson himself; and Nicholson, though an Episcopalian, was suspected of Catholic sympathies.

As soon as Nicholson received news of the declaration of war, he took steps to guard Fort James and stationed sentinels on Coney Island to report the approach of French ships. In the midst of these preparations a consignment of wine arrived from Europe for Jacob Leisler, a well-known wine merchant. Leisler refused to pay the duty, on the ground that the collector of the port was a Roman Catholic and that since James's flight there was no duly constituted government in New York. Leisler was a German, born at Frankfort-on-the-Main. After coming to New York, he became a prosperous merchant, and married a connection of Bayard and Van Cortlandt. Bold and cunning, Leisler had some of the characteristics of a successful demagogue, though he lacked in judgment. On the other hand, in business he was noted as a man of integrity, and it is said he was kind-hearted and generous. It was perfectly evident, however, that he was just the man to be influenced by the condition of affairs in New York at this critical time. He was dominated principally by two ideas, namely, his hatred of Popery and his dislike of aristocratic tendencies, whether exemplified in social or political life.

Nicholson himself precipitated the insurrection by a most injudicious exclamation. On May 30th, having entered into an altercation with a lieutenant in one of the train-bands, he rashly exclaimed: "Who commands this fort, you or I? . . . I would rather see the city on fire than take the impudence of such fellows as you." Already suspicious of Nicholson's intentions, the people were now certain that he meant to betray the city to the French. A movement was immediately set on foot, the result of which was the capture of the fort. Leisler, himself a captain of one of the train-bands, took command. Leisler thereupon drew up a declaration, which was signed by some of those who had assisted him in seizing the fort. This declaration referred to "Dongan's Popish" government and charged Nicholson with having threatened to set the city on fire. It announced further that the possession of the fort would be retained until the existing rulers of England sent properly qualified persons to receive it. To all objections to his revolutionary conduct, Leisler replied: "What, do you talk of law? the sword must now rule." A week from the day that this announcement was read to an applauding multitude, on the 10th of June, Nicholson sailed for England.

Leisler and four other captains then sent an address to William and Mary, in which they gave a detailed narrative of recent events and promised entire submission to their majesties' pleasure. Leisler next invited each of the counties and the neighboring towns to send delegates to New York on the 26th of June, to form a Committee of Safety. In response to his invitation some of the counties and towns sent delegates. New York, Brooklyn, Flatbush, Flushing, Newtown, Staten Island, Orange, Westchester, and Essex in New Jersey, each sent two. Not a third of the inhabitants of the province registered their votes in the election. Most of the towns in Queens County and in New Jersey, and all in Suffolk, Ulster, and Albany Counties, refused to take part in it.

On the 26th of June, 1689, Leisler's convention assembled at the fort in New York. Two of the delegates soon withdrew, perceiving that the main drift of the convention was to make Leisler commander-in-chief. Ten remained, and these formed themselves into a Committee of Safety. The next day this committee signed a commission appointing

Leisler captain of the fort at New York until further orders from England. Furthermore, the people of the city and county were required to render him all aid and assistance in suppressing any foreign enemy and in preventing all disorders which might develop.

Leisler, having succeeded in placing himself at the head of affairs in New York, next tried to assume authority over the inhabitants of other parts of the province. He met with resistance at Albany. The people of that town readily proclaimed William and Mary, but refused point-blank to recognize Leisler's authority. They declared "they were not in any wise subordinate to the city of New York, nor the power then exercised therein." Leisler, galled at this defiance of his authority, sent Jacob Milborne with an armed force to take possession of the fort at Albany. He arrived on November 9, 1689, and demanded admission to the fort. This was refused by Mayor Schuyler, who had been placed in command of the fort. For two days Milborne occupied his time making speeches in the City Hall, on the streets, or, in fact, in any place where he could get people to listen to him. He declared he had been appointed by the authorities of New York to assume charge of affairs at Albany. His speeches having little effect on the people, he determined to take bolder methods to gain his desire. He collected his forces, marched to the fort, and again demanded its surrender. Upon being met with a second refusal, he withdrew his company within the city gates. Upon the Mohawks' threatening to make common cause with the Albanians against him, Milborne was compelled to dismiss his men. On the 16th of November Leisler's baffled emissary returned to New York, having utterly failed in his mission.

Although Leisler failed at first to bring Albany under his authority, his power in New York increased daily. He had diligently caused rumors of Popish plots to be circulated. He had seized special letters addressed to "such as may bear rule for the time being," egotistically assuming that they were meant for himself. Those he read, and acted upon the orders contained in them. He caused Councillor Bayard and William Nicolls to be arrested, claiming that the former was the instigator of a plot against the peace of New York.

The Committee of Safety, who were mere tools of Leisler, signed a commission delivering over to the latter the government of the entire province. He was empowered to administer oaths, to issue warrants, and, moreover, to do anything he thought advisable for the preservation and protection of the peace of the inhabitants. The only qualification was that he should consult with the military and civil authorities, as occasion should require. Even the Albany authorities, in the following spring, being annoyed by domestic troubles and the fear of Frontenac's movements, by the advice of Connecticut, acknowledged Leisler's authority.

Leisler soon found himself without revenues to defray the expenses of the province. He proclaimed the statute of 1683 as still in force. This turned the people against him. They tore down the proclamation, and the merchants refused to pay the duties. Leisler resorted to fines, imprisonments, confiscations, until his popularity was turned first into distrust and then into hatred.

The unsuccessful expedition of Milborne against Albany occurred in November, and Frontenac had arrived in Canada just before. He determined to send war parties against the exposed English frontier towns along the Mohawk and the Hudson. Three raiding parties were sent out,—the first was ordered to Hudson River, the second into New Hampshire, and the third into Maine. There were about two hundred and ten men in the first party—one hundred French Canadians and ninety-six Indians. They were led by Frenchmen of quality, among whom was Le Moyne d'Iberville.

The raid of the Five Nations upon Montreal in 1689, to which reference has been made, was the immediate cause of Frontenac's sending these three expeditions against the

English. The first expedition resulted in the frightful massacre of the sleeping citizens of Schenectady on the night of the 8th of February, 1690. The village might have been amply protected by troops and fortifications. In fact, the Albany committee expected an attack. Then why were the gates of the village open, no sentinels stationed, no scouting parties in the vicinity, and no adequate garrison stationed in the town? The answer is, Schenectady, like Albany, was rent by party spirit, the inhabitants being divided into Leislerians and anti-Leislerians—or the "short-hairs" and the "swallow-tails," as they were called.

The Schenectady horror had two very important results—one permanent and the other merely temporary. They were, the calling of the first American Congress and the strengthening of Leisler's authority. A few words concerning each will be in place.

The intelligence of the burning of Schenectady spread through the colonies like wildfire. The Governor of Massachusetts urged in letters to other colonies the necessity for immediate action to provide for the common defence. The General Court of Massachusetts, wishing to organize a joint effort of the colonies, proposed to hold a congress. The call was dated March 19, 1690. It stated that, in view of the atrocities that had been committed against the English by the French and Indians, the neighboring colonies, and Virginia, Maryland, and the parts adjacent, should be invited to meet at New York to determine upon suitable methods for assisting each other for the safety of the whole land. The Governor of New York was desired to transmit this invitation to the Southern colonies. This was the first call for a general congress in America. "It is free from narrowness, liberal in its spirit, simple in its terms, and comprehensive in its objects."

Thomas Hinckley, Governor of Plymouth, appointed a commissioner to the congress, though the General Court was not in session. He was zealously in favor of the congress. Henry Bull, the Quaker Governor of Rhode Island, said, though the time was too short to convene the Assembly for the purpose of appointing a commissioner, yet he promised the aid of that colony to the utmost of its ability to resist the French and Indians. The head of the convention of Maryland wrote that it was the design of the Assembly to send arms and men to aid in the general defence. President Bacon, of Virginia, replied that the proposition would require the action of the Assembly, and that nothing could be done until the arrival of the daily expected governor. Commissioners from Massachusetts, Plymouth, Connecticut, and New York colonies met at New York.

The results of the congress were unanimously effected. On May 1st an agreement was signed by five colonies—Maryland promising to coöperate—to raise eight hundred and fifty-five men to strengthen Albany and, "by the help of Almighty God," to subdue the French and Indian enemies. Of this force, New York was to furnish four hundred; Massachusetts, one hundred and sixty; Plymouth, sixty; Connecticut, one hundred and thirty-five; and Maryland, one hundred. In addition, the Iroquois sachems were to equip one thousand eight hundred warriors. Massachusetts was to provide most of the naval armament. The lieutenant-governor of New York was to name the commander of the force, and that force was not to be employed on any other service without the consent of the five colonies. Officers were to preserve among their men good order, punish vice, keep the Sabbath, and maintain the worship of God. Efforts were made to obtain additional aid from New Jersey, Pennsylvania, and Rhode Island. No proposition seems to have been entertained for a permanent organization.

Another direct though temporary result of the massacre of Schenectady was the strengthening of Leisler's power, as is evidenced by the final surrender of Albany to his authority. But the untenable character of his position was exposed, as we have seen, upon his attempting to summon a legislature for the purpose of raising money for the expenses of the government. Some persons refused to pay taxes, on the ground that Leisler was a usurper. Likewise, some towns, notably the Yankee towns on Long Island, refused to send representatives to the Assembly.

The immediate cause, however, of the waning of Leisler's authority may be traced to the failure of the expedition sent out against the French and Indians in Canada as a result of the congress at New York. The naval expedition sailed up the St. Lawrence under Sir William Phipps and laid siege to Quebec. The allied forces under Fitz-John Winthrop, of Connecticut, marched from Albany toward Montreal; but the forces merely "marched up the hill and then marched down again." Frontenac had outwitted them. Dissension in the confederate army, however, was the immediate cause of failure. Leisler lost prestige by the miscarriage of this expedition, and the dissatisfaction that had been hidden up to this time began to assert itself. Complaints were made upon every side, and protests against his government were sent to England. The Assembly did not meet until October, but when it did it put itself on record as being the most despotic Assembly that had met in any colony.

The inhabitants of Hempstead, Jamaica, Flushing, and Newtown met and wrote to the king's secretary of state. They complained of the tyrannical acts of Leisler, Milborne, and their accomplices. They said Milborne was famous for nothing but infamy. That he had plundered houses, stripped women of their apparel, and sequestered estates. They begged the king to break this "heavy yoke of worse than Egyptian bondage." They said the crimes that Leisler had committed would force him to take shelter under Catiline's maxim—"the ills that I have done cannot be safe but by attempting greater."

Matters went from bad to worse. The new year, 1691, dawned gloomily. The wrath of the people was held in check only by the fort. Leisler resorted to the most extreme measures for the collection of taxes. Even Leisler's friends began to desert him, for they could not restrain him.

He lost popularity rapidly. "The dominies came in and rebuked him in the name of the Lord. Old women taunted and defied him on the street, and the mob threw stones at him and called him 'Dog Driver,' 'Deacon Jailer,' 'Little Cromwell,' 'General Hog,' and other choice epithets." It was evident that the great demagogue had fallen from honor.

On September 2, 1689, the king appointed Colonel Henry Sloughter Governor of New York. Sloughter probably secured this post through the influence of some of William's corrupt courtiers, for it has been said that he was utterly destitute of every qualification for government, that he was licentious in his morals, avaricious, and poor.

Finally, after a great many delays, on December 1, 1690, Sloughter set sail for New York in the frigate *Archangel*, which was to convoy the *Beaver*, the *Canterbury*, and the storeship *John and James*. Two companies of soldiers were in the expedition, one under the command of Sloughter, and the other under the command of Major Richard Ingoldsby, the lieutenant-governor, "a rash, hot-headed man," who had formerly served in Holland and had just returned from victorious service under William in Ireland. The little fleet was separated by severe storms, and the *Archangel*, carrying the governor and his company, ran ashore on one of the Bermuda Islands. This necessitated a delay for repairs. The other three ships, however, were able to proceed to their destination. On the 29th of January, Ingoldsby arrived in New York. He immediately sent a message to Leisler, demanding the fort and its stores for the king's soldiers. Leisler refused to yield the fort unless Ingoldsby should produce written orders from the king or the governor. The lieutenant-governor had no documents in proof of his official standing, they being on board the *Archangel*. Leisler took him to be a Catholic conspirator who wanted to seize the colony for James. Ingoldsby quartered his troops in the City Hall, and wrote to the New England governor for advice. He was urged to bear with Leisler until the governor should arrive to simplify matters. But proclamation and counter proclamation, threat and counter threat, passed between the two factions until affairs came to a crisis on March 17, 1691. Leisler, goaded on by opposition and popular discontent, fired upon the king's troops as they stood on parade. Other shots were fired, and several soldiers were wounded and two were killed. These shots were answered, but, safely intrenched behind the breastworks, Leisler's forces did not suffer.

Ingoldsby put himself on the defensive, and was relieved, March 19th, by the intelligence that Sloughter had arrived. As soon as he heard of the condition of affairs at New York, Sloughter hastened to the City Hall and read his commission. After swearing in the new councillors, he sent Ingoldsby to the fort to demand of Leisler its surrender. Leisler refused to comply with the demand, but sent Milborne and De la Noy to make terms with Sloughter. The governor imprisoned the messengers, and for the third time demanded the surrender of the fort. Leisler now saw that it was useless to hold out longer, and surrendered on Friday, the 20th of March. All the men were promised a pardon except Leisler and his councillors, who were imprisoned. The Assembly, which had been summoned on the day of Leisler's arrest, met in April. One of its first acts was the declaration that Leisler was guilty of an act of rebellion. A packed jury was drawn and the trial began on March 30th. The prisoners were charged with treason and murder. Eight of the prisoners pleaded "not guilty." Leisler and Milborne refused to plead, and they were tried as mutes. After eight days, the jury pronounced them guilty, together with six others. Two were acquitted. Chief Justice Joseph Dudley pronounced the sentence of death upon the eight condemned men. The prisoners petitioned for a reprieve until the king's pleasure should be known, and it was granted.

All the condemned men, save Leisler and Milborne, were pardoned. The governor could not resist the flood of petitions that came in, demanding the execution of these two.

It has been said that the governor was offered large sums of money to sign the death warrants, and that his wife, from sheer covetousness, forced him to do it. The historian Smith says Sloughter was a guest of the worst enemy of Leisler, Colonel Bayard, and when overcome with wine was prevailed upon to sign the death warrants, and before he recovered his senses the prisoners had been executed. This can hardly be true, inasmuch as the warrants were signed on Thursday and the execution took place on the Sunday following. Dominie Schyns was the messenger sent to break the terrible news to the unhappy men. They petitioned Sloughter for a reprieve, but it was not granted. On the 15th of May, 1691, Leisler and Milborne were hanged near old Tammany Hall, in New York.

The event was variously judged. Some jurists pronounced the whole proceedings perfectly lawful. Others held that there were extenuating circumstances which were not allowed to appear at the trial. Concerning Leisler himself, opinions differ just as widely. He has been held up as a champion of Dutch democracy against English aristocracy, of Protestantism against Romanism, of republicanism against monarchism. On the other hand, Broadhead can see no good in Leisler, and stamps his efforts as " the selfish attempt of an upstart demagogue to obtain a local importance, which neither his own character nor the circumstances of the province warranted." In spite of these conflicting opinions, however, there can be little doubt as to the honesty of Leisler's purpose. He may have been arbitrary and tyrannical, and the hatred of him may have been very well founded, but to say that he was an "upstart demagogue" is not at all consonant with the facts in the case. Regarded in the light of those disturbed months immediately following the arrest of Andros and the flight of Nicholson, the conduct of Leisler may be satisfactorily explained, if not altogether condoned. He very naturally assumed that the deposition of James II. and the accession of William III. meant the overthrow of the government of the former in

# By His Excellency

*Richard Earl of Bellomont*, Captain General and Governour in Chief of His Majesties Province of *New-York*, &c.

## A PROCLAMATION

WHEREAS it is of abſolute Neceſſity for the Good and Proſperity of this Province, that our Principal and firſt Care be in Obedience to the Laws of God, and the wholſom Laws of *England*, to ſhake off all ſorts of Looſeneſs and Prophaneneſs, and to unite and joyn in the fear and Love of God, and of one another, by a Religious and Virtuous Deportment and Behaviour, every one in his reſpective Station and Calling, to the end that all Heats, Animoſities and Diſſentions may vaniſh, and the Bleſſing of Almighty God accompany our Our Honeſt and Lawful Endeavours, and that we joyn Our Affections in the true Support of His Majeſties Government over us, who has ſo often and ſo generouſly expoſed His Sacred Perſon to eminent Dangers, to Redeem us from the growing Power of Popery and Arbitrary Government, and has by the Bleſſing of God procured Our Deliverance, and an Honourable Peace, and is a great Example and Encourager of Religion and Virtuous Living. I have therefore thought fit, by and with the Advice of His Majeſties Council for this Province, and I do hereby Strictly Prohibit all Inhabitants and Sojourners within this Province from *Curſing, Swearing, Immoderate Drinking, Sabbath Breaking* and *all ſorts of Lewdneſs* and *Profane Behaviour* in *Word* or *Action*. And for the true and effectual Performance hereof, I do by and with the Advice aforeſaid, Strictly Charge and Command all Mayors, Aldermen, Juſtices of the Peace, Sheriffs, Conſtables, and other Officers within this Province, that they take care that all the Laws made and provided for the Suppreſſion of Vice and encouragement of Religion and Virtue, particularly the Obſervation of the *Lords Day* be duely put in Execution, as they will anſwer the Contrary at their Peril.

*Given at New-York the Second Day of April, 1698. and in the Tenth Year of the Reign of Our Sovvraign Lord,* WILLIAM *the Third, by the Grace of God, of* England, Scotland, France *and* Ireland, *King, Defender of the Faith,* &c.

Bellomont.

## God Save the KING.

---

*Printed by* William Bradford, *Printer to the Kings Moſt Excellent Majeſty in the City of* New-York, *1698.*

Proclamation by Governor Bellomont regarding cursing, swearing, Sabbath-breaking, etc., dated April 2, 1698. *From the original in the New York Public Library, Lenox Branch.*

New York. Consequently, he merely took up the reins of government where the representatives of James had dropped them. No doubt, he did so with the intention of turning them over to the properly accredited representatives of the new monarchs when they should make their appearance. Leisler's action was most patriotic. He refused to surrender the fort, because Lieutenant-governor Ingoldsby had arrived, as we have seen, without any official documents with which to support his pretensions to the government. Leisler was naturally suspicious of Ingoldsby's claim, thinking it to be the trick of a Stuart refugee to gain possession of New York. The former's willingness to surrender authority to the officially deputed representatives of the Protestant monarchs relieves him of the imputation that he was himself desirous of obtaining possession of the government. Whatever view we may take of Leisler and his policy, his execution, as well as Milborne's, was a frightful blunder—impolitic is too weak a word. The attainder against Leisler and Milborne was reversed by Parliament in 1695. The convictions, moreover, were annulled and the estates of the two men were restored to their families.

We must now turn our attention to the condition of affairs in Maryland that resulted from the overthrow of James II. Lord Baltimore was visiting in England when William and Mary ascended the throne, and he was instructed immediately to proclaim the new sovereigns in his province. Accordingly, he despatched a messenger to carry the order to his Council. Unfortunately for him, the messenger died on the way. The proclamation was delayed long enough to give the proprietor's enemies ample time to hatch new plots and to vitalize old ones against him. The Marylanders knew of William's succession, for he had been proclaimed in Virginia and in New England. The delay to proclaim him in their province they chose to consider intentional and to construe as a device on the part of the Catholics to gain control of the colony. The proprietor's enemies had for years circulated reports of Romish plots, and now the failure of his Catholic government to proclaim the Protestant king gave them just the opportunity for which they had been looking.

A second messenger was sent out by Lord Baltimore, but he reached Maryland too late to prevent the impending revolution. Reports of a conspiracy among the Indians, French, and Catholics to exterminate the Protestants were now diligently circulated by the malcontents. Exaggerated accounts reached the settlers, from different sources, of attacks being made by an armed force. When investigation proved the report false in one place, another report sprang up in a different place. After all rumors were run down and proved utterly baseless, an uprising for the time being was prevented.

The peace thus secured was only temporary, however; for a few months later, in July, trouble broke out anew. This time the opposition was headed by John Coode, a captain of militia, assisted by Blackiston, one of the collectors of customs, and an unrelenting enemy of Baltimore. Others joined them, and together they marched on to St. Mary's. Here the officers had been able to gather only a small force, and they were compelled to surrender without even a show of resistance. The government thus changed hands without bloodshed.

In the meantime, Coode and his associates had organized themselves into what they called a Protestant Association. After the surrender of St. Mary's, they set forth in a paper an explanation of their action. Their sole excuse for taking up arms was the persistent rumors of Popish plots to annihilate the Protestants. These reports had been proved false, and there is little doubt but that Coode and Blackiston had contributed a fair share to their circulation. It is certainly true that the declaration they issued was signed by men who had investigated the rumors and had declared them to be false.

Coode now took the title of "General," and promised his followers high dignities as a reward of merit for their insurrectionary acts. The Associators were not emphatically supported, even by all the Protestants. Yet they proclaimed William and Mary the new sovereigns. Furthermore, they called an Assembly and filled all offices with Protestants. Then followed address after address directed to William, in which all the counties save Anne Arundel declared themselves in sympathy with Coode and his movement. Counter addresses were also sent, discounting the charges against the proprietary and declaring Coode and his followers a set of "factious knaves." The Associators, having the approval of William, conducted the affairs of the government much as they saw fit. Officers were commissioned, property was plundered, and all those who should essay to stay them in the accomplishment of their purposes were threatened with death.

During the reign of James II., *quo warranto* proceedings against the Maryland charter had been in progress, but his flight from England practically put an end to the suit. The charter remained unimpaired and the proceedings were not resumed. However, William was now anxious to gain every advantage that would aid him in his fight with Louis XIV. Consequently, he was by no means loath to take Maryland under the direct protection of the crown, when that course was advised by his Council and urged by the colonists themselves.

The king at first decided to proceed against the charter by way of *scire facias;* but as this was a very slow and tedious method for the accomplishment of the object sought, Chief Justice Holt was requested to render an opinion as to whether the government of the province could be taken over in any other way. In June, 1690, the chief justice gave the following opinion: "I think it had been better if an inquisition had been taken, and the forfeitures committed by the Lord Baltimore had been therein found before any grant be made to a new governor. Yet since there is none, and it being a case of necessity, I think the king may by his commission constitute a governor whose authority will be legal, though he must be responsible to the Lord Baltimore for the profits. If an agreement can be made with the Lord Baltimore, it will be convenient and easy for the governor that the king shall appoint. An inquisition may at any time be taken if the forfeiture be not pardoned, of which there is some doubt." The council next ordered the attorney-general to proceed against Lord Baltimore's charter, it being claimed that assumption of the government by the king was the only means of preserving the province. After the counsel on both sides had been heard, Lord Baltimore was deprived of all governmental powers, without, however, loss of his territorial rights. From being a free palatinate, Maryland now became a royal colony, and continued as such for the next twenty-three years. The Church of England was established by an Act of Assembly, and the people were taxed for its support.

Title-page of the first American Bible, and portrait of Robert Aitken, the publisher of it. *From the originals in possession of the Historical Society of Pennsylvania.*

## CHAPTER XIII

*THE MIDDLE COLONIES AFTER THE FLIGHT OF JAMES II., 1692–1714*

As in the case of all revolutions, that of Leisler was followed by a period of reaction. Leisler was called by certain of his democratic enemies "Little Cromwell," and there is much in the appellation that was not intended by its authors. There are, indeed, points of similarity between this New York revolution of 1689 and its great prototype, the English Revolution of 1640. Likewise, there are decided points of similarity between the New York reaction of 1691 and the English reaction under Charles II. in 1660. Of course, the New York revolution of 1689 was but the faint echo of the English Revolution of 1688, when James II. was driven out of England, but 1688 itself was but the continuation and consummation of the great revolution under Cromwell. Leisler had all the bigotry of Cromwell and none of his breadth of character. Both were fanatically religious, and both hated the Roman Church. Both started out by being democratic and ended by being tyrannical. They were creations of the times, and the times demanded such creations. Leisler lost his life, and Cromwell did not, but we do not know what would have happened had the latter lived a decade longer. But to draw a parallel between Leisler and Cromwell is like comparing a frog pond to the great Atlantic—one neither shows the importance of the former nor the greatness of the latter. Leisler had, no doubt, some of the characteristics of Cromwell, but only in miniature. The points of resemblance lie rather in the times than in the men. As in England in 1660, so in New York in 1691, a reaction against liberal democracy set in and an aristocracy that accomplished nothing but discontent was firmly established in power.

We come now to a period of puppet governors, with but one or two exceptions. "History," says Roberts, "often turns on the character and conduct of the rulers. At this period New York affords no wide field of that sort. Its governors moved over the stage almost as rapidly and with little more substance than the Scottish kings who appeared to Macbeth. Their terms were more brief than those in other colonies. While Virginia had twenty governors in the century before the Revolution, Massachusetts twenty-one, and Pennsylvania twenty-five, the executive authority in New York underwent thirty-three changes, counting the lieutenant-governors serving temporarily as heads of the government." After the execution of Leisler, New York was in a most critical condition. It was rent by internal factions and threatened by foreign warfare. Louis XIV. was fully bent upon the chastisement, if not indeed the conquest, of the people who in alliance with the Five Nations had made desolate his Canadian territory. Everything that French ingenuity and cunning could suggest was employed to induce the Iroquois to break with their English allies.

Sloughter went to Albany on May 26, 1691, to negotiate with the Mohawks for the purpose of counteracting the influence brought to bear upon them by the French. The troubles of the Leislerian period had well-nigh caused the loss of the sympathy and allegiance of the friendly Iroquois, for the wily Frenchman had employed his time to the greatest possible advantage. No time was to be lost, and Sloughter appreciated this fact. On his arrival at Albany, he found the Mohawks waiting for him. Mayor Schuyler, of Albany, and Robert Livingston managed the negotiations. The former had brought gifts from England, and these were presented to the Indians with the pomp and ceremony suggestive of a much more formidable list of valuables than the following: one dozen stockings, six shirts, three bags of powder, sixteen bars of lead, thirty strings of wampum, three runlets of rum, three rolls of tobacco, and some coats of duffels to the "chief on the sly."

To restore the confidence of the Indians, an aggressive campaign into Canada was decided upon. Mayor Schuyler was put in command of the expedition and left Albany on the 21st of June with four hundred men. Five-sixths of these were Indians. The expedition, though gallantly conducted, met with only negative success, save that it stimulated the Iroquois to further aggressive efforts against the French.

When the expedition left Albany, Sloughter left also— but in the opposite direction. While the valiant Schuyler and his forces were fighting the French and Indians, Sloughter no doubt was making vigorous and repeated assaults upon his rum barrels. In this he excelled, for in the midsummer of 1691 he died in the agonies of a complaint resembling delirium tremens.

Chief Justice Dudley, the person to assume control of affairs in an emergency of this kind, was in Curaçoa, and the Council declared Ingoldsby commander-in-chief until the king's pleasure should be known. About the only good accomplished by Sloughter was the establishment upon a firm foundation of a representative body. The first thing he did after the arrest of Leisler, in fact, was to issue writs for the election of an Assembly. It was made up of the pronounced opponents of Leisler—of the party of aristocrats. It met in a tavern on Pearl Street, on the 9th of April, 1691, and marked the beginning of "continuous constitutional government in New York."

Ingoldsby's characterless rule was to last but little over a year and a month. In response to a request for help against the French and Indians, William appointed Colonel Benjamin Fletcher governor. Fletcher arrived on

August 29, 1692, and was given a brilliant reception that cost £20! The new governor was a "soldier of fortune," zealous and energetic, but very avaricious and wholly unfit to rule a province. One of his first acts was to make a trip to Albany. He spent weeks as the guest of Peter Schuyler and with him made a trip into the Mohawk country, where he was entertained by the Indians in their famous castles. They called him the "Great Swift Arrow." He pried into their character, habits, and strength, and learned something of their language. The Indians called Schuyler the "Great Brave White Chief," and well they might, for he was easily the equal of Frontenac in his skill in dealing with the red men. To Peter Schuyler more than to any other man is due the cementing of the Iroquois friendship.

Fletcher soon found that the bed of a governor was not one of roses. The Leislerians and the anti-Leislerians —the democrats and the aristocrats—fought continually. They lost sight of the commonweal in the intensity of their petty bickerings. Then, again, Fletcher demanded some very doubtful things: first, he wanted to establish the Protestant Episcopal Church and support it from the revenues; and secondly, to get the revenue voted for the lifetime of the reigning king. Matters reached a crisis on a revenue bill that had been amended by the governor and supported by the Council. The Assembly voted it down and passed the original bill. This exasperated Fletcher so much that he took it upon himself to rebuke the Assembly, after which he immediately declared it prorogued. He described the people of New York as "divided, contentious, and impoverished." By his opposition he drove them into a still more stubborn resistance to his plans.

William added to Fletcher's burdens by revoking in 1693 the proprietary grants of Pennsylvania and Delaware to William Penn and adding them to New York. The Jerseys and the Connecticut militia had already been put under his control. Immediately after his appointment, Fletcher summoned the Pennsylvania Assembly and required all its members to take the oaths prescribed by Parliament. He utterly disregarded the quarrels between the Upper and Lower Counties, and summoned representatives of both. As in the case of the New York Assembly, Fletcher requested that of Pennsylvania to pass measures for the defence of the Canadian frontier. But the Quakers were totally opposed to granting war supplies, and the new governor at once came into conflict with their Assembly. After repeated and unsuccessful attempts to secure a war grant, in which he first threatened and then cajoled the Quakers, Fletcher was compelled to acknowledge himself thoroughly outwitted and beaten. He dissolved the Assembly and returned to New York. The additional load of Pennsylvania was too much for Fletcher's weak back, and he prayed the king to relieve him. His request was granted in the following year.

Penn, who had been deprived of his province for nearly two years, now prepared a petition to the king, praying to be reinstated in his rights. The petition was referred to the Privy Council, which, after having made a thorough examination of the case and finding nothing against the petitioner, recommended the restoration of the province. Penn now became a man of influence at court. He appointed Markham as his deputy, who was to be assisted by Samuel Carpenter and John Goodson. In 1700, Penn himself visited the colony, but his brief stay of two years was not very agreeable to him. There was constant friction between the Assembly and himself on the issue of money grants for the defence of the northern frontier. Furthermore, the Assembly was so pertinacious in its demands for a new charter that Penn finally gave a reluctant consent.

This new charter consisted of nine articles, the first of which dealt with religious liberty. Fletcher and Markham had required all office holders to subscribe to the English Toleration Act of 1689, but Penn was broader-minded. This first article of the new charter accorded the Catholics the privilege of holding office. The king, however, did not sustain Penn in the matter, and required the Pennsylvania Assembly to enforce the Act. Consequently, Catholics, Jews, and "unbelievers" were shut out from office until the American Revolution. The second article of the charter granted a larger representation from the counties, made the Assembly an entirely independent legislative body, and took away from the Council the legislative powers that it had enjoyed. Certain articles provided for local government. The last article declared the charter void should its provisions be violated by Penn or any of his heirs.

At this time Pennsylvania politics assumed a triangular character. The three parties in the field were the Proprietary, Churchman, and Lloyd. The last-mentioned party was, in many respects, the most unique. At its head stood David Lloyd, formerly a Welsh lawyer and a captain in Cromwell's army. He was a man of great ability, but obstinate and revengeful. He became a member of the Provincial Council, and in 1686 was appointed attorney-general by William Penn. For thirty years Lloyd was a prominent figure in the Assembly, and many of the laws of Welsh coloring passed by that body were due to his influence. On the other hand, his obstinacy caused the defeat of many salutary laws and measures. At first a friend of the proprietor, he later became the leader of the party that bitterly opposed all measures of the administration. On Penn's departure for England, Andrew Hamilton, who had been Governor of East Jersey, was appointed Governor of Pennsylvania. Hamilton shortly afterward died, and John Evans, a Welshman, was appointed in his place. James Logan became provincial secretary. Logan was a shrewd politician and a faithful supporter of the proprietary. From his boyhood he had paid much attention to scientific studies, and he, David Rittenhouse the astronomer, John Bartram and his son William the botanists, Thomas Godfrey, who shared with John Hadley the honor of inventing an improved quadrant, and Benjamin Franklin stand foremost among the scientists of Pennsylvania's early history.

Lloyd began to be a power in Pennsylvania politics about 1704. The administration greatly dreaded his ascendency and used every effort to check his rise in power, but without success. A very good idea of his character as judged by the administration may be had from the following letter of James Logan to William Penn, under date of 1704: "David Lloyd being recorder of the city and likely in all probability to be speaker of the next Assembly, from his temper, so well known, there seems but little good to be anticipated. The generality, however, are honestly and well inclined and out of the Assembly are very good men, but when got together, I know not how, they are infatuated and led by smooth stories. David himself makes as great a profession as any man, but we can see no good effects from it."

Lloyd was made speaker of the Assembly of 1704, and immediately set about attacking the proprietor and Governor Evans. In the Assembly of 1705, he probably had a hand in defeating revenue bills and urgent measures in the interest of the proprietor. In this opposition his hands were undoubtedly strengthened by the unpopularity which the Proprietary party had incurred by reason of its attempt to levy an impost on commerce. Nor was that unpopularity lessened by the childish insistence on the part of the administration officials upon minor and petty matters of official etiquette. The following instance is in point and will suffice as a typical example of other instances. Upon one occasion, Lloyd neglected to rise while speaking. The governor commanded him to stand, but Lloyd refused point-blank, claiming " to be exempted from this tribute of respect in conference where equality was indispensable and was sanctioned by precedent." Lloyd claimed to represent the people, but inasmuch as the governor claimed to represent the queen the latter doggedly insisted on his point. The House, " fearing the difference might terminate in unseemly language," withdrew in a body.

One of Lloyd's most powerful antagonists was James Logan. Lloyd was not so learned as Logan, but was far more pleasing in his manner. Besides, he was skilful in debate, and championed popular rights. Lloyd and his party accused Logan of trying to deprive the people of their rights, and articles of impeachment were drawn up, but they failed in their issue. Governor Evans was next attacked for his immoral conduct. Unfortunately, most of the accusations were true, and it was necessary for Penn to admonish his representative before the latter mended his ways.

The administration next attempted to turn the tables upon Lloyd, who had just been reëlected speaker of the Assembly of 1709. This time, Logan, through Governor Charles Gookin, the successor of Evans, preferred charges against Lloyd for certain alleged misdemeanors. But the charges were examined into and declared false. Matters finally came to a crisis when Logan was arrested by order of the Assembly, but was released by the governor on the ground that the Assembly had no authority to make arrests outside its own body. Later, Logan went to London, where he favorably presented his case to the proprietary. These petty disputes so vexed Penn that he threatened to sell out to the government unless the Assembly showed a disposition to improve. The people then realized their danger, and in the following election not a single member of the old Assembly was returned, not even Lloyd. This Assembly, without Lloyd, it is said, "ceased to live on quarrels." Nevertheless, Lloyd was returned by the voters soon after, and was even elected speaker, but it was as a chastened man. His defeat had taught him the emptiness of popularity. He ever afterward worked in the interests of the public, and after his death, when critical measures came up before the Assembly, that body felt deeply the loss of Lloyd's wise counsels.

The Lower Counties or "Territories" on the Delaware had never worked harmoniously with the main province of Pennsylvania. At this time the Territories and the main province each comprised three counties. To preserve the balance of power between the two sections, each had

James Logan.
After the painting now in Independence Hall, Philadelphia.

David Rittenhouse.
From the painting by Charles Willson Peale, in possession of the American Philosophical Society.

an equal number of representatives in the Council. Inasmuch as the latter was much larger than the former, the political balance could not be maintained much longer. Disagreement between the two territorial divisions dates from almost the time when the Territories came into the possession of Penn—1685. Thenceforward, the trouble continued to grow more acute, until finally the six members of the Council from the Territories proceeded to appoint and commission justices without the concurrence of the whole Council or of its president, Thomas Lloyd. The Council protested in 1690 against these unconstitutional measures, but the members from the Territories not only paid no attention whatever to its protests but even took further arbitrary steps.

The Territories continued to be jealous of the province, and matters did not mend. For purposes of conciliation, October 14, 1700, Penn convened the Assembly at New Castle. In his address to the Assembly the proprietor urged amity and concord between the two contesting factions, but without the desired result. The members from the Territories claimed the right to withdraw from the Assembly when they pleased, and even refused to recognize the authority of the proprietary unless a mutual understanding was arranged. They admitted that the crown had the right to establish a form of government, but specifically demanded an equal representation in the General Assembly. If this were not accorded them, they saw that the rapid growth of the province would soon put them in the minority. If an equal representation could not be secured, the recalcitrant members believed the Territories would fare better under a separate government. Nevertheless, the plan of equal representation was rejected by Penn and the province.

An agreement was finally reached, by which no law of interest to the Territories was to be enacted unless by a vote of two-thirds of the members from the Territories and of a majority of the members from the province. It was likewise agreed that the latter should pay £1,575 and the former £425 for the support of the proprietor and the governor. Furthermore, by another Assembly the Territories were permitted to dissolve their union within three years from the date of the new charter, if they so desired.

This agreement did not settle the dispute, for after the departure of Penn to England trouble again developed. The representatives of the Territories refused to meet in an Assembly with those of the province. They also refused to accept the new charter, which had been signed by Penn on October 25, 1701. It was the turn of the province now to ask to be relieved from political union with such cantankerous counties. Governor Andrew Hamilton tried his best to preserve the union, but the province was firm in its demand for separation. The final separation occurred in October, 1702, when Pennsylvania convened its legislature apart from the Territories. The two colonies were never again united, and the Lower Counties became almost an independent republic. They were not included in the charter, and the executive power of the Governor of Pennsylvania over them was too feeble to restrain them. The proprietors of both Pennsylvania and Maryland claimed jurisdiction over the Lower Counties, and between the two disputes the foundation for the sovereign State of Delaware was established.

An important law regulating suffrage was passed during the administration of Governor John Evans. Qualified voters had to be the owners of fifty acres of land or possessed of £50 in money. No person could vote unless born or naturalized in England or in the province. Residence in the province for two years before the election was likewise required. The sale or purchase of votes was punished by a fine and loss of the right of suffrage for a period of time. Penalties were likewise provided for other electoral irregularities. Each county was accorded eight representatives, while Philadelphia was given two.

The matter of war grants probably gave the provincial governors of Pennsylvania more trouble than anything else.

Queen Anne made a requisition upon the Assembly for one hundred and fifty men, besides officers, for the expedition against Canada. Governor Gookin knew the conscientious scruples of the Quakers against war grants, and proposed that a grant of £4,000 for the support of the government be made. The matter was taken under consideration, and an attempt at a compromise is shown in the following reply of the Assembly: "the raising of money to hire men to fight (or kill one another) was a matter of conscience to them, and against their principles": but not to appear disloyal they would appropriate £500 as a present to the queen. The governor objected to the smallness of the amount, and refused to pass several bills until the grant was increased. Not until the next Assembly was the sum raised to £2,000, and then only in the form of a present to the queen. The composition of this Assembly was completely different from the preceding one. It worked harmoniously with the governor and attended strictly to business. A better and ampler revenue system was established, the revenue came into the treasury with greater regularity, and there was less bickering and quarrelling between rival political factions. The harmony between the executive and the Assembly was due in no small degree to Gookin himself. He had learned the value of docility toward the legislators, and by yielding to many of their whims secured at least an outward harmony.

In New York, Governor Fletcher and his Assembly continued to quarrel, until the Leislerians, through tact and diplomacy, brought about his recall. They accused Fletcher of at least receiving bribes or hush money from pirates, if not, indeed,—as some asserted,—of being in complicity with them. It is difficult to say how much truth there was in their accusations, if, in fact, there was any. Piracy had long been in existence, and was even encouraged rather than otherwise by the European governments. During the time of war, armed private vessels, with or without licenses, roved the seas and plundered almost at pleasure. They did not stop with preying upon the enemy's commerce, but soon turned their attention to the commerce of neutrals or even to that of their countrymen itself. In so far as Fletcher was concerned, the Leislerians saw their chance to bring about his downfall by connecting him with these piracies, and were not slow in grasping the opportunity. Fletcher always resented the charges most indignantly, and, it must be said, they were never really proved.

It is true, he had issued commissions for sea captains to raise men and equip privateers against the French, but this was in line with the common practice in England. He had probably accepted bribes and had promised protection, but not to known pirates. Nevertheless, commissions were found in the possession of sea robbers like Coates, Hoare, Tew, and others, that seemed to implicate the governor in their crimes. He maintained that they had turned pirates after receiving their commissions as privateers, with the exception of Tew, who had promised not to engage in piracy again. Tew was an agreeable and companionable fellow, whom he had often entertained at his table and had taken to drive. He wished to convert the former pirate from the "error of his ways and especially to cure him of the vile habit of swearing." With this end in view, he had presented him with a book on the subject and had made him a present of a gun of some value. Tew, in return, the governor said, had presented him with a curious watch. It was also claimed that he had presented Mrs. Fletcher and her daughters with valuable jewels. Tew shortly afterward showed to what extent he had been converted from the error of his ways through the governor's missionary zeal by proceeding to the Indian Ocean and harboring himself with others of his kind among the creeks of Madagascar. Here he "plundered and murdered until humanity," says Mrs. Lamb, "refuses to blot the pages of history with his deeds." Fletcher was not the only citizen of New York implicated in piracy. Some of the wealthiest and hitherto most respectable citizens were likewise accused of profiting

THE
# MODEL
OF THE
## GOVERNMENT
OF THE
## PROVINCE
OF
## EAST-NEW-JERSEY
IN
## AMERICA;

And Encouragements for such as Designs to be concerned there.

*Published for Information of such as are desirous to be Interested in that place.*

## EDINBURGH.

Printed by *John Reid*, And Sold be Alexander Ogston Stationer in the Parliament Closs. Anno DOM. 1685.

---

*Good Order Established*
IN
Pennsilvania & New-Jersey
IN
## AMERICA,

Being a true Account of the Country; With its Produce and Commodities there made.

And the great Improvements that may be made by means of 𝔓𝔲𝔟𝔩𝔦𝔠𝔨 𝔖𝔱𝔬𝔯𝔢-𝔥𝔬𝔲𝔰𝔢𝔰 for 𝔥𝔢𝔪𝔭, 𝔉𝔩𝔞𝔵 and 𝔏𝔦𝔫𝔫𝔢𝔫-𝔠𝔩𝔬𝔱𝔥; also, the Advantages of a 𝔓𝔲𝔟𝔩𝔦𝔠𝔨-𝔖𝔠𝔥𝔬𝔬𝔩, the Profits of a 𝔓𝔲𝔟𝔩𝔦𝔠𝔨-𝔅𝔞𝔫𝔨, and the Probability of its arising, if those directions here laid down are followed. With the advantages of publick 𝔊𝔯𝔞𝔫𝔞𝔯𝔦𝔢𝔰.

Likewise, several other things needful to be understood by those that are or do intend to be concerned in planting in the said Countries.

All which is laid down very plain, in this small Treatise; it being easie to be understood by any ordinary Capacity. To which the *Reader* is referred for his further satisfaction.

---

By *Thomas Budd.*

---

Pr nred in the Year 1685. H

---

Title-pages of two important early works relating to the Provinces of New Jersey and Pennsylvania.
*From the originals in the New York Public Library, Lenox Branch.*

by the spoils. The remarkable increase in the number of strangers in the city, the sale of the richest oriental goods, the unusual circulation of the gold coins of the East, not to speak of the rapidity with which expensive buildings were erected, all pointed to illicit and unusual sources of wealth.

It mattered little whether the charges made against Fletcher by his enemies were true or false, they had sufficient foundation in circumstances to bring about his recall. We must recollect in his defence that he had not lived in peace with his legislative Assembly, and it is altogether likely that this fact may have lent strength to the accusations against him. The Assembly did not support him in his endeavors to secure an established ministry, a revenue for the king during life, repairs for the fort, and the erection of a chapel. One act of Fletcher's, however, must not be passed over in silence. In his zeal for the good of a State church, he had built a small chapel in the fort in 1693, for which the queen sent plates, books, and other furniture. It was burned with the other buildings in 1741, and but little is known of its history. One church, however, of his creation remains a monument to his administration to this day. Fletcher granted what was known as the King's Farm to Protestant Episcopal churchwardens for the site of a new edifice. A building was at once projected, and in course of a few months was completed. A charter, bearing date May 6, 1697, was granted by an Act of Assembly, approved and ratified by the governor and Council. This was Trinity Church, the foundation of the vastly rich and powerful Trinity parish of to-day.

Richard Coote, Earl of Bellomont, the new governor, though appointed in June, 1697, did not arrive in New York until April 2, 1698. His coming was a great event in the colony. He was greeted by a committee of prominent citizens from both political parties and crowds of people. Four barrels of gunpowder were burned in the salute of welcome, and a pretentious dinner was served in his honor. Bellomont was to serve likewise as Governor of Massachusetts and New Hampshire. He had been created earl by William in recognition of his services as treasurer and receiver-general of Mary and as the confidential friend of the king. He was a man of pure life and strict honor, and much above the average type of the colonial governor. He belonged to the aristocracy of England, yet believed in popular liberty and was not averse to political equality. He frequently championed the cause of the common people, and thus won the enmity of the aristocratic element of the colony. Largely for this reason his administration proved to be a stormy one. In addition, he had to contend with political corruption among public officials.

Immediately upon his arrival, Bellomont took up the cause of the Leislerians. He had the body of Leisler buried again with honor, and restored the estates of Leisler and Milborne to their families. This caused trouble, for many innocent persons had bought up parts of these estates. The new governor attacked land grants and even proposed bills preventing anyone from owning over one thousand acres of land. He ousted the Bayards, who were accused of complicity with the pirates, and appointed Leislerians in their places.

In the election of 1699 the aristocracy was completely defeated, and the Leislerians secured all the offices. This caused somewhat of a panic, for the rumor was spread broadcast that an attempt would be made by the Leislerians to get compensation for the property they had lost several years before. In 1700, just prior to the death of Bellomont, an act was passed favorable to the claims of the Leislerians. The aristocracy thereupon petitioned the crown. Charges of treason were then brought against Bayard, and a packed jury found him guilty. He, with Hutchings, was sentenced to be disembowelled and quartered, while others in the so-called treason suffered confiscation of estates. However, upon the arrival of Lord Cornbury, the new governor, May 3, 1702, Bayard and Hutchings were liberated and their lands restored to them. The Leisler Act was repealed, and the policy of neutrality adopted by the new governor very much allayed the ill feelings between the contesting factions.

For years piracy had been imperceptibly growing. It reached its height after England and Holland put an end to Spain's supremacy. Privateering against Spanish-American commerce had the air of respectability, but it soon degenerated into piracy. Then, again, tariff regulations had much to do with fostering the practice, for the people were eager to purchase goods from the pirates on account of the low price for which they were sold. Another cause of the remarkable growth of piracy during the seventeenth century was undoubtedly the more rapid expansion of commerce than the growth of naval facilities for protecting it. The chief haunts of the pirates were in the Indian Ocean, off the coast of Madagascar. Frequently, however, they would bring their stolen goods to New York and swear they had captured them from the French. Then, again, New York merchantmen would meet them at Madagascar and trade rum for their gold and East India goods. Finally, the trade prospered to such a degree that it became difficult to suppress it.

Chief among those engaged in this unlawful trade was Captain Kidd, a cultivated and attractive mariner, and an honest man during the early part of his life. He is said to have been the son of a Presbyterian minister in Scotland, and frequently styled himself "gentleman." In 1691 Kidd received an award of £150 from the Council of New York for services he had rendered the colony.

The pirates became so arrogant that the king determined to suppress them, and with this object in view a naval force was fitted out to be sent to the eastern seas. Kidd was recommended for the captaincy of one of the ships, and he, Robert Livingston, and Lord Bellomont entered into a private partnership to put down piracy. They subscribed £6,000 among themselves, and Kidd was given letters of marque, authorizing him to capture French vessels. Ten per cent of the proceeds was to be given to the king, the rest to be divided among the three partners. Kidd left New York for Madagascar in 1697. Nothing was heard of him for some time, until the rumor came that he himself had turned pirate. Such a report placed Bellomont in a precarious position, a fact of which his enemies were not slow in taking advantage. Shortly afterward, Bellomont received a message from Kidd, saying he had returned to Narragansett Bay and had prizes to the amount of £10,000 on board. He denied he had ever turned pirate.

How Kidd is supposed to have become a pirate is one of the most interesting, though perplexing, historical romances that the history of New York presents. Let us follow his career in the eastern seas for a brief space, for about it centres the history of the colony for almost a decade. In fact, the reputation of Bellomont and of Robert Livingston suffered considerably by reason of their intimacy with Kidd. The politics of the colony and even of England were tainted with the suspicion that those high in authority were in league, not only with Kidd, but with all the prominent pirates and privateers, buccaneers and maroons, of that piratical age.

Captain Kidd was furnished with two commissions: first, letters of marque and reprisal, authorizing him to capture French vessels—England being at that time at war with France; secondly, special commission for the arrest of pirates, confiscation of their property, and for bringing them to trial. With these two commissions he sailed out of Plymouth for New York, May, 1696, in the *Adventure,* a galley of thirty-six guns and eighty men. After increasing his company to one hundred and fifty-five men and taking on additional stores at New York, he sailed at first for Madeira, and after his departure from there the civilized world saw nothing of him for more than two years. He reached Madagascar in February, 1697, just nine months from his sailing from Plymouth. Finding no pirates in those parts, he tried his fortunes on the coast of Malabar. His provisions were every day wasting, and his ship began to need repairs very seriously.

At first it does not appear that he had the least design of turning pirate. His first depredation was at a place called Mabber, on the Red Sea, where he took some "Guinea corn" from the natives by force. After this he is said to have acceded to his starving crew's demands to turn pirate. Happening to talk of the Mocha fleet, it is claimed he said: "We have been unsuccessful hitherto; but courage, my boys, we'll make our fortunes out of this fleet." Soon the fleet appeared, convoyed by one English and one Dutch man-of-war. This he attacked, though without success. One attack led to another, until he and his crew imperceptibly took up the life of pirates. However, for a while they confined themselves to attacking the vessels of the heathen, but afterward those of Christian nations were likewise attacked.

The *Adventure* proving old and leaky, Kidd transferred his goods to a captured Moorish merchantman, the *Queda*, but lost all except forty of his men—some going with the *Resolution*, another pirate ship, and others deserting. He next touched at Amboyna, one of the Dutch spice islands, where he received the unwelcome intelligence that he had become notorious in England and had been declared a pirate. His piracies, in fact, had so alarmed the English merchants that a motion passed Parliament to inquire into his commission and to discover the persons who had fitted him out.

In the meantime, a royal proclamation was issued granting pardon to all pirates who would surrender themselves. Kidd and another pirate, Avery, were excepted. This was to throw off all suspicion that his partners, well-known in English and American politics at that time, might incur. The Tories exaggerated Kidd's deeds for the purpose of undermining the influence of the Lord Chancellor, who was a Whig. When Kidd left Amboyna he knew nothing of this proclamation, otherwise he would surely never have sailed right into the jaws of danger. He relied upon his interest with Lord Bellomont, the showing of a French pass or two found on board ships he had captured, and a division of the rich booty he had secured, to hush the matter up and to ensure that justice would but wink at him.

Kidd had, however, made an enemy of the one man of whose friendship he stood most in need. Bellomont may have had his shortcomings, but they were not in the direction of a lack of zeal for the public good. Then, again, Kidd had wounded his pride—for the governor had a very keen sense of his own honor. Kidd had been sent out for the special purpose of clearing the American coast of pirates, but had turned pirate himself. Bellomont was eager for revenge.

In the meantime, Kidd had bought a small sloop at the island of Curaçoa, in which he put his spoils of immense value. He left the *Queda* at Santo Domingo and proceeded to New York. There he learned that the governor had gone to Boston. Kidd was joined by his wife and children at Block Island. At Narragansett Bay, he sent the message to Bellomont informing him of his arrival with goods worth £10,000. He declared himself entirely innocent of the acts of piracy with which he had been charged. Bellomont, in reply, promised him protection if he could establish his innocence. Accordingly, on July 1st, Kidd landed in Boston, made the governor's wife a present of jewels, and recited his story. The governor not being satisfied with it, Kidd was arrested a few days later and finally was sent to London. Here he was imprisoned more than a year, while evidence was being collected against him in the East Indies.

Kidd was tried in May, 1701, at the Sessions of Admiralty held at the Old Bailey, on the two charges of piracy on the high seas and the murder of one William Moore, a gunner. When Kidd was asked what he had to say why sentence should not be passed against him, he answered that "he had nothing to say, but that he had been sworn against by perjured, wicked people." When sentence was pronounced, he said: "My lord, it is a very hard sentence. For my part, I am the innocentest person of them all [referring to other pirates on trial, some of whom had been acquitted], only I have been sworn against by perjured persons." On May 12, 1701, Captain Kidd and six others were executed at Execution Dock. Their bodies were hung in chains, at intervals down the river, and there exposed for several years. The verdict was undoubtedly predetermined; but a few years before, Kidd's exploits would have been applauded rather than condemned. "Under ordinary circumstances," says Doyle, "Kidd, instead of becoming an ogre of legend, might have ended his days as a respected citizen, and his bones, instead of bleaching on a gibbet, might have rested under a stone where he would be described as an exemplary husband and father, a brave seaman, and a pious Christian."

We must turn our attention now to affairs in the Jerseys. In the spring of 1692 the proprietors had appointed Colonel Andrew Hamilton Governor of West Jersey, where he arrived in September of the same year. His personal popularity led the people to accept the resumption of a proprietary form of government without complaint. The Assembly was convened on September 28th, at Perth Amboy, and all laws passed subsequent to 1682, with but few exceptions, were either reënacted or amended. In addition, a war grant was made to assist New York in defending her frontiers against French and Indian invasion. A similar grant was refused in 1696, unless New York were actually invaded. Later, legislation was passed to improve foreign trade, to regulate the courts, and to construct better roads.

With an increase in population and the growth of settlements, the people of East Jersey began to feel pressing need of more schools and schoolmasters. The first action of importance in East Jersey in this direction was in 1693. In the records of a meeting of the Council held at Perth Amboy, October 20, 1693, we find the following: "A message from ye house of Deputyes with two bills past ye house, one Intitled for setling a School and School Master in every town in and throughout ye province, the other a bill for regulation of ordinaries." In fact, the records of the period are replete with evidence of the determination of the people to establish a suitable school system.

By an Act of Parliament in 1697, all proprietaries were compelled to submit the names of their appointees to governorships to the king for approval. Inasmuch as no one but native-born Englishmen could hold such offices under this act, Governor Hamilton was ineligible, being a Scotchman. Accordingly, he was dismissed on October 12, 1697, and Jeremiah Basse was put in his place. Though commissioned on July 15, 1697, the latter did not arrive until the spring of 1698. Dissatisfaction with him immediately developed, and West Jersey refused to recognize him. The dissatisfaction with Basse grew more and more pronounced, until in August, 1699, the authorities were compelled to dismiss him and reinstate Hamilton. This was made possible through the opinion of the king's attorney-general and solicitor-general that a native of Scotland was eligible as governor of a province. He retained the position for but a short time. Opposition developed against him, in turn, and Andrew Bowne was commissioned in his place. He, likewise, was not recognized. As a matter of fact, the Jerseys politically were in a state bordering on anarchy. The proprietors had become scattered throughout England, Scotland, and America. For years they had received but little proceeds or emoluments from the province. Conflicting reports soon came before the crown of the condition of affairs in the Jerseys, and the final result was a surrender of the patents of both East and West Jersey to the crown.

Negotiations leading to this event lasted from July, 1699, to August, 1702. On August 17, 1702, Queen Anne accepted the surrender of the two charters. The surrender was absolute, with the exception of a retention by the proprietors of certain land privileges, such as quitrents.

At the same time, the distinction between East and West Jersey ceased, and the two were united and placed under the governorship of Edward Hyde, Lord Cornbury, the newly commissioned Governor of New York. In her instructions to Lord Cornbury, Queen Anne established a General Assembly for the consolidated Jerseys. It was to sit alternately first at Perth Amboy in East Jersey and then at Burlington in West Jersey. Cornbury's commission was dated July 25, 1702. There were one hundred and three articles in his instructions, one of which granted liberty of conscience to all except Papists.

In New York, the death of Governor Bellomont in 1701 threw matters into confusion. The sadness occasioned by his death was more than counteracted by the clash of political interests that followed immediately. There was no one on the spot who had a clear constitutional right to succeed the dead governor. In this lay the danger. There were a number of claimants, but upon none of these could those in authority agree. Lieutenant-governor Nanfan, who, according to the charter, should have taken up the reins of government immediately upon the decease of his superior, was in Barbadoes. Colonel William Smith, the senior member of the Council, was away, but hastened to New York immediately upon hearing the news.

For over a year New York was in a state of continuous political turmoil. But events, in the meantime, were moving in kaleidoscopic fashion. William III. died, March 8, 1702, after a reign of over thirteen years, and was succeeded by Anne, the younger daughter of James II. Two months after, May 3d, Lord Cornbury landed at New York, with considerable ceremony, as governor of the province. The usual banquet was served. The new governor was a first cousin of the queen, and had been appointed governor by William. He had been engaged in military affairs for nearly twenty years, but of political power he had little or no conception. Of tact and discretion he had none, nor did he have any sympathy with the idea of popular rights.

In the late autumn of 1703, Cornbury met the New Jersey Assembly at Perth Amboy. He explained the constitution and stated his purposes to the Council and Assembly. He then demanded a revenue for the government. The Assembly thanked him for his kind expressions, but refused to comply with his demands with reference to the revenue. The governor thereupon prorogued the Assembly, declaring that it would not legislate for the good of the province. Practically the same farce was repeated the next year, when the Assembly met at Burlington. This time, however, the governor demanded an appropriation for the defence of the province. He had already asked for £2,000 per annum for twenty years to defray the current expenses of the government. The Assembly agreed to grant but £1,300 per annum for three years, and was forthwith dissolved for its contumacy. By having three of the new representatives who opposed him rejected, Cornbury secured a more pliant Assembly in November of the same year. The £2,000 was voted, a militia established, and the rights of suffrage granted to all freeholders.

By his arrogance and extravagance, Cornbury found himself in difficulties not only with the New Jersey Assembly but likewise with that of New York. The former in 1707, under the leadership of Samuel Jennings as speaker, resolved itself into a committee of the whole and decided to lay its grievances before the queen. Jennings read these grievances to the governor, in spite of the latter's frequent interruptions. In New York he had become thoroughly discredited by reason of his attempt to establish the Protestant Episcopal Church in that province to the exclusion of all other denominations.

Protests against his administration in both provinces continued to be received by the government in England in such numbers that his fitness for his position was seriously discussed by the authorities. The people of New Jersey and New York were disappointed in him. They were attracted at first by his rather handsome face and courteous manners, but they soon experienced his inefficiency. He bore a striking resemblance to his cousin, Queen Anne, and made himself ridiculous by bedecking himself with magnificent and costly millinery, like a lady of the court. When these petitions for his removal came in rapid succession and were supported in every instance by the signatures of men of character and influence throughout the two colonies, the government acted with commendable promptness. Baron Lovelace of Hurley was appointed in his place, and arrived at New York on the 18th of December, 1708.

In the midst of the festivities occasioned by the event of the arrival of the new governor, Cornbury was seized by his numerous hungry creditors and lodged in the debtor's prison. Here he was confined until he became Earl of Clarendon through his father's death. He then paid his debts and left New York, with few friends, if any, to mourn his departure. "He carried with him to England," says Lamb, "the memorable distinction of having been one of the most disreputable of all the New York governors." The new governor fell ill shortly after his arrival, and died in the following May. He was succeeded temporarily by Lieutenant-governor Ingoldsby, who appeared not to have the confidence of anyone.

In New Jersey, Ingoldsby's brief rule was characterized by the emission of £3,000 in bills of credit to maintain an expedition against Canada, under Colonels Nicholson and Vetch. Three bills were prepared: first, one for raising £3,000; secondly, one to enforce its currency; thirdly, to encourage volunteers to go on the expedition against Canada. As a result of the second bill, paper currency made its appearance in New Jersey. The legislature took care in this, as well as in all the succeeding emissions, to establish a sinking fund to provide for its ultimate withdrawal. New bills were to be substituted as the old ones became ragged and torn, and no reëmissions on any account whatsoever were to be permitted. This issuance of paper money was undoubtedly a very unwise step, in spite of the precautions taken by the legislature against inflation. It was, in fact, but a few years before (June 18, 1704) that Queen Anne had issued her famous proclamation regulating the value of coins. The colonial governments met in New York for the purpose of making effective Anne's law. The values of all coins in circulation were fixed, and there were hopes that a stable monetary system would be the result. Such was not the case, however; money grew even scarcer, and the colonies resorted to paper currency.

Ingoldsby was succeeded by Robert Hunter, a Scotchman, who proved himself to be one of the best governors New York had during the colonial period. He was liberal, wise, refined, and congenial. He was most enthusiastically received by the people upon his arrival. He soon won the good will of the Council, but differences regarding the revenue always stood as an insuperable barrier to a complete understanding between himself and the Assembly. Conflict of opinion arose between the Assembly and the Council as to the relative status of each; the latter claimed to be the upper house, like the House of Lords, and considered the Assembly as only an advisory board. The Assembly, in turn, kept a check upon both Council and governor by doling out funds for the support of the government in yearly instalments.

In Maryland, we have seen that the English Revolution of 1688 had its counter effect in the overthrow of Lord Baltimore's proprietary government. This occurred in 1691, and the next year Sir Lionel Copley assumed the reins of government. His first act was to dissolve the convention and call an Assembly which immediately proclaimed William and Mary. By another act, the Church of England was established, and the principle of taxation for its support was recognized. Annapolis was made the capital of the province. In 1700 an act was passed establishing uniformity of worship throughout the province. The influence of the Dissenters in England, however, prevented its acceptance by the crown. This most sensible use of the veto by the crown did not, unfortunately, benefit the Roman Catholics. They were denied the privilege of celebrating Mass publicly. Furthermore, no teacher of the young could be a Roman Catholic, and very often the property of members of that faith was confiscated.

During the whole period that Maryland was a royal province the Assembly enjoyed a most unusual degree of power. The delegates refused to establish a permanent revenue, and put a tax on imported negroes for the purpose of obstructing their importation. The Assembly was not successful, however, in engrafting English rights and liberties on the colony. Several times the attempt was made, but on every occasion it met with scant courtesy at the hands of the crown. Free schools and libraries were established. In 1710 there were nearly thirty thousand free persons in the province, but progress was by no means rapid.

Before leaving this period, let us turn for a moment to a consideration of what was at times called the negro insurrection of 1712, to distinguish it from the more serious plot of 1741. The importation of negroes at this date was perhaps more lucrative than any other kind of commerce. The importance of the traffic is clearly evidenced by the establishment of a slave market at the foot of what is now Wall Street, in New York. The traffic continued to prosper until, as a result, right in the midst of the despair caused by the failure of a second Canadian expedition, alarming symptoms began to manifest themselves. Nearly half the population of New York City in 1712—then about six thousand—was "black." All the wealthy families owned slaves, there being in some establishments as many as fifty. The ignorance and stupidity of the slaves and the lack of unity among them seemed to preclude most effectually any possible danger from them. It is claimed however, that a number of those negroes who had received some hard usage from their masters planned a scheme of revenge. They were to kill as many citizens as possible, without regard to whether they had been injured by them or not. Meeting at midnight in an orchard not far from the present Maiden Lane, they armed themselves with guns, swords, hatchets, and butcher knives. Their first criminal act was to set fire to an outhouse for the purpose of alluring their unsuspecting victims. The ruse was successful, and as a result nine men were murdered in a most brutal manner and six were seriously wounded.

Those who escaped gave the alarm, and the governor sent a detachment of soldiers from the fort at double-quick time. Before the soldiers arrived, the negroes had taken to the woods. Sentinels were stationed at all the ferries to prevent their escaping from the island, and on the following day they were all captured. Six committed suicide, but the others were brought to trial. Twenty-one were condemned and executed. Of these, several were burned at the stake, others were hanged, one was broken on the wheel, and one hung in chains to die of starvation. A large number of others were arrested on suspicion of being implicated in the crime. They were afterward released for lack of sufficient evidence to convict, or were pardoned by the governor.

## CHAPTER XIV

### GROWTH OF AN ARISTOCRATIC COLONY, 1714–1754

HUNTER'S wise administration of nine years marks a period of steady growth and prosperity in New York. The increase in population following the Leislerian rebellion was slow, due undoubtedly to a large extent to the continuous exodus of young men to New Jersey and Pennsylvania. Then, again, the French and Indian wars and the consequent danger of invasions from Canada prevented the settlement of the interior of the province. Still, in 1720 New York province had a population of approximately twenty-seven thousand whites and four thousand blacks. From 1693 to 1720, the strength of the militia had increased from two thousand nine hundred and twenty-three to six thousand.

The only bar to a thoroughly healthy social growth during this period was the alarming increase of servitude of all kinds, but especially that of the negroes. The lower stratum of society, or the servile class, of New York was the same in kind as in the other colonies, especially Virginia. There were indented white servants and negro slaves. The indented white servants were either: first, convicts shipped from Great Britain to get rid of them; or secondly, poor men and women kidnapped and sold into servitude; or thirdly, redemptioners, who were to pay their passage money by servile labor after arriving in the colonies. Owing to the fact that the great landed estates of New York were cultivated largely

by free tenant farmers, servile labor was by no means the
rule there, as it was in the Southern provinces. Negro slaves
and indented white servants were far less numerous than in
the South. Nevertheless, the rapid increase of both classes
in New York during this period was a matter for serious
apprehension.

Negro slaves were probably first brought to New Amsterdam in 1625, and from that time on throughout the
colonial period the traffic afforded remunerative returns to
those who were engaged in it. The average price for slaves
of both sexes was from £30 to £50. They were assigned
all kinds of tasks, agricultural and domestic, from plowmen
to valets. The slaves appear to have been fairly well treated
and were not overworked. Mrs. Grant asserts, in her
*Memoirs of an American Lady* (i, 51), that among the people
of Albany "even the dark aspect of slavery was softened
into a smile." The existence of the "bad" negro made it
necessary, however, to enact laws restricting considerably
the privileges of all the others. They were not permitted
to congregate in numbers exceeding four, and they could
not carry weapons of any description, under a penalty of ten
lashes at the whipping post. Another act provided that no
slave could go about the streets after nightfall anywhere
beyond a certain limit without a lighted lantern, "so as the
light thereof may be plainly seen." In 1746, New York
City had a population of eleven thousand seven hundred and
twenty-three, and of this number two thousand four hundred and forty-four were slaves. John Cruger, a slave dealer
from 1712 to 1733, was an ex-alderman of New York, and
afterward served four consecutive terms as mayor of the
city. This shows how the traffic was viewed in New York
at this period. The negro slave trade was regarded somewhat in the same light as we consider the immigration traffic
of to-day. The profits from the trade were too great and
the social odium incurred in engaging in it too insignificant
for the thrifty New York merchants to resist the temptation
of embarking in the business. There were, in addition to the

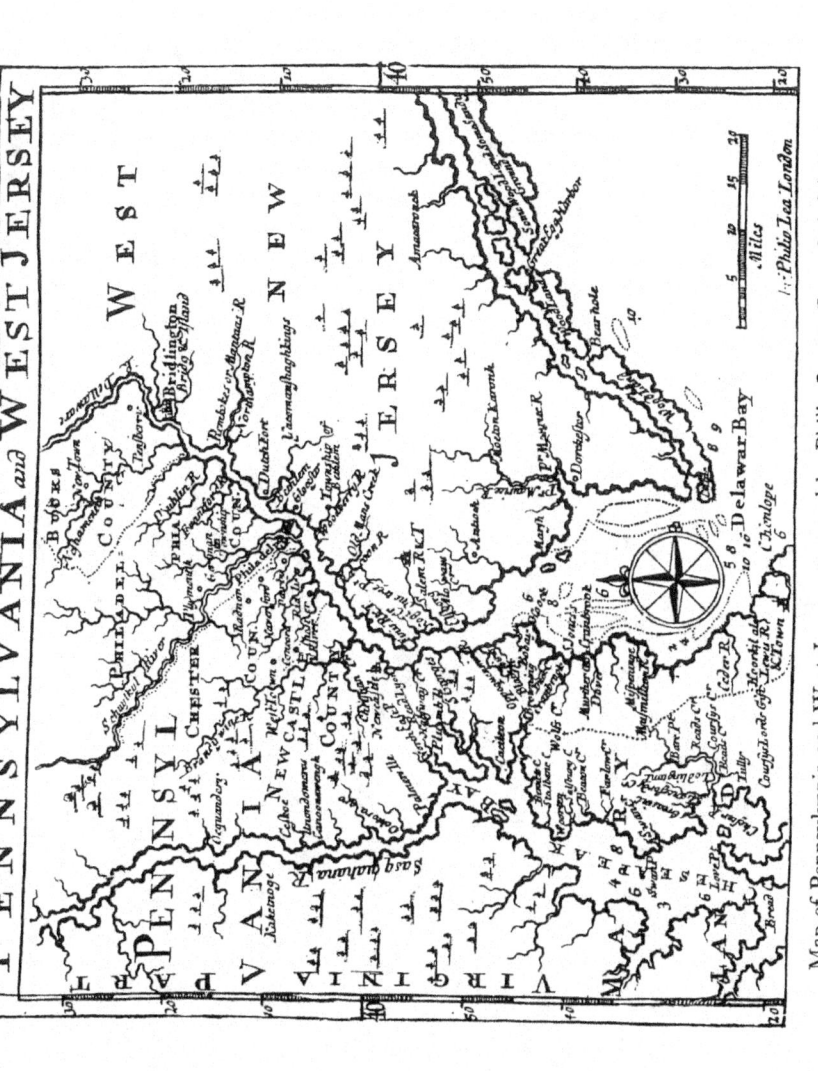

Map of Pennsylvania and West Jersey, engraved by Philip Lea. From Gabriel Thomas's "*Account of Pennsylvania,*" the original of which is in the New York Public Library, Lenox Branch.

negro slaves, also Indian slaves. On November 30, 1711, we find that the following law was passed: "All negro and Indian slaves that are let out to hire within the city do take up their standing in order to be hired at the market house at the Wall Street Slip."

Commerce naturally expanded with the increase in population. Especially was this true in regard to the trade with the Indians. The exports of the province far exceeded the imports. From 1717 to 1720, the former amounted to about £52,000 per annum, and the latter, £21,000. The navigation laws had not benefited the British merchants so much as they expected, although attempts were made to enforce the laws rigidly. It was the aim of British merchants to restrict manufactures in the colonies and in this way compel the colonists to purchase their goods in England. There is an interesting letter from Caleb Heathcote to the Lords of Trade, written in 1708, that throws some light on this policy of the British merchants: "My proposal was to divert the Americans from going on with their linen and woollen manufactories, and to turn their thoughts on such things as might be beneficial to Great Britain. They are already so far advanced in their manufactories that three-fourths of the linen and woollen, especially of the coarser sort they use, is made amongst them." The British merchants likewise planned the development of a business in naval stores. We have seen how Hunter tried to carry out this idea by importing the Palatines, and how signally he failed in that attempt.

Though there were many minor occurrences during the remainder of Governor Hunter's administration, there is but one matter of importance we need stop to consider. That is the constant bickering between him and his Assembly. Let us bear in mind that this was not particularly characteristic of Hunter and was in no sense due to any peculiarity of his. Every colonial governor had very much the same experience, though not every one was so nearly free from blame as was he. There were constant struggles in all the colonies between the governors and their Assemblies relative to the money question. The royal governors insisted that their salaries and the funds for the support of the colony should be voted once and for all and at a fixed rate. The Assemblies insisted on voting salaries and supplies every year or at every meeting of the legislature. In this way they hoped to retain a firm control of the public purse. The colonies realized that just as soon as they voted fixed sums for long periods they would cease to have a check upon the arbitrary will of the governors. The latter were helpless as long as the Assemblies controlled the public purse. The people understood this full well, and consequently guarded their interests jealously. But it brought on constant strife and occasioned much bad feeling. The different royal and proprietary governors made the question one of " privilege." They maintained that the action of the Assemblies was an invasion of the rights and privileges of the king. The colonies claimed, on the other hand, the English right of voting their supplies periodically. They demanded absolutely the right of self-taxation just as it was enjoyed by the English people through the House of Commons.

During the reigns of Anne, George I., and George II., the colonies were entirely successful in retaining this privilege in its integrity. The monarchs, on the other hand, through their representative governors, were as yet too weak to make a successful attack upon this claim of the colonies to self-taxation. This was due, no doubt, to the fact that Anne had not the energy and strength of a man. George I. and George II. were foreigners, and were thus compelled to hand over the actual management of home and colonial affairs to their ministers and representatives. When George III. came to the throne, this condition of affairs became changed. That monarch made the great mistake of the century in trying to coerce the colonies, where other monarchs or their gubernatorial representatives had merely threatened, browbeaten, cajoled, bribed, or begged. The result in general we know, the result in New York we shall see in due time. We may repeat, therefore, that the troubles Governor Hunter experienced were neither unusual nor due to his own peculiarities. In many respects he was the best governor New York had had for years.

Early in 1719, Hunter began to make preparations to return to England. He did this quietly, because he greatly feared that the news of his intention might occasion intrigues, if it should be known that he was to resign his government. No one knew of his decision until June 24th, when he summoned the House before him, and, after transacting the special business for which they had been called, he arose and addressed them in the following words: "May no strife ever happen among you, but that laudable emulation who shall approve himself the most zealous servant and most dutiful subject of the best of princes, and most useful member of a well-established and flourishing community of which you have given a happy example." The Assembly replied: "You have governed well and wisely, like a prudent magistrate, like an affectionate parent." He returned to England, but was soon appointed Governor of Jamaica, where he died in 1734.

"No governor ever left New York with greater *éclat* or carried with him more substantial tokens of good will and affection" than Hunter. He sailed in July, 1719, and the chief command of the province devolved upon Peter Schuyler as the oldest member of the Council. His short administration was marked by very few events of note. A little over a year from the time of Hunter's farewell to New York, on the 17th of September, 1720, Schuyler was relieved from executive duties by the arrival of Governor William Burnet.

Two men stood out prominently in the affairs of the colony during the early years of the eighteenth century. They were Peter Schuyler and Robert Livingston. For eight years Schuyler served as Mayor of Albany, having been designated to fill that position in the charter granted by Governor Dongan. He was the leader of the movement against Leisler, and was a member of the Provincial Council during Fletcher's administration. In 1700, he was appointed colonel of the Albany County militia, and as a soldier stood foremost in the colony. He had the confidence of the Iroquois, whom he frequently led in attacks upon the French and Indians. He treated the red men as his brethren, and frequently invited them to visit him at his home, to sit at his table. The confidence with which he inspired the Indians made him a valuable man in all the political conferences between them and the whites. He was known to the Indians familiarly as "Brother Quider." His knowledge of the impending dangers from Canada came from the red men. To convince the British government of such dangers, he, with five Iroquois chiefs, made a memorable visit to England at his own expense. The presence of such strangers in England was an unusual event and created a sensation throughout that country.

To raise funds, Schuyler hit upon the novel idea of exhibiting his five warriors before the public. It was during this visit that the Iroquois warriors came upon the half-starved Palatines and out of sympathy and commiseration offered them some of their lands along the Schoharie. Schuyler's arguments were heeded by the British court, but out of neglect or jobbery on the part of the ministry the expedition fitted out at that time proved a failure. Later, however, his policy was carried to a triumphant end.

Among the noted families into which the Schuylers had married was that of the Livingstons. Robert Livingston was closely allied to Schuyler in his opposition to Leisler, and favored Leisler's execution. He received the manor of Livingston through a grant obtained from Governor Dongan and confirmed by George I. in 1715. He afterward became Mayor of Albany, was a member of the Provincial Council, and often sat in the General Assembly. His descendants have played an active part in the affairs of the country.

Governor William Burnet began his administration on September 17, 1720. He was the son of a bishop, famous as a historian. Burnet himself was a man of learning and accomplishments. He had lost money in the South Sea Bubble, and thought to retrieve his fortunes by exchanging with General Hunter the office of comptroller of customs in London for the governorship of New York. He allied himself with the friends of Governor Hunter, and further strengthened his position in the colony by a marriage with a daughter of a prominent Dutch merchant—Abraham van Horne. He had no difficulty whatever in securing a grant of revenue for five years, which afterward was extended to eight years. Throughout his administration he was zealously supported by the colonists in the chief measures for the good of the colony.

Burnet deemed it advisable to meet the Indian sachems in Albany during the summer of 1721. He treated them kindly, and soon won their friendship and their promise to agree to his terms of peace. On his part, he promised to establish an English settlement in their wild country. They referred to his marriage with an American girl with considerable felicity, and presented the bride with a few beavers for pin money. They furthermore added most significantly that it was "customary for a brother upon his marriage to invite his brethren to be merry and dance." Burnet took this suggestion in good part and thanked them for their good wishes. He then distributed presents, and ordered several barrels of beer to be given them "to rejoice with and dance over."

Nevertheless, in 1722, the very next year, the Five Nations were reported as making frequent inroads into Virginia, contrary to a treaty of long standing. In Pennsylvania, a quarrel between the whites and some Indians of the Five Nations had resulted in bloodshed. Fearing that other colonies were tampering with the Indians, Burnet deemed it advisable to see the sachems himself and expostulate with them for their conduct. The Indians, in their turn, promised that if representatives from Virginia would meet them they would renew the covenant chain and keep clear of the Virginia territory in all their future hunting and warlike expeditions. Burnet interpreted this to mean that fine presents would refresh their memories, and so wrote to the Lords of Trade.

He furthermore proposed a congress of governors and commissioners from all the colonies to meet the Indian chiefs at Albany. His ostensible object was to confirm treaties; but his real object was to show the Indians that the English could act in unison as well as the French. This congress met in September, 1722. Governor Spotswood, of Virginia, attended the congress and frankly submitted all the propositions that he had made with the Indians up to that time. Sir William Keith, of Pennsylvania, presided over the congress, while Burnet acted as agent for Boston. The session lasted several days and terminated satisfactorily to all parties.

This congress memorialized the English government to grant funds to erect trading posts and forts throughout the Indian country. In this way the encroachments of the French could be anticipated. Had the government acted upon this advice, millions of dollars and thousands of lives would have been saved; and furthermore, the great French and Indian War might not have been precipitated. England, however, paid little attention to the appeal, and the project was reluctantly abandoned.

Burnet had taken possession of Oswego and in 1722 established a trading post there. This annoyed the French, who feared the trade from the upper lakes would be drawn thither and diverted from Montreal. Securing the consent of the Onondagas, the French restored their trading post and fort at Niagara. The other members of the confederacy objected, however, and their representatives met Burnet in council at Albany in 1726. They said: "We come to you howling, and this is the reason why we howl, that the Governor of Canada comes upon our land and builds thereon." The governor, in response, promised much, but could perform little. The merchants of New York and Albany profited by the illicit trade in Indian goods with Montreal, and opposed the governor in his Indian policy. He could do very little for the protection of the Indians.

On June 11, 1727, George I. died and George II. ascended the throne of England. Contrary to his desire, Burnet was removed in 1728 from the government of New York to that of Massachusetts and New Hampshire. He was escorted with much ceremony on his journey from New York to Boston, and carried with him the good will of the colonists. On the borders of Rhode Island he was met by a committee from Boston. A member of this committee was a Colonel Taylor, who made a rather facetious reply to a complaint by Burnet of the long graces said at the meals where they had stopped along the road. The governor inquired when they would shorten. "The *graces* will increase in length until you get to Boston; after that, they will shorten till you come to your government in New Hampshire, where your excellency will find no grace at all," replied Taylor. One important event, at least, characterized his administration of New York. He renewed the ancient covenant chain with the Indians. This was extremely seasonable, for the next spring the French prepared to make further encroachments upon the English borders. Burnet's successor was Colonel John Montgomery, a gentleman of honor to George II. while he was Prince of Wales. Montgomery's great aim was to get money. He avoided contests with the legislature by giving way to that body in all things. His administration was a short one. He died in office, July 1, 1731, and it may be said that it was but a faint shadow that the event cast upon the colonial horizon. Three important events occurred, however, during his administration that we must not fail to record: the establishment of a public library in New York City in 1729; the granting of a new charter to the city in 1730; and the settlement of the Connecticut-New York boundary dispute on May 14, 1731.

Rip van Dam succeeded Montgomery, as acting governor. He was the oldest member and the president of the Council, and "one of the people of figure." For thirteen months he filled the position with dignity until relieved by Colonel William Cosby, who arrived in New York on August 1, 1732. Cosby's administration is particularly remembered by reason of the great money dispute with Rip van Dam. It led to a trial which created the most intense interest throughout the English colonies. The Assembly considered Cosby a friend of the people, and followed the popular wish by readily granting a revenue to support the government for six years. This included a salary for the governor of £1,500, together with certain emoluments amounting to £400. In addition, £150 was voted to pay his expenses on a journey to Albany, besides a sum to be expended in presents for the Iroquois. Afterward £750 was voted him as a present in recognition of his services in helping to prevent the passage of legislation detrimental to the interests of the colony. Chief Justice Smith said: "All this did not satisfy the colonel, who had come to New York to make a fortune, and had not sense enough to see that it was his interest to improve the popularity which attended, or rather preceded, his arrival. Meeting Mr. Morris, who had a seat in the Assembly, he, on hearing of the gratuity voted by the Assembly, exclaimed, 'Damn them! why did they not add shillings and pence?'"

But Van Dam, the merchant, caused still fiercer ire in the breast of the choleric colonel when a settlement of accounts was called for. While Rip van Dam was in the chair he, of course, received the salary of governor. But Colonel Cosby brought with him the king's order, dated May 31, 1732, for an equal partition between himself and the president of the Council of the salary, emoluments, and perquisites of the office, from the time Van Dam first administered the government to that at which Cosby relieved him. The opinion of the Assembly was asked as to whether the whole salary should be paid to the acting governor or only a part of it. The Assembly refused to deliver an opinion and referred the question to the Council. The Council consented that the warrants should be drawn for the whole sum.

After the Assembly adjourned, Cosby produced his order from the king. Van Dam knew that the governor had received while in England, upon various pretences, sums of money which exceeded what had been paid to himself by over £2,400. Consequently, he stated his receipts at £1,975 7s. 10d., and those of the governor as £6,407 18s. 10d. The English governor demanded half of the former amount; the Dutch merchant agreed, provided he received half of the latter amount. He would retain his salary, if his opponent was content; otherwise, he appealed to the order for an equal division of receipts between them. The governor created a court of exchequer to compel the Dutchman to refund. Van Dam retaliated by trying to institute a suit at common law. Cosby dreaded this because Van Dam was popular and the jury would no doubt declare in his favor. Van Dam's plea to be tried at common law was overruled, and he was compelled to make his defence before the judges in equity. His counsel were William Smith, father of the historian, and James Alexander, father of William Alexander, Lord Stirling, both eminent lawyers. They made exception to the court resorted to by the governor. Chief Justice Morris supported the exception. The two associate justices, James De Lancey and Aldophe Phillipse, voted against the plea. Morris published his opinion and sent a copy with explanation to Cosby on the latter's demand. Cosby was so irritated as a result of the publication that he removed Morris from office after twenty years of unimpeachable service. De Lancey was appointed in his place. The governor took this action without consulting either the Assembly or the Council. The case was subsequently dropped without settlement, and

Cosby never recovered any of the money. But the proceedings created two violent parties and the most bitter feelings. The democratic, or popular, side was with Van Dam, while the aristocratic side was with Cosby. The opposition to Cosby took head rapidly, and in 1734 it was decided to send Morris to England with the object of securing the removal of the governor. The utmost secrecy was deemed advisable.

Out of the Van Dam-Cosby dispute grew another trial, which excited interest throughout the English colonies and stirred New York from centre to circumference: namely, the trial of John Peter Zenger for publishing a libel.

In 1693, William Bradford came from Philadelphia and brought with him the "art of printing." He was born in Leicestershire, England, May 20, 1663, and sailed with Penn for America, September 1, 1682. The first sheet printed by Bradford in Philadelphia was an almanac in 1685, and the first book was written by George Keith, teacher of the first school establishment in Pennsylvania. This book reflected upon the Quakers, and their wrath drove the printer to New York. Here, October 16, 1725, he commenced the first newspaper published in that province. It must be borne in mind that the earlier governors sent from England had instructions not to permit to be erected such a "pestiferous engine" as a printing press. Bradford became printer for the governor, and his newspaper was, to some extent, a government organ.

One of Bradford's apprentices was John Peter Zenger, born in Germany in 1697. He came from the Palatinate with his widowed mother, a brother, and a sister, in 1710. He was one of the party of Germans brought over by Governor Hunter at the expense of Queen Anne's government. In 1711, he was apprenticed to Bradford, whose paper was called the *New York Gazette.* Later, November 5, 1733, Zenger started an opposition paper, calling it the *New York Weekly Journal.* Bradford's paper was in the hands of the governor and his friends exclusively. Zenger's paper was taken up by the "patriots"—the supporters of Van Dam and Morris. The *Journal* was filled with witticisms directed against the government officials. Bradford replied in the *Gazette*, but he was not equal to his adversary in sarcasm. Cosby and his councillors were driven almost to madness.

Further trouble was caused by Zenger's paper taking up the accusation against Francis Harrison, one of the councillors. Harrison was accused of having written a letter threatening James Alexander and his family with bodily injury unless a certain sum of money were paid. Harrison indignantly denied the imputation, but suspicion continued to rest upon him, though he was exonerated by his fellow councillors. The affair was industriously fomented by the *Journal*, and out of it, in part, grew the imprisonment and trial of John Peter Zenger.

Chief Justice De Lancey called the attention of the grand jury in October, 1734, to certain low ballads in the *Weekly Journal*, which he designated as "libels." He said, in substance: "Sometimes heavy half-witted men get a knack of rhyming, but it is time to break them of it when they grow abusive, insolent, and mischievous with it." The ballads were ordered to be burned by the common whipper. Later, attempts were made by the Council to discover the author of certain other libels. The governor was requested to have the printer prosecuted. The communication was sent to the Assembly, but was laid upon the table. On November 2, 1734, numbers 7, 47, 48, and 49 of Zenger's *Weekly Journal* were pronounced by the Council "as containing many things tending to sedition and faction, and to bring his majesty's government into contempt, and to disturb the peace thereof." These numbers of the newspaper were condemned to be burned near the pillory by the common hangman on Wednesday, the 6th instant, between the hours of eleven and twelve in the forenoon. It was also ordered that the mayor, Robert Lurting, and the rest of the city magistrates should attend the burning. The court, however, would not suffer the order to be entered, and the aldermen protested that it was arbitrary and illegal. As recorder, Harrison made a lame effort to justify the Council by citing the example of the Lords in the celebrated Sacheverell case (1710). He also made reference to the proceedings against Bishop Burnet's pastoral letter. The city authorities refused to attend the ceremony, and ordered their hangman not to obey the order. It is said that the papers were burned by a negro slave of the sheriff, and that the spectators were limited to the recorder and a few dependents of the governor.

Zenger writes in one of the numbers of the *Weekly Journal* that the "Attorney General then charged me by Informations for Printing and publishing Parts of my Journals No. 13 and 23 as being *false, scandalous, malicious, and seditious.*" The Council next issued an order to the sheriff to arrest Zenger for printing and publishing the alleged libellous papers. The arrest was made on Sunday, the 17th of November, and Zenger was committed to prison. A writ of *habeas corpus* was issued, in order to secure either his discharge or his liberation on bail. The hearing was held in the presence of some hundreds of the inhabitants. Among the citations made were Magna Charta; The Petition of Right (3 Carolus I. c. 1, June 7, 1628); The Habeas Corpus Act of 31 Carolus II. c. 2, 1679; 2 Hawkins, Chapter 15, Section 5; The Case of the Seven Bishops, Temp. Jacobus II. (1688). Needless to say, the defendant was admitted to bail upon furnishing bonds to the extent of £400. In his paper of November 25th, the editor apologized for not issuing the last *Weekly Journal*. The governor, he said, had put him in jail, but he now had the liberty of speaking through a hole in the door to his assistants. He would consequently supply his customers as heretofore. His dictations, however, were carefully watched.

The grand jury found no bill against Zenger. Nevertheless, on the 28th of January, 1735, Bradley, the attorney-general, filed an information against him for false, scandalous, malicious, and seditious libels. This could be done and the defendant practically indicted without the intervention of the grand jury. The trial excited the attention of all America. It began in July and occupied the entire summer. It was an important feature in the early history of the press of New York. It has been styled "the germ of American freedom and the morning star of that liberty which subsequently revolutionized America."

The specific libel which brought Zenger into trouble was his declaration that "the people of New York think, as matters now stand, that their liberties and properties are precarious, and that slavery is likely to be entailed on them and their posterity, if some things be not amended." Cosby was particularly referred to when the *Journal* further declared: "We see men's deeds destroyed, judges arbitrarily displaced, new courts erected without consent of the legislature, by which, it seems to me, trials by juries are taken away when a governor pleases; men of known estates denied their votes, contrary to the received practice of the best expositor of any law. Who is there in that province that can call anything his own, or enjoy any liberty longer than those in the administration will condescend to let him do it?"

Zenger was defended by James Alexander and William Smith, of New York, and Andrew Hamilton, of Philadelphia, three of the most prominent lawyers in America at that time. The services of Hamilton were not actually enlisted until after the other two counsel for the defence had been disbarred by Chief Justice De Lancey. Alexander and Smith immediately attacked the jurisdiction of the court itself by aiming at the legality of the commissions of Chief Justice De Lancey and Judge Phillipse. These lawyers claimed that the commissions of the judges read "during pleasure" instead of "good behavior" and had been granted by the governor independently of the Council. These facts, they maintained, made the commissions void. This attack upon their commissions was considered a gross contempt of court, and Chief Justice De Lancey, addressing Smith, said: "You have brought it to that point, sir, that either we must go from the bench or you from the bar." He thereupon ordered the names of the two counsel stricken from the rolls, thus excluding them from further practice. This caused almost a panic. The court then assigned John Chambers as counsel for the printer, who pleaded "not guilty" for his client and obtained a struck jury.

Hamilton, who had come forward in the meantime and offered his services free of charge in the defence of Zenger, admitted the publication of the articles charged in the "information." Bradley, the attorney-general, then demanded that the jury find a verdict for the king. "By no means," exclaimed Hamilton. "It is not the bare printing and publishing of a paper that will make it a libel; the words themselves must be libellous, that is, false, scandalous, seditious, or else my client is not guilty." Bradley said "the truth of a libel could not be taken in evidence." Hamilton held that an untruth made the libel, and challenged Bradley to prove the facts charged to be false, in which case he would acknowledge them scandalous, seditious, and a libel. To save trouble, however, he offered to prove the papers true. Chief Justice De Lancey informed Hamilton that he could not be admitted to give the truth of the libel in evidence, as the law was clear that a libel could not be justified. He held, furthermore, that it is "far from being a justification of a libel that the contents thereof are true, or that the person on whom it is made had a bad reputation, since the greater there is of truth in any malicious invective, so much the more provoking it is." Hamilton's address to the jury was full of sarcasm. He said: "You are the best judges of the law and the fact, and are to take upon yourselves to say whether the papers are false, scandalous, and seditious."

Chief Justice De Lancey charged the jury that they were judges of the fact, but not of the law, and that the truth of the libel was a question beyond their jurisdiction. This ruling did not have the least effect upon the jury. Hamilton's arguments had exerted a tremendous influence upon them, while those of the attorney-general had been swept aside like chaff. They returned a verdict, after only a few minutes' deliberation, of "not guilty." A great shout of applause went up after the verdict was known. This angered the judges, and one of them indiscreetly threatened the leader of the tumult with imprisonment, if he could be discovered. Captain Norris responded that huzzas were common in Westminster Hall, and were somewhat loud at the time of the acquittal of the Seven Bishops. The next day the corporation of the city tendered Hamilton a public dinner. The corporation, likewise, voted the freedom of the city in a magnificent gold box, "for the remarkable service done to this city and colony, by his defence of the rights of mankind and the liberty of the press." In referring to this trial, Gouverneur Morris is reported to have said that "instead of dating American liberty from the Stamp Act, he traced it to the persecution of John Peter Zenger, because that event revealed the philosophy of freedom, both of thought and speech, as an inborn human right."

As a result of the Zenger trial, the scribblers of the day took courage and wrote more impudently than before. The public prints were filled with squibs and ballads and serious charges against high officials. Zenger's acquittal was considered "the great triumph of the age." The democratic party, which stood behind him and supported him, considered the decision a victory for itself. It was, indeed, a personal victory for Alexander, Smith, Van Dam, and the other leaders of that party. The opportunity for retaliation now presented itself. Alexander and Smith proceeded against the judges before the next session of the Assembly for depriving them of their practice.

Cosby, in the meanwhile, seemed to lose no opportunity of gaining the detestation of both friends and neutrals and of increasing the hatred of his enemies. He treacherously destroyed deeds belonging to the city of Albany, and in consequence caused almost a panic. He decided to resurvey all the old patents on Long Island, and, as many of them had been drawn up by the Indians and early settlers without much regard for accuracy, the greatest consternation was caused by his decision. Even De Lancey could not support him in this decision, and remonstrated with the governor. The only reply he received, however, was: "What do you suppose I care for the grumbling rustics?"

Time, however, was shortly to work a way out of the difficulty. Cosby grew seriously ill during the winter of 1736. Upon being told that his life was in danger, he determined to take his last revenge upon him whom he considered his worst enemy. He summoned a few of his councillors to his bedside, and secretly suspended Van Dam to prevent his assumption of the government as president of the Council. Cosby died on March 10, 1736, and when his death was announced there was little outward manifestation of sorrow, but a very considerable inward feeling of joy. The people, who were fearing a daily attack upon their land patent rights, rejoiced greatly at being rid of the tyrant. Cosby had been received joyfully, but was relinquished with much more joy. The democratic party was in high glee over the prospects of Van Dam's speedy occupancy of the chair of state. Their triumph had come, thought they, but in that they were doomed to disappointment. Early the next morning the Council met and administered the oath of office to George Clarke, who was next to Van Dam in the order of age. Van Dam demanded the great seal of the province and the instructions of the king from Clarke, but the latter refused to surrender them and quoted the act of suspension by which Van Dam's claim was annulled. Van Dam contested the validity of Cosby's act of suspension, claiming that the former governor was delirious and irresponsible. He claimed, furthermore, that Cosby's authority ceased with suspending him from the Council and that such suspension could not debar him from assuming the powers of government after the governor's death. At all events, Van Dam claimed that his suspension could not continue after Cosby's death and that the Council had no authority to qualify Clarke. The sympathy of the

# By his Excellency

*William Cosby,* Captain General and Governour in Chief of the Provinces of New-York, New-Jersey, and Territories thereon depending in America, Vice-Admiral of the same, and Colonel in His Majesty's Army.

## A PROCLAMATION.

Whereas Ill-minded and Disaffected Persons have lately dispersed in the City of New-York, and divers other Places, several Scandalous and Seditious Libels, but more particularly two Printed Scandalous Songs or Ballads, highly defaming the Administration of His Majesty's Government in this Province, tending greatly to inflame the Minds of His Majesty's good Subjects, and to disturb the Publick Peace. And Whereas the Grand Jury for the City and County of New-York did lately, by their Address to me, complain of these Pernicious Practices, and request me to issue a Proclamation for the Discovery of the Offenders, that they might, by Law, receive a Punishment adequate to their Guilt and Crime. I Have therefore thought fit, by and with the Advice of his Majesty's Council, to issue this Proclamation, hereby Promising *Twenty Pounds* as a Reward, to such Person or Persons who shall discover the Author or Authors of the two Scandalous Songs or Ballads aforesaid, to be paid to the Person or Persons discovering the same, as soon as such Author or Authors shall be Convicted of having been the Author or Authors thereof.

*GIVEN under My Hand and Seal at Fort-George in New-York this Sixth Day of November, in the Eighth year of the Reign of Our Sovereign Lord GEORGE the Second, by the Grace of GOD of Great- ritain, France and Ireland, KING, Defender of the Faith, &c. and in the year of Our LORD, 1734.*

*By his Excellency's Command,*
Fred. Morris, *D. Cl. Conc.*

**W. COSBY.**

## GOD Save the KING.

Proclamation relating to two scandalous songs or ballads. *After the original in the New York Public Library, Lenox Branch.*

## A Song made upon the Election of new Magistrates for this City.

*To the tune of, To you fair Ladies now on land*

To you good lads that dare oppose
  all lawless power and might,
You are the theme that we have chose,
  and to your praise we write:
You dar'd to shew your faces brave
In spight of every abject slave;
      with a fa la la.

Your votes you gave for those brave men
  who feasting did dispise;
And never prostituted pen
  to certify the lies
That were drawn up to put in chains,
As well our nymphs as happy swains;
      with a fa la la.

And tho the great ones frown at this.
  what need have you to care?
Still let them fret and talk amiss,
  you'll shew you boldly dare
Stand up to save your Country dear,
In spight of usquebaugh and beer;
      with a fa la la.

They beg'd and pray'd for one year more,
  but it was all in vain:
No wolawants you'd have, you swore;
  By jove you made it plain:
So sent them home to take their rest.
And here's a health unto the best;
      with a fa la la.

## A Song made upon the foregoing Occasion.

*To the Tune of, Now, now, you Tories all shall stoop.*

Come on brave boys, let us be brave
  for liberty and law,
Boldly despise the haughty Knave,
  that would keep us in aw.
Let's scorn the tools bought by a sop,
  and every cringing fool.
The man who basely bend's a sop,
  a vile insipid tool.

Our Country's Rights we will defend,
  like brave and honest men;
We voted right and there's an end,
  and so we'll do again.
We vote all signers out of place
  as men who did amiss,
Who sold us by a false adress.
  I'm sure we're right in this.

Exchequer courts, as void by law,
  great grievances we call;
Tho' great men do assert no flaw
  is in them; they shall fall,
And be contemn'd by every man
  that's fond of liberty.
Let them withstand it all they can,
  our Laws we will stand by.

Tho' pettyfogging knaves deny
  us Rights of Englishmen;
We'll make the scoundrel raskals fly,
  and ne'er return again.
Our Judges they would chop and change
  for those that serve their turn,
And will not surely think it strange
  if they for this should mourn.

Come fill a bumber, fill it up,
  unto our Aldermen;
For common-council fill the cup,
  and take it o'er again.
While they with us resolve to stand
  for liberty and law,
We'll drink their healths with hat in hand,
  whoraa! whoraa! whoraa!

The two scandalous songs which figured in the Zenger-Cosby trouble.
After the original in the New York Public Library, Lenox Branch.

community was, of course, with Van Dam. The people trusted him and believed in him. They considered him grievously wronged and were disposed to support his claims by force if necessary.

Just at this crisis, despatches arrived from England clearly establishing Clarke in the presidency of the Council and making him commander-in-chief of the province, and later, July 30th, lieutenant-governor. Clarke now tried to conciliate all parties. He brought about a reconciliation between the judges and Alexander and Smith. Their right of pleading before the bar was returned to them. Clarke's action in the matter was commendable, but it lost him the confidence of the most influential members of the aristocratic party. De Lancey especially was not pleased.

Let us turn for a moment from the course of the narrative to consider that most curious manifestation of popular panic known as the Negro Plot of 1741. It is especially interesting in that it shows into what excesses people ordinarily conservative and normally sane may be led by mob influences. The psychology of panics and mobs is a subject in practical sociology extremely interesting, but up to the present little studied and far less understood. History affords overwhelming proof to substantiate the fact that the wisest of men may give way to these subtle influences when the circumstances are peculiarly favorable. For purposes of illustration, we have but to refer to the following manifestations of a tendency to return to the social status of the brute: the New England and old England "witchcraft" delusions; the various lynchings that characterize parts of the United States at present; the stampedes in burning theatres or the mad rushes in time of peril; the senseless runs on banks; and the violence of a mob. All point to the fact that men in groups are subject to influences entirely different from those that govern them as individuals. Cotton Mather, the New England divine of "Magnalia" fame, was one of the wisest and most self-possessed men in the New England of his time. Nevertheless, he was drawn into the vortex of fanatical persecution that swept over New England during the last decade of the seventeenth century.

It must be admitted, however, that in the case before us there was indeed a very solid foundation for the uneasiness that manifested itself on the part of the inhabitants of New York City in the year 1741. Ever since the unfortunate affair of 1712, the citizens of New York had been more or less afraid of an outbreak on the part of the negro slaves, who comprised so large a part of the population. Laws were enacted from time to time to keep them under thorough control. Forty lashes on the bare back was the penalty if more than two negroes were seen together, or if a negro was seen walking with a club in his hand outside of his master's grounds. Mention has been made of the fact that English traders flooded New Amsterdam with negro slaves, regardless of the remonstrances of the authorities. The province was upon the point of enacting a stringent set of laws against this practice when the colony was delivered over to the English. Under Dutch rule the slaves had not been abused, but, on the contrary, had been treated mildly and gently. In consequence, they regarded no punishment worse than a threat to sell them to other masters. After the English conquest, however, the colonial records are full of the arrangements made by the English government to impose slaves on its colonies. Many members of the government had large interests in the slave trade, and it was their policy to encourage the traffic. Lord Cornbury's instructions were to encourage the importation of slaves into New York province, notwithstanding the efforts of the colonists to stop it.

On February 28, 1741, the denizens of New York were terrified at the knowledge that a robbery had been committed at Robert Hogg's, a worthy tradesman of the middle class. Pieces of silverware, coins, linen, and other articles were stolen. Suspicion fell on some negroes who had been in the habit of meeting together at a tavern on North River. The keeper of the tavern was a man named Hughson.

His wife had a white servant named Mary Burton, a girl of only sixteen years of age, with very low tendencies. This girl was at once suspected of being an accomplice of the negroes, and was arrested. In order to screen herself, she implicated her master, his wife, his daughter, some of the negroes who had been seen in the tavern, and several other persons. Pleased with the notoriety which she had thus gained for herself, she proceeded to invent a tissue of lies that threatened to inculpate persons of a much higher social standing than those she had at first drawn into the plot. She used all the low cunning she possessed to encourage the idea that a negro uprising was contemplated. The whole community was thoroughly alarmed. One of the negroes, John Varrick, was proved by witnesses to have concealed some of the stolen property on his master's premises and was immediately thrown into prison. Mary Burton next implicated a woman of bad character called Peggy Carey.

Rumors now became rife that the negroes intended to attack their masters and burn the town, hoping thus to set themselves free. The following month, March 18th, a fire broke out in a house within the enclosure of the fort. This caused the terror of the inhabitants to be excited to the highest pitch. No one felt safe; the citizens secretly formed organizations for self-protection. To allay the fears of the public the governor sent a communication to the legislature, stating that the fire in the fort had been started by a plumber while repairing the roof of one of the buildings. But other fires followed in quick succession, and although one was caused by sparks from a tobacco pipe, and another by a foul chimney, nevertheless, the citizens, now thoroughly demoralized, traced everything to the negro slaves. This can be more readily understood when we realize that there were at the time over two thousand slaves in a city that contained but a total population of ten thousand. Add to this the fact that there had lately arrived from one of the Spanish colonies a large cargo of negroes, who were believed to be particularly desperate characters. They had been free negroes, but had been captured and sold into slavery and were, in consequence, very restive in their captivity. A rumor that these slaves had determined to rebel added considerably to the general state of uneasiness. Another cause for alarm was given by a report that the Jesuit priests in Canada were inciting the Indians on the northern borders of the province to revolt; furthermore, that they were to be aided by a negro revolt in all the towns, the idea being the subjection of the colony by the French. The fright while it lasted was indeed real, and many people left town. As a consequence, the abandoned houses were robbed of what goods had been left behind. At the same time, gangs of roughs insulted respectable citizens or indulged in street fights with each other. The "Fly Boys" and the "Longbridge Gang," for example, had frequent battles on the neutral grounds of the common, now City Hall Park.

On April 21, 1741, a most notable group of the merchants of New York was called to compose the grand jury. Mr. Phillipse was the foreman of the jury and charged it to summon the arch-disturbers of the peace. Mary Burton, her former master, the innkeeper Hughson, and the unfortunate outcast Peggy Carey were summoned to appear. The testimony against the negroes proved them dishonest, but not conspirators. Nevertheless, two negroes were condemned to be hanged on Monday, May 11, 1741. These were Prince, who had led such a disorderly life that the community was undoubtedly well rid of him, and Cæsar Roosevelt. The latter was hanged on the gibbet near the present site of the intersection of Centre, Chatham, and Pearl Streets. Other trials followed during the whole summer of 1741, and thirteen negroes were burned at the stake, eighteen hanged, and seventy transported. The tavern keeper Hughson, his wife, and maid were convicted of being receivers of stolen goods and of keeping a thieves' meeting place. A French priest and school teacher, John Ury, owed his conviction as much to his inability to speak English as to any real complicity in crime. He was accused of conspiracy and of officiating as a priest. The law under which he was convicted and executed had been passed during the administration of Lord Bellomont, about 1700. The prejudice against the Roman Catholics at that time had been very strong. These executions were absolutely unwarranted—especially that of the priest. But the majority of the citizens were insane with terror and suspected the priest of persuading their negro slaves to rise up against them.

The excitement was somewhat allayed by the enactment of severe laws against negro meetings. These rigorous laws soon fell into abeyance. Within ten years the negroes were admitted to the rights and privileges of free subjects; and more care was taken as to the class of negroes imported. It is unjust to the people of New York of that day to condemn without reserve their action in this matter. We may see very clearly from our exalted position of to-day that no alarm need have been felt either of an uprising of the negroes or of an invasion of the Indians, but such was not the case in 1741. The terror caused by both of these fears was real. The people of New York had for years dreaded outbreaks from both quarters, and it must be admitted that many alarming incidents had occurred from time to time to confirm them in their fears. Furthermore, the false testimony of the worthless girl, Mary Burton, was at that time accepted without reserve.

That part of the War of the Austrian Succession called in America King George's War was not formally declared until March, 1744. Nevertheless, actual hostilities had broken out in the colonies before the end of Lieutenant-governor Clarke's administration. In this war, England was arrayed against both France and Spain, and the colonies of the respective countries were involved. New York was, of course, particularly exposed to ravages by the French and Indians down through the Champlain, Mohawk, and Hudson valleys.

Renewed attempts were now made to cement the union with the Iroquois. But it was not Clarke and his counsels that were chiefly instrumental in winning the friendship of these Indians. That credit belongs to a man well known in the history of the Mohawk valley—a man second only to Arendt van Corlear. This man was Sir William Johnson, the nephew of Admiral Sir Peter Warren.

Johnson was an Irishman of high birth, coming originally from Warrentown, County Down. He had settled in the Mohawk valley, not far from the site of Schenectady, and had been successful from the start in the management of his family estates and in his relations with the Iroquois, whose confidence and affection he early acquired. He formed a settlement upon the estate of his uncle, and took every opportunity of visiting the sachems in their castles and the common people, both whites and Indians, in their huts. The following story is related of Sir William Johnson, which illustrates exceedingly well the tact and diplomacy characteristic of all his dealings with the Indians.

At one time a Mohawk chief coveted a new scarlet coat trimmed with gold lace, which Sir William had just received from London. He hesitated only a day or two before calling at Johnson Hall in the familiar manner which Johnson had inaugurated, and said he had dreamed a dream. He had dreamed that the grand knight gave him his fine red coat. Sir William understood the significance of the hint, and, in "tender consideration of his own popularity," it is said, gave the chieftain the much desired treasure. But Sir William, too, presently dreamed a dream. He went to see the chieftain, and related it to him. He had dreamed that the chieftain and his council gave him a large tract of land, the boundaries of which Sir William designated with geographical precision, from such a tree to such a rivulet. The gift was made, but the old Indian said: "Ugh! I no dream any more. White chief dream better than Indian."

The advisability of appointing a governor for New York had been considered for some time. Clarke's administration had lasted seven years, but had terminated rather ingloriously. His important concessions to the Assembly relative to the disposition of the revenue only whetted its appetite for other privileges. The Assembly next demanded the right to appoint its own treasurer. When this was conceded, the privilege of choosing the auditor-general was claimed. Failure to secure this led to the withholding of the salary of that officer and estrangement between the Assembly and the lieutenant-governor. Clarke was succeeded by Admiral George Clinton, who arrived in New York on September 22, 1743. He was the second son of the sixth Earl of Lincoln, and has been described as a "man of talent and liberality." He troubled himself little beyond taking measures to repair his fortunes, and allowed himself to drift along smoothly in the direction of least resistance.

We will recall that even before the beginning of Clinton's administration the conditions in Europe were most threatening. France again began to assume an attitude of hostility toward England. News, however, of the formal declaration of hostilities did not reach New York until early in July of 1744. There was great alarm, for it was well known that the city and colony were almost defenceless by land and sea. Suddenly and without warning, the news came that the enemy was moving up the northern border and that the English traders had retreated from Oswego precipitately. This created a very unfavorable impression upon the minds of the Indian allies, who were not slow in detecting any evidences of a want of courage on the part of the English. Many of the Indians had come long distances for the purpose of trade, and when they found Oswego deserted they were naturally very much vexed. To prevent disaffection among the Indians, Oswego was then reinforced and special sums of money were voted for the defence of Albany and Schenectady.

In many respects, the most important event of this war in America was the capture of Louisburg by the colonial troops. The discussion of the question of ways and means for the defence of the province broke the harmony that had hitherto existed between the governor and the Assembly. New England was making preparations to attack Louisburg, which was the strongest fort in America north of the Gulf of Mexico—the veritable Gibraltar of the continent. Clinton received an urgent letter from Governor Shirley, of Massachusetts, "recommending a closer bond of union between the colonies" in order that the war might be pressed to a more successful conclusion. When Clinton urged such proceedings on the part of New York, he was reminded of the liberality of the various appropriations and told that the taxes of the people were already too great and ought not to be increased except for purposes of defence. The Assembly treated the governor very uncivilly—refused to answer his questions and delayed or refused war appropriations, holding that the conquest of Canada belonged exclusively to the crown. As long as Louisburg remained in the hands of the French, the peace of New England and New York was in constant danger of being disturbed. Great Britain herself was not likely to take an active part in the reduction of Louisburg, for fear of a threatened invasion from France. On the other hand, the colonists had for some years urged the British government to seize the fort and to invade Canada, and had even promised to bear the larger part of the expense. The British government finally assented, but failed signally to fulfil its promise.

It soon became evident that the home government did not intend to assist materially in the capture of Louisburg; accordingly, the colonists determined to bring about its capture through their own efforts. The proposal of an expedition against the stronghold first came up before the General Court of Massachusetts and was adopted by a majority of one vote. Circular letters soliciting aid were sent to the other colonies. The matter came up before the New York Assembly, and after a long and spirited debate £3,000 of the local currency was granted for the expedition. This seemed to the governor a niggardly grant, so he set about raising assistance by private subscriptions. He also sent ten eighteen-pounders from the king's magazine; yet, notwithstanding the aid granted by the other colonies, Massachusetts was forced to bear most of the expense of the undertaking.

An armed fleet set sail from Boston in April, 1745; and after being joined by several vessels from the West India fleet, the combined ships proceeded to attack Louisburg. Five attempts were made to silence an island battery which protected the harbor, but all were failures. Several days prior to these attacks, supply vessels for the fort had been captured by the colonial fleet. Many of his troops becoming mutinous, the commander of the fort saw that all further resistance was useless, and capitulated on June 17th. By the terms of capitulation, six hundred and fifty regular soldiers and one thousand three hundred inhabitants of the town were to be shipped to France. In the siege the loss was about one hundred and fifty, but many of those left to garrison the fort perished afterward from sickness. Johnson, in his *History of the French War*, says: "Though it was the most brilliant success the English achieved during the war, English historians hardly mention it." Nevertheless, it was one of the most splendid achievements of the age. Europe was astonished at the successful issue of the expedition, and the American colonies were awakened to a realization of their power. The officers in charge of the expedition were handsomely rewarded with promotions and distinctions. There was a strange reluctance, however, on the part of the crown to reimburse the colonies for the heavy expenses they had incurred; but the claim was prosecuted with diligence, and the colonies finally, in 1749, obtained £183,649, which was equitably divided among them. Notwithstanding the importance of the capture,

Louisburg was given back to the French by the Treaty of Aix-la-Chapelle, October 7, 1748.

During the autumn of 1745, Saratoga was destroyed by a party of French and Indians from Crown Point. More than thirty families were massacred and many persons taken into captivity. The utmost consternation prevailed at Albany. Families from the Mohawk-Hudson valley fled precipitately from their homes, loudly condemning the government that had permitted such a condition to exist. The colony was aroused and showed a certain spasmodic desire to correct its omissions. But as every appropriation of money precipitated fresh quarrels, little was in reality accomplished.

Hardly anything of importance characterized the period 1746 to 1754 except the constant bickering between the governor and the Assembly. Early in the spring of the year 1746, Clinton asked to be allowed to return to England for the recovery of his health. He was heartily disgusted with New York. But the French were so active and the affairs of the colonies in so critical a condition, that he could not be relieved at that time. In October, 1748, the peace of Aix-la-Chapelle was proclaimed. From the outbreak to the close of hostilities the war had lasted nearly five years, and things were about the same at the end as at the beginning. It took another war of seven years to settle definitely the dispute between England and France.

The quarrels between Clinton and the Assembly are important historically, because it was during his administration that the new doctrine of Parliamentary supremacy in American colonial affairs was first practically tested. It should be remembered that during the early part of their history the colonies held that they were under the domination of no outside authority, unless it were that of the king. Furthermore, that his power over them was limited, because he had delegated it to others through charter grants. Certainly, they claimed, Parliament had no authority over them.

As soon as Parliament gained the upper hand under the ministerial form of government of the Hanoverian monarchs, just so soon did Parliament begin to assume supreme control of the colonies. Also, what is more to the point, Parliament began to devise schemes for carrying that assumption into practical effect.

The ministry now decided that it would be the proper course to experiment upon New York. It deemed the return of peace to be a most favorable time to make the experiment. There would not be the danger of lukewarmness on the part of the colonists in waging the war against England's enemy. Nor would there be the graver danger of the colonies going over to that enemy, as there would have been during the war just ended. Consequently, the ministry resolved to extort from the Assembly two prerogatives that had always been claimed by the central government, but which had never been admitted by the colonies; in fact, these prerogatives had been denied the home government by the colonial Assemblies from the very beginning. They had always evinced the most decided determination never to yield an inch. These two prerogatives were: first, the privilege of demanding fixed salaries for all regal officers of whatever character without a periodic voting of the same, whether yearly or otherwise; secondly, the privilege of having a permanent revenue at the royal disposal to be disbursed as it best pleased the authorities, without rendering any account whatsoever to the representatives of the people. It is very evident that these two prerogatives as claimed on the part of the home government were the crux of the whole trouble between the governors and the colonial legislatures. They were likewise the causes of all the quarrels as between the king and the colonial legislatures and as between Parliament and the colonial legislatures. And finally, it may be held with a considerable degree of historical exactness that they were the great underlying causes of the American Revolution. In this particular New York experiment, Parliament determined to gain these prerogatives by a process of bulldozing and extortioning; or, if this failed, by craftily managing affairs in such a manner that by producing extreme disorder in the province the interposition of Parliament would be certain.

Unfortunately for Clinton, he was the unwelcome instrument by which the disciplining process was to be accomplished. This policy on the part of the British ministry to compel New York to acknowledge these two prerogatives led to still further differences among Governor Clinton, his Council, and the Assembly. A legislative deadlock would have been ultimately the consequence, had not a change in the administrative head of the province been first effected. Clinton consequently became increasingly impatient to return to England. On a trip to the Indian country, July 4, 1753, Clinton revealed the secret that he was daily expecting a successor and that upon his arrival he would sail for England.

On Sunday, October 7th, Sir Danvers Osborne, the new governor, once a member of Parliament for Bedfordshire, and brother-in-law of the Earl of Halifax, arrived. De Lancey, amid popular huzzas, received the commission as lieutenant-governor. Osborne was inaugurated on Monday, and was considerably disturbed by one passage in the city's address to him: "We are sufficiently assured that your Excellency will be averse from countenancing, as we from brooking, any infringements of our estimable liberties, civil and religious." Osborne turned to Clinton and remarked: "I expect like treatment to that which you have received before I leave this government." On Tuesday, Osborne seemed gloomy. He convened the Council, and said he was enjoined to insist upon a permanent revenue and asked opinions as to the prospect of gaining it. The reply was most emphatic: "The Assembly of New York would never submit to such a demand." William Smith, when directly appealed to by the governor, insisted: "That no such scheme could ever be enforced." The governor looked sad and remarked: "Then what am I sent here for?"

The next day, Wednesday, the city was startled by the shocking intelligence that the governor had hanged himself! The decision of the jury was that he had destroyed himself in a moment of insanity. De Lancey now became acting governor, and his instructions were unqualified. He was to insist upon "a permanent revenue, solid, indefinite, and without limitations." This put De Lancey in an embarrassing position, inasmuch as he had most strenuously advised never to give in to this very demand of the home government. Nevertheless, he grasped the situation in a most tactful and masterful manner. Each year the Assembly passed an annual appropriation bill. De Lancey would then return it, but at the same time he would secretly advise the ministry to give in to the people. This it did finally, September 24, 1756, through Sir Charles Hardy, who succeeded Osborne as governor in September, 1755. Thus through De Lancey's tact the Assembly won a most important legislative victory.

Before bringing the account of New York during this period to a close, reference should be made to an important event in the history of education. A bill passed the Assembly on October 22, 1746, granting permission to establish a college by means of the lottery system then much in vogue. The raising of £250 by lottery was the humble start of King's College, now known as Columbia University. In November, 1751, the funds thus collected were vested in a board of trustees. In 1752, the college was enlarged by a gift of land from Trinity Church. In November, 1753, Dr. Samuel Johnson, of Connecticut, was invited to be its president, which position was accepted by him, but not until after the passing of the charter. This took place in 1754, and in July of the same year instruction of the youth was begun in the schoolhouse belonging to Trinity Church. The charter was definitely granted on October 31, 1754, from which time the existence of the college is to be properly dated. The early history of the institution was marked by an unfortunate controversy between the Presbyterians and the Episcopalians. The latter attempted to secure the supervision of the college, and as a result its supporters were divided into two hostile parties.

In connection with the foundation of King's College, it will not be out of place to mention an event of equal historical importance from an educational point of view that took place in the neighboring province of New Jersey. On October 22, 1746, a charter was granted the College of New Jersey. The foundation of the college was due largely to the religious enthusiasm attending the progress of George Whitefield through the colonies. The institution was first located at Elizabethtown, and its first president was Jonathan Dickinson. Its firmest supporter in early times, however, was Governor Jonathan Belcher. In a letter to his cousin, William Belcher, the governor writes as follows:

"SIR—This is a fine climate and a Country of great plenty tho' but of Little profit to a Governour. The inhabitants are generally rustick and without Education. I am therefore attempting the building of a college in the province for Instructing the youth in the Principles of Religion in good Literature and Manners and I have a Reasonable View of bringing it to bear.

"*Burlington N. J. Sept, 1747.*
"I am Sr
Your Friend and Very humble servant
J. BELCHER."

The college was rechartered in 1748 and was soon removed to Newark. In 1757 it was again removed and located finally at Princeton. It was quite successful during the colonial period. Money was raised by private contributions, by lotteries, and by general collections authorized by the churches of the Presbyterian faith in Great Britain and America. The Rev. William Tennent was very successful in his efforts in behalf of the college, having collected £1,500 in England, in addition to books and mathematical instruments. A large proportion of the earlier graduates entered the ministry.

In 1766, Governor William Franklin, of New Jersey, granted a charter for a college to be called Queen's College. Upon this foundation Rutgers College at New Brunswick was erected. The reasons for its establishment were twofold: first, the fear of encroachments by the Church of England; and secondly, the difficulty of obtaining ministers for the Dutch Reformed Church.

## Beskrifning Om De swenska Församlingars Forna och Närwarande Tilstånd,

uti

Det så kallade **Nya Swerige**,

Sedan

**Nya Nederland,**

men nu för tiden

Pensylvanien, samt nästliggande Orter wid Älf-wen De la Ware, Wäst-Yersey och New-Castle County uti Norra America;

Utgifwen

af

**ISRAEL ACRELIUS,**

För detta Probst öfwer de Swenska Församlinngar i America och Kyrkoherde uti Christina, men nu Probst och Kyrkoherde uti Tidingehyra.

✸✸✸✸✸✸✸✸✸✸✸✸✸✸✸✸✸✸✸✸✸✸✸

**Tryckt hos HARBERG & HESSELBERG,**

1759.

## Kort Beskrifning Om PROVINCIEN **Nya Swerige**

uti

AMERICA,

Som nu förtiden af the Engelske kallas

**PENSYLVANIA.**

Afsatte och trowärdige Mäns Skrifter och berättelser thopsatte och sammanskrefwen, samt med åtskillige Figurer utzirad af

THOMAS CAMPANIUS HOLM.

Stockholm, Tryckt uti Kongl. Boktr. hos Sal. Wankijfs Efterlefwerska, af J. H. Werner. Åhr MDCCII.

*From the originals in the New York Public Library, Lenox Branch.*

Title-pages of two very early works relating to the settlements on Delaware River.

# CHAPTER XV

## *GROWTH OF A DEMOCRATIC PROVINCE, 1714-1754*

THE tact which Governor Hunter displayed in the government of New Jersey brought about a friendly understanding between himself and the Assembly. His message to the Assembly that convened on December 7, 1713, reveals a bit of interesting flattery. He expressed himself as being glad to see them after so long an absence, and believed they were not sorry to "meet him in so good company." He urged them to support heartily the queen's government; to provide for past arrears; to discountenance vice and immorality; to improve trade; and to encourage agriculture. He furthermore explained that the members of his Council entertained no views or interests different from those of the representatives of the people, and that all were working for the best interests of the province. He urged frequent and amicable conferences between the two legislative bodies as the best means of settling the affairs of the province in a wise and economical manner. He disclaimed any intention on the part of the Council to support certain disgruntled persons in their contention that the representative legislative body was no Assembly at all.

The reply of the Assembly was couched in the same friendly terms as characterized the message of the governor. It promised to endeavor to do all in its power to bring to a successful issue all the queen's wishes. Following up these good intentions, the Assembly passed a bill enabling Quakers to act as jurors and to hold offices of trust upon their solemn affirmation and declaration and exempting them from taking the oath. Other beneficent laws were passed, and the Assembly wound up its affairs to the mutual satisfaction of itself and the governor. "I hope," said the governor, in his speech proroguing the Assembly, "my conduct has convinced the world (I cannot suppose you want any further conviction) that I have no other view than the peace and prosperity of this province; if such a few as are enemies to both, are not to be reduced by reason, I shall take the next best and most effectual measure to do it."

Between the years 1713 and 1716 we find nothing of striking importance in the affairs of the province to merit special treatment. In the conduct of his government, Governor Hunter sought continually to bring about a better understanding between all parties. The people were not only satisfied with his administration, but were even pleased with it. The old quarrels and grievances disappeared, and for a time peace and harmony prevailed.

Unfortunately, this era of good feeling was not continued altogether undisturbed to the end of Governor Hunter's administration. Colonel Daniel Coxe was elected speaker of the Assembly which Governor Hunter convened in the spring of 1716. In March, 1710, an act had been confirmed designating Burlington and Perth Amboy alternately as the places of meeting of the Assembly. In 1716, the Assembly should have met at Burlington, but for reasons of State the governor convened it at Perth Amboy instead. The Assembly remonstrated against this action of the governor as being an infringement of the law of 1710. Hunter urged in support of his action the fact that there were certain things of great weight which made it impracticable to hold the Assembly at Burlington at that time. The Assembly allowed the matter to drop, but the harmony of the previous three years was considerably disturbed. Coxe disliked the governor, and used his influence to prevail upon other members of the Assembly to oppose Hunter and the measures he desired to have adopted.

Only nine members appeared at the meeting of the Assembly held on May 14, 1716, at Perth Amboy. These nine sent a message to Hunter, urging him to adopt such measures as would compel the attendance of the absentees. Warrants were sent out, and as a result four others made their appearance; but Coxe continued to absent himself. The governor ordered the thirteen to meet and to elect a sergeant-at-arms, who should compel the other absent members to attend. John Kinsey was elected speaker. In the governor's message to the Assembly, Coxe was referred to in the following words: "As the conduct of that gentleman who last filled the chair sufficiently convinced you of a combination between him and his associates to defeat all the purposes of your present meeting: I hope, and cannot doubt but it will open the eyes of all such as by his and their evil acts, and sinistrous practices, have been misled and imposed upon; so that for the future, here they will not find it so easy a matter to disturb the peace of the country." The House then took up the case of the absent members. The speaker and his associates were severally expelled for "contempt of authority and neglect of the service of their country." It was furthermore decided that if they were returned again at a new election, they should not be permitted to hold their seats in the Assembly. Nevertheless, some of the expelled members were reëlected, but, pursuant to the action of the preceding Assembly, they were not permitted to retain their seats. Coxe appealed to the king, but was not sustained in the appeal.

In 1719, Hunter was succeeded as Governor of New York and New Jersey by William Burnet. When the new governor visited New Jersey he found it heavily in debt. The colony was experiencing the bad results of a depreciated paper money, the value of which had been rendered uncertain by inflation. Nor did the Assembly profit by experience. Bills of credit were issued to the amount of £40,000 for the purpose of increasing the circulating medium of the province. Burnet continued to administer the government of New York and New Jersey until 1728, when he was transferred to Massachusetts.

John Montgomery succeeded Burnet as Governor of New York and New Jersey, April 15, 1728. During his administration greater efforts were made to separate New Jersey from New York. Montgomery died in office, July 1, 1731, and then Lewis Morris acted as Governor of New York and New Jersey until relieved by Colonel William Cosby in September, 1732. Immediately upon his assumption of authority in New Jersey, trouble with the Assembly developed. He was utterly unfit for the government of that province. Men of his type were likely to drive the colonies from the control of the mother country. If he could not bend the judges to his way of thinking, he would have them removed without cause. We have already referred to his quarrel with Chief Justice Lewis Morris and the consequent removal of the latter. Likewise, we have seen what a stir he created by reason of his new land surveys and land grants. He died in 1736, and was succeeded in the government of New Jersey by John Anderson, the president of the Council. Anderson died about two weeks afterward and was followed as acting governor by John Hamilton, who was the son of Andrew Hamilton, governor of the province in the time of the proprietors.

The separation of New Jersey from New York was first proposed during the administration of Burnet. The question continued to be further agitated until 1730, when a petition was sent to the king, urging the separation of the two provinces. Another petition pressing for similar action was sent to the king in 1736. From a maritime point of view the separation was advisable, because New Jersey vessels were required to be registered in New York at the cost of £10. Those who favored separation argued that commerce would receive fresh impetus; that this would redound to the benefit of the mother country, for a large number of men would be required in the manufacture of tar, pitch, and turpentine. Then, again, immigrants, especially the Palatines, refused to settle in New Jersey because of its dependence upon New York. Furthermore, salaries paid to officials in New York were spent outside of New Jersey. Very often writs were delayed in execution, and meetings of the Council were not held in New Jersey. Finally, the petitioners summed up their arguments in the following words: "The heart burnings among the Inhabitants, and the Grievances of the Country are not known and understood, or at least never regarded, the governor being free from the Noise and Clammor of them, at New York." The petition was granted, and in the summer of 1738 a commission came to New Jersey and separated that province from New York. Lewis Morris was appointed Governor of New Jersey. He published his commission at Amboy on the 29th of August, 1738, and at Burlington several days later.

The appointment of Morris was received with great enthusiasm on the part of the popular party. Nevertheless, he constantly complained of the "insincerity and ignorance among the people," and objected to what he termed the "meanest of citizens" trying to direct the government in its affairs. It was not long before he quarrelled with the Assembly about money matters. That body refused to support the government, unless he acceded to its demands. Before a compromise could be effected, Morris died on the 21st of May, 1746, and was succeeded by John Hamilton, at that time president of the Council. Before a commission could be issued to a new governor, Hamilton died on June 17, 1747, and his place was taken by John Reading, the next oldest councillor. Reading held the office until the summer of 1747, when Jonathan Belcher arrived as commissioned governor.

Belcher had been Governor of Massachusetts. He was a scholar and a man of affairs, but his views were of the Puritan type. He published his commission in Amboy, but resided at Burlington for several years. He was a follower of George Whitefield. He refused to worship in Burlington on Sundays, on account of that town's ungodly

Sabbath. On some Sundays he could be seen driving his coach and four along the road to Philadelphia, there to worship in the Presbyterian church. He had scruples about taking this drive on the Sabbath, and soon abandoned it. While attending commencement at the College of New Jersey, he was seized with a paralytic stroke. Benjamin Franklin sent him an electric apparatus which he hoped might work a cure. Belcher never recovered from the stroke, and died on the 31st of August, 1757. His friend, the Rev. Aaron Burr, president of the college, preached the funeral sermon. Although Belcher quarrelled at times with the Assembly concerning the appropriations for the support of the government, yet his administration was a most successful one. He would often say: "I have to steer between Scylla and Charybdis; to please the king's ministers at home, and a touchy people here; to luff for one and bear away for another."

The lieutenant-governor, Thomas Pownall, succeeded Belcher. Inasmuch as the former was at the same time Governor of Massachusetts, the active duties of the executive once more devolved upon John Reading, president of the Council, until the arrival of Francis Bernard on June 15, 1758. Bernard was a Royalist, and was selected as Governor of New Jersey by Lord Halifax. He courted favor by formulating plans to enlarge the royal power in the colony. The most important event of his administration was the treaty with the Indians made at Easton, Pennsylvania, October, 1758. In all, five hundred and seven Indians—men, women, and children—attended the conference. This treaty, among other things, provided for a settlement with the Indians by which they might continue to live in New Jersey under certain restrictions. The conference closed on the 26th of October, and the records state that "some wine and punch were called for, and mutual healths were drunk and the conferences were concluded with great satisfaction." Bernard was removed from New Jersey to Massachusetts in 1760, and was succeeded by Thomas

Boone. The latter remained in office but one year, whereupon in 1761 he was removed to South Carolina. His successor was Josiah Hardy, who served less than two years. It had been decided that every American judge should keep his appointment during the royal pleasure, but Hardy issued a commission whose term was to last during good behavior of the judge. Having thus violated his instructions, he was promptly dismissed in 1762; but he was afterward appointed to the consulship at Cadiz, Spain. He was succeeded in the governorship of New Jersey by William Franklin, an illegitimate son of the great philosopher. He secured his appointment through the influence of Lord Bute, and was the last of the royal governors.

During this rapid succession of governors and the consequent kaleidoscopic changes of politics, New Jersey was rapidly developing in population and material resources. In 1738 the population was about forty-seven thousand, and of these four thousand were slaves. Seven years later this had increased to sixty-one thousand, making an addition for the period of fourteen thousand people. The increase of the population of some of the counties in West Jersey between 1699 and 1745 was found to be more than sixfold. The prosperity of the colony was doubtless due to the virtuous and industrious character of the settlers. Perhaps New Jersey's most notable progress lay in the direction of the rapid development of its schools and churches. The development of the two, as in New England, went hand in hand—the Congregationalists and the Presbyterians being the chief factors in the development of the former. The origin of the schools may be traced undoubtedly to the coming of the Dutch and the Swedes. During the early period, the time of the settlers was almost entirely consumed in defending themselves from the attacks of the Indians and in wresting a scanty livelihood from the primitive soil. As a result, the task of educating the youth fell to the lot of the pastors of the settlements. This practically explains the close relationship between the Church and the school.

Education at that time was quite as much religious as secular. No doubt, however, many New Jersey youths attended the Collegiate Church School founded at New Amsterdam in 1633, which afforded secular instruction. The first school in New Jersey of which we have record was established at Bergen in 1664. Engelbert Steenhuysen, a church clerk, was the schoolmaster. Instruction was given from eight o'clock until eleven in the forenoon, and from one o'clock until four in the afternoon. Steenhuysen taught reading, writing, spelling, and even arithmetic when the maturity of the student's mind permitted such an "intellectual pursuit." The Swedes along the Delaware also furnished secular instruction, but as their efforts to colonize New Jersey were never successful they played but a minor part in the instruction of New Jersey youth. Each nationality in the province endeavored to confine its children to the language of the mother country. The Dutch were partially successful in this attempt; the Swedes failed utterly. The Bible and the Catechism were the chief sources of educational inspiration. A "little Latin and less Greek" perhaps topped off the student's elementary knowledge. Scientific studies were little taught, and, in fact, were even tabooed, because in certain minds they were associated with witchcraft and the occult arts.

The progress of the educational movement was greatly accelerated by the coming of the Scotch and English colonists. In 1664 we find Governor Carteret's charter to Bergen containing a provision for a church and "free school." They were to be supported from the proceeds realized from a tract of land exempted from taxation. In other towns land was set aside, the income from which was to be applied to the support of schools. The East Jersey legislature first made provision for education in 1693, declaring that "the cultivation of learning and good manners tends greatly to the good and benefit of mankind." Towns were accorded the privilege of electing three men, who should determine the schoolmaster's salary and fix other rates.

Just as we find the Congregationalists and the Presbyterians in East Jersey eager to establish schools, so we find similar good intentions on the part of the Quakers in West Jersey. Legislative acts were passed for the betterment of the school system. One Thomas Budd advocated a rather novel plan of education. It was compulsory attendance at the "publick school" for seven years. His plan was to establish such schools in all towns and cities, while "persons of known honesty, skill, and understanding should be yearly chosen by the governor and General Assembly to teach and instruct boys and girls." The curriculum was to embrace "true English and Latin . . . reading and fair writing, arithmetick, and book-keeping." In addition, the boys were to be instructed in "some mystery or trade, as the making of mathematical instruments, joynery, turnery, the making of clocks, and watches, weaving and shoemaking." The girls, on the other hand, were to be taught "spinning in flax and wool, the knitting of gloves and stockings, sewing and making of all sorts of needle work, and the making of straw work as hats, baskets," etc.

It must not be understood, however, that education in New Jersey was general. Unfortunately, there was, on the contrary, much illiteracy, as is proved by the letters of the missionaries sent by the Society for the Propagation of the Gospel in Foreign Parts. Wherever schools were conducted under the auspices of different sects, usually only children of that sect received instruction. During the time New Jersey was under royal government, no great stride was made in the advancement of education. Prior to the middle of the eighteenth century, no public library existed in New Jersey. Books were accessible only to clergymen and the rich. There were likewise very few newspapers. To remedy the evils resultant upon a lack of general educational facilities, private schools soon made their appearance. The schoolmasters of these early private schools were similar in many respects to the early Methodist preachers. They gave instruction at the houses of their pupils, receiving board and lodging in part payment for their services. They usually journeyed from one locality to another until a favorable opportunity opened the way for their establishment in a permanent school wherein they might, perhaps, locate for the rest of their lives. Frequently these itinerant schoolmasters were graduates of Harvard and Yale, and later of Princeton. Women did not teach in schools. The rod was frequently employed. The scholar made his own pen from a goose quill, and ink was manufactured from vegetable products. The temperature of the schoolroom varied little from that without its walls—being hot in summer and cold in winter. " Much of the instruction was given by questions and answers, and woe betide the boy who did not learn verbatim his Bible verses, although the master might be redolent with gin when he heard the verbatim."—(Lee, *New Jersey as a Colony and as a State*, i, 358.) The education of the girls was sadly neglected. A knowledge of reading and writing was considered sufficient for all their needs. In this respect, the Quakers were more liberal than their contemporaries. As far as higher education is concerned, we have already noticed its beginning in the establishment of Princeton College in 1746.

During the period under consideration, the number of churches increased rapidly until about 1765, when there were forty-one Presbyterian churches in East Jersey and fourteen in West Jersey. The Quakers had thirty meeting houses in West Jersey, while the Episcopalians had twelve churches in East Jersey and nine in West Jersey. The Baptists had nineteen churches, and in addition there were churches supported by the Dutch and Swedish inhabitants of the province. The churches were substantially built and located in central spots, but they had neither adornments nor embellishments. The shed for horses was an early and necessary adjunct to the church building.

The legal profession was quite late in being placed upon a substantial and legitimate basis. Among the early settlers there was an element of undesirable persons, adventurers and the riffraff of European society. Following close in their wake came worthless lawyers, who quickly availed themselves of the unsettled condition of the times; but in the course of time men of ability appeared. Those who showed any marked degree of legal talent speedily rose to distinction. It is a remarkable fact, however, that from 1704 to 1776 there were only two chief justices of New Jersey who were attorneys licensed by the courts of the province. Laymen not infrequently held the office of attorney-general.

The houses of the first settlers were mostly of the Dutch type of architecture. On the exterior were the angular, zigzag gables, with long, projecting gutters. The stoops, or porches, were considered necessary to the comfort of the home. Within, a distinctive feature was the scrupulously clean Dutch kitchen. There were no stoves, but instead the enormous fireplace extending along the width of the house. It was the most characteristic feature of the household economy of the early settler. These settlers were a fairly sober class of people, indulging principally in the drinks peculiar to the Dutch. Buttermilk and bread were their staple food. In the winter the family collected around the old folks at the fireplace, while in summer the young folks sat on the stoop and chatted and gossiped to their hearts' content. The cattle and pigs wandered around the streets of the settlement almost at will.

New Jersey was agricultural, and the farmer was the dominant figure of the period. The Dutch kept their land in a high state of cultivation. Their houses in East Jersey were usually of stone or brick, but the homes of the settlers along the seashore were mostly built of wood, and those along Delaware River were for the most part of brick. The higher classes could afford candles for illumination, but the average person had to be content with the smoky and uncertain light of pine knots in the fireplace. In the summer very little illumination was needed; the members of the household retired soon after sunset to get the needed rest for the arduous duties of the next day. Carpets were a luxury, as were also wall paper and curtains, while in all New Jersey there was probably not a bath tub. The "best" room of farmhouses was kept dark and tight and opened only to visitors, or when a funeral or a marriage occurred in the family. The farmers worked hard during the summer, but the coming of winter brought them relaxation. Early rising was considered one of the cardinal virtues. Salted meat, especially pork, and vegetables formed the principal diet, while rum, gin, tea, and coffee afforded them ample liquid refreshments. An icehouse was considered a luxury. Naturally, the dull monotony of the farms soon became distasteful to the youth, who frequently sought employment in the merchant marine or entered counting houses in the towns and cities.

In the towns, the ubiquitous tavern was the place of rendezvous every evening for the men. Frequently, the keeper was a man of considerable influence in his neighborhood. Sometimes he acted as an arbitrator in disputes. He was intimate with the lawyers and was the fountain head of information on current events and incidents around town. He kept his eyes open for runaway slaves. The choicest viands of the season, such as venison, bear, and wild fowls, were served at his table. Legislative acts made it compulsory for towns to have inns through which to supply the needs of strangers. Inns were centres of drunkenness, swearing, and general disorder, and it became necessary for the legislature to enact a set of restrictive acts. Every innkeeper was required to take out a license, and none was permitted to retail more than two gallons of liquor at a time to any one person except under a special license.

The colonists were sociable in their instincts and lively in their manner. There were weekly evening clubs in the village, and balls and concerts in the cities. French influences and taste were particularly noticeable in those parts of the province inhabited by the Huguenots. They stimulated the growth of the Protestant religion, and brought with them their native refinement and their love of the beautiful. In fact, they contributed to the life of the province those sentiments so strikingly lacking in the English character of that day. It may be said that the influence of the French was subjective rather than objective. They contributed a romance element which appears picturesque when contrasted with the Teutonic habits of the other settlers. They contributed likewise their skill as craftsmen, merchants, professional men, and scholars (Lee).

## CHAPTER XVI

### GROWTH OF A QUAKER COMMONWEALTH, 1714–1754

DURING the administration of Governor John Evans, of Pennsylvania, the vexed question again arose as to whether the Assembly had power to adjourn. The governor opposed most strenuously the assumption of any such prerogative on the part of the Assembly. This attempt to limit its cherished privileges angered that representative body, and a sharp remonstrance was sent the governor in the form of an address. Inasmuch as the members were in a hurry to return to their homes, the writing of this remonstrance was intrusted to a committee of eight men, of which David Lloyd was chairman. Only two of the eight committeemen, Joseph Wilcox and David Lloyd, had much to do with drafting the address. When finished, the address as a specimen of defamatory literature was indeed remarkable, for Wilcox is said to have incorporated in it all the scurrilous and scandalous reflections that he could produce. This address was denounced by Logan, in a letter to Penn, as "a piece of unparalleled villainy that needs no observation or remark to aggravate it."

Evans was sustained by Penn in his condemnation of the claim of the Assembly that it possessed the power to adjourn at pleasure. Furthermore, the proprietor wrote feelingly of the ingratitude of the members of the Assembly and applied strong terms to their address. "If that letter," said he, "be the act of the people, truly represented, it was sufficient to cancel all his obligations of care over them; but if it were done by particular persons assuming to act for the whole, he expected the country would purge itself, and take care that due satisfaction was given to him." In the spring of 1706, Logan, in reply, wrote Penn with reference to the intended prosecution of Lloyd: "'Tis in vain, I believe, to attempt it; he carries so fair with our weak country-people, and those that long looked upon him to be the champion of the Friends' cause in government matters in former times, that there is no possessing them. In the Assembly the most judicious were for having business done first, lest quarrelling with him should prevent doing it, and throw them into confusion; for his party is strong as that of the wicked and foolish."

This attack upon the proprietor aroused the indignation of the citizens of the province, who, in spite of their determination to preserve popular power, could not forget totally Penn's great service. For a while Lloyd seemed to lose popularity, and there was much less noisy obstruction. The reaction in favor of Penn was interpreted by Evans to be a signal justification of his own conduct, and his spirit rose as that of the Assembly sank. One of the members who had dared to speak disrespectfully of the executive was sued and threatened with being "kicked out" unceremoniously. The member pleaded his privilege, inasmuch as the offence had been committed during a session of the Assembly. The decision of the court was against the offender. The Assembly then threatened to impeach the judges and the sheriff for a breach of privilege. A demand of the governor for the expulsion of the member was likewise refused, and the claim was set forth that the Assembly could not expel a member for words spoken outside "of that body. The Assembly furthermore claimed that service of a legal process on a member for any other cause than treason, felony, or breach of the peace was a violation of privilege" (Bolles).

Three incidents well illustrate the character of Evans and show by what actions he first lost the support of the people and in the end merited their contempt. He disliked

Early issues of New Jersey, New York, and Delaware paper currency, including an indented bill. *From the originals in the New York Public Library, Lenox Branch.*

the religion of the Friends and was by no means careful to disguise that dislike. Trouble soon developed as a result of the disinclination of the Friends to enact a militia law. Evans thought the danger from actual invasions occasioned by the war that had broken out between France and Spain would dispel the unwillingness on the part of the Friends to resort to arms. There being no immediate danger of an invasion of Pennsylvania, the artful governor thought it advisable to create an artificial one. Following out this determination, it is said he concocted a plan with a man named French, of New Castle, and others, by which an alarm of actual invasion by the enemy was to be spread broadcast. At the time of the holding of the annual fair at Philadelphia, the governor received an urgent message from French announcing the presence of the enemies' ships in the Delaware. The intelligence was immediately made public. Evans mounted his horse, rushed through the streets with drawn sword, and commanded the populace, of whatsoever political or religious creed, to rally for the defence of the province. A panic was the result. Shipping was withdrawn from the wharves, and valuables of all kinds were concealed. Before nightfall the ruse was discovered, and the reaction against the authors of the false report was so violent that they were compelled to seek safety in flight. The experiment, in so far as it was a test of the martial spirit of the Friends under imminent danger of invasion, was a ridiculous failure. They were attending their religious meetings at the time, and only four of their sect came out armed ready to meet the attack of the phantom enemy.

Not content with thus bringing his popularity to the lowest possible ebb, Evans immediately proceeded to force the incoming tide of popular hatred of him toward its flood. In 1706, he erected a fort at New Castle, to protect the river, as he claimed, but in reality, says Bolles, "to vex the trade of the province." All ships navigating the Delaware were required to report and pay a toll of £5 and a fixed sum for any gun fired to compel such payment. Some

Quakers determined to test the governor's authority thus to interfere with the free navigation of the Delaware. They proceeded down the river in a vessel, and when near the fort two of them went ashore and informed the commander that their vessel had been regularly cleared, and requested that they be not interfered with in their passage down the river. This request was refused; and as the vessel passed, a shot was fired through its mainsail. This drastic action not being successful in bringing the vessel to, the commander followed in a little boat. It was a case of catching a Tartar, for the Quakers, instead of permitting themselves to be captured, quietly imprisoned the commander and proceeded to Salem. Evans had, in the meantime, followed by land to New Castle and succeeded in overtaking the vessel before it reached Salem. Here all fell into the custody of Lord Cornbury, who was Governor of New Jersey as well as of New York and claimed likewise the vice-admiralty of the Delaware in addition to his other honors. The commander was taken before Cornbury, and that pompous official reprimanded him. Nor did he spare Evans, who was likewise the recipient of sentiments not at all of the neighborly stamp.

The third of the acts which were particularly responsible for bringing Evans into contempt with the people was concerned with the administration of justice. Penn had sent his eldest son, William, to America in company with Evans. William had sown more than his share of wild oats, and his banishment to America, where he was to reside upon an estate of seven thousand acres presented by his father, was an effort on the part of the latter to prevent his son and heir from reaping the usual plentiful harvest of tares. In intrusting the welfare of the young man to his old friends in Pennsylvania, the proprietor frankly wrote: " He has wit, has kept top company, and must be handled with much wisdom." For a while James Logan succeeded in keeping him under proper control, but the companionship of Evans in the end proved more attractive and, we may add, more disastrous for

William. Evans and young Penn soon entered upon a career of dissipation. They frequented low taverns, started unseemly rows in the streets, and masqueraded in female attire. In one of the carousals, a constable was beaten while performing his duty, and the city guard was called out to restore order. Young Penn was among those arrested, but Evans escaped. The former was brought before the mayor and reprimanded. He claimed exemption from interference on the part of the officers; and he was supported in this contention by Evans, who annulled the proceedings of the court. The Friends were now thoroughly aroused and had the young man indicted. The matter was dropped, however, upon the proprietor's recalling his son to England. Evans, however, remained to witness to a still greater extent the increasing hatred of the people.

Largely as a result of these acts of Governor Evans, the tide that had been setting in toward favor of the proprietor now retreated and the popular party was once more restored to all its former powers. Lloyd was again chosen speaker of the Assembly, and Evans was finally succeeded as governor of the province by Charles Gookin (February, 1709). During Gookin's incumbency Lloyd continued to be the ruling spirit among the people and was several times elected speaker of the Assembly. The governor had "mild manners and economical ways," and Penn therefore thought that he might prove acceptable to the people. He was born in Ireland, and, having entered the army, rose to a captaincy in Earle's Royal Regiment. The colonists called him "Colonel." No sooner had he put his foot upon the soil of Pennsylvania than he was petitioned for a redress of grievances. Nor did the victorious popular party stop at this negative way of showing their dislike for Evans. The former governor was charged with high crimes and misdemeanors, and demands were made for his criminal prosecution. Gookin claimed he had no authority to proceed to such radical measures. He became more than ever dependent on the Assembly for support, and under Lloyd's leadership that body took advantage of the needs of the governor, to extend its own powers. As a result of this policy of the governor, an unusual harmony between himself and the Assembly was maintained, at least outwardly, for several years. This happy state of affairs was not destined to continue to the end of the governor's administration. He lost popularity by neglecting to punish some rioters who tried to prevent the arrest of a clergyman indicted for a serious offence; also, by interpreting a Parliamentary statute in such a way as to disqualify Quakers from giving evidence in criminal cases, from serving on a jury, and from holding office. Furthermore, evidences of mental infirmity made their appearance. The governor accused Isaac Norris, Mayor of Philadelphia and speaker of the Assembly, and James Logan of being disloyal to the English government and well-disposed toward the cause of the pretender James. The Council asked for the governor's recall, and a successor arrived in May, 1717. Gookin could not prove his charges against Norris and Logan and was compelled to withdraw them most ignominiously, ascribing his conduct to mental weakness. Gookin's successor was Sir William Keith. During Keith's rule the quarrels between the executive and legislative bodies were much fewer. The people were too busily engaged in their own private affairs to pay much attention to politics, and the Assembly was not well attended. Nevertheless, for this very reason the control of the Assembly fell into the hands of a few bold and fearless leaders of the opposition, of whom David Lloyd was for years the acknowledged leader. Lloyd died in 1731.

Keith was the first and last governor of Pennsylvania to possess a title. He was a Scotchman, without fortune, and probably sought the governorship of Pennsylvania for the money he thought he could get out of it. During Queen Anne's reign he had been appointed surveyor-general of customs for the American colonies. Having lost that position upon the accession of George I., he turned a covetous

SOME
ACCOUNT
OF THE
PROVINCE
OF
PENNSILVANIA
IN
AMERICA:
Lately Granted under the Great Seal
OF
ENGLAND
TO
William Penn, &c.

Together with Priviledges and Powers necessary to the well-governing thereof.

Made publick for the Information of such as are or may be
disposed to Transport themselves or Servants
into those Parts.

---

LONDON: Printed, and Sold by *Benjamin Clark*
Bookseller in *George-Yard Lombard-street*, 1681.

Two rare works on Pennsylvania. From the originals in the New York Public Library.

---

Umständige Geogra-
phische
Beschreibung
Der zu allerletzt erfundenen
Provintz
PENSYLVA-
NIÆ,
In denen End-Gräntzen AMERICÆ
In der West-Welt gelegen/
Durch
FRANCISCUM DANIELEM
PASTORIUM,
J.V. Lic. und Friedens-Richtern
daselbsten.

Worbey angefüget sind eini-
ge notable Begebenheiten / und
Bericht-Schreiben an dessen Herrn
Vattern
MELCHIOREM ADAMUM PASTO-
RIUM,
Und andere gute Freunde.

---

Franckfurth und Leipzig/
Zufinden bey Andreas Otto. 1700.

eye toward Pennsylvania. Hannah Penn was finally persuaded to appoint him governor on the recommendations of the Provincial Council, of William Penn the Younger, and of Secretary Logan. This support was seconded likewise by the chief inhabitants of Philadelphia and their London friends. She was probably also influenced by Keith's professed interest in the proprietor's affairs. She said of him in a letter to Logan: "He has given me such assurance of his care and zeal in our affairs as give us room to hope you may safely consult with him for your own ease and our benefit in cases of property."

Keith had hardly been settled in his new position, when news came of the approaching end of the proprietor. William Penn was then (1718) over seventy-three years old, yet had partially recovered from the first stroke of paralysis, which had in a measure dethroned his reason. A second and a third stroke now followed in rapid succession, and the great proprietor was laid low. He had left his home in Rushcombe-near-the-sea for a visit to Bristol on July 27, 1718. His hard labors in his province and in England now produced their legitimate results. The treatment he had received from those who owed almost everything to him and the wildness of his son William had quite broken his spirit. Early on the morning of the 28th of July, Penn died. He was buried at Jordans.

Whatever view we may hold with regard to Penn's government of his province, we must admire his steadfastness of character and his "unflinching devotion to what he believed to be the highest truth." The prospective loss of powerful friends at court and the loss of high social and political honors which it was in their power to bestow did not cause him to flinch in the slightest degree from the performance of a duty for which he felt divinely called. Perhaps the best estimate of his character is that given in the obituary memorial issued by the Friends of his own monthly meeting. Let us quote a brief extract from it: "In fine, he was learned without vanity; apt without forwardness, facetious in conversation, yet weighty and serious—of an extraordinary greatness of mind, yet void of the stain of ambition; as free from rigid gravity as he was clear of unseemly levity; a man—a scholar—a friend; a minister surpassing in speculative endowments, whose memorial will be valued by the wise, and blessed with the just."

Penn's "Holy Experiment" was the "most ideal political experiment ever attempted." It was a realization of some things of which Harrington in his *Oceana*, Plato in his *Republic*, and More in his *Utopia*, never dreamed. From a material point of view the experiment was a most decided success. Had it been possible for Penn to continue to reside in the province, the many troubles and dissensions to which we have had occasion to refer, and which undoubtedly retarded the growth of the colony, might never have arisen. Penn himself never made a truer statement than when he said: "Though good laws do well, good men do better; for good laws may be abolished or evaded by ill men; but good men will never want good laws, nor suffer ill ones." During Penn's absences those who were evilly disposed toward him took every advantage, and even his friends allowed the interests of the province to be assailed too often by reason of their own selfishness and quarrelsome disposition. His policy of friendliness and kindness toward the Indians was a signal success, from whatever point of view we examine it. However unselfish his career, his character has not altogether escaped attacks by Macaulay and Franklin. Macaulay was undoubtedly in error; and Franklin, by reason of his practical cast of mind, was never in a position to judge the motives of an idealist such as Penn was in very many respects. The purity of his motive cannot be impugned, even though one may notice here and there evidences of self-interest.

Pennsylvania was prosperous from the very beginning of its settlement. Even those settlers who were most outspoken in accusing Penn of harshness were more successful in material affairs than their contemporaries in the other colonies. Penn's province was more widely, better known in Europe than any of the other colonies. Consequently, a more cosmopolitan population settled within its boundaries. At the time of Penn's death the population had reached, approximately, fifty thousand, and Philadelphia had taken such strides that it was then the largest city on the continent. This growth made Pennsylvania one of the most prosperous of the English colonies in America.

Penn left a widow and six children—a son and a daughter by his first wife, and three sons and a daughter by his second. His land was encumbered by a mortgage, and he had entered into an agreement with the crown for the sale of his proprietary rights. His will had been made prior to this agreement. His English and Irish estates he devised to his son William and his daughter Letitia Aubrey—children by his first wife, Gulielma Maria Springett. These estates returned an annual revenue of £1,500 and were counted far more valuable at that time than his possessions in the New World. To his widow and her children he left his American possessions after his debts were paid out of them. To the Earls of Oxford, Mortimer, and Pawlet he intrusted the government of the province and Lower Counties, to be sold by them to the crown or to any other prospective purchaser. They were given authority likewise to place upon the market as much land as might be necessary for the complete satisfaction of his debts. His daughter Letitia and the three children of his son William were made recipients of ten thousand acres of land each. His widow was appointed the sole executrix and legatee of the estate, and the remainder of the lands in America were to be given to her children at her discretion and subject to an annuity to herself of £300.

Several vexed questions now arose concerning the nature of the government under the will. As between the respective rights of the crown, the heir-at-law, and the widow in the government of the province, the whole question was so thoroughly muddled that the trustees would not assume the responsibility of acting. They consequently appealed to the Court of Chancery to determine their rights. For this purpose an action was begun that was not decided until 1727. In the meanwhile, Penn's widow assumed the direction of the provincial affairs until the decision was rendered establishing the proprietary's will. The embryonic agreement with the crown was not sustained, and in consequence the proprietary rights devolved first on William Penn the Younger. At his death they devolved on his son Springett conjointly with John, Thomas, and Richard, the three sons of the proprietor's second wife, Hannah Callowhill.

Soon after Keith's arrival in the province, he met the Assembly of the Lower Counties at New Castle. Through the exercise of considerable tact he was successful in brushing aside the haze that had hitherto clouded the proprietary's claim to the government of that territory. The legality of that title was now unreservedly admitted by those most interested. The settlement was indeed most opportune, for by reason of the disputed title to governmental prerogatives and of the errors of the preceding governors a movement was on foot to petition the crown for the appointment of a royal governor. Fresh from his successful negotiations with the Assembly of the Lower Counties, Keith proceeded to Philadelphia, more confirmed than ever in his determination to be a tactful and politic executive. Here he made his first address to the Assembly of the province. This address is so thoroughly typical of the character of the man, and so well illustrative of the character of his entire administration, that we cannot refrain from quoting portions of it at some length. The portions selected will not be given verbatim, but in the paraphrased form in which they have been quoted by Bolles in his *Pennsylvania* (i, 232):

He announced "his tender regard for their interests. He should always endeavor to make the time they must necessarily bestow on the public service as easy and pleasant to them as he hoped it would be profitable and satisfactory to the country. The warmth of his inclination towards them might be inferred from his application during the last year, to introduce to the prince regent the humble address of the Assembly to the king, which had been so graciously received by his exertions; by the diligence and expense with which he had obtained his commission, without other prospect or advantage than that of serving them; and by the fatigue he had already undergone to promote their service. But these things were trifles compared with their indispensable obligation to support the dignity and authority of the government, by such a reasonable and discreet establishment as the nature of the thing and their own generosity would direct; and whatever they might be disposed to do of that kind, he hoped might no longer bear the undeserved and reproachful name of a burthen on the people; but that they would rather enable him to relieve the country from real burthens, by empowering him to introduce a better economy and more frugal management in the collection of taxes, which were then squandered by the officers appointed to assess and collect them."

Keith was quite as successful in his dealings with the Indians, from the very beginning of his administration, as he had been with the people of the province. He visited the Governor of Virginia, and together they drew up an agreement with respect to certain boundary disputes with the Indians that were threatening to become serious. The agreement proved satisfactory to the Indians of Pennsylvania and of the Five Nations, and was ratified at Conestoga. Keith showed his insight into the Indian character and illustrated his tact and diplomacy by using all the pomp and ceremony he could devise. He set out upon the journey accompanied by seventy horsemen, with the intention of impressing the natives. He was altogether successful in his mission.

Keith's great popularity made it possible for him to float another important measure, a militia law. This had always been repugnant to the Assembly, which had constantly opposed military measures; but there was now a real and pressing need of it, since the French were rapidly encroaching upon Pennsylvania territory. These encroachments of the French were such that in 1732 it was revealed that they claimed all the territory drained by rivers and streams whose mouths were in their territory. It is interesting to speculate as to the real causes of Keith's unprecedented popularity during the first year of his administration. We find him always on the side of the people, always lenient toward the Quakers, decidedly favorable to rigid religious codes, and always friendly disposed toward the Indians. These were undeniable virtues, and no doubt sufficiently account for his popularity. The other governors had invariably cast their lots with the proprietors, either from political motives or from a strict sense of loyalty and of obligation to their employers. But Keith, meditating upon the shortness of the administrations of his predecessors and the turbulence of their official careers, determined to profit by their unhappy experiences. Consequently, from the first he posed as friend and protector of the people. His rule, in consequence, was longer than those of his predecessors, but his end proved to be also more disastrous—with one possible exception.

Keith succeeded where both Evans and Gookin had signally failed. He convinced the Assembly that a court of equity was a necessity and that he himself as governor could lawfully perform the duties incident to the office of chancellor.

During the administration of Keith's predecessors the criminal jurisprudence of the province had been allowed to drop into a condition of chaos. Murderers had been allowed to escape, or had been kept in prison for years without being brought to trial. During Gookin's administration two murderers had been allowed to escape by reason of the governor's denial of the qualification of jurymen who would not take the oath to sit in judgment of capital cases. The boast was made that these murderers could not be tried on a capital charge. Nevertheless, Keith showed commendable vigor in having them indicted and tried. They were convicted and sentenced to death by a jury, eight of which were Quakers. Finally, the colony became thoroughly alarmed at this critical condition of affairs, and the Assembly became eager to obtain any regular administration of justice consistent with its fundamental rights. At the suggestion of Keith, an act was passed adopting those penal statutes of England best adapted to the existing needs of the province. This act likewise contained a provision securing the right of affirmation to those who were conscientiously opposed to taking an oath. In addition to unnatural crimes, high and petit treason, murder and manslaughter, "witchcraft and conjuration," robbery and burglary, rape and arson, malicious maiming, and every other felony except larceny, were declared to be capital on a second conviction. The province continued under the English criminal code until after the War of the Revolution, when it returned to the more humane code set forth by Penn.

It must not be lost sight of that Penn had established a most admirable criminal code in the first year of the province. This body of laws had as its fundamental principle the reformation of the criminal rather than his punishment, and was far in advance of any criminal law of that time. These laws were "animated by the spirit of philanthropy, and the punishments were designed to tie up the hands of the criminal; to reform and repair the wrongs of the injured party; and to hold up an object of terror sufficient to check a people whose manners he endeavored to fashion by provisions interwoven in the same system." The only capital offence was wilful and premeditated murder. The offences, in great number, for which death was exacted in Great Britain at the time were not capital in Pennsylvania. Such, for instance, were robbery, burglary, arson, rape, unnatural crimes, forgery, and treason of all degrees. Imprisonment at hard labor, flogging, fines, and forfeitures were inflicted upon offenders, with varying severity depending upon the degree of the crime. Even a premeditated murderer could not be convicted except upon the testimony of two witnesses. After conviction, execution was stayed until the executive had had the opportunity of carefully reviewing the case. Should he deem it advisable, he could pardon the offender or commute the punishment.

The provisions of Penn's charter required that all laws enacted by the Assembly should be transmitted to England within five years for the royal approval or veto. The queen in Council vetoed every one of the provisions of Penn's criminal code. The Assembly, however, reënacted and enforced them, and for a while the English authorities, for some reason or other, seemed to connive at this defiance of authority. Then came the period of confusion during the administration of Gookin, which was ushered in by the repealment of the laws permitting affirmation in the place of taking oaths. This was the result of a law, passed during the first year of the reign of George I., declaring that no person could qualify for office or take part in criminal proceedings except upon taking an oath. As a result, judges belonging to the Society of Friends refused to sit in criminal cases, and, because from the Friends most of the judges were chosen, the administration of justice was practically suspended.

One of Keith's laws permitted the wives of men at sea to take legal action as if unmarried. Certain municipal regulations were also enacted requiring the appointment of city surveyors. These officials were to decide upon certain building regulations and were intrusted with the responsibility of having them enforced. There is one act of Keith's that brought him considerable popularity at the time, but that must now be condemned as the most pernicious policy of his whole administration. He first initiated the colonists into the mysteries of a paper currency. Not that the discredit should be laid solely at his door—it was an epidemic that was destined to take possession of the province in time, just as it had of Massachusetts more than thirty years before, and just as it did every one of the thirteen colonies before the overthrow of the English rule. But Keith

The armor portrait of William Penn. *From the painting presented to the Historical Society of Pennsylvania by Granville Penn in 1833.*

led the way and advised the introduction of the fiat money, thinking it would supply the woeful lack of a metallic currency and thus cause the wheels of industry to move rapidly where hitherto they had been seriously clogged. The lack of a supply of money sufficient to meet the legitimate demands of a growing commerce had indeed become a most serious question. Specie had been so scarce from the beginning of the settlement of the colony, that the people were compelled to use the products of the soil for paying their debts. By an act of the Assembly, wheat, rye, Indian corn, barley, oats, pork, beef, and tobacco, as in other colonies, were made legal tender at their market prices. Even taxes were made payable in produce at current local rates, and the proprietary quitrents might be paid in wheat by special arrangement with the proper authorities. As the colony grew, this method of barter became embarrassing and awkward and the whole commercial system became disarranged. There were some coins in circulation, but their value was by no means stable and their quantity was exceedingly limited. To relieve the situation, some of the colonies had already resorted to the printing press. Massachusetts was the first to issue paper money, taking the initiative in 1690. By Keith's time the question in Pennsylvania had become the all-important one, and the governor was never averse to tickling the "popular fancy." He considered the time ripe for a popular move on his part, and recommended the Assembly to consider the expediency of adopting a paper money system.

Two men in the province, however, were wise enough to appreciate the dangers from the financial heresy. James Logan and Isaac Norris both opposed the issuance of paper money, and transmitted to the Assembly their reasons for their opposition. They opposed the plan on the ground of its probable disapproval by the Privy Council. Seeing, however, the determination of the people to have paper money at any cost whatsoever, these two men next did their best to render the movement as harmless as possible. They

suggested that the sum issued should be small, "sufficient
to pass from hand to hand;" that it should continue in circulation no longer than five years if not approved by the
crown; and that its final retirement should be absolute, and
justly and equitably provided for by a well-devised sinking
fund. Keith replied to these objections, at the same time
stating his reason for supporting the plan. Popular sentiment was with the governor, and a system of paper currency
was shortly matured.

Of the £15,000 in bills of credit first issued, £2,500
went toward the payment of the public debt, £1,500 was
distributed to some of the counties as a loan; and the remainder was lent to individuals at interest and on certain
approved security. All the last-mentioned loans were
secured by sterling plate or real estate. The maximum
period before maturity of the loans on plate was one year
and on lands eight years, and the interest demanded was
four per cent. The amount of the loans could not be less
than £12 or more than £100. There was one exception
made to this rule—if all the bills had not been lent four
months after the opening of the loan office, the former
applicants could increase their borrowings to a maximum
of £200. The kinds of land that might be offered as
security for a loan were carefully defined by the laws.
Failure to liquidate within two months after the maturity
of an instalment subjected the borrower to be proceeded
against by the province for the absolute possession of the
security thus forfeited. All bills were to be destroyed upon
their return to the loan office. The act contained a legal
tender provision, and all persons who refused to accept the
bills at their par value in full payment of all debts in real
and personal estate transactions were fined. The loan
office was in charge of four trustees, and the bills were
signed by persons specified in the act. The workmanship
of the bills was so poor and crude that they were counter-
feited almost immediately. Many of the counterfeits were
made in Ireland, and the counterfeiters carried on a most

remunerative business. A law was passed making the penalty for counterfeiting the clipping of ears, flogging, and fine, which, if not paid, made the offender liable to be sold for a period of seven years to anyone who would pay for his labor. Of course, this did not stop counterfeiting, and in 1753 the punishment was made "death, without benefit of clergy."

To keep the paper currency out of the hands of the speculators, the act provided that the lands could not be divided and that no fictitious titles could be created. Every proper precaution was taken to protect the currency, both in the examination of titles and in the rigid adherence to the provisions of the law governing loans to individuals. The loans made to the province toward the payment of the public debt were to be liquidated from the customs and excise tax. The counties were to repay their loans from the proceeds of an annual tax of a penny a pound added to the customary county rate. Within a few months the thing happened that usually characterizes the issuance of bills of credit. The bills were so popular that £30,000 more were soon emitted, under an act which extended the maximum period of maturity to twelve years. Some few changes were made in the provisions of this second act, but in all essential principles the changes were unimportant.

Logan, as we have seen, protested vigorously against the issuance of paper money, and after that measure had been passed he watched the results with keen interest. Although he had ceased to be a member of the Council, he was still clerk of that body and secretary of the province. He and the governor watched each other closely, knowing full well that a conflict between them was inevitable and that open hostilities might be precipitated at any moment. An error on the part of Logan furnished the governor with the opportunity which he had been eagerly awaiting for some time. The former assumed the personal responsibility of inserting in the minutes of the Council an account of its proceedings which had not been formally approved. Keith thereupon removed him from his office. The affair did not rest there, for Logan went to England and complained to Mrs. Penn of what he considered his bad treatment. Mrs. Penn had always had the utmost confidence in the secretary and was considerably exasperated at the governor's action. She wrote to Keith and accused him of neglecting the proprietary interests, and threatened his removal unless he mended his ways. He was ordered peremptorily to reinstate Logan in his office and to put him in possession of the seal of the province.

Two of the trustees sent Keith a letter, in which they strongly disapproved of his recent behavior and told him that his remaining in office depended altogether on his compliance with the instructions he had received from Mrs. Penn. This letter did not mince matters, but was concise, frank, and right to the point. It was a stinging rebuke to the governor. "The care of the Province," they wrote, "devolving in some measure upon us as trustees, we have been obliged to consider the late conduct in it, which has been so far from giving content to the Friends, who expected a very different account of it, that we might have very justly proceeded to a change. But the widow of our worthy friend, our deceased proprietary, is still willing thou mayest have further trial, and be continued longer; the only terms of which are thy strict compliance with the instructions given in the foregoing letter. Thou mayest suppose, perhaps, that the powers of government are not directly lodged by the will in our said friend, the widow; and, therefore, that it may not belong so immediately to her to direct in affairs of government; but, as the interest of the family is principally concerned in the welfare and prosperity of that Province, it can become no other person better to take care of it; and if ever the propriety of this proceeding be questioned, thou mayest easily be convinced, there is sufficient power to end all disputes with thee about it."

Keith was not the man to act supinely in an affair where his own personal pride was involved. He sent a spirited reply to Mrs. Penn, in which he justified his acts, although

## Im Nahmen und zur Ehre GOttes!

Wir Unterschriebene urkunden und bekennen hiemit/ demnach wir zusammen fünff und zwantzig tausend Acker/ Englischer Maß/ unvertheilten Lands/ in der Americanischen Provintz Pennsylvania, gesampter Hand gekauffet/ auch jeglicher sein Antheil nach Außweiß darüber besagender Rechnungen würcklich bezahlt haben: Nemlich

| | | |
|---|---:|---:|
| Jacob von de Walle | 2500 | |
| und Caspar Merian 2500. jetzund Jacob von de Walle | 833⅓ | 5000. |
| und Daniel Behagel | 1666⅔ | |
| Lt. Johann Jacob Schütz | 4000 | |
| Johann Wilhelm Uberfeld/ jetzund Frantz Daniel Pastorius | 1000 | 5000. |
| Jacob von de Walle | 1666⅔ | |
| Georg Strauß/ jetzund Johanna Eleonora von Merlau/ | | |
| M. Johann Wilhelm Peters Haußfrau | 1666⅔ | 5000. |
| Daniel Behagel | 1666⅔ | |
| Dr. Gerhard von Masricht | 1666⅔ | |
| Dr. Thomas von Wilich | 1666⅔ | 5000. |
| und Johannes le Brun | 1666⅔ | |
| Balthasar Jawert | 3333⅓ | 5000. |
| Johannes Kemler | 1666⅔ | |

Summa 25000.

Daß wir wegen sothaner Güther/ vor uns/ respective unsere Haußfrauen/ Kinder und Erben/ im Nahmen GOttes eine Gemeinschafft oder Societet angetretten und geschlossen haben/ auff Art und Weiß als hiernach folgt:

1. Obbesagte Ländereyen/ wie und wo sie uns sampt und sonders angewiesen seyn/ oder uns künfftige angewiesen werden mögen/ selbsten auch die über obig specificirtes/ uns competirende Stadt loß/ nämlich die vier oder sechs Plätze in der Stadt Philadelphia zum Auffbauen neuer Häuser / und incirca beyläufftig 300. Acker in der Stadt Gerechtigkeit und Freyheit vor und umb Philadelphia gelegen/ und das neulichst/ zur Ziegelbackerey/ an Schollkiel/ erkauffte Land/ sampt allen und jeden/ an allen Orten und Enden in gantz Pennsylvanien auffgerichteten und künfftigen Gebäuen und anderen meliorationen, auch dahin gesendete/ dorten gekauffte oder sonsten erlangte Victualia, Kauffmanns Wahren/ Viehe/ Haußgeräth/ etc. erlangte und künfftige Real-Rechten und Gerechtigkeiten/ sollen jetzt und künfftig/ in gleichen Rechten gemeinschafftlich seyn und bleiben/ nach eines jeden obspecificirtem Antheil/ so er in derselben Compagnie hat.

2. Alles und jedes/ was zu deren cultivirung und Anrichtung/ zu Gebäuen/ item zu Uberschickung der Dienstbotten/ Pacht-Leuten und andern Personen/ auch der Kauffmanns-Wahren/ Lebens-Mitteln/ Werckzeuge etc. und dorten im Lande an Handwercker und Taglöhner etc. Summa an allen Kosten/ wie die Nahmen haben mögen/ in America und Europa hiebero angewendet worden ist/ oder künfftig auff hierbedicht benahmte Weiß/ verwendet werden möchte/ soll auff gemeine Kosten geschehen pro rato eines jeden Antheils.

3. Dargegen auch alle Nutzungen/ Gefäll/ was daselbsten erworben/ gebauet/ gepflantzet/ fruchtbar gemacht/ und gezeuget wird/ es sey an Erd-Gewächs/ leibeigenen Menschen/ Viehe/ Manufacturen etc. nichts überall außgenommen/ sollen unter allen Interessenten/ pro rato der Ackerzahl/ gemein seyn.

4. Was dieser Compagnie Angelegenheit betrifft/ sollen die fünff Haupt-Stämme (jedes 5000. vor ein Haupt-Stamm gerechnet/ oder wie man sich künfftig etwan anders vergleichen

12. Im unverhofften Fall über kurtz oder lang zwischen uns/ unseren Erben und Nachkommen/wegen dieser Güter und deren dependencien einiger Mißverstand oder Anlaß zum Streit vorfallen möchte/ soll solches zwischen den Gliedern der Geselschafft/ oder dafern diese von beyden Theilen nicht gantz unpartheyisch gehalten würden/ durch andere von den uneinigen Partheyen/einmüthiglich erwehlte zwey redliche Persohnen/ mit Macht/daß diese zwey erwehlte Persohnen/ die dritte/ wann sie es nöthig achten/ zu sich nehmen/ auff Art und Weiß/ als jetzt beschrieben wird/ geschlichtet werden: Nemlich die erwehlte Schieds-Freunde sollen auff bestimpten Tag und Orth/ in Beywesen der mißhelligen Partheyen/ oder dero Bevollmächtigten/ nach Anruffung Göttlichen Beystands/ und reifflicher der Sachen Überlegung/ das Werck nach ihrem besten Verstand und Gutdüncken durch ihre Urtheil/ wann sie die Partheyen nicht vergleichen können/ entscheiden. Jm Fall aber diese drey nicht einig werden/ oder die meiste Stimmen nicht außfinden könten/ so sollen sie sich bey ein oder zweyen Haupt-participanten Raths erholen/ und darnach die Urtheil verfassen und außsprechen: Wogegen hernacher auff keine Weiß oder Weg etwas ferner gethan/ gehandelt oder admittiret werden soll/ auff keine Weiß oder Weg/ mit Recht oder mit Gewalt/ von keinem Richter oder Menschen/ der gantzen Welt/ in Europa oder America. Und dafern jemand hiergegen sich zu setzen anmaßen wolte/ soll er eo ipso seines gantzen Antheils verlustig/ und darzu des Orts/ wo er wohnet/ allgemeinen Allmosen-Kasten mit einer Straff/ von 200. Rthl. ohne alle exception, auch ohne fernere declaration, ipso facto verfallen seyn.

Alles treulich und sonder Gefährde: Dessen zu wahrer Urkund ist gegenwärtiger nach reifflicher Überlegung von allen Interessenten einmüthiglich beliebter Brieff/ unter aller und jeder eigenhändigen Unterschrifft und vorgetrucktem Jnsiegel zwölffmahl außgefertiget/ und jeglichem dessen ein exemplar zugestellet/ auch eines zu den gemeinschafftlichen documentis geleget worden. Welcher gegeben zu Franckfurt am Mayn/ den 12. Novemb. anno 1686.

First and last pages of the prospectus of the Frankfurt Company. *From the original in possession of the Historical Society of Pennsylvania.*

at the same time he tactfully professed his readiness to obey all legal instructions. Furthermore, he maintained most vigorously his rights as governor to act in certain matters independently of the proprietary. Nor did he allow the matter to rest there. He sent all the correspondence to the Assembly, including Mrs. Penn's instructions and his own letter in reply. Logan replied to Keith by a memorial in which he presented the arguments of the dissenting members of the Council. That body, as a whole, however, was on the side of Keith and considered his cause their own cause. Logan's memorial aroused the latent ire of David Lloyd, which had until then been sleeping peacefully under the dignified robes of the chief justiceship. The "agitator," Logan's ancient adversary, threw off all official dignity and came to the defence of popular rights. He adduced proof after proof that in the exercise of his prerogatives the governor was totally unresponsible to the Council. Keith was completely sustained by the Assembly, and Mrs. Penn was informed of the fact by letter. Keith was furthermore pledged the support of the Assembly in resisting the proprietary's specific instructions (Bolles).

The usual reaction set in shortly afterward. Keith and the Assembly had gone a step too far, and none realized the fact better than the members of that legislative body. Rumors of Keith's early removal became rife, and his popularity lessened in direct proportion to the credibility of those rumors. Those whose object it was to be always on the winning side deserted him at once. They were soon followed by others, until the stampede to the proprietary side became general. As the ultimate fate of the governor developed into a certainty, the members of the Assembly treated him with coldness or, worse, with indifference. He now underwent the usual experiences of a popular hero fallen from favor. His unpopularity became as great as had been his popularity in the palmy days of his prosperity. Even those whom he had served most faithfully, and for whom he had risked the breach with the proprietary, turned against him when they were convinced that the end of his power was at hand. The Assembly refused him anything more than a half-hearted vote of confidence. His stipend for the current year was cut more than in half, and the £400 that the Assembly allowed him was voted in a grudging manner.

Keith was finally removed in 1726, after having been in office more than nine years. He clung to the hope that he would be ultimately recalled, and as there were still many of the colonists who supported him his hopes were not without seeming foundation. He became the centre of the opposition to the new administration, and let no opportunity pass without adding to its difficulties. He was elected to the Assembly, and at first exerted considerable influence upon its deliberations. Later, however, upon the exposure of what were supposed to be his ulterior motives, either to secure his reappointment or the overthrow of the proprietary government, his influence was reduced to almost zero.

Keith's sole ambition was to be popular, and he tried to accomplish this in every way possible, either by fair or foul means. He made promises when cornered which he knew he could not keep. This plan for a while proved successful, but in the end brought about his ruin. Success turned his head so completely that he fancied himself not only superior to Logan in ability but even more powerful than the proprietary itself. His disputes with Logan brought about his downfall, and after his sceptre had departed his popularity soon followed.

Keith remained in the province until the spring of 1728, when he was obliged to leave secretly to avoid prosecution for debt, into which his lavish style of living had involved him. Shortly after his return to England, he published a pamphlet on the state of the colonies. He is said to have been the first person to suggest to the crown the advisability and practicability of taxing the American colonies. This was in 1739. A sad end overtook the ex-governor. He died in the Old Bailey, where he had been imprisoned for debt.

However severely we may condemn Keith's personal failings, we are compelled to recognize the fact that the colony prospered under his zealous support of the popular party as it had never prospered before. He has been condemned severely—and justly so—by Pennsylvania historians for his treacherous conduct of the proprietary's interest in the province. But in their eagerness to blacken his character, they have failed either to give him the little personal credit that is due or to recognize the beneficent results of his alliance with the popular party. Keith undoubtedly had selfish interests to serve in assuming the championship of the popular cause, but we cannot believe that his attitude toward that cause was one totally devoid of principle. He was ambitious, he was selfish, and he was not always particular as to the means he adopted to accomplish his ends; but his faults were committed in the defence of the popular rights rather than in the enhancement of the aristocratic power. That fact does not by any means excuse his errors, but it does put him in a relatively better light when he is compared with other colonial governors who shared his faults but, unlike him, did nothing for the cause of popular government.

Patrick Gordon, who succeeded Keith (1726), was most successful in winning the respect of the people. He had been a soldier in the English army and had served from his youth to the close of Queen Anne's wars. He was born in the same year as William Penn, 1644, and had fought in Europe at a time when the English armies were commanded by Marlborough. In his first address to the Assembly, he assured the members that the frankness acquired in the camps would be continued in the executive chair. He disclaimed any intention of resorting to "refined or artful" politics in the discharge of his duties and reiterated his determination to be candid in all his dealings with the Assembly. As Keith profited by the mistakes of his predecessors, so, as the sequel proved, Gordon profited by the errors of Keith. He restored the Council to its former prerogatives and struck a happy balance between the interests of the proprietaries and those of the people. In fact, he tried to make the two seemingly conflicting interests identical. Soon after Gordon became governor, news was received of the death of the king; and the Assembly sent a congratulatory address to his successor, George II.

Shortly afterward, Gordon addressed a communication to the Assembly on the subject of bills of credit. The five years' limit having been reached, the paper money acts were submitted to the Privy Council. The Committee of the Council on Trade and Plantations had warned the Pennsylvania Assembly of the dangers incident to its paper money policy. Nevertheless, in recognition of the fact that the currency had already become widely circulated among the people, permission was given to continue it temporarily. It was specifically understood, however, that no further issues should be made and that all outstanding bills should be withdrawn as rapidly as possible. Gordon agreed entirely with the point of view of the committee, until by actual observation of the operation of the currency in Pennsylvania he was led to change his opinions. He then expressed his belief that the bills of credit had been a benefit both to the province and to England. Importations from England had greatly increased; more ships had been built; and the currency itself, far from depreciating in value as it had in the other colonies, had actually risen in value. He showed, likewise, that the drain of gold and silver to England had been somewhat checked by the establishment of iron furnaces and by the cultivation of hemp; that these, likewise, would enhance the value of the paper money and make it secure until it could be dispensed with altogether. For this reason, he thought the Privy Council would overlook any little breach of its instructions.

In fact, there was already a noisy demand for another issue of the currency. The colonists thought it a great convenience to trade, and credited the existing stagnation of business to the fact that many of the bills had been redeemed and that the supply was not equal to the drain

Richard Penn, the Proprietary.
*From the painting by Robert Wilson.*

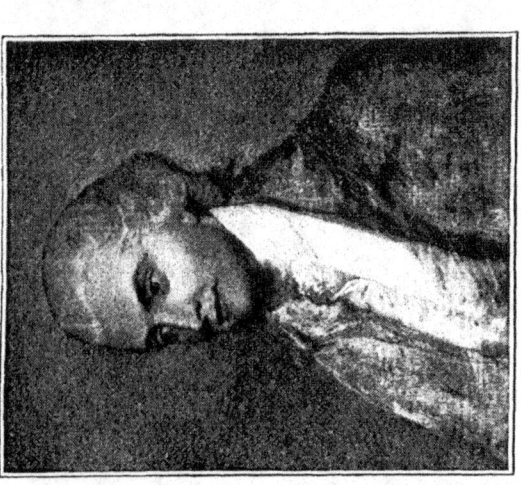

John Penn, son of Thomas Penn.
*From the painting by Robert Edge Pine.*

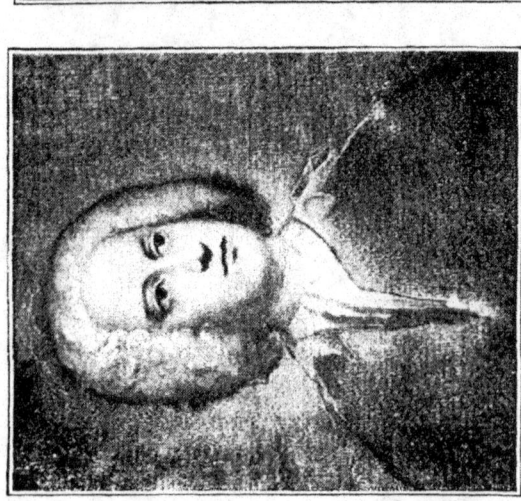

John Penn, called the American.
*From the painting attributed to Sir Godfrey Kneller.*

*The originals of which are now in possession of the Historical Society of Pennsylvania.*

of gold and silver to England. Merchants were overstocked with goods, navigation was discouraged, and shipyards were idle. The Assembly prepared an address to the Privy Council, in which the old arguments in favor of paper money were repeated and the specific plea entered that Pennsylvania was not like other colonies; that Pennsylvania had secured the bills by requiring the pledging of valuable concrete property; that the issues were not made solely on the credit of the government, as had been done in other colonies. The Assembly thereupon prepared a bill reissuing the amounts already authorized and adding an issue of £30,000 to be repayable by instalments in sixteen years. The whole sum current thus became £75,000, and the last issue was to continue current until 1739.

In 1733, William Penn's second wife, Hannah, died. Penn's estate at the time of his death had been so greatly reduced that his widow's last days were clouded by the lack of sufficient means to live according to her station. William Penn's grandson Springett, son of William Penn, Jr., had died two years before (1731), and Dennis in 1722. The Assembly then questioned Gordon's authority to act as governor. However, a new commission was sent him, signed by John, Robert, and Richard Penn, in whom the government was then vested. The appointment was approved by the crown, which, however, reserved the right to govern the Lower Counties on the Delaware. John Penn, known as the "American," because he was born in Philadelphia during the founder's second visit, came out to the colony during the administration of Gordon. He returned in a few months to checkmate Lord Baltimore, who was planning a settlement of the disputed boundary between Maryland and Pennsylvania altogether in his own interests. Thomas Penn resided in the colony from 1732 to 1741 and was a member of the Council. By reason of his narrow and somewhat selfish policy, he failed to win the esteem of the people.

Governor Gordon died in August, 1736, in the ninety-second year of his age. The ten years of his administration had been a decade of peace and prosperity. Personally, he was able to say "that the oftener he met the Assembly, the more their confidence in each other was increased." The governor was held in the highest esteem by both the people and the proprietary. His frankness had commanded the regard of all. "The dissension between the 'proprietary and popular parties was scarce remembered; the unanimity of the Assembly, the Council, and the governor, gave an uninterrupted course of prosperity to the Province. During this period the colony increased greatly in population and in wealth."

Another governor was not appointed for two years. During that period, James Logan, as president of the Council, acted in the place of the executive. Few matters of importance characterize Logan's exercise of the executive function, except the boundary dispute with Maryland. This dispute was more than seventy-five years old and now culminated in a quarrel accompanied by some bloodshed. A detailed account of the dispute will be given in the succeeding chapter, on the " Development of Maryland." Logan had never been beloved by the people of the province. They claimed that he had always been opposed to their interests and favorable to those of the proprietary. We might have expected a reasonably tumultuous interregnum as a result of Logan's accession to power. But such was not the case. The two years passed with scarcely a ripple upon the surface of the provincial waters. "The annals of the time consist of those dull, ordinary events that are a true indication of a people's happy existence."

The state of the province upon the arrival of the new governor, George Thomas, in 1738, is an interesting contrast to what it was at the meeting of the Assembly in 1682. Great changes had come to the colony during the years that had intervened. At the first settlement of the province, the people were profoundly grateful to Penn for the haven he had afforded them from the religious persecution of the mother country. In 1738, however, Penn was dead and the regard which had been shown for him and his family had disappeared. In its place had grown up indifference and even disregard, while the Assembly felt under no obligation to anyone for anything. The supremacy of the people was thoroughly established. The representatives made the laws and consulted no interest other than that of the people. The only check to the Assembly's complete control of all legislative matters was the veto power of the governor and the Privy Council.

This condition of affairs was due to the fact that generations that knew not Penn or his family had sprung up in the province. The attractions the colony had to offer, religious, political, and material, were such that wave after wave of emigrants came from many countries of Europe. Most of them had never heard of Penn, and those who had heard of him did not cherish any particular sentiments with respect to him or his family. They knew of no reason why they should act differently toward his family than they did toward others of the proprietary class. By far the most numerous of the people who finally settled in Pennsylvania were the Germans. We have already recurred to the fact that the Germans, oppressed and persecuted at home, learned with delight from Penn of his project to found a colony where all should be free. Most of them came to Pennsylvania, and prominent among them was Francis Daniel Pastorius, who, as agent of the Frankfort Land Company, composed of wealthy persons, chiefly Pietists, in Germany and Holland, settled a colony at Germantown in 1683. After that, the number of German settlers increased rapidly, many of them coming from Heidelberg. They knew more about Pennsylvania, because Pastorius had written concerning the colony in his circulars, which had been spread broadcast throughout the old country. Profiting by the unhappy experience of the Palatine Germans during the administration of Governor Hunter, many of the later emigrants avoided New York and came directly to Pennsylvania. The Mennonites, persecuted at their homes in the cantons of Zurich,

Bern, and Schaffhausen, went to Alsace in 1672. Later, they came to Pennsylvania, where they settled on land now a part of Lancaster County. They were similar in religious belief to the Friends. Many Moravians also came from Georgia at the beginning of the Spanish war, owing to the fact that their religion forbade their taking up arms. Many German emigrants settled in Bucks, Berks, Montgomery, Lancaster, and York Counties. By the time of the Revolution, they had spread over a very considerable portion of the province, but the centre of the German population was in Berks and Lancaster Counties.

For the most part, the Germans were very friendly disposed toward the Quakers. They always expressed their gratitude for the kindness and protection they had received at their hands. They claimed they had not experienced equally kind and liberal treatment in any other English colony. Consequently, when it came to a political contest, the Germans always voted in support of Quaker control when the struggle assumed the character of an anti-Quaker movement. Governor Thomas, on the contrary, always maintained that this support of the Germans was won by the Quakers' representing that the militia law was well calculated to reduce them to the slavery they had experienced in their own country and from which they had so happily escaped; furthermore, that this militia law, which was supported by the anti-Quaker party, was intended to drag them from their farms to work on the fortifications of the province.

In addition to the Germans, there was a large number of Scotch-Irish who came to Pennsylvania. They were so called because they were descendants of Scots who had taken up their residence in the north of Ireland. They were bold, enterprising, and hardy, and favored a frontier life in preference to settling in the more thickly populated portions of the province. They disliked the Pope as heartily as they venerated Calvin and Knox. They had left Ulster in Ireland because of religious bigotry, commercial jealousy, and oppression by the landlords. The Scotch had been persuaded to take up at very low rentals the lands forfeited by the Irish. By industry and frugality, they prospered where the Irish had eked out but a bare subsistence. This prosperity aroused the avariciousness of the landlords, who, upon the expiration of the leases, demanded higher rents. The Scotch refused to submit to this species of extortion, while the Roman Catholics, eager to regain their old lands upon almost any conditions, readily agreed to pay the higher rentals. The Irish bid higher for the lands than did the Scotch, and the latter were dispossessed. Many of the first Scotch-Irish emigrants settled in Bucks, Chester, and York Counties, and later in the Kittatinny valley.

The Quakers had not been called upon for twenty-five years to contribute toward the expenses of an actual war with a foreign nation. During that period, the province had increased in wealth, its commerce had developed unassailed by French privateers, and it had not been burdened with taxes to support the wars of the mother country. In October, 1739, however, war was declared between England and Spain, and privateers were soon scouring the seas. This was the "War of Jenkins's Ear," which was followed shortly by the great War of the Austrian Succession. Governor Thomas at once made a request for aid from the Assembly. The reply was returned that: "The Quakers do not (as the world is now circumstanced) condemn the use of arms in others, yet are principled against it themselves." They admitted, however, that those who thought it right to fight had "an equal right to liberty of conscience with others." In recognition of this fact, they would not oppose any movement on his part to organize a voluntary militia outside of the laws and without a consultation with the Assembly. In his attempt to force the Assembly to give up what he considered their foolish scruples, the governor was completely defeated. Finally, on the advice of the Duke of Newcastle, he permitted an officer of the regular army to recruit volunteers. Seven hundred men were thus raised, although the quota from Pennsylvania was only four hundred. As many of these volunteers were redemptioners, a new cause for complaint was lodged against the governor. He was offered £3,000 by the Assembly if he would prevent the enlistment of these servants, who still had considerable time to serve. The governor declined the offer and raised the necessary funds on the credit of the British government. The Assembly appropriated at least £2,500 to indemnify the masters who had lost their servants.

By his impolitic manner of dealing with the Assembly, the governor soon developed an anti-governor party. The clash came at the election in the autumn of 1742. There was considerable rioting at the polls, and over fifty of the disturbers of the peace were locked up in the jail. The Quakers were entirely successful in the election, and all the old members of the Assembly were returned. The governor acknowledged himself completely defeated, and agreed to the bills the Assembly demanded. He was rewarded by having all his back pay granted him. The war with France had been renewed in the meantime, and the governor showed his change of heart by enlisting men only from the combatant portion of the people and by making no requisition upon the Assembly for money.

In this effort to recruit soldiers, Thomas was ably assisted by Benjamin Franklin. He wrote pamphlets on the subject and called a meeting of the people, at which he urged them to form an association for defence. As a result of his efforts, ten thousand volunteers were enrolled, and armed and equipped at their own expense. They were called "Associates," and the militia of Pennsylvania retained that name for years afterward. This was the second time Franklin had appeared before the public, but it was the first time he had contributed to the province a real service. Born in Boston, January 17, 1706, he was apprenticed to his brother James, who was a printer. During his apprenticeship he contributed to his brother's paper several anonymous articles that were warmly commended. Having quarrelled with his brother, at seventeen years of age he came to Philadelphia, where he continued in the printing trade. Here he became acquainted with Governor Keith, who sent him back to Boston, to his father, with strong recommendations that he be made a master printer. His father paid no attention to this advice. Next, at the instance of Keith, he went to London, expecting the governor to furnish him with letters of credit and introduction that would enable him to return a master printer. After reaching London, he discovered that Keith had thoroughly deceived him. He had but fifteen pistoles in his pockets, but set out to look for work. Finally, he was employed at a printing house in Bartholomew Close, where he stayed a year, during which time he earned good wages and "squandered them on idle companions, lewd women, treats, and shows."

In 1726 he returned to Pennsylvania, and with the assistance of some friends he established himself in business. Three years later he came before the public for the second time. Franklin had made his first appearance in political life in Pennsylvania during the paper-money controversy of the administration of Governor Gordon. He wrote a pamphlet on *The Nature and Necessity of a Paper Currency.* Franklin was at that time only twenty-three years old, had been in the province only six years, and was still a foreman in the printing shop of Samuel Keimer. He was the recipient of unstinted praise for the ability displayed in this pamphlet. It was considered a "remarkable production, in advance of his time, and an enlightenment of the Province." As a matter of fact, it was a very inferior production. It was full of the most mischievous fallacies and was overrun with the rankest financial heresies. He tried to show what a great stimulant to trade and prosperity is an abundance of money. The land bank scheme was as attractive to him as had been John Law's Mississippi Company commercial stock to the French public prior to the bursting of the bubble in 1720—just nine years before. Furthermore, he spoke of the paper currency "as coined land," and maintained that anyone who possessed land should have the privilege of coining it into the new currency. Franklin argued, likewise, that the land pledged as security should be "coined" up to its full value. He held that there was no danger in this radical action, because land in Pennsylvania was steadily increasing in value. Also that the issuance of the bills on the pledged lands, by stimulating trade and industry, in turn augmented the value of those lands. It was a species of financial reasoning in a circle that was well worthy of the times, but not of the man. He showed a woeful lack of insight into human nature by arguing that no man would be so foolish as to borrow more of the paper money than his land was worth and thereby impair the value of the very money he was borrowing.

Franklin did not go to the extreme of advocating an unlimited issue of paper money, but he did believe it should be issued in very large amounts and that it should be kept equal at least to the advancing value of land. This he considered the very acme of conservatism and far within the limits of safety. Franklin always believed the pamphlet exerted a great influence upon the people at that time and had much weight in the final decision of the matter. It may have had some influence upon those of the rank and file of the colonists who cherished the fond delusion that something could be created out of nothing and that they themselves were to become the happy recipients of the wealth thus created. The pamphlet had probably no influence whatever, either upon the members of the Assembly or upon the influential people in private life. By these classes it was either ignored entirely or its faults excused "for the sake of a certain power of statement it displayed, which gave promise of better things." In a part of his autobiography, written in 1771, Franklin himself, writing of paper money, admitted that he had arrived at the opinion that "there are limits beyond which the quantity may be hurtful."

In 1730 Franklin married Miss Deborah Read, with whom he had become acquainted before his departure for England. The year before, he had become the editor and

Patrick Gordon, Governor of Pennsylvania. *From the painting now in possession of the Historical Society of Pennsylvania.*

proprietor of the *Pennsylvania Gazette*, of which he made a decided success. In 1732 he began the publication of what was commonly called *Poor Richard's Almanac*. It was purported to be by " Richard Saunders." Both the almanac and the paper he sought to make vehicles of useful information for the people. They inculcated especially the virtues of frugality and industry. Whatever may have been the financial heresies of his youth, Franklin was always on the side of every enterprise which in his judgment would make for the public good. Both to his personal efforts and to his pen is due the credit of the foundation of the Philadelphia Library in 1731. His wisdom, foresight, and public spirit gained an almost immediate recognition. " By his talents, prudence, and integrity, he continued to rise in the estimation of the community in which he lived, until he was deemed worthy of the highest honors which the country could bestow."

In 1736 Franklin became clerk of the Assembly, which office he accepted probably from the "double motive of serving the public and also himself." By accepting the political office he thought some of the public printing might fall to his lot. He was not disappointed in his hopes. He was chosen for the same position the following year, though at first opposed by a member of the Assembly, who put forward a candidate "whose merits were compared with Franklin's failings." Franklin gained the support of this member by borrowing and duly returning a curious book. The member through this means became better acquainted with Franklin, and later became his friend. Franklin was made postmaster of Philadelphia in 1737, and deputy postmaster-general for the British Colonies in 1753. In 1757 he was sent to England as agent of the Assembly to plead the cause of the people in opposition to the claim of exemption from taxation on the part of the proprietaries. He was entirely successful in his arguments before the Privy Council, which decided that the estates of the proprietaries should bear their due proportion of the public burdens. He received the thanks of the Assembly on his return for his able and faithful presentation of its cause. In 1752 he made the experiment with the kite by which he brilliantly proved the identity of lightning and electricity. The accounts of his early experiments read before the Royal Society attracted but little attention. "The paper," says Franklin in his autobiography, "which I wrote for Mr. Kinnersley, on the sameness of lightning with electricity, . . . was laughed at by the connoisseurs." These papers soon attracted the attention of the French, however, and later were again brought before the notice of the Royal Society. "They soon made me," says Franklin, "more than amends for the slight with which they had before treated me." He was made a member of the society without any application being made on his behalf and without the payment of the customary dues on admission, amounting in all to twenty-five guineas. They also honored him with the Copley gold medal (1753), and presented him with a set of the *Transactions* without charge. The Universities of Edinburgh and Oxford conferred upon him the degree of Doctor of Laws, in 1762, before his return to America. A similar honor had been conferred upon him by the Scottish University of St. Andrews in the spring of 1759. In speaking of Franklin's account of his electrical experiments, Sir Humphry Davy says: "A singular felicity of induction guided all his researches, and by very small means he established very grand truths: the style and manner of his publication are almost as worthy of admiration as the doctrines it contains. . . . He has written equally for the uninitiated and for the philosopher."

In 1749, Franklin wrote a pamphlet entitled *Proposals Relating to the Education of Youth in Pennsylvania*. This led to the formation of an association by some prominent citizens of Philadelphia for the purpose of establishing an institution of learning higher in standard than any in the city at that time. They selected the financially embarrassed Charitable School which had been founded in 1740, and raised it to the dignity of an academy. A board of trustees was constituted, and on May 14, 1755, a charter was secured from the proprietaries Thomas Penn and Richard Penn. The first commencement was held on May 17, 1757, when seven students received the degree of Bachelor of Arts. The Rev. William Smith, M. A., the first provost, went to England in 1761 and succeeded in raising a considerable sum of money for the college. In 1779, the legislature confiscated all the rights and properties of the college and bestowed them on a newly chartered institution called the "University of the State of Pennsylvania." This was the first university in the United States. Ten years later, the act of confiscation was rescinded and the rights and properties were restored to the original institution. In 1791, the old college and the new university were amalgamated by an act of the legislature under the name "The University of Pennsylvania." The medical school, the oldest in America, was founded in 1765 and the law department in 1790.

Before continuing the thread of our narrative, it would be well to mention at this point some events of interest in the early history of printing and publishing in Pennsylvania. William Bradford set up the first printing press in Philadelphia in 1685. An almanac by Daniel Leeds, a student of agriculture, was one of the earliest books published. Most of the books and pamphlets published were of a religious character. The first exception to this rule was a book of travels by Jonathan Dickinson, entitled *God's Protecting Providence*. Certain it is that the title of this book of itself does not prove the exception. The typography is described as wretchedly executed and disfigured by constant blunders. The Bradfords supplied Philadelphia with printers for over one hundred years. They printed the first newspapers in both New York and Philadelphia. Andrew Bradford, son of William Bradford, printed at Philadelphia, December 22, 1719, the *American Weekly Mercury*, which was the first newspaper published in the province. The same printer, as we have seen, removed to New York and brought out the *New York Gazette*, the first newspaper printed in that city, in October, 1725. Franklin planned the *Pennsylvania Gazette*, and in 1729 became its proprietor. He made the first copperplate printing press used in America. The printers usually combined their business with bookbinding and book selling, and in some instances even dealt in groceries and fancy goods. Some, likewise, served the public as importers of books on law, medicine, and history, those books being most in demand at that time. In 1782, Robert Aitken printed at his shop in Philadelphia the first Bible in English published in America. Among other printers was Christopher Saur, the publisher of *Der Hoch-Deutsch Pensylvanische Geschicht-Schreiber*, who printed the Bible in German.

In 1749 the money question was again brought prominently before the people. The circulation of the bills of credit had been diminished greatly by reason of the payment of the former loans. For this reason the Assembly desired to issue additional paper money at a lower rate of interest and in larger amounts to individuals. The plan was to issue £80,000, payable in sixteen years by annual instalments. Whatever amounts were repaid were to be reissued for the remainder of the period. The maximum amount that could be lent to individuals was allowed to remain the same as in the last issue, and the interest was placed at five per cent. Governor Thomas strongly objected to the bill, insisting that it was unfair to the proprietaries. After a heated discussion of the subject, a compromise was finally arranged by which the proprietaries agreed to accept a fixed sum to cover fluctuations in the value of the currency. These difficulties being overcome, the bill became a law, and the sum of £80,000 was kept in circulation.

As a result of the careful investigation into the operation of the paper-money systems in the different colonies, Parliament passed a bill in 1751 prohibiting the northern colonies from issuing or reëmitting bills of credit except for extraordinary emergencies. Through the efforts of its agents and of the proprietaries, Pennsylvania was not included within

PHILIP JOHN SCHUYLER

*From the miniature by Trumbull, in possession of Yale University.*

the scope of this bill. The following year, the Assembly wished to issue £40,000 more of the currency, but later reduced it one-half owing to the opposition of the governor. That opposition not being withdrawn, a committee to consider and report on the currency was appointed. As chairman of this committee, Franklin showed the benefit of the paper money by pointing to the great internal improvements, the great increase in manufactures and in population. In 1730 the number of vessels clearing the ports of the province was one hundred and seventy-one, in 1734 the number had increased to two hundred and twelve, while from 1749 to 1752 it had averaged over four hundred annually. The population had nearly doubled in twenty years. Commerce had extended westward, until it included remote Indian tribes. Agriculture was flourishing, and the loan office made the purchase of land easy. "Yet, great as these benefits were," reported the committee, "they might have been much greater had this easy method for the purchase and improvement of lands kept pace, as it ought to have done, with the growing numbers of the people. Even at this time, though application had been greatly discouraged through failure of success, there were not less than one thousand on the list, waiting their turn to be supplied."

Governor Thomas resigned in the summer of 1746, and his place was assumed temporarily by Anthony Palmer, president of the Council. Thomas's departure was greatly regretted. He had at first opposed both proprietary and Assembly and had regarded particularly the king's interests; but he soon profited by experience and seldom clashed with the popular legislative body. Palmer was shortly compelled to call the attention of the Assembly to the bold privateering attempts of the French and the Spaniards. They did not hesitate to enter the bay and plunder the inhabitants along the shores. In fact, a Spanish privateer commanded by Don Vincent Lopez sailed up the river, under the English flag, almost as far as New Castle and committed depredations upon small shipping. But the Assembly would not move in the matter. The treacherous channel of the Delaware and the dangers incident to its navigation, the members thought, would protect the city and province from serious injury by the privateers.

The reason for this inactivity by the Assembly was the latent Quaker opposition to hostilities, either offensive or defensive. Logan and some other prominent Quakers believed in defensive war and always lent their aid to the governor. They favored the erection of a battery below the city. Some of them were rich and exercised considerable political power. The influence of the Scotch-Irish Presbyterians was felt likewise. They were becoming more numerous and important, and their arguments in favor of defence no doubt had some credit with the young Quakers. The little subterfuges resorted to in making appropriations illustrate this silent approbation of defence by many Quakers. Franklin cites two cases that very well illustrate this state of mind. The Quaker members of a fire company allowed money to be appropriated for purposes of defence by not appearing at the meeting when the money was voted. Franklin estimated that nineteen out of every twenty Quakers favored the war. When the Assembly was asked to contribute to the expedition against Louisburg, £4,000 was voted "to be expended," they said, "in the purchase of bread, beef, pork, flour, wheat, or other grain." Franklin held that the words "other grain" were inserted by the Assembly for the specific purpose of allowing the governor to purchase gunpowder. When urged to demand a better bill, the governor replied he knew what the Assembly meant. The gunpowder was purchased and no objection was urged. The first proprietary himself appointed a professional soldier governor of the colony and gave him authority as a captain-general to levy war. Another time, he is said to have requested the king to furnish men-of-war to protect Pennsylvania from the French. It was a common practice for Quaker merchants to employ convoys for the protection of their ships. In fact, it may be said that the scruples of the Quakers against war were more fancied than real.

James Hamilton, the son of Andrew Hamilton the eminent lawyer, was appointed lieutenant-governor in November, 1748. He did not take up the duties of his administration under the most auspicious circumstances. The war just closed, the War of the Austrian Succession, had lasted nine years and had been brought to a close by the Peace of Aix-la-Chapelle in 1748. Pennsylvania had contributed little in money and soldiers toward the war, and had suffered but little loss from the depredations of the enemies. The northern colonies had borne the brunt of the war, while Pennsylvania was left in peace to cultivate its soil and to develop its commerce. But Pennsylvania, likewise, was to experience the hardships of warfare. The Peace of Aix-la-Chapelle had satisfied neither party, and it was in reality nothing more than a truce. In America, in fact, it did not even amount to a cessation of hostilities. All felt that the great struggle was postponed but a few years at most. All saw that the renewal of hostilities was inevitable.

Eager to extend their territories, and to connect their northern possessions with Louisiana, the French had projected a line of forts and military posts along the Mississippi and the Ohio. The latter river was explored, and the lands upon both sides were occupied. Leaden plates with inscriptions declaratory of their claims to the river and the lands adjacent thereto were buried in many places. They established themselves at Presque'Île, and, proceeding southward, they erected a fort at Au Bœuf, and another at the mouth of French Creek, known as Fort Machault. By the end of 1753 they had completed a chain of forts from Montreal to French Creek. Major Washington was sent in December, 1753, to warn the trespassers to retire. Governor Hamilton appealed to the Pennsylvania Assembly for assistance to help the Virginia authorities to expel the French. Hamilton tried to prove that the enemy was really on Pennsylvania soil, but the Assembly stoutly maintained that Virginia soil only had been as yet invaded and that the Virginians should be left to attend to their own affairs. Washington was defeated at Fort Necessity, and Hamilton again made a fruitless appeal for an appropriation. This time he would have secured it had he been tactful. In fact, the Assembly voted an appropriation; but upon the governor's insisting on his power to amend, the bill was withdrawn entirely. These events were leading rapidly to that great final duel between England and France known in the American colonies as the Old French and Indian War and in Europe as the Seven Years' War or the Third Silesian War.

## CHAPTER XVII

### *DEVELOPMENT OF MARYLAND, 1714-1754*

THE first royal governor, Sir Lionel Copley, arrived in Maryland in 1692 and the government was handed over to him by the colonial Convention. His Council was appointed largely from among the "Associators," in whose hands was the government. His first Assembly was presided over by Kenelm Cheseldyn as speaker. Mention has been made of the fact that the Assembly's first move was the recognition of the title of William and Mary, to whom an address was presented thanking them for deliverance from "a tyrannical Popish government under which they had long groaned." This same Assembly made the Protestant Episcopal Church the established Church of the province. The ten counties were divided into parishes, and an annual poll tax of forty pounds of tobacco was imposed for Church purposes. In 1702 a toleration clause was added to the act exempting Protestant Dissenters and Quakers from penalties and disabilities. They were given permission to have separate meeting houses, provided they had paid the poll tax to which reference has been made. This exemption did not extend to Roman Catholics, who, on the contrary, were treated more severely. The oath of "abhorrence" was required in addition to the oath of allegiance, and no Roman Catholic attorney was given permission to engage in his profession. This severe action against the Roman Catholics was due largely to the state of international politics. Marlborough had been dismissed, and Louis XIV. was making formidable preparations to compel the reinstatement of James. The French and Indians were threatening Albany, and it was rumored that parties of them were even hovering about the head of Chesapeake Bay.

Governor Copley died in 1693, and, after a "brief and violent interval" of Sir Edmund Andros, was succeeded by Francis Nicholson, late Governor of Virginia. The capital of the province was changed from St. Mary's to Annapolis, in spite of the remonstrances of the inhabitants of the former place. This act of the governor, in connection with other unpopular acts, caused a certain amount of disaffection that found a ready response in John Coode. This is the same Coode who played an important part in the Fendall revolt of 1681. He was arrested, tried, and acquitted; nevertheless, even during his trial, he continued to sit as a delegate. He next made his appearance at the head of the forces that captured St. Mary's, overthrew the proprietary government, and proclaimed William and Mary King and Queen of England. In 1696 he had been elected to the Lower House, but Governor Nicholson refused to qualify him on account of his clerical orders, holding that once a priest always a priest and that a repudiation of the priestly robes did not of itself change the circumstances. Smarting under this defeat, Coode got together some men of the baser element and threatened that having pulled down one government he could pull down another. He failed utterly in his efforts to stir up disaffection, and was ultimately indicted by the grand jury. However, he escaped to Virginia, where he lived under the protection of Governor Andros until in 1701, after having presented an abject petition, he was pardoned. He regained much of his old popularity, and in 1708 he sat in the Assembly as a delegate. Browne (*Maryland*, 188) presents him to us in any other than a favorable light. He says: "In throwing off the clerical habit Coode seems to have renounced religion, morality, and even common decency; he was a blatant blasphemer, railing openly at Christianity and the Bible; he had raised a fund to build a church, and appropriated a great part of it; and on one occasion he was so drunk and disorderly during divine service that Governor Nicholson caned him with his own hand."

On January 2, 1698, Nicholson was transferred to the government of Virginia, and his executive mantle fell upon Nathaniel Blakiston. In 1703 the latter resigned, and the office passed to John Seymour. Maryland was affected very little by the early colonial wars, not being situated in close proximity to the borders. During King William's War the province had sent a gift of £100 to the Governor of New York for defence against the French and Indians, but was unable to send any troops. A quota of men and supplies was demanded by the king in 1694.

Queen Anne's War broke out in 1702, but though French ships of war cruised in Chesapeake Bay almost as far north as Annapolis, Maryland did not suffer as a result of it. The coast was infested by pirates, who were aided and protected, some say, by the Pennsylvanians. Of course, the name of Captain Kidd appears foremost in the list of pirates. Several of them were captured in Maryland and were sent over to England for trial, until courts of admiralty were established in the province. In 1704 the people of the colony were brought into close touch with the war through the exploits of Richard Johnson, in command of a brigantine. He was captured off Martinique by a French privateer. Before reaching the French port for which the captor headed, he, with another Englishman, took possession of the privateer through strategy, threw the captain overboard, and then reached Maryland in safety, where they had their prize condemned and sold.

A war with France always seemed to be considered by the authorities a just cause for greater severity in the treatment of the Roman Catholics. Queen Anne's War was no exception to the rule, for the alarm was spread that the people of that faith in the province were planning to assist the French. The priests were not permitted to say Mass or exercise any priestly function, on penalty of fine and imprisonment. Furthermore, should any Roman Catholic teach or even board young persons, he was to be transported to England for trial. The incoming of Irish Romanists was discouraged by the imposition of a poll tax of twenty shillings. It is instructive to note that the same duty was laid on negroes, who were now being imported in large numbers direct from Africa, whereas formerly they had been imported for the most part from the West Indies. It was estimated that there were eight thousand negroes in the province in 1712, out of a population of forty-six thousand.

Edward Lloyd, president of the Council, acted as governor during the interim between Governor Seymour's death in 1709 and the appointment of John Hart. The new governor was appointed through the influence of Benedict Leonard Calvert. The latter having abjured the Roman Catholic faith had been admitted into the Church of England. He was the son and heir of Charles, third Lord Baltimore and second proprietary, and, needless to say, his abjuration of the faith of his family was a great blow to the elder Calvert. The yearly allowance of £450 was withdrawn, and the son was compelled to appeal to Queen Anne for assistance. He was granted a pension of £300 by the queen during the lifetime of his father, and by a settlement with Governor Hart he received £500 in addition. Upon his accession in 1714, George I. renewed all these favors. On February 20, 1715, Charles, Lord Baltimore, died and was succeeded in his titles and estates by his son. The latter, however, likewise died on the 5th of the following April, and was succeeded by his minor son Charles, who became fifth Lord Baltimore and fourth proprietary. Because he was a Protestant, the province was restored to the young proprietary, " to give encouragement to the educating of the numerous issue of so noble a family in the Protestant religion."

Almost the last and one of the best contributions of the royal government to the development of the province was the thorough revision of the laws. These had fallen into considerable confusion by reason of many illogical changes, and the Assembly took up the revision of the whole code in 1715. The work was done very satisfactorily, and the code adopted served the province during the rest of the colonial period and furnished the fundamental principles of the law of the State of Maryland. In 1722 a dispute was precipitated which ended ultimately in defining the exact relationship between the English common and statute law and the provincial laws and practices. The Upper House and the proprietary contended that, in their application to provincial jurisprudence, the English statutes should be restricted to those most suitable to the province and those that infringed least upon the chartered rights of the proprietary. The Lower House, on the contrary, demanded the introduction of all the statutes or the submission of the question of selection to the courts. The contest lasted for years and was finally decided in favor of the Lower House. The law of the province was to be made up of its own acts and usages, but when they were silent the laws and statutes of England were to be applied. The benefits of the English law were to be secured without the abandonment of the right to self-government.—(Browne, *Maryland*, 204–207.)

Charles Calvert, uncle of the proprietary, succeeded Governor Hart, who had been removed in 1720. At the death of the former in 1726, Benedict Leonard Calvert, brother of Lord Baltimore, was appointed governor. The latter resigned in 1731 on account of ill health and was succeeded by Samuel Ogle. Very few events of importance characterize this period of the history of Maryland. The colonists lived quietly at their country seats and directed the cultivation of their lands.

Maryland was thoroughly Southern in the character of its settlements. Municipalities did not thrive on its soil as they did in New England and to a lesser extent in New York and Pennsylvania. The two colonies upon the tributaries of Chesapeake Bay were settled by an entirely different type of people from that which settled the New England colonies. The environment, furthermore, was entirely different. The early settlers of Maryland and Virginia were cavaliers, or country gentlemen. They settled in a most delightful climate, where the soil was rich and where both land and water combined to furnish them a livelihood upon the easiest terms imaginable. The numerous long, broad, and deep rivers, flowing lazily and quietly toward the great Chesapeake, furnished every planter a natural highway at his very door. This environment, combined with the colonists' natural love for the independence of a country life, led the early settlers of Virginia and Maryland to take up their plantations in favorable localities along the banks of the navigable rivers. The swiftly moving streams of New England favored the development of manufacturing, which necessitated town life. The Southern rivers favored the development of agriculture of the large plantation type, which in turn necessitated group isolation. In New England, therefore, we find the town the important unit of local government, while in Maryland and Virginia it is the county. As we have a blending of the two extremes of character and environment in the Middle colonies, so we find a mixture of the two types of local government. In New York, New Jersey, Pennsylvania, and Delaware, both the town and the county are found to have importance.

Queen Anne tried to develop artificially what character and environment had failed to develop. She expressed a wish that towns should be founded in Maryland, and the Assembly reluctantly erected them "by batches." In 1706, forty-two had thus been created, but hardly one passed beyond the surveying stage of stakes and stones. Lots were offered for sale, rights of entry and clearance were given the ports, and everything, in fact, was done officially to make the places more than paper towns. Only one minor detail of successful town making was always lacking, namely, the inhabitants.

For ninety years after the first settlement of the colony, St. Mary's and Annapolis divided the honors of being the only real towns. Then came Joppa, upon Gunpowder River, which for fifty years or more prospered, while St. Mary's gradually declined. But Joppa was destined to fall before a greater rival; for, as Browne poetically puts it, Baltimore came and "drew off her trade, and she gradually dwindled, peaked, and pined away to a solitary house and a grass-grown graveyard, wherein slumber the mortal remains of her ancient citizens."

The increase in trade enjoyed by the planters along the banks of the Patapsco suggested the pressing need of a convenient port in that locality. The first steps for the "erection" of a town on the Patapsco, to be called "Baltimore Town," were taken in 1729, when the Assembly was petitioned for an enabling act. The act was passed, and sixty acres bordering on the northwest branch of the river were purchased for forty shillings an acre from Charles and Daniel Carroll. In January of the following year the site was cut up into half-acre lots, and streets were laid out. The harbor was spacious and secure and had a depth of at least twenty feet. The water-front lots were purchased almost immediately, and the town started out upon its career much more auspiciously than its two predecessors in name of the century before. Of the shadowy and almost mythical Baltimores of 1683 and 1693, there was never enough of material existence to afford a moment's pleasure to the most hopelessly confirmed student of antiquarian proclivities. A Baltimore was laid out on Bush River, Baltimore County, in 1683, and another in Dorchester County a decade later. Certain it is that they died, if they can be said ever to have lived, "unwept, unhonored, and unsung."

The Baltimore of 1729 was fortunately located in many respects, the site being at the head of tidewater and navigation on Patapsco River, about fourteen miles from Chesapeake Bay and nearly two hundred miles up from the ocean. The river at this point is a broad estuary, while above it dwindles rapidly to a small and swiftly moving stream that was capable of furnishing water power to many prospective mills and manufactories. In substance, its mild climate, its varied soils, its central location, its excellent harbor, furnished it with all the natural qualifications for a great city. Yet its growth at first was very slow, not having been greater than twenty dwellings and one hundred inhabitants during the first twenty years. In 1752 it contained twenty-five houses and two hundred persons, while in 1765 the number had increased to fifty houses. After this the growth was much more rapid, and in 1775 the population had risen to five thousand nine hundred and thirty-four, and there were five hundred and sixty-four houses. The town was incorporated as a city in 1797.

Practically the only serious disturbance that arose to annoy the colony during the period under consideration was due to the territorial encroachments of Pennsylvania. The history of Maryland could easily be written from the point of view of the establishment of her boundaries. The urgency of the Virginia-Maryland border difficulties was one of the immediate causes of the assembling of those conventions and congresses that led finally to the formation of a more perfect union in 1789. In turn, the adoption of the Federal Constitution made possible a peaceable settlement of the boundary disputes. The unsettled condition of the territorial limits of Maryland was an inheritance which naturally came from the vagueness of colonial grants and charters. In some instances these overlapped, and in other cases an intervening neutral space was left that afforded ground for disputes. In most cases, however, the disputes arose from a misunderstanding with reference to the exact location of some natural object,—a tree, a stone, a hill, a tributary, or a cape. The boundary question vexed the wisdom and temper of many governors, both of Maryland and Pennsylvania.

The order of the Privy Council dated 1685 had determined Maryland's eastern boundary by dividing Delaware between Lord Baltimore and William Penn. The northern boundary had been definitely fixed in the grants of the two proprietaries. The southern boundary of Penn's grant was the fortieth parallel, while the northern boundary of Baltimore's grant was the same parallel. For a long time, however, Penn had refused to coöperate with Baltimore in definitely determining that parallel. He realized fully, no doubt, that it was decidedly to his advantage to keep the matter unsettled. And so it proved; for after the fortieth parallel was surveyed, both Chester and Philadelphia were found to be located well south of it. They were thus within the limits of Maryland, as prescribed by the original charter grants of both Lord Baltimore and William Penn.

William Penn was one of the shrewdest proprietors that ever held a grant for a rood of land on this continent. He had Quaker forbearance and British pugnacity, and with this happy combination of virtues he very seldom entered upon a territorial dispute without coming out the victor. And, one might add, there was not a square foot of territory upon which he had the ghost of a squatter's claim but that he backed that claim with all the cunning, force, and influence at his command. When cunning would serve his purpose better than anything else, he used it as few others could. When force was necessary, there was no one who could strike harder and more effectually than he. These two qualities, together with his influence with the English king, made him a power to be feared. All three weapons he used in defence of his boundary pretensions. Had it not been for the strength of Lord Baltimore's position, combined with some excellent qualities of character possessed by that individual himself, William Penn would undoubtedly have grabbed all of Maryland that Virginia might have graciously left. William Penn found Lord Baltimore a "foeman worthy of his steel;" and if the former usually won his point, the victory was diminished to such an extent that it was but little more than a defeat. Furthermore, it was not a victory won in every case because of the better diplomacy of Penn so much as because of the unpopularity of the faith represented by Lord Baltimore. For was not religious toleration first exemplified in Maryland?

In no event are the characteristics of Penn shown better than in the establishment of the boundary between his possessions in the peninsula and those of Lord Baltimore. The disputed territory in this case was what is now called Baltimore Hundred, in the southeastern part of Delaware. The name of the hundred is indicative of Lord Baltimore's claim. The right to Baltimore Hundred was in dispute for nearly a century and was not determined until 1775, when it was settled in favor of Delaware. Land warrants issued prior to this settlement claimed this district as being in Worcester County, Maryland. In 1682 William Penn occupied this disputed territory and claimed as its southern boundary Fenwick's Island, then called Cape Henlopen. The present cape of that name was at that time called Cape Cornelius and later Cape Inlopen. Prior to 1682, Baltimore Hundred was embraced in several patents issued by the Duke of York.

Disputes soon arose between William Penn and Lord Baltimore as to what cape was meant in the grants, and these disputes were continued until the final official settlement in 1775. The method Penn employed to gain possession of a part of the disputed territory will illustrate his shrewdness. On March 4, 1683, he ordered a survey to be made of a tract of ten thousand acres for a manor for the Duke of York. The location suggested was "a rich ridge at the head of the Murderkill Creek, near Choptank road." But instead of locating it anywhere near the place indicated, it was surveyed on what is now Fenwick's Island. This survey gave weight to the claim of Penn's successors to this territory when the question came up for final adjudication. For over a half-century the territory continued in dispute. Overt acts of aggression and resistance frequently marked the progress of the quarrel. A petty boundary warfare was carried on.

After the death of Penn in 1718, his sons, who had jointly inherited the proprietorship, continued their father's dilatory tactics. In 1732 they succeeded in securing a written agreement from Charles Calvert, Lord Baltimore, by which they obtained all that they had demanded. The boundary line was to run due north through the middle of the Delaware peninsula until it touched the circumference of a circle having a radius of twelve miles from the town of New Castle as its centre. From this point of intersection the line followed the circumference of the circle north and east until a point in Delaware River was reached fifteen miles south of Philadelphia. Thence the boundary was to run due west to the extent that the two provinces were conterminous.

Baltimore visited Maryland in 1732 for the purpose of examining personally the facts in the boundary controversy. He appointed his commissioners provided for by the agreement to which reference has already been made. The Pennsylvania commissioners failed upon two occasions to meet the Maryland commissioners at New Castle. Joppa was next proposed as the meeting place, but the suggestion was not accepted. The condition of affairs now grew too serious for the question under dispute to be permitted to continue longer unsettled. On May 14, 1734, the Pennsylvania Council, sitting at Philadelphia, was informed that Maryland had acted in a very unneighborly manner; that some inhabitants of Pennsylvania who lived on the border were constantly annoyed by Marylanders, some of them, in fact, having been carried off and imprisoned. Furthermore, it was asserted that the Marylanders had laid claim to some land by extending their border further than ever had been done before. In order to come to an understanding, Messrs. Hamilton and Georges were appointed commissioners to bring about some agreement between the proprietaries and Lord Baltimore in regard to "laying out lines, limits, and boundaries." After visiting Annapolis, they returned and presented a report of their work. It was not satisfactory, however, and the Pennsylvania governor directed a letter to the justices of the counties of Chester, Lancaster, New Castle, Kent, and Sussex, reviewing the situation.

They were advised of the necessity of protecting persons along the border, and of preventing citizens of other provinces from encroaching upon Pennsylvania territory. They were to make frequent visits and tours along the border, promising the inhabitants aid whenever it should be needed.

The disturbances, indeed, became quite serious. Some fifty or sixty families of Palatines who had settled in Baltimore County, Maryland, were promised exemption, it is said, from militia duty and the poll tax of forty shillings if they would declare their allegiance to Pennsylvania and refuse to pay the Maryland tax assessments. Sheriffs' posses representing both the proprietaries invaded the debatable territory and made arrests. Armed bands prowled round the county, beating men of the opposite side or carrying them off to prison. The following incident, as related by Browne, is typical of many others that occurred during this period of border warfare: "Sheriffs on both sides summoned posses and made inroads into the debatable territory, arresting and carrying off prisoners; houses were attacked by armed bands, and men on both sides beaten or dragged off to prison. Sheriff Buchanan, of Lancaster County, with a party, enters the house of a Dutchman, one Loughman or Lachmann, a Marylander, and beats him unmercifully. His wife interposes, and the discourteous sheriff beats her, until Lachmann consents to go with him as his prisoner. But on the way they meet five Dutchmen, who, seeing the plight of their countryman, set on the sheriff, rout his posse, and carry him off into captivity." Mention might also be made of Thomas Cresap, one of the most violent of the Maryland partisans. His house was burst into by a party of Pennsylvanians, who threatened to burn the house and hang the owner. At another time, their threat to burn the house was put into effect, and the inmates were fired upon as they tried to escape. One man was killed, and Cresap, who was among those wounded, was carried off a prisoner to Philadelphia, where he was lodged in jail. Strenuous efforts were made by Governor Ogle, of Maryland, to have

Cresap released. Failing in his efforts to accomplish this end, he ordered the arrest of a dozen of the principal participants in the riot. This was done successfully by a party of Marylanders. Then followed a period of border warfare interspersed with proclamations, peaceful and warlike, on the part of the governors of the two provinces. The land was constantly harried by sheriffs' posses from both provinces and by unauthorized bands led by adventurous leaders who took advantage of the riotous times to ply successfully their border brigandage.

The condition of affairs grew so alarming that appeal was finally made to the king by the governor and Assembly of Maryland, requesting assistance in bringing an end to the border warfare. The crown thereupon issued an order in Council commanding an observance of the peace on the part of both contesting parties. The proprietaries were likewise enjoined not to make any new grants in the disputed territory until the whole boundary question could be adjusted. Furthermore, for the sake of temporary peace, the governors of both Maryland and Pennsylvania agreed to the establishment of a provisional boundary line. This line was to be accepted by the inhabitants actually in possession of the disputed territory as valid in all their relations. In the words of the compromise, then, it was agreed "that the respective Proprietaries should hold and exercise jurisdiction over the lands occupied by themselves and tenants at the date of the agreement, though such lands were beyond the limits thereinafter prescribed, until the final settlement of the boundary lines, and that the tenants of the one should not interfere with the other." This arrangement was to last until a final adjustment of the boundary could be made by the English Court of Chancery.

Finally, the opposing parties came together and appointed commissioners to settle the boundary dispute. In 1739 Colonel Levin Gale and Samuel Chamberlain were appointed commissioners to represent Maryland, and Richard Petets and Lawrence Growden to represent Pennsylvania.

The entire boundary line between Maryland and the Lower Counties (*i. e.*, Delaware) was to be settled. By the terms of agreement of 1732, the transpeninsular line was to begin at Cape Henlopen. This, of course, precipitated the vexed question as to the exact location of this cape—whether it was where Cape Henlopen is now situated or on Fenwick's Island. A difference in the method of spelling the name of the cape gave rise to this controversy. By the early Swedish settlers the cape now known as Henlopen was called "Inlopen," and the "exterior or false cape" at Fenwick's Island "Henlopen" or "Hinlopen." The Swedish aspirate letter " H " prefixed to the word " Inlopen " changed it from "interior" to "exterior" cape. The matter in dispute was referred to the Lord Chancellor of England, who decided that the terms of agreement should be interpreted as fixing the beginning of the line at the exterior cape, or Fenwick's Island. In this manner the long-standing boundary dispute was definitely settled.

The line was not surveyed, however, without much difficulty, not to speak of danger and privation. These difficulties are recorded by one John Watson in a most interesting manner. He was one of the surveyors appointed by the Pennsylvania commissioners to assist in the survey of 1750. He kept a careful diary, and it is from this diary that we get some interesting information with regard to the details of the survey. In the first place, he tells of the ridiculous controversy that arose between the commissioners concerning the manner in which the twelve miles' radius establishing the northern boundary of what is now Delaware should be measured. The Maryland representatives held that it should be measured upon the surface of the earth, while those from Pennsylvania held just as stoutly that it should be made by "horizontal measurement," and not by following the inequalities of the earth's surface. The former method would have been, of course, to the advantage of Maryland, and the latter to the advantage of Pennsylvania. This was the occasion of the scholastic dispute. The question was referred to the courts, and the Pennsylvania point of view was sustained.

What concerns us more particularly in this place is Watson's account of the difficulties and inconveniences the surveyors experienced in projecting the boundary line from Fenwick's Island to Chesapeake Bay. It seems that they were frequently in imminent danger of drowning by the tide overflowing "Phœnix Island" [Fenwick's Island] while they were encamped upon it. This can be readily understood when we recall the fact that in 1831 a great tidal wave swept over the entire island, drowning all the cattle as well as several persons who happened to be upon it at the time.

After much wrangling as to details, the survey was begun and the line projected several miles. But on January 8, 1750, the surveyors were compelled to discontinue work by reason of the great accumulation of ice on the marshes and lowlands. The next spring, on April 29, 1751, the work was resumed, and the line was advanced thirteen miles. Then an unexpected obstacle was encountered. The men assisting the surveyors struck for higher wages. The work was delayed, but in the end the surveyors were compelled to accede to the demands of the strikers, for it was impossible to secure other assistance. The work was thereupon continued without further delay, except that incident to the swampy condition of the soil. On June 15, 1751, the line was completed to Chesapeake Bay, a distance of sixty-nine miles two hundred and ninety-eight perches from the starting point on Fenwick's Island.

The long strip of coast line, fortified by sand dunes and backed by Assawoman Bay and broad stretches of marsh, called Fenwick's Island is indeed an island. But this was not the case in former years. In 1682, when William Penn assumed possession of his purchase in the peninsula, this strip of territory was connected with the mainland. During the early part of the nineteenth century, however, a ditch was dug on its landward side. Through the action of the tide this ditch has become a channel. The island is about forty miles long and a mile wide, one-third of it being in Delaware and the rest in Maryland. In former years the abundance of wild celery made it the feeding grounds for canvas-back ducks, but the entrance of the ocean through the artificial channel killed the wild celery at the head of the bay. Now the only game the island affords is quail and beach birds.

A word or two concerning the later history of this scene of one of the most interesting surveys in the records of the two provinces of Maryland and Pennsylvania may not prove altogether uninteresting. The point where the boundary line between Maryland and Delaware cuts the coast is marked approximately by the Fenwick's Island lighthouse. This lighthouse is a tower eighty feet high, showing a flashing light. It was erected in 1857, to protect shipping from the shoal that extends out into the ocean about twelve miles. Many vessels had been driven upon the shoal in foul weather, and the place had come to be considered dangerous. There may be seen at present old hulks upon the beach in different stages of decay, silent proofs of the former dangers of the coast. Yet, notwithstanding the existence of the lighthouse and a lightship and a foghorn on the shoals, the International Line steamship *Rhynland* ran ashore near this spot in the winter of 1898.

There are some of Maryland's sons whom history has failed to give the importance due them. There are others deserving of notice who have not been mentioned at all. Among the latter is Thomas Fenwick, from whom Fenwick's Island derived its name. He was one of those restless, adventurous men who emigrated from England to Maryland during the latter part of the seventeenth century, but not to worship according to the dictates of their conscience. His object was the betterment of his very much impaired fortunes. He had the fibre of a man, but not the making of a martyr. He was one of those practical, close-grained pioneers who made possible a successful struggle

James Hamilton, Governor of Pennsylvania. *From the painting by Benjamin West, now hanging in Independence Hall, Philadelphia.*

with the forests and savages of the New World. Both kinds of men were necessary for the successful establishment of the colony—men who would sacrifice their lives for the sake of conscience, and men who were not afraid to lose their lives in pursuit of their fortunes. Colonial Maryland developed men of both types.

Fenwick took up a grant of land between what is now Little Assawoman Bay and the ocean. At that time, and up to a century ago, this narrow strip of land fringing the ocean was cut by three inlets. The northernmost was called the Little Assawoman Inlet, the southernmost Green River, and about midway between these was Sinepuxent Inlet. All three have been filled up for nearly a century. It seems, in fact, that the island is gradually rising. Fenwick's Island lighthouse stands very near the centre of this grant secured by Thomas Fenwick.

Fenwick was a prominent man in local affairs and is frequently mentioned in the records of Sussex County, Delaware, and Worcester County, Maryland. It must be recalled that his grant lay at the centre of that territory the possession of which was hotly disputed by Lord Baltimore and William Penn. Under the proprietorship of the latter, Fenwick held the positions of sheriff and notary public, and filled several minor offices. During the latter part of his life he took up his residence at Lewestown, Delaware, where he died and is supposed to have been buried. At his death the island passed into the possession of his daughter, Mary, who married William Fassett about 1735.

This Fassett was a bold, seafaring man, and in one of his ventures was captured by the pirates that thickly infested the coast during the latter part of the seventeenth and the early part of the eighteenth centuries. These pirates made coastwise traffic dangerous and frequently made raids upon the coast, as several chainballs discovered on Fenwick's Island early in the last century testify. When just off this island, and not far from shore, the pirates threw Fassett overboard to avoid the expense of keeping him.

The beach being sandy, and Fassett being a good swimmer, he succeeded in getting ashore, after an exhausting battle with the tide and surf. Tradition has it that upon landing Fassett vowed he would spend the rest of his life in endeavoring to become the possessor of the island upon whose hospitable beach he had been cast. Fortune smiled upon him far more graciously than he had ever dreamed it would. He married Mary Fenwick and secured the island. On the mainland, not far from Fenwick's Island, are the scenes of the childhood of Stephen Decatur, the great American commodore. He was born at Sinepuxent, Maryland, January 5, 1779, and was killed in a duel with Commodore James Barron, in March 22, 1820, at Bladensburg, Maryland. Likewise, the Hon. John Middleton Clayton, who negotiated the famous Bulwer-Clayton treaty with the British, was born at Dagsborough, Sussex County, Delaware, July 24, 1796. Dagsborough was a part of General John Dagworthy's grant and for that reason it was so called. In deeds recorded prior to 1785 it was called Blackfoot Town.

After the close of Queen Anne's War by the Peace of Utrecht in 1713, there was a long peace of over a quarter of a century, during which the ocean was free from privateers and the borders of the colonies were not threatened by the French and the Indians. The next war began in 1744 and was called King George's War. It grew out of the dispute as to the Austrian succession and ended with the treaty of Aix-la-Chapelle in October, 1748. Maryland suffered some little disturbances during this war, as a result of actual and threatened attacks of the French and Indians upon unprotected English colonial border settlements. Three companies were sent to Albany to coöperate in the proposed conquest of Canada. The crown made the usual requisition for money. This time the money was demanded to pay the Maryland troops until Parliament could defray the whole bill. The Assembly declined to make the appropriation, on the ground that the province had raised troops, provisioned, and transported them.

Charles Calvert, fifth Lord Baltimore, died in April, 1751, and was succeeded by his son Frederick, the sixth and last baron. Frederick had none of the good qualities of his family, but was degenerate in character to such an extent that his acts bordered very closely upon the criminal. He regarded his province merely as a source of revenue for the satisfaction of his low pleasures. He never visited Maryland. The population of the province at this time was approximately ninety-four thousand, not including thirty-six thousand negroes. Iron furnaces had been set up, and pig iron was shipped to England. Tobacco, corn, furs, and lumber were the staple exports. About twenty-eight thousand hogsheads of tobacco and one hundred and fifty thousand bushels of wheat were annually exported. At the outbreak of the French and Indian War the province may be said to have been in a fairly prosperous condition. But the Treaty of Aix-la-Chapelle was merely formal and did not even amount to a complete cessation of hostilities in America. France continued her aggressions along the river valleys of the north and the west, and in 1755 the colonies were precipitated into what is known as the Old French and Indian War. The following year hostilities broke out in Europe, where this war was known as the Third Silesian, or Seven Years' War.

Shortly after the dispute concerning the English statutes was settled in favor of the people, Maryland experienced a marked industrial improvement. Prior to about 1735, the planter had raised tobacco almost exclusively, but after that date wheat and corn were grown somewhat extensively. Settlements were made in the remote parts of the province, roads were cleared, bridges were built, towns sprang up, and the "facilities for a social and commercial intercourse were thereby greatly increased." Prior to this industrial change, the homes were few and scattered, and the inhabitants lived by themselves with their servants. Except along the water front, the people held little communication with each other. Later, everything was very much changed.

There were the county seats, where the courts met and where men gathered together and exchanged ideas. Here they discussed the latest news and reviewed experiences concerning many things. This, of course, had a tendency to develop the social side of their natures and to make them something more than the isolated planters of former years.

Like some of the other provinces, Maryland was settled by different nationalities. Not only did the English come, but likewise the Germans, Swedes, Italians, and French, drawn there no doubt by the mild climate and by the absence of religious persecution. Some of them were educated and some were not. Many of them were "indented servants," who, after their term of service, became free, took up land, and mingled to a certain extent with the other inhabitants. This varied population undoubtedly presented strongly marked peculiarities. There was a fairly well-marked contrast and distinction in classes, which developed an aristocracy, somewhat tempered and subdued, however, by the constant infusion of material derived from the redemptioners. The aristocratic landholder kept somewhat aloof from the lower classes and did not mingle with them socially. There was some little distinction, even in dress. Nevertheless, underneath all this class distinction there seems to have been a general sense of equality.

Although a few of the first colonists were educated, that was not, generally speaking, characteristic of the province as a whole during the colonial period. Those who wanted their children educated and could bear the expense usually sent them to England. There were very few libraries, even among the higher classes. William Rind kept a circulating library at Annapolis, in 1764, but it was not well patronized. Among the swamps and in the backwoods illiteracy was particularly prevalent. Governor Nicholson took the lead in affording the opportunities of a better education. His zeal for education had led him to found William and Mary College in Virginia. He had no sooner taken up the duties of the executive in Maryland than he urged the Assembly to establish free schools. As a result of his efforts and liberality, King William School was founded at Annapolis in 1696. An export duty was laid on furs for the maintenance of schools.

The charter which Lord Baltimore formulated for Maryland planted an almost feudal system in America. The proprietary was to be at its head, with almost kingly prerogatives. Under him were the planters, who usually possessed a large retinue of slaves and servants. Of the latter there were three classes,—convicts, indented servants, and free willers. Those called "indented servants" are sometimes spoken of as "redemptioners." By the term was meant persons who in lieu of their passage money to America bound themselves over, by contract, to serve a certain number of years. The population of the colonies was greatly increased by this system. The term of service varied in different States. The term of indented service in Maryland was limited by the act of 1715, unless an express contract had been entered into. Servants above the age of twenty-five were obliged to serve five years; between eighteen and twenty-two, six years; between fifteen and eighteen, seven years; and if under fifteen years, they were to serve until they reached the age of twenty-two. Upon the expiration of their term of service they became freemen. Their servitude was usually of a very mild character until the introduction of slavery, when in some instances they received even harsher treatment than the slaves. When their days of service were over, the master was compelled to give them fifty acres of land, corn enough to serve a year, three suits of wearing apparel, and tools with which to work. The female redemptioners were eagerly sought in marriage as soon as their term of service was completed. The fact that they had been servants was not counted against them in any way. Many citizens who became distinguished in after years had been redemptioners, or descendants of redemptioners.

The words "transported" and "apprenticed servant" during the colonial period had nothing of their present meaning. Genealogists are sometimes misled by them, but by reason of insufficient examination. The methods of English colonization in the seventeenth century are fairly well understood. A commercial company, an association, or an individual secured from the monarch a charter, grant, or patent for certain lands the boundaries of which were usually very ill defined. In some instances, the monarch himself undertook the colonization of his public domains, giving the direct supervision of affairs to a trusted friend, who later became the royal governor. Thus, although colonies were settled under royal charter or under proprietary auspices, yet the methods of inducing people to emigrate were very much the same in all cases. Where the settlements were not made in consequence of religious, political, or social persecution, they were made under the pressure of special pecuniary inducements. In the case of Maryland, Cecilius Calvert, the lord proprietary, offered special advantages to those who brought settlers. Of course, with the first expeditions came gentlemen of culture and families who sought the betterment of their fortunes. These men in turn frequently took advantage of the liberal offer of the proprietary to superintend other expeditions, for which they received grants of land with special privileges. Captain Thomas Cornwallys was one of these men. He was one of the "nearly two hundred gentlemen adventurers and their servants" who embarked on the *Ark* and the *Dove* with Leonard Calvert, the governor, and George Calvert, his brother. He and Jerome Hawley were mentioned as counsellors.

Cornwallys almost immediately took advantage of the liberal offers to those who superintended the settlement of colonists. Some he brought from England and others from the Virginia colony. In many cases he advanced the money for transportation and the costs of settlement. In consideration of this "transportation" the colonists bound themselves to serve Cornwallys as "apprenticed servants" for a stated length of time—usually for four or five years.

Some of those thus apprenticed were gentlemen of reduced fortunes, who were perfectly willing to serve in this manner until they had cancelled their indebtedness. Consequently, to have "transported apprenticed servants" meant in many cases merely to have advanced the costs of colonization for services of this kind. The ancestors of some of the most prominent Maryland families came with Cornwallys and under the same conditions. A man would frequently record that he "transported" his wife. This was done that he might take advantage of the land offers of the proprietary.

Another interesting element in the population of early colonial Maryland were the "rangers." They were bands of adventurous spirits under popularly chosen leaders. They frequented the remote parts of the province—beyond tidewater, about the falls of the Potomac or the heads of the Patapsco and the Patuxent, or toward the north along the banks of the Susquehanna. They enjoyed the border life, watched the Indians, took up strayed or unmarked cattle, captured runaway servants and fugitives from justice, and challenged all suspicious persons entering or leaving the province by land. Later, their place was taken by the backwoodsmen.

The practice of sending convicts to Virginia began in the reign of James I. It was gradually extended to the other colonies, and was later regulated and legalized by Parliament. These convicts were called "seven-year passengers," or "king's passengers." They were usually sent over by private shippers, and sold at an advantage. They were not all hardened criminals; frequently, they were men who had committed minor offences. Some were political offenders whom George I. sent over because, as he observed, servants were few and hard to get in the colonies, and by their labor and industry could increase the value of the province.

It was estimated in 1767 that for thirty years past at least six hundred convicts a year had been imported into Maryland. The number increased so rapidly that it was found necessary to make the testimony of one convict good against another.

The number of murders and robberies committed in the year 1751 by these convict servants became alarming. This led to orders by the courts of Baltimore and Anne Arundel Counties that £50 security should be given for every convict imported. These orders were later set aside, and in 1769 the Assembly passed an act relating to the bad practice. Every master of a ship transporting felons was required to produce a copy of the record of conviction. Upon the sale of the felon, this record had to be deposited with the county clerk by the seller. The purchaser, likewise, was compelled to go before a justice of the peace in his county and give security to the extent of £20 currency for the good behavior of the convict. This security did not become void until after the convict had kept the peace during the time for which he had been transported or during his residence in the province.

Imprisonment for debt was of frequent occurrence. The law was modified in 1732 by an act which provided for the release of debtors upon their surrendering all their property upon oath. Toward the latter part of the proprietary period, from fifty to over one hundred debtors were released at every session of the Assembly. Later, by reason of the great increase of imprisoned debtors, the county courts were given the power to release them.

Another class of people which gave the authorities and the people of the colony constant trouble was the paupers, whose ranks were constantly being recruited by servants, who, having served their terms, were sent out to shift for themselves. The required present of fifty acres of land and other gifts upon the expiration of their terms of servitude were usually squandered in a short time. After that, the former servants frequently became so poor that the county had to care for them. In the year 1753 the counties were allowed six hundred and forty-seven thousand and twenty-seven pounds of tobacco for the support of the poor. Fourteen years later, an almshouse was established in each of the several counties.

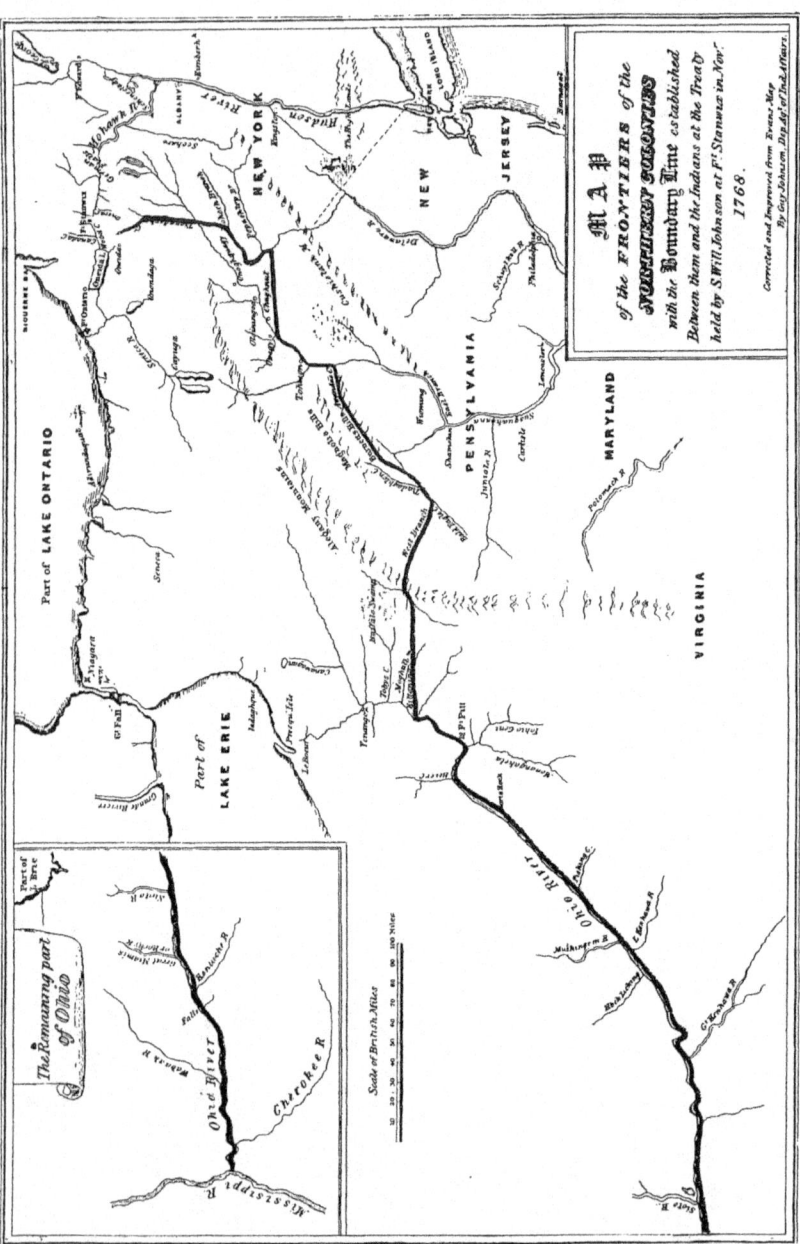

Map of the frontiers of the northern colonies, with the boundary line established between them and the Indians in the treaty made by Sir William Johnson at Fort Stanwix in 1768. *From the collection of George Barrie, Jr.*

## CHAPTER XVIII

### *THE FRENCH AND INDIAN WAR, 1754–1763*

THE Peace of Aix-la-Chapelle, which had been concluded in October, 1748, was not satisfactory to either the French or the English. The English colonies were particularly dissatisfied because Louisburg remained in the possession of the French. They realized fully that as long as this was the case English trade and fisheries on the northeast coast would be in jeopardy. Nor were the French, on the other hand, better satisfied, for one of the stipulations of the treaty was the removal of the people of Acadia. This, indeed, was a very bitter draught for the French. It is not astonishing, therefore, that we find French and English settlers, notwithstanding a so-called declaration of peace, continually at strife. Boundary lines were fruitful causes of dispute. Neither the French nor the English believed that the peace would be lasting. Everything, in fact, portended an early renewal of the conflict, and wise men advised Governor Clinton, of New York, to secure the dominion of Lake Ontario by forts and by an armed sloop.

Upon the approach of such a crisis, it was perfectly evident to all those in authority that the Iroquois should be conciliated. Brave, enterprising, shrewd, and occupying as these Indians did a small country of the highest strategic importance, their friendship was a matter of the greatest value to the English. The policy of the English in their treatment of the Indians had been, for the most part, one of irritation and insult. The policy of the French colonists, on the contrary, had been to let no opportunity pass to conciliate the Algonquins in every way possible. Consequently, the latter Indians, who outnumbered their hereditary enemies the Iroquois six to one, were the natural allies of the French at the outbreak of the war. Nor was it absolutely certain that the powerful Iroquois would be unanimous in the espousal of the English cause. Under ordinary circumstances, they would have allied themselves with the English, without question, to fight their old enemies the Algonquins. The bad treatment and encroachments of the English on their territory had, however, almost driven the Iroquois over to the enemy. The French, on their part, lost no opportunity of employing their diplomacy and tact in widening this breach between the allies. The French were upon the point of bringing their diplomacy to a successful issue, when they were partially thwarted by Sir William Johnson.

Sir William imitated the French in his Indian policy, and by kindness and honesty in his relations with the Iroquois finally won their lasting friendship. The Mohawks adopted him and gave him the rank of "Sachem." He exerted his influence over them against the French, and would have succeeded admirably in his efforts to win them completely to the English had not the narrow policy of the colony thwarted him. This change of the colony's Indian policy occurred in 1753, and had the effect of angering the tribes upon whom the English were most dependent for the protection of the border against the attacks of the French and Indians. Johnson, however, applied himself most assiduously to bring about a reconciliation, which he realized better than anyone else was the one thing necessary to prevent an English disaster in the war that everyone knew must come sooner or later. He was entirely successful in his efforts, and managed to propitiate the savages at the famous Onondaga council fire. The next year saw him a delegate to the colonial congress at Albany, to which we shall now turn our attention.

The convention at Albany met at the prompting of the Board of Trade, which instructed the royal governors to treat with the Six Nations and concert general measures of defence with reference to the impending French war. The convention met on June 19, 1754, and its sessions continued until the 21st of September following. New Hampshire, Massachusetts Bay, Rhode Island, Connecticut, New York, Pennsylvania, and Maryland were represented in the convention by twenty-five delegates. Virginia was represented by Lieutenant-governor James De Lancey, of New York. In addition to the desire to treat with the Six Nations with regard to a mutual defence against the French, there was likewise a somewhat vague expectation on the part of the delegates that plans for a closer union between the English colonies in North America would be presented. The avowed purpose of the union would be, of course, the stronger defence of the colonies against all enemies, especially the French; and the better negotiation of treaties with the Six Nations.

The representatives of the Six Nations were slow in arriving, but quick at rebuking the English for their neglect, and, worse, their bad treatment of them. They favored union and peace, nevertheless, but found fault with the colonists for their lack of action. "You desire us to speak from the bottom of our hearts, and we shall do it," said Hendrick, the great Mohawk chief. "Look at the French, they are men, they are fortifying everywhere—but, we are ashamed to say it, you are all like women, bare and open, without any fortifications. 'Tis your fault, brethren, that we are not strengthened by conquest, for we would have gone and taken Crown Point, but you hindered us. We had concluded to go and take it, but we were told it was too late, and that the ice would not bear us. Instead of this, you burnt your own fort at Saratoga and ran away from it, which was a shame and a scandal to you. Look about your country and see: you have no fortifications about you, no, not even in this city; 'tis but one step from

Canada hither, and the French may easily come and turn you out of your doors." The disaffection of the league of the Six Nations was inversely as the number of their representatives in attendance at the conference. Although the colonies had provided presents in great abundance and had invited all the tribes, yet there were but one hundred and fifty warriors present. Half of the Onondagas had been won over to French influence, and even the Mohawks were in a disaffected mood. The convention prepared a very careful address, which was delivered to the Indians. It seems to have had the desired effect, for they left in a much better frame of mind than they came.

Never had the colonies witnessed an assembly of more prominent men. There were present from New York, Lieutenant-governor James De Lancey, who acted as president of the convention, Joseph Murray, John Chambers, William Smith, Colonel William Johnson, and Colonel Myndert Schuyler, chairman of the Indian commission. From Massachusetts Bay there were Thomas Hutchinson, Samuel Wells, John Chandler, Oliver Partridge, and John Worthington; from Connecticut, Lieutenant-governor William Pitkin, Elisha Williams, and Roger Wolcott; from New Hampshire, Theodore Atkinson, Richard Wibbird, Meshach Weare, and Henry Sherburne, Jr.; from Rhode Island, Stephen Hopkins and Martin Howard, Jr. Maryland sent Benjamin Tasker and Abraham Barnes; while Pennsylvania sent John Penn, Richard Peters, Isaac Norris, and Benjamin Franklin, the "most benignant of statesmen." At the Friday morning session, June 21st, De Lancey suggested that to avoid all disputes about the precedency of the colonies, they should be named in the minutes according to their situation from north to south. This suggestion was accepted unanimously. It is said, however, that in the convention hall the delegates sat in the order of their individual social rank. Peter Wraxall was chosen secretary of the convention at this session, and took the oath of office three days later—June 24th.

Sir William Johnson.
*From the painting in the Château de Ramezay, Montreal.*

After a consideration of the Indian trouble, in which the Iroquois in a most frank manner charged the English with neglect and rapacity, the convention considered a plan of union of the different colonies. All the members felt the pressing necessity of some sort of union for the defence of the interests of the people represented. On Monday afternoon, June 24th, all the representatives being present, including the president of the convention, Lieutenant-governor De Lancey, a motion was passed unanimously that opinions be delivered as to whether a union of all the colonies was not at that time absolutely necessary for their security and defence. It was then agreed that a committee should be appointed, composed of one delegate from each colony represented at the convention. This committee was to prepare and receive plans or schemes for the union of the colonies. Furthermore, that the committee should have the power to digest these plans into one general plan for presentation to the convention. Each colonial delegation was to select its own representative on the committee. The following men were accordingly selected: Thomas Hutchinson, Massachusetts Bay; Theodore Atkinson, New Hampshire; William Pitkin, Connecticut; Stephen Hopkins, Rhode Island; Benjamin Franklin, Pennsylvania; Benjamin Tasker, Maryland. The selection of New York's representative was left to the lieutenant-governor. He appointed William Smith. At the Friday afternoon session of the convention, June 28th, the committee distributed among the delegates "Short Hints" of a plan of union. The following afternoon, these "Hints" were the subject of considerable debate, but the convention was unable to arrive at any conclusion with regard to them. On the following Monday morning, July 1st, another motion was passed, authorizing the same committee to draw up a representation of the state of the colonies at that time. The committee made a full report on the subject on the following Saturday morning, July 6th. The report was laid upon the table until the following Tuesday afternoon, when it was adopted. At the morning session on Tuesday, July 9th, the plan of the union was debated and agreed upon, and Benjamin Franklin was requested to make a draft of it. On Wednesday morning, July 10th, Franklin reported the finished draft, which was read and considered paragraph by paragraph. After some amendments had been agreed upon, the plan was accepted by all the commissioners except those of Connecticut.

Franklin had some time prior to the convention formulated a plan, which had been favorably spoken of by some friends in New York. This plan, which he called "Hints," served as the foundation for the completed plan which the convention finally accepted. The union was to include New Hampshire, Massachusetts Bay, Connecticut, Rhode Island, New York, New Jersey, Pennsylvania, Maryland, Virginia, North Carolina, and South Carolina. These were all the British colonies at that time in North America, except Georgia and Nova Scotia. Another plan had been proposed in the convention, which included only New Hampshire, Massachusetts Bay, Connecticut, Rhode Island, New York, and New Jersey. Furthermore, it would seem by the "Hints" communicated to Mr. Alexander, of New York, by Franklin, that the latter himself did not at first contemplate anything more than a union of the northern colonies.

The plan as finally adopted provided for one general government. Each colony, however, was to retain its own domestic constitution, except in certain particulars. At the head of the general government there was to be a president-general, who was to be appointed and supported by the crown. In conjunction with him there was to be the Grand Council. Its members were to be chosen by the House of Representatives of the Assemblies of the different colonies. In this popular body, Massachusetts Bay was to have seven representatives, New Hampshire two, Connecticut five, Rhode Island two, New York four, New Jersey three, Pennsylvania six, Maryland four, Virginia seven, North Carolina four, South Carolina four,—a total of forty-eight.

These numbers could be changed after the union was in force for three years, but should never exceed seven, nor be less than two, for each colony. Philadelphia was to be the temporary seat of the proposed federal government, on account of its central location. It was thought that the representatives could reach Philadelphia even from New Hampshire and South Carolina in fifteen or twenty days. The time of the meeting was left to the president-general. There was to be an election for the Grand Council every three years. That body was to meet once a year, but oftener if the executive head should deem it necessary. It was to choose its own speaker and was not to sit longer than six weeks at any one time, except by its own volition or by the special command of the crown. Nor could it be prorogued or dissolved, except in the same way. Each member was to be paid ten shillings sterling per day while the Assembly was in session. Likewise, during the journey to and from the place of meeting—twenty miles being reckoned as a day's journey. In case of the president-general's death, the speaker of the Grand Council was to act in his place until the crown appointed a successor. The separate duties of the president-general and Grand Council, and likewise their mutual duties, were carefully outlined.

The provisions of the plan presented a compromise between the prerogative and popular power. The president-general was to have a negative on all laws, but the origination of all bills was left with the Grand Council. The representation of each colony in the Grand Council depended upon its contributions, but, as we have seen, a maximum and a minimum representation were established. All military officers were to be nominated by the president-general, subject to the advice of the Grand Council. All civil officers, in turn, were to be nominated by the Grand Council. It required the joint order of the president-general and the Grand Council before money could be issued. It was, however, to regulate all relations of peace or war with the Indians, land purchases outside of the particular colonies, and matters of trade. Furthermore, it could establish, organize, and temporarily govern new settlements; it could raise soldiers, equip war vessels, make laws, and levy just and equal taxes.

The plan as thus finally drawn up was reported to the Board of Trade and to the Assemblies of the colonies for adoption. England considered it too democratic, and hence the Board of Trade did not approve of it. Neither did the Assemblies adopt it, as they considered that it embodied too much royal prerogative. Franklin remarked upon one occasion that he thought his plan must have been just about right, inasmuch as both England and the colonies rejected it, for diametrically opposite reasons. He says in his autobiography: "Its fate was singular: the Assemblies did not adopt it, as they thought there was too much prerogative in it, and in England it was judged to have too much of the democratic." Although the plan failed of adoption, it was most productive of good results. It no doubt helped to cultivate the idea of union among the colonies, which germinated at that time and took root and grew until years after it developed into maturity during the Revolution.

The colonies rejected Franklin's plan of union for very much the same reason that they paid little or no attention to the plan of union of William Penn in 1697, and opposed the Andros consolidation scheme of 1688. The times were not ripe for such a radical intercolonial project. America had been settled by people of too diverse nationalities and religions, and their settlement had been too recent, for them to have overcome entirely all their national prejudices. Many colonists still maintained to a certain extent the customs, preconceptions, and religions of their native lands. It would take time to soften the characteristics of the different nationalities and make them one in their love for their adopted country. Besides, there was the ever present fear of Parliamentary and royal tyranny, either direct or through representative governors. And, more to the point, there were the numerous jealousies between colony and colony.

Mount Johnson June 13th 1755

Sir

This Moment I rec'd information from some Mohawk Indians, that this Morning they had mett Eight or ten Onagungue Indians laying on the Watch with 2 Miles of my House on this Side the River. Who also informed them that another party of ab.t 10 of the said Nation were lurking near Albany, on the opposite side of the River.

I directly sent out fifteen of my own People and am in hopes they may come up with them, as they knew where they lodged last night. A party of the Militia are gone into the Woods at the back of them. I also dispatched Orders to Col.o Glen, & Ransleer to send two Parties from each of their Battallions on the Scout, about their respective districts. also a Brisk Officer and 30 picked Men to cutt off the Indians retreat to their Canoes. I have heard of no mischeif as yet, but dread soon may. this will drive all the remaining out Inhabitants from their Settlements. and I hope it will rouse up the Spirit and indignation of this Colony in particular, as well as the neighbouring ones to act with that vigorous, and generous unanimity in the intended measures ag.t our implacable (and if they would do so) I might add our contemptable Enemies. If unhappily a narrow spirit of frugality &c should retard or defeat the Schemes w.h have been agreed upon, Surely Sir we must appear in a bad light in the eyes of the World. I am most respectfully, S.r your Most Obt & Most humble serv.t
W.m Johnson

Governour Delancey —

    Letter in relation to Indian affairs written by Sir William Johnson to Governor James De Lancey of the Province of New York, June 13, 1755. *From the original in the Emmet Collection.*

All feared the possible encroachments of Parliament or the crown, and each envied all the others any signs of unusual prosperity. Jealousy and penuriousness were the two really potent causes of the downfall of the New England Confederation. They had likewise considerably to do with bringing about the rejection of Benjamin Franklin's plan.

Desire for a relatively greater power in the Assembly of the New England Confederation on the part of each colony, combined with a relatively decreasing inclination to bear a proportional share of its financial burdens, brought about the Confederation's downfall. In the last analysis, the intercolonial jealousies that were instrumental in defeating Franklin's plan were founded upon similar causes. These jealousies, combined with the diversities of nationality, made the consolidation of the English colonies at that time and under those circumstances impossible. But Franklin was not discouraged. His plan of union broadened as he grew older, until it comprehended "the great country back of the Appalachian Mountains." He said: "In less than a century it must become a populous and powerful dominion."

The Albany convention was held none too soon, and the league of the Six Nations was conciliated none too effectually. The relations between England and France were so strained in North America by reason of conflicting interests that a formal declaration of war was not necessary to precipitate hostilities. The very next year (1755), a year before war was formally declared, witnessed the threatened outbreak. In May, 1756, Austria and France completed a defensive alliance, and England found herself allied with Frederick of Prussia, who was opposed by very nearly all the powers of northern Europe. The English plan of campaign against France in America was the organization of the three expeditions, one to operate against Fort Du Quesne, another against Niagara, and a third against Crown Point. Acadia, or Nova Scotia, was to be put into such a condition of defence as to render it proof against capture.

The English government, aroused by the defeat of Washington in the Ohio country and his capitulation to the French on July 4, 1754, had determined to take more vigorous means of protecting itself against the encroachments of the French. It sent two regiments to America under the command of Major-general Edward Braddock. He sailed from the Downs for Virginia, on the 21st of December, in the *Centurion*, a ship almost as famous among English sailors as Nelson's *Victory*. It was to be followed as soon as possible by the main body of the fleet. The intelligence of Braddock's arrival was at first received with enthusiasm by the colonies of Maryland, Virginia, and Pennsylvania as the signal for speedy defeat of the French. Braddock was a thoroughly well-seasoned soldier, but knew as little about the methods of warfare with savages as he knew much about the set forms of continental warfare. His first official act on reaching Virginia was to summon the governors of the colonies to meet him in congress at Alexandria. Here, the governors of New York, Massachusetts, Pennsylvania, Maryland, and Virginia assembled in April, pursuant to the call, and proceeded to discuss plans for the summer's campaign. Much indignation was expressed by Braddock at the failure of the Assemblies to raise the money required for the campaign. The governors explained the difficulties they always experienced in persuading the Assemblies to appropriate money for the common defence. They furthermore volunteered the opinion that the people would not take action of their own accord, but would acquiesce in a tax laid upon them by Parliamentary act. Inasmuch as the English government had long since determined upon the policy of raising in the colonies a general fund for the immediate necessities of the impending war, this advice of the governors is extremely significant when viewed in the light of subsequent events.

Braddock seemed to be incapable of acting in a tactful manner. Every move he made was well calculated to arouse the resentment of the colonists. One of the most fertile causes of disaffection was his enforcement of a regulation that had been promulgated before his arrival. It was that the general and field officers of the American militia should have no rank when those of the regular British army were in the field. He likewise declared that the savages might put to flight the raw American troops, but that they would make no impression upon the seasoned, well-disciplined British regulars. This attitude on the part of Braddock was not calculated to bring harmony into the ranks of his forces. He also found considerable fault because progress had not been made on the road which he expected would be cut from the Susquehanna, below the junction of the Juniata to the forks of the Youghiogheny. He was depending upon this road for the transportation of flour and other stores from Philadelphia for the support of the army. Finally, the Pennsylvania Assembly, realizing the advantage it would be to have direct communication with Fort Du Quesne, began the work of construction. Even then, however, the Assembly was not willing to pay half the amount it cost to construct the road.

Braddock now proceeded to prepare a plan for the campaign. The troops were to be mobilized at Fort Cumberland, and it was expected that the Forty-fourth and Forty-eighth Regiments would be increased to seven hundred each by enlistments from Pennsylvania. This expectation never materialized. Governor Morris, of Pennsylvania, was requested to offer a bounty of £3 to everyone that enlisted. The governor did what he could to assist the campaign, but he was greatly handicapped by the half-hearted measures adopted by the Assembly. For this reason, many of the Pennsylvanians enlisted under northern commanders or offered themselves for service in Virginia and New York.

Before starting out on his campaign, Braddock carefully inspected the commissary arrangements made for his army. The disclosures were indeed disheartening. He had expected Maryland and Virginia to furnish twenty-five hundred horses, two hundred and fifty wagons, and eleven hundred beeves. Instead, he found that only twenty wagons and two hundred horses had been sent, and the provisions furnished by Maryland, on inspection, proved to be utterly worthless. Through the energy of Benjamin Franklin, the deficiency was finally made up from Pennsylvania. Braddock set out from Alexandria with his army on the 8th and 9th of May. On account of the roughness of the roads, the route originally determined upon was somewhat changed. On the 20th of May he collected all his forces at Will's Creek. The ranks of the Forty-fourth and Forty-eighth Regiments were increased by men from Maryland and Virginia. In addition to these forces there was a troop of provincial light horse and a detachment of sailors with a half-dozen officers. The light horse troop had formerly served as Braddock's bodyguard, and the sailors and their officers were furnished by Commodore Rapel. The sailors were to assist in building bridges. The strength of the force was two thousand and thirty-seven, in addition to the company of light horse, the sailors, and the Indians. The number of the savages was a very uncertain quantity, as but few remained with Braddock to the end. There were about two hundred sailors, which made the grand total two thousand two hundred and fifty. The army was ill supplied with provisions, the officers sharing with the men the scantiness of food. Through Franklin's influence, some of the money which had been appropriated by Pennsylvania was used to supply the subalterns with camp supplies. The Lower Counties on the Delaware contributed fat oxen and sheep for the support of the army.

At Will's Creek, or Fort Cumberland, as Braddock named the place in honor of his patron, the troops were put under rigorous discipline. Much time was spent in drilling and making preparation for the one hundred and thirty miles of wilderness that must be penetrated before Fort Du Quesne could be reached. Trees had to be felled, roads made, and bridges constructed. The confluence of the Monongahela and the Youghiogheny was finally reached, and the river was forded at the mouth of Turtle Creek on the 8th of July. The severest military discipline was exacted, even in these wilds where the path was but twelve feet from the river bank to the hillside. Flanking parties and guides had been provided, but the one important thing needed in the wilderness was lacking—namely, scouts.

When Contrecœur, the commandant, saw the English advance, fifteen hundred strong, right at hand, he was for giving up and retreating immediately. One of his captains, however, Beaujeu by name, asked permission to go out with a company to prepare an ambuscade for the English. Contrecœur consented, and Beaujeu won the support of the Indians by reproaching them with cowardice. Early on the morning of July 9, 1755, the two hundred and thirty French and Canadians and the six hundred and thirty-seven red men left Fort Du Quesne under command of Beaujeu, Dumas, and Ligneris.

The meeting between the French and English forces was unexpected to both. The Indians threw themselves flat on the ground or got behind trees or rocks, and remained almost invisible to the foe during the whole engagement. The English, on the other hand, foolishly followed the Old World military tactics, and in their bright scarlet uniforms and compact ranks presented a fine target for the unerring bullets of the Indians. The militia fought bravely, although greatly exhausted by the long marches and the unaccustomed discipline. The officers showed great courage, the general himself having had four horses shot under him before succumbing to his wounds. Washington, who was serving on Braddock's staff, was shot through his coat four times and had two chargers killed under him. He was practically the only active officer toward the end of the engagement. By the latter part of the afternoon, the English were surrounded, and ammunition had almost failed, yet still Braddock refused to surrender. But further resistance proved futile. Every aide except Washington was incapacitated, and a large majority of the officers and nearly two-thirds of the army were killed or wounded. Braddock then ordered a retreat, which soon developed into a headlong flight. "Despite all the efforts of the officers to control," said Washington, "they ran as sheep pursued by dogs, and it was impossible to rally them." Braddock himself had received a mortal wound and died several days after, and was buried by the wayside. On hearing of the disaster, Dunbar destroyed all his stores and ammunition at Fort Cumberland and abandoned the place. The defeat caused consternation in England and brought the colonies to a realization of their perilous position. The Virginia House of Burgesses voted £40,000 and the Pennsylvania Assembly £50,000 for the defence of the colonies. Other colonies promised men and arms, according to their ability. The defeat, moreover, caused those Indians who had been wavering in their allegiance to the English to declare for the French.

In 1758 a second, and this time a successful, attempt was made to capture Fort Du Quesne. John Forbes, who had been appointed the year previous brigadier-general, was transferred to Pennsylvania for the purpose of retrieving the ground lost by the defeat of Braddock. His forces numbered about seven thousand men. Washington commanded the forces from Virginia, Maryland, and North Carolina; while Lieutenant-colonel Henry Bouquet, a Swiss, commanded the regulars, and the men from Pennsylvania and Delaware. Forbes, who was detained in Philadelphia on account of illness, did not reach Raystown, or Fort Bedford, until September. His weakness had been increased by the long journey, but he went on until he reached the camp of Loyalhanna, November 5th. After a council of war was held, it was decided to go no further. Later, however, upon learning that many of the Indians had deserted the French in the fort, and that the commandant, Ligneris, on account of lack of provisions, had sent some of his men away, this decision was reversed. In spite of the fact that the provisions were nearly exhausted, Forbes decided to send Washington to take the fort. The French, of five hundred men, finding themselves far outnumbered and destitute of means to defend themselves against a siege, set fire to the fort and decamped. When Washington arrived the next day, there was nothing left but a smoldering ruin. A stockade was then built and all the provisions that could be spared were collected, and two hundred men were detached from the troops and left behind to take charge of the fort, which Forbes had renamed Fort Pitt. Early in December, Forbes began his march eastward. He succeeded in reaching Philadelphia, but died in the following March.

Braddock's defeat was indirectly responsible for the failure of a contemplated expedition against the French fortress at Niagara. This fort was weak and partly dismantled, but owing to its strategic situation it was important that it should fall into the hands of the English. It was a centre of the fur trade and touched hands with both the east and the west. To William Shirley was assigned the duty of taking the fort, and it was expected that, after a victory at Fort Du Quesne, Braddock's army would join him at that place. Braddock's defeat, however, combined with obstacles in the way of the project, both natural and artificial, led to the abandonment of the attempt in October, 1755. Oswego was rebuilt and garrisoned.

The reverses of 1755 were partly balanced by the successes of William Johnson. His objective was the capture of Crown Point, which commanded the highway into New France. The Marquis de Vaudreuil, realizing the importance of holding Crown Point, gave Dieskau seven hundred regulars, one thousand six hundred Canadians, and seven hundred Indians for a garrison. Johnson had about three thousand four hundred raw colonial troops and Indians. The opposing forces met on September 8th, on the shores of what is now known as Lake George, but at that time Lac Saint-Sacrement. Only one thousand four hundred of the French and one thousand of the English were in the engagement. The English colonial troops fought bravely, and the French were completely defeated. The French regulars were annihilated, and Dieskau was wounded and captured. Johnson built (1755) a strong fort on the shore of Lake George. He named it Fort William Henry and gave Fort Lyman the name of Fort Edward, both names being given in honor of two of the king's grandsons. The English government showed its appreciation of Johnson's success by granting him £5,000 and conferring upon him the title of baronet. The year following (1756), the Earl of Loudon was put in command of the military forces in America, with Major-general Abercrombie as second in command. They were given power independent of the colonial governors and had authority to quarter soldiers without the consent of the colonial Assemblies.

Great Britain made a formal declaration of war on May 18, 1756, and in June Abercrombie arrived and at once quartered his troops on the people of Albany. Loudon did not arrive until late in July. Montcalm had been in the meantime put in command of the French interests, and with the Chevalier de Lévis, the second in command, and the adjutant Bougainville had reached Quebec in May. Montcalm showed commendable energy by laying siege to and capturing on August 14th the English post at Oswego. Loudon replied to this French challenge by retreating almost precipitately to New York. Cautious man that he was, he took care to protect his retreat from a force half as large as his own by throwing the trunks of trees across the trail. His conduct was in marked contrast to that of Captain John Armstrong, a Scotch-Irish Covenanter of Cumberland. At the head of a party of colonists, he penetrated the wilderness and almost exterminated a force of Delaware Indians that had been ravaging the frontiers of Pennsylvania. The ammunition the savages had stored was destroyed and eleven white captives were rescued.

Loudon next planned an expedition against Louisburg. By June of 1757, he arrived at Halifax, where during the

Hendrick, chief of the Mohawk Indians in alliance with the British forces, after an engraving issued in London *circa* 1750. *From the original in the Emmet Collection.*

next month he was joined by a squadron from England with additional forces. It was then learned that the French were at Louisburg, in force prepared to meet the expected attacks. Again Loudon turned toward New York, this time at the head of ten thousand troops and sixteen ships and frigates. This expedition was the main cause of the horrible massacre of the English garrison at Fort William Henry; for, learning of it, Montcalm gathered an army of eight thousand Indian, Canadian, and French troops, and on August 1st set out from Ticonderoga. Four days later the investment of Fort William Henry was begun. Colonel Munro, of the Thirty-fifth Regiment, was in command. His garrison numbered some two thousand two hundred and sixty-four men—a force not much more than a fourth as strong as that of the attacking French.

The garrison was able to hold out five days, having in the meantime suffered a loss of three hundred killed and many more disabled by wounds and by an epidemic of smallpox. On the 9th of August, not having received aid from Colonel Webb, who with upward of four thousand troops was within relieving distance, Munro surrendered. He received honorable terms, and the garrison marched out of the fort with the honors of war. Montcalm used every effort to hold the Indians to the terms of capitulation, but as soon as they got within the walls of the fort they began their own horrible war practices. The sick and wounded of the English were murdered; and not being satisfied with this shedding of blood, the Indians turned their fury upon the English soldiers. Montcalm and the French officers succeeded in keeping the savages in check for a time, but later they broke all bounds and continued the massacre. The Indians killed about seventy, including sick and injured, and made prisoners of about two hundred men. Most of the captives the French redeemed later.

Loudon, as the head of English military affairs in North America, had proved himself an absolute failure. He spent most of his time in making plans for great campaigns or planning how he could best keep an enemy of half his own strength from successfully preventing his retreat. At last his inefficiency became clearly apparent to all, and he was recalled. Under his leadership the "depth of degradation had been sounded." Said Pitt: "Nothing is done, nothing is attempted. We have lost all the waters; we have not a boat on the lake. Every door is open to France." The French controlled most of the continent. Upon Loudon's recall, Abercrombie, the second in command, took his place. Aided by Wolfe and Amherst, he was to conduct the operations in the north. Louisburg was to be reduced, and this success was to be followed up by the capture of Quebec. Ticonderoga was to be destroyed, thus relieving the northern colonies of the constant danger from invasion, and the way westward was to be opened by the capture of Fort Du Quesne.

The man who infused this new life into English colonial affairs was William Pitt. In 1757, he had strongly opposed the Hanoverian policy of the king and was deprived of office. But king, aristocracy, and people soon discovered that the nation could not do without him, and he was again placed in power. The people enthusiastically supported him, because he stood for everything opposed to the narrow, venal policy of the Duke of Newcastle, and because he had constantly in mind the interests of the people and the welfare of the nation. He laid his plans for the betterment of affairs in America, and a change was soon apparent. As we have seen, he immediately placed capable men in charge of the war in the colonies.

Pitt rejected the coercive policy adopted by his predecessor toward the colonies, and invited New England, New York, and New Jersey to raise as many troops as possible. He expressed himself as believing that they were well able to furnish at least twenty thousand for the expedition against Montreal and Quebec. Pennsylvania and the Southern colonies were to assist in the conquest of the west. It was thought that England would provide arms, ammunition, and tents, and in time might be prevailed upon to grant a proper compensation for any advance made by the colonies. Nothing was to be required of the colonies but "the levying, clothing, and pay of the men." He furthermore obtained an order from the king making every provincial officer not above the rank of colonel equal in command with the officers of the regular army, "according to the date of their respective commissions." Pitt's fair and liberal treatment of the colonists had its immediate satisfying results. The contributions from the colonies, especially from those of New England, even exceeded the premier's expectations.

Early in the spring of 1758, Pitt sent a fleet in command of Admiral Edward Boscawen, with Amherst and Wolfe. It consisted of twenty-two line-of-battle ships, fifteen frigates, and about ten thousand effective troops. After a long and stormy voyage, the expedition reached Halifax on May 28th. On June 7th Louisburg was reached, and on July 26th it was taken.

While the fleet was before Louisburg, a large army was being mobilized on the shores of Lake George. There were six thousand three hundred and sixty-seven British regulars and nine thousand and twenty-four American provincials, mostly from New England, New York, and northern New Jersey. The nominal commander-in-chief of this force was Abercrombie, but the moving spirit of the enterprise was Viscount Howe. On the 5th of July, the armament moved down the lake. After the foot of the lake was reached, a four miles' advance upon Ticonderoga was begun. In the very first skirmish Viscount Howe was killed, and from that moment the life of the expedition seemed to have departed. Abercrombie was timid and irresolute. The attack upon the enemy's intrenchments resulted in a criminal slaughter of nearly two thousand brave English soldiers. Montcalm had but a fourth the number of Abercrombie's army, and yet, owing to the cowardice of the latter, won a complete victory. Abercrombie did not stop his retreat until the lake was between himself and Montcalm, and until the artillery and ammunition were safely lodged at Albany.

The only redeeming feature of the defeat was a negative one. It led to the capture of Fort Frontenac on the 26th of August. This, in turn, rendered Fort Du Quesne virtually untenable and led later, on the 25th of November, to its evacuation and destruction by the French. The capture of Fort Frontenac was effected by three thousand provincials, of whom more than eleven hundred were New Yorkers, including the brothers James and George Clinton. Both these distinguished themselves as military leaders in the American Revolution and later in the political affairs of the State of New York. James was the third son and George the youngest son of Colonel Charles Clinton. James Clinton greatly distinguished himself in the French and Indian War and later in the American Revolution. He was the father of De Witt Clinton. He became fourth Vice-president of the United States, and held the office of Governor of New York, by successive reëlections, for eighteen years. In 1801, he was elected for an additional term of three years.

In the year 1759, England seemed to have reached the very "apogee of her military grandeur." From every quarter of the world came news of the success of the British arms. In America, Pitt was loyally supported by every colony north of Maryland. New York and New Jersey were particularly active in volunteering support. Although New Jersey had lost a thousand men, yet it voted to raise an additional thousand, and taxed itself for the war yearly an amount equivalent to about £1 from each individual. The campaign in America for the year was laid out on a far-sighted and masterly plan. General Stanwix was to secure and hold the frontier between Pittsburg and Lake Erie; Sir William Johnson and Brigadier Prideaux, with what Indians they could collect, were to have Montreal as their objective point, advancing by Niagara and Lake Ontario. General Jeffrey Amherst, the newly appointed

General James Clinton.
*From the pastel by James Sharpless, now in Independence Hall.*

commander-in-chief, was to advance with the main army as far as Lake Champlain and unite with the army of the St. Lawrence for an attack upon Quebec if a favorable opportunity offered itself. The capture of Quebec was the salient feature of the whole plan.

The first move in the campaign was against Niagara. Two regiments of English troops with artillery, a battalion of royal Americans, and two battalions of New York provincials, were under the command of Prideaux. In addition to these forces, there were Iroquois under Sir William Johnson. After detaching garrisons to supply Fort Stanwix and Oswego, the expedition sailed for Niagara early in July. The fort was soon invested, and the assault was begun. Prideaux was killed early in the attack by the bursting of a small mortar, and Johnson took his place. A relief party of one thousand one hundred whites and two hundred Indians having been completely routed, the garrison was compelled to surrender.

The French now began to give way on all sides. They had lost the whole upper valley of the Ohio; their forts at Presqu'Île, Venango, and Le Bœuf had been destroyed by themselves. Fort Du Quesne, Oswego, and Niagara had fallen into the hands of the English, and now, on the 26th of July, Ticonderoga and, on the 1st of August, Crown Point were evacuated. Stupidity is too weak a word to characterize Amherst in his disposition of his forces after the successes at Ticonderoga and Crown Point. Let us put him in the class with Loudon and Abercrombie; the association cannot injure the reputation of the latter two, and will fairly well characterize the standing of Amherst. He should have coöperated with Wolfe before Quebec, where Montcalm had gathered practically the whole effective fighting force of Canada.

Quebec surrendered on the 18th of September, 1759. After its fall, the French became demoralized. An attempt in 1760 to recapture Quebec failed. The French, under the Chevalier de Lévis, fell back upon Montreal. Here they made their last and ineffectual stand. On the 7th of September, 1760, the city was surrounded, and surrendered the next day. The Peace of Paris was not signed until three years after (February 10, 1763), but the fall of Montreal practically marks the close of the great struggle in America. The French power was completely overthrown, and the English colonies were introduced to a new era of colonial history.

The contrast between the Northern, Middle, and Southern colonies in the interest displayed in the war is indeed most marked. There was not a battle fought during the years 1759 and 1760 without men from New England, New York, and New Jersey being found in the ranks. Comparatively speaking, Pennsylvania and Maryland took but slight interest in the progress of the war, after the occupation of Fort Du Quesne. Further south than Maryland, the interest was still more languid.

A great deal of money was needed to finance the war, and the different colonies employed different methods of raising the necessary funds. Great Britain made large contributions, but so heavy were the burdens of the war that it is no disparagement of the mother country to say that the colonies were obliged to depend for the most part on themselves. Some provinces levied taxes, but in Pennsylvania the money was raised by issuing bills of credit. Varying amounts of these were authorized from time to time. The issuance of these bills was the occasion of numerous quarrels between the Assembly and the governors. Apart from objecting to the paper currency on principle, the governors were required to oppose it in royal or proprietary colonies by special orders of their superiors. They were instructed not to sign any bills of that character for any reason whatever. From the first emission, in 1723, to the last instalment during the provincial administration, the issues of bills in Pennsylvania aggregated £1,316,650. In most of the colonies the value of these bills of credit depreciated greatly. As to what that depreciation was in Pennsylvania, where the paper money was fairly well protected by tax levies, it is most difficult to get a fair estimate. Franklin held that there had been no depreciation whatever. He admitted, however, that the Philadelphia merchant was compelled to pay very large premiums for the specie he was required to transmit to the foreign merchants in payment of his importations. Nevertheless, this was due, said Franklin, to the scarcity of specie and did not prove a depreciation in the value of the paper money. As compared with the value of labor and commodities, no safe conclusion may be drawn. As compared with silver, there is no question of the relative depreciation of the Pennsylvania bills of credit, but it was much less than in other colonies issuing paper money. Even in the case of silver, however, it is difficult to form an estimate of this depreciation. There was hardly enough specie in the colony to serve as the basis of a fair comparison of values after foreign obligations were cancelled.

On account of the policy of non-resistance which the Quakers held from the very beginning of the French and Indian struggle, Pennsylvania became very much disliked by the other colonies. They did not relish the idea of being compelled to bear Pennsylvania's share of the burden of war. Robert Hunter Morris, the Governor of Pennsylvania, did everything he could to stir the Assembly to a sense of its duty, but the Quaker influence predominated and little was done by that body at the beginning of the struggle, either to raise money or troops for the expeditions.

After the defeat of Braddock, the Indian allies of the French broke all bounds and massacred even women and children. The accounts of one horrible massacre after another finally aroused those who had hitherto either given half-hearted aid or no aid at all, and they quickly made plans for defence. A Militia Bill was passed without amendment, which "encouraged and protected voluntary associations for public defence." The northwestern frontier was assigned to Franklin, who was given full power to commission officers. With the assistance of his son, who had served in the army against Canada, Franklin easily succeeded in raising five hundred men. Franklin immediately began to erect forts and proceeded to complete his plans for the military association. He was elected colonel of a regiment in Philadelphia composed of one thousand two hundred men.

In addition to Franklin's efforts to protect the borders, the Germans and Scotch-Irish joined forces to compel the Assembly to take more positive measures. They drew up a petition and presented it to the Privy Council. A committee was appointed to look into the charges, which finally condemned the too peaceful policy of the Assembly. A further declaration was made that it was the duty of that body "to support the government and protect its subjects; that the measures enacted by the Assembly for that purpose were inadequate; and that there was no hope for more effective ones so long as the majority of that body consisted of persons whose avowed principles were opposed to military service, although they were less than one-sixth of the population." The report, being adopted, caused a stir among the Quakers, a number of whom retired rather than give assent to a vigorous military policy. Thus matters were left in the hands of those who did not hold the principle of non-resistance.

In Maryland, Governor Horatio Sharpe tried again and again to get the Lower House to vote an appropriation for the common defence. First, that body refused unless the revenue should be taken from a tax on licenses. To this the governor refused to accede, inasmuch as it was an infringement upon the prerogatives of the proprietary. Next, an appropriation of £7,000 was made on condition that £4,000 of it should consist of a new issue of bills of credit. Sharpe refused to sign the bill, and another deadlock was the result.

The news of Braddock's defeat reached Annapolis on July 15th. The settlers were reported flying in all directions, and it was feared that Frederick County would be entirely depopulated unless some immediate action were taken for its defence. The Indians were striking terror into the hearts of the border settlers. The Assembly finally came to terms on the threat of the enraged settlers of Frederick County to march upon Annapolis with Thomas Cresap at their head and compel action. The proprietary agreed, however, that his own manors should be taxed. A bill finally passed the Assembly, issuing £40,000 in bills of credit. It was to be used in "building forts, raising troops, securing the alliance of the southern Indians, and paying bounties on Indian scalps." Additional taxes and duties provided a sinking fund for the redemption of the bills. Among these was a tax on bachelors, as "men who were derelict in a citizen's first duty at a time when it was most imperative."

As soon as the seat of war was transferred to the north, and when it was evident that it would stay there, the Maryland Assembly once more refused to pass supply bills. Sharpe succeeded in raising some volunteers, who contributed most effective services against the Indians. The evacuation of Fort Du Quesne freed the whole province from danger, and likewise eradicated from the Assembly the little inclination it had to help the common cause. The Maryland troops engaged in the expedition were voted £1,500, and then the matter stopped short. There is no disputing the niggardliness of Maryland's conduct in this war. It was not equalled by that of Pennsylvania. It is fortunate that the safety of the American colonies did not depend upon the generosity of the Maryland Assembly.

Shortly after the settlement of the long-standing boundary dispute between Pennsylvania and Maryland in 1760, the northern boundary was likewise established. The first agreement, we recall, was between Lord Baltimore and Thomas and Richard Penn. It was reached on the basis of the agreement of 1732. In 1763, Charles Mason and Jeremiah Dixon, two well-known English mathematicians, began the determination of all those parts of the boundary not completed at that time. They were employed by the proprietaries. First, they determined the northeastern angle of Maryland, which was to be the starting point, and then ran a line westward upon the latitude 39° 43′ 26.3″ north. The Indians interrupted the survey in 1767, after it had been carried two hundred and forty-four miles from Delaware River. This was only thirty-six miles east of the terminus sought. The line was marked by milestones, and on every fifth stone the arms of Baltimore were cut on one side and those of the Penns on the other. Where cut stones could not be conveyed, cairns were substituted. The part of the line left unsurveyed was fixed in November, 1782, by Colonel Alexander McLean, of Pennsylvania, and Joseph Neville, of Virginia. It was verified and permanently marked in 1784. The survey was revised in 1849 by commissioners appointed by Maryland, Pennsylvania, and Delaware. The boundary stone at the northeast corner of Maryland had been removed accidentally. The survey was made by Lieutenant-colonel James D. Graham, of the United States topographical engineers. The work of Mason and Dixon was confirmed, and Maryland gained less than two acres. This Mason and Dixon Line, as separating the Northern from the Southern States, was destined to play a very important rôle in the politics of the nation.

The accession of Lieutenant-governor James De Lancey to executive control in New York was a fortunate occurrence upon the eve of the French and Indian War. Governor George Clinton had been succeeded by Sir Danvers Osborne, who arrived on October 10, 1753. Shortly after, however, Osborne committed suicide, and two days later (October 31st) De Lancey entered upon the executive authority. He was superseded in that position when Sir Charles Hardy arrived at New York on September 3, 1755, but continued to exercise the real power of the office. New York had to bear much of the brunt of the struggle, and did it nobly. At the outbreak of the war in 1755, the Assembly voted £45,000 in paper money and authorized a levy of eight hundred men. Shortly afterward, £48,000 was added to this amount and the force was increased to one thousand seven hundred men. In 1759 the quota was further increased to two thousand six hundred and eighty, and a bounty of £15 was offered. Likewise, £100,000 in paper money was ordered, which was to be cancelled in nine annual instalments.

These provisions were but a slight part of the burdens the people of the province bore. Troops were billeted upon the citizens, and time and time again the war swept over the borders, carrying with it all the losses incident to a French and Indian invasion. New York was, in a large measure, the battlefield of the war. Armies moved across the province from New York to Lake Champlain and from Albany to Niagara. Settlements were broken up, manufactures were interrupted, and agriculture and commerce were checked. The strain upon the province cannot well be exaggerated. The effects of the war were evident in the following statistics for the year 1756: the white population was eighty-three thousand two hundred and thirty-three, and the black, thirteen thousand five hundred and forty-two. Out of these numbers two thousand six hundred and eighty were kept constantly in the field. The war debt in 1762 was more than £300,000, and a tax of £40,000 a year was assessed to meet it.

At the outbreak of the war, Governor Belcher, of New Jersey, addressed the Assembly on the relations between the home government and France. The House replied, through its committee, that New Jersey had no available money with which to aid the frontier colonies in their expeditions against the French or their defences against the Indians. The failure of the expedition against the French on the Ohio and the return of the troops from Fort Necessity, however, awoke the Assembly to a realization of the great danger threatening all the colonies. On April 24, 1755, the governor issued a proclamation stating that the Assembly had provided for "Pay, Cloathing, and Subsistence of five hundred Men," to be under the command of Colonel Peter Schuyler.

The colony seemed thoroughly aroused. Funds were appropriated by the Assembly, voluntary contributions were made, and by May 12th four out of five of the New Jersey companies were nearly completed. By June, 1756, the Assembly had appropriated £75,000 and had seven hundred and fifty men in the field. The New Jersey troops met with a disaster on the 21st of July, 1757, when Colonel John Parker lost all but seventy-five men of a party of three hundred and fifty in a water attack upon Fort Ticonderoga. The excitement in New Jersey was intense. It was feared the whole Hudson valley would be wrested from England.

In 1758 New Jersey recruited a thousand men, and in 1760 still another thousand, while in 1761 a force of six hundred men were recruited for service on the Canadian border. New Jersey troops were represented in many of the important battles of the war. They were at the fall of Quebec and were among the levies of 1762, 1763, and 1764. No colony acted with greater promptness and with more genuine unselfishness in providing means for the common defence than did New Jersey when finally aroused to the seriousness of the struggle.

George II. died suddenly on October 25, 1760, and was succeeded by his grandson, George III. The new monarch had been taught by his mother two things: "to be an Englishman and to be a king." He made changes in the cabinet immediately, by way of emphasizing his determination to rule as well as to reign. He made personal appointments in the army and the Church, and likewise controlled many important civil offices in the court and government. In this way he surrounded himself with men so completely dependent upon him that they were willing to do anything and everything he wished. They were truly the "king's friends." Through his influence, the Newcastle ministry, of which Pitt was the real head, was forced to resign in May, 1762. Pitt had already resigned on October 5th of the preceding year.

The Seven Years' War of Europe,—the French and Indian War of America,—which had cost so much money and so many lives, was brought to a formal close by the Treaty of Paris. The British nation, on the whole, was opposed to its terms. Pitt fought against the clause that gave France a share in the fisheries of Newfoundland and the St. Lawrence. In fact, he was strenuously opposed to anything that might possibly result in the restoration of French maritime power. The terms of the treaty were briefly as follows: first, all Canada was ceded to the British; secondly, Nova Scotia, Cape Breton, and dependent islands were likewise given to the British, with the exception of a share in the fisheries and the possession of two islets, Saint-Pierre and Miquelon, as a shelter for French fishing vessels; thirdly, the boundary was to be the middle of Mississippi River from its source as far as the river Iberville, the middle of the latter river from Lakes Maurepas and Pontchartrain to the sea; fourthly, France ceded to Spain New Orleans and all Louisiana west of the Mississippi; fifthly, England acquired Senegal in Africa and the command of the slave trade; sixthly, in Europe, each country took back its own—Minorca reverting to Great Britain.

The colonists had gone into the war in a disunited condition, each colony and province for itself. Those that were not immediately affected by the conflict cared little how it terminated. The war did not bring them together exactly, but it taught them that they had numbers, wealth, and ability, which, when united, could be used with telling effect. The growing sentiment of independence, now that the fear of the French despotic ideas was removed, had almost untrammelled opportunity for development. Affection for the mother country had not been increased by the war. During its course, the British had constantly irritated the colonists and their troops by the overbearing and contemptuous manner of the generals sent from England. The constant threat of Parliamentary control of American finances added to the distrust of England that the war had intensified.

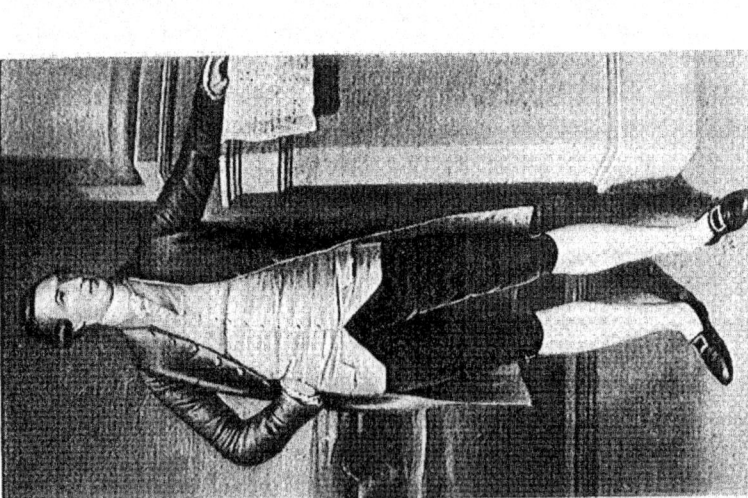

WILLIAM PACA  
CHARLES CARROLL OF CARROLLTON

After the painting by John B. Bordley. After the painting by Thomas Sully.
From the originals in the State House, Annapolis.

## CHAPTER XIX

*ASSUMPTION OF PARLIAMENTARY CONTROL, 1763-1765*

WHEN the sagacious Vergennes, the French ambassador at Constantinople, heard of the conditions of the Treaty of Paris, he uttered a prophecy in these words: "The consequences of the entire cession of Canada are obvious. England will well near repent of having removed the only check that could keep her colonies in awe; they stand no longer in need of her protection; she will call on them to contribute toward supporting the burdens they have helped to bring on her; and they will answer by striking off all dependence." Said the equally sagacious Choiseul: "We have caught them at last." He believed fully that the cession of Canada would lead to the independence of North America.

The fear of France once removed, the conflicting ideas with regard to the power of Parliament over the colonies were bound to clash. The records of the colonial Assemblies are one continuous protest against Parliamentary, royal, or proprietary interference with the right to initiate money bills. The difficulties experienced by royal and proprietary governors were in nearly every instance due to disagreements with the colonial legislatures with regard to appropriations. The governors would insist on a stipulated salary fund for a period of years, or an unitemized budget, and the Assemblies would just as often oppose it. In nearly every instance the Assemblies finally won a complete victory. Control of colonial purses in turn gave them control of almost all important legislation.

The fight was kept up, as we have seen, during the French and Indian War, when it caused much hard feeling between the representatives of the mother country and the colonial legislatures. There was lack of interest on the part of the Southern colonies, almost criminal negligence on the part of Maryland and Pennsylvania, and a stubborn liberality by New York, New Jersey, and New England. To undiscerning persons, the close of the war seemed to promise a cessation of the struggle of the people for the control of their revenues. As a matter of fact, however, the war was the most important cause of its continuation. Indeed, the struggle was to grow even more bitter than before and was to lead shortly to the great American Revolution. Instead of contesting with royal and proprietary governors, the colonies had now to deal with Parliament itself. The colonial side of the dispute also became changed. The great question at issue tended to bring the colonies closer together, and Parliamentary tyranny brought about a union between them. Formerly, the colonies fought their battles individually, because the power that essayed to infringe upon what they termed their inalienable rights differed in the several colonies. But after the Seven Years' War, the one great threatening power was Parliament; and the colonies, realizing this, slowly but surely united in their opposition to its encroachments.

The French and Indian War was the immediate cause of Parliamentary aggression upon the control by colonial Assemblies of their own revenue. This war, begun by England for the acquisition of the Ohio valley, doubled the British national debt, thus increasing it to the amount of £140,000,000. The national supplies during the first year of peace amounted to £14,000,000. The nation's lands and industries were overburdened by public charges to such an extent that the people were afraid to increase the debt. In America, the northern colonies likewise were quite exhausted by reason of their expeditions and their losses.

To reimburse the colonies for at least part of the losses they had suffered, Parliament passed an act appropriating £150,000 in specie for distribution among the colonies, Pennsylvania receiving £26,000 as her first year's grant. The Assembly of that colony sent a resolution to its governor, continuing Franklin and Charles as its agents in England and enabling them to receive the money. The governor refused to agree to the clause authorizing the agents to receive the money granted by Parliament. Nevertheless, the Assembly ordered its agents to take the money and to deposit it in the Bank of England subject to the drafts of the province. The money was finally paid to Franklin, who invested it in English funds. New Jersey received £5,000, and the Lower Counties [Delaware] somewhat over £3,000. Of the latter amount, the agent was allowed to retain one-half of one per cent, while one-half of the remainder went to New Castle County, three-tenths to Kent, and the remaining two-tenths to Sussex. The money was employed in liquidating the debts contracted in consequence of the war.

On account of the large national debt of England, her people thought America should assist in carrying the burden, particularly as much of it had been created in defending the colonies. Again, Pontiac's war (1763-1764) had definitely shown that the frontier still needed protection. England's plan was to supply troops to be distributed along the frontier, for the support of which the colonies were to be taxed. The British idea was that the colonists in America were subject to the powers of Parliament; furthermore, that Parliament could yield them more or fewer powers of self-government for a time and then withdraw them at will. It was claimed that the colonists had representation in Parliament, for the reason that the members of the House represented the whole British Empire rather than a mere section of it. On the other hand, the colonists claimed that Parliament had no more to do with the colonies than the Assemblies in the colonies had to do with Parliament.

At this time (1765), the revenues from the colonies amounted to about £1,900 per year, which cost upward of £9,000 to collect. The government now determined to get a substantial revenue. There were no longer to be "requisitions from the king," but instead the British legislature was to put a tax on the colonies. Hereafter, all royal officers, not inferior in rank to the executive, were to be subject to the will of the king. The crown was to appoint them and fix their salaries. They were to sustain the authority of Great Britain. The Navigation Acts were to be rigidly enforced. Finally, it was determined that twenty regiments should be maintained in America, to be supported by the crown the first year, but afterward by the colonies.

These various policies toward the American colonies caused several political parties to spring up in England. At first there were two Whig factions, but when in 1762 Lord Bute was made prime minister, and George Grenville secretary of state, their attempts to create a court party drove the Whig factions together. These two Whig factions now united, and, having the support of the people, bitterly opposed the court party. Bute withdrew on April 8, 1763, and Grenville became prime minister, with Charles Townshend as first lord of trade. Townshend and Grenville did not agree in their opinions, although in the same ministry; and the former, perceiving that the fall of the ministry was near at hand, resigned. Thereupon George III. put the government in the hands of a triumvirate consisting of Grenville, Egremont, and Halifax. Grenville was no great favorite of George, but he was selected because he was dependent on the court. The idea of George and his friends was that all parties should come together, and out of this coalition the king could choose his ministry.

Parliament was at a loss what tax to impose on the colonies, but it was of the unanimous opinion that foreign and intercolonial commerce should first be taxed. This, however, would not supply the government's needs. A poll tax would hardly be fair to the colonies, for some of them would be taxed more than others, especially those in which slavery was prevalent. The colonists would never endure a land tax like quitrents. An excise was held in reserve, but was not adopted at this time. Exchequer bills for currency would be illegal, owing to the Acts of Parliament which prohibited the use of paper money in the colonies. Parliament had to take into consideration two things: first, how to raise money, and, secondly, how to raise enough.

A bill for raising money for the depleted English treasury from colonial revenues was brought before the ministry in 1763. The resignation, however, of Charles Townshend from the cabinet caused its postponement. Grenville, the foreign secretary under Bute, did not regard the colonies as royal dominions. He considered them subject to the crown, but with independent parliaments. To him they only existed as benefits to British trade. He believed that the internal taxes were just the same in principle as the external taxes which Parliament had been collecting. Grenville's great object was an American revenue that would divide the public burden between England and her colonies.

In 1763, Grenville convened the colonial agents in London and explained his plan. A stamp tax was to be laid on the colonies by Act of Parliament. These agents were to inform their respective Assemblies of his plans, and, if those plans were not suitable, to suggest a more agreeable tax. On September 22, 1763, the three lords of the treasury, Grenville, North, and Hunter, met to consider the matter of presenting such a bill before Parliament. Charles Jenkinson was ordered to write to the commissioners of the stamp duties to " prepare the draft of a bill to be presented to Parliament for extending the stamp duties to the colonies." These instructions were carried out. The tax bill was not brought before Parliament at once. There were several motives, in fact, that caused Grenville to feel reluctant to present the bill at this time. One of them was the opposition of the Bedford party. He therefore postponed the tax for a year, although stating that he would

surely bring it up at the end of that time. When Parliament
assembled in 1764, Jenkinson urged Grenville to present
the American Stamp Act, but it was not until early in 1765
that the bill came up before the House of Commons in its
final form.

The tax proposed by Grenville was no new scheme.
Nearly forty years before the passage of the Stamp Act,
Sir William Keith, the late Governor of Pennsylvania, had
presented an elaborate scheme to the king, proposing the
extension of the stamp duties to the colonies by Act of
Parliament. Dunbar, during his brief but exciting career
in New Hampshire, had advised the same plan. In April,
1734, Governor Cosby suggested to the New York Assembly "a duty upon paper to be used in the Law and in all
conveyances and deeds." He urged it as an experiment
which might bring a considerable amount of money into
the treasury. A like proposition was made by Lieutenant-
governor Clarke to Governor Clinton in 1744. In the first
case the Assembly objected, and in the second case Clinton
did not deem the scheme expedient. Both Governor Sharpe,
of Maryland, and Governor Dinwiddie, of Virginia, had
advised it at the time of the abortive attempt to unite the
colonies in 1754.

The king and the lords favored Grenville's scheme, in
spite of the opposition raised in several quarters. Grenville, however, was not at all sure that subjects ought to be
taxed without representation. Nevertheless, he thought policy, commerce, and finance demanded it. He held that the
colonies existed, in a way, for exploitation,—for the improvement of trade. The colonies had disregarded the Acts
of Navigation and had thus robbed England. He increased
the number of customs officers and instructed them to enforce vigorously the navigation laws. The governors were
ordered to suppress illicit trade. All civil, naval, and military officers in America were ordered to coöperate. The
commander-in-chief was to place troops at the service of
the revenue officers, if necessary. Likewise, the executive

Andrew Hamilton. *After the painting by Adolf Ulrik Wertmüller.*

head of the navy, whose officers held custom house commissions with authority to enter harbors and seize suspected persons or cargoes, was required to do the same.

In June, 1764, news was received that a Stamp Act would be introduced into the House of Commons the following year. The people of New York were thoroughly aroused by the intelligence. Said one person: "I shall wear nothing but homespun;" "I shall stop drinking wine," said another; "I shall dress in sheepskins with the wool on," said a third. The English statesmen believed New York would be loyal, even if all the other colonies rebelled. They were wrong. The New York Assembly convened in September (1764), and adopted a memorial address to the House of Commons, in which it was said: "The people of New York nobly disdained the thought of claiming liberty as a privilege . . . but founded the exemption from ungranted and compulsory taxes, upon an honorable, solid, and stable basis, and challenged it, and gloried in it as their right." The New York agent in England was communicated with by a committee appointed for the purpose, and instructed to do all in his power to prevent the passage of the proposed laws. New York put itself on record as considering a "violation of her rights and privileges, even by Parliament, an act of tyranny," and that it would abhor the power which might inflict it; and, as soon as able, would cast it off, or perhaps try to obtain better terms from some other power. Lieutenant-governor Cadwallader Colden was acting governor. He did his best to carry out the designs of the king, and got himself heartily despised in consequence.

Grenville presented before the House fifty-five resolutions embracing all the details of the act. His argument was that Parliament had to defend the colonies, hence Parliament could exact duties from the colonies to help to pay for this defence. Beckford, a friend of Pitt, replied to Grenville's argument. He urged other means besides the Stamp Act. Colonel Isaac Barré, Wolfe's companion before Quebec, taunted the House with ignorance of American affairs. Charles Townshend, who thought that he knew all about such affairs, arose, and, after an exhaustive argument concerning the equity of the proposed taxation, ended with this peroration:

"Will these American children, planted by our care, nourished up to strength and opulence by our indulgence, and protected by our arms, grudge to contribute their mite to relieve us from the heavy burden under which we lie?"

Barré responded quickly, in a speech known to every schoolboy:

"*They planted by your care!* No; your oppressions planted them in America. They fled from your tyranny to a then uncultivated, inhospitable country, where they exposed themselves to almost all the hardships to which human nature is liable; and, among others, to the cruelties of a savage foe, the most subtle, and I will take it upon me to say, the most formidable of any people upon the face of God's earth; and yet, actuated by principles of true English liberty, they met all hardships with pleasure, compared with those they suffered in their own country from the hands of those who should be their friends.

"*They nourished by your indulgence!* They grew by your neglect of them. As soon as you began to care about them, that care was exercised in sending persons to rule them in one department and another, who were, perhaps, the deputies to some members of this House, sent to spy out their liberties, to misrepresent their actions, and to prey upon them,—men, whose behavior on many occasions has caused the blood of those *sons of liberty* to recoil within them; men promoted to the highest seats of justice; some who, to my knowledge, were glad, by going to a foreign country, to escape being brought to the bar of a court of justice in their own.

"*They protected by your arms!* They have nobly taken up arms in your defence; have exerted a valor, amidst their constant and laborious industry, for the defence of a country whose frontier was drenched in blood, while its interior parts yielded all its little savings to your emolument. And believe me—remember I this day told you so—the same spirit of freedom which actuated that people at first will accompany them still. But prudence forbids me to explain myself further. God knows that I do not at this time speak from motives of party heat; what I deliver are the genuine sentiments of my heart. However superior to me in general knowledge and experience the respectable body of this House may be, yet I claim to know more of America than most of you, having seen and been conversant in that country. The people, I believe, are as truly loyal as any subjects the king has; but a people jealous of their liberties and who will vindicate them, if ever they should be violated. But the subject is too delicate; I will say no more."

The speech was extemporaneous, and was regarded as merely a hit at Townshend. In the gallery sat Jared Ingersoll, the agent of Connecticut. He sent a report of the speech to New London. It was printed in the newspapers of the town. It spread rapidly throughout New England, and all America—even Canada, where it was translated into French. The people seized upon "Sons of Liberty" as a slogan.

But it was of no use—petitions and prayers were of no avail. "We might," said Franklin, "as well have hindered the sun's setting." On February 7, 1765, the act was ordered to be brought in. Petitions against it were sent in, but the House ruled "to receive no petition against a money bill." The petition of Virginia, however, was debated upon, whether to receive it or not. It was not received. Finally, the bill was passed in the House, with an opposition of about fifty votes. An insignificant minority that betrayed the general lack of interest and comprehension of the issues! "The affair passed with so very little noise that in the town they scarcely knew the nature of what was doing." On the 27th of February, the bill came before the House of Lords. On the 8th of March, the bill was agreed to by the Lords, without having encountered an amendment, debate, protest, division, or single objection. On the 22d of March it received the royal assent and became a law. It was not to go into effect until the 1st of November following.

"The Stamp Act provided for the payment, by British subjects in America to the English exchequer, of specified sums, greater or less, in consideration of obtaining validity for each of the common transactions of business" (Palfrey). By its terms, newspapers, almanacs, marriage certificates, law documents, and other papers had to be stamped. It was expected that this would bring to the English treasury about £100,000 annually. It is an open question who was responsible for the Stamp Act. Jenkinson, being only private secretary to the Earl of Bute, could not have been responsible for it, although while acting in that office he proposed such a scheme. Jenkinson himself says: "If the Stamp Act was a good measure, the merit of it was not due to Grenville; if it was a bad one, the ill policy did not belong to him." Bancroft is of the opinion that Grenville himself was not the responsible person. The latter even doubted, as we have seen, the wisdom of taxing the colonies without representation.

Grenville thought to soothe the feelings of the colonists by appointing as stamp officers native Americans. Said he: "Now, gentlemen, take the business into your own hands; you will see how and where it pinches, and will certainly let us know it; in which case it shall be eased." No one thought the tax would be resisted; Fitch and Hutchinson were quite sure that Parliament had a right to tax, and even Otis and Franklin did not dream of active resistance—let alone armed resistance.

The tax seemed ideally perfect. It would collect itself —without the stamps, marriages would be void, notes valueless, transfers of real estate invalid, inheritances irreclaimable, mortgages unregistered. The English statesmen applauded the tax; the Americans received it with disgust. Said William Smith, Jr., son of the historian: "This single stroke has lost Great Britain the affection of all her colonies; what can be expected but discontent for a while, and in the end open opposition?" John Watts voiced the same sentiment when he said: "The task may seem easier in theory than prove in the execution; I cannot conceive there will be silver or gold enough in the colonies to carry this act through."

The colonists throughout the length and breadth of the country showed a commendable zeal. Many associations known as Sons of Liberty were organized, and the growth of a most ominous feeling of unity was apparent. Each colony adopted the method best to its liking of showing its opposition to the policy of the Parliamentary party in control of affairs. There were all degrees of opposition, from the defiant attitude of Massachusetts to the outward calm of New York. The Virginia Assembly put itself on record to the effect "that the inhabitants of that dominion inherited from the first settlers equal franchises with the people of Great Britain; that their rights had never been forfeited or given up; that the General Assembly of Virginia had the sole right and power to lay taxes on the inhabitants; and furthermore, that no man in the colony was bound to yield obedience to any tax law other than those made by their own General Assembly, and whosoever should, by speaking or writing, maintain the contrary was an enemy to the colony." Otis, of Massachusetts, suggested a most radical step. He proposed an American congress to consider carefully the Acts of Parliament. His suggestion took practical form in a circular letter sent to all the colonial Assemblies proposing a congress to meet at New York on the second Tuesday in October.

In the meantime, the printing press was being put to a good use. The Stamp Act was reprinted and sold on the streets of New York under the caption *The Folly of England and the Ruin of America*. Outspoken denunciation of the English government appeared in nearly every issue of the newspapers; and open threats were made in numerous pamphlets. In this mass of denunciatory material, there was one rather sober, well-balanced essay, signed "Freeman." It is supposed to have been written by John Morin Scott. Several quotations from this essay may prove interesting:

"It is not the tax, it is the unconstitutional manner of imposing it, that is the great subject of uneasiness in the colonies. . . . The absurdity of our being represented in Parliament is so glaring that it is almost an affront to common sense to use arguments to expose it. The taxation of America is arbitrary and tyrannical, and what the Parliament of England has no right to impose." The English constitution was analyzed and declared to have within itself the principle of self-preservation, correction, and improvement. "If the interests of the mother country and her colonies cannot be made to coincide, if the same constitution may not take place in both, if the welfare of England necessarily requires the sacrifice of the most natural rights of the colonies,—their right of making their own laws, and disposing of their own property by representatives of their own choosing,—if such is really the case between Great Britain and her colonies, then the connection between them ought to cease; and sooner or later it must inevitably cease. The English government cannot long act toward a part of its dominion upon principles diametrically opposed to its own, without losing itself in the slavery it would impose upon the colonies, or leaving them to throw it off and assert their own freedom. There never can be a disposition in the colonies to break off their connection with the mother, so long as they are permitted to have the full enjoyment of those rights to which the English constitution entitles them. They desire no more; nor can they be satisfied with less." This essay was copied by the newspapers of the country and was read by the people.

Inasmuch as the stamp collectors were the material embodiment of what the colonists saw fit to consider the tyrannical policy of Parliament, they were the first objects of the popular indignation. The question was very shortly debated whether or not the stamp collectors should be tolerated at all. The English ministry seemed to irritate the colonists in direct proportion to the extent that it attempted to placate them. Grenville appointed prominent Americans as stamp collectors, but the claim was immediately made that such men would make the worst possible officers. The analogy was drawn between them and negro overseers, who were always the most cruel taskmasters although of the same race. The names of the stamp collectors were first published in Boston on August 8th. The temper of the colonists can be fairly well tested from the character of a conversation that is supposed to have been carried on between a friend of Jared Ingersoll, of Connecticut, and another colonist. Ingersoll had just arrived from England, duly qualified as a stamp collector. "Had you not rather these duties should be collected by your brethren than by foreigners?" asked the former. "No, vile miscreant! Indeed we had not," exclaimed Daggett, of New Haven. "If your father must die, is there no defect in filial duty in becoming his executioner in order to secure the hangman's fees? If the ruin of our country is decreed, are you free from blame for taking part in the plunder?"

Affairs in New England now rapidly came to a crisis. In less than a week after the names of the stamp collectors were published in Boston, Andrew Oliver, the Massachusetts official, was hanged in effigy from a tree near Boston. Before the sheriff could remove the effigy, the people had secured it and placed it upon a funeral pyre in front of the collector's house. Chief Justice Hutchinson, who favored the tax, now decided to take a hand in the proceedings. He ordered the drum beat for the purpose of summoning loyal citizens to quell the mob. But no one was bold enough to obey his command. He then tried to disperse the throng, but found himself suddenly compelled to flee for his life. Oliver discreetly resigned his collectorship next day. Nor did the lawless element stop here. They burned Hutchinson's house, destroyed his furniture and books, and scattered his plate and ready money. His manuscript history of Massachusetts was thrown into the gutter and came near being injured beyond repair. It must be added that the better element of Boston denounced the excesses of the mob.

These lawless acts were not confined to Boston. The stamp collector of Rhode Island was compelled to resign; and when Jared Ingersoll reached Connecticut he was met by five hundred mounted men from New London and Windham Counties. He was thus compelled to resign by the time he had reached Wethersfield. He rode a white horse; and it is said someone asked him, jocosely, what he was thinking about. "Death on a pale horse and hell following," said he. He was led to the court house, where he read his resignation within the hearing of the legislature. Then, swinging his cap above his head, he shouted three times: "Liberty and Property!" The stamp collectors of New Jersey and Pennsylvania resigned shortly afterward. The Southern colonies, Jamaica, St. Christopher, Nova Scotia, New Brunswick, and Canada at first contented themselves with passing resolutions to resist the law. Later, however, resistance in the Southern colonies was not confined to resolutions. After the Stamp Act went into effect, lawless deeds were committed in different parts of the South—notably in North Carolina.

Interest now became centred upon New York as one of the most important cities of the continent and the headquarters of the British forces in America. Stamps were sent to New York, but James McEvers, the stamp distributor, sent in his resignation rather than subject himself to the dangers of receiving them. In fact, the generally disordered state of affairs in the city led Lieutenant-governor Colden to demand of General Thomas Gage sufficient military force to suppress the sedition. The lieutenant-governor was assured that he would be provided with a military force sufficiently strong to put down all possible disorder. Relying upon this promise, he boldly asserted that he would do everything in his power to have the stamped paper distributed at the time appointed by the Act of Parliament.

These were bold words, for, in the meantime, the Sons of Liberty had been at work. So well had their task been done, that on the 7th of October, 1765, the Stamp Act Congress assembled in the City Hall at New York. Its deliberations lasted through nearly three weeks. Colden declared the congress "unconstitutional, unprecedented, and illegal." Ships of war were moored at the wharves, and the fort was ordered to prepare for any emergency. The commander of the fort, Major James, rashly declared he "would cram the stamps down the throats of the people with the end of his sword." But it is well said that while he was giving utterance to such bellicose expressions, the people were splitting those same throats with the yell: "Unite or Die!" —taken from a motto on a device representing a snake cut into parts, to represent the colonies. Furthermore, it was not long before James was compelled to swallow his own words through the force of public indignation. Colden fumed with rage at what he considered the lawlessness of the people, but to no avail. The merchants displayed wonderful self-possession and quietly prepared an agreement to send no new orders for goods or merchandise, to countermand all former orders, and not even to receive goods on commission, unless the Stamp Act were repealed.

Judge Robert R. Livingston, Major John Cruger, Philip Livingston, Leonard Lispenard, and William Bayard represented New York in the Stamp Act Congress. Delegates were present at the congress from nine of the colonies. Four of the colonies sympathized with the movement, though they did not find it convenient to choose representatives. These were Virginia, New Hampshire, North Carolina, and Georgia. "Here," says Frothingham (*Rise of the Republic of the United States*), "several of the patriots, who had discussed the American question in their localities, met for the first time. James Otis stood in this body the foremost speaker. His pen, with the pens of the brothers Robert and Philip Livingston, of New York, were summoned to service in a wider field. John Dickinson, of Pennsylvania, was soon to be known through the colonies by *The Farmer's Letters*. Thomas McKean and Cæsar Rodney were pillars of the cause in Delaware. Edward Tilghman was an honored name in Maryland. South Carolina, in addition to the intrepid Gadsden, had in Thomas Lynch and John Rutledge two patriots who appear prominently in the subsequent career of that colony. Thus this body was graced by large ability, genius, learning, and common sense. It was calm in its deliberations, seeming unmoved by the whirl of the political waters." Timothy Ruggles, of Massachusetts, a Tory, was made chairman of the congress, and John Cotton, clerk. Before the organization of the congress, the Massachusetts delegation called upon Lieutenant-governor Colden, but found him in no mood to give the slightest official countenance to the proceedings. In fact, he assured them of his unalterable determination to execute the law to the letter.

Nevertheless, in spite of this rebuff, the congress proceeded to organize itself, and continued its sessions as if completely oblivious of the proximity of the lieutenant-governor or the existence of his threats. The rights, privileges, and grievances of the colonists were the subjects under consideration at the second day's session. It took eleven days' debate before the congress could agree upon a declaration of rights and grievances. Finally, with the exception of Timothy Ruggles, of Massachusetts, and Robert Ogden, of New Jersey, the delegates present from six of the colonies signed it. The delegates from Connecticut, New York, and South Carolina had not been authorized to agree to such a declaration. Notwithstanding this, the document was accepted—each colony having one vote—and was ordered inserted in the journal.

The congress adjourned on the 25th of October, and arrangements were made for transmitting the proceedings to those colonies that were not represented. The Assemblies of most of the colonies represented heartily approved of the support given the document by their representatives.

The speaker of the General Court of Massachusetts severely rebuked Ruggles for his failure to sign the declaration; and Ogden, of New Jersey, was hanged in effigy by the people of that colony, so incensed were they at his want of loyalty to the common cause. Meanwhile, the newspapers of the day kept the colonists in touch with the action of the different colonial Assemblies. At the same time, the Sons of Liberty took a most radical step in advance by outwardly supporting, through their Committee of Correspondence, a continental union of all the colonies. They followed up this interest by publishing what support might be counted upon in case of necessity. A stolid determination to resist the Stamp Act at all hazards was clearly evidenced upon every hand.

These preliminaries were not attended to a day too soon; for, about ten o'clock at night on October 23d, two days before the adjournment of the Stamp Act Congress, a ship laden with stamped paper was reported off Sandy Hook. A man-of-war anchored in the harbor announced the arrival of the ship by the firing of a cannon. The next day the ship proceeded up the bay, accompanied by a man-of-war and a tender. There was every evidence of suppressed wrath on the part of the populace. No overt act for the time being was committed, but there were numerous signs of a growing storm. The next morning the following notice was found posted in many conspicuous places:

<blockquote>
Pro Patria

The first Man that either distributes or makes use of Stampt Paper, let him take care of his House, Person, and Effects.

Vox Populi.

We dare.
</blockquote>

There was no mistaking the temper of the people now—all were determined to resist the landing of the stamps, come what might. The congress—still in session—said: "We will no more submit to Parliament than to the Divan of Constantinople." Colden knew not what to do, and in his extremity summoned his Council for advice. But only three out of the seven responded to his summons, and they had no advice to offer other than that he had better move in the matter very carefully. Otherwise, he might be subjected to civil suits by those merchants of the city having merchandise in the ship on the grounds of detention of their goods. In his dilemma, the lieutenant-governor wisely decided that it was the better part of valor to retire within the walls of the fort, where, in case of necessity, he would be well prepared to crush at its inception any outbreak on the part of the populace. On the 31st of October the colonial governors subscribed to the oath necessary to enforce the provisions of the act. For the time being, however, no governor was bold enough to take the initiative.

Thousands of people now swarmed into New York, and the conditions were growing more threatening day by day. Open threats were made by the more outspoken element of the crowd, while others contented themselves with singing ballads more martial in their character than poetic. One of these ballads seems to have been a special favorite. It contained thirteen verses, one of which will be sufficient to indicate the character of the other twelve:

> "With the beasts of the wood, we will ramble for food,
> And lodge in wild deserts and caves,
> And live poor as Job, on the skirts of the globe,
> Before we'll submit to be slaves, brave boys,
> Before we'll submit to be slaves."

We are indebted to Mrs. Lamb (*History of New York City*) for a most vivid and interesting account of the Stamp Act riot in that city:

On the evening of October 31st, the day before the Stamp Act was to go into effect, the merchants of New York met at Burns's tavern for the purpose of signing a non-importation agreement. Said Judge Robert R. Livingston: "England will suffer more by it in one year than the Stamp Tax or any other—should others be imposed—could ever recompense.

Merchants have resolved to send for no more British manufactures, shopkeepers will buy none, gentlemen will wear none; our own are encouraged, all pride in dress seems to be laid aside, and he that does not appear in homespun, or at least in a turned coat, is looked upon with an evil eye. The lawyers will not issue a writ. Merchants will not clear out a vessel. These were all facts not in the least exaggerated; and it is of importance that they should be known."

This evening witnessed no rioting whatever. To be sure, a large number of boys and sailors got together in front of the house where the merchants were gathered, thinking there was to be a "burial of liberty" or some other equally foolish ceremony. When, however, they saw the merchants separate peaceably, they marched through the streets hurrahing and whistling, but did no damage other than to break a few windows. Many of these merchants belonged to the Sons of Liberty, and, in order to secure a coöperation of merchants throughout the colonies, they resolved to appoint a special Committee of Correspondence. Those first appointed withdrew their names, fearing the consequences. Finally, however, the following fearless, radical, energetic men accepted: Isaac Sears, John Lamb, Gershom Mott, William Wiley, and Thomas Robinson. The names of the Philadelphia merchants were not added until November 14th, and those of Boston not until December 9th.

The 1st of November witnessed most unusual demonstrations against the obnoxious Stamp Act. Pennants were hoisted at half-mast, and bells were tolled continuously. During the day notices were posted in prominent places, giving warning that any recognition by a citizen of the validity of the stamps in current business transactions would result in injury to his person and his property. A placard was addressed to Lieutenant-governor Colden and delivered at the fort toward evening, warning him of his fate if he did not that night make solemn oath before a magistrate, and publish it to the people, that he would not execute the Stamp Act. Things seemed ominous. The crowds increased toward evening. Sailors came from the harbor, countrymen from the surrounding districts. The fort was strengthened by the arrival of troops from Turtle Bay; a strong guard was placed in the jail; and the cannon of the merchants of Copsy Battery, near the foot of Whitehall Street, was spiked by order of Colden. This last act did not tend to allay the anger of the populace. About seven o'clock an organized band of the Sons of Liberty, led by Isaac Sears, marched to the common and hung upon a gallows, rigged temporarily for the purpose, an effigy of Colden and one of the Devil whispering in the former's ear. In the hand of the Devil was a boot—being a satire upon the Earl of Bute, one of the staunch supporters of the Stamp Act. From the gallows they marched down Broadway to the fort, accompanied by a most formidable mob carrying candles and torches.

Another mob constructed an effigy of Colden and placed it upon a chair, which they paraded through the streets, at every other step riddling the effigy with bullets, by way of making it feel at home. When they arrived at what is now Wall Street, they stopped in front of the house of McEvers, the stamp distributor who had resigned, and gave three cheers. This mob swung the effigy within ten feet of the fort gate, and then called to the guard to fire. They then hurled bricks, stones, and epithets at the fort, yet without any result. Not a word was returned, Gage having very wisely given orders to that effect. The mob then broke into the lieutenant-governor's coachhouse, took out his coach, and paraded it to the common and back.

The fort fence facing Broadway had been torn down by the soldiers, to expose any assailants to the fire from the fort. This inflamed the mob. The boards were gathered together in a pile, and upon them were thrown coach, chair, gallows, effigies, and every movable thing that could be found in the stables, and the whole set on fire. It was intended that violence should end here, but no mob ever stops where the leaders intend it should stop. The rioters became unmanageable.

They broke into the house of Major James, who had been unwise enough to boast what he would do under given conditions, brought out everything that was in the house, and burned the whole in front of the door. They broke into his wine cellar, and drank to the dregs all it contained; the doors, partitions, and windows were knocked to pieces. They destroyed his conservatory and trampled down his fine gardens.

This practically ended the violence of the night. But next day the lieutenant-governor was informed that unless he surrendered the stamps the fort would be attacked that evening. He finally agreed that he would distribute no stamps but would leave the matter to be regulated by the governor, Sir Henry Moore. He stated, likewise, that he was willing to place them upon a man-of-war, if Captain Kennedy would receive them. This the captain declined to do, not wishing to offend the people. In a speech to the mob, Sears said: "We will have the papers within twenty-four hours." An assault was planned for Tuesday, November 5th, and the notices of such an assault were signed "The Sons of Neptune." They were going to attack the fort. Colden summoned Mayor Cruger and some of the more prominent citizens to the fort. A conference was held, and as a result the following placard was posted conspicuously:

"The governor acquainted Judge Livingston, the mayor, Mr. Beverly Robinson, and Mr. John Stevens, this morning, being Monday, the 4th of November, that he would not issue, nor suffer to be issued, any of the stamps now in Fort George.

ROBERT R. LIVINGSTON,<br>
JOHN CRUGER,<br>
BEVERLY ROBINSON,<br>
JOHN STEVENS.

The Freemen, Freeholders, and Inhabitants of this city, being satisfied that the stamps are not to be issued, are determined to keep the peace of the city, at all events, except they should have other causes of complaint."

Before night, however, notices were posted directly under the above, in all the public places, inviting a meeting in the "Fields" on Tuesday evening, November 5th, and requesting every man to come round for the purpose of storming the fort. On Tuesday morning, November 5th, Colden wrote the Marquis of Granby: "I expect the fort will be stormed this night,—everything in my power is done to give them a warm reception. I hope not to dishonor the commission I have the honor to bear, and I trust I may merit some share of your Lordship's regard."

Mayor John Cruger came forward as the compromiser. Colden was urged to hand the stamped paper over to the corporation of the city. A deputation of merchants waited upon him to receive his reply. He hesitated, pleading his oath to the king and the great contempt into which the government would fall by concession. He was advised to yield. By four o'clock, a large crowd had collected about the City Hall to learn results. The mayor and the aldermen went to the fort and warned Colden of the danger of further delay. Colden appealed to General Gage for counsel. Gage replied that a fire from the fort would be the signal for an insurrection and the beginning of a civil war. Colden promised that the stamped paper should be surrendered to the corporation. The mayor and aldermen, accompanied by a prodigious concourse of people of all ranks, soon after proceeded to the fort gate, and received the papers. Three cheers were given by the crowd, after seeing the paper taken to the City Hall, and peace was restored to the city.

When the news of the passage of the Stamp Act reached Maryland, the Assembly was not in session. Governor Sharpe deemed it advisable not to summon a meeting of that body, fearing the radical action it might take. Nevertheless, the people found a medium for the expression of their feelings in the *Maryland Gazette*, then the only newspaper in the province, and Charles Carroll of Carrollton, William Paca, and other distinguished citizens vigorously

Mary White Morris.

Robert Morris.

*From the original paintings by Charles Willson Peale, now in Independence Hall, Philadelphia.*

opposed the act. Zachariah Hood, a native of the colony, while in England had been appointed stamp distributor. When he arrived at Annapolis, he received much the same reception that stamp distributors had met with in other colonies. He was "flogged, hanged, and burned in effigy" in several towns and in other ways insulted. In spite of this unmistakable evidence of the temper of the people, Hood persisted in retaining the office. The mob tore down his house in Annapolis, and he was compelled to flee to New York. Governor Sharpe admitted to Lord Halifax that it would require a military force to protect Hood and that if the stamps were then to arrive an attempt would be made to burn them.

Sharpe asked military protection of General Gage for the stamp distributor, but the Sons of Liberty moved more rapidly than the governor. Hood was captured and taken before a magistrate. He was made to swear to resign and never take part in the execution of the Stamp Act. The stamped paper for Maryland arrived shortly afterward on the sloop-of-war *Hawke*, but as there was no authorized person to receive it, and as the populace was threatening, it was shipped back to England.

Sharpe next called an Assembly. A proposition from the Assembly of Massachusetts for a general congress of representatives from the colonies to consider the existing state of affairs and join in a memorial to England was unanimously approved by both houses and the governor. Furthermore, on the 28th of September, a committee of the Assembly reported a set of resolutions in the nature of a bill of rights. It was declaratory of "the constitutional rights and privileges of the freemen of the province." There is no mistaking the drift of these resolutions. They are short, but right to the point, and assert unequivocally the claim of the colonists of Maryland to the privileges and immunities of British subjects guaranteed in 1632 by the charter of Charles I. to Cecilius Calvert, Lord Baltimore. We have omitted the lengthy quotations from this charter appearing at the end of the third resolution. The resolutions were as follows:

I. *Resolved, unanimously*, That the first adventurers and settlers of this province of Maryland brought with them and transmitted to their posterity, and all other his Majesty's subjects since inhabiting in this province, all the liberties, privileges, franchises, and immunities, that at any time have been held, enjoyed, and possessed, by the people of Great Britain.

II. *Resolved, unanimously*, That it was granted by Magna Charta, and other the good laws and statutes of England, and confirmed by the Petition and Bill of Rights, that the subject should not be compelled to contribute to any tax, tallage, aid, or other like charges not set by common consent of Parliament.

III. *Resolved, unanimously*, That by royal charter, granted by his Majesty, king Charles I., in the eighth year of his reign and in the year of our Lord one thousand six hundred thirty and two, to Cecilius, then Lord Baltimore, it was, for the encouragement of people to transport themselves and families into this province, amongst other things, covenanted and granted by his said Majesty for himself, his heirs, and successors, as followeth . . .

IV. *Resolved*, That it is the *unanimous* opinion of this House, that the said charter is declaratory of the constitutional rights and privileges of the freemen of this province.

V. *Resolved, unanimously*, That trials by juries are the grand bulwark of liberty, the undoubted birthright of every Englishman, and consequently of every British subject in America; and that the erecting other jurisdictions for the trial of matters of fact, is unconstitutional, and renders the subject insecure in his liberty and property.

VI. *Resolved*, That it is the *unanimous* opinion of this House, that it cannot, with any truth or propriety, be said, that the freemen of this province of Maryland are represented in the British Parliament.

VII. *Resolved, unanimously,* That his Majesty's liege people of this ancient province have always enjoyed the right of being governed by laws to which they themselves have consented, in the articles of taxes and internal polity; and that the same hath never been forfeited, or any other way yielded up, but hath been constantly recognized by the king and people of Great Britain.

VIII. *Resolved,* That it is the *unanimous* opinion of this House, that the representatives of the freemen of this province, in their legislative capacity, together with the other part of the legislature, have the sole right to lay taxes and impositions on the inhabitants of this province, or their property and effects; and that the laying, imposing, levying or collecting, any tax on or from the inhabitants of Maryland, under cover of any other authority, is unconstitutional, and a direct violation of the rights of the freemen of this province.

When the 1st of November came and there was no stamped paper in the province, some persons were very much exercised as to how business was to be transacted legally. The Frederick County court settled that question in a peremptory way. It declared that its business could be transacted without the stamped paper. The clerk, out of form, declined to comply with the orders and was committed to prison for contempt of court. He was released, however, very soon after by purging himself of contempt. This example was followed by other courts, and there was no further interruption of business. A mock funeral was conducted in Fredericktown, at which the Stamp Act was the deceased, and an effigy of Hood, the late stamp officer, was the sole mourner. Burlesque addresses were delivered, and then both the deceased and mourner were buried.

When news of the probability of the passage of a Stamp Act by Parliament reached America, Pennsylvania resolved to send Benjamin Franklin to London as a colonial agent. There was some opposition on the part of the proprietary party to his going, and it was asserted that at least three-fourths of the inhabitants opposed it likewise. However, when the question was put to the people, he was elected. He immediately sailed for England. When the Stamp Act was brought up, he, with other representatives of American colonies, appealed to the minister and remonstrated against the tax.

During his presence in England on this mission, Franklin was summoned before a committee of the House of Commons. In answer to questions, he told them that the provisions of the Stamp Act requiring gold and silver in payment of stamped paper worked an injury to the colonists, inasmuch as gold and silver were scarce. Furthermore, the inacessible roads would prevent taking stamped paper into the interior country. He declared, furthermore, that the late war was really a British war, made in defence of British trade and commerce, and that the colonies had borne their just proportion of the expenses. He stated emphatically, also, that the whole attitude of America toward Great Britain before the enactment of the Stamp Act was one of friendliness and good will. He urged the repeal of the tax, if only to regain this good will.

He was asked whether the people of America would submit if the act were moderated, and replied that they would not submit. "May not a military force carry the Stamp Act into execution?" he was asked. His reply to this question was: "They will find nobody in arms. They cannot force a man to take stamps. They will not find a rebellion; they may, indeed, make one." He also made it clear to them that the Americans would refuse any kind of internal tax. He was asked what the colonists would do if an external tax were laid on the necessities of life. To this he replied: "I do not know a single article imported into the northern colonies but what they can either do without or make themselves." Franklin labored earnestly to prevent the law's being enacted, and when it was passed he wrote to a friend: "The sun of liberty is setting; you must light the candles of industry and economy."

Later, Franklin, having been asked to recommend a man for distributor in Pennsylvania, named his friend John Hughes. The latter was still acting in that capacity when the *Royal Charlotte* reached Philadelphia bringing stamped paper for Pennsylvania, Maryland, and New Jersey. Her arrival created considerable disturbance among the inhabitants. As she sailed up Delaware River, all the vessels in the harbor put their colors at half-mast, and the citizens draped the buildings throughout the city in mourning. Immediately thousands of people assembled to devise ways and means of preventing the distribution of the stamps. It was suggested that the resignation of Mr. Hughes should be requested. He was at once waited upon by a committee of gentlemen, but flatly refused to resign his office. Had it not been for illness in his family, the distributor might have been subjected to mob violence. He gave assurances, however, that he would not carry out the duties of his office until requested to do so by the people. The *Royal Charlotte* spent the winter in the Delaware, without unloading her cargo of stamps.

On the 31st of October, the day before the Stamp Act was to go into effect, the newspapers put on signs of mourning. The editors had resolved to discontinue their publications until means could be devised to avoid incurring the penalties incident to publishing without the necessary stamps. On November 7th a small sheet was published at the office of the *Pennsylvania Gazette*. It had no title or mark of distinction, and was headed merely *No Stamp Paper to be Had*. On November 14th another paper appeared, entitled *Remarkable Occurrences*, and on the 21st of the same month the regular publication of the paper was resumed. The public offices were closed in Pennsylvania from the 1st of November until after the news had been received in the following May of the intended repeal of the act. A number of merchants in Philadelphia signed the non-importation agreement, although such action was decidedly detrimental to their business interests. Prominent among these patriots was Robert Morris, of the prosperous firm of Willing and Morris. Although devotedly attached to the mother country, Morris staunchly opposed the Stamp Act.

The news of the passage of the Stamp Act had an effect upon the people of New Jersey entirely different from that which we have noted in the cases of other colonies. No outward show of lawlessness was made, and Governor William Franklin—illegitimate son of Benjamin Franklin—advised the crown officials that the spirit of resistance, though not manifesting itself in mob violence, was nevertheless alert and determined. The chief stamp officer, William Coxe, resigned, and the local stamp officer for Salem was forced out of office. Furthermore, the lawyers of New Jersey organized, and at Perth Amboy, on the 19th of September, before the Stamp Act was to go into effect, they resolved that they would not make use of the stamps for any purpose or under any circumstances. They furthermore resolved that they would not practise their profession until April 7, 1766.

The Sons of Liberty were organized in New Jersey by February, 1766, and they euphemistically advertised their determination to resist the Stamp Act by swearing to "support the British Constitution." The representatives and members of this organization from the eastern and western divisions of that province requested the lawyers "to proceed to business as usual without stamps." They requested them likewise to use their influence "to open the courts of justice as soon as possible." The lawyers replied that they would resume their practice by the 1st of April, if they did not hear from Parliament by that time. Furthermore, that unless the Stamp Act were repealed or suspended, they would unite with the Sons of Liberty in their opposition to it.

The Grenville ministry had fallen in July, 1765, and had been succeeded by that of Rockingham. Parliament met on December 17, 1765, when Grenville and Bedford strongly urged the continuance of the tax and insisted that no relaxation or indulgence should be granted to the colonists. Pitt, on the other hand, rose from a sickbed and urged the repeal. Conway, who had all along fought the Stamp Act, was now secretary of state for the colonies. He brought in a bill for the repeal of the act on the ground that it had interrupted British commerce and jeopardized British merchants. He also told Parliament that unless the act were repealed, Spain and France would declare war. Jenkinson urged modification of the act. After Edmund Burke had answered Jenkinson, Pitt arose and delivered a speech of extraordinary eloquence, which had great effect on both sides of the Atlantic.

Arrayed against the repeal were the king, the queen, the princess-dowager, the Duke of York, Lord Bute, and other influential personages of the kingdom. Bedford predicted the defeat of the ministry. On the day of voting, the lobbies of the House were crammed. Three hundred merchants waited anxiously for the resolution of the House. Repeal would mean greater business; a continuance of the tax might jeopardize their very livelihood. When the vote was taken on the first reading of the bill for repeal, February 22, 1766, two hundred and seventy-five were for and one hundred and sixty-seven against repeal. After the result was announced, "the roof of St. Stephen's rung with the long continued shouts and cheerings of the majority." Conway was surrounded by the joyous populace as their deliverer, while Grenville, mortified, passed in a rage, amid the hisses of the people. Pitt was the god of the hour. In the final vote on March 17, 1766, two hundred and fifty were for, while one hundred and fifty were against repeal. The next day the bill was brought before the House of Lords, where it was finally carried. All those who voted for repeal did so at the cost of the king's favor. Bedford declared: "We have been beaten, but we made a gallant fight." Burke described it as "an event that caused more universal joy throughout the British dominions than perhaps any other that can be remembered."

Coincident with the repeal of the Stamp Act, Parliament asserted in the strongest and most unrestricted form the sovereignty of the British Legislature. This was done first of all by resolutions and then by a Declaratory Act. The latter affirmed the right of Parliament to make laws binding the British colonies "in all cases whatever." The votes of the colonial Assemblies which had denied Parliament the right of taxing them were condemned as unlawful. When the news of the repeal of the Stamp Act, March 18, 1766, reached New York, the joy of the people was unbounded. On June 23d the Assembly ordered a statue erected in Wall Street in honor of William Pitt. It was to serve as "a public testimony of the many eminent services he had rendered to America, particularly in promoting the repeal of the Stamp Act." George III. was to be honored, likewise, by an equestrian statue, and John Sargent, agent of the colony in London, by a piece of plate. The king's statue was erected on the Battery on August 21, 1770, and remained there until 1776. In the disturbance of that year it was pulled down and cast into musket-balls for the defence of liberty against the assaults of the one in whose honor it had been erected.

June 4, 1766, the king's birthday, was celebrated by the erection of a mast or liberty pole "to his most gracious Majesty, George III., Mr. Pitt, and Liberty." The provincial officials, civil and military, from the governor down, mingled with the people in their festivities. "An ox was roasted on each side of the common; a large stage was built up, on which were placed twenty-five barrels of strong beer, a hogshead of rum, with sugar and other materials to make punch. At another part of the field were preparations for a bon-fire; twenty-five cords of wood surrounded a pole, on the top of which were affixed twelve tar-barrels. At the upper end of the field were placed five-and-twenty pieces of cannon; a flag displayed the colors of Great Britain, and a band of music played *God save the King*."

In Philadelphia, the master of the ship bringing the good news was presented with a gold-laced hat. Bonfires illuminated the town, and the people generally showed their joy by consuming vast quantities of beer. A banquet was held, the governor and other dignitaries being present. It is significant that it was not until at the close of the banquet that the diners voted unanimously that, on the 4th of June, the king's birthday, everyone should give his homespun to the poor, and dress himself in clothes of British manufacture. In the Lower Counties [Delaware], the rejoicing at the repeal of the act was but "equalled by the depression upon its passage." A somewhat florid address to the king was drawn up by Cæsar Rodney and Thomas McKean. The announcement of the repeal of the Stamp Act in Maryland was celebrated, as in other colonies, by bonfires, the firing of guns, and the giving of banquets. The healths of Pitt, Barré, and Camden were drunk in "portentous quantities of punch," and even Zachariah Hood was permitted to return to Annapolis and ply his legitimate vocation.

The passage of the Stamp Act and its subsequent repeal are two of the most important events in the history of Great Britain in her relation to the American colonies. The passage of the act was the natural result of the French and Indian War; its repeal was but the postponement for less than a decade of the final clash between two opposing theories of governmental control. From the point of view of George III. and his ministry, it would have been better by far not to have repealed the Stamp Act. The claim of Parliament to the prerogative of taxing the colonies for their own support was bound to clash with the opposing claim of the provincial Assemblies to be themselves the sole depositories of that prerogative. The surrender of Parliament on March 18, 1766, but made its position in 1775 the more difficult. Had Parliament not surrendered in 1766, the issue would have been met at that time fairly and squarely. It is impossible to prophesy what would have been the result had the American Revolution been precipitated in 1766 instead of 1775. And, in fact, there is no great certainty that the opposition to the Parliamentary claim to sovereignty in colonial taxation would have gone to the extent of open rebellion. The position of England, however, at the former date was relatively much stronger than at the latter date, and that of the colonies relatively weaker.

The Middle colonies were destined to play a most important part in the struggle for independence. Centrally situated on the Atlantic seaboard, they were to serve as so many territorial links connecting the New England with the Southern colonies. For this reason, largely, they were to become the theatre of war and were to bear the brunt of the conflict. Early in the struggle, possession of the Champlain-Hudson valley was to be the object sought by the British forces. Once this strategic line could be secured, it would be only a short time before New England and the Southern colonies would be defeated in detail. The Middle colonies once secured and the two extremes of the disaffected territory separated, resistance to the victorious armies of the invader could not be long sustained.

We have traced the development of the Middle colonies from their first settlement to the repeal of the Stamp Act. We have seen how diverse were the social elements entering into the life of these colonies. Notwithstanding this fact, we have observed how readily they combined to offer a united opposition to the Stamp Act in 1765. During the next ten years, this germ of national unity developed with remarkable rapidity until it reached its second state in the Declaration of Independence. An account of the events of this period, however, forms a logical part of the history of the American Revolution.

From the point of view of the colonies, the repeal of the act was a great victory and carried with it momentous results. The colonial opposition to the act was only in line with a long series of precedents. It mattered not what external forces claimed the prerogative of laying taxes upon the colonies, the Assemblies were in duty bound to oppose that claim. It was well for them that the final crisis did not come until a later date. The decade intervening was one of important developments. The Declaratory Act, the Trade Acts, and finally the Boston Port Bill, gradually alienated the colonies from the mother country. What is more to the point, they slowly but surely furnished the motive for a closer union. Again, the colonies were much stronger in 1775 than in 1766, and the successful ending of Pontiac's war had removed the last semblance of danger from an external foe. During the decade a truce was patched up between the two contending theories of governmental control; but it was not to be of long duration. The French and Indian War had served as a military training school for men who were to play the most important rôles in the drama of the American Revolution. The period from 1766 to 1775 furnished them with the opportunity of perfecting themselves in the parts they were to play in the struggle from which were to emerge " The United States of America."

# CHRONOLOGICAL TABLE

| DATE | | PAGE |
|---|---|---|
| 1609. | Hudson entered North River of New Netherland . . . . . . . . . . . | 6 |
| 1610. | Dutch fur trade established on the Hudson . | 7 |
| | Sir Samuel Argall visited and named Delaware Bay . . . . . . . . . . | 40 |
| 1611. | Block established a trading station on Manhattan Island . . . . . . . . | 7 |
| 1613. | Dutch title to Manhattan first disputed by England . . . . . . . . . | 8, 60 |
| 1614. | "New Netherland" first so named . . . . | 8 |
| | Forts Nassau and Amsterdam erected in the Hudson . . . . . . . . . . | 9 |
| | Trade monopoly granted to United New Netherland Company . . . . . . | 40 |
| 1617. | Treaty of peace made between the Dutch and the Five Nations . . . . . . . | 10 |
| | Bergen, New Jersey, founded . . . . . | 242 |
| 1620. | New Jersey included in the patent of the Council for New England . . . . . | 241 |
| 1621. | England disputed Dutch occupancy of the Hudson and Delaware valleys . . . | 60 |
| 1623. | Fort Nassau (Gloucester, New Jersey) erected | 15 |
| | Dutch established a colony on the Delaware | 41 |
| | The Walloons settled in New Netherland | 15, 180 |
| 1625. | Negro slaves first imported into New Amsterdam . . . . . . . . . . | 336 |
| 1626. | Manhattan Island purchased by the Dutch . | 16 |

509

| DATE  | | PAGE |
|---|---|---|
| 1626. | The Dutch attacked by the Mohawks . . . | 17 |
| 1629. | Patroonship established in New Netherland . . . . . . . . . . | 21, 41 |
| 1630. | Staten Island purchased . . . . . . . | 23 |
| 1631. | Dutch settlements on the Delaware destroyed | 235 |
| 1632. | Charter granted to Lord Baltimore of Delaware and part of Pennsylvania . . . | 60 |
|       | Charter of Maryland granted to Lord Baltimore . . . . . . . . . . . | 214 |
| 1633. | Roman Catholic colony settled by Lord Baltimore in Maryland . . . . . . . | 196 |
| 1634. | Troubles between the Dutch and the Raritan Indians composed by treaty . . . . | 26 |
|       | Charter of Long Island, New Jersey, Maryland, Delaware, and Pennsylvania granted | 61 |
|       | The first colonial settlement made in Maryland, at St. Mary's . . . . . . . | 217 |
|       | New Jersey included in the Palatine grant of New Albion . . . . . . . . . | 241 |
| 1635. | First naval engagement fought on inland waters of America . . . . . . . . . | 221 |
|       | First Assembly of Maryland met . . . . | 224 |
| 1638. | Swedish colony established on the Delaware at Christina (Wilmington) . . . . . | 45 |
|       | New Haven colonists founded Milford (Newark) New Jersey . . . . . . . | 248 |
| 1640. | Dutch colony settled under Swedish patronage on the Delaware (New Castle County) | 47 |
|       | New Haven colonists acquired lands on the Delaware . . . . . . . . . . | 243 |
| 1641. | Colony of New Englanders settled on the Delaware at Varkin's Kill (Salem) and Passayunk (Philadelphia) . . . . | 49, 63 |
|       | Jesuits discriminated against in Maryland . . | 197 |
| 1642. | The Dutch expelled the English colonists on the Delaware and the Schuylkill . . . | 63 |

## CHRONOLOGICAL TABLE

| DATE | | PAGE |
|---|---|---|
| 1642. | Puritan refugees from New England migrated to New Netherland | 183 |
| 1643. | Indians at Pavonia and Corlear's Hook slaughtered by the Dutch | 33 |
| 1645. | Peace treaty signed by Dutch and Indians at Fort Amsterdam | 35 |
| | Baltimore's government overthrown in Maryland | 223 |
| 1646. | First Swedish church erected in America, on Tinicum Island | 52 |
| | First Lutheran church built in Pennsylvania | 192 |
| | Lord Baltimore regained government of Maryland | 229 |
| 1647. | Popular representation established in New Netherland | 94 |
| 1648. | The Swedes attacked the Dutch settlement on the Schuylkill | 103 |
| 1649. | Roman Catholic worship prohibited in Maryland | 198 |
| | Providence (Anne Arundel) settled by Congregationalists | 228 |
| | Toleration Act passed in Maryland | 229 |
| 1650. | Treaty made between New Netherland and New England as to rights of settlement on the Delaware | 69 |
| | New Netherland gained popular rights from the States General | 124 |
| | Boundary between New Netherland and New England defined | 132 |
| | Bicameral legislature established in Maryland | 233 |
| 1651. | New Haven Delaware colonizing expedition arrested by Dutch at New Amsterdam | 69, 86 |
| | Lord Baltimore's rights to Maryland disputed by Cromwell | 230 |
| 1653. | Municipal government established for New Amsterdam | 125 |

| DATE | | PAGE |
|---|---|---|
| 1654. | The Swedes captured Dutch fort (Casimir) on the Delaware. | 107 |
| 1655. | The Swedish power on the Delaware overthrown by the Dutch | 111 |
| | Long Island revolted against the Dutch | 131 |
| | Dutch colonists massacred by Algonquins | 151 |
| | Jews allowed to settle in New Netherland | 194 |
| | Insurrectionary battle fought in Maryland | 231 |
| 1657. | Quakers expelled from Boston settled in New Amsterdam | 187 |
| | The Lutherans opposed by the Dutch authorities of New Amsterdam | 192 |
| 1658. | Maryland adopted repressive measures against Quakers | 188 |
| | Lord Baltimore's proprietary rights in Maryland restored | 232 |
| 1660. | Second emigration made by Walloons to the New World | 180 |
| 1662. | Mennonites established on South River | 190 |
| | Waldenses settled on Staten Island | 195 |
| 1663. | Dutch colonists of Esopus massacred by Indians | 151 |
| | First settlement of Quakers in New Jersey | 188 |
| 1664. | New Netherland surrendered to England | 144 |
| | Treaty of peace made between Dutch and Algonquins | 152 |
| | Boundary between New York and Connecticut defined | 161 |
| | New Jersey granted to Lord John Berkeley and Sir George Carteret | 241, 245 |
| | Elizabeth Town patent granted | 244 |
| | First school established in New Jersey | 376 |
| 1665. | Witchcraft persecution discouraged in New York | 159 |
| | New Jersey government constituted | 246 |

## CHRONOLOGICAL TABLE

| DATE | | PAGE |
|---|---|---|
| 1667. | New Netherland finally ceded to English by Treaty of Breda . . . . . . . . | 158 |
| 1668. | The Dutch "burgher" distinctions abolished in New York province . . . . . . | 163 |
| | First Assembly of New Jersey met . . . | 250 |
| 1670. | Long Island towns rebelled . . . . . . | 165 |
| 1672. | Mail service established between New York and Boston . . . . . . . . . | 170 |
| 1673. | New York surrendered to the Dutch . . . | 167 |
| | Quaker proprietorship of New Jersey acquired | 188 |
| | New Netherland obtained New Jersey settlements . . . . . . . . . . | 252 |
| 1674. | New York province restored to England . . | 169 |
| | Retrocession of New Jersey settlements to England . . . . . . . . . . | 252 |
| | Sir George Carteret received new grant of New Jersey . . . . . . . . . | 253 |
| | Penn and his associates acquired half-interest in West Jersey . . . . . . . . | 254 |
| 1675. | Salem, New Jersey, founded . . . . . . | 188 |
| 1676. | East and West Jersey created independent provinces . . . . . . . . . . | 252, 255 |
| 1677. | Burlington, New Jersey, founded by Quakers | 189 |
| | Popular government established in West Jersey . . . . . . . . . . . | 256 |
| 1680. | New York claimed control of New Jersey . | 241 |
| | Duke of York relinquished all claim to New Jersey . . . . . . . . . . | 253 |
| | The Jerseys became independent of New York . . . . . . . . . . . | 259 |
| 1681. | Charter of Pennsylvania granted to Penn . | 189, 265 |
| | Penn and others purchased East Jersey . . | 255 |
| | Penn's first colonists arrived in the Delaware | 267 |
| 1682. | The "Territories" on the Delaware separated from New York . . . . . . | 160 |
| | First church erected in New Jersey . . . | 244 |

| DATE  |                                                                                  | PAGE |
|-------|----------------------------------------------------------------------------------|------|
| 1682. | Penn's government established . . . .269,                                        | 270  |
|       | Penn's treaty made with the Delaware Indians                                     | 273  |
|       | Penn's first Assembly held at Chester. . .                                       | 274  |
| 1683. | First legislature met in New York province 155,                                  | 176  |
|       | First permanent Society of Friends in North America established at Germantown .  | 191  |
|       | Colony of Labadists settled in Maryland. .                                       | 196  |
|       | First school established in Pennsylvania . .                                     | 278  |
|       | Germantown colony, Pennsylvania, established . . . . . . . . . . .               | 407  |
|       | Boundary between Maryland and Pennsylvania disputed . . . . . . . .              | 450  |
| 1685. | Boundary line between the grants of Penn and Baltimore fixed . . . . . . .       | 239  |
|       | First printing press operated in Pennsylvania                                    | 415  |
|       | Eastern boundary of Maryland determined .                                        | 428  |
| 1687. | Boundary line established for East and West Jersey. . . . . . . . . . .          | 255  |
| 1688. | Proprietary rights in New Jersey surrendered to the crown . . . . . . . . .      | 261  |
|       | New York and New Jersey incorporated in United New England . . . . .             | 286  |
|       | Peace conference held at Albany between the English and the confederacy of the Five Nations . . . . . . . . . | 288  |
| 1689. | The "Lower Counties" of Pennsylvania separated from the province . . . .         | 281  |
|       | Political union of New York and New Jersey severed . . . . . . . . .             | 293  |
|       | Maryland revolted against the proprietary government . . . . . . . . .           | 306  |
| 1690. | People of Schenectady massacred by French and Indians . . . . . . . . 33,        | 299  |
|       | Congress of English colonial delegates for united defence against the French and Indians held at New York . . . . | 300  |

CHRONOLOGICAL TABLE 515

| DATE | | PAGE |
|---|---|---|
| 1691. | Maryland transferred to the crown of England | 239 |
| | Leisler and Milborne executed in New York | 304 |
| | New York engaged in military operations against Canada | 311 |
| 1693. | Pennsylvania and Delaware politically annexed to New York | 312 |
| | East Jersey enacted a general school law | 328, 376 |
| | Bradford established his printing place in New York | 346 |
| 1695. | Pennsylvania restored to Penn's proprietorship | 313 |
| 1696. | Roman Catholic disabilities imposed in Pennsylvania | 196 |
| | King William School founded at Annapolis | 441 |
| 1697. | Trinity Church, New York, founded | 321 |
| 1700. | Religious disability enacted in Maryland | 332 |
| 1702. | New Jersey annexed to New York | 242 |
| | Pennsylvania severed political union with the Lower Counties (Delaware) | 318 |
| | East and West Jersey became a royal province | 328 |
| | Religious toleration enacted in Maryland | 421 |
| 1709. | Paper money issued in New Jersey | 331 |
| 1710. | The Palatines settled on the Hudson and in New York | 202 |
| | Palatines first settled in Maryland | 205 |
| 1712. | Negro insurrection occurred in New York | 333 |
| | Population of Maryland estimated | 424 |
| 1715. | Laws of Maryland codified | 425 |
| | Term of service of indented servants regulated in Maryland | 441 |
| 1717. | Palatine colony first settled in Pennsylvania | 205 |
| 1719. | First newspaper published in Pennsylvania | 415 |
| 1720. | Population of New York province estimated | 335 |

| DATE | | PAGE |
|---|---|---|
| 1722. | Trading post established at Oswego | 342 |
| | Conference of colonial governors with sachems of Five Nations at Albany | 342 |
| 1725. | First newspaper published in New York | 416 |
| 1729. | Public library established in New York City | 343 |
| | Franklin advocated a paper currency | 411 |
| | "Baltimore Town" founded | 427 |
| 1730. | New city charter granted to New York | 343 |
| 1731. | Connecticut and New York boundary settled | 344 |
| | Philadelphia Library founded | 413 |
| 1732. | Franklin began the publication of *Poor Richard's Almanac* | 413 |
| 1734. | Moravian settlement made in Georgia | 208 |
| 1735. | Freedom of the press vindicated in the trial of Zenger in New York | 349 |
| 1738. | New Jersey separated from New York | 373 |
| | Population of New Jersey | 375 |
| 1739. | Governor Keith, of Pennsylvania, advised taxation by Great Britain of American colonies | 402 |
| 1741. | Maryland proprietary rights restored | 239 |
| | New York terrorized by negro plot | 353 |
| 1742. | Mühlenberg appointed to the head of the Lutheran Church in Pennsylvania | 192 |
| 1745. | Louisburg captured | 361 |
| | Saratoga destroyed by the French and Indians | 362 |
| 1746. | Population of New York City enumerated | 336 |
| | Charter granted for the College of New Jersey | 366 |
| | Princeton College established | 378 |
| 1748. | Jews granted extended privileges under the British in New York | 194 |
| | Louisburg retroceded to France | 362 |
| 1751. | Academy (later the University of Pennsylvania) for higher education founded in Philadelphia | 415 |

| DATE | | PAGE |
|---|---|---|
| 1751. | The British Parliament restricted the issuing of bills of credit in the northern colonies | 416 |
| | Boundary disputes between Maryland and Pennsylvania adjusted . . . . . . | 434 |
| 1752. | Population and houses of Baltimore . . . | 428 |
| 1754. | King's College (Columbia University) chartered . . . . . . . . . . . | 365 |
| | Conference of colonial governors with Six Nations at Albany . . . . . . . | 447 |
| | A plan of colonial union adopted at Albany . . . . . . . . . . . | 450 |
| | French victory over British under Washington at Fort Necessity . . . . . . | 454 |
| 1755. | The Acadians removed to Maryland . . . | 207 |
| | Braddock defeated at Monongahela River . . | 457 |
| | French defeated at Lake George . . . . | 460 |
| 1757. | College of New Jersey finally located at Princeton . . . . . . . . . . | 366 |
| | Massacre of the garrison of Fort William Henry . . . . . . . . . . . | 461 |
| 1758. | Treaty with Indians made by Governor of New Jersey at Easton, Pennsylvania . | 374 |
| | Fort Du Quesne captured from the French . | 458 |
| | Louisburg captured . . . . . . . . | 463 |
| 1759. | Fort Niagara captured . . . . . . . | 465 |
| | Quebec surrendered . . . . . . . . | 465 |
| | Ticonderoga and Crown Point evacuated by the French . . . . . . . . . | 465 |
| 1760. | Montreal surrendered . . . . . . . . | 466 |
| | Boundary settlement made between Pennsylvania and Maryland . . . . . . | 469 |
| 1763. | Mason and Dixon line surveyed . . . . | 470 |
| | Plan of taxation of American colonies considered by British Cabinet . . . . . | 479 |
| | Colonial agents advised of proposed taxation of colonies . . . . . . . . . . | 480 |

| DATE | | PAGE |
|---|---|---|
| 1764. | News of proposed Stamp Act reached the colonies | 481 |
| | New York Assembly protested against the proposed Stamp Act | 481 |
| | Franklin sent to England to protest against Stamp Act legislation | 499 |
| 1765. | Census of churches in New Jersey | 378 |
| | American Stamp Act passed | 484 |
| | Middle and Southern colonies opposed the Stamp Act | 488 |
| | The New England stamp distributors forced to resign | 488 |
| | Stamp Act Congress assembled in New York | 489 |
| | Non-importation agreement signed by New York merchants | 492 |
| | Philadelphia and Boston merchants signed non-importation agreement | 493 |
| | Citizens of New York compelled the lieutenant-governor to surrender the stamps | 496 |
| | The Maryland Assembly answered the Stamp Act by a declaration of rights | 497 |
| 1766. | Charter granted for Queen's College (Rutgers) | 367 |
| | The Stamp Act repealed | 503 |
| | George III. and Pitt honored by statues in New York in commemoration of repeal of Stamp Act | 504 |
| 1769. | Law enacted in Maryland as to transported felons | 444 |
| 1782. | First Bible printed in America, at Philadelphia | 416 |
| 1797. | Baltimore incorporated as a city | 428 |

# LIST OF ILLUSTRATIONS

## VOLUME IV

FACING PAGE

Hannah Penn. *Water-color facsimile after the original painting by Joseph Wright in Independence Hall, Philadelphia* . .

William Penn. *Water-color facsimile after the original painting by Joseph Wright in Independence Hall, Philadelphia* . . *title*

Letter stating that Manhattan Island had been purchased from the "wild men" for the value of sixty guilders. *From the original in the Royal Archives at The Hague, Holland* . . 16

Document signed by Peter Stuyvesant. *From the original in the Myers Collection, Lenox Branch of the New York Public Library*. . . . . . . . . . . . . . . 33

Nicolas J. Visscher's map, issued about 1655, showing the second published view of Manhattan Island as it appeared in 1640. *From the original in the New York Public Library, Lenox Branch* . . . . . . . . . . . . . . . 37

Engraved copy of Lindström's map of New Sweden. *The original of which is in the Royal Library, Stockholm* . . . . 49

Fenwick's address to those minded to plant within his Colony of New Cesarea, or New Jersey. *From the original in possession of the Historical Society of Pennsylvania* . . . . 64

Map of the town of Mannados, or Manhattan, as it was in September, 1661. The earliest extant English map of New York, known as "The Duke's Plan." *From the MS. in the Geographical and Topographical Collection in the British Museum* . . . . . . . . . . . . . . 81

## MIDDLE STATES AND MARYLAND

FACING PAGE

First engraved view of New Amsterdam, showing Manhattan Island as it was in 1630. *From a copperplate published at Amsterdam in 1651, now in the New York Public Library, Lenox Branch* . . . . . . . . . . . . . 97

Title-page of the *Charter of Liberties and Exemptions*, dated 1629, which attempted to transplant to America the feudal tenure and burdens of Continental Europe. *From the original in the New York Public Library, Lenox Branch* . . 112

Title-pages of the earliest separate printed account in English of New York, and of the first comprehensive account of the colony. *From the originals in the Columbia University Library*. . . . . . . . . . . . . . . 117

Document, dated 1673, relative to the surrender of New York to the Dutch. *From the original in the New York Public Library*. . . . . . . . . . . . . . . . 124

Peter Stuyvesant. *From the painting in possession of Peter Stuyvesant, Esq.* . . . . . . . . . . . . . 144

Early broadside relating to King William's War, issued September 12, 1696. *From the original in the New York Public Library*. . . . . . . . . . . . . . . . 160

Map of Maryland in 1635. *From the original in the New York Public Library, Lenox Branch* . . . . . . . . . 181

Title-page of Alsop's *Character of the Province of Maryland. From the original in the New York Public Library, Lenox Branch* . . . . . . . . . . . . . . . . 188

Sir George Calvert, first Baron Baltimore. *From a copy in the State House at Annapolis after the original by Daniel Mytens the Elder, now in possession of the Earl of Verulam at Gorhambury, England* . . . . . . . . . . . . 192

Broadside: a law of Maryland concerning religion (the Maryland Toleration Act). *From the original in the New York Public Library, Lenox Branch* . . . . . . . . . . . 197

Autograph letter, dated January 13, 1755, from Horatio Sharpe, Governor of Maryland, to Robert Hunter Morris, Governor of Pennsylvania. *From the original in the Emmet Collection* 204

Charles Calvert, third Lord Baltimore. *From the painting by Thomas Sully after an original attributed to Van Dyke, but probably by Kneller, now in the Philadelphia Academy of the Fine Arts. The Sully is now in possession of the Maryland Historical Society* . . . . . . . . . . . . 213

## LIST OF ILLUSTRATIONS

FACING PAGE

Letter of Frederick Calvert, sixth, and last, Lord Baltimore. *From the original in possession of the Historical Society of Pennsylvania* . . . . . . . . . . . . . 220

Letter of Cecil Calvert, second Lord Baltimore. *From the original in possession of the Historical Society of Pennsylvania* . 229

Augustine Hermann. *From the original painting in possession of Mrs. Hermann Massey* . . . . . . . . . 236

Early German map, dating probably from the latter part of the seventeenth century, showing the division line between East and West Jersey. *From the original in the private collection of Julius F. Sachse, Esq.* . . . . . . . . . . 241

Title-pages of one of the earliest tracts, and of the first comprehensive account of New Jersey. *From the originals in the New York Public Library, Lenox Branch* . . . . . 257

William Franklin, Governor of New Jersey. *From the original painting in possession of Dr. Thomas Hewson Bache, of Philadelphia* . . . . . . . . . . . . . 272

Mrs. Franklin, his second wife. *From the original painting in possession of Dr. Thomas Hewson Bache, of Philadelphia* . 272

Title and first page of Penn's *Frame of Government*. *From the original in possession of the Historical Society of Pennsylvania* . . . . . . . . . . . . . . 277

Sir William Keith, Governor of Pennsylvania. *Photogravure after the miniature presented to the Historical Society of Pennsylvania by W. A. Whitehead, Esq.* . . . . . . 284

Lady Keith. *Photogravure after the miniature presented to the Historical Society of Pennsylvania by W. A. Whitehead, Esq.* 284

Manuscript list of debtors to the estate of Colonel Francis Lovelace, signed by Sir Edmund Andros. *From the original in the Emmet Collection* . . . . . . . . . . . 289

Proclamation by Governor Bellomont regarding cursing, swearing, Sabbath breaking, etc., dated April 2, 1698. *From the original in the New York Public Library, Lenox Branch* . . 304

Title-page of the first American Bible, and portrait of Robert Aitken, the publisher of it. *From the originals in possession of the Historical Society of Pennsylvania* . . . . . 308

James Logan. *After the painting now in Independence Hall, Philadelphia* . . . . . . . . . . . . . 317

## MIDDLE STATES AND MARYLAND

FACING PAGE

David Rittenhouse. *From the painting by Charles Willson Peale, in possession of the American Philosophical Society* . . . . 317

Title-pages of two important early works relating to the provinces of New Jersey and Pennsylvania. *From the originals in the New York Public Library, Lenox Branch* . . . . 321

Map of Pennsylvania and West Jersey, engraved by Philip Lea. *From Gabriel Thomas's "Account of Pennsylvania," the original of which is in the New York Public Library, Lenox Branch* . . . . . . . . . . . . . . . 336

Proclamation relating to two scandalous songs or ballads. *After the original in the New York Public Library, Lenox Branch* 353

The two scandalous songs which figured in the Zenger-Cosby trouble. *After the original in the New York Public Library, Lenox Branch* . . . . . . . . . . . . 353

Title-pages of two very early works relating to the settlements on Delaware River. *From the originals in the New York Public Library, Lenox Branch* . . . . . . . . . 369

Early issues of New Jersey, New York, and Delaware paper currency, including an indented bill. *From the originals in the New York Public Library, Lenox Branch* . . . . . . 384

Two rare works on Pennsylvania. *From the originals in the New York Public Library* . . . . . . . . . . 389

The armor portrait of William Penn. *From the painting presented to the Historical Society of Pennsylvania by Granville Penn in 1833* . . . . . . . . . . . . . 396

First and last pages of the prospectus of the Frankfurt Company. *From the original in possession of the Historical Society of Pennsylvania* . . . . . . . . . . 401

John Penn, called the American. *From the painting attributed to Sir Godfrey Kneller. The original of which is now in possession of the Historical Society of Pennsylvania* . . . 405

John Penn, son of Thomas Penn. *From the painting by Robert Edge Pine. The original of which is now in possession of the Historical Society of Pennsylvania* . . . . . . . 405

Richard Penn, the Proprietary. *From the painting by Robert Wilson. The original of which is now in possession of the Historical Society of Pennsylvania* . . . . . . . . 405

# LIST OF ILLUSTRATIONS

FACING PAGE

Patrick Gordon, Governor of Pennsylvania. *From the painting now in possession of the Historical Society of Pennsylvania* . 412

Philip John Schuyler. *From the miniature by Trumbull, in possession of Yale University* . . . . . . . . . . 416

James Hamilton, Governor of Pennsylvania. *From the painting by Benjamin West, now hanging in Independence Hall, Philadelphia* . . . . . . . . . . . . . . 436

Map of the frontiers of the northern colonies, with the boundary line established between them and the Indians in the treaty made by Sir William Johnson at Fort Stanwix in 1768. *From the collection of George Barrie, Jr.* . . . . . 445

Sir William Johnson. *From the painting in the Château de Ramezay, Montreal* . . . . . . . . . . . 449

Letter in relation to Indian affairs written by Sir William Johnson to Governor James De Lancey of the province of New York, June 13, 1755. *From the original in the Emmet Collection* . 453

Hendrick, chief of the Mohawk Indians in alliance with the British forces, after an engraving issued in London *circa* 1750. *From the original in the Emmet Collection* . . . 460

General James Clinton. *From the pastel by James Sharpless, now in Independence Hall* . . . . . . . . . . 464

William Paca. *After the painting by John B. Bordley. From the original in the State House, Annapolis* . . . . . . 475

Charles Carroll of Carrollton. *After the painting by Thomas Sully. From the original in the State House, Annapolis* . . 475

Andrew Hamilton. *After the painting by Adolf Ulrik Wertmüller* 480

Mary White Morris. *From the original painting by Charles Willson Peale, now in Independence Hall, Philadelphia* . 497

Robert Morris. *From the original painting by Charles Willson Peale, now in Independence Hall, Philadelphia* . . . . 497

# INDEX

ABERCROMBIE, 462-463
  Maj-Gen 460
ACRELIUS, 62
ADAMS, Sheriff 203
ADOLPHUS, Gustavus 44 79
  82 110 235
AITKEN, Robert 416
ALEXANDER, 351 353 James
  345 347 349 Mr 450
  William 131 219 345
ALRICKS, Jacob 195
ALTHAIN, John 216
ALVA, 78
AMADEUS, Victor 294
AMHERST, 462-463 465
  Jeffrey 464
ANDERSON, John 372
ANDRINGA, Joris 169
ANDROS, 87 172-176 188 283
  286-289 292-294 Edmund
  171 241 253 261 285 291
  422 Gov 254 262
ANNE, Queen 319 328-329
  331-338 346 388 403 423-
  424 426 438
ARGALL, 14 Capt 60 Samuel
  8
ARLINGTON, Lord 157 162

ARMSTRONG, John 460
ASHMORE, William 221
ASPINWALL, William 66
ATKINSON, Theodore 448-
  449
AVERY, 325
BACKARUS, Dominie 124
BACON, President 300
BAILEY, John 244
BAKER, John 244
BALTIMORE, 218 227 229-
  230 233 239 427 470 Lord
  57-58 63 159 183 196-198
  209 212-214 216-217 219-
  221 223 231 235-236 238
  275 306 308 332 405 425
  428-431 437 439 441 497-
  498
BANCROFT, 484
BARCLAY, Robert 259
BARNES, Abraham 448
BARRE, 482 505 Isaac 481
BARRON, James 438
BARTRAM, John 314 William
  314
BASSE, Jeremiah 328
BAXTER, 126 131 George 68
  125 127 129-130 236

BAYARD, 295 322 Col 286 304
    Councillor 298 Judith 93
    Nicholas 93 172 203
    William 489
BEAUJEU, 457
BECKER, Joseph 208
BECKFORD, 481
BEDFORD, 502-503
BEEKMAN, William 172
BELCHER, 374 Gov 471
    Jonathan 366 373 Thomas
    29
BELLOMONT, 322 324 Gov
    329 Lord 323 326 357
BELLSON, John 221
BENNETT, 184 198 231-232
    Justice 186 Richard 230
BERGEN, 376
BERKELEY, 169 246 253
    John 188 241 244 Lord 251
    William 228 233 245
BERNARD, Francis 374
BERRY, John 251
BEVEREN, Sieur 5
BIKKER, 108-109 Gerrit 107
BINCKES, Jacob 166
BLACKISTON, 306
BLACKWELL, John 280
BLAKE, 119-120
BLAKISTON, Nathaniel 423
BLANCKE, Capt 53
BLINCKES, Jacob 252
BLOCK, 59 Adrian 7-8 40 134
BLOMMAERT, 42 Samuel 23
    41
BOES, Capt 252
BOGARDUS, 36

BOGARDUS (Cont.)
    Dominie 31 35 124
    Dominie Everardus 25
BOLLES, 384-385 392 401
BOONE, Thomas 375
BOSCAWEN, Edward 463
BOUQUET, Henry 458
BOWENSEN, Tymen 17
BOWNE, Andrew 328
BRADDOCK, 207 455-459
    467-468 Edward 454
BRADFORD, 347 Andrew 415
    Gov 18 William 346 415
BRADLEY, 348 350
BRADSTREET, Simon 68
BRENT, Giles 223
BREWSTER, William 181
BROADHEAD, 161 291-293
    304
BROCKHOLLS, 176 Anthony
    175
BROOKE, Lord 134
BROWNE, 226 231 422 425
    427 432
BUCHANAN, Sheriff 432
BUDD, Thomas 377
BULL, Capt 172 Henry 299
BULWER, 438
BURKE, Edmund 503
BURNET, 342-343 372 Bishop
    165 348 Gov 204 William
    339 341 371
BURR, Aaron 374
BURROUGHS, John 172
BURTON, Mary 355-357
BUTE, 479 Lord 375 478 503
BUTLER, 146

BYLLINGE, 258 Edward 188 254-255 257
CABOT, 13 40 John 4 57 Sebastian 4 57 59
CALLOWHILL, Hannah 278 392
CALVERT, Benedict Leonard 424-425 Cecilius 60 196 212 214 216 238-239 442 497-498 Charles 205 238-239 424-425 431 439 Frederick 439 George 60 196 212 216 233 432 Gov 222-223 228 Leonard 196 216 220-221 224 229 432 Philip 232-233 236 238
CALVIN, 408
CAMDEN, 505
CAMPANIUS, 192 John 51 Thomas 52
CAMPBELL, Neil 261
CAREY, Peggy 355-356
CARLETON, Dudley 60
CARLYLE, 3
CARR, Robert 145 159
CARROLL, Charles 427 496 Daniel 427
CARTERET, 169 246 250 259 Elizabeth 245 George 174-175 188 241 244-245 251-253 255 Gov 248-249 376 James 251 Lady 175 Philip 174 241 245 247 260
CARTWRIGHT, 160 Col 159 George 145
CATHARINE, Of Aragon 78

CECILIUS, Lord Baltimore 232
CHALMERS, 246 253
CHAMBERLAIN, Samuel 433
CHAMBERS, John 350 448
CHAMPLAIN, 10 173
CHANDLER, John 448
CHARLES, 140 169 214 245 477 King 156 165 219 238
CHARLES I, 19 58 60-62 87 131 159 230 497 King 498
CHARLES II, 78 118 133 139 141 146 150 162 166 169 178 230 253 257 260 264 284 309 King 259
CHARLES V, 5 12 78 81
CHARLES X, 110
CHESELDYN, Kenelm 421
CHOISEUL, 475
CHRISTIAN IV, King Of Denmark 81
CHRISTIANSEN, 9 Hendrick 7-8 40
CHRISTINA, Queen 45 110 Queen Of Sweden 104
CLAIBORNE, 184 198 219-223 225 228 231-232 William 214 218 230
CLARKE, 353 358-359 George 352 Lieut-Gov 357 480
CLARKSON, 272
CLAYTON, John Middleton 438
CLINTON, 360 362 Dewitt 464 George 359 464 470 Gov 364 445 480 James 464
CLOBERRY, 218

CLOSE, Bartholomew 411
COATES, 320
COBB, 201
COLDEN, 489 491 494-496
   Cadwallader 481 Lieut-
   Gov 488 490 493
COLE, 188 Josiah 187
COLUMBUS, 4
COLVE, 168-169 Anthony 167
   252
CONTRECOEUR,
   Commandant 457
CONWAY, 503
COODE, 307 John 306 422
COOTE, Richard 321
COPLEY, Gov 422 Lionel 332
   421
CORNBURY, 330-331 Lord
   322 354 386 Viscount 242
CORNWALEYS, Capt 224
   Thomas 221
CORNWALLYS, 443 Thomas
   442
COSBY, 345-347 349 351-352
   Gov 480 William 344 372
COTTON, John 490
COUCELLES, 173
COXE, 371 Daniel 370
   William 502
CRESAP, 433 Thomas 432 469
CROMWELL, 82 118 120 127
   138 198 230-231 245 263-
   264 280 309-310 314 Oliver
   3 137 139 183 Richard 139
   162
CRUGER, John 336 489 495-
   496

CRYGAR, Martin 72
D'IBERVILLE, Lemoyne 298
DAGGETT, 487
DAGWORTHY, John 438
DANKERS, Jasper 195
DAVENANT, William 230
DAVERRAZANO, Giovanni 4
DAVY, Humphrey 414
DAWSON, William 221
DEBOGARDT, Jost 48
DECATUR, Stephen 438
DEHORST, William 47
DELABADIE, Jean 195
DELAET, 42
DELAMONTAGNE, Jean 28
   103
DELANCEY, 352-353 364-365
   Chief Justice 347 349-350
   James 345 447-448 470
   Lieut-Gov 449
DELAWARE, Lord 61
DELAWARR, Lord 40
DELEVIS, Chevalier 465
DEMILT, Anthony 172
DENTON, Daniel 170 244
DEPEYSTER, Johannes 172
DERAZIER, Isaac 19
DEREDDEN, Gothardt 47
DERUYTER, 120 156-157 166
DESILLE, Vice-Director 111
DEVAUDREUIL, Marquis 459
DEVRIES, 27 29-33 41 43 46
   52 61 David Pieters 42
DEWITH, Capt 40
DEWITT, Cornelius 157
DICKINSON, John 489
   Jonathan 366 415

DICKSON, Jonathan 206
DIESKAU, 459-460
DINWIDDIE, Gov 480
DIXON, 470 Jeremiah 469
DONGAN, 197 286 296 Gov 340 Thomas 176 285
DORSEY, Maj 228
DOUGHTY, Francis 183
DOWNING, 148 George 147
DOYLE, 327
DRAKE, 81
DRISIUS, 191-192
DUBOIS, Louis 181
DUDLEY, Chief Justice 311 Joseph 290 303
DULANEY, Daniel 205
DUMAS, 457
DUNBAR, 458 480
DURAND, Mr 228
DURFORD, 229
DYER, William 175 253
EARLE, 387
EATON, 136 Gov 67 69-70 76
EDWARD, VI 78
EELKENS, Jacob 10
EGREMONT, 478
ELIZABETH, Queen 78 81-82
EVANS, 384-386 394 Gov 315-316 387 John 314 318 383
EVELYN, George 222
EVERTSEN, Cornelius 166 252
FAITHORNE, 237
FASSETT, 438 Mary 437-438 William 437
FENDALL, 132 188 233 Gov 236 Josiah 232

FENWICK, 254 256 John 188 253 Mary 437-438 Thomas 436-437
FERDINAND, 83
FISKE, 161
FITCH, 484
FLEETE, Henry 217
FLETCHER, 312-313 320-321 340 Benjamin 311 Gov 319 Mrs 320
FLOWER, Enoch 278
FORBES, 459 John 458
FORRESTER, 132 Andrew 131
FOX, 186 Christopher 185 George 185 188 209 258
FRANCIS, I 59 I Of France 4
FRANKLIN, 390 411-414 416-418 452 467-468 477 483-484 500-501 Benjamin 88 206 314 374 410 448-450 453 456 499 502 Deborah 412 James 410 William 367 375 502
FREDERICK, III 199 Of Prussia 453
FRONTENAC, 283 298 301 312
FROTHINGHAM, 489
FULLER, 233 William 184 231
GABRY, 235
GADSDEN, 490
GAGE, 494 Gen 496-497 Thomas 488
GALE, Levin 433
GEORGE I, 338 340 343 388 396 424 443

GEORGE II, 338 343 404 472
GEORGE III, 338 472 478 504-505
GEORGE, King 357 438
GEORGES, Mr 431
GERRITSEN, Hon Mr 25 Wolfert 23
GILBERT, Humphrey 57 Matthew 248
GODFREY, The Merchant's Man 64 Thomas 314
GODYN, 42 46 Samuel 23 41
GOETWATER, Ernestus 192
GOODSON, John 313
GOOKIN, 388 394 396 Charles 316 387 Gov 319
GORDON, 404-405 Gov 411 Patrick 403
GRAHAM, James D 470
GRAHAME, 260
GRANT, Mrs 336
GRASMEER, Dominie 105
GREENE, Thomas 229
GRENVILLE, 479-481 484 487 502-503 George 478
GROWDEN, Lawrence 433
GUSTAF, Karl X 110
HADLEY, John 314
HALIFAX, 478 Lord 374 497
HALL, 159 Mary 158 Ralph 158
HAMILTON, 261 350-351 420 Andrew 314 318 327 349 372 419 Gov 328 James 419 John 372-373 Mr 431
HARDY, Charles 365 470 Josiah 375

HARRINGTON, 390
HARRISON, 348 Francis 347 Mr 227
HART, Gov 425 John 424
HARVEY, Gov 219-221 John 218
HAWLEY, Jerome 61 442
HAZARD, 52
HEATHCOTE, Caleb 337
HEEMSKERK, Jacob 6
HENDRICK, Willem 167
HENRIETTA, Maria Queen 60 196 214
HENRY, IV 184 VII Of England 4 VIII 78
HERMAN, 236 Augustine 195 235 237 Ephraim 195
HEYES, Pieter 42
HEYM, Peter Petersen 20
HEYN, Peter 42
HINCKLEY, Thomas 299
HINNOYOSSA, Alexander 159
HOARE, 320
HOCKHAMMER, Henry 47
HODGSON, Robert 187
HOGG, Robert 354
HOLLENDER, Peter 48
HOLT, Chief Justice 307
HOOD, 499 Zachariah 497 505
HOPKINS, Stephen 448-449
HOSSET, Gillis 23
HOSSETT, Gillis 42
HOWARD, Lord Admiral 81 Martin Jr 448
HOWE, Viscount 463
HUBBARD, 131 James 130

HUDDE, 54 83 103-104
  Andreas 53 Commissary
  102
HUDSON, Henry 6 11 40 59
HUGHES, John 501
HUGHSON, 354 356
HULFT, Peter Eversen 16
HUNTER, 203-205 335 371
  479 Gen 341 Gov 202 337
  339 346 369-370 407
  Robert 201 332
HUTCHINGS, 322
HUTCHINSON, 484 Anne 31
  183 Chief Justice 487
  Thomas 448-449
HUYGHENS, Hendrick 54
  103
HYDE, Edward 329
INDIAN, Chief Hendrick 447
  Chief Pacham 32 Chief
  Pemenatta 105
  Krieckebeeck 17 Krol 18
  Onas 272 Pontiac 477 507
  Sindacksegie 288
  Taiminent 273 Wappan-
  zewan 105
INGERSOLL, Jared 483 487-
  488
INGLE, 228-229 Richard 222
INGOLDSBY, 303 311 332
  Lieut-Gov 305 331 Richard
  302
INNESS, 170
IRVING, 24-25
JACQUET, John Paul 114
JAMES, 261 285 289 291-292
  295 302 422 King 182 284

JAMES, Duke Of York 141
  238
JAMES, Maj 489 495
JAMES I, 14 59-60 181 213
  286 443 I Of England 41
JAMES II, 78 178 197 234 239
  260-262 281 283 286 290
  293 304-305 307 309 329
  King 238
JANSEN, Antoine 29 Jan 45
  53 63-64 66
JENKINSON, 480 484 503
  Charles 479
JENNINGS, 258 Samuel 257
  330
JOHN, III 79
JOHNSON, 361 460 Richard
  423 Samuel 365 William
  358 446 448 459 464-465
JONES, William 259 266
JOPPA, 427 431
JORIS, 16 Adrian 180
KEIMER, Samuel 411
KEITH, 389 392-403 George
  278 346 Gov 205 411
  William 342 388 480
KENNEDY, Capt 495
KIDD, 324-326 Capt 323 327
  423
KIEFT, 28-32 34-36 45-46 54
  69 91-96 122-123 132 150
  152 Director 149 Director-
  Gen 75 183 Gov 49 64 67
  William 27
KINNERSLEY, Mr 414
KINSEY, John 371
KIP, Jacob 172

KLING, Moens 48 103
KNICKERBOCKER, 170
    Diedrich 93
KNOX, 408
KOCKERTHAL, Clergyman
    200
KUYTER, 121 Joachim 36
LACHMANN, 432
LAMB, 331 John 493 Mrs 320
    492
LAMBERTON, 64 76 George
    49 65 242
LAMBRECHTSEN, Chevalier
    148
LAURIE, Gawaine 189 254-
    255 261
LAW, John 411
LAWRENCE, Gov 207
LEBLEEUW, Francois 130
LEE, 378 381
LEEDS, Daniel 415
LEISLER, 197 293 296-305
    309-311 322 340 Jacob 159
    185 295
LENNOX, Lord 57
LEVERETT, John 138
LEVERMORE, 250
LEWGER, Secretary 198 225
LEWIN, John 175
LIGNERIS, 457 Commandant
    458
LINDSTROM, Peter 108
LISPENARD, Leonard 489
LIVINGSTON, 205 Philip 489
    Robert 174 201-202 310
    323-324 339-340 Robert R
    489 492 495

LLOYD, 279 316 384 387
    David 280 314-315 383 388
    Edward 424 Thomas 278
    317
LOE, Thomas 264
LOGAN, 316 383-384 399-400
    402 418 David 401 James
    314-315 386 388 397 406
    Secretary 389
LOPER, Jacob 37
LOPEZ, Don Vincent 417
LORD, Baltimore 305 469
LOUDON, 460-462
LOUGHMAN, 432
LOUIS, 166 295 XIII 19 XIV
    19 165 184-185 195 199 283
    290 294 307 310 422 XIV
    Of France 157
LOVELACE, 163 166-167 170-
    172 Baron 331 Francis 162
    192 Gov 164 Lord 200
LUCAS, Nicholas 189 254-255
LURTING, Robert 347
LUYCK, Aegidius 172
LYNCH, Thomas 490
MACAULAY, 390
MACK, Alexander 208
MANN, Abraham 274
MANNING, 172
MARKHAM, 281 313 Col 272-
    273 William 268 279
MARLBOROUGH, 422
MARY, 78 162 296-297 305
    307 322 332 421 Princess
    290 Queen 292-294 Queen
    Of England 422
MASON, 470 Capt 71

MASON (Cont.)
　Charles 469
MATHER, Cotton 353
　Increase 289 292
MAURICE, Prince 182
MAVERICK, 162 Samuel 160
MAY, 59 Capt 41 Cornelius 40
　Cornelius Jacobsen 8 15
　180 Peter 45
MCEVERS, 494 James 488
MCKEAN, Thomas 490 505
MCLEAN, Alexander 470
MEGAPOLENSIS, 191-192
　Dominie 111-112 144
　Dominie Johannes 31
MELYN, 37 121-122 Cornelius
　36 124
MILBORNE, 298 301 303-305
　322 Jacob 172 297
MINUIT, 28 45-46 Director 18
　Director-Gen 23 Gov 41
　Peter 16 24 48 61
MOLL, John 274
MOLOCK, Anthony 5
MONTANUS, Arnoldus 170
MONTCALM, 460-461 463 465
MONTGOMERY, 344 John
　343 372
MOORE, Chief Justice 279-
　280 Father 198 Henry 495
　Nicholas 274-275 277
　William 326
MORE, 390
MORRIS, 346-347 Chief
　Justice 345 Gov 351 455
　Lewis 372-373 Mr 344
　Robert 502

MORRIS (Cont.)
　Robert Hunter 467
MOTT, Gershom 493
MUHLENBERG, 193 Henry
　Melchior 192
MULGRAVE, Lord 57 241
MUNRO, Col 461
MURRAY, Joseph 448
NANFAN, Lieut-Gov 329
NEGRO, Prince 356
NELSON, 454
NEVILLE, Joseph 470
NICHOLSON, 288 293-296
　304 Col 203 331 Francis
　228 262 287 422 Gov 423
　440
NICOLLS, 142 144 156-157
　160-162 164 169 171-172
　251 Col 145 Gov 153-155
　158-159 245 247 250 253
　Richard 141 143 152 244
　William 298
NORRIS, Capt 351 Isaac 388
　397 448
NORTH, 479
O'CALLAGHAN, 30 95 101
　146-147 163
OGDEN, 491 John 244 Robert
　490
OGILBY, John 170
OGLE, Gov 432 Samuel 425
OLIVE, Thomas 258
OLIVER, Andrew 487
OSBORNE, 365 Danvers 364
　470
OTIS, 484-485 James 489
OXENSTIERN, Axel 110

OXENSTIERN (Cont.)
    Chancellor 44 47 John 62
PACA, William 496
PALATINE, Elector 195
PALFREY, 484
PALMER, Anthony 417
PAPPEGOYA, John 106
PARKER, John 472
PARTRIDGE, Oliver 448
PASTORIUS, Francis Daniel
    191 407
PAUW, Michael 23
PEARSON, Thomas 271
PENN, 190 239 256 267-268
    270-281 286 292 313 316-
    318 346 383-384 390 395-
    396 406-407 470 Dennis
    405 Gulielma Maria 391
    Hannah 278 389 392 405
    John 392 405 448 Lady 265
    Letitia Aubrey 391 Mrs
    400-401 Richard 392 405
    415 469 Robert 405
    Springett 382 405 Thomas
    392 405 415 469 William 58
    160 185 188-189 191 209
    234 238 254-255 258-259
    263-266 269 312 314-315
    386-387 389 391-392 403
    405 428-430 435 437 452
    William Jr 405
PEPYS, 158
PETERS, Hugh 31 Richard
    448
PETETS, Richard 433
PETRI, Laurentis 79 Olaus 79
PHILIP II, 77 79 81

PHILIP II (Cont.)
    Of Spain 5 King 83 173
PHILLIPSE, Aldophe 345
    Judge 349 Mr 356
PHIPPS, 294 William 292 301
PIERSON, Abraham 248
PITKIN, William 448-449
PITT, 463-464 472-473 481
    503 505 William 462 504
PLATO, 390
PLOWDEN, Edmund 58 61
    132
POWELSON, Jacob 46
POWNALL, Thomas 374
PRIDEAUX, 465 Brigadier
    464
PRINCE, Thomas 68
PRINTZ, 51-55 64-67 83-84
    103 105-107 Gov 102 John
    48 50 104
RAPEL, Commodore 456
READ, Deborah 412
READING, John 373-374
REDMAN, 66
RICHELIEU, 19
RIND, William 440
RITTENHOUSE, David 314
ROBERTS, 310
ROBINSON, Beverly 495 John
    181 Patrick 279 Thomas
    493
RODNEY, Caesar 490 505
ROELANDSON, Adam 25
ROOSEVELT, Caesar 356
RUDYARD, Thomas 260
RUGGLES, 491 Timothy 490
RUPERT, Prince 171

535

RUTLEDGE, John 490
RYSINGH, 108-109 111-114
  John 107
SACHEVERELL, 348
SAINTJOHN, 117
SALOMON, Haym 193
SALTONSTALL, Lord 134
SARGENT, John 504
SAUNDERS, Richard 413
SAUR, Christopher 416
SAYE, Lord 134
SCHUTE, 112 Swen 108 111
SCHUYLER, 340 Mayor 297
  310-311 Myndert 448 Peter
  33 312 339 471
SCHYNS, Dominie 304
SCOTT, John 140 John Morin
  486
SEARS, 495 Isaac 493-494
SEDGWICK, 139 Robert 138
SELE, Lord 134
SEYMOUR, Gov 424 John 423
SHARPE, 469 Gov 480 496-
  497 Horatio 468
SHERBURNE, Henry Jr 448
SHIRLEY, Gov 360 William
  459
SLOUGHTER, 303-304 310-
  311 Gov 197 Henry 302
SLUYTER, Peter 195-196
SMIDT, Derck 111 114
SMIT, 32 Claes 31
SMITH, 242 304 351 353 Chief
  Justice 344 John 220
  Richard 183 Thomas 221
  225 William 329 345 349
  364 415 448-449

SMITH (Cont.)
  William Jr 484
SPOTSWOOD, Gov 342
SPRINGETT, Gulielma Maria
  391
STANDISH, Miles 138
STANWIX, Gen 464
STEENHUYSEN, Engelbert
  376
STEENWYCK, Cornelius 172
STEIN, Hans 32
STEVENS, John 495
STIRLING, 132 Lord 141
STONE, 231 Gov 184 William
  229
STUART, 118 139 305
STUIJVESANT, Peter 34
STUYVESANT, 37 68-70 77
  79-80 82-83 85-86 94 96 98-
  112 114 120-138 140-143
  145 149 151-152 158 163
  187 191-192 194-195 235-
  236 Balthazar 92 144 Gov
  72 Judith 93 Peter 34 36
  55 67 76 91-93 148 243
TASKER, Benjamin 448-449
TAYLOR, Col 343
TEMPLE, 166
TENNENT, William 366
TEW, 320
THICKPENNY, John 64
THOMAS, 410 George 406
  Gov 206 408-409 416-417
THOMPSON, Richard 223
THROGMORTON, John 31
  183
THRUSTON, 188 Thomas 187

TILGHMAN, Edward 490
TIM, The Barber 64
TORKILLUS, Reorus 45 192
TOWNSHEND, 483 Charles 478-479 482
TREAT, Robert 248 250
TUCKER, William 214
TUDOR, Mary 78 81
TURNER, Capt 49 243 Robert 267
UNDERHILL, John 34 134
URY, John 356
USSELINCX, 44 William 10 43
VANBRUGH, Johannes 172
VANCORLEAR, Arendt 152 174 358
VANCORTLANDT, 295
VANCURLER, Jacob 134
VANDAM, 345-346 351-353 Rip 344
VANDERDONCK, 30 126 Adrian 123
VANDINCKLAGEN, 99 103 123-124 Lubbertus 27
VANDYCK, 99 151 Hendrick 150
VANELSWYCK, 112-114 Hendrick 109
VANHORNE, Abraham 341
VANRENSSELAER, 24 42 Kilian 23 25
VANSLECHTENHORST, 100-101 Brant 99
VANTIENHOVEN, 107-108 124-125 135 Cornelius 123 Secretary 32 104

VANTROMP, 119-120 Cornelius 166
VANTWILLER, 26-27 Wouter 24-25 124
VANVLEECK, Tielman 243
VANVOORST, 32
VANZYLE, Capt 252
VARRICK, John 355
VASA, Gustavus 79
VAUGHAN, William 212
VERGENNES, French Ambassador 475
VERHULST, William 16
VERRAZANO, 57 59
VETCH, Col 331
VETELLESETIS, Mutius 217
VINCENT, 54 61
VNDERDONCK, 133
VOLKERSTEN, Capt 40
VONDERDONCK, Adrian 236
VONWALLENSTEIN, Albert 235
WALDRON, Resolved 235-236
WARREN, Peter 358 Ratcliffe 221
WARWICK, Lord 134
WASHINGTON, 420 454 457- 459 Maj 419
WATSON, 435 John 434 Luke 244
WATTS, John 485
WEARE, Meshach 448
WEBB, Col 461
WEISLER, 203
WELLS, Samuel 448
WEST, Francis 214
WESTON, Thomas 224

WHITE, Andrew 216 Father 217 223
WHITEFIELD, George 366 373
WHITEHEAD, George 258
WIBBIRD, Richard 448
WILCOX, Joseph 383
WILEY, William 493
WILLETT, Thomas 68 138
WILLIAM, 78 162 296-297 302 305 307 311-312 322 332 421
WILLIAM, John 199
WILLIAM, King 84 292-293 423 King Of England 294 422
WILLIAM, Of Orange 262 290
WILLIAM III, 239 262 304 329
WILLIAMS, Elisha 448
WILLING, 502
WILLOUGHBY, Lord 118
WINDEBANKE, Secretary 61
WINSLOW, Edward 71 86
WINTHROP, 142 161 169-170 Fitz John 168 Fitz-John 301 Gov 65 76-77 82 160 Lord 134 Mr 143
WISE, John 289
WOLCOTT, Roger 448
WOLFE, 462-463 465 481
WOOLLEN, 65 John 64
WORTHINGTON, John 448
WRAXALL, Peter 448
YORK, Duke Of 244
ZEH, Magdalena 203
ZENGER, 348-350 John Peter 201 346-347 351

www.ingramcontent.com/pod-product-compliance
Lightning Source LLC
Chambersburg PA
CBHW071215290426
44108CB00013B/1183